Some reviews of **Mask of Treachery**

He has established beyond reasonable [...]
the first man, and the moving spirit am[...]
a changed picture of Anthony Blunt. [...]
recruited Burgess. The major key to h[...]
network of homosexual contacts within [...]
Blunt who wormed his way into British intelligence and inserted Communist
agents in the State Department and OSS; as a result the CIA hired agents who
in fact were working for the Soviet Union. When Blunt was in MI5, he had
the job of rifling the diplomatic pouches of Allied embassies. From
information Blunt gave the Russians from this source they were able to
liquidate nationals in Eastern Europe who were hostile to them. Then in 1951
Blunt helped Burgess and Maclean to escape and covered their tracks.

But Costello's book is no mere biography of Blunt. It covers the activities of
all the British spies as well as the upheavals in America aroused by the
testimony of Elizabeth Bentley and Whittaker Chambers. The
documentation is prodigious. Costello's editor told him to dig in the archives
before he interviewed sources, and he did both to considerable effect. His
book is a formidable achievement, as comprehensive a review as exists of the
operations and exposure of the pre- and postwar Soviet spy rings. Whatever
reservations I have about his methods and conclusions, no praise can be too
high for his research.

Noel Annan
The New York Review

Costello's book is, as he puts it, 'the first documented dossier on Blunt, MI5
and Soviet subversion', and as such is researched indefatigably.

Costello takes a sweeping historical view of his subject and places Blunt
within the larger context of subversion of Western governments by Russian-
directed communist agents and cells in the 1920s and 1930s. He deals
exhaustively with both the Comintern and the Homintern. The result is a
book packed with information, much of it shattering in its revelations of our
national vulnerability to Soviet intelligence operations . . .

Costello has unearthed a mass of material of the greatest interest with praise-
worthy energy and acuteness. Its full implications will take time to assess . . .

Anthony Curtis
Financial Times

John Costello sets out to reconstruct the treasonable activities of Anthony Blunt . . . and other associates in the . . . Cambridge spy ring . . . contains a great deal of fascinating material.

Its great virtue is the amount of new material that Mr Costello has assembled. His biggest haul comes from American archives – the files of the State Department, where he tracked down a large volume of British MI5 (counterintelligence) reports.

John Gross
The New York Times

. . . in 1979 I cornered and flushed out the then Sir Anthony Blunt, a smooth, tough and seasoned spy if ever there was one. Now *Mask of Treachery*, John Costello's . . . biography . . . still causes my heart to miss a beat or two. I doubt if any rival could match his thoroughness and determination. This Anglo-American contemporary historian has uncovered some revealing insights.

Andrew Boyle
Daily Telegraph

. . . new and explosive material emerges about the post-war activities of Anthony Blunt.

Costello, by diligently seeking out intelligence files now available in the US, shows how the old spy became a homosexual mole for Stalin inside Buckingham Palace . . . when he carried out a secret mission to Hesse in the American occupation zone of Germany on behalf of King George VI. Blunt recovered royal family papers from the castles of the German cousins and the belief is that among the documents was hard evidence about the dangerous political flirtation between the Duke of Windsor and Hitler. As a reward Blunt became Keeper of the King's Pictures and allegedly used his position to provide Stalin with information from the pinnacle of the British establishment.

This fascinating book asserts that Blunt's knowledge provided him with a gold-plated insurance policy. For years his threat to reveal the royal secret saved him from exposure.

Ronald Payne
Daily Mail

To describe *Mask of Treachery*, John Costello's long and comprehensive examination of Anthony Blunt's career, as closely researched is almost an understatement. He has not only ransacked every available written source in Britain, but has also broken new ground by gaining access to British evidence in the US National Archives, which has yet to be released in this country. The written evidence has been cross-checked with many valuable interviews of those who knew Blunt at Cambridge in the 1920s and 30s, in his varied roles as a member of the Apostles, an early authority on Poussin, an open Marxist as well as a concealed agent and talent-spotter for Soviet intelligence, and others who served with him during and after the war in MI5.

Nigel Clive
Times Literary Supplement

. . . the last word on the subject of Blunt, Philby et al . . . lucid, thorough and written with the easy fluency John Costello brought to his fascinating study of Second World War mores, *Love, Sex and War*.

. . . a vividness which animates its cast of spies, and aesthetes, and reminds us yet again how mightily the British establishment strove to protect its brazen disloyalties.

Henry Pugh
The Standard

Mask of Treachery presents a well-written and beautifully documented case history of Soviet espionage . . . it will stand as the most comprehensive portrait to date of an enigmatic spy who played for both teams . . . and survived to have others tell the tale.

Nigel West
Catholic Herald

. . . John Costello comes closer to solving the enigma than most of his predecessors.

. . . a sensitive and well-documented biography.

Michael Hartland
The Times

. . . there is much in Costello's account of the original Soviet recruitment drives of the 1920s and 1930s which is thorough and fascinating. He uses these original spores as laboratory specimens, showing convincingly the way they connected together and fanned out across Britain and into America.

Paul Greengrass
Sunday Times

Costello's book combines the work of the intellectual and the detective. It is the most detailed account available of the Cambridge spy ring. However, it goes beyond the narrow confines of mere investigation to describe the numerous attempts, through both politics and espionage, to infiltrate the British and American intelligence services in the UK and the USA.

Frankfurter Allgemeine Zeitung

John Costello has written the definitive work on the scandal of the century: the Soviet infiltration of the British security organizations.

Börje Isakson
Dagens Industri

Compared to John Costello's *Mask of Treachery* the accusations of *Spycatcher* come down to a gentle whisper.

Lennart Ljunglöf
Aftonbladet

Mask of Treachery

John Costello read Law and Soviet Economic History at Cambridge University, where he was Secretary of the Union and Chairman of the Conservative Association. A former LWT and BBC television producer, he is author of *The Pacific War* and *Love, Sex and War*, and co-author of *D-Day*, *The Battle of the Atlantic*, *Jutland 1916*, *The Concorde Conspiracy*, and the prize-winning US bestseller *And I Was There: Pearl Harbor and Midway – Breaking the Secrets*. Researching and writing *Mask of Treachery* has taken four years of transatlantic commuting between London, Washington DC and New York.

John Costello

Mask of Treachery

Pan Books
in association with Collins

Originated and first published in the United States
by William Morrow & Co. Inc., New York

First published in Great Britain 1988 by
William Collins Sons & Co Ltd

This revised edition published 1989 by
Pan Books Ltd,
Cavaye Place, London SW10 9PG
in association with Collins

9 8 7 6 5 4 3 2 1

ISBN 0 330 30992 7

Photoset by Parker Typesetting Service, Leicester
Printed and bound in Great Britain by
Richard Clay Ltd, Bungay, Suffolk

For
Robin and Julia

Author's note

This paperback edition of *Mask of Treachery* has been edited, revised and updated to take account of new information which has come to light since the hardcover edition of the work has appeared.

Contents

Preface

Shortly after I started my investigation of the Cambridge spies, two bizarre encounters provided a foretaste of just how tortuous the trail of Blunt would become.

First, an extremely reticent former member of the thirties' Communist cell in Trinity College quickly agreed to see me. It was only after he had talked frankly about the cell's activities that he found out that I was not the son of a former comrade of the same name. With that the interview quickly came to an end. On the second occasion my name proved a drawback when I tried to contact a reclusive senior figure in the American counter-intelligence community. He, too, believed mistakenly that I was the son of Desmond Patrick Costello.

The little-known case of this New Zealander of Irish extraction illustrates the problems confronting a historian.

The facts of Desmond Patrick Costello's academic history and subsequent career in World War II military intelligence conform to the classic pattern of the Cambridge moles. After graduating in classics from the University of Auckland in 1932, Costello arrived at Trinity that same year on a traveling fellowship. He became active in the Trinity Communist cell before becoming an assistant lecturer in classics at Exeter University in 1936. After joining the army he quickly made a name for himself as an intelligence analyst when the Germans drove the British forces out of Greece and Crete in 1941. General Freyberg, the New Zealand forces commander, appointed Costello to be his divisional intelligence officer during the subsequent campaigns in North Africa and Italy.

That Costello was a 'bit left-wing' did not deter the New Zealand prime minister from appointing him in 1944 as second secretary to their legation in Moscow with the cheery assurance: 'It won't hurt to have one or two Communists in Moscow.'

After six years in the Soviet Union, during which he taught himself Russian and made many Russian friends – including the writer Boris Pasternak – Costello served in the New Zealand diplomatic service at the Paris embassy until 1955. He then accepted an appointment as professor of Russian at Manchester University.

Professor Costello first came under MI5 suspicion as a result of information given by Anatoli Golitsyn, the senior KGB officer who defected in 1961. His debriefing revealed that it was 'Paddy' Costello who had provided New Zealand passports for Peter and Helen Kroger (the former New York Communists Morris and Lena Cohen), who were convicted as members of the so-called Portland Spy Ring for stealing anti-submarine-warfare secrets.

The Manchester University academic was put under surveillance by the watchers of MI5. He was observed meeting suspected Soviet agents. But this was not enough to charge a professor of Russian literature with espionage. Not until *after* Anthony Blunt confessed to his own treason in April 1964 did Blunt provide Peter Wright with the confirmation that Costello had indeed been another Cambridge recruit. But it was too late to confront Professor Costello with his treachery. According to his *Times* obituary, Costello had 'died unexpectedly at the age of 52' on February 24, 1964. It does not seem a coincidence that Blunt 'burned' Costello only after he was dead.

What justification is there to conclude that Costello was a Soviet spy? There is no confession, no primary source evidence, and no declassified MI5 investigation or other official documentation that proves he was yet another Soviet mole recruited at Cambridge. The case against Costello rests on information given in defiance of the Official Secrets Act by the former MI5 investigating officer Peter Wright to Harry Chapman Pincher, the veteran British journalist with a reputation for accurately relaying intelligence information. Although Wright's book *Spycatcher* makes no mention of Costello, Pincher confirmed that he made notes about Costello during his 1981 interviews with Wright in Tasmania.

Further confirmation that Paddy Costello was a long-term Soviet agent was provided to me on a nonattributable basis by a senior American intelligence source who cited his own debriefing of Golitsyn. This still begs the question of absolute proof, but it does provide credible corroboration that Costello was another Soviet spy whose career appears to have begun in the peculiar circumstances of Cambridge in the thirties.

For the historian, the problem of charting the progress of an espionage network is the lack of documentary proof. Intelligence officers who have devoted a lifetime to counterespionage operations repeatedly stress that without a confession, or the arrest of a spy in the act of passing secret information to a hostile power, the lack of evidence is what makes espionage such a difficult crime to prove.

Yet counterintelligence case officers also emphasize that espionage networks do not grow spontaneously: they must be directed and managed. This basic truth is supported by the reports and investigations that intelligence services – especially the British – are loath to declassify. This is because documentary records that span a long time frame establish a paper trail – the essential spoor of counterintelligence methodology that the case officer talks about, but for which he has no hard proof. Nonetheless, if one studies the paper trail of Soviet intelligence efforts, one finds that they betray themselves by their remarkable consistency of purpose and operational technique – especially when supplemented by the minutiae provided by defectors from Moscow's intelligence apparatus.

At an early stage in the course of my work on this book, I was fortunate to locate part of that historic paper trail: a large volume of British MI5 reports in the confidential archives of the US Department of State. Supplemented by FBI reports that I obtained under the Freedom of Information Act and buttressed by files that had escaped the official 'weeders' of the British Foreign Office and Home Office, this significant new document-ation leaves no doubt about the scope of the secret Anglo-American 'special relationship' that began during World War I. It also reconstructs the elusive spoor of Soviet operations – especially in the context of the Cambridge spies.

Working from the clues presented by these documentary records, it is now possible to examine – for the first time from a case officer's viewpoint – an accurate picture of the pattern of Soviet subversive operations against Britain and then the United States from the mid-1920s onward. By using the documents to cross-check the testimony of British and American participants in this secret war, fresh interpretations of events emerge. We can now understand for the myths that they are the self-serving accounts promoted both by the British government and by those, such as Kim Philby, who betrayed it.

Like all skillful disinformation, the corrosive fabrications pro-moted by Anthony Blunt himself, echoing those orchestrated from Moscow by Burgess and Philby in their books, and Philby's final interviews just before he died in 1988, all were constructed around a connective tissue of truth. Where I have chosen to rely on statements by Blunt, Philby or Burgess, or others in the conspiracy, it is because these particular statements can be cor-roborated by documents or other reliable intelligence sources. Where suspect sources conflict with events as they can now be documented, I have endeavoured to make that fact clear with supporting analysis in the source notes.

The Official Secrets Act has necessarily restricted the attrib-ution of certain information contributed by former MI5 and MI6 officers. But such conclusions as I reached have been drawn only after considerable documentary analysis and many hundreds of hours of discussion of my findings with informed opinion on both sides of the Atlantic.

Just as the case officer is responsible for his judgement calls, I take full responsibility for the conclusions arrived at in this work. They cannot be complete and unequivocal, but they were reached after the careful weighing of new documentary evidence and in the spirit of historical objectivity. Some of my distinguished fellow countrymen, who have made it clear that they regard the freedom of speech enshrined in the American Constitution as a dangerous threat to the profession of intelligence, may find some of my conclusions contentious, and possibly offensive.

I would, however, remind those who challenge my thesis and my conclusions with special pleading of their access to 'informed sources' that the faintest ink is usually a more reliable foundation for historical analysis than the strongest memory. I acknowledge that I have not seen every MI5 report, but I cannot apologize for the message conveyed by the documents I studied, nor for the assessments given me by informed sources. So if that portion of the MI5 record that provides the core of this book speaks falsely, then would it not be appropriate for the British government to declassify the remainder of these secret-service records that are half a century old?

The *Spycatcher* debacle, and the mass of secret data from Britain now openly available to historians in the United States, argues that the time has now come for Parliament to pass a Freedom of Information Act appropriate to a democratic nation. Yet in a policy decision that challenges one of the most basic of Western freedoms, the right to know, the British government hustle Parliament into legislation that amended the Official Secrets Act in a way that will make it impossible for historians ever to have access to intelligence officers or their secret archives. Under the new 1989 law, interviewing MI5 or MI6 officers, even off the record as I have had to do, would attract criminal prosecution.

When it comes to the verdict of history, it is ironic how official secrecy continues to hold Britain's leaders in thrall. It was an obsession that Blunt and his associates so effectively turned to the Soviet advantage, and it flies in the face of Shakespeare's time-tested axiom:

Time's glory is to calm contending kings,
To unmask falsehood, and bring truth to light.

Acknowledgments

This project would not have come to fruition but for the very considerable individual contributions made by three people behind the scenes, contributors who deserve equal billing with the author:

Bruce Lee, my editor at William Morrow, whose expertise as a former newsman not only inspired, sustained and drove this project, but whose singular editorial skills, wisdom and patience have fashioned the final result.

Robert T. Crowley, whose encyclopedic study of the KGB and knowledge drawn from firsthand experience have made sense of the many multiple images as he guided me through the 'wilderness of mirrors'.

Andrew Lownie, whose Cambridge historian's training and intellectual stamina have been tested and vindicated by four years of persistent spare-time interviewing and rigorous archival research.

My reasons for gratitude to these three unsung contributors may not be immediately apparent to the reader, but the text and source notes also reveal that this book would not have been possible without the personal testimony and insights that flesh out the book's documentation. To some of those I cannot name I owe my deepest debt of gratitude.

To Lord Annan, Andrew Boyle, Robert Cecil, Robert J. Lamphere, Verne Newton, Harry Chapman Pincher, Michael Straight and Nigel West (Rupert Allason, M.P.) I owe a special word of thanks. Not only have they afforded both Andrew Lownie and me many hours of interviews, but in long transatlantic telephone discussions and correspondence over many years, each has unhesitatingly permitted me to tap his fund of personal knowledge, reminiscence and perceptive analysis. They may not agree with all my conclusions, but their advice was indispensable and most carefully considered.

More than a hundred others contributed directly or indirectly to my research, either by letter or interview, or by supplying photographs or information. I should like to single out for special thanks:

In the United Kingdom: Dr Christopher Andrew, Alan Berends, the late Professor John Bowle, Professor R. Braithwaite, Dr Anita Brookner, Dr Christine Carpenter, Mrs Robert Cecil, the late Sir John Colville, John E. C. Costello, Mr and Mrs F. Cowgill, Professor Dan Devin, Lady Mary Dunn, Sydney Elwood, Rachel Gould, Peter Fairbarn, Professor Henry Ferns, Bruce Fireman, Sir Charles Fletcher-Cooke, Sir Dudley Forwood, Dr Martin Gilbert, Jean and Peter Gimpel, Dr Anthony Glees, Sir Ernst Gombrich, Hugh Gordon, Paul Greengrass, Robert Harbinson, Duff Hart-Davis, Margot Heinemann, Jack Hewit, Charles Higham, Mr and Mrs John Hilton, Professor Sir Harry Hinsley, David Irving, Timothy and Mrs Kemball Johnston, Tyler G. Kent, Dr George Knuppfer, Rosamond Lehmann, David Leigh, Peter J. Liddell, Alan Liddell-Hart, Mr and Mrs Alastair MacDonald, Sir Dennis Mahon, Patricia Meehan, Mr and Mrs Arthur Martin, Dr Janet Morgan, Mr and Mrs Donald McCormack, Leonard Miall, the late Joan Miller, Malcolm and Kitty Muggeridge, Alexis Racine, Guy Rais, John Richardson, Michael Robertson, Dr A. L. Rowse, Kenneth Rose, Andrew Roth, Andrew Rothstein, James Rusbridger, Brian Sewell, Andrew Sinclair, Professor Jon Stallworthy, Professor George Steiner and Dr Zara Steiner, Malcolm Turnbull, Lord Thurlow, W. J. West, Jasper Wight, Christopher Wright, Philip Ziegler; and a cordial acknowledgement to Mrs Cherry Hughes.

Harold J. Ketzer of Frankfurt and Hansruedi Zellweger of Zurich provided hospitality and valued assistance with research in Germany.

In the United States, I should like to thank: Professor James Barros and his son Andrew, Emily Crowley, Laughlin Campbell, Dr George Carver, Dr Ray Cline, George Constanedes, Dr Robert Conquest, Dr John Dziak, Professor Sydney Hook, Stephen Koch, Robert Haslach, John Hawkins, Hayden Peake, the late Rear Admiral Edwin T. Layton and Mrs Layton, Janetta Lee, Nicholas Lawford, John Loftus, Judge Robert Morris, Desmond MacCrae, Captain and Mrs Roger Pineau, Walter Pforzheimer, Professor Ronald Radosh, William Rusher, Dr Arnold Kramish, Dr Wilfred Basil Mann, Stephen J. Koch, Timothy Naftali, Daniel J. Mulvenna, the late Dr Karl Wittfogel, John Saxon, Professor Robert Chadwell Williams, Professor Simon Schama, Thomas S. Troy, Professor Robin W. Winks, Natalie Grant Wraga.

I must also acknowledge the supportive mosaic of indirect contributions made by the other writers whose works have provided valuable background detail and anecdote. Their books are identified in the appropriate source notes, which also serve as the bibliography.

The documentation that provided the telephone underpinning of this book would not have come to light without the patient help provided by the archivists and staff of the National Archives in Washington. John Taylor has, for over a decade now, been both counsellor and guide in the excavation of new data to fuel and inspire my historical writing. I would like to take this opportunity to add my own endorsement to numerous accolades paid to this unique historical resource at a model national institution. Among its informed, ever-willing and helpful staff who have been of particular assistance to this book are John Butler, Terri Hammett, Dane Hartgrove, William H. Lewis, Wilbur Mahoney, Timothy Nennigan, Richard von Doenhof, William Harris, Sally Marks, Katherine Nicastro, Edward R. Reese and Ronald Swerczek.

Special thanks are also extended to Dr Michael J. Halls, the archivist of King's College, Cambridge, for considered and insightful guidance to the affairs of the Bloomsberries. Also to the librarian of Trinity College; Marion Stuart and the staff of the Churchill College Archives; the Manuscripts Division of the Cambridge University Library and the Bodleian Library, Oxford; the archivist of Christ Church, Oxford; the staff of the Cambridge County Library; the chief clerk of the Cambridge Union Society; and the archivists of Eton College, Marlborough College and Westminster School.

Thanks are due to the staff of the Public Record Office, Kew; the Foreign Office Library; the Courtauld Institute; the Beinecke Rare Book and Manuscript Library, Yale University; the Hoover Institute, Stanford, California; the London Library; the New York Public Library; and the Library of Congress, Washington, D.C.

Robin and Julia Wight have made many major contributions to the project through their sustaining friendship, generous hospitality and logistical support. I thank my parents and many friends on both sides of the Atlantic, especially John Alston, Patricia Greenwood, John and Kari Hegarty, Gerald P. Jantzi, David Kagan, Kenneth Nichols, Laurence Pratt, Chauncey Smith and Milo O'Sullivan and all the others on both sides of the Atlantic who by hospitality, chauffeuring or sympathetic attention have shared in some of the trials and triumphs of a four-year research project – and to Sharon and Stak Aivaliotis and Peter Jones, for improving my image.

Gary Lazarus, Frederic M. Schulman and Fred Biehl in New York, with the diligent assistance of Anthony Rubinstein, Julia Palca and Simon Olswang in London, have helped shepherd this complex project through some very tangled legal thickets. But this book would not have been possible at all without my publishers, who nurtured this project with all the patience and skill of a parent raising a temperamental and sometimes rather wayward child. My gratitude is extended to the house that first signed up this book, William Morrow, and all its staff, but especially to Abigail Stackpole, John Harrison, Andy Ambraziejus, Cheryl Asherman, Joan Amico, Bernard Schleifer, Mark Stein and John Wahler, my heartfelt thanks. Roger Schlesinger brought William

Collins into the project in midstream and to him and Ariane Goodman, Simon King and Juliet Annan, who have acted as parents for the English edition – and to Teresa Sacco of Pan Books – again my grateful thanks.

New York
London
August 1988

The publication of *Mask of Treachery* – belatedly in November 1988 – was a small victory, although the battle against the British government's determination to entomb the full record of Britain's secret services in Official Secrecy was lost in Parliament five months later. That it has been published at all in Britain was in no small measure due to the efforts of the journalists of *The Times*, *The Daily Telegraph*, *The Daily Mail*, *The Evening Standard*, *The New York Times* and *ITN News* who gave timely publicity to the efforts by the government's D Notice Committee to vet the manuscript even as the book was coming off the presses in the United States.

My thanks are also due to the editors of *The Times*, *The Times Literary Supplement* and the *New York Review of Books* who provided space for the debate of some of the more controversial results of my research. New information and comments gleaned from the hundreds of letters my publishers have received from readers and correspondents as a result of the controversy generated by publication, have been incorporated to revise and update this edition.

I am particularly grateful for the helpful critiques and comments on the original edition supplied by Lord Annan, Dr Ralph Bennett, Andrew Boyle, Nigel Clive, Andrew Davies, John Gross, Jack Hewit, Robert Lamphere, Dr A. N. May, Martin Simmonds, Michael Straight, Raymond Rocca, Professor Robert Winks and Sir Dick White. To those who have supplied additional information and help, but especially to Robbie Dunwoodie of the *Scotsman* and Peter Hull of Pan Books, my grateful thanks.

Despite the constraints of the new Official Secrecy laws which would now make it impossible to have researched and written *Mask of Treachery*, I trust this account will not be the final exposure of the astonishing cover-up of the true extent of the betrayal of Britain by Anthony Blunt and his privileged contemporaries in the British Establishment.

June 1989

List of Illustrations

List of Documents

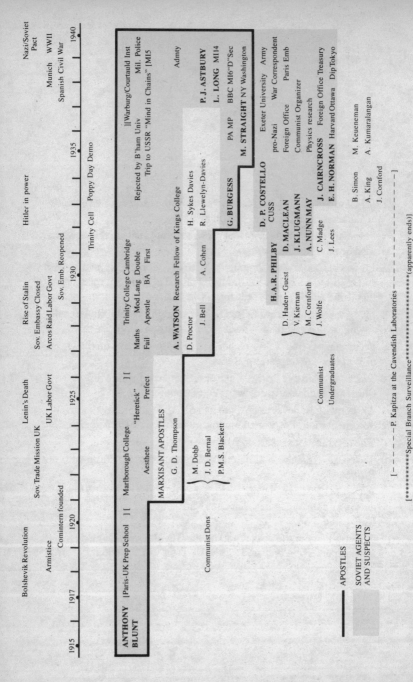

Timeline (1940 – 1969)

- 1940 — Dunkirk / Hitler's Attack on Russia
- 1945 — Hiroshima / Defeat of Nazis
- USSR A Bomb
- 1950 — Korean War / Burgess & Maclean
- Stalin's death
- 1955 — Suez Debacle
- 1960 — Cuban Crisis
- Philby Defects
- 1965 — Blunt Confesses
- 1969

Person	Timeline events (left → right, c.1940 → 1969)
BLUNT	"C" MI5 "B"; SHAEF; Surveyor Royal Art & Courtauld Director; Contacted by Modin; Knighted; Queens Gallery; Immunity Deal
WATSON	Admiralty Research; Royal Missions; Interrogated no confession
ASTBURY	Radar research with Blackett; Sonar and NATO anti-sub warfare research; Refused interrogation
LONG	Military Intel; London University; Physicist CERN Nuclear Accelerator Geneva; Named and confesses
BURGESS	USA; BBC; Germany; Foreign Office; Columbia Pictures UK; USA Defects; "New Republic"; Moscow/Driberg book; dies
STRAIGHT	State Dept; USAAF; Confesses to FBI and MI5
COSTELLO	Army Intelligence ULTRA; Contacts Burgess; NZ Embassy Moscow; NZ Embassy Paris; Professor Russian Manchester; Dies and named by Blunt
PHILBY	SOE; MI6 Sec "V"; "IX" Turkey; USA MI6; Interrogated; Exonerated; MI6 rehires Beirut; Defects; "My Silent War"
MACLEAN	Foreign Office; Washington; Cairo; London Defects; Moscow Press Conf. Soviet Foreign Ministry
KLUGMANN	SOE; Balkans Ops; Communist Party; Physics professor in Ghana; Suspected by MI5 Dies
NUNN MAY	Atomic Bomb project; Exposed and convicted; Retires under suspicion to live in Rome
CAIRNCROSS	GCHQ ULTRA; MI6; Treasury; Named and confesses
NORMAN	Tokyo; Ottawa; Assistant to MacArthur in Japan; Ambassador Egypt; Suicide after Communist accusations in Congress

1 'How Can You Ever Forgive Me?'

At 10:30 every weekday morning, a dapper man in his mid-fifties emerges from London's Chancery Lane underground station and hurries through traffic-clogged Fleet Street on his way to work. His neat gray moustache, stylish suit and black briefcase give the impression that he belongs to the legal profession. Well it might be, for Guy Rais's journalistic beat is the High Court of Justice, which deals with the most important civil cases in England. But his real 'office', as he prefers to call it, is the bustling newsroom of *The Daily Telegraph*.

On Tuesday morning, 12 February 1980, Rais arrived at his desk expecting an assignment to cover a major libel case that would be bread-and-butter reading for the British public. But before he could check the assignment roster, his telephone rang. It was a tipster who calmly said: 'A man has jumped from the top floor of Portsea Hall.'

The deep male voice on the other end of the line told Rais the address of the incident: a block of luxury flats just north of Marble Arch. The man politely declined to identify himself and hung up. At first Rais believed it was just a crank call. 'People ring up with the most ridiculous tip-offs,' he told me, 'and half of them don't lead to stories.' But after some seconds of reflection, this call aroused his interest.

Portsea Hall was the address of some newsworthy names. Among them was the flamboyant former foreign secretary, Lord George Brown. It was also the home of Anthony Blunt, a self-confessed spy, notorious homosexual, and recently-forced-to-retire surveyor of the Queen's pictures.

Three months earlier, Prime Minister Margaret Thatcher had made a sensational statement in the House of Commons and confirmed for the first time that Blunt had been a Soviet agent. Rais had covered the story. The Prime Minister's disclosures scandalized England. Blunt had been made a Knight Commander of the Royal Victorian Order for his service to the royal collections and was a courtier at Buckingham Palace for nearly forty years. He was a third cousin of the Queen Mother. He had extensive connections and influence. He was a former Slade professor at London University, a long-serving director of the world-famous Courtauld Institute of Art, and an honorary fellow of Trinity College, Cambridge. But he was also linked to three college contemporaries who had defected to Moscow. They were the so-called Cambridge traitors: one the former senior British intelligence official Kim Philby, and two renegade diplomats named Guy Burgess and Donald Maclean.

Immediately after Thatcher's disclosure, the Queen had stripped Blunt of his knighthood. The spy had gone into seclusion at his flat at Portsea Hall. But by using a journalistic trick, Rais had managed to telephone Blunt and interview him.

'Are you still a Communist, Sir Anthony?' Rais had asked.

'No, of course I'm not,' Blunt replied in a plummy voice. 'In the thirties, you know, it was not unusual to be strongly anti-Fascist.' It was the self-serving statement that Rais had expected. But he used it anyway in his article.

Now he told the assignment editor of the suicide tip and ran for a taxi and the twenty-minute cab ride to the six-story, brick-and-concrete building that was the scene of the incident. As his taxi swung past Connaught Square into Portsea Place, Rais saw there were two police cars parked at the Art Deco front entrance of Portsea Hall.

He asked the police what had happened but did not get anything helpful except confirmation that an elderly man had fallen from the sixth floor early that morning. Rais was gratified that his telephone informant had his facts straight. But once he stepped inside the door he realized that the story was not his exclusively.

Other Fleet Street reporters were gathered at the doorman's semicircular desk underneath the chandelier in the lobby.

The doorman, William Druce, was adamant. Only a tenant could enter the building and use the elevators. So Rais decided to pull an end run. He located the doorman's flat and approached his wife.

Gladys Druce was a stoutish woman in her fifties, and proved eager to describe the early-morning drama. The Druces lived in the back, in a basement flat at the foot of the fire escape. She had been woken 'just before five o'clock by a terrific thump. At first we thought some masonry had fallen from the roof. My husband went out in his nightclothes and found this man outside our daughter's bedroom window.'

Her husband identified the victim as a Mr Gaskin, who had lived with Anthony Blunt ever since the two men had moved into Flat 45 five years earlier. 'It was a miracle that Mr Gaskin was still alive,' she said. Indeed, it was miraculous that anyone could survive a sixty-foot fall from the tiny iron balcony above. Mrs Druce also told Rais she had heard the injured man gasp: 'I came out for a breath of fresh air.'

Gaskin proved to be doubly lucky. St Mary's Hospital was only half a mile away, and the ambulance crew, along with a fire engine, arrived just a few minutes after Mrs Druce called the 999 emergency number. After that the police arrived in force, including plainclothes detectives.

'Where is Blunt? Rais asked.

Mrs Druce said that he had left around half past seven, 'very upset and very concerned'.

Rais had been a reporter too long to accept this at face value. 'It was their duty to protect the residents,' he told me. 'At first I thought he was still there.' So he went off to find the nearest telephone and dialed Blunt's number. When the familiar voice did not answer, he set off up the Edgware Road toward Paddington Station.

At the grimy Praed Street entrance of St Mary's Hospital, Rais joined the other reporters milling around the entrance. A hospital spokesman appeared and read a short statement. He confirmed that a patient identified only as William John Gaskin was making 'satisfactory progress', recovering from an emergency operation for 'internal bleeding and treatment for a number of fractures'. The only concession to the press was the doctor's admission that it was 'amazing' that the fall had not killed the sixty-five-year-old man.

'Hospitals never do give out much useful information because they protect the privacy of patients,' Rais observed. In such circumstances, he explained, reporters suspend their normal cut-throat competition. 'We leaned on each other,' Rais said, recalling how the reporters spread out to question every doctor and nurse in sight. 'Persistence is what counts. Someone let slip, "I was in the operating theater", another that "Dr So-and-so was in charge", and so we pieced the story together.'

The reporters learned that the injured man was originally from Belfast, was a former Irish guardsman, and for thirty years had been Blunt's live-in lover. They joked that the two men had probably had 'a rough night of it'. One man from the *Daily Express* provided a more dramatic slant to the story. He said that a woman living in the fifth-floor flat below Blunt had claimed that she had been woken around five by loud noises and people shouting. Then, it had 'stopped, all of a sudden'.

'When anyone falls from a balcony in such curious circumstances there is a great deal of speculation,' Rais said. The question was whether it was a simple suicide or if Blunt had pushed Gaskin over the balcony in the heat of a blazing row.

'Speculation is all very well,' Rais continued, 'but it seemed to me that to hang around at the hospital was just banging our heads against a wall.' So he returned to Portsea Hall to take another look at the site. From the far side of the Edgware Road he could see that the fire-escape railings were well above waist height. Another puzzle was why an elderly man should go outside during the chill midwinter dawn. And if Gaskin needed a breath of fresh air, why had he picked the cramped iron fire escape when he could have used the large sheltered balcony opening off the flat's front room with its view over tree-lined Connaught Square?

Rais then checked Metropolitan Police Headquarters for an official comment. The Scotland Yard press office would say only that detectives had taken fingerprints from the balcony and had found nothing suspicious. There was no evidence of a struggle. Blunt had made a sworn statement that he was 'sound asleep' at the time of the incident. And when Gaskin regained consciousness he insisted he had missed his footing and fallen. The matter was to be logged as an accident. No further investigation would be made. Criminal charges were not contemplated.

Rais went back to his office and typed up the hard facts. No responsible newspaper would publish unsubstantiated rumors and risk a libel suit. Still Rais was not satisfied. After filing his story with the copydesk he went back to Portsea Hall.

No lights were visible in Flat 45 when he came by at seven. So Rais headed on to St Mary's Hospital. Reporters and several cameramen were still staking out the main entrance. They believed that Blunt would make a bedside visit to his injured friend. There were bantering comments about 'how to spot an old queen', but the joke was wearing thin.

'I took the view that with all the trouble Blunt was in, a public appearance at the hospital was the last thing he would do,' Rais said. 'After all, what could a visit achieve that a phone call could not, especially if his friend was so badly hurt?'

Rais then departed for home, leaving his colleagues to keep the vigil. He later heard some Fleet Street gossip that Blunt had disguised himself as an old woman and given the press the slip while visiting his lover. The idea was not quite so outlandish as it seemed. There is a Cambridge photograph that shows a girlish-looking, young Anthony Blunt languidly posing in ringlets and gown in imitation of the romantic Victorian poet Elizabeth Barrett Browning.

The truth of the matter is that the former surveyor of the Queen's pictures did *not* get up a 'drag act' to visit Gaskin. I have been assured of this by one of Blunt's close friends, who told me exactly what Blunt *did* to elude the reporters that night.

'Nobody, but nobody spotted him going into the hospital,' my source insists. He is a respected international art consultant. On condition that his name would not be mentioned, Blunt's friend agreed to see me in his New York City townhouse on the Upper East Side. Amid an impressive collection of art, he offered cocktails and proceeded to tell me what he knew.

A short time after Gaskin's mysterious fall, he lunched with Blunt at Portsea Hall. He recalled: 'It was an unusually hot day for early March, but every window in the apartment stayed tightly closed. Finally I had to say, "God! Anthony, the heat is unbearable!"'

'I haven't been able to go near a window since John's accident,' Blunt replied. 'Would you mind opening it for me?'

The art consultant said that Blunt swore that he had been fast asleep when Gaskin fell. He was awakened by a door banging in the wind. 'I left the bedroom,' Blunt explained, 'but couldn't find John anywhere.'

According to the New York art consultant, the strain of living with Blunt had proved too much for the former Irish guardsman. Another of Blunt's confidants, Brian Sewell, a former pupil from the Courtauld Institute, agreed. Alluding to the incident, which some of Blunt's circle still darkly referred to as the 'Defenestration of Portsea Hall', Sewell said that the couple's domestic affair had been falling apart for some time.

'While in no way camp,' he told me, 'Gaskin was both wife and manservant. He cooked for Anthony and put out a clean shirt for him every morning.' But Sewell said that Gaskin also 'greatly distressed Anthony' with his early-morning domestic chores and fetish for spending hours slicing carrots paper thin. 'Food meant nothing beyond eating to Anthony,' said Sewell, and Blunt was never generous with his praise for Gaskin's cooking. 'Lady John would often launch into his "I slave-my-guts-out-for-you" routine like a regular harridan, and a dreadful row would simmer on for days like a bad soap opera.'

The publicity that followed Blunt's exposure proved to be the final straw. Gaskin became increasingly paranoid and was drinking too much. 'John was fanatically loyal and protective,' the art consultant said. 'He felt terribly destroyed when all the espionage business came out because he realized that for all those years Anthony had excluded him from his confidence. Gaskin, he believes, was suicidal.

'John was from lower-class Belfast,' Blunt's art consultant friend observed, sniffing disdainfully. 'He was not unattractive physically, but was of limited intelligence.' He said that Blunt had fallen for the former Irish guardsman when he was a handsome, muscular thirty-year-old.

'Anthony chased soldiers and "rough trade" out of sheer naughtiness,' said Blunt's New York friend. He revealed that Anthony preferred sexual adventures with lower-class men. Even after he had been knighted by the Queen, he continued to pick up soldiers by night in the bars and public lavatories frequented by the men who guarded Buckingham Palace by day. The suave expatriate Englishman explained that paid liaisons with soldiers in the Guards and Household Cavalry regiments were a common practice in London's upper-crust homosexual scene.

'The key to understanding Anthony,' the New York consultant told me, 'is to know the tremendous charge he got out of living his life on many different levels.' Blunt, he said, obtained an immense satisfaction from escorting the president of France around the Queen's pictures at Buckingham Palace, knowing that at six o'clock he had a rendezvous with his Russian controller and could then go on to a homosexual encounter with a guardsman. 'Anthony skipped nimbly from one role to the other. All the time I knew him he was drinking heavily to keep his hideously complicated life together.' Blunt was cold and emotionless, but could be surprisingly loyal to his friends. That was why he appeared filled with remorse when he discussed the incident over lunch. Blunt had been determined to get into the hospital to see his injured friend and had managed to slip in through a side entrance to spend an hour at Gaskin's bedside.

Blunt regarded his coup against the press as a personal triumph. So did his inner circle of friends. As the New York art consultant polished off his tumbler of whiskey, he assured me with a nod of approval: 'Now it takes an old spy to get away with that!'

What precisely had the 'old spy' got away with? How did he do it? What type of man was he? What was the significance of the roles he lived and played? These questions have been the focus of a three-year search involving hundreds of interviews and the sifting of thousands of documents in archives on both sides of the Atlantic. Many attempts have been made to piece together the Blunt story from inadequately sourced interviews that cannot be cross-checked. The accounts obtained for this book – even when given by 'confidential sources' – have been checked for consistency by intelligence experts with firsthand experience of Soviet cases on both sides of the Atlantic.

More important, many of the facts that emerged in these interviews have been checked against contemporary MI5 reports, which the British government never intended should become available to researchers. For example, in this account are published, for the first time, organizational charts and personnel lists of Britain's wartime intelligence services. Contemporary 'Most Secret' reports shared with the American government in the twenties are reproduced here which show that early warnings about Soviet efforts to penetrate the university system had been picked up long before Anthony Blunt reached Cambridge.

Despite all that had been written about Blunt, it was difficult to distinguish fact from fiction, gossip from truth. 'Anthony himself remains a shadowy figure' was the considered opinion of Robert Cecil, a former British diplomat who interviewed Blunt extensively before his death. I had approached Cecil in the early stages of my research and he was convinced that the old spy remained a figure of shadows and speculation – precisely because he was so successful at compartmentalizing and concealing his life. To find the real Blunt, I would have to open each compartment of his secret lives.

Blunt's impassive masklike countenance was his primary asset.

It was a throwback to his Norman ancestors, and his face camou-flaged a ruthless intellect. Its glacial self-assurance enabled Blunt to pursue a fifty-year career of high scholarship and low treach-ery. Of all the people I interviewed who believed they knew Blunt well, there was only one who could recall seeing more than one side of his multifaceted personality. This was Rosamond Leh-mann, one of Britain's most distinguished novelists. She was able to penetrate Blunt's mask to catch glimpses of the intensely vulnerable and guilt-ridden rebel who hid his real face from everyone else. Now in her mid-eighties, Miss Lehmann nonethe-less looked no older than a comfortable sixty on the autumn afternoon when she opened the door of her pink-stucco London townhouse in a quiet backwater of Kensington.

Self-spoken and hesitant at first, Miss Lehmann apologized for not being able to see properly after her recent eye operation. But when she had settled down in her cozy front room surrounded by the mementos of a lifetime of literary success, she quickly relaxed. Unprompted, she seemed to anticipate my questions and began to pour out her vivid memories of that lost hothouse world of Cambridge intellectuals of which she and Blunt had once been a part.

'It doesn't seem possible that we're living in the same country as the one I knew before the war,' Rosamond Lehmann sighed. Her first novel, *Dusty Answer*, was published to enormous critical success in 1927. Set in post-World War I Cambridge, it is a personally revealing account of a young woman's struggle to come to terms with the emotional complexities of her adult love for childhood boyfriends, and her yearning to understand the realities of homosexual attachments. The heroine of *Dusty Answer* sets out to 'dissect him and make notes, learn him by heart and marvel at' the mysteriously attractive boy in her life. But she never does, and finally she leaves Cambridge, which 'had disliked and distrusted her and all other females'.

Talking with Rosamond Lehmann about the Cambridge she knew and wrote about so brightly, I could see clearly that time had not dimmed the psychological insight that made her an international literary celebrity before she was twenty. Blunt, she recalled, had been introduced to her by her brother, John, in 1928 or 1929, when he was an undergraduate at Trinity College. The two often encountered one another in later years as they both shared friends in intellectual circles of the so-called Bloomsbury group. Miss Lehmann explained that most of the brilliant Cambridge graduates of her generation gravitated towards this loose but influential group of writers, artists and thinkers who were challenging the conventional English cultural, political and artistic values.

The center around which this celebrated circle of friends and lovers revolved was novelist Virginia Woolf and her husband, Leonard, an active socialist and publisher who ran the Hogarth Press. The stellar throng included novelist E. M. Forster, economist John Maynard Keynes, biographer Lytton Strachey, artist Roger Fry, art critic Clive Bell, and Vanessa, his artist wife, who was Virginia Woolf's younger sister. On the periphery hovered the philosopher-mathematician Bertrand Russell and the expatriate American poet T. S. Eliot.

'Bloomsbury' was synonymous with a style that was outspoken, iconoclastic, and well to the left of the political center. But Miss Lehmann could not recall any occasion when Blunt ever mentioned politics. 'In fact, I never thought of him as anything other than a rather aloof and erudite academic,' she said. She was aware that he was fond of her because he always singled her out. 'But I never really liked him,' she added firmly. 'I always found Anthony too aloof and too coldly intellectual.'

Miss Lehmann struck up close relationships with many of Blunt's Cambridge friends. The outrageous and sharp-witted Guy Burgess was her particular favorite. 'In contrast to Anthony, Guy was not only brilliant, but very affectionate and warm-hearted,' she explained. 'I was very fond of him.' He was a welcome weekend guest at her country home near Oxford. 'He'd bathe in the river,' she recalled, 'then sit up very late talking politics to anybody who would listen.'

Blunt, Burgess and many other friends of Rosamond Lehmann's

were intellectual Marxists. She explained that many of them sympathized with the Communists because they were violently opposed to appeasement of Hitler. In 1928 she had married Wogan Philipps, on Oxford graduate and an old Etonian who went off to Spain in 1936 to drive an ambulance for the Republicans. After her husband was wounded, he made a Pauline conversion to communism. They were divorced before Philipps succeeded to the title of Lord Milford in 1962. As Britain's first publicly declared Communist baron, he took his seat in the House of Lords only to demand the abolition of that hereditary chamber. The writer and critic Cyril Connolly, who was also a friend and admirer of Rosamond Lehmann, compared her, with her own moderate political views, to 'the Alcazar of Toledo, an irreducible bastion of the bourgeoisie entirely surrounded by Communists'.

'I was probably the first person outside those immediately involved to know that Anthony was involved in some way with spying or treason,' Miss Lehmann told me. The first inkling of his treachery came from Goronwy Rees, a promising young fellow of All Souls, Oxford's elite graduate college. Rees was also a close associate of both Blunt and Burgess. Miss Lehmann revealed that Rees arrived 'awfully flustered and stressed' one afternoon toward the end of 1936. He insisted on a confidential talk.

'Goronwy said that he had just had the shock of his life,' Miss Lehmann recalled. 'His staggering news was that Guy Burgess had told him that he was a Comintern agent and had tried to recruit him to the Communist cause.

'Goronwy was very fond of me. He said he needed to tell somebody and he thought that I was discreet. But if I ever mentioned it to anybody, he said he'd strangle me.' Miss Lehmann quickly added: 'He said it in such an alarming way that I knew that he meant it.'

'Have they recruited you too, Goronwy?' Miss Lehmann said she asked him. 'Are you going to work with Guy Burgess?'

'Goronwy gave me an ambiguous answer,' she said. Looking back she was sure that he had not told her the truth.

'Goronwy was a thumping liar,' Miss Lehmann added quite

forcefully. 'But at the time I buried it deep inside me.' She admits that she wanted to believe Rees. She explained that his deviousness and fascination for women were well portrayed by novelist Elizabeth Bowen. Rees appears in thin disguise in her *Death of the Heart*, a novel published in 1938, which describes the fatal love affair between a teenage girl and an 'arriviste' philanderer named Eddie. 'It is not an entirely accurate portrait of Goronwy because no novelist makes a portrait as a journalist would,' Miss Lehmann cautioned. 'But Eddie's manners, his emotion, and his treachery capture Goronwy very well.'

So by the mid-1930s, Miss Lehmann knew that Burgess was a Communist agent. She suspected Rees, and wondered about the involvement of their friend Blunt. But it was not until Burgess defected to Moscow in 1951 that an incident convinced her that it was Blunt, not Burgess, who had been at the center of the web of treachery that had ensnared her friends.

Miss Lehmann explained that Blunt was always solicitous whenever he encountered her after 1938. He finally blew his cover in 1956, after Guy Burgess and another diplomat, Donald Maclean, had appeared at a press conference in Moscow. Blunt immediately sought her out at a small cocktail party at a mutual friend's flat in Eaton Square.

'Can I give you a lift home?' Blunt asked after a few moments of polite conversation. Miss Lehmann thought his offer strange. He knew that she lived only two hundred yards away at the other corner of London's grandest residential area. But he pressed her to accept, explaining that he had arranged a car to take him on to a dinner engagement.

'The moment I got into the cab, Anthony burst into tears,' she said. 'He covered his face with his hands and muttered in a choked voice, "Can you forgive me? Can you ever forgive me?"'

'"Forgive you for what?" I asked. "Whatever's the matter, Anthony?"' He kept shaking his head until the cab drew up to her front door.

'Anthony sort of waved me away, so I got out.' She remembers watching him with his face over his hands, shaking with sobs, as she shut the door and the cab drove away. 'It was an extra-ordinary scene.'

At the time, Miss Lehmann thought Blunt was very drunk. But twenty years later, after Blunt's public exposure as a spy, she learned two important facts that caused her to revise her opinion: the British government revealed that Blunt had been repeatedly subjected to rigorous interrogation throughout the fifties, and Blunt's eldest brother, Wilfred, told her that around the time of his brother's tearful breakdown in the cab, their mother had also become worried about his strained and gaunt appearance. Miss Lehmann is now convinced that in 1956 Blunt was on the verge of cracking under the strain and had tried to appeal to her in a moment of intoxicated weakness in the cab.

'Anthony wanted me to forgive him for something for which he was deeply, deeply guilty. But it was something that he just could not bring himself to reveal.' Miss Lehmann believes she caught sight of a tortured man that evening in Eaton Square, a man who had lived so long behind the mask of treachery that he was permanently trapped by his own deceit.

'After that I did not see Anthony again for over twenty years,' Miss Lehmann mused. Then, a few weeks after his exposure, he telephoned her out of the blue and asked whether he could come over. 'As he was an old friend, I thought it would be kind, but I could not think why he should want to come and see me.'

After Blunt arrived, they chatted inconsequentially while she poured him drink after drink. Not until he had consumed what Miss Lehmann described as 'an immense quantity of gin', did he explain the real reason for his visit.

'I came to tell you that there was not a word of truth in anything Goronwy Rees said,' Blunt blurted out. Miss Lehmann told me that she thought at first he was referring to Rees's deathbed confession to author Andrew Boyle, whose book *The Climate of Treason* had blown Blunt's cover once and for all. But on reflection she believes Blunt may have suspected all along that Goronwy had told her about Burgess's attempt to recruit him. 'I confessed as soon as I knew all my friends were safe,' Blunt assured her. But he was also careful to assert that he was of far more use to the British than he ever was to the Russians.

'Anthony then got up, gave me a kiss, and said, "I must go now." ' Miss Lehmann asked him to visit her again. 'He said he would, but he never even telephoned me. I think Anthony was anxious to discover how much I knew about him from Guy and Goronwy. He was really only checking up on me. He wanted to know how much I knew about him and whether, in any sense, I could still be dangerous to him.'

The silences between my questions and Rosamond Lehmann's answers grew longer. 'This is going to be a very difficult book for you to write, because you will have to tell the story of an enigma.' She paused, then offered a final bit of advice: 'The only way you will be able to make sense of Anthony Blunt's story is to treat it like a psychological thriller.'

Our discussions had evidently stirred many memories. When I left that evening I worried that I might have raised too many ghosts. My concern was allayed when I heard a few days later that she had told her grandson that our afternoon had brought her closer to a new understanding of a man she believed to be 'a very alarming personality'.

It is one thing to unravel a psychological thriller of fiction. But it is an entirely different matter when it comes to real life. It had taken a long, long time to reach the point where my research could prompt someone as knowing as Rosamond Lehmann to tell a confidant that I was on the right track. I had been dealing with the results of hundreds of interviews, and over a period of years, I had found discrepancies in people's stories that complicated the story of Blunt in unexpected ways, which raised the problem, of course, of what twist or turn was the proper lead for me to follow.

I had discussed these problems with my editor, a heartless man in terms of his response to these complexities, because he insisted that I locate *documents* on Blunt. 'There is always a paper trail' was how he put it. 'You have to take the paper trail and build a chronology of Blunt's life. Lawyers would call this charting. It's what a good case officer would do in intelligence. It takes time. It's hard work.' Once this chronology was done, then I could return to my interviewing. The paper trail would give me the necessary checks and balances to help evaluate the leads of what people were telling me about Blunt. And in some cases, seemingly innocuous pieces of paper would force truly telling new information from people who had never spoken for the record.

I believed at first that documents would be nearly impossible – if not totally impossible – to find. To the best of my knowledge, other authors writing on British intelligence had always told me that their work was always hampered by an almost total lack of documents in the British archives. But I had been given my marching orders, and I began to dig into the US archives in Washington. To my surprise a large body of British material surfaced. I began cross-checking the sources. In one instance there amounted to thousands of pages of documents and reports on Communist agents and associated countersubversion. In England my researcher Andrew Lownie, a Cambridge history graduate, found more documents, including letters, official records and writings that had never been analysed by other historians. This documentation enabled me to go back to sources to ask for confirmation or denial of what existed on paper.

Here, I faced a new problem. The more I worked with this new documentation, the more I cross-checked it with interviews, the more I became impressed with the mask of treachery that Blunt had built as a shield for his operations.

I came to the conclusion that Blunt had lived his whole life as a lie. Unfortunately, as time passed, the lies of Blunt's life had come to be accepted as truth by the public. For the real story of Anthony Blunt's life shows how a superbly sophisticated Soviet intelligence operation exploited the failures of British society for Soviet purposes. The Blunt story would not have been possible but for the problems of the British educational system, the ambiguities of its political system and the weakness of its intelligence operations. It is also possible to conclude that these flaws in the British system, which were so skillfully manipulated by the

Soviets, were so great that they explain why for so many years the British government has never allowed the story of Anthony Blunt to be told. Unraveling of the psychological-thriller aspects of Blunt's life therefore has great significance for the governments on both sides of the Atlantic.

Today, it is common knowledge that the British security services suspected Blunt's treason in the 1950s. As far as the public was concerned, however, the first break in the case occurred in 1979 when British journalist Andrew Boyle concluded a series of remarkable investigative interviews and published his shocking book, *The Climate of Treason*. (It caused an immediate sensation in London and was published a short while later in America under a new title, *The Fourth Man*.) Boyle made the case that there had to have been a Fourth Man in a ring of upper-class English spies that the Russians had recruited from Cambridge University. That spy ring had come to light when Guy Burgess and Donald Maclean had defected to Moscow in 1951. The 'missing diplomats', as they became known, were assumed to have been the First Man and Second Man in the ring. Their Cambridge contemporary, Kim Philby, had also come under suspicion of being their accomplice. Many years after official exoneration, the former high-ranking British intelligence officer confounded his investigators by identifying himself as the so-called Third Man when he fled to Moscow in 1963.

That same year Blunt's secret career was uncovered, and in return for immunity from prosecution, he confessed to MI5 in 1964 and became the Fourth Man. It had taken Boyle years to overcome what he described as 'Britain's highly restrictive Official Secrets Act and the natural deceitfulness of spies' to build his case. Britain's stringent libel laws prevented him from naming Sir Anthony Blunt as the Fourth Man in the first edition of his book. But Boyle's work provided sufficient pointers to the real identity of the person he code-named 'Maurice' for the press and members of Parliament to force the government's hand. Prime Minister Margaret Thatcher surprised everyone, including Boyle, by not attempting to sweep the whole matter under the carpet of official secrecy. On 15 November 1979, in a statement to the House of Commons, she named Blunt as a former Soviet spy.

The prime minister's revelation that, for sixteen years, Blunt had been kept safe from exposure under a secret immunity deal shocked the nation almost as much as her confirmation that the Queen's art adviser was a self-confessed Russian spy. But Boyle's success in piercing the cocoon of official silence to expose Blunt did not bring the full disclosures he had hoped for. The government quickly reimposed its traditional bureaucratic secrecy. It refused a parliamentary commission of inquiry and did not make any comment beyond the Prime Minister's brief statement. A week later, the veil of official secrecy became a veil of official hypocrisy. Blunt, without so much as a blush, invoked the Official Secrets Act to avoid answering questions at his one and only press conference.

Outraged newspaper editors condemned Blunt's brief appearance as a 'cynically stage-managed Establishment set piece'. It was not insignificant that Blunt had said that the British system was 'better than the American'. His preference was not simply an admission of his antipathy toward the United States. Blunt knew that he could rely on British law to protect him from the full consequences of his treacherous secrets. Whereas, if he were an American citizen, congressional inquiries and the Freedom of Information Act would have enabled journalists and elected officials to root out the real extent of his treachery and the conspiracy behind the subsequent official cover-up.

Criminal prosecution and imprisonment threaten anyone in Britain who publicly discloses or passes to an unauthorized person any bureaucratic document or fact that the government deems officially secret. Ever since 1911, when the fear of German subversion and Irish nationalism panicked Parliament into passing the all-embracing Official Secrets Act, this draconian law has muzzled debate and screened from public access information on many sensitive issues. Newspapers and book publishers can be prohibited from printing facts obtained by anyone from government documents or officials. In other words, there *are* limits on the free press in England. The government has the absolute right to withhold any fact or document it does not choose to release or declassify under the so-called thirty-year rule.

British official secrecy also goes to extreme lengths to protect the two principal intelligence and security organizations: MI5, the Home Office's internal-security network, and MI6, the Foreign Office's overseas Secret Intelligence Service (SIS). So secret is MI6 supposed to be that no government official knowingly admitted to its existence. The London headquarters of both organizations, though well known to journalists, are an official secret not to be printed in newspapers. Although both MI5 and MI6 have been in existence since before World War I, no records of either organization have ever been formally declassified. Furthermore, current or former members of MI5 and MI6 who communicate intelligence information to outsiders do so at the risk of criminal prosecution. So do those who 'incite' them to give information, or anyone who publishes it.

Despite all these deterrents, the skeletons in closets have continued to rattle; disturbing information about Blunt and his associates has continued to leak out. Many former British intelligence officers, who played a key role in Blunt's case, are more concerned about the continuing governmental cover-up than possible prosecution. They have continued to leak information that suggests Soviet penetration of Britain's intelligence services has been – and perhaps still is – far more serious than officially admitted.

In response to these and other charges, the government has been forced to acknowledge that Britain's security services conducted a series of intensive secret internal investigations. These officially unproductive inquiries were intended to root out longterm Russian penetration agents like Blunt, Burgess, Maclean and Philby, who because of their deep cover were dubbed 'moles'. 'Mole hunting' has become a lucrative field for British journalists, writers and even academics.

Circumstantial evidence has surfaced to suggest that the most important Soviet mole of all was the late Sir Roger Hollis, the head of MI5 from 1956 to 1965. The charges were made by Peter Wright, MI5's former 'mole-hunter-in-chief', who wrote his memoir *Spycatcher* from retirement in Australia, where he is safe from imprisonment under the Official Secrets Act.

The British government, perhaps fearing that Wright's disclosures would set a dangerous precedent and encourage other intelligence officers to spill even more politically damaging revelations, took the issue of confidentiality of its former intelligence agents to the courts in Australia, England, Scotland, New Zealand and Hong Kong. In the furor the legal battle provoked, writers and journalists who had consulted with former intelligence officers were threatened with prosecution, and stern official letters of warning were sent to all surviving MI5 and MI6 officers reminding them of their lifetime oath of secrecy. Newspaper were injuncted and intelligence officers were banned from publishing their memoirs. When the government lost the final round of their two-year legal battle against Peter Wright in October 1988, a new Official Secrets Act was introduced into Parliament. Despite protest, it was steamrollered into law in the spring of 1989 and it effectively prohibits any past or present British intelligence officer from discussing even historic cases without permission – and it imposes a criminal sanction for publishing such information in the UK *even it is already in print abroad*!

The government in Britain may be able to muzzle its own citizens, but it cannot silence former American intelligence officers. These professionals have long shared the belief of their British colleagues that it is time for the full truth to be told. In the United States, former CIA and FBI agents can speak more freely on the record than their British counterparts.

Among the readily accessible and hospitable network of retired intelligence officers centered on Washington there exists a group with strong British connections and interests. This group was led, until his death in 1986, by James Murphy, the London chief of the OSS (Office of Strategic Services) counterintelligence section known as X-2, which had access to the most sensitive British wartime secrets. Murphy was the mentor of the CIA's legendary spycatcher, the late James Angleton, who liaised with Kim Philby in London and later in Washington. Angleton shared a Ryder Street office at MI6 headquarters in London with Norman Holmes Pearson, a Yale professor of English, the unofficial American representative on Sir John Masterman's XX Committee (Double-Cross Committee), running German double agents. Also in this group is Robert J. Lamphere, a former FBI counter-intelligence agent who provided the British security services with the information that led to the exposure of the atomic physicist Klaus Fuchs and Donald Maclean.

The constraints of the Official Secrets Act make such frank disclosures about the real nature of Soviet operations impossible in Britain. Former MI5 and MI6 agents cannot go on the record. But the information they have provided me has helped their American colleagues construct a professional reinterpretation of the Blunt case. Thanks to their help it has been possible to make sense of the clues that lie at the heart of the case.

This analysis shows that Blunt must have been a much more dangerous Russian agent than the British government has revealed.

'Blunt's true importance to his Russian masters,' said Robert Crowley, a former senior member of the CIA, in a wide-ranging interview, 'can be determined from the fact that he was the only identified, native-born Briton known to have achieved a supervisory level in directing and controlling his fellow countrymen. By that I mean people who were supporting and servicing Soviet intelligence.'

Crowley bases his assertion on his solid professional knowledge of Soviet undercover operations. He can dissect the arcane minutiae of KGB operations with the incisiveness and detail of a Harvard Law professor. His mental card index of Russian agents is phenomenal. His years at the CIA studying Soviet operations have given him an encyclopedic knowledge of the KGB.

Tall and contemplative, Crowley projects a courtliness that belies his many years in the tough world of military intelligence. His patient courtesy and ability to detect the vital connections in an enormous volume of data made him a formidable counter-intelligence officer and debriefer of Soviet defectors. Crowley's authority is highly respected by the former MI5 agents who know him. So while they may be legally constrained from speaking on-the-record for themselves, they have concurred with much of Crowley's thoughtful reconstruction of the Blunt case.

The first point that Crowley made to me – and he made it very strongly – was that he does not believe that convincing answers have yet been given to three central questions:

1 Why did Blunt and his contemporaries from the privileged English class turn traitor?
2 How did the Russians recruit and expand their Cambridge network so rapidly?
3 What was the full extent and nature of Soviet penetration?

'It is difficult to find a Soviet anywhere in the Blunt story as it has been told so far,' says Crowley. 'They are the missing players in the drama.' The reason, he speculates, is the nonavailability of MI5 surveillance records from the twenties and thirties. Without an accurate picture of the Russian presence in Britain at the time, it has been impossible to identify how the Soviets might have recruited, trained, directed, disciplined, sustained and rewarded their British spies.

'It's a simple fact of life that major Soviet espionage networks are not spawned in a laboratory dish. Their spies are initiated, organized and run by Soviet case officers.' Therefore, Crowley suggested, any self-respecting counterintelligence officer taking on the case would start by trying to establish the How? When? and By Whom? of Blunt's recruitment.

'No one has yet come up with an explanation of Blunt's recruitment that fits what we know about Soviet operational practice,' Crowley declares. 'Everyone has accepted Blunt's version and, at best, that is highly suspect.' He points out that Blunt and Philby were the only two members of the spy ring to have gone on the public record and that both have been taken at their word. That, suggests Crowley, was astonishing; spies invariably try to conceal the roots of their treachery with false justifications.

'Focus on *how* the Russians carried out their recruiting of the Cambridge ring,' Crowley advised, 'and then you will discover how the seemingly disconnected pieces of the Blunt case come together.'

Thanks to the guidance of Crowley and others, I turned up a remarkable number of new pieces of the puzzle in still secret British documents that have been uncovered in the United States. The Official Secrets Act does not extend offshore and these discoveries contradict assertions made in other books whose writers had to rely on unsupported interviews.

For example, new information on Burgess, Maclean, Philby – and Blunt – has been culled from FBI files obtained under the US Freedom of Information Act. A hoard of 'Most Secret' British MI5 reports in the files of the US Embassy in London was gathering dust for years on the shelves of the National Archives in Washington. These reveal the secret counterintelligence data that was provided to the United States on a regular basis by the British between the wars. It shows, for the first time, that the extent of the Soviet penetration effort was indeed recognized by the British authorities at an early stage in the 1920s. Then there are the papers of Professor Norman Holmes Pearson at Yale. They include not only the diaries he kept while an intelligence officer during World War II, but also many confidential reports on the inner workings of the British counterintelligence services. Taken all together, the material reveals the weakness that enabled Russian moles like Philby to take control of a whole section of MI6 in 1945.

Assembly of these intelligence snapshots in chronological order illuminates both the details *and* the broad picture of the clandestine Soviet assault on Britain and the United States. The documents reveal that the nature if not the objective of the Russian subversion *was* known to the British authorities – and *was* communicated to the United States – even before Blunt and his associates went up to Cambridge. This must raise serious questions of either negligence or criminal high-level conspiracy within the British security services years before MI5 opened its doors to Blunt, Philby and Burgess.

A more alarming overall picture of Soviet penetration emerges from the new evidence. Many of its aspects confirm the dire warnings issued by MI5's former mole-hunter Peter Wright: 'The British establishment has never accepted that it was, en masse, penetrated by the Russians.' But now that it has been documented that this penetration began earlier, went deeper and was more extensive than previously recognized, it supports Wright's conclusion that 'it was simply not correct to say that the extent of the penetration was thoroughly investigated.'

With documents to work from, with interviews that cross-check the documents, it is now possible to view the recruitment of Anthony Blunt in the same way a professional counterintelligence officer would do it. (One of the questions I will discuss later is the failure of MI5 and MI6 to create a Research and Analysis Department [R&A] prior to the 1970s, and the effects of this failure.) Using as a starting point the close examination of Blunt's background and character, it becomes obvious why he was such a potentially valuable agent for the Russians. In turn, this gives new insight into how the Russians recruited him, why he was trusted by Moscow with a supervisory role, whom else Blunt recruited and their importance, and what information Blunt betrayed.

Building the case step by step, certain patterns and hitherto unappreciated facts emphasize the critical importance of the Blunt case. They include:

- One of Lenin's first acts after coming to power in Russia in 1917 was to order two émigrés in London, Maxim Litvinov and Theodore Rothstein, to set up a network of subversion. They were funded by diamonds smuggled into England.

- By 1920, the Soviet Union had a trade delegation in London. It was led by Leonid Krassin, who imported all the tools and talents necessary to establish a far-reaching intelligence underground in Britain.

- From the outset, the Soviet Union has been sophisticated and successful in penetrating the British ruling establishment and government on many levels. The case of Anthony Blunt is a perfect example of the cleverness with which the Soviets have manipulated the idiosyncrasies of the British system.

- There were two waves of Soviet penetration in England before Blunt was recruited in the third wave. This wave was the agents recruited in the late 1920s not only at Cambridge and Oxford but also, and possibly even more importantly, at Birmingham and other universities that specialized in electronics, mathematics and engineering.

- Contrary to popular belief, there were Marxists in the secret society of the Apostles of Cambridge before Anthony Blunt joined their ranks. In terms of treason, however, Blunt was not the Fourth Man. He was the First Man, the primary agent.

- Also contrary to popular belief, Guy Burgess did *not* recruit Anthony Blunt.

- A major key to Blunt's success was sexual blackmail and his network of homosexual contacts within the British establishment.

- With the outbreak of World War II, Soviet agents were slipped into positions of power in MI5 and MI6 with special attention being paid to the infiltration of the counterespionage divisions. This was deemed vital to Moscow, because such penetrations were the best way to keep tabs on the success of Soviet operations. They also allowed Moscow to monitor the intentions of the principal enemies of the Soviet state, Great Britain and the United States.

- Blunt personally recruited agents who penetrated British intelligence according to the guidelines established by Moscow.

- Blunt also recruited agents at Cambridge who penetrated the administration of President Franklin D. Roosevelt.

- The Cambridge moles associated with Blunt helped insert Communist agents into the State Department and the wartime Office of Strategic Services (OSS), the predecessor of the CIA.

- Blunt's personal handling of diplomatic pouches belonging to Allied embassies during World War II helped facilitate the Soviet takeover of Eastern Europe at the conclusion of the war.

- Scientists associated with the Cambridge network played a critical role in stealing the secrets of the atomic bomb and passing them to Moscow.

- The Blunt network in MI5 falsified legends so that after World War II the CIA hired, for covert operations, agents who were allegedly anti-Communist but who were, in reality, working for the Soviet cause.

- Instead of protecting documents that compromised the pro-Hitler activities of the Duke of Windsor and the Duke of Kent, Blunt passed this damaging information to the Russians.

- Blunt was always one step ahead of MI5 because of help he received from one of the most senior officers within MI5, who has so far escaped investigation for being a Soviet mole.

- Blunt remained 'an agent of influence' for the Russians long after he was suspected by the British of being a Soviet spy.

- In 1951, Blunt orchestrated the escape of Burgess and Maclean to Moscow.

- In 1957, Blunt was reactivated to contact Philby and six years later was the principal beneficiary of Philby's defection to Moscow.

- Blunt left two deadly legacies: the first involved the fact that the Blunt case embarrassed both American and British intelligence agencies so that both governments had a vested interest in preventing the Blunt story from being told. More important, the Blunt case soured the relations between the American intelligence-operations people and their British counterparts. This distrust continues today.

2 'French Leanings'

'You must admit,' Anthony Blunt bragged to his elder brother Wilfrid, after his treason had been made public, 'I'm a very good actor.'

Published six months before his death in December 1986, Wilfrid Blunt's memoir reveals just how good an actor Anthony was. Despite Wilfrid's close, lifelong relationship with Anthony, he never suspected that his brother was a Soviet agent. Anthony, he insisted, withheld the 'whole ghastly truth' until after the Prime Minister exposed him in the House of Commons.

Wilfrid Blunt's account shows that he, like other writers, accepted Anthony's explanation as to how he became a Marxist and 'was ensnared by the machinations of Guy Burgess'. (Anthony had read and by implication approved that draft of Wilfrid's memoir before his own death.) We also know now that Anthony went to considerable lengths, both privately and publicly, to portray Burgess as his recruiter and to implicate his friend as being the First Man in the Cambridge spy ring. In his only post-exposure press statement, Blunt insisted: 'I was persuaded by Guy Burgess that I could best serve the cause of anti-Fascism by joining him in his work for the Russians.'

Close scrutiny, however, shows that Blunt had carefully worded his only public pronouncement so as to minimize his role in the Cambridge spy ring. He declared that he had become a Marxist 'in the mid-1930s', when the Western governments were appeasing Hitler, and it had seemed to him 'that the Communist Party constituted the only bulwark against Fascism'. Guy Burgess was 'one of the most remarkable, brilliant people I had ever known,' Blunt said. Burgess also had persuaded him 'that the Marxist interpretation was right'.

Blunt portrayed Burgess as the mastermind of the Cambridge Communists. And by inflating his friend's influence, Blunt successfully diminished the public's idea of his own role in the conspiracy, describing it merely as being an impulsive response to his friend's 'brilliant' appeal to 'assist' him to defeat the forces of Fascism.

When questioned by reporters, Blunt said that it had been Burgess's idea that he should become the resident Soviet talent spotter in Cambridge. Blunt then said that after the war he realized what he called 'the true facts about Russia' and that helping the Soviets had been 'a huge mistake'. But, Blunt declared, he had put his conscience before his country. For this reason he had not warned the authorities about Burgess because he 'could not denounce my friends'.

To believe Blunt's story – and to date too many have taken him at his word – is to accept that Guy Burgess was his Marxist mentor. But on closer examination it is Burgess who emerges as Blunt's scapegoat.

Blunt went to great lengths to ensure general acceptance of his account. And one reason why no one has yet challenged it is that Blunt – and the British government – have shared a continuing interest in creating a smokescreen that hid the real story. As we shall see, Blunt and British intelligence combined forces to keep the truth from the public and England's allies.

So far, no published accounts have challenged this official cover story. Peter Wright's *Spycatcher* and every British writer who has followed Andrew Boyle's ground-breaking analysis of the Cambridge Comintern appear to have accepted Blunt's version of events.

Wilfrid Blunt, in his memoir (endorsed by his brother), says that Burgess did not recruit Anthony until the winter of 1936, *after* he and Anthony had both returned from a summer trip to the Soviet Union. But London *Sunday Times* reporters Simon Freeman and Barrie Penrose, in their *Conspiracy of Silence*, disputed Blunt's public assertion that he 'became a communist, or more particularly a Marxist, in 1935–36'. They concluded Blunt was 'attempting to disguise the fact that, by the beginning of 1934 at the latest, he was, like his friend Guy Burgess, communist.'

Yet despite the wide variety of dates for Blunt's actual recruitment, there has been a truly remarkable agreement that Burgess's recruitment preceded and was instrumental in determining Blunt's own decision to become a Soviet agent. It has been echoed with surprising unanimity by such disparate authorities as Peter Wright in *Spycatcher* and Kim Philby himself in 1988. But Philby, it has to be assumed, was speaking from Moscow under the KGB's direction and was out again to deceive. He refused to be drawn on 'operational details', but encouraged British journalist Phillip Knightley to infer that Burgess was indeed the 'mastermind', with a Delphic assertion that Burgess was the one 'who maintained all the links with all of us'.

The real facts, according to the documented record that has now been uncovered, are very different. Taking these into account a counterintelligence officer would point out that:

1 Blunt was a self-confessed Russian agent who liked to boast about his ability to deceive.

2 None of the dates given for Blunt's conversion are consistent.

3 The Russians would not have employed a newly graduated Burgess with his mercurial temper to recruit Blunt, an aloof research fellow who was six years his senior.

Blunt's apparent inability to recall the pivotal date of his supposed 'Damascus Road' conversion to Marxism is a glaring flaw in his alibi. Did it take place in 1935, as he insisted after his exposure – or was it two years earlier, as he suggested in a farewell lecture in 1972 to the Courtauld Institute? More significant still is how such a meticulous mind as Anthony Blunt's could have forgotten so momentous a milepost in his career. The logical conclusion is that Blunt went to his grave an unrepentant spy.

American authorities on Soviet undercover operations have

always been skeptical about the role ascribed to Guy Burgess. They point out that he was an undergraduate until the summer of 1933 and then failed to obtain even a junior fellowship at Cambridge. Blunt implied that he was homosexually infatuated with the younger Burgess. But the presumption that the Russians would have trusted Burgess to sign up an agent so many years his senior does not match with what they know about Soviet operations. Moreover, Home Office files have come to light that show that by the mid-twenties Moscow was operating a highly sophisticated network of Soviet nationals and sympathizers in Britain and at various universities. Under these circumstances, they would not have been likely to use Burgess as a recruiter. More importantly, they never recruited any of their important agents overnight, as Blunt's own account asks us to believe.

Blunt's version of events was not swallowed hook, line and sinker by those MI5 officers who were assigned to handle his case. Arthur Martin wrote to *The Times* of London and complained that he had been hampered by higher authority in his investigations of Soviet moles. Peter Wright, who in 1965 took over the task of hunting them down, testified in 1986, 'It is simply not correct to say that the extent of penetration was thoroughly investigated.'

The British authorities dismissed Wright's assertions in *Spycatcher*, but still refused to release, even for an Australian judge, the results of their top-secret investigations. But the Most Secret British contemporary documents that have come to light while researching this book reveal that MI5 knew about Russian subversion in British universities in the early 1920s – long before Blunt was ensnared. This new documentation undermines the credibility of the convenient cover story that it was not until a decade later that Guy Burgess became the prime recruiter of the so-called Cambridge moles.

Blunt, in the supposedly full and frank confession that he made in 1964 in return for a secret immunity deal, was careful to overplay Burgess's importance. According to Arthur Martin, however, who first obtained Blunt's confession, Blunt never told him the whole truth. Martin remains skeptical about how truthful Blunt was with him. Although Martin did not himself investigate all the Cambridge connections, he considered it significant that not until the year after Burgess's death in the Soviet Union was he able to persuade Blunt to confess.

Dead men tell no lies. They cannot contradict the living. Given the extent to which it has become clear that Blunt lied and obfuscated about his career as a Russian spy, it would be more plausible to assume that his excuse that he 'could not confess until all my friends were safe' was purely self-serving.

Blaming a friend for leading you astray is the oldest ploy in the book. But it worked for Blunt because everyone believed his eldest brother's account that Anthony's recruitment by Burgess occurred in 'late 1935 or early 1936'. The British government wanted the public to believe Blunt's story about the late date of his recruitment almost more than the old spy himself did. So no one bothered to check the available records inside and outside the United Kingdom. These put quite a different interpretation on the sequence of events – and how the Russians *really* went about recruiting spies at Cambridge.

The question now becomes this: if Guy Burgess was *not* the so-called First Man, as has been believed for so long, who was?

The clues emerge from Blunt's attempts to deflect attention from the real culprit.

Cambridge University was, and still is, an intensely hierarchical society. The same holds true for Russia's secret service, the KGB. Therefore, when it was desired to recruit a senior member of the university such as Blunt, no one would have known better than the Russians that this was not a task for an undergraduate. Nor would they have picked as their number-one recruiter in Cambridge a drifting postgraduate student like Burgess. If he was as brilliant as Blunt claimed, Moscow would have asked why he could not secure tenure at any college. Counterintelligence experts repeatedly stress that the Soviets ran a highly disciplined and centrally controlled network. They believe that Moscow would not have given any authority to someone with Burgess's disreputable character and notorious lack of self-discipline because he would have been difficult, if not impossible, to control.

'On the basis of extensive research of Soviet operational practice,' ex-CIA specialist Crowley told me, 'Blunt, rather than Burgess, emerges as a more probable First Man.' Crowley contends that with Blunt at the center instead of the periphery of the Cambridge net, the inconsistencies with Soviet practice which he sees in the 'official' account, disappear. The most important of these inconsistencies, he stresses, is the supposedly central role of Guy Burgess. 'From what is known about Burgess,' Crowley says, 'he appears an increasingly unlikely candidate for the Cambridge recruiter.' Moscow could not have failed to note all of Burgess's failures and personality weaknesses. 'All these add up,' Crowley concludes, 'to a negative argument against the recruitment of Burgess as prospective "principal agent."'

'Blunt on the other hand,' Crowley explained, 'would have impressed the Russians as very sound agent material.' American counterintelligence specialists leave no doubt that both the FBI and the CIA concluded Blunt must be considered the most talented, and therefore the most dangerous, of all the Cambridge group.

'The Soviets are thorough and cautious in the process of agent selection,' Crowley explains. He stresses the endless patience that the Russians take in vetting foreign recruits and believes that it could not have taken place in the brief period allowed by Blunt's chronology.

Crowley believes that the Soviet officers who identified Blunt as a potential recruit would have given him high marks for his icy self-control and his obvious intelligence. As a rising young academic, he had promising access to potentially valuable information and people in authority. Blunt's well-connected family would also have been of interest to Moscow because it held the promise of even greater access.

'Access leads to information, and information was what Moscow wanted,' Crowley says. 'But make no mistake about it –

they would also have taken endless trouble to satisfy themselves that the brilliant young Blunt was driven by a commitment: a commitment that they could divine and one that made him susceptible to discipline and control.'

To establish whether Blunt's commitment was controllable, the Russians would have examined the minutiae of his family background and school career. They would have been looking for clues to 'his personality, his prejudices and motivations'.

To conduct an analysis of Blunt as Crowley believes the Soviets would have done, the details of his early life and parental influence provided by his eldest brother Wilfrid must be more carefully examined than has been done to date.

The real story of Anthony Blunt's extraordinary life begins during an unseasonal heat wave on 26 September 1907, in the vicarage of Holy Trinity Church, Bournemouth. Anthony was born on this date into an upper-middle-class family that already consisted of two brothers: Christopher, a chubby two-year-old, and Wilfrid, who was six.

The Reverend Arthur Stanley Vaughan Blunt was a solid, hearty man, well attuned to the conventional propriety of his parishioners. Bournemouth was a south-coast town that was the very model of Edwardian respectability; it was a favorite with retired Indian Army officers and convalescents.

The Reverend Blunt, who preferred to be called Stanley, was the son of the suffragan bishop of Hull. Like his father, Stanley considered himself a 'broad evangelical' in the mainstream of the Church of England. He had a deep suspicion of Roman Catholics and distrusted anything 'popish' such as Baroque architecture. He pronounced God as 'Guard' in accordance with established Church of England practice. A good social mixer, he was just as much as home on the tennis courts as in the pulpit.

According to Wilfrid, his father was a 'good man' but regarded by his sons as 'hearty' and 'distant'. There is a suspicion that there was a resentment of the cold showers and daily family prayers that their father considered part of the regimen necessary to build a Christian character. Wilfrid also noted that their parents both 'tacitly assumed we would all eventually want to be ordained'.

Mrs Blunt was a puritanical teetotaler who forbade the consumption of strong drink under her roof and fussed about her husband's pipe-smoking. Wilfrid describes his mother as a 'woman of infinite goodness and almost puritanical simplicity, incapable of telling the whitest of lies'. A reserved woman, her natural shyness was exaggerated by her deafness in one ear.

Hilda Violet Masters was ten years younger than her bridegroom when Stanley Blunt married her at the turn of the century. As the youngest daughter of an iron-willed matriarch, she had been well trained on how to rule over a household that eventually consisted of maids and governesses in addition to her husband and three sons. She had also brought some needed money and aristocratic connections to the Blunt family. Both were essential to maintaining an upper-class social status on a vicar's modest stipend.

Burke's Landed Gentry, the indispensable guide to England's leading families, listed the Reverend Blunt and his heirs until 1922. But then they were dropped because their closest aristocratic relative was judged 'politically and morally unsound'. He was the Victorian poet, diplomat and adventurer Wilfrid Scawen Blunt. A kind of latter-day Lord Byron, Scawen Blunt had devoted his life to writing passionate verse and martyring his popularity to a campaign for Irish, Indian and Egyptian independence. But it was his seductions of titled ladies that really scandalized Victorian society. According to Wilfrid, his parents never once mentioned the family's second cousin whose name he bore.

If cousin Scawen Blunt's immorality so offended Hilda's highminded piety, what would she have thought if she had lived long enough to see her favorite son denounced as a traitor? She doted on her intelligent sons, who soon learned the importance of concealing from their overbearingly strict mother their secret childhood transgressions. Anthony became her 'Benjamin', and Hilda cosseted him because she was convinced that he was a 'delicate' infant who needed frequent doses of proprietary nursery tonics.

Anthony returned his mother's affection; they remained devoted to each other until the end of her life. This strong maternal bond may well have contributed to Anthony's ability – and determination – to conceal that for most of his life he had systematically betrayed the most cherished ideals and standards of this patriotic, puritanical mother.

The Masters family claimed an aristocratic lineage superior to that of the Blunts. Hilda Masters was a second cousin of the Earl of Strathmore, whose daughter, Lady Elizabeth Bowes-Lyon, became the consort of King George VI and mother of Queen Elizabeth II. According to Wilfrid's recollections, royal connections were also important to the family because of their maternal grandmother's close friendship with the Duchess of Teck.

Grandma Gertrude Emma Masters was the personification of a Victorian matriarch. Although a semi-invalid with a bad leg, she ruled over her family from her pramlike invalid carriage, waving her smelling salts and thumping her silver-topped ebony cane. A formidable campaigner on behalf of temperance and a supporter of Christian charities, she was an 'alarming' figure to her grandsons. By contrast, they held their white-bearded grandfather in special affection. A mild-mannered man, he had served as colonial magistrate in Madras, and retired early from India to a genteel if unostentatious house near the River Thames at Richmond.

Finding herself conveniently close to the Duke and Duchess of Teck's residence at White Lodge in Richmond Park, the redoubtable Grandmama Masters toadied with enthusiasm her aristocratic neighbor's heavy round of Christian charity and temperance work. A punctilious correspondent, she once dispatched a servant with paper and pen to White Lodge when the Duchess failed to respond to one of her letters. But the two remained on warm terms. Their daughters learned to skate together on the park's ponds, and the Blunt boys' Aunt Mabel became a close friend of the Tecks' daughter Princess Mary.

Mary later married George, Duke of York, the oldest surviving son and heir of Edward VII.

When King George V succeeded to the throne in 1910, the Blunts proudly counted the new queen of England as a family patron and friend. According to Wilfrid, his Aunt Mabel and his mother had become confirmed 'royalty snobs'. The whole family went en masse to cheer the coronation procession. Aunt Mabel bound the family's royal correspondence in leather, and for many years his mother and aunt were the honored recipients of hand-me-down dresses, hats and parasols from the royal wardrobe. This was a great family confidence – and one of the 'state' secrets that Anthony never divulged.

The Blunts' royal connections may have been responsible for a dramatic transformation in their lives that took place in 1911. The Reverend Blunt applied to become chaplain of the British embassy church in Paris, and Wilfrid recalls his father announcing matter-of-factly at breakfast one April morning that the family was moving to France. And so the stage was set for the pivotal educational experience that led the Reverend Blunt's youngest son into a career of treachery.

In Anthony's own words, Paris 'coloured the whole of my future development'. The city's effect on Anthony was far-reaching and dramatic. It aroused and shaped his precocious interest in art and architecture. During the formative childhood decade when his home was in the cosmopolitan French capital, he became more and more alienated from what he perceived as the stuffy conventionalities and philistinism of Britain and the British way of life.

Anthony's father had become a person of some importance in the embassy in Paris. The splendor of being part of the most glittering outpost of the British Empire in Europe would have been apparent to Anthony when the king and queen made a state visit to Paris in 1912.

Even the Reverend Blunt's hearty sermons seemed more bearable. Obliged to attend two services each Sunday, Anthony and his brothers now had more to hold their attention than the musty hymnbooks and dull congregation of Holy Trinity Church, Bournemouth. The worshipers at St Michael's were colorful and intriguingly cosmopolitan.

A short walk from the chaplain's residence past the mouth-watering *pâtisseries* was the domed Greek temple guarding the entrance to the Parc Monceau. This grandest of all Parisian gardens has the cultivated rusticity of the classical vistas so beloved of the French sixteenth-century painters. It is easy to imagine you are stepping out of the traffic of the Rue de Cour-celles into a painting by Claude Lorrain or Poussin. The greensward leads to gravel paths that meander through the middle distance like the roads of the Roman *campagna* into groves of trees shading a dark lake where a waterfall, framed by frag-mentary Doric columns, tumbles past the stony stare of carved nymphs. This must have been a magical world for the six-year-old Anthony Blunt and his brothers accustomed to the municipal geranium borders and geometric rose beds of Bournemouth.

'Paris was gloriously and endlessly exciting,' Wilfrid wrote. He must have communicated his own sense of adventure to his youngest brother, for whom he became role model, confidant and guide. Keeping up spurred Anthony's physical and intellectual development. At the age of six he was too tall for the mark painted on Parisian trams that showed who had to pay full fare. The switch in 1912 from age to height caused much anguish to the self-righteous Hilda Blunt. She carried a copy of Anthony's birth certificate in French to persuade the skeptical Paris tramcar con-ductors that her son rode at half fare.

'My earliest recollection connected with works of art is that I can just remember going to the Louvre before the 1914–18 war,' Anthony recalled half a century later. He could not remember which pictures had impressed him, but we have Wilfrid's word that he was soon collecting picture postcards of religious paint-ings. The eldest brother's detailed account of their childhood trips of exploration to Versailles, Malmaison and Saint-Cloud reveal how close he and Anthony became as a result of their shared interest in art.

Christopher, their middle brother, was the odd boy out. According to Wilfrid, he showed no interest in painting or architecture and appears to have rather deliberately distanced himself from them with his single-minded pursuit of coin collecting. Childhood photographs of the three invariably show Christopher scowling. Wilfrid's pointed references to his middle brother's reputation for 'naughtiness' suggest that, as often occurs in sibling trios, the eldest and youngest Blunt may have ganged up on him and seen to it that Christopher was unfairly blamed for their mischievousness. Wilfrid also recounts how they played elaborate practical jokes such as dangling coins attached to virtually invisible black threads out of their windows, and rigging up their father's Pianola to startle visitors with ghostly music.

World War I left a special imprint on Anthony's intellectual and artistic development. When the guns roared out of the crystalline summer skies in 1914, the Blunt brothers were on vacation with relatives in England. Wilfrid, much to his regret, was packed off to his preparatory school. Not until October, after the German advance on Paris had ground to a halt along the banks of the River Marne, was it considered safe for Anthony and Christopher to rejoin their parents in Paris.

Anthony's formal education began when he left his nursery governess and joined Christopher at L'École Villiers, a nearby Parisian day school. He quickly became fluent in French, and although the war had closed the city's museums, he continued his exploration of Paris architecture when Wilfrid came home for vacations. Anthony recalled how he had been 'compelled to look at architecture' and so began a lifelong fascination with the structure, form and decoration of buildings.

Summer holidays in wartime were spent on economical bicycling holidays with the whole family pedaling through Normandy, the Auvergne and Fontainebleau. Wilfrid provides a revealing insight of Mrs Blunt's 'materfamilias' role in his account of how they lodged at the simplest – and presumably cheapest – hotels. But the accommodation was never settled until their mother had been upstairs to 'vet the lavatories'.

Wilfrid also related how they had already begun to compare the frugality of their own home with the generous hospitality of their adopted aunt, an American named Vandervoort. 'Vandy', as she liked to be known, lived in a smart residence in the Boulevard Malesherbes. She was an expatriate with a fortune to match her ample figure. Expensive presents, trips to the circus and drives in the Bois de Boulogne were usually followed by sumptuous teas at Pré-Catelan. It was at Vandy's insistence that the Blunt brothers took their first deliciously sweet sips of Château d'Yquem. When Hilda Blunt found out that her sons had tasted the forbidden liquor, she fretted about Vandy's harmful influence on her sons.

'The chaplain's house,' as Wilfrid wryly observed, 'was not a good jumping-off point for Bohemia.' But thanks to Vandy the Blunt boys began to develop a taste for the pleasures of the world and, perhaps, secretly to question the puritanical values imposed on them at home.

Wilfrid admits that from an early age he fostered Anthony's developing artistic consciousness as a shared reaction against the worthy dullness of their home. Their parents' principal cultural artifacts were wishy-washy Victorian watercolors and shelves of blue-bound devotional works such as *The Psalms in Human Life*.

In 1916, Anthony's parents considered him mature enough to join Christopher at a preparatory school in Sussex, one of the more successful of a number of smallish private schools at Seaford. The two brothers traveled to and from England by train and the Channel steamers that braved drifting mines and prowling U-boats. Wartime travel set the brothers apart from their classmates, whose only experience of the great conflict was sticking pins marked with flags into schoolroom maps.

The Blunts took it for granted that their children had embraced the family's Christian beliefs. But Wilfrid's memoir and the recollections of Anthony's schoolfriend Louis MacNeice reveal that both brothers had begun to question their parents' religiosity at an early age. But neither dared give any voice to their advancing skepticism. They appear to have unconsciously redirected their nascent rebellion against puritanical Christian values into a more acceptable form: a personal crusade against the cultural values of their parents. Yet a strong emotional bond tied Anthony to his mother. Throughout his life, according to Wilfrid, his youngest brother appears to have gone to considerable lengths to avoid hurting his mother's feelings. Rosamond Lehmann had also noted Anthony's deep concern. But the need to preserve that tie also demanded a degree of deviousness and self-concealment on Anthony's part that can only have intensified and deepened his rebellion.

There are clues in Wilfrid's account of their boyhood suggesting that there existed other reasons for Anthony's lifelong rebellion against conventional English life. In 1916, the three brothers, who by that time were all at school in England, spent the Christmas season at the Lancashire estate of their uncle Sir Ralph Assheton. He was a member of Parliament and managed to maintain the life of an Edwardian country gentleman throughout the war.

The liveried footmen, shooting parties, English country-house life alternately fascinated and offended Anthony and his brothers. The snobbish Asshetons, with their obsession with their ancient pedigree and the rows of ancestral portraits lining Downham Hall, made their visiting cousins feel unwelcome. The Eton-educated Asshetons constantly reminded the Blunts of their 'poor-relation' status. Wilfrid noted how they had been made to 'feel inferior, ungrateful and even rebellious'.

The Assheton snubs, both real and imagined, made a deep impact on Anthony. Although he never regarded himself as anything other than a member of the English privileged class, the Asshetons' unbearable snootiness appears to have reinforced his growing conviction that everything in France was more sophisticated and vastly superior to what he knew of in England. 'I developed a very strong French leaning,' Anthony would write, 'which has coloured my whole attitude toward things ever since.'

The first recorded manifestation of Anthony's rebellion was against his father's preference for Gothic architecture. 'At that time my taste was extremely conventional,' Anthony later conceded, noting that this was because his father 'did not encourage him to look at anything later than medieval architecture.' The Reverend Blunt considered seventeenth-century Baroque churches 'vulgar and decadent' expressions of 'popishness' and 'idolatry'. Wilfrid recalled that he was 'rapped over the knuckles for enticing Anthony away from the Gothic which alone it was respectable to admire.'

The values Anthony increasingly rejected were those of his parents. He owed a bigger debt to brother Wilfrid, 'who was six years older and was becoming a painter by the time I was growing up, and had far closer contacts, naturally, with the artistic world.'

Wilfrid set Anthony an example of how to be a cultural and social rebel. Confounding the Reverend Blunt's expectations, his eldest son showed no inclination for the Church. Then he abandoned Oxford for a brief spell to become apprentice painter in a Paris atelier. The irony is that while Wilfrid, through unconventionality and talent, eventually found himself a niche teaching art, Anthony managed to climb to the pinnacle of the art world by dint of conventional scholarship.

3 'Sexual Politics'

'Anthony Blunt had that special ability to enter any role and play it marvelously well,' Robert Cecil said. 'He was a languid man, certainly, but he had a very acute brain.'

Interviews with Blunt at his London flat shortly before his death reinforced Robert Cecil's impression of Blunt as a calculating and ruthless man. As he poured out a sherry before the lunch that punctuated our daylong conversation, Cecil observed how he invited Blunt down to his home. He had offered to drive Blunt over to his brother Wilfrid's nearby home afterward. But Blunt always politely declined.

'I got the impression Anthony would have been most uncomfortable accepting my hospitality,' Cecil observed. 'It would have put him under an obligation to me.'

The setting, we speculated, would have discomfited Blunt. The Cecils' house is on the outskirts of a Hampshire village where cricket matches have been played on the local green since the seventeenth century. Its windows look out past Mrs Cecil's lush flower beds, to cows grazing on the gentle downland slopes beyond the rosebushes. It was the home of a diplomat who retired after a career devoted to preserving the very English values that Blunt set out to destroy. The careers of the two men may have been very different, but they sprang from similar social backgrounds and shared a common heritage and education.

After postwar service in embassies in Europe, Cecil headed the British information services in New York and the Cultural Relations Department. Then he retired to make a second career as a university lecturer and writer of books and articles on contemporary history. When Blunt was publicly unmasked as a Soviet agent, Cecil's intimate knowledge of Blunt's wartime operations caused him to wonder what kind of man could have betrayed so much.

Like Blunt's, Cecil's courteous yet authoritative manner is deeply rooted in the traditions of Britain's privileged class. His family connections are woven more tightly than Blunt's into the fabric of British history. Lean and bespectacled, Cecil still maintains in his mid-seventies the upright bearing of the urbane and confident young diplomat who in 1945 joined his friend Donald Maclean as a first secretary at His Britannic Majesty's Embassy in Washington. He had known Maclean at Cambridge and has written his own book on him.

Recalling Maclean and his own experience in Washington, Cecil explained that Blunt shared, along with Philby and Burgess, a peculiarly British hauteur toward the United States. Cecil speculated that this traditional upper-class British attitude may have played a part in prompting his Cambridge contemporaries to look toward the east rather than west. In the thirties a few intellectuals had begun to sense that the British Empire was on the decline. The United States, by contrast, was a power on the rise. So was the Soviet Union. This was a source of inspiration to young people with leftist sympathies. Cecil's generation had expected to grow up to inherit and rule an empire on which the sun never set. But the cataclysmic upheaval of the First World War had upset that comfortable notion. It had also provided – for those who cared to read it – the writing on the wall that Britain's imperial power was envied by America and hated by the Soviet Union.

'The mistake that Maclean and the others made was to pin their colors to the Russian mast because of the latent anti-Americanism that infected so many of my generation,' Cecil said. 'Englishmen went to the United States not to a foreign land, but to a country they regarded as populated and run by a race of socially inferior Englishmen.'

Blunt's calculated and cold-blooded inhumanity puzzles and

still concerns Cecil. He was as interested as I was in discovering what motivated the man's treachery. He did not believe that there had been sufficient attention paid to why Blunt's Cambridge contemporaries, Maclean, Burgess and Philby, all highly intelligent members of Britain's privileged class, so readily betrayed their country. Their university experience and the seeming impasse of contemporary British politics played their part, of course. But Cecil believed there might have been a more sinister Soviet involvement in which Blunt had an important role.

Cecil pointed out that Cambridge played a part in Maclean's conversion to Marxism, and he admitted that he, too, had once been almost hooked. He recalled that after a long political discussion with Marxist friends, he had returned one evening to his rooms almost convinced that the future hope of mankind was the great Soviet experiment.

'Fortunately,' Cecil said with a wry smile, 'when I woke up the next morning, I realized that my commitment to communism had not survived the night.'

Maclean, Cecil believes, became a Marxist because he was genuinely committed to change society. He at one point wanted to abandon Cambridge for the Soviet Union and drive a tractor on a collective farm. 'Donald became involved in the student rights movement,' Cecil recalled, 'because he genuinely believed in the struggle of the masses.'

Consideration for the proletariat was not, Cecil believes, Blunt's motivation for becoming a Communist. He was driven by a different set of values than Maclean. The only aspect of Marxism that appealed to Blunt, Cecil believes, was his determination to obtain access to the power that came with being on the side of the future.

'The welfare of the masses did not interest Anthony. His objective was to effect some major change in British society which would leave him on top.' Whatever that change was to be, Blunt would not work for it by selling copies of *The Daily Worker*, or passing resolutions at a meeting. Anyone could do that. Politics on this level was boring: beneath the dignity of a member of the intellectual elite such as himself.

'Secret power, I am sure, was the real appeal to Anthony for becoming an undercover Communist agent,' Cecil said. He reached this conclusion during his interviews with Blunt. Cecil believes Blunt's desire for social change was also rooted in the nature of his peculiarly personal vendetta against British society.

'As Blunt rose higher in public and academic esteem, all the time Anthony was privately laughing at everyone,' Cecil observed. He also agrees that Blunt's dislike of British society must have been triggered by a reaction to his family's puritanical Christianity and his boyhood experience in France. He said that Blunt's school career was instrumental in giving direction to reinforcing that rebellion.

'You have to grasp that Anthony was a very exceptional character, not merely another traitor,' Cecil advised me. It is impossible to make sense of Blunt, he believes, unless it is appreciated how exceptionally talented a manipulator he was. Furthermore, the intricacies of his quite astonishing character reveal that he had a unique ability to gain power over people and make them trust him.

Blunt made no specific admissions during his three interviews with Cecil, who theorized from his own educational experiences that Blunt must have learned the lesson at his public school that if you want to have power over people you first have to gain control over someone else.

The British public schools are not 'public' – except in the sense that they were open to any boy whose parent could afford the fees and who could pass the entrance examination. Cecil explained that his public school, Wellington College, had the same reputation for toughness as Marlborough, where the three Blunt brothers were educated. The pupils at Marlborough and Wellington, like those at the more famous Eton and Harrow, represented a cross-section of British middle- and upper-class society. The prefects and athletes were the privileged class. They lorded their juvenile authority over the other boys with brutal thrashings administered by thin bamboo canes.

Anthony discovered the secret of obtaining power over people at an early age,' said Cecil, 'when he found out that the way to beat the system was to gain control over a prefect or a senior boy.' What Cecil alluded to was sexual blackmail.

Today, when one walks through the school quadrangle by a girl and boy chatting eagerly about classwork as they hurry with their rackets on the way to the tennis courts, it is difficult to visualize just how rugged an establishment Marlborough College was in the 1920s. (The admission of female students is a relatively recent innovation.) The red-brick Georgian buildings have a warmth that belies the schools' earlier reputation for toughness. Even the institutional Victorian buildings and the austere Gothic-revival chapel are softened by the clinging red creeper and framed by the spreading branches of beech and lime trees.

Marlborough College was founded in 1843 and what it lacked in prestige and ancient heritage it quickly compensated for with its glowing record of academic success – thanks to the many intelligent and industrious vicars' sons it attracted. Church of England clergymen received a discount on the tuition, and that is why it became the Blunt brothers' school. Their father could not afford to send three boys to Eton.

In the five years he was there, Anthony Blunt grew to know and love the picturesque setting, if not the school itself. Situated at the north end of the one-street market town of Marlborough, the college is within easy bicycling distance of some of the most beautiful countryside in England. To the north rears Martinsell Hill and the wild Wiltshire downs with their beech coppices and prehistoric burial mounds. South up the hill from the small town were the mysteries of the ancient oak forest of Savernake with its herd of deer. It was not the idyllic location of Marlborough College or its surrounding countryside that impressed arriving new boys as they walked warily down Granham hill from the railway station. It was the school's harsh reputation. Their fears were soon realized when they found themselves assigned to a dormitory in an ugly Victorian building. New boys were told Junior House was the work of the same architect who had designed London's notorious Wormwood Scrubs prison. This was a bit of local folklore, but for those boys who worked, ate and slept in this great square building, the similarity of their life to prison was painfully real.

According to Wilfrid Blunt, 'any modern gaol would seem a paradise' compared with Junior House, where new boys lived 'in constant fear of infringing petty regulations laid down by our oligarchy of tyrants'. His contemporary T. C. Worsley also noted that 'Marlborough prided itself on its toughness'. He wrote that 'life was lived on the barest of bare boards, at the smallest and hardest of desks, in the coldest of cold classrooms, in the total absence of any possible privacy. One was always cold, usually hungry.'

Recalled the poet Louis MacNeice, Anthony's contemporary, 'physical discomfort and futile ritual – those were the first things I noticed.' For up to a year they stayed in Junior House, supposedly being hardened before transfer to Upper School. 'Boys of that age being especially sadistic,' MacNeice noted ruefully, 'life in the Junior House was more uncomfortable than the supposedly more frightening life we moved on to.'

The shock of incongruous tribal rituals did not hold much terror for the fourteen-year-old Anthony Blunt when he arrived at Marlborough in January 1921. He had learned about the school's peculiar customs from his older brothers. But no amount of foreknowledge could have spared him from the humiliating duty of 'fagging' for senior boys. Bullying was also institutionalized and tolerated by the masters as a necessary part of the hardening-up process in the Junior House, where the length of stay depended on sexual development rather than educational accomplishment. Junior housemasters made periodic bathroom inspections to watch for the sprouting pubic hair, the signal for a boy's promotion to Upper School.

Most Junior House boys faced the prospect of their promotion with considerable apprehension. It meant that in the two years before they became members of the sixth form, they ran the constant risk of beatings and sadistic rituals. Recollections of Upper School still chill the memories of those who endured it. Wilfrid Blunt remembered the hall that contained nearly two hundred desks where the boys of fourteen to sixteen worked day and evening as a 'brutal, junior hell'. Worsley described it as 'a cold and barbarous barn'.

A single master aided by six junior prefects selected primarily for their athletic prowess – and their ability to wield a cane – maintained strict discipline. 'The only law was a jungle law of force; and the special sufferers were the individualists and non-conformers,' recalled Worsley. He avoided the worst of the bullying because his ability at sports earned him rapid promotion to junior-prefect status. Seniority and physical strength established the bullying order among the members of Little Fire and Big Fire, the two large grates on either side of the hall. Every evening the prefects came marching up and down the rows of desks lashing out with their canes. The most junior boys cleaned up the day's litter and deposited it into an enormous wastepaper basket.

This receptacle also served to imprison the unfortunate boy whom the prefects every once in a while singled out for Marlborough's supreme disciplinary penalty – the much-feared 'basketing'.

'They would seize him,' MacNeice wrote, 'tear off most of his clothes and cover him with house paint, then put him in the basket and push him round and round the hall.' As a finale a rope would be produced and the basketed victim hauled thirty feet into the air.

'Government of the mob, by the mob, and for the mob' was how MacNeice described the scene. He roundly condemned what the deliberately absent masters considered 'a fine old tradition' as 'a perfect exhibition of mass sadism'.

Sadism was also encouraged in the thrashings administered by older boys on their juniors for the most minor transgressions. Those who were beaten, and most of those doing the beating were prudishly ignorant of the sexual undertow of such escapades. One critic coined the term 'sexual concentration camps' to describe Britain's public schools. Recent research has shown that sexual activities, from widespread masturbation to actual cases of rape of junior boys, were not uncommon in Britain's public schools. But it was not until after World War II that serious medical and psychological investigations into human sexual behaviour revealed the contradictions inherent in segregating boys in boarding schools.

Instead of lessening the pent-up sexual energies of the boys, the standard public-school regime of physical exercise actually fanned the flames of the healthy young libidos. In these segregated environments, boys who were sent away from home from the age of eight inevitably transferred their affection to members of their peer group. In English public schools, romance was, by physical necessity and educational inspiration, homosexual.

Much of the Greek literature used as set texts in schools emphasized that the love of man for man was on a higher plane than the carnal love of a man for a woman.

Platonic admiration of male youth and prowess on the games field were socially and legally acceptable only as long as they remained 'unsullied'. As the homoerotic cult blossomed in public-school boys, the British Parliament voted in 1885 to make homosexual acts a criminal offense. The conflicting currents of law and morality generated a unique state of confusion and anxiety. 'Beautiful sins,' quipped Oscar Wilde, 'are the privilege of the ruling class.' The furor that erupted with Wilde's trial for sodomy in 1895 was symptomatic of this collective fear and guilt about 'the love that dare not speak its name,' a term coined appropriately by Wilde's one-time lover, Lord Alfred Douglas.

On the basis of many confidential interviews, the author of a recent British study, *The Public School Phenomenon*, believes that an average of a quarter of the boys attending Britain's public-school system during the first decades of this century engaged in regular sexual contact. More than 90 per cent owned up to 'fact or fantasy' love affairs with other boys. The majority were purely romantic affairs like the distant passion for another Marlborough boy recalled by John Betjeman. A year ahead of Anthony Blunt, the future poet laureate of Britain 'never dared touch anyone' because of his fear that he 'would have gone to gaol – and hell'.

Betjeman, like many public-school boys, found his intense amorous feelings for a fellow Marlburian both frustrating and confusing. And Wilfrid Blunt recalled that the headmaster's advice on sex to his confirmation class was that 'if we treated all women as we would our mothers and sisters we would never go far wrong.'

Some public-school boys learned to fear and even despise the opposite sex; many more grew up confused and hostile toward women. Their dilemma became the butt of a smutty Eton joke, about a laundress who raised her skirt to expose her passion for a young student.

'There! What do you think of that?'

'Gosh, ma'am,' said the astonished boy. 'If you wait a minute I'll run to my room, get my cricket bat and come back and kill it.'

Marlborough housemasters treated the onset of puberty as 'a sort of disease like measles.' Wilfrid Blunt, like most homosexuals who became teachers, considered any physical contact with a pupil to be a violation of trust. Some did not. The Reverend Blunt's godfather, Dean C. J. Vaughan, resigned the headmastership of Harrow under the threat of exposure by one of his former pupils.

While Britain's public-school system may not have increased significantly the incidence of homosexuality in the national population, it instilled subconscious homoerotic attitudes in successive generations of middle- and upper-class males. And their shared proclivities in public school resulted in the development of extensive underground 'old boy networks' of practicing homosexuals. In turn, because the law made practicing homosexuality a criminal offense punishable with a harsh jail sentence, the homosexual networks among the British elite offered great opportunities to any blackmailer – or spy – who gained admission.

Not every homosexually inclined boy managed to gain admission into the magic ruling circle. Wilfrid claims to have been so

sexually immature that he was ignorant of 'the pleasure of masturbation' and therefore 'did not really understand those whispered,
sniggering references to certain arcane practices alleged to take
place in the denser thickets of Manton Coppice.'

The more precocious boys at Marlborough rendezvoused for
illicit sexual practices in the woodlands half a mile from the
school, but they did not always have enough regard for the
secrecy that was essential for their protection. Indiscretion was
the downfall of one group. Their conversation offended the pru-
dish Cuthbert Worsley and he reported them. Much to his surprise, he wrote of how an investigation resulted in the expulsion
of three senior boys.

Rumors about 'The Cult of Priapus', as MacNeice termed it,
spread quickly in a closed institution. What Anthony Blunt made
of the gossip about Manton Coppice is not recorded. But we do
know from his close friend MacNeice that 'nearly all the elder
boys had their mild homosexual romances – an occasion for
"billets" and giggling and elaborately engineered rendezvous.'
He admitted writing a poem to 'a dark-haired boy of sixteen who
had large grey feminine eyes'. Blunt criticized the verse as too
heavily influenced by Tennyson.

MacNeice insisted that this was his only flirtation with another
boy, but Blunt's liaisons were more serious, according to their
mutual friend John Hilton. He told me of an incident during their
final year when, on a pouring wet day, he had been waiting under
the arcade across from the dining hall, waiting for it to open.

'Anthony, who as a prefect had an umbrella, suddenly darted
forward and I darted with him,' Hilton recalled. 'It turned out
that he had seen a "love object" and intended offering "it" a share
of the umbrella – he was very, very angry.' The boy could well
have been 'the Beautiful Basil' whom MacNeice refers to frequently in letters to Blunt that date from their last year at school.
Their homoerotic tone suggests that Anthony was involved in a
series of such liaisons. Other Marlborough boys referred to only
by their first names are cryptically described as members of the
'Elect'.

In one letter to Blunt, MacNeice signed off, 'I wish you dreams of Edward's eyes. I am afraid they are not pure.' Another contained a reference to a boy called John: 'I should say the satisfactory end for violent affection is a break.'

On the evidence of this correspondence Blunt appears, at the very least, to have formed a number of romantic attachments to other boys during his senior year. Other members of his circle were certainly doing so; their contemporaries remember at least one boy was expelled from Marlborough after being caught indulging in homosexual practices.

It is impossible to do more than speculate about the origins of Anthony Blunt's homosexuality, but a parallel can be drawn with the experience of another of his contemporaries, Thomas Driberg. He also was the son of a distant older father and dominant middle-class mother. Driberg graphically described in his memoir *Ruling Passions* how he became homosexually active before going to public school. Like Blunt, Driberg became a Communist. For many years he was a member of Parliament and a Russian agent who also fed information to MI5.

Also like Blunt, Driberg was an aggressive homosexual who relished the danger involved in searching for sexual partners in public lavatories. They shared a preference for servicemen, a common trait of Britain's privileged classes in search of illicit sex partners. The services of a whore or lower-class male pickup could be paid for, and this made the relationship less inhibiting because the unequal social status of the participants did not induce feelings of guilt.

So if Blunt's initial homosexual experience was with a soldier in a public lavatory, it would explain why the scenario always had a powerful erotic fascination for him. There would have been plenty of opportunity for such an encounter during his trips back and forth to Paris. (His family did not move back to England until the end of 1921, when his father became rector of St John's Paddington, a dowdy middle-class parish north of Hyde Park, near the Great Western Railway's London terminal.)

Anthony Blunt was then in his first term at Marlborough

College and he considered himself vastly superior to his contemporaries. His foundation scholarship attested to his intellectual ability. He spoke French better than any master and had amassed a precocious knowledge of art. But he was also intensely cynical toward the hearty Christianity and orthodox Britishness that Marlborough considered its duty to instill in all its boys.

Blunt, who had acquired from his brothers a useful insider's survival guide to the school's rules and tribal rituals, would have become an obvious target for bullying and cutting down to size by more senior boys. Forty-five years later, when Sir Anthony Blunt – as he then proudly was – recalled for the benefit of two Marlborough boys how 'perfectly beastly' were his first terms, he said he 'lived in perpetual fear' that he might be 'basketed'.

'My life,' Blunt declared, 'was made a misery for me for two terms by the bullying of one boy.' He did not elaborate, nor did he explain how or why the bullying ceased. But his admission that it did not continue beyond the second term of the school year suggests that something might have made the bully desist.

How did Blunt manage to neutralize the bully? Robert Cecil wonders. Why had such an obviously offensive junior boy managed to escape a ritual basketing?

Drawing on his own background knowledge of the similarities between Wellington and Marlborough, Cecil believes that Blunt obtained some hold over the prefects and senior boys to relieve him of the bully's wrath.

'Sexual politics,' Cecil said. 'That is the only way I can describe it.' He believes Blunt discovered that sex was the key to survival in a society where adolescent boys were alternately beating or competing with each other for favors and privileges. Cecil speculates that Marlborough, like Wellington, would have had its share of homosexual witch hunts to root out what the headmasters euphemistically described as 'vice'. Invariably the senior boy faced expulsion but not the younger boy. The presumption was always that the junior partner in a sexual crime would have been bullied or corrupted against his will. A junior boy could therefore entice an older one to his advantage in the game of 'sexual politics'.

'You see,' Cecil said, 'Anthony would have been attractive to the older boys because he could turn on considerable charm.' When bullied he would, after a term or so, have learned how to get his own back in a peculiarly feminine way.

'At Wellington,' Cecil explained, 'the athletes, despite the rules against fraternizing with the juniors, would have their friendships with smaller boys.' Although protective of their favorites, they were terribly exposed because of the other seniors. According to Cecil, although prefects may also have been protecting a young chap on the side, they were not going to let anyone who was caught breaking the rules off the hook.

'Anthony was clever enough,' Cecil believes, 'to exploit this complex web of sexual entanglement to escape sadistic bullying.' Blunt might have found himself a protector, Cecil theorizes, or even provoked an overtly homosexual encounter to entrap the bully who might have been trying to force his attentions on him. 'Now I'm going to the housemaster, or else!' would, Cecil believes, have been a powerful threat. If the blackmail worked – and it seems it did – it would explain why Blunt was no longer threatened by senior boys. Other would-be bullies, forewarned that the youngest Blunt boy was dangerous, would not molest him. Cecil also points out that Blunt would thereby have acquired an enormous contempt for the system as a result of his own ability to bend its weakness to his advantage.

'In later life,' Cecil emphasized, 'Anthony knew that much of Britain was run by former prefects vulnerable to the same kind of blackmail.' Cecil's theory explains why Blunt was so important to the Soviets. He knew how to manipulate the semisecret homosexual networks that were extensions of public-school system.

'Anthony Blunt became a spy because he wanted to get back at the establishment,' said Oxford historian John Bowle. 'There is no doubt in my mind about that.'

A year senior to Blunt at Marlborough College, Bowle ended

his career as a fellow of Wadham College. The wispy white-haired professor was the very image of a crusty old don who made little effort to conceal his personal animosity toward Blunt. Yet, during our interview, Bowle provided a revealing insight into Blunt's character. Personal experience of Blunt and his recollections of similarly precocious boys during his own career as a history master at Westminster School and Eton had convinced him he was right.

'Intense conceit,' Bowle declared firmly. 'That was the secret of Blunt's personality.' He explained that Blunt was a brilliant scholar who easily won academic honors. This, however, was not enough for him. He wanted to prove his superiority by excelling at everything. He yearned to be a leader at school. But he faced a major hurdle. Blunt did not excel at team sports. At Marlborough, as at the other British public schools, the real test of leadership potential came on the playing fields.

'Blunt felt ostracized and slighted because he was bad at games,' explained Bowle. 'He was not the brilliant all-rounder that he thought he was.' The resulting wound to his self-esteem was deep and permanent. According to Bowle, Blunt tended to harbor grudges. This, Bowle believed, fired Blunt's personal insurrection against the public-school system, a rebellion that underpinned his secret antiestablishment work for the Soviets.

Bowle's firsthand view of Blunt as a precocious adolescent rebel who translated his personal insurrection against his school into a betrayal of his country in later life coincides almost exactly with the independent assessment of his motivational impulse made by Robert Cecil.

That Blunt was immensely conceited about his intellectual abilities squares with the Marlborough records, which reveal him as a scholastic high flier. He excelled in mathematics and steadily climbed up the academic ladder, winning a great many prizes and scholarships until he became the undisputed top of his class in his final year. He was so fluent in French that one master let him take over the class. But Blunt's arrogance often grated on his contemporaries. John Hilton recorded in his diary how 'that terrible boy

Blunt came to ask for the key of the classroom and of course had to stay to tea and monopolized the conversation.'

Blunt's unshakable self-assurance was apparent even at four-teen. 'Old for his years in the knowledge of the world and knowledge of where he was going,' according to his closest friend at Marlborough, Louis MacNeice, who described him as 'a domi-nating figure both in his assurance and incandescent spirit and with his imposing height and large handsome, long-haired head.' Blunt became 'the dominant intellectual' of his generation while making a reputation for a 'precocious knowledge of art and an habitual contempt for conservative authorities'.

'Socially and in power terms, these boys carried no weight at all,' Cuthbert Worsley wrote in his memoir of Marlborough. 'Public approval among the masters as well as boys was reserved for the athlete.' The Marlborough motto, 'Virtu, Studio, Ludo,' might more appropriately have reversed the order of 'Study' and 'Play' to acknowledge the preeminence of games.

Games were compulsory for all. On afternoons when it was too wet to play, the whole school was sent on cross-country runs. The hated 'Sweats' sent straggling lines of miserable boys toiling over the windswept downs with prefects clocking them along. Dawdlers and those who took shortcuts were beaten. Games worship reached its peak in the summer term with cricket 'a kind of pagan religious rite,' according to Worsley, who spoke with the authority of a member of the Marlborough First XI, the school's top team.

Blunt himself admitted that he 'hated compulsory games'. Certainly it was not because of any physical incapacity, because at Cambridge he played hockey and he is also on record as saying how he enjoyed running 'rather slowly over long distances' across the downs.

Blunt, it seems, was psychologically ill-equipped to be a team player. Those who would not accept him on his own terms, he despised. He grew his hair long, causing the local barber to remark to MacNeice that he 'didn't think THAT gentleman would be any good at games because his hair would get in the way.' Shortly afterward the bursar issued instructions to the hairdresser to cut all boys' hair shorter. 'He couldn't have people going about like a lot of poets,' MacNeice reported home. 'The Bursar doesn't like poets.'

Blunt was delighted to be regarded as an aesthete. He liked to recall how he showed contempt for the athletes by playing catch with a large, brightly colored ball right across their game.

'We went out of the way to be irritatingly provocative,' Blunt admitted in a 1967 interview with the two schoolboy editors of *The Marlburian*, the college's magazine. He recalled how he and his friends delighted in ostentatiously taunting the prefects by flouting nonexistent rules as they flaunted blue silk handkerchiefs from their wristwatches in chapel. He also told the Marlborough boys how he helped organize a more adult and focused 'revolt against the absolute dominance of games.'

In these published recollections, Blunt portrayed himself as one of the leaders, along with John Bowle and John Betjeman, of a group of more senior boys who systematically mocked Marlborough's sacred code of athleticism. By calling themselves aesthetes and associating themselves with the 'art for art's sake' sentiments of Oscar Wilde, they deliberately set out to shock. Betjeman was the leading spirit of this cult of aesthetic dilettantism. His hoarse laughter and childish behavior included rolling a hoop around the school while wearing a green feather behind his ear. It infuriated the hearties. The future poet laureate's eccentric passion for Gothic-revival architecture, Victorian trams and Methodist chapels Blunt regarded as contrived, because he dismissed them as a 'wilful passion' and a 'joke'.

Blunt had more respect, it seems, for John Bowle, whom he claimed to have rescued from marauding hearties. 'He used to come into my study, absolutely terrified, and say: "Can you give me shelter, they're trying to throw me in the swimming pool."'

Bowle thereby put himself under an obligation to the younger boy, who thereby gained an entrée to the circle of older Marlborough aesthetes. Blunt said he became a member of the group who founded 'a paper called *The Heretick*, which was intended to express our disapproval of the Establishment generally.'

John Bowle said this was a typical Blunt fabrication. Blunt had nothing to do with founding the magazine. *The Heretick*, he said, was his brainchild. Betjeman had thought up the magazine's name. Blunt had not even helped with the magazine; he had merely contributed two articles. Bowle angrily recalled how the tactlessness of Blunt's second piece had been instrumental in closing down *The Heretick*.

The Heretick, according to Bowle, was not nearly as anti-establishment as Blunt claimed. Bowle and Betjeman edited a more literary alternative to the school magazine, which was dull and devoted too much space to games reports and obituaries of old Marlburians. The first issue of *The Heretick* in March 1924 proclaimed 'Upon Philistia Will I Triumph' above Bowle's cover drawing of a scowling hockey player taunted by a mischievous faun.

Far from declaring open war on the school establishment, Bowle revealed that the headmaster himself had encouraged and supported the publication. Dr Cyril Norwood was a reformer who tried to strike a balance between the classroom and the games field by reforming the curriculum and giving more emphasis to science.

Norwood's support for *The Heretick* collapsed when the second issue appeared in June 1925. The games master violently objected to the opening article, which attacked the 'ludicrous pomposity' of the belief that 'the foundations of our mighty Empire are laid on the playing fields of our schools'. But it was Blunt's provocative piece on the Wildean theme of art and morality that caused an uproar. 'To call a work of art immoral is like calling an ink spot sympathetic,' he wrote, adding that: 'To say that a painting is immoral merely shews a lamentable incapacity for appreciation.' Blunt later claimed that his housemaster had provoked him to write the piece because he 'thought that the Matisse and Rouault which I had in my study were indecent.' This was confirmed by Hilton, who remembers that Blunt was 'at loggerheads with his housemaster over books picturing unclothed and amorous persons'.

'A typical Blunt piece of work,' Bowle snorted. 'Priggish, boring and conceited.' Considering his later espousal of Marxism, it is surprising that at the age of nineteen he insisted that 'great artists could not be moral reformers'. Nevertheless, one Marlborough parent found this whiff of the scandalous Oscar Wilde so offensive that he wrote to the headmaster threatening to remove his son from the school. Norwood thereupon banned *The Heretick*.

Bowle blamed his magazine's demise on Blunt's 'intense conceit'. But Blunt, predictably, told a different story to the *Marlburian* editors in 1967. He made no mention of the furor provoked by his article, merely stating that the second issue went into debt because it was 'duller than the first' and did not sell. 'A fitting end for such an ephemeral production' was Blunt's haughty comment.

Blunt's conceit was so great that it seems he found it difficult ever to accept responsibility for his own mistakes. Whether it was the folding of the school magazine, the attribution of a painting or his conversion to communism, Blunt always had to pass the blame to someone else. The trait is particularly evident in his repeated insistence that he was never interested in politics. The Marlborough record is very revealing when weighed against the picture Blunt contrived to present of himself as having been always the naïve, detached, apolitical academic.

'Politics was simply a subject never discussed at all at Marlborough,' Blunt is on record as telling his Courtauld students in a farewell lecture. Since it was later published under the title of 'From Bloomsbury to Marxism', Blunt presumably approved and corrected it before he retired in 1973. When Blunt gave his talk about the influences of Marx and Bloomsbury, he had already given MI5 his secret confession blaming Guy Burgess for recruiting him to the Communist cause. He therefore found it convenient to stress his youthful political naïvety to reinforce assurances that his espousal of Marxism was an aberration of his Cambridge years.

Yet Blunt's own rebellion against the athleticism of Marlborough was a consciously political act, especially when considered against the social and political upheavals of World War I which shattered the verities of the Victorian generations. The new social and political realities that had swept away the comfortable Edwardian England also undermined the shaky economics of Britain's imperial legacy. In Europe the old order was under siege. Socialism, with its emphasis on the rights of the masses rather than the privileges of the few, had become a major political force in Germany and France. The Russian Revolution of 1917 had given birth to a Communist state dedicated to the worldwide subversion of capitalism. Even in Britain the whiff of revolution was in the air. The enfranchisement of women in 1918 and the expansion of organized labor unions, together with the growth of bureaucracy and business during wartime, presented an increasing challenge to the traditional ruling class. In the wake of a succession of postwar economic crises and deepening industrial unemployment, the rise of socialism among the working class threatened the traditional division of parliamentary rule between the Liberal and Conservatives parties.

The Labour party preached class war by way of industrial strikes and the ballot box. When Liberal wartime Prime Minister David Lloyd George's coalition government broke up in 1922, the Conservatives returned to power. Labour emerged from the election for the first time as the radical opposition in a Parliament that included two Communist members. Labour's leader, Ramsay MacDonald, became Britain's first socialist prime minister when he formed a minority government at the beginning of 1924. But this was not the dawn of the socialist revolution so many conservatives feared. Overwhelmed by economic problems and their decision to give official recognition to the Soviet Union, the Labour government collapsed after only eight months.

The Conservatives swept back to power in the fall elections of 1924. With their avuncular pipe-smoking champion Stanley Baldwin as prime minister, the former public-school prefects were once again firmly in charge of the British government. The politics of nostalgia, however, did nothing to arrest Britain's economic decline.

Despite Baldwin's soothing reassurances, the bitterness released by a rising unemployment rate deepened the sense of collective class-guilt in a growing number of British intellectuals. There was increasing disenchantment with the 'headmasterly' prime minister and the 'prefect' mentality of Britain's ruling class. The public schools themselves had responded to the postwar political and economic upheavals with reaction and retrenchment. But while zealous headmasters banned from school libraries subversive works like Alec Waugh's *The Loom of Youth* that assailed the homosexual hypocrisy and games worship of the public schools – and even the *Daily Herald*, Britain's young socialist newspaper – they could not prevent boys from reading them during their vacations.

The changing British political landscape and increasing disenchantment among the educated elite were also reflected in the cultural shock of Bloomsbury. New forms of literature, poetry and art, fomented in the drawing rooms of the quiet London district, were soon reaching from the universities down to the public schools like Marlborough, where the embryo intellectuals like Blunt were smoldering with unfocused discontent. Impressionable young minds, already in reaction against starchy parental values, devoured Lytton Strachey's anti-establishment assault on *The Eminent Victorians*. Another catalyst for young minds groping for a new definition of cultural values was the powerful fragmented imagery of T. S. Eliot's *The Waste Land*.

Like many of his contemporaries, even the precociously bright Anthony Blunt may not have fully grasped the scope of one of the twentieth century's seminal works of poetry that Eliot himself described as the portrayal of 'the immense panorama of futility and anarchy that is contemporary history.'

The Waste Land nonetheless had a powerful impact on a generation of rebellious young intellectuals intent on toppling the towers of the old cultural order in their quest for the elusive 'city over the mountains'.

*

'We were very much aware of the Eliot movement,' Blunt recalled, 'and we all knew *The Waste Land* off by heart.' Strachey's histories 'justified', he said, his schoolboy 'hatred of the Establishment'. This antipathy found its chief expression through his ardent championship of modern art. He explained that his 'great desire to proselytize' was because of a 'genuine admiration of the new' and his determination to preach the decadence of the old order. But art for the young Blunt was also a political cause; a vehicle for self-promotion. He himself admitted as much in a rare movement of self-revelation, saying that his intention was to 'exasperate the other boys and masters at school'.

Blunt had been laying the foundations of his crusade ever since the autumn term of 1923, when he finally escaped from the brutality of Upper School. Emerging with distinctions in the school-certificate examinations, he entered the sixth form and shared a study. He stocked it with his growing collection of art books and decorated the walls with modern prints. He set himself up as Marlborough's revolutionary prophet of modernism and began lending out books and prints of French paintings that many masters and boys considered shocking and subversive.

The first Post-Impressionist exhibition had outraged London in 1910. Roger Fry, the painter and Bloomsbury art critic, had organized the first showing of Cézanne, Matisse, Gauguin and van Gogh. As director of painting at the Metropolitan Museum of Art in New York from 1905 to 1910, Fry had introduced Americans to the brightly colored paintings. But the staid British cultural establishment had violently rejected the art, which was already popular in the United States. *The Times* warned that paintings such as van Gogh's *Sunflowers* were a 'bad influence on the younger generation', and the conservative *Morning Post* compared the show to a plague and demanded that 'the source of infection ought to be destroyed'. Ironically, it was Blunt's second cousin Wilfrid Scawen Blunt, who had taken the lead in denouncing the canvases of the Post-Impressionists as 'a pornographic display'.

A decade later Blunt appreciated that after the outcry over Fry's prewar London exhibition, French Impressionist paintings were still considered shocking and that Picasso's Cubist canvases represented a frontal assault on staid British taste. Paintings, rather than political slogans, therefore became the banners of Blunt's schoolboy rebellion.

Louis MacNeice, who became the principal lieutenant of Blunt's attack on the bastions of Marlborough's aesthetic conventionality, provides an arresting image of the sixteen-year-old rebel. He described Blunt as 'very tall and very thin and drooping, with deadly sharp elbows and the ribs of a famished saint'. He particularly noted his friend's 'cold blue eyes, a cutaway mouth and a wave of soft brown hair falling over his forehead'. According to MacNeice, Blunt had not yet learned the knack of concealing his emotions. Whenever he became angry, MacNiece observed how it affected Blunt's 'pre-Raphaelite beauty'. He would pout and stick out his lip and 'his good looks vanished and the sulkiness was all'.

'Anthony was an austere hedonist,' wrote John Hilton, another contemporary, who described Blunt as 'living for gratification of the senses, with an eye for social esteem and seeking anchorage in a system of scholarly detail.' A fellow member of the mathematical sixth form, Hilton was keenly aware of the sharp difference between his two friends. MacNeice he described as 'a ribald seer, an anarchic and mocking seeker after the deep springs of action and faith'.

MacNeice, who was in the classical sixth, was a husky, untidy youth, who was remembered as Blunt's sidekick and proselytizer among the 'hearties', to whom he had an entrée because he played a useful game of rugby. MacNeice had a ferocious Celtic talent for words that made him a gifted poet and orator. He shared with Blunt the common revolt against their clergyman fathers, whose moral values 'were a delusion, and politics and religion a waste of time'. The boys concluded that 'the only values were aesthetic', which appears to have been the way they both disguised from their parents their rejection of Christian values as they immersed themselves in what MacNeice described as 'the bacchanalian chorus of adolescence'.

MacNeice and Blunt both separately insisted that their mutual attraction was not physical. 'It is important that you understand that Louis was always totally, irredeemably heterosexual,' Blunt assured Oxford Professor Jon Stallworthy, MacNeice's biographer, shortly before his death. But Stallworthy agrees that MacNeice's letters to Blunt suggest that Louis was aware of his friend's preferences because of many overt homosexual references in their decade-long correspondence.

Blunt seems to have found in MacNeice's creative brilliance the necessary grist for honing his razor-sharp analytical intelligence. Blunt nonetheless was 'infinitely more intelligent than MacNeice' but 'not nearly such a genius,' observed their mutual friend Hilton. But there can be no doubt that it was Blunt's dominant personality that drew the trio together at Marlborough. He drilled them in the need to display their intellectual superiority over other boys who were merely clever.

'Anthony was usually the nucleus of a cloud of circling electrons,' Hilton said. According to Blunt, his circle proved their intelligence 'avidly and extremely widely but in a very eccentric manner.' Their cultural philosophy reflected their chorus master's deep-seated anti-authority prejudices. They rejected Shakespeare as 'part of the establishment' in favor of Marlowe; Shelley and Keats were romantic and passé. They devoured Voltaire's philosophical novel *Candide* because it attacked established institutions. They despised the high Victorian Tennyson but approved Gothic horror stories. Grimms' fairy tales together with the prose and limericks of Edward Lear became props for a child-cult. They admired the contemporary verse of T. S. Eliot and the Sitwells. They read Gertrude Stein aloud 'up and down the dormitories to exasperate our neighbors'.

'Anthony and I went in for eclectic reading,' MacNeice wrote in later life. 'It was either stark and realistic or precious and remote and two dimensional.' Blunt, he noted, had 'a flair for bigotry' and 'every day he blackballed another musician.' They liked Bach, Handel and Mozart, but despised Wagner, who according to Blunt was 'establishment, romantic, all the things that we thought were most wicked.'

Blunt's presumptuous confidence in his aesthetic sense came from his familiarity with the Post-Impressionist pictures he had seen in the Paris galleries. His brother Wilfrid, then an art master of Haileybury school, kept him informed about the latest trends, eventually introducing Anthony to Roger Fry. Blunt reinforced his juvenile preconceptions about modern painting with technical expositions that he had gleaned from his growing collection of art books. His aesthetic bible in his formative years was a slim volume by the Bloomsbury critic Clive Bell.

Art, as it was simply titled, was the first English book to attempt a modern definition of the essential aesthetic values of painting. 'Significant Form' was the label Bell coined to define the combination of lines, colors and spatial relationships that 'stir our aesthetic emotions'. What he had read in these art books may well have influenced Blunt's decision to specialize in mathematics at Marlborough. 'Art transports us from the world of man's activity to a world of aesthetic adulation,' Bell had written, suggesting that the 'pure mathematician rapt in his studies knows a state of mind which I take to be similar, if not identical.'

Bloomsbury's principal artistic theorist may have therefore well been responsible for Blunt's pursuit of mathematics, but there can be no doubt at all that Anthony embraced Bell's belief in significant form and employed it to discount the representational elements in painting. Pure form became a dogmatic obsession for Blunt. Even MacNeice recorded how reluctant he had been to challenge Blunt's fixed opinions by liking the 'jugness of the jug and bowlness of the bowl' in the colored print of a Picasso still life on the wall of the study they shared. For Blunt, 'anything else but Pure Form was out.' MacNeice wrote, 'literary content was wrong or irrelevant, and naturalism was an insult'.

Form, rather than representation, remained an article of faith for Blunt. So was everything French. Paris was the standard by which he judged everything else. He admitted he was 'extremely snooty about all English art' because he considered it 'either literary or derivative'. The only exception was William Blake and his passion for the mystical artist-poet was a lifelong enthusiasm. But Blunt accommodated his prejudices, if it suited his proselytizing purposes, as it did in 1925 when there was a public outcry at sculptor Jacob Epstein's primitive *Rima*. Despite his belief that Epstein 'was not a good sculptor' he boldly defended the statuesque relief 'because it was Modern Art'.

Blunt's youthful bigotry revealed a great deal. He justified his single-mindedness as the result of 'a great desire to proselytize'. But his use of religious terms to describe his challenge to the old aesthetic gods and identification with the new was especially significant. It shows that he realized that he was aligning himself with a revolution in the visual arts as sweeping as any since the Renaissance. Recognition that the French Cubist and Post-Impressionist painters 'were still regarded as dangerous revolutionaries' reinforced Blunt's sense of mission. He knew that their preoccupation with abstraction and nonrepresentational form challenged the most basic assumptions of Western art. It was in its way no less 'revolutionary' than Marx's political doctrine that challenged the fundamental human need for material possessions.

Cubism, and particularly Picasso's pre-World War I still lifes, had special appeal for Blunt. Their bold planes and sharply defined, colorful forms lent themselves to a mathematical rationalization about art that appeared 'scientific'. This appealed to his keenly analytical mind just as he later found his sympathies drawn to the 'scientific' approach of Marxist political dialectic. Blunt himself later admitted that his youthful approach to art was too formularized and dogmatic. He accepted many of his juvenile attitudes as misconceptions, especially his dismissal of the High Renaissance art that became central to his professional career. In his later years he excused his blinkered views as the enthusiasm of youth for clearcut definitions. But such was Blunt's conceit that he blamed his teenage errors of judgement on the 'wrong ideas' perpetrated by the artists themselves.

'Blunt does not like Cubism very much except the theory,'

MacNeice noted perceptively, after an impromptu exposition had left the school's Astronomical Society 'quite lost'.

At Marlborough Blunt was uncritically accepted as the leader of the circle of rebellious aesthetes. 'We traipsed along eagerly with him,' John Hilton wrote, acknowledging that Blunt was 'far ahead of us in sophistication.' Blunt also showed his political skill by contriving to get himself elected secretary of the school debating society. This coup especially impressed Hilton because Blunt had 'hardly ever attended a debate before'.

The debating society, however, proved an inadequate launching pad for Blunt's grandiose plan for demolishing Marlborough's bastions of philistinism. He was scheming to set up a more influential cultural forum, one that would involve sympathetic masters and senior boys. But Blunt's proposal for a full-fledged Art Society ran into opposition from the art master, Christopher Hughes.

'I did not get on well with Hughes,' Blunt recalled in his Courtauld lecture fifty years later. He said this was because Hughes 'believed all art stopped at the pre-Raphaelites.'

His contempt for Hughes became a vendetta after the master tried to block his plans. He first tried to outflank the art master by inviting Clifford Canning, a boyish-looking master who had been a friend to all the Blunt boys, to become president of the Art Society. Canning had taken holy orders in 1924, but this did not faze MacNeice and Blunt. They regarded him, in contrast to their clerical fathers, as an 'intelligent Christian'. Many of the disciplinarians in the staff common room thought Canning was too close to his boys. In particular they criticized the way he had turned his rooms into a salon and a refuge for budding aesthetes.

Blunt's society quickly became a staff-room issue. His housemaster, Dr Guillebaud, who evidently had little sympathy for the one boy in C3 House who caused him more problems than any other, supported Hughes. The art master insisted that if there was going to be an Art Society at Marlborough, then he was going to be president. That did not suit Blunt. But with Canning's help he outmaneuvered the opposition by calling his forum the

'Anonymous Society' and enlisting George C. Turner, a sympathetic senior master (who the following year succeeded Dr Norwood as headmaster) as its nominal president.

'I've been bullied by Blunt into joining his society,' John Hilton wrote to his parents. It was not, he took care to reassure them, 'really eccentric' because masters as well as members of the school teams were members.

Blunt's objective for his new society was anything but the promotion of eccentricity. He wanted to project his influence and authority with the aid of members of the Marlborough establishment. Besides Canning and G. C. Turner, the senior classics and science masters were regular participants. Thanks to MacNeice's contacts among the athletes, three leading school-team players were also persuaded to join up.

The prestige of Blunt's Anonymous Society as a forum in which boys joined with masters for stimulating discussion rapidly eclipsed the school's established Literary Society, which was 'rather dull' by comparison. Within a year it had become a kind of juvenile Bloomsbury. Marlborough's brightest intellects plied each other with philosophical debate while they munched on the egg sandwiches provided by the hospitable Canning at his house, the Priory, off Marlborough High Street. Formal presentations ranged from the lighthearted paper given by MacNeice on 'The Mailed Fist of Common Sense and How to Avoid It' to avant-garde piano recitals of Debussy by Dr Goad, the science master, and a succession of Blunt's precocious dissertations on modern art.

Blunt was relentless in his campaign against Hughes. In debating such topics as the rival merits of Picasso and Michelangelo, he wrote his opponents down with long perorations supported by prints and quotations from his many art books. His sheer persistence and mastery of detail usually demolished his opponents.

'I remember reading a paper proving that art went underground at the end of the Renaissance,' Blunt recalled, 'reemerged at El Greco, and then submerged again until Cézanne and the Impressionists.' Hughes was 'so roused' at Blunt's polemic that he insisted on giving an answering paper. The feud between them was worsened the following month when Hughes refused to allow Wilfrid Blunt to exhibit a still life in the annual exhibition of paintings by Old Marlburians.

'It was unworthy of a pavement artist,' fumed the art master. To which Blunt remarked that the art master's paintings 'seemed to have been scrubbed with soft soap.'

The January meeting of the Anonymous Society, when Hughes set out to get his own back on the scornful Blunt, was, according to MacNeice, 'very tense'. But Hughes's blustering defense of Pre-Raphaelite painting became so confused that Blunt collapsed into sarcastic laughter. The art master could stand the humiliation no longer.

'You've hurt me many times, and now I'm hurting you,' Hughes blurted out. According to Blunt's recollection, this 'delightful' confrontation reduced the art master to tears of frustrated rage.

Such triumphs greatly enhanced Blunt's self-esteem. The importance and respectability of 'Blunt's Society' was never higher. It even included the senior prefect and rugger XV team player Michael Robertson. Most of the school's other leading lights participated, including James Mason, the future film star. Younger boys emulated Blunt, grew their hair long and called themselves aesthetes. He established himself as a prominent figure and did his best to live up to his reputation. He and his circle strove to appear avant-garde as they strolled around the school, posturing as though to admire the details of an imaginary Baroque church.

'Sometimes I was conscious that Anthony and I were spending too much time being "enfants terribles",' MacNeice admitted. But Blunt's career received its final accolade in 1926 when he won a scholarship to study mathematics at Trinity College, Cambridge. Blunt self-effacingly said that he topped the candidates' list in *The Times* only because of alphabetical order. But the scholarship fixed his star securely in the school firmament. Winning a highly competitive Trinity College scholarship had marked him out as one of the brightest young men of his age in Britain, and a recruit for the ruling elite. The aesthete rebel became, overnight, a respectable school hero, helped by a newspaper article on the examination results that noted, 'Marlborough is not a public school, it is a miracle.'

'I think it is less cruel to people with minds than any other public school,' MacNeice assured his mother in a letter in January 1926 announcing that his friend Blunt had been made a senior school prefect. 'There are so few prefects with any intelligence,' MacNeice observed.

To impress his circle with his newfound prefectorial authority, Blunt proposed adding an art magazine, *The Apollo*, to the sixth-form papers. This infuriated his fellow prefects who objected to the 'horrible' journal. But it was impossible to keep the new school hero down. Marlborough boys paid tribute to the rebel's success by adapting verses of the school song: 'Yes, We Are Collegiate' became 'Yes, We Are Aesthetic', with Blunt's name linked to MacNeice's and Hilton's in the refrains. Even *The Marlburian* satirized his success as a cultural revolutionary. But it is doubtful whether Blunt liked the reference to his 'inane though slightly malicious smile' or 'the wave of hair of which I am not a little proud'.

For his final two terms Blunt basked in the esteem of his schoolfellows and lorded it over them as prefect. According to MacNeice, who had won a classical scholarship to Oxford, they had little to do in their final two terms at school except 'amuse ourselves and infuriate everyone else'. They made long bicycle rides to sleepy Wiltshire hamlets, where they rang the East Kennet church bells in anticipation of the coming freedom. 'Anthony says this really is the best country in the world,' MacNeice wrote after a trek gathering wild-apple blooms and bluebells.

During the late-spring days, when Britain teetered on the brink of civil disorder during the 1926 general strike, Blunt and Mac-Neice lazed naked in the buttercups beside the chalky banks of the meandering Kennet. According to Blunt, the strike was treated very largely 'as sort of joke, when one's elder brothers and one's parents were and did curious things.'

Anticipation of their coming triumph at Cambridge and Oxford was celebrated with tea parties for their friends. At the very last one they stuffed themselves on walnut cake and solemnly dispatched the tea service, piece by piece, out of the window to smash against the wall opposite. 'We kept the best till last,' MacNeice recorded. 'The sugar bowl, still full of lumps, burst on the wall like a round of machine-gun fire and the large teapot sailed to its doom trailing tea from the spout. "Ruins of Carthage", we said and washed our hands of Marlborough.'

In the Prize Day speeches of 28 June 1926 Anthony Frederick Blunt was singled out as Marlborough's top scholar. The crowning moment of Blunt's school career came when the headmaster put him at the top of the list to be congratulated for the scholarship he had won to Trinity College. But this was only by way of an introduction to his remarks about 'Blunt's propaganda of Modern Art'.

'I cannot refrain from congratulating him also,' said Turner, 'on his persistent efforts to interest an incurably sentimental society in modern aims in art and literature.'

A discernible snicker snaked around the huddled ranks of boys as the headmaster confessed, with a smile, that he found Blunt's 'world of angles, dissonance and mis-shaped objects' a 'very odd one.'

Anthony Blunt sat proud and detached. Junior boys, accustomed to hearing praise lavished on cricketers and rugby players, looked around to glimpse this unusual school hero. Their housemaster, Dr Guillebaud, 'was enraged' according to MacNeice. Any nineteen-year-old would have found his head swelling with pride. But before the rush of self-satisfaction must have reached Blunt's toes, he was stung by a sharp rebuke. 'Blunt and some others may go image breaking, but' – the headmaster paused – 'that is no bad thing so long as the hammer is swung fair and square at the image and not the heads of rival worshipers.'

Laughter erupted throughout the hall. Blunt had been cut

down to size in his moment of glory. The headmaster had touched a raw nerve by publicly exposing Blunt's willingness to turn his high-minded championship of the cause of modern art into personal vendettas.

The moment brought some satisfaction to Christopher Hughes. The art master had already turned down 'nearly all' the paintings Blunt and MacNeice had submitted for the Prize Day exhibition. Blunt had fired off a final scornful salvo entitled 'De Cubismo,' which appeared in *The Marlburian*. 'Modern art,' Blunt declared, 'should be judged by the same standards as Persian rugs,' which, he insisted, were the 'formal qualities of pattern and color'. He attacked the 'evil tradition' of 'purely imitative' pictures and storytelling painting, singling out the art master's cherished Pre-Raphaelites as exemplifying a 'peculiarly English failing'. The French, Blunt claimed, had 'revolutionized the art of all European countries, except England'.

Hughes had the last word. 'Unless the critic grasps something of that feeling for nature,' Hughes wrote in the next issue of the school magazine, 'it is easy to understand how he missed the finer points of Art.' This parting shot struck Blunt's exposed flank. For all his pedestrian aesthetic values, Hughes was a creative artist who had instinctively put his finger on Blunt's great failing: he had little artistic ability himself, and this lack of understanding of the creative impulse flawed his critical judgements.

Did Blunt harbor a resentment against art and artists because of an inferiority complex? Blunt's lack of ability on the games field appears to have been a contributory factor in spurring his rebellion against the Marlborough athletes. Could the recognition of his lack of artistic ability have prompted him to take a similar revenge on art?

MacNeice's recollections reveal that he and Blunt had experimented with painting in the style of the artists they admired. Together they daubed watercolors of Matisse-like goldfish and painted Picasso-style still lifes. On one occasion an angry bathing master confronted Blunt when he set up his easel at the school swimming moat. Anthony managed to get permission to continue his canvas by assuring the master it was not the naked boys he wished to record for posterity but the corrugated-iron bathing shed.

Unfortunately, neither this nor any other Blunt picture survives, in the original. But research for this book turned up a photograph of his work. It suggests that Blunt's inability to draw may have prompted his passion for objects rather than people, and also his fanaticism for Cubist art. The only known genuine Blunt is preserved for posterity in a photograph of his Marlborough study. It is propped up against the wall over his desk. An enlargement reveals a still-life watercolor of a small urn atop a pyramid of books. The painting probably dates from September 1925, when a MacNeice letter mentions that Anthony had brought 'a superb piece of lustre ware' from his summer trip to Belgium. But Blunt's effort clearly did not do justice to the urn. The painting's clumsy composition and lack of form confirms that the young critic was a poor artist whose dogmatic, intensely analytical approach to art ignored the emotional qualities of a painting. It also suggest that Blunt was determined to set himself up as the arbiter of cultural values to compensate for his own lack of talent.

On the eve of his departure for university life, Anthony Blunt was already a deadly combination in terms of his psychological profile. He was prepared to rebel and strike out against the society in which he lived. He was blessed with a superb intelligence that allowed him to spot the weak points in people and organizations. He had learned the secrets of sexual blackmail. He was capable of manipulating his peers and his teachers. And, as Robert Cecil has pointed out, he was cold blooded enough, calculating enough, that he could achieve his goal of secret power over other people's lives. And since Blunt's 'acute brain' ensured his success at an early age, the only questions were: how would he achieve his adult goals, and who would help him achieve them?

4 'Exporting the Revolution'

Two years before Anthony Blunt went to Marlborough College and discovered his talents for manipulating people, momentous events were being played out on the world's stage that would have a dramatic impact on his adult life. In March 1919, Vladimir Ilyich Lenin, chairman of the people's commissars and virtual dictator of the emerging Soviet Union, summoned foreign sympathizers to the motherland of communism to discuss the future of the Revolution.

It would take another two years for the Bolsheviks to win the bloody civil war and secure total control of all Russia, but Lenin was planning with deadly precision. With Leon Trotsky standing at his side, Lenin gave his overseas battalions their marching orders: he announced the Third Communist International, or Comintern as it came to be known. Lenin thereby proclaimed that the Bolsheviks were the leaders of the world socialist movement, and the Comintern would be the agent by which the dreaded enemy known as capitalism would be destroyed. What Lenin and Trotsky intended was a global revolution that was to be coordinated and directed by Moscow.

Trotsky drew up the plan of battle: it called for applying every means – legal and illegal – to undermine and abolish all other forms of government, including democracy. When it came to establishing the so-called dictatorship of the proletariat, the end justified the means. In a ringing recasting of Marx's famous phrase, Trotsky called on the workers of the world to unite in the name of the Comintern, telling them they had 'nothing to lose but your chains'.

A principal target for the Comintern was Great Britain. Over the years, the pattern of the onslaught can be seen as three successive waves of subversion, each one more dangerous than the last. Simply put, the first wave would call for spontaneous combustion, the explosion of hatred created by the British class system. The second wave would involve trade; by opening these lines of communication, Moscow hoped to infiltrate and suborn the labor movement. The third would be the most dangerous of all to the British government because Moscow had learned from its previous failures. It would take a new tack and spend years infiltrating the system from within to gain control of the British government's counterintelligence system. This was the sophisticated plan that activated Blunt and the Cambridge spies.

To understand the story of Blunt, one has to go back to the abdication of Tsar Nicholas II in March 1917, an event that was warmly welcomed by British radicals. The subsequent overthrow of Kerensky's socialist provisional government by the Bolshevik Revolution in November of that year cooled their ardor somewhat and the Parliamentary Labour party declared itself opposed to Lenin's dictatorship of the proletariat.

British socialists nevertheless protested against the launching of military expeditions by Allied forces (British, American and Japanese) to Archangel and Siberia in March 1918. The declared objectives of these operations were to protect Allied war matériel against capture by the Germans, with whom the Bolshevik government had just signed a peace treaty. Then the Labour party joined its voice to Moscow's furious protests at the invasions by capitalist powers in support of the White Russian armies who were fighting to overthrow the six-month-old Revolution. Britain was also suspected of complicity in the August assassination attempt on Lenin. (The shots that wounded the architect of the Bolshevik Revolution were actually fired by a disaffected Russian socialist named Dora Kaplan.) In a retaliatory move, Moscow arrested Robert Bruce Lockhart, a Foreign Office envoy, along with two of his officers. The British government responded in kind by detaining Maxim Litvinov and several other Russians who were serving as the Bolsheviks' unofficial emissaries in London. This practical demonstration of the realpolitik of Anglo-Soviet relations may have lacked the traditional niceties of diplomatic protocol, but it produced a speedy exchange of prisoners.

As a trusted member of the Bolshevik old guard, Litvinov had been living in exile in London since the 1905 abortive uprising against the tsar. He had fled after taking part in 'expropriation raids' – a Soviet euphemism for robbing Russian banks of millions of rubles. Litvinov had married an English girl, Ivy Low, and had become an accomplished socializer and an astute exploiter of class conflict. His polished manners and many connections in British left-wing circles had earned him Lenin's respect and a key role in organizing the Soviets' subversion and intelligence apparatus in Britain.

Litvinov's abrupt repatriation to Moscow – where he eventually became Stalin's commissar for foreign affairs in 1930 – obliged Lenin to make some significant changes in his scheme for exporting the Revolution to Britain. Litvinov's mission was taken over by Theodore Rothstein, another resident Russian émigré with extensive contacts with the left wing. His mission was to unite the fractious and splintered British Marxist groups into a coherent revolutionary movement. It proved to be an uphill struggle and in the 1919 'Referendum on Socialist Unity', the British Marxists rejected the call to form a single Communist party.

Historically, the writing of Marx had made little impact on either the workers or the intellectuals of the capitalist nation. Dialectical materialism aroused little enthusiasm in British socialists who regarded themselves as heirs to the older radical tradition of the seventeenth-century Leveller sects and the nonconformist Christian Methodism of the eighteenth century. Violent revolution was also alien to the moderate views of the genteel socialists in the Fabian Society, which, since its foundation in 1884 by middle-class intellectuals, had been guided by economists Sidney and Beatrice Webb and critic and writer George Bernard Shaw.

British socialists believed in achieving social reform by 'permeation' of existing political institutions, and a querulous alliance between the trade-union movement and socialist intellectuals gave birth to Britain's parliamentary Labour party, which won twenty-nine seats in the 1906 general election.

The Marxist hardliners refused to give up and World War I was seen by true Marxist believers as ushering in the final crisis of capitalism as predicted by the Second International which had resolved in 1889 'to accelerate the fall of the bourgeoisies'. But the Labour party, which had rashly affiliated itself with the International in 1908, broke its pledge to oppose 'an imperialist war'. It declared in support of the British government, as did the Trades Union Congress, which called for an 'industrial truce'.

The socialist leaders on Clydeside defied the truce and fomented a series of strikes. By 1917, the government was obliged to intervene to halt the spread of industrial anarchy that threatened to disrupt the war effort. The enormous expansion in Britain's counterintelligence organizations during World War I enabled the government to move surely against the homegrown Marxist revolutionaries to contain the Communist menace. By 1918 this activity overshadowed their original mission to round up German sympathizers and spies.

The Secret Service Bureau, formed in 1909, was divided into two departments: one responsible for domestic counterintelligence and the other for overseas operations. In 1916, as a direct reflection of their particular wartime responsibilities to the Military Intelligence department in the War Office, they were renamed MI5 and MI6 (pronounced M-eye-five and M-eye-six). They were headed by two powerful personalities who possessed a uniquely British talent for combining eccentricity with ruthlessness: Captain Vernon Kell and Commander Mansfield Smith-Cumming.

Kell, a mustaschioed army officer and veteran of the Boxer Rebellion in China, was every bit as talented a bureaucratic empire builder as Cumming, a naval officer with a passion for fast cars. Cumming was known simply as 'C', a title inherited by succeeding directors of MI6. His spies – who included the roman-ticized Sidney Reilly – attracted considerable fictionalized atten-tion as spy literature became a fashionable genre. But it fell to the less glamorous MI5 to maintain the mundane filing cards in the Central Registry. These, as we shall see, made by far the greater contribution to the empire's security. By 1917, Kell's department had grown from 19 people to 844, and its register of suspicious characters had increased to a quarter of a million cards. These were constantly updated by 130 trusted female clerks.

By the end of the war, the Central Registry had become the heart of MI5's operations; its alphabetized 'Special Intelligence Black List' index was coded by nationality, credentials and a suspect's subversive activities. The data on these cards were collected from the chief constables of the British police services, and the Special Branch – the elite undercover force of London's Metropolitan Police, founded in 1887 to counter Irish Fenian terrorism – carried out investigations and arrests on behalf of MI5. Dominion and Indian police, informants, port disembark-ation records and government censors – who monitored all tele-graphic and postal communications – also contributed their reports to MI5; additional intelligence was obtained from wartime allies.

The rapid expansion of MI5's Registry was eyed enviously by Sir Basil Thomson, assistant commissioner of the Metropolitan Police and head of Scotland Yard's Criminal Investigation Divi-sion. The Bolshevik takeover of Russia's provisional socialist government convinced Thomson that undercover Marxist revolu-tionaries would soon replace German spies as the new enemy. He regarded Bolshevism as a 'sort of infectious disease, spreading rapidly but insidiously, until like a cancer it eats away the fabric of society and the patient ceases to wish for his own recovery.'

Thomson cast himself in the role of the surgeon summoned by destiny to rid Britain of the Communist cancer. In 1919, the specter of a 'Triple Industrial Alliance' among miners, rail-waymen and transport workers was threatening a general strike that could paralyse the country. As head of the Home Office's newly formed Directorate of Intelligence, Thomson had authority rivaling that of MI5, which had suffered a peacetime staff cut and loss of the Passport Control Service (through which it operated under cover) to the Foreign Office. But the assistant commissioner of the Metropolitan Police still had to rely on Kell's MI5 Registry for the intelligence on which he based his weekly report for the Cabinet.

Stamped SECRET, the early copies of 'Revolutionary Organizations in the United Kingdom' reports in the declassified British Cabinet records, as supplemented by the later reports in the US State Department files, reveal the extent and depth of the surveillance operation run by MI5, Special Branch, and the local police forces in Britain during the twenties and thirties. From Communist activities on 'Red Clydeside', to the Irish Sinn Feiners, to information on Moscow's devious efforts to fund the financially strapped socialist *Daily Herald* newspaper, and the plans for a Youth International to infiltrate schools and universities, Thomson's weekly reports suggest that Scotland Yard was anything but complacent when it came to monitoring Comintern subversion in Britain.

Secret reports received from the Hungarian commander in chief in Budapest revealed that Lenin had ordered fifty million rubles deposited in Berlin banks in November 1919 to fund Comintern subversion overseas. As a result, Thomson called for tough new antirevolutionary legislation, modeled on that already introduced in the United States and Canada, to make it a criminal offense to advocate the overthrow of the government by force, and to accept financial support or propaganda from the Soviets.

Prime Minister Lloyd George's coalition government of Liberals and Conservatives balked at introducing these measures. Thomson was fettered by having to work within the existing sedition and conspiracy laws to monitor the Comintern operations against Britain. In contrast to Commander Cumming and Admiral Sir Hugh Sinclair, who succeeded him as 'C' in 1923, neither MI5 nor Special Branch underestimated the skill and ruthlessness of the opposition they faced.

Feliks Edmundovich Dzerzhinski, C's principal adversary in Moscow, was a spymaster of very different mettle from 'Quex' Sinclair, who continued the tradition of recruiting Britain's spies from the upper-class members of London gentlemen's clubs. Handpicked by Lenin in December 1917 to head the All-Russian Extraordinary Commission to Combat Counterrevolution and Sabotage (Vserossiyskaya Chrezvychaynaya Komissiya or VChK), better known as the feared Cheka secret police, Dzerzhinski was was a veteran Bolshevik. His goatee and beady blue eyes gave him a gnomelike appearance. There was nothing benign, however, about the Polish revolutionary who had already spent over eleven of his forty years in the tsar's jails or Siberian exile.

An instinctive master at predicting human behavior, Dzerzhinski was an awesome interrogator. According to one of his victims, his 'eyes made you feel that he could see into your very soul.' He proudly bore on his wrists the scars of handcuffs as evidence of the apprenticeship that uniquely qualified him to carry out Lenin's orders 'to Combat Counterrevolution, Speculation and Sabotage'. Dzerzhinski founded a ruthless secret-police system, whose mission was both offensive and defensive: to be the 'Sword and Shield' of the Revolution.

The Cheka became the weapon by which Lenin and his Bolshevik minority swiftly imposed their authority on the Russian civilian populace and the Red Army. At the same time the Cheka branched out into overseas espionage to counter the threat posed to the Revolution by White Russian émigrés. The organization that Dzerzhinski built discharged its functions so thoroughly that it grew in numbers and authority. Soon it was an indispensable part of the Soviet *apparat* that, after a succession of name changes, became the State Security Committee (Komitet Gosudarstvennoy Bezopasnosti), the all-pervasive KGB.

In the 1920s Bolshevism was perceived as an immediate threat on both sides of the Atlantic. During the final year of World War I, the British and Americans entered into a secret treaty for sharing counterintelligence information. The treaty is still in force, although this particular 'special relationship' has never been officially acknowledged on either side of the Atlantic. While the British Empire was Moscow's principal target in the interwar years, English-speaking Soviet agents were often switched between the two countries and subversion on both sides of the Atlantic was linked and coordinated by the same directorate in the Comintern's Moscow bureau.

The secret MI5 and Special Branch reports in the National Archives in Washington reveal how wartime exchanges on German spies quickly gave way to peacetime swapping of information about Bolshevik revolutionaries and subversion. The United States was better equipped to meet the Communist subversion when J. Edgar Hoover became director in 1924 of what became the FBI – and assistance was provided by British reports passed via the US embassy in London. They were circulated by the State Department to the Justice Department and thence to military and naval intelligence organizations which, when the situation required, called on the services of the local police forces to arrest spies and subversives.

Commencing in February 1920, the Special Branch reports listing 'prominent revolutionaries in the United Kingdom', along with digests of Thomson's weekly reports on subversive activities, were hand-carried to the first secretary of the US embassy in London by senior Special Branch officers. The State Department's initial lack of security and facilities for handling such sensitive information very nearly ended this unique secret collaboration only a month after it began. In March, information from one of Thomson's reports appeared in *The New York Times*, which printed details of Britain's secret emergency plans to meet a Communist-inspired national strike. Investigation by the Justice Department confirmed the leak had occurred despite a Strictly Confidential classification. It was only after Washington tightened up security in May that Thomson proposed setting up with the Americans 'a Clearing House in London for all undesirable Bolsheviks'.

While the Clearing House operation was never made official, it is obvious that it went into effect because of the volumes of documentation under 800 B 'Bolshevik' in the State Department records in Washington. These reveal that American requests for data from the Central Registry were being met on a regular basis. In turn, the Americans supplied information for the MI5 files on the Comintern. As mutual confidence and trust developed between MI5 officers and their contacts in the US embassy, cooperation extended way beyond exchanging visa applications from known and suspect Communists. The details of Comintern personnel, organization and operations that appear in the US records are documentary testimony – where none is available in Britain – of the remarkable early success of MI5 in intercepting Moscow's secret communications and penetrating the evolving Communist organizations.

A sobering realization confronts any researcher delving into the indigo leather-bound confidential London Embassy files. They contain actual MI5 and Special Branch reports that represent only the tip of the iceberg of data that remains locked away by the British Official Secrets Act. How this intelligence (still top secret in Britain) was used remains a matter for speculation. But the scope and detail of the files that were passed to the Americans were so extensive that it is difficult to see how MI5's expertise and early success could have been squandered in such appalling later failures.

The British security services were, as the new documentary evidence shows, more than a match for the primitive Soviet efforts to subvert Britain from within and without. After Litvinov's abrupt repatriation in 1918, it is clear that both Kell of MI5 and Thomson of Special Branch quickly discovered that his mission and his authority had passed to Theodore Rothstein, on whom they had already an extensive dossier.

A long-standing member of the British Socialist party, Rothstein had funneled Soviet funds to and sought to impose Moscow's direction upon the British revolutionary organizations. The breakthrough came in June 1919 with the arrest of Jacob Novosivitsky, an American Bolshevik, at Liverpool. After interrogation he was 'turned' into a double agent and his confession to working for Rothstein as a trusted courier enabled Special Branch to monitor Comintern orders to and contacts with Ludwig C. A. K. Martens, the self-proclaimed Soviet representative in New York. The secret Anglo-American exchanges led to Martens's deportation from the United States in January 1921, along with forty members of his staff, for advocating the overthrow of Congress.

The Special Branch report on Rothstein provides a detailed picture of how he ran the Soviet underground network in Britain from his mother's house in Highgate. His summer home was a converted railway Pullman car near Lake Windermere, situated conveniently near the shipyards, mines, and factory areas of the industrial north of England. His son Andrew, who, according to the secret report, 'assists him', was a Brackenbury Scholar at Balliol College, Oxford. (Andrew Rothstein was later to become the first English-born member of the Soviets' London-based Communist cell while managing Moscow's news agency in Fleet Street.)

Theodore Rothstein, MI5 had established by 1921, communicated with Moscow mainly by courier. The British had learned – through infiltrators and by censoring his mail – that he used a secret password with trusted contacts in the British Socialist party. He also employed a code for his secret cables to the Comintern, of which, Thomson reassured the Cabinet, 'the Authorities possess a copy'. MI5 monitored how the Comintern's principal agent in Britain received the substantial funding to pay subsidiary agents, contribute to the former suffragette leader Sylvia Pankhurst's organization, and even dole out funds to Italian Bolsheviks.

'Among the remittances received by Rothstein from Russia,' the Special Branch report noted, 'was a packet of diamonds.' These were not industrial diamonds, but gems looted from tsarist nobles. Mrs Rothstein, according to the British report, enjoyed adorning herself and her daughter with diamond necklaces, earclips and brooches. The most surprising revelation was that

Rothstein had worked until 1919 for MI7, a branch of Britain's military intelligence. This made him one of the first Soviet moles because he had used his position of trust to feed reports from Russian newspapers to George Lansbury, editor of the *Daily Herald*, and to supply Sylvia Pankhurst with information for her People's Russian Information Bureau.

Rothstein's 'contempt for Sylvia Pankhurst's intelligence and discretion' was also revealed to MI5. In January 1920 Pankhurst appealed directly to Lenin to recognize her Workers Socialist Federation as the 'Communist Party (British Section of the Third International)' after attending a secret convocation in Holland of European Comintern leaders. Unfortunately, the militant suffragette's opposition to Communists' standing as parliamentary candidates conflicted with Lenin's ruling that 'Soviet propaganda can and ought to be carried on from within the bourgeois parliaments.'

Without a united British Communist party to take the lead, the threat of imminent revolution was remote. The British revolutionary groups indulged in 'too much theatrical cloak and dagger' for Thomson to believe that their secret meetings constituted 'a real menace'. But Thomson did not hesitate to caution the Cabinet against underestimating Lenin's capacity for 'composing quarrels' and 'dictating policy'. Thomson's real concern was with the next wave of Comintern activity. This he believed would automatically follow the diplomatic recognition of the Bolshevik regime because Prime Minister Lloyd George had a naïve belief that opening commercial activity with the Soviet Union was the best way to blunt Moscow's subversion.

'The moment trade was established Communism would go,' declared Lloyd George with a myopic miscalculation that belied his reputation as a *realpolitiker*. An invitation was issued to the Soviets to send a delegation to London in the spring of 1920 to begin talks about a trade treaty. The fear of MI5 and Special Branch that the Soviets would exploit this diplomatic overture proved justified that May. The British trades unions rallied to the 'Hands Off Russia' campaign instigated by London dockworkers, who refused to load ships with munitions destined for the Polish army in the final phase of the Russian civil war.

When the official trade delegation from Moscow arrived in London, Winston Churchill, the secretary of state for war and air in Lloyd George's coalition government, absented himself from the formal reception for the Soviets rather than 'shake the hands with a hairy baboon'. But Leonid Krassin, the tall and elegantly spoken Soviet commissar for foreign trade, was the exact opposite of a primatelike Bolshevik revolutionary. As head of the delegation he promised that members of his staff would not 'interfere in any way in the politics or internal affairs of the country.'

It gave Thomson, however, a certain grim satisfaction to report that Krassin's assistant, N. K. Klisko, had wasted no time in contacting 'Communist elements' immediately after the delegation's arrival. When Rothstein 'attached himself' to the delegation despite written Soviet assurances not to interfere in Britain's domestic politics, MI5 was confirmed in its belief that such promises were not worth the paper they were written on. Thomson's predictions about Lenin's determination to impose his authority on the fractious British Communists was also borne out. When their leaders attended the Second Congress of the Third International in Petrograd authority was conferred on the dozen delegates to unite into the Communist party of Great Britain (CPGB). At a conference in London at the end of August, some 154 delegates of the CPGB adopted the Soviet leadership, the dictatorship of the proletariat, and adherence to the Comintern's revolutionary objectives. Communications intercepted by MI5 revealed that Rothstein was secretly designated CPGB 'chairman appointed by Moscow Executive'. He was promptly barred from reentering Britain after Thomson dryly acknowledged he should be credited 'for such unity as was achieved' because 'he supplied the funds'. But the failure of the British party to attract intellectual supporters ensured that it was a worker-led organization, a factor that played its part in leading the Soviets to attempt an alternative penetration of Britain's ruling elite.

So while the CPGB played an important part in the first wave of the Soviet assault on Britain, it was doomed to a minority appeal after the four million strong Labour party – the largest socialist body in Europe – rejected affiliation with the 'intellectual slaves of Moscow'. MI5 informants relayed the details of Zinoviev's plan for infiltrating the armed forces and the trade unions with Communist cells 'to fan the already existing flames of discontent, to foment revolt, and finally to bring about revolutionary action.' The distinctive cut of Russian diamonds smuggled into Britain in Soviet diplomatic bags helped derail the Trade Delegation's efforts to fund their subversive plans.

Comintern agents were multiplying in Britain, but MI5 and Special Branch possessed a secret weapon needed to contain and counter Communist subversion.

Since 1917 British code breakers had been able to read the Soviet cipher traffic. The Bolsheviks' disdain for all things tsarist had prompted them to reject the sophisticated codes of the imperial government, replacing them with a simple transposition system in plain Russian. With the assistance of F. C. Fetterlein, one of the leading cryptanalysts of the ousted regime, and his team of émigré women translators, British intelligence was kept abreast of the Kremlin's most secret exchanges as its envoys fanned out to export the Revolution.

'We were able to attack their systems step by step with success from the days of Litvinov's first visit to Copenhagen, of Kamenev as their first representative in London, followed by Krassin, until the famous Arcos raid in 1927', recalled one of the codebreakers.

The discovery in the archives of Churchill College, Cambridge, of a detailed and uncensored history of the Government Code and Cipher School code-breaking establishment blows a large hole in the British government's coy refusal to acknowledge the extent of its peacetime code-breaking effort. Denniston headed the secret organization for over two decades. This authoritative insight comes from the private papers of Commander Alexander Denniston, the head of Britain's top-secret GC&CS which operated in a ten-story Westminster office block known as the Broadway Buildings. A wiry Scot with a quizzical expression, Denniston had been a member of the Royal Navy's famous World War I code-breaking team in Room 40 of the Admiralty.

Led by the legendary code breaker Captain (later Rear Admiral) William Reginald 'Blinker' Hall, the GC&CS staff had broken the German foreign minister's cable to the German ambassadors in Washington and Mexico City that signalled Berlin's imminent intention to begin unrestricted U-boat warfare. After the contents of the notorious 'Zimmermann' telegram was leaked to the press, public opinion in America hardened in favor of entering the war against Germany in 1917. This demonstration of the value of 'signal intelligence' in twentieth-century diplomacy convinced the British government of the necessity for continuing and expanding its eavesdropping operations after the war. Accordingly GC&CS was set up under Foreign Office control.

Its most spectacular triumph was the breaking of the German Enigma machine codes in World War II, to provide the Allies their so-called Ultra secret. Denniston's paper, moreover, reveals that while he was put in charge of GC&CS to 'advise on the security of codes and ciphers', its real objective was 'to study the methods of cipher communications by foreign powers'. In his 1944 memoir, Denniston concedes Britain made a priority of eavesdropping on its allies: French ciphers were read with ease, and 'good progress' had been made in penetrating the American diplomatic ciphers.

Denniston, however, reported that the 'only real operational intelligence' GC&CS provided in the twenties came from the Soviet traffic. It was his code-breakers who kept the British government abreast of the Russian Trade Delegation's clandestine mission of subversion and spying during Britain's lengthy negotiations with Krassin in 1920–21. The intercepted telegrams reveal how the Soviets began the talks with a typically hard line. 'That swine Lloyd George has no scruples of shame in the way he deceives,' Lenin warned Krassin. 'Don't believe a word he says and gull him three times as much.'

The British government, with the advantage of knowing its

opponent's hand, held firm with their demands for Moscow to repay the Russian loans repudiated by the Bolsheviks and for an end to subversive activities against the British Empire. The ability to monitor the instructions sent to Krassin after he returned in July with Lev Kamenev (chairman of the Moscow Soviet and the new head of the delegation) kept MI5 and Special Branch aware of the developing threat. They warned the prime minister of the trade delegation's central role in the 'plot to create red revolution and ruin in this country'.

Lloyd George decided, nevertheless, that despite the 'flagrant breach of the conditions' by the trade delegation, there was an 'undoubted advantage' in 'our being able to tap these messages as it gives us real insight into Bolshevist interests and policy.' He wanted to keep the Soviet trade deal alive because he hoped it would stimulate the faltering British postwar economy and bring votes for his ailing Liberal party.

The prime minister adopted a stick and carrot approach. He confronted the Russian delegation on 10 September 1920, and accused Kamenev, who was due to depart for Moscow next day, of a 'gross breach of faith'. He made it clear that the head of the Moscow Soviet would not be readmitted to Britain. But his deputy Krassin would be permitted to remain, provided he adhered strictly to the agreement not to engage in subversion. The government arrested leading Communists after an October miners' strike persuaded the Cabinet to pass an Emergency Powers Act authorizing MI5 to step up action against civilian subversives.

The British government's public crackdown against Communist subversion was not lost on Lenin. His regime was struggling to stave off a collapse of the Soviet economy. Trade was seen as a vital road to economic rejuvenation after the debilitating period of 'war communism', so talks with the British resumed in November. By January 1921 Leonid Krassin took a draft agreement back to Moscow. With Lenin's New Economic Policy putting a high priority on exporting products for badly needed foreign capital, the Soviets 'capitulated' to the British terms, and the Anglo-Soviet Trade Agreement was signed on 16 March 1921. Three months later the Russians, despite their devastated economy, invested a third of a million pounds in one of the City of London's most expensive office buildings at 49 Moorgate.

Renamed Soviet House, it served as Russia's London headquarters for three years until Moscow was granted the right to maintain an embassy in Britain. Meanwhile, its trade delegation enjoyed limited diplomatic immunity, which the Comintern turned to its advantage by launching into a new course of subversion, propagandizing the British trade unions to affiliate with the Profintern, the so-called Red International of Labor Unions.

Ironically, shortly after the Foreign Office opened a file headed 'Violations of the Russian Trade Agreements', the activist Sir Basil Thomson was sacked and his Intelligence Directorate disbanded. This came after Lloyd George's shaky coalition government was faced with charges by the Labour party that Special Branch had become a 'system of domestic espionage' aimed at the working class. General Kell welcomed the demise of the powerful assistant commissioner of the Metropolitan Police because it removed a rival whose authority had been forcing MI5 into a subsidiary role.

If the Intelligence Directorate had survived, it could have provided Britain's security services with the coordination necessary to deal with the increasing sophistication of the second Soviet assault. The new beachhead was the All Russian Co-Operative Society – better known as Arcos Limited – a £1 million limited liability company formed in London. With an Anglo-Soviet board of directors and a staff that grew in five years to more than two hundred Russians, Arcos was ostensibly engaged in conducting commercial operations. But behind the commercial front, Arcos was a cover for the operations of the Soviet intelligence service and representatives of the control commission who supervised the CPGB.

The majority of Arcos managers were handpicked officers of Soviet Military Intelligence – the GRU (Glavnoye Razvedyvatelnoye Upravleniye). Their mission was to be industrial espionage agents, and their role was indicative of the importance that Lenin gave to rehabilitating and modernizing the Soviet economy. Obsolete Russian factories needed technology and know-how that could only be bought at inflated prices for hard currency from greedy capitalist businessmen. The trade delegation quickly became the cover for the systematic GRU-masterminded theft of Western technology with only a minimum investment in legal trade. This soon developed into an industrial-espionage operation on a global scale. It was managed under the auspices of the Commissariat for Foreign Trade, Narkomvneshtorg, NKVT, whose Torgpredstva (or trading delegations), nominally offshoots of Arcos in Britain, sprang up in every European capital by the end of 1921.

The Soviets had to wait three years before the United States – Russia's biggest potential market – permitted any direct trading because Congress had passed a law prohibiting any trade with the Soviets after they had repudiated their war debts. But Ludwig Martens – with the help of sympathetic American bankers, businessmen, Marxists and smuggled diamonds – functioned as the 'unofficial' Soviet ambassador and trade representative in New York until his deportation in 1921.

One of Marten's closest associates was a doctor of medicine, a Jewish émigré from Odessa named Julius Hammer. According to State Department records, Hammer was a generous contributor to the US Socialist party and 'believed to be at present part of the Bolshevik regime'. That explained why he was 'one of the first to establish one of the "fronts"', corporations and purchasing agencies' that were in reality controlled by 'Soviet Jewish elements under the direction of the Soviet Government of Russia.' Hammer, with Abraham Heller – 'a notorious Bolshevik' and associate of Martens – was the founding partner in the Allied Drug and Chemical Company. A State Department investigation revealed that this company, incorporated in 1917 with Martens holding half the stock, was 'utilized by the Soviet Government in starting trade with the United States'.

Dr Armand Hammer, the youngest son of Julius, and a

graduate of Columbia University Medical School, began his business career as company secretary for Allied Drug. The international philanthropist and octogenarian head of the Occidental Petroleum conglomerate has actively championed trade with the Soviet Union throughout his long and remarkably successful career. Armand Hammer has counted among his personal acquaintances every Soviet leader. He met Lenin in Moscow in 1921. This was after his father's business career had been curtailed by his father's arrest and conviction for manslaughter after the death of a woman for whom he had performed an illegal abortion. Lenin was evidently impressed that Julius Hammer's letter introducing his son Armand was written from a Federal penitentiary. The Soviet revolutionary leader seems to have felt that the capitalist system had harshly punished the good doctor not for medical malpractice but for his socialist convictions. As a gesture of goodwill to Julius for his commitment, Lenin awarded his son one of the first foreign concessions and put private railroad cars at Armand's disposal. Feliks Dzerzhinski, the head of the Cheka, was appointed to head the commission administering the concessions. This suggests that industrial contracts were not regarded by the Soviets as mere business transactions, but as an integral part of the subversive strategy.

It appears significant, moreover, that Armand Hammer's trip to Russia, which included a stopover in London, also aroused the interest of MI5. On 8 July 1921, the US embassy in London was alerted that his father, Dr Julius Hammer, was 'noted on our files as having been a close associate of Trotsky and later of Martens'. While there is, however, no concrete evidence that the youngest Hammer son shared his father's commitment to the Bolshevik cause, the Hammers' concession to mine asbestos in the Urals was signed by Maxim Litvinov, the Soviet trade commissar. The original contract was made with Allied Drug and Chemical, but this corporation had 'disappeared as an active institution'. On Armand's return to the United States in December 1921, his brother Harry J. Hammer and three business associates had formed the Ural-American Refining and Trading Company, which changed its name to the impressive-sounding Allied American Corporation in 1922. Nor does it appear insignificant that Allied American became the first Soviet-American trading agency or that one of its subsidiaries, Allied American Fur Sales Company, maintained what State Department officials called its 'real' bank account at the Midland Bank in London, 'where it receives the supervision of certain individuals connected with the Russian government'.

The 'individuals' in question were officials of Soviet House. Documents discovered by Special Branch in the possession of an Arcos employee named Anton Miller linked payments of $5,000 made by Harry Hammer in 1925 to Joseph Moness and Julius Heiman. The pair were Comintern agents known to be involved in channeling funds to the American Communist party. But the demands of espionage and subversion in the United States outstripped the resources of a single trading corporation. In 1921 orders came from Moscow to expand the American operation. Allied American was then obediently merged with two smaller Soviet-controlled trading fronts: Products Exchange Corporation (Prodexco) and the All-Russian Textile Corporation (Derutra).

The amalgamation gave birth to Amtorg – American Trading Organization – with its 'home offices' at 14 Kuznetsky Most, Moscow. The attorney who engineered the deal, Charles Recht, had acted as legal adviser to Ludwig Martens. He contrived to set up Amtorg as a 'licensee' of Russian goods with a charter of incorporation that artfully circumvented the congressional ban on direct trade with the Soviet Union. But once in operation, Amtorg sponsored an influx of Soviet managers and 'inspectors' to conduct its licensing operations. As with Arcos, its key personnel were GRU officers trained in espionage, who worked alongside officials of the GPU and control commission posing as commercial agents. Amtorg's secret mission was to fund a network of Communist groups using the cover of legitimate business. Its officials practised some highly creative accounting, drawing its funds from Arcos in London and then shunting the transfers around its numerous accounts in Canada and the United

States. In this way Amtorg disguised the huge sums it fed to the Soviets' North American espionage and subversion network.

The establishment of Amtorg in 1924 coincided with the controversial decision by Britain's first Labour government to grant full diplomatic recognition to the Soviet Union.

This Red Letter year for the Communist Revolution opened with Lenin's death in January and a struggle for power among Joseph Stalin, Leon Trotsky and Grigori Zinoviev. The triumvirate that Lenin designated as his titular successor and guardian of the Revolution was quickly dominated by Stalin, who gained the upper hand by allying himself with the chief of the secret police.

Feliks Dzerzhinski had consolidated the real behind-the-scenes power in the Kremlin two years earlier, when Lenin authorized the transformation of the Cheka into the State Political Administration, the GPU (Gosudarstvennoye Politicheskoye Upravleniye). Through his able lieutenant, Mikhail Abramovich Trilisser, who became the chief of the GPU Foreign Department, Dzerzhinski gained the power to veto Comintern activities when they affected security, and to coopt the services of foreign Communist parties for intelligence gathering.

Stalin, who believed in 'building socialism in one country' before exporting the revolution, was a pragmatist. He did not share the messianic belief of Trotsky or Zinoviev in the immediacy of the global Communist revolution. After the Comintern's disastrous failure to precipitate a workers' uprising in Germany in 1923 cost Zinoviev a further loss of authority, his power waned. It was already on the line when the British, citing wholesale violations, threatened to cancel the trade agreement. The rapidity with which the Kremlin agreed to renew promises 'not to support with funds' or 'spread discontent or to foment rebellion in any part of the British Empire' indicated the value, both covert and commercial, that the Soviets put on the trade agreement.

Yet neither Lenin nor his successors had any intention of sticking to their agreements. They believed that to achieve the goals of communism, the end justified any expedient, especially when it came to taking advantage of the fact that Britain's first Labour administration was all for granting Moscow full diplomatic recognition.

This was one of the first acts of Ramsay MacDonald's short-lived government. After some initial concern about his trustworthiness, Britain's security-service chiefs concluded that MacDonald was 'loyal and straightforward' – but not enough, it seems, to have access to his own Special Branch file! After a wave of strikes, MI5 chief Kell set up a Committee on Industrial Unrest to ascertain 'whether any appreciable percentage of the unfortunate aspects of these strikes was due to Communist activity.'

MI5 was able to inform the Cabinet it had 'irrefutable evidence' that the Communist party received weekly financial payments from the Russian Trade Delegation. The CPGB had been brought firmly under Comintern direction in 1922 when it adopted a report on organization, prepared by two members of its executive: Harry Pollitt and Rajani Palme Dutt. Pollitt, a Lancashire boilermaker of rare oratorical skill, and Dutt, an austere Anglo-Indian theoretician who had graduated from Balliol College, Oxford, formed a partnership that led the party on an unswerving course dictated by Moscow for more than two decades.

The Labour government's apprehension about firm action against Communist subversion for fear of prejudicing the signing of commercial treaties with the newly established Soviet embassy helped bring down MacDonald's government. The prime minister's decision not to release John Campbell, a Communist journalist arrested under the Incitement to Mutiny Act for writing seditious articles aimed at the military, cost the Labour party its Liberal support in Parliament. After losing a vote of confidence on 8 October 1924, MacDonald's minority government resigned.

The Red Menace issue dominated the general election, whose outcome was never in any doubt after the *Daily Mail* of 25 October printed a letter leaked from MI5 purporting to have been sent by Comintern chief Zinoviev on 15 September. It ordered the British Communist party to 'strain every nerve' to ensure that the government accept the Anglo-Soviet trade treaties. The instructions to the CPGB to step up 'agitation-propaganda work in the armed forces' made it appear that Moscow was preparing to unleash the Red Revolution in Britain.

Genuine or not, the Zinoviev letter gave Stanley Baldwin's Conservatives a landslide victory. Ironically, Trotsky and Zinoviev welcomed the downfall of Britain's first socialist government. To them it was an article of faith that true socialism could be achieved only by bullets, not by ballots. But the affair brought more discredit to the Comintern, as Stalin and his ally Dzerzhinski called for concentrating the GPU's efforts on internal control rather than dissipating resources on fomenting world revolution. The split in the Soviet leadership widened the following year, allowing Stalin to engineer Trotsky's dismissal as war commissar. This enabled Dzerzhinski to extend the authority of the GPU over the foreign operations of the Comintern.

Baldwin's second Conservative administration also consolidated the authority of Britain's counterintelligence services by halting general circulation of Soviet intercepts and Special Branch reports to the Cabinet. But despite continuing evidence of subversive activities from Soviet House in Moorgate and the new Soviet embassy in Belgravia, the prime minister accepted the Foreign Office view that continuing peaceful relations with Moscow were preferable to 'a definitely outlawed Russia' that would increase its efforts at secret subversion.

It was not simply a matter of clandestine subversion. 'The Bolshevization of the British Trade Union Movement has begun,' announced *The Times* of London in April 1925 after the Profintern announced a Joint Anglo-Soviet Advisory Committee. The hardline anti-Bolshevik home secretary, Sir William Joynson-Hicks, and Sir Wyndham Childs, who had succeeded Thomson as chief of Special Branch, believed it was only a matter of time before the Soviets would have to be sent packing. Rising unemployment and industrial unrest were the background to intercepted Comintern communications to the CPGB and the

Profintern-sponsored National Minority Movement. These claimed ten thousand trade-union members should be 'prepared to fight' in a civil war for 'the seizure of power by the working class'. Communist agitators were told to educate Britain's sailors and soldiers to 'turn their guns on the masters as the workers of Russia had done'.

In response to the growing economic crisis Prime Minister Baldwin declared: 'All the workers of this country have got to take a reduction in wages.' The trade-union movement rallied behind the militant miners, who refused to accept the savage wage cuts threatened by the private colliery owners in order to make their coal prices competitive on the international market. The Cabinet postponed the inevitable confrontation by offering the miners a nine-month pay subsidy until the Royal Commission reported on the crisis the following May. The Conservative press accused Baldwin of a sellout.

To demonstrate the government's resolve, the Prime Minister called on the Home Secretary to make preparations for combating subversion and beating a general strike. Sir William Joynson-Hicks, 'Jix', as he was known in the popular press, was an iron-jawed reactionary who had stepped up police raids on London's fashionably notorious nightclubs. But it was not cocaine-snorting flappers or brothel madams whom Scotland Yard's Special Branch was looking for on 13 October 1925, when they raided the headquarters of the Communist party of Great Britain. They arrested the leading party officers and carted off a large haul of documents and propaganda leaflets. Sedition charges resurrected from the 1797 Mutiny Act enabled the government to try Pollitt and eleven other executive members of the CPGB. They were found guilty and sentenced to prison terms of six months to a year. This was a precedent-setting punishment since it signaled that political opinions rather than demonstrable subversive acts would be used to secure convictions in the courts.

As the showdown with Britain's labor unions edged closer in the spring of 1926, the Comintern communications intercepted by MI5 disclosed that Moscow expected the confrontation with the miners to spark the 'gigantic struggles' of the British working class. 'Only a well-organized strike movement can prepare the way for active revolutionary struggle,' Zinoviev advised the CPGB in February.

Well in advance of the impending showdown, the British took care to keep the Americans fully briefed on Arcos and its connections with Amtorg via Captain Guy Maynard Liddell of Special Branch, who proposed visiting Washington in April. When Liddell delivered his 27 March report to the US embassy in Grosvenor Square, he suggested that his forthcoming marriage to Calypso Baring, the sister of Lord Revelstoke, a leading London banker, offered the perfect cover for him 'to meet some of the men in the [State] Department who are interested in the same sort of work', while on his honeymoon trip. Liddell was a Special Branch officer who had liaised with US embassy officials. The State Department was advised that he was 'one of the cleverest and most intelligent of "our friends".'

Liddell's photographic memory and ruminative brain had taken him to the top of Scotland Yard's section responsible for tracking Communist subversion. The thirty-four-year-old son of an army captain and a professional violinist, Liddell was a gifted cellist whose promising musical career was cut short by World War I when he joined the field artillery. After winning the Military Cross for bravery under fire on the Western front, he had been selected for Special Branch by Metropolitan Police Commissioner Thomson in 1919. For thirty-three years, Liddell was at the heart of Britain's counterintelligence operations, working with MI5, the armed forces, MI6 and the code breakers of GC&CS. It is now clear that his visit to Washington resulted in closer Anglo-American cooperation to secretly combat Soviet subversion.

The Americans were kept posted, through their London embassy, of Moscow's efforts to exploit the industrial unrest and create all-out class warfare on the streets. When the general strike erupted in Britain on 3 May 1926, after the miners refused to accept the pay cuts recommended by the Royal Commission, the government proved better prepared than the Comintern and its CPGB agitators. The Conservative Cabinet did not send in troops, as Zinoviev predicted it would, when the transport and dock workers joined the striking miners in an all-out bid to bring the country to a halt. Instead, with calm headmasterly authority, Baldwin rallied his Tory supporters in the middle class to keep essential transport services running. This tactic took the Comintern and its British agents by surprise. With no barricades for the proletariat to man, there was no class warfare in the streets. No workers were shot and within a week the general strike collapsed.

Even Moscow's attempts to fuel the British strike with funds was met by rejection. The Trades Union Congress was so apprehensive of charges of bribery by 'Red Gold' that it returned the strike donations sent by the Profintern and the Soviet Union. Not even the rabidly anti-Bolshevik home secretary could substantiate his initial claim that Moscow was 'providing money on the first day of the general strike for financing'. Joynson-Hicks buttressed his convictions, however, by publishing a so-called Blue Book of selected documents seized from Communist party headquarters. These included a message to Comintern headquarters referring to 'transmitting money by the secret channel'. Only after the general strike collapsed did the locked-out miners openly accept a £1.25 million supposedly donated by their Soviet counterparts.

When the striking miners began drifting back to work in September 1926, the Red Menace appeared defeated. But far from giving up, the Soviets renewed their subversive assault by extending their efforts to India, where a rejuvenated Communist party with funds from Moscow began fomenting political and industrial unrest. In Britain, despite a stiff warning delivered to the Soviet ambassador in February 1927, Foreign Secretary Austen Chamberlain informed the Cabinet a month later of 'highly secret information' he had received about 'the activities of the Soviet Union in this country'.

What exercised the Cabinet's concern was the growing threat of espionage and subversion networks operating out of Arcos. The arrest in March of Soviet spy Ethel Chiles had alerted MI5 to this danger. The twenty-five-year-old German Comintern agent, whose real name was Kate Grüssfeld, had used a forged British passport for her work for International Workers' Relief. This was a Comintern front organization that MI5 described as 'a flagrant case of fraudulent perversion'.

The secret reports supplied to the US State Department reveal that Chiles was part of the ring run by Jacob Kirchstein, an elusive Comintern agent whom British and American authorities had spent two years trying to track down. Grüssfeld remained tight-lipped under interrogation and refused to name any American associates. The extent of Kirchstein's espionage network was only revealed after addresses found by Special Branch at Arcos headquarters led New York police to raid the headquarters of the Moness Chemical Company at 426 Broome Street in Manhattan. There, papers stuffed in a stove confirmed that Moness had received substantial loans over the signature of Harry J. Hammer.

MI5 reports in the US Archives show that the Grüssfeld/Kirchstein case played an important part in persuading the British government to curb such blatant violations of the Anglo-Soviet trade treaty. But before the home secretary could authorize any direct move against Arcos headquarters, MI5 had to find a pretext that would allay Moscow's suspicions that the raid was a result of breaking their codes or penetrating their British operations.

In a curious twist of fate, it was an old boy of Marlborough College named George Monckland who provided the evidence that Special Branch needed to justify a raid on Soviet House. A Lloyd's underwriter, Monckland told Special Branch how in March 1927, a man by the name of Wilfred Macartney had approached him in an illegal Mayfair gambling club and offered a retainer of £50 a month to supply the Soviets with information on arms shipments obtained in the course of his work at Lloyd's. On 22 March Macartney produced a letter from a man named K. J. Johnson. He claimed that Johnson was 'the superior Russian spy agent in the country', telling Monckland that in an emergency he could call on the Soviet military attaché and say he was 'one of the firm'.

Monckland evidently was not cut out for spying. A week later he informed the authorities about Macartney. An MI5 officer identified only as 'Peter Hamilton' persuaded him to become a double agent with the code name of 'M2'. His role was to provide Special Branch with the justification for mounting a surprise raid on Soviet House when, at the end of April, MI5 supplied Monckland with a manual titled 'Regulations for Training Flying Personnel of the Royal Air Force'. Monckland's instructions were to pass this manual to Macartney. It was prominently marked SECRET even though sources in the RAF knew it was out of date. Macartney returned the manual to Monckland a few days later, saying it was 'no good because it was obsolete'. MI5 therefore knew that a Soviet agent familiar with RAF operating procedures must have read the manual and that it would certainly have been copied in the Arcos headquarters.

A foolproof trap had been set by MI5. But the carefully planned 'sting' operation went awry on 11 May 1927, after the Home Secretary advised the Cabinet that the secret report was in the trade delegation. The RAF manual supplied to Macartney was obviously intended to provide the cast-iron evidence of espionage that could be 'discovered' to send the whole Soviet delegation packing.

The Home Secretary was able to persuade the Prime Minister to authorize the raid only because the British secret service had an informant *inside* Soviet House who *tipped off* MI5 that a copy of that secret RAF report had been made. That much is obvious from an original draft of Baldwin's announcement stating that the Soviets had been caught redhanded. It has come to light in declassified British Cabinet records and specifically refers to a 'missing' document of 'an official and highly confidential nature, so marked' that the government knew 'from information voluntarily furnished by a person lately in the employment of Arcos' had been 'conveyed to 49 Moorgate and there reproduced by means of photographic apparatus'.

On the strength of this assurance from the Home Secretary, the Cabinet agreed on the afternoon of 11 May to authorize a police search of the Arcos premises.

The meticulously planned raid began at 4:30 the following afternoon. A squad of blue-uniformed policemen converged on 49 Moorgate, just north of the Bank of England. Within minutes, fifty plainclothes detectives of Special Branch emerged from the nearby underground station, having traveled from Scotland Yard on the Circle Line so as not to attract suspicion. They raced up the steps into the main entrance of 49 Moorgate, the office building that served as headquarters for the four hundred staff members of Arcos and the thirty-five diplomatically accredited members of the Soviet Trade Delegation.

Brushing aside the angry protests of Soviet officials, the detectives fanned out according to a rehearsed plan. One detachment headed downstairs to the basement, which they found barred by a massive locked steel door. Upstairs, panic broke out. Secretaries shrieked hysterically at the sight of detectives' pistols as the plainclothes police officers hustled them into corridors and demanded keys to locked filing cabinets and safes. In one office the manager barred the door in an effort to gain time to contact the Soviet chargé d'affaires at Chesham House. But the telephone lines had been cut off.

Acrid smoke began curling up from a ground-floor office window and the clanging bells of fire engines added to the chaos and confusion in the narrow city streets. The stench of burning paper drifted into the corridor outside the office of the head of the trade delegation, who happened to be away in Geneva. When Special Branch officers burst into the locked code room, after threatening to shoot the door down, they saw through the choking smoke two men and a middle-aged woman feeding a small bonfire with the contents of a large dispatch box on the table. The detectives stamped out the flames, rescuing charred documents. From the pocket of one of the men fell a roll of papers that confirmed he was Anton Miller, the trade delegation's cipher clerk. In his possession he had lists of names and addresses of Comintern agents across the world.

When the police broke into the underground room with its battery of photographic apparatus they did not find the copy of the secret RAF manual they had been told was there. They did arrest an illegal immigrant, Robert Kolling, who acted as a courier between Soviet House and the Russian legation on Chesham Place. Under interrogation, Kolling later confessed to using a whole string of aliases in his assignments as an official of the Russian Seamen's Union and a full-time Red agitator.

Despite protests from the Soviet embassy, the intensive police search of Arcos headquarters continued late into the night and all through the next day. The enormous steel doors in the basement of 49 Moorgate had to be cut down with pneumatic drills and the oxyacetylene torches that had been brought in to open the many safes to which keys had mysteriously vanished. When the police broke into the vault they found stacks of files, propaganda films, and crates of guns that the Soviets disingenuously claimed were hunting rifle 'samples'. The floor-to-ceiling search went on through the weekend, yielding two truckloads of material, which were driven off to Scotland Yard.

Not a single page of the planted RAF manual was found among the quarter-million documents that took more than a week of round-the-clock sifting by a team of translators from the Foreign Office supervised by MI5 officers. While the search for the incontrovertible evidence of espionage continued, a major diplomatic and parliamentary row erupted. Maxim Litvinov, the assistant commissar for foreign affairs, protested that diplomatic relations with Britain and millions of pounds in trade had been put at risk 'in the grossest and most insulting manner' by the police raid, which he called 'a most serious hostile act'.

The failure to come up with the proof of redhanded espionage gave the British government fits. The Cabinet had resolved to break diplomatic ties with the Soviet Union and send the trade delegation packing. But without blowing the secret interception of the Soviet cable traffic, they lacked the hard evidence to justify such a radical course of action. More than a week passed while the parliamentary row grew worse. Labour members sympathetic to Moscow's propaganda accused the British government of engineering the Arcos raid as a diplomatic insult, timed to discredit the opposition to the government's pending trade-union legislation.

All the Home Secretary would tell the House to quell the storm of Labour criticism was that he was 'satisfied that a certain official document was or had been improperly in the possession of a person employed in the premises occupied by Arcos.' His subsequent admission that the document could not be found prompted another noisy outburst from the opposition benches. Weakly, Joynson-Hicks assured the House that 'the police have taken possession of certain papers which might bear upon the case.'

The US military attaché reported to Washington that a War Office source had said that the postponement of a full statement by the Prime Minister on the raid was because the 'situation demanded the most careful handling'. Lacking the military manual to prove a Soviet espionage ring operated from Arcos, the British government took twelve days to decide there was no choice but to reveal some of the intercepted secret Comintern messages.

When the Prime Minister rose to address the House of Commons on 24 May, his carefully worded statement justified the raid because of 'information secured, and supported by documentary evidence' that led the government to believe that a missing War Office document 'had been conveyed to Soviet House and there reproduced by means of a photo-static apparatus, the exact character and location of which were described.' What Baldwin did not describe was the RAF manual, or how it reached the Soviets, or the existence of a British mole on the Arcos staff. In his most imperturbable manner he merely referred to 'secret staff records' and 'other documents' that it was 'unnecessary to describe'.

To bolster the government's contention that the Soviets had violated the terms of their trade agreement, the Prime Minister read verbatim the text of three secret Soviet telegrams, two to Moscow from the Soviet chargé d'affaires in London. These official communications left no doubt about the degree to which the Soviets had been abusing the terms of their trade agreement by using their officials in London to conduct subversive and propagandizing activities. Although Baldwin did not identify the source of the cipher cables that had 'come into the possession of HM government', Moscow must have been alerted that their ciphers had been broken.

The Labour opposition spokesman protested that none of the documents seized in the Arcos raid nor the Soviet telegrams provided conclusive proof of the government's charges of 'both military espionage and subversive activities'. With a cavalier disregard for security that horrified the British code breakers, the Home Secretary wound up the six-hour debate by reading four more incriminating communications that Rosengolz had recently sent to Moscow.

The House of Commons voted overwhelmingly in favor of the expulsion of the Russians and the abrogation of the Anglo-Soviet Trade Agreement. But the GC&CS code breakers were left wringing their hands in frustration since their opponents now knew beyond any doubt that their ciphers had been broken.

The Arcos raid, which the Conservative government regarded as a major victory in its undeclared war against socialism and communism, in fact proved to be a strategic disaster in the long run. The Soviets, as Denniston and the GC&CS code breakers predicted, promptly changed their code system to one-time pads that were theoretically unbreakable. The failure to find the RAF manual in Soviet House cost MI5 and Special Branch the one sure weapon with which to fight the second wave of Moscow's penetration and subversion in Britain.

Why the carefully planted evidence was not at Arcos headquarters did not emerge until the trial of Macartney in December 1927, a month after his arrest along with a German named Georg Hansen, who had arrived in London as an undercover Comintern agent after the Soviet diplomats had returned to Moscow.

Monckland testified that Macartney had telephoned and warned him to 'get rid of any incriminating documents' *at the very hour* the raid on Soviet House was actually in progress. Macartney had also boasted that 'he had been warned that the raid would take place and that he had been able to warn the people at Arcos.'

Under cross-examination, Macartney denied that he had alerted the Soviets. It is possible that Monckland, as the Crown's witness, was primed to provide an 'official' and plausible explanation of why the copy of the RAF manual that triggered the raid was never found. But only five people outside the Cabinet knew the day before that the operation against Arcos had been set for the following afternoon. This suggests that a ranking MI5 or Special Branch officer tipped off the Soviets. A joint MI5-Foreign Office investigation into the leak never produced a culprit; and the official report on the affair is still an Official Secret.

So, too, are the contents of the two truckloads of Soviet paperwork seized by the British in the Arcos raid. Only six examples were given in a special government White Paper titled 'Documents Illustrating Hostile Activities of the Soviet Government and the Third International Against Great Britain'. But the counterintelligence value of the largest haul of Soviet documents ever taken in the West has now become evident from one report on the Arcos files that found its way into State Department archives via the US embassy in London.

We now know that the raid provided the British with extremely valuable information about Soviet methodology and operations. Seized documentation ranged from the code system 'used between the Soviet authorities and the Workers (Communist) Party of America' to MI5's assessment of an interlocking network of Moscow-directed Communist cells radiating out from Arcos.

'The Constitution and Duties of Russian Communist Party (VKP(b)) Cells Abroad' – a post-Arcos report still an Official Secret in Britain – illustrates the insights MI5 obtained in 1927 on Soviet objectives and the interrelation between the GRU's foreign industrial espionage, the GPU's undercover operations and the Comintern-directed CPGB. The heart of this network of spying, propaganda and subversion was the Vsesoyuznaya Kommunisti-cheskaya Partiya (Bolshevikev) – All Union Communist Party (Bolshevik) – or VKP(b) 'cell'.

The secret British report on the VKP prepared for the Americans explained the key role played by the primary cell based in Soviet House, which had been 'confirmed from papers obtained during the raid on 49 Moorgate'. Documents showed that it 'consisted of members of the staff of Chesham House, The Russian Trade Delegation and of Arcos, and its subsidiary companies.' The cell's function was 'to increase its circle through conversion of others to Communist ideas and to carry out any special instructions that may be received from its own Central Committee through its Party Executive.'

This report is pivotal. It conclusively shows that, contrary to later official British assertions, MI5 had unraveled the 'genetic code' of the Soviet virus by 1927. The mechanism by which the 'disease' of communism was transmitted was known even as the repercussions of the Arcos raid were felt in Moscow. One of the most important outcomes was to hasten the takeover of the Comintern by the GPU for the second wave of Soviet clandestine war against Britain. American counterintelligence experts confirm that the thirty-page VKP memorandum reveals that the British authorities had compiled a very detailed dossier on the direction and depth of this second assault on the political system, trade unions, armaments factories, and intellectual elite.

MI5, for example, was by 1927 fully aware that the Comintern had set up and used the Society for Cultural Relations as a front organization for recruiting Communist and left-wing sympathizers in the universities as part of a coordinated scientific and technological espionage. The evidence contained in this section of the report suggests that Special Branch had not only penetrated the SCR, but appreciated how the scientific research at Cambridge made it a special target for the Soviets.

Six years earlier, when MI5's prime concern was sedition in the armed forces and subversion of the trade unions, a brilliant young

Russian electrical engineer from the Petrograd Polytechnic Institute had obtained a visa for Britain even though Germany and France had refused him entry visas on suspicion that he was a Bolshevik agitator. By 1927, Peter Kapitza was associated with the leading members of the brilliant band of pioneering nuclear physicists at Cambridge's renowned Cavendish Laboratory.

In 1920, Kapitza was called on by Abram Joffe, the Soviet Union's leading physicist, under whom he had studied at Petrograd, to join a delegation of scientists. The Soviet Scientific Mission was set up with the ostensible objective of establishing links between Russia and the scientific community in the West and as a purchasing agent for laboratory instruments, supplies and machine-shop equipment. But, as with the trade delegation, its members were also expected to spy out useful research and act as Communist proselytizers for the Soviet Union as the world's first 'scientific' political system.

Kapitza himself would later deny that the efforts he made to join Lord Rutherford's team at the Cavendish were motivated by anything other than the purest scientifc ambitions. But the historical record shows that Soviet scientists, whose skills Lenin ranked as important state assets, were never permitted to leave unless they could be trusted to continue serving the Revolution abroad. Nor can there be any doubt that Kapitza was singularly persistent and successful in establishing himself as one of Cambridge's most prominent scientific figures.

Kapitza's arrival in England shortly after the setting up of Arcos is also significant because it was under its auspices that he first contacted Rutherford as a purchaser of scientific equipment. Moreover, by 1927, when the Soviet Trade Delegation was sent packing, the undercover GRU officers engaged on scientific intelligence would have assembled a clear picture of the advanced work being done at Cambridge into radioactivity, X-ray crystallography and nuclear physics. What Kapitza learned from his participation with the team working at the Cavendish Laboratory (which within seven years would split the atom) gave Russian nuclear physics a major boost.

Even if Kapitza himself was as reluctant a Soviet repatriate as he protested from Leningrad in 1934 when his exit visa was withdrawn, he nonetheless served as part of the first and most successful of the Soviet Union's scientific penetration operations. American intelligence sources are aware that the GRU considered Cambridge such an important scientific target that it maintained a resident control officer there. This confidential disclosure to the author confirms the documentary evidence that the Soviet intelligence apparatus was already in place at Cambridge when Anthony Blunt entered Trinity College as a first-year Scholar in October 1926.

5 'Boys of Rough Trade and Laddies of Leisure'

While Moscow was doing its best to spread socialist revolution throughout Great Britain – and the world – Anthony Blunt arrived at Cambridge University. He signed the Trinity Admissions Book on 26 September 1926, after his tutor, Reginald Vere Lawrence, a historian fellow who was then the junior bursar.

To Blunt, as to most freshmen who came up from the politically cloistered public schools, socialism – if it was of any concern at all – seemed doomed after the Conservative government's defeat of the general strike only six months earlier. The general strike had pricked the social conscience of the student body. But as one undergraduate wryly commented: 'Even the most hardened socialist was apt to break down before the lure of realizing at last a latent but long cherished desire to drive a real train.'

However, the current of left-wing sympathy among senior members of the university – known as dons from the Latin *dominus*, 'master' – was more consistent. A hundred of the more radical, led by Trinity College fellows, had publicly urged the government to negotiate with the TUC. Among them was a young fellow from Pembroke College named Maurice Dobb, who after a visit to Moscow in 1925, made no bones about his Communist sympathies. A frequent speaker in the Union Society, the undergraduate debating forum modeled on the House of Commons, Dobb tirelessly reminded those who would listen how science and art were flourishing under the 'aristocracy of intellect' in the Soviet Union.

Six years earlier, the secretary of the Heretics Club, a radical discussion forum founded in 1904, had told the president: 'I wish we could all be Bolsheviks quick and have done with it.' This enthusiastic supporter of the Soviet Union was Dora Black, a don from Girton – one of only two women's colleges – who was to marry Bertrand Russell, the left-wing philosopher-mathematician whose wartime imprisonment for pacifist pamphleteering had cost him his fellowship at Trinity College. Nor was the future Lady Russell the only member of the Heretics infatuated with the bold new socialist experiment in Russia. Preoccupied with such diverse issues as psychology, art, science and economics, the Heretics, during Blunt's time at Cambridge, became one of the principal centers in the university for intellectual socialist debate and the promotion of the 'social relations of science movement'.

'The Russian experiment has aroused very great interest inside the university,' observed Claude W. Guillebaud of St John's College, who noted how undergraduates seemed 'less conservative' than previous generations. The intellectual fascination with Marxism was spreading beyond the more progressive members of the Economics Faculty such as Dobb. The supposedly 'scientific' rationale of dialectical materialism held an immediate appeal to the Cambridge physicists, biologists and chemists who were responsible for the university's illustrious reputation as one of the world's foremost centers of scientific research.

Cambridge's preeminence in science was confirmed in 1874 with the founding of the Cavendish Laboratory under the first professor of experimental physics, J. Clerk Maxwell, the pioneer of electromagnetic theory. His successor, Professor J.J. Thompson, was the discoverer of the electron, and his experiments set the course for modern physics before World War I demonstrated the potential destructiveness of twentieth-century technology.

'We are living in the heroic age of physics,' Sir Ernest Rutherford declared in 1923, four years after taking over from Thompson. The New Zealand-born Nobel laureate, who discovered the atomic nucleus, presided over the Cavendish's golden age. In the laboratory complex built on the site of the friary where England's Protestant reformers had assembled more than two and a half centuries before, Rutherford was gathering the most talented concentration of physicists the world had yet seen. Cambridge's professor of astronomy, Arthur Eddington, and P. A. M. Dirac had forged the theoretical link between Einstein's theory of relativity and quantum mechanics. But it was at the Cavendish that Rutherford's team conducted the experiments that led to the splitting of the atom and ushered mankind into the nuclear age.

The scientific rationalism generated by the Cavendish powerhouse even invaded lectures in English literature. Ivor A. Richards, the iconoclastic literary critic from Magdalene College, was given to drawing electrical circuits on the blackboard to illustrate his lecture on Shelley's 'Ode to the West Wind'. Richards' razor-sharp intellect and his 'scientific' approach presented a stark contrast to the Victorianism of Sir Arthur Quiller-Couch, professor of English Literature, a celebrated novelist whose lectures were notable for his wearing full morning dress and refusal to acknowledge the presence of female undergraduates.

Meanwhile, Professor George Edward Moore, a pioneer of the linguistic approach to philosophy, was emphasizing the importance of asking the right question in order to elicit the right answer. His assertion of the moral value of the 'pleasures of human intercourse and the enjoyment of beautiful objects' had exercised a profound influence on the turn-of-the-century generation of undergraduates. Neoplatonism, and Moore's teachings that common sense was a valid criterion for weighing moral certainties, had provided the philosophic underpinning for such eminent Cambridge disciples as Bertrand Russell, Leonard Woolf, John Maynard Keynes, Roger Fry, Lytton Strachey and E. M. Forster. They had forged the intellectual, moral and social reaction to Victorian liberal Christianity that became known as Bloomsbury.

Bloomsbury embodied the essence of Cambridge's questioning, liberal-humanist tradition. The skepticism of its prominent intellectuals produced the debunking histories of Lytton Strachey, the revolt against literary realism in Virginia Woolf's novels, and the rationalistic view of modern art of Clive Bell and Roger Fry. The upsurge of scientific rationalism persuaded many of the group that moral imperatives could be reduced to simple equations and that theology would eventually become a branch of anthropology. This notion prompted Bertrand Russell's aphorism that the Ten Commandments, like a Cambridge examination paper, required that 'only six need be attempted'.

'Life at Cambridge,' Blunt once boldly declared, 'was to an extraordinary extent for me an extension of life at Marlborough.' But the actual record – and the recollections of his undergraduate friends – suggest otherwise. Like other freshmen who had glittered brightly in their public-school environment, Blunt did not measure up immediately to the brilliance of the intellectual competition at Cambridge. Although he had been a dominant figure at Marlborough, his self-esteem suffered a severe shock at finding he was outshone by such contemporaries as Bronowski and Empson, who were more brilliant and creative.

At Marlborough, modern art had been the vehicle for Blunt's remarkably successful protest against the system. At the university, he found that French Post-Impressionist painting had long ago lost its novelty value. His fellow undergraduates hung prints of Van Gogh and Cézanne in their rooms. Many of the dons were followers of Bloomsbury and just as familiar as Blunt with the finer points of Cubism. The tutorial system, which supplemented lectures with 'supervisions' where teachers and undergraduates exchanged ideas and criticism on a one-to-one basis, made it more difficult to find a target for extending his schoolboy aesthetic rebellion.

When it came to flamboyance, Blunt also discovered that he would need more elaborate props than the toy balls and hoops he had used at Marlborough to make an impression. The elegant Steven Runciman was Trinity College's resident aesthete, cutting elegant poses with a parakeet perched on his heavily ringed fingers and his hair cropped in an Italianate fringe.

Competing with Runciman's parakeet and 'aesthetic' banquets featuring costly delicacies like plover's eggs was far beyond

Blunt's financial resources. To be an aesthete at Cambridge or Oxford required wealthy parents. Neither the Reverend Blunt's stipend nor Hilda Blunt's small independent income permitted Anthony to live luxuriously. His £100-a-year scholarship covered less than half the cost of his university admission, tuition and examination fees, books and lodging. Because he was a scholar, Blunt enjoyed a large set of rooms in Bishop's Hostel, known as 'The Ritz'. But his small allowance would not stretch to scarlet walls and vodka parties like those of the Etonian aesthete in Jesus College who ventured out only in a hired Daimler, which he referred to as 'my barouche'.

To be an aesthete, social status was as important as scholastic attainment. Learning 'was what the grammar school boys did' according to Blunt's bosom friend MacNeice, who wrote from Oxford scornfully of 'those distorted little creatures with black teeth who held their forks by the middle and were set on making a career.' Public-school boys went to university 'either for sport and beer drinking', or, according to MacNeice, 'for the aesthetic life and cocktails'.

Public-school boys and the attitudes of the privileged class dominated Cambridge. A 'good' second-class 'Oxbridge' degree, respectable family connections and an 'old school tie' were the standard passport for future success in Britain's legal, financial, political and academic institutions. And since the undergraduate population turned around every three years, the ambitious freshman with an eye to making lifelong friends and connections was under pressure to establish himself in the Oxbridge pecking order during his first year.

What is surprising about Blunt is that his first year was such a disaster. He had no platform to speak from or attack. Nor did he join any of the undergraduate societies such as the Union from which he might have dazzled his contemporaries with his theories about art.

Unlike MacNeice, who threw himself into Oxford life with gusto, playing rugger for his college, writing poetry for *Cherwell*, the university newspaper, and beagling with the Christ Church pack, Blunt lost out in the undergraduate status race. He sought only the company of a select few of his school friends; one of the closest of these was Michael Robertson, who had been one of Marlborough's senior prefects and a star rugger player.

A measure of their attachment was that Blunt was best man at Robertson's wedding in 1931 and godfather to his eldest son – a fact that Robertson proudly pointed out when he received me at his timbered country cottage deep in the heart of East Anglia's 'Constable country'. A tall, diffident man wearing a tweed jacket and plus-four breeches, Robertson insisted he 'wasn't frightfully bright like Anthony', when recalling how he had come up to read law and history. He still held an intense loyalty toward Blunt, admitting that he continued seeing him even after his exposure as a spy. This feeling may have accounted for his difficulty in recalling details of his Cambridge friendship with Blunt, but he vividly remembered how their Marlborough circle was dismayed at the overbearing attitude of the old Etonians who dominated Trinity.

Alastair MacDonald, who had been in the Anonymous Society and was now in Gonville and Caius College reading history, remembers being flattered that during their first term, he and Blunt regularly received invitations to dinner at Mrs Granville Gordon's musical evenings. A large, somewhat overbearing lady whose grating voice was accentuated by loose false teeth that flapped as she talked, Mrs Granville Gordon's passions were music and claret.

'Mrs Granville Gordon used to refer to us as the Three Marlborough Musketeers, although we never discovered which one of us she thought of as her D'Artagnan,' MacDonald told me with some amusement. 'We were all three of us rather poor so none of us dressed up in dinner jackets. We simply turned up in the gray flannel bags and jackets that we wore all the time.'

MacDonald's recollections of how much they prized these regular invitations to dinner from a prominent Cambridge hostess at whose table they could talk knowledgeably with dons suggest that Blunt had not yet found a mentor to replace Clifford Canning of Marlborough. He found himself at odds with his subject and his mathematics supervisor. This would not be surprising. Blunt's principal lecturer and examiner was Ralph H. Fowler, a large, hearty golfing Trinity don who was Cambridge's first professor of physical mathematics. A survivor of the beaches of Gallipoli during World War I, Fowler had done his most original theoretical work, a paper on improving the flight of spinning projectiles, while recovering in the hospital from serious shrapnel wounds.

Blunt's dislike of heartiness, his distaste for all things mechanical, could not have endeared him to Fowler. According to John Hilton, 'Anthony was the best pure mathematician at Marlborough.' But his penchant was not for analysing the dynamics of artillery shells, or for the physics or optics problems that accounted for fully half the Cambridge first-year maths syllabus. Blunt was attuned to the symmetry and order of pure mathematics, which he identified with the aesthetic principles of modern art. But he also knew that his academic standing, his status as a Trinity scholar, *and* his financial security depended on getting high marks.

'Mathematics enjoys the advantages, and suffers the penalties of being a secret doctrine,' cautioned one of Blunt's lecturers in a contemporary student handbook. Mathematics as it was taught at Cambridge in the twenties was a stern and uncompromising discipline. It required intellectual toughness for staying the three-year course. More than half of every first-year class dropped out, or switched to other subjects, rather than face two more years of an intellectual obstacle course in which 'pure maths' – algebra, trigonometry, calculus and analytical geometry – required additional study for the 'applied maths' of dynamics, elementary electricity and optics. Even so, Part I of the Cambridge Maths Tripos was not much more taxing than the examinations in which Blunt had excelled at school. As one of a dozen undergraduate scholars in his first-year class of 132, Blunt might have been expected to sail through his first-year exam with distinction.

On 14 June 1927 Blunt's failure to do justice to his scholarship became public when the first-year tripos examination results were ceremonially posted on the west wall of the Cambridge Senate House.

'Blunt, A. F.' was not among the candidates who were on the first-class list. He was among the also-rans, who received an undivided second. It was the first time he had failed to acquit himself with distinction in a mathematics examination. To make his fall from academic grace even harder to live down, the relative easiness of the Part I papers permitted more than 40 per cent of the examinees to get firsts.

What went wrong?

Why had Marlborough's star pupil failed to live up to his schoolboy reputation as one of his generation's ablest mathematicians?

The most obvious explanation for his second-class performance was the result of mediocre grades in the applied-maths subjects: dynamics, optics and elementary electricity. That Blunt's poor grades caused a deep personal sense of failure was evident from his refusal ever to acknowledge that his Cambridge degree was anything other than a double first in modern languages. This was in keeping with his desire to portray his career through school and university as an uninterrupted success story. Alastair MacDonald believes, however, that 'Anthony was very much disturbed during his first year and was unable to concentrate.'

I finally discovered, in the archives of King's College, Cambridge, evidence that confirms just how unsettled and unhappy Blunt was during his freshman year.

Halfway up a worn stone staircase marked PRIVATE, MEMBERS OF THE COLLEGE ONLY, a landing leads off to a Gothic portal. An iron-bound wooden door opens on to a long library where tall stacks of books flank tables polished by the sleeves of generations of students. Through the mullioned windows, a placid green lawn washes up from the River Cam and laps the pale grey stones of King's College chapel, one of the architectural masterpieces of the Tudor age.

In the library, as nowhere else in the university, there exists the interplay of concentrated scholarship and glorious environment that is the very essence of the Cambridge mystique that inspired E. M. Forster to observe: 'Body and spirit, reason and emotion, work and play, architecture and scenery, laughter and seriousness, life and art, these pairs which are elsewhere contrasted were fused together into one.'

This distillation of the Cambridge spirit in the handwriting of the Bloomsbury novelist, one of the most celebrated of King's College's literary sons, can be read, 'by appointment only', in a small air-conditioned annex at the end of the library. Here too are kept the original manuscripts of *A Passage to India*, *A Room with a View*, and *Maurice*, books that have made one of the twentieth century's most reclusive novelists into a posthumous box-office success.

Royalties from the Forster films help maintain the Modern Literary Archives. Knowledgeably managed by Dr Michael Halls, a surprisingly youthful archivist, his vault contains many of the letters, papers, diaries and manuscripts of other Bloomsbury members for whom King's was a spiritual home. But sharing shelf space in a vault lined with boxes of the voluminous correspondence of Virginia Woolf, Forster and John Maynard Keynes are four cartons of letters deposited in 1969 by Anthony Blunt. His scrawled notes on the brown paper envelopes state that he wanted them sealed until after his death. The collection consists of postcards and letters sent to Blunt over the course of ten years by his friend Louis MacNeice, the Oxford poet. These letters provide a revealing, intimate and sustained insight into a close friendship that did not break up until 1936, the eve of the Spanish Civil War.

The MacNeice letters are tantalizingly incomplete. Like so much else about Blunt. But they provide fresh insights and clues to his elusive character, but they also raise as many questions as they answer. The evidence of the postmarks suggests that Blunt withheld, or destroyed, some of the letters. Nor did a search of the MacNeice Papers at the Bodleian Library at Oxford turn up a single one of Blunt's replies. Nevertheless, MacNeice's letters provide far more information than Blunt ever did about his early aspirations and frustrations and his circle of intimate friends and lovers during the first decade of his enigmatic career.

The picture the letters give contrasts sharply with Blunt's own autobiographical accounts, on which other investigators have had to rely. The MacNeice correspondence reveals how undergraduate life shattered the daydreams of two teenage rebels who had set out from their public school full of confidence that their scholarship and wit would bring them the glittering prizes. The many references to their schoolmaster mentor, Clifford Canning, and to Blunt's homosexual attachments, suggest they both had great difficulty cutting their emotional ties to Marlborough.

'You are really rather sublime, I can imagine you preaching to a spellbound Cambridge Anonymous Society,' MacNeice wrote encouragingly in the summer of 1926 before Blunt arrived at Cambridge. Blunt was then in Italy, where his father had taken a temporary summer chaplaincy that provided his family with an economical vacation at Stresa, on the northern shores of Lake Maggiore.

'My dear child,' MacNeice wrote affectionately two weeks later, assuring his friend that he looked like Apollo and admitting he himself was 'still averse to women'. A Poussin painting MacNeice had seen in the Dublin Art Gallery left him 'rather taken with that paint like golden tea with milk'. Blunt later borrowed this simile when writing about the painter, who became a lifelong passion.

At the age of fifteen, Blunt, according to Marlborough contemporary Ellis Waterhouse, had become convinced that Poussin was a figure of immense stature waiting to be rediscovered. As a schoolboy, Blunt may have calculated – like other art historians before him – that by dedicating his own lifetime to the patient rediscovery of Poussin, he could achieve a lasting and posthumous glory from the greatness of his chosen artist.

Reference to *Crime and Punishment*, Dostoevski's novel about a student's psychological struggle to overcome social and academic rejection, these early MacNeice letters suggested that Blunt was suffering from some underlying insecurity. 'Are you sure you'll bear Cambridge all right?' MacNeice wondered, suggesting a concern that rolling hoops and trailing blue handkerchiefs were not sufficiently 'adult' manifestations for an undergraduate aesthete. 'And how is your toy?' he quipped. 'I am thinking of getting a wooden dog on wheels to draw after me at Oxford.'

Once at Oxford, even MacNeice found that the undergraduate decadence satirized by Evelyn Waugh in *Brideshead Revisited* was fading. But MacNeice was neither surprised nor 'altogether displeased' when the Merton College hearties attacked him and tore his trousers off. He assured Blunt it was an aesthete's duty to be 'tastefully insane, inanely obscene and obscenely tasteful', insisting that 'the banner of Intelligence had to be kept flying'. But his Cambridge friend, however, had already abandoned any pretense of being a flamboyant aesthete. 'But my dear Anthony, you must not become a hypochondriac,' MacNeice pleaded. 'University is really rather amusing.'

Evidently Blunt did not find Cambridge that amusing. After little more than a month, his disillusion had reached a critical point, and he drove across England to Marlborough with two school friends to see Clifford Canning. On the way back they stopped at Oxford unannounced. While his friends changed a flat tire, Blunt sought out MacNeice. Anthony was in a 'black mood' when they encountered one another outside Merton College hall. The hurried meeting did little to resolve Blunt's personal crisis. From the explicit nature of the letter MacNeice sent after their talk, it is evident that Blunt's tangled homosexual relationships contributed to his insecurity at Cambridge.

'I hope you did not go away enraged,' MacNeice wrote. 'Your appearance was so meteoric.' He advised Blunt that the 'continuing of this affection' for a mutual school friend then at Oxford was 'quite hopeless', except for 'a little emotion which might be called platonic'. Blunt's passion for another boy at Marlborough, called Edward, was 'far superior in every way'. But concern that Basil, his other Marlborough favorite, was too involved with another boy called Colin, MacNeice said was altogether unfounded, because that relationship was 'platonic from Basil's standpoint'.

'I still believe in the idea of mutual affection,' MacNeice reassured Blunt, 'but have never yet seen two people capable of it.' Anticipating that his advice would upset his friend, he apologized for 'a brutal letter' and for being a 'didactic and moralizing pig'. But the correspondence suggests that Blunt was in the midst of a serious emotional crisis by the end of his first term when MacNeice wrote on 6 December that 'Canning is very worried about your hatred of Cambridge and wouldn't believe me when I told him it was probably exaggerated.'

Blunt's 'hatred' of Cambridge appears to reflect the insecurity that haunted him throughout his first year – a symptom of the frustration that he felt. He believed himself to be a superior person, but had as yet received no such recognition from his undergraduate peers.

Furthermore, Blunt's inability to break away from his immediate circle of Marlborough contemporaries may also have encouraged his growing disillusionment with Cambridge. His friend at Oxford also found that the hoped-for intellectual stimulation had fallen short of expectations. MacNeice complained of the 'jargon and false profundity' of dons who 'caught little facts like flies in a web of generalization'. They were so detached that they 'might just as well have been at Cambridge'.

And to raise Blunt's spirits MacNeice planned a midsummer canoe trip up the Kennet to the scene of earlier triumphs.

'The Prince of Wales will declare open the first Phallic procession to the accompaniment of Marine bands,' MacNeice enthused. 'We shall skip through the hoops of the seven spheres and sway by our toes upon the balls of heaven.' He assured Blunt: 'Out of you will come a great Boreas searing the earth to a perfect nudity.' These flights of language with their allusions to Blake's poems were, it seems, calculated to bolster his friend's flagging self-confidence.

'In the new Jerusalem, what will happen when the sea suddenly vanishes?' MacNeice wondered in an April letter. It was mailed to

Downham Hall in Lincolnshire, where Blunt was spending the Easter vacation with his snobbish Assheton cousins. Blunt's earlier 'hatreds' seem to have been mellowing at the prospects of lazy summer afternoons punting down the willow-hung River Cam, to be followed by a summer job as a paid tutor in Italy. His good fortune impressed MacNeice, who wrote home explaining that his friend's tutoring might be 'a menagerie' but at four pounds a week it was 'highly lucrative'.

Blunt's dreams then came crashing down at the end of May, after he had labored through three-hour exam papers on such taxing subjects as orthogonal geometry and the behavior of magnetic fields. Even before he had handed in his final maths paper, he must have known that he had failed to get a first. He would, therefore, have anticipated the summons from his tutor to explain why his performance fell below the standards expected of a Trinity Foundation scholar. He would be warned that he had to improve or he would lose his scholarship status and the hundred pounds a year grant.

To limit the damage to his reputation and career, Blunt moved with a swiftness that suggests he had expected his poor examination results.

'Anthony got a second in his schools, he is going to drop Maths and do Modern Languages,' MacNeice informed his parents matter-of-factly. Blunt's decision to switch to French came as a surprise to his parents, who believed that a degree in maths was a more secure passport to the academic career their youngest son was contemplating. Was it possible for an immensely conceited twenty-year-old like Blunt to swallow his pride and concede that his mental apparatus was not, after all, up to the rigorous demands of the Cambridge Maths Tripos? Or did he see his stumble as another failure of the 'system' to accord him the distinction he believed was his due?

Blunt now had to live with the public verdict of Professor Fowler and his four examiners. They had judged him not to be a first-class mathematical intellect. To someone as convinced of his own superiority as Blunt, this was the unkindest cut of all. He had set his sights on an academic career and had stumbled at the first hurdle. His self-esteem had suffered a double blow: having to live down a second-class examination result when the majority of his class had firsts was galling enough. Blunt's friend Hilton, who himself 'felt the lack of a pilot in Oxford's mathematical seas,' says that Blunt blamed the Marlborough maths master, who 'spoon-fed us'.

Whatever the reason for his failure, to an aspiring academic accustomed to top-dog status, the public announcement of his lackluster performance added further injury to his pride. He could imagine the Marlborough masters he despised gloating, as they read the tripos listings in *The Times*, which showed how the examiners had finally cut Blunt down to size.

Blunt, as his contemporaries attested, harbored grudges. He would not easily forgive the Cambridge mathematicians for what he believed to be vicious snub. And it contributed to Blunt's decision to take a unique revenge against the British system as a whole.

Blunt's egotism ruled out any attempt to salvage his reputation as a mathematician. Nor was his decision to switch subjects simply because, as others suggested, he 'thought that languages would be more relevant than the mental gymnastics of pure mathematics.' If that were the case, he could have read for Part II of the Modern Languages Tripos. His fluency in French and his general facility with languages made this a 'soft' option. But Blunt's belief that he was a first-class intellect did not permit half-measures, and obliged him to wipe his academic slate clean by starting afresh and devoting his second year to another Part I. This meant writing off his entire first year and joining a new freshman class the following October. It would not only set him back from his peer group, but would cost him an additional year of study. That was the price Blunt decided to pay for a crack at the coveted 'double first'. (Only by the award of first-class results in *both* Part I and Part II could a Cambridge undergraduate aspire to the university's highest academic accolade and an open door to a fellowship.)

Blunt put the best possible construction on his academic set-back. But he did not fool MacNeice, who now characterized their Marlborough trip as 'a Wake up the river'. The exam results were evidently still grating on Blunt when he journeyed to Oxford a week after the public announcement because John Hilton noted in his diary how Blunt's arrival 'further upset the universe'. Supper at the Trout Inn at Godstow in the company of the Marlborough clique restored his humor for the trip to the old school the next day. After punting up the Kennet for a picnic amid the moonlit downs, Blunt stayed on with the Canning household. That he conducted a serious review of his future is evident from MacNeice's letter to his mother, in which he said that it was agreed that he should become a writer. 'Anthony is wavering in his decision to be a schoolmaster,' MacNeice observed. 'I expect his tutoring in Italy will finish that off.'

The three boys whom Blunt had agreed to tutor were the sons of Réné Gimpel, who was a friend of one of the Reverend Blunt's more well-to-do parishioners. The Gimpel galleries were among the most famous in London. Gimpel had married the daughter of Edward Duveen, the wealthy British collector who had built up an art empire selling old masters to American millionaires. Blunt set off for Menaggio with high hopes that he would make influential friends who could help him establish himself in the art world.

At the Hotel Victoria, a grand-luxe establishment on the picturesque shores of Lake Como, Blunt first met his charges. The three Gimpel brothers – Jean, nine; Peter, twelve; Charles, fourteen – proved more of a menagerie than he had anticipated.

'We must have been quite difficult,' Jean Gimpel recalled to me with a smile. There was no actual academic tutoring, he explained, but Blunt supervised them during the day: swimming, walking or sailing on the lake. Jean told me that their mother was most upset when Blunt did not carry out his duties properly by swimming with his charges. Since there is no evidence that Blunt actively disliked the water, his refusal may have had more to do with retaliating for the affront delivered to his pride by the Gimpel parents.

'My father was a 'grand bourgeois', Jean explained. 'He did not believe it was proper for servants – which is how he regarded Anthony – to be seen eating with us in the evenings when everyone dressed up for dinner.' Looking back, Jean reflected that their young Cambridge tutor would have taken his father's action as a personal slight.

Blunt wasted no time in paying back the snub. When the Gimpels returned to London, they discovered that he had put it about that the boys had behaved badly. 'We took a long time to forgive him for that,' Jean Gimpel said. The experience taught him to be suspicious of men like Blunt, who he said 'cultivate art as a compensation for their lack of creativity.' Many years afterward, Jean recalled, during an interview with his son at the Courtauld Institute, Professor Blunt had tartly remarked: 'My goodness, how you have changed.'

Jean Gimpel also pointed out that Blunt later went to great lengths to cast doubt on the authenticity of a self-portrait of Poussin the family owned. Jean and his brother Peter believe this was another retaliation for their father's refusal to admit the young tutor to the dinner table. This gave Blunt a grudge against the family. 'It may even have helped make him a Marxist,' he said, only half seriously.

There may be more truth than Jean Gimpel realized in his statement. Having had his ego badly wounded by his first year at Cambridge, Blunt would have magnified out of all proportion any personal slight by the Gimpels. The snub Blunt felt he suffered by his exclusion from the dining room of the Hotel Victoria – and his subsequent spreading of vindictive rumors about the three brothers – dashed his hope for a friendship with an influential figure in the art world. And it could only have added another smoldering ember to his determination to get even with the Establishment.

Anthony Blunt liked to convey the impression that the Bloomsbury set welcomed him with open arms. 'Their ideas were very firmly planted in all of us,' he once said, 'so that going to Cambridge and coming into direct contact with these people was only a direct extension.' Apparently content to take their cue from Blunt, those who have written about him have portrayed his Cambridge career as a meteoric rise to academic and aesthetic distinction. But the record shows this to be another myth.

Blunt had failed to take Cambridge by storm in his first year, and so began his second year a long way short of the freshman most likely to succeed. He also knew that it would be more difficult to win admission into the Apostles, the elite intellectual fraternity with close associations with the charmed Bloomsbury circle. He had already discovered that members of this society played a dominant role in the intellectual life of Cambridge because most of Bloomsbury's founding members had sprung from the patrician worldliness of Trinity and King's College, where John Maynard Keynes was now the bursar. While Keynes formulated the theories that were to transform the global economy, he acted as a father-figure for the Apostles and made the college the spiritual home of what was known as Bloomsbury-on-Cam.

When Blunt returned to Cambridge at the beginning of October 1927, to join that Michaelmas term's intake of freshmen reading modern languages, he worked doubly hard to make his mark, spurred on by the failure of his summer tutoring in Italy.

MacNeice tactfully referred to this setback in a letter. 'I want to hear more about your Italian Purgatory and your Bavarian Paradise,' he wrote, referring to his friend's bitter experiences with the Gimpels and subsequent recovery amid the baroque architecture of Munich, which he visited with Wilfred Blunt on the way back to England. MacNeice strove loyally to bolster Blunt's self-esteem. 'I am writing a novel featuring you,' he informed Blunt in December. 'I hope you don't mind, but I am giving you dark hair and some athletic prowess.' Blunt must have been flattered and amused to hear about his appearance as the white-flanneled hero of a public-school cricket team. The opening line was: 'Downs dozing in the distance was all he could remember and the light beneath them.'

Regrettably, the manuscript of MacNeice's first novel has not surfaced among his papers in the Bodleian Library. His letters indicate that he sent the finished draft to Blunt the following year with an appeal to help find a publisher. John Hilton, his Oxford and Marlborough compatriot, read the manuscript and pronounced it memorable chiefly for its 'very brilliant portrait of Anthony'.

Tantalizing glimpses of the youthful Blunt emerge in the letters MacNeice sent him. 'You might have been a cardinal, but I fear you missed your epoch,' MacNeice wrote teasingly to his friend. 'However, you lighten up this one a good deal, like a water-snake of bright colours come by mistake out of the bathroom tap.'

'Lots of luck in your schools,' MacNeice wrote to Blunt before his 1928 examinations. 'I feel it would be superfluous to wish you mental agility.' It was. Already fluent in French, Blunt had made an Easter vacation trip to Vienna 'to improve his German'. This time Blunt easily managed a French first class and a respectable 2:1 in German in Part I of the Modern Languages Tripos. His translations and essays in both received As from the examiners, who praised his understanding of the 'literature, history or institutions of the country concerned'.

Blunt had redeemed his academic reputation and saved his Trinity scholarship. He was back on course for a double first as he began studying for Part II of the tripos, which was concerned not so much with languages as with European 'literature, history and thought'. The 1930 Cambridge Register records that Blunt took a first class in the Part II Modern Languages examinations with a distinction for his special papers. After a false start, he could now proudly claim to have achieved his goal of a double first, a success that Trinity recognized by awarding him a research scholarship and an Allhusen Scholarship.

The following year the university awarded him the coveted Allen Scholarship; a Trinity fellowship was now a foregone conclusion. He was elected the next year for his dissertation on 'The History of Theories of Painting with Special Reference to Poussin' – essentially the same thesis on which he was to be awarded his doctorate degree in 1935.

The university register also discloses, however, that Blunt had actually graduated a year earlier. Regulations permitted his Part I in the Mathematics Tripos to count with his Part I Modern Languages to qualify for the degree of bachelor of arts. The reason for Blunt's decision to take his degree at the end of the third year appears in the MacNeice correspondence. In 1929 Blunt was considering applying for a graduate vacancy as a curator at Cambridge's art museum. 'Is it a good job at the Fitzwilliam?' MacNeice enquired that May. 'I am going to be a colonial professor I expect,' he declared flippantly, adding: 'My life hangs on getting a first at the moment.'

A more serious family crisis seems to have prompted Blunt's decision to equip himself without delay for a junior curatorial post in the Fitzwilliam Museum art department. His father's health was failing. If Trinity did not renew his scholarship for a fourth year of undergraduate studies, he might have to get a university job in order to complete his studies.

Fortunately, the college awarded Blunt a senior scholarship. But that summer the fifty-nine-year-old Stanley Blunt was stricken by his worsening stomach complaint. An exploratory operation in September 1929 revealed cancer. Surgery followed, but the doctors found the disease had spread too far to be operable. That November Hilda Blunt was left a widow. 'What a loss he will be,' Queen Mary wrote condolingly to Blunt's mother. 'Why should he have been taken, who was doing such good work on earth, when such useless, evil people are allowed to live?'

It has been speculated that Reverend Blunt's death was a pivotal event in turning his youngest son into a Soviet agent. No evidence has yet been uncovered suggesting his father's death provided the psychological release that sent Blunt down the slippery path to treachery. Neither Anthony nor his brothers had been especially close to their father, and as Wilfred has made clear, his father's death intensified the bond between his mother and her favorite son. The most important point that has emerged from an investigation of the facts behind the Blunt myth is that very little about his career allows for such a superficial explanation. This is especially true of published accounts of his homosexual affairs. According to one recent story, Blunt's 'first love affair' was with a college contemporary called Peter Montgomery, a second cousin of British World War II hero Field Marshal Bernard Montgomery.

The Trinity Register, however, reveals that Peter Montgomery, who became a music director with the BBC after serving as a wartime army-intelligence staff officer, did not come up to Cambridge until Blunt was in his second year. Friends confirm Montgomery did indeed become one of Blunt's longtime homosexual lovers, but the MacNeice letters make it clear that Montgomery cannot have been the first.

Analysis of the published record shows that reminiscences provided by Cambridge contemporaries *after* Blunt's exposure as a spy in 1979 are also suspect. This is especially true in the case of some distinguished figures whose memories of Blunt have been blurred so as deliberately to distance themselves from the self-confessed traitor. For example, the late Sir Michael Redgrave, who actually came up to Magdalene in 1927, described himself in his autobiography as a 'University aesthete' who 'thought of himself as a socialist'. Redgrave would have us believe that he arrived in Cambridge in 1928, the year he teamed up with Blunt – a 'young postgraduate student [sic] at Trinity' – to edit a literary magazine called *The Venture*.

According to Redgrave it was his friend the undergraduate poet Robin Fedden 'who suggested we should have a third editor'. But Redgrave must have already known Blunt for a year because he was a classmate of Blunt's in the 1927 Part I Modern Languages lectures. Yet Redgrave, perhaps anxious to allay suspicions about his own left-wing leanings (which had led to his wartime ban from the BBC for signing a 1941 antiwar pro-Soviet manifesto), insisted: 'I never got to know Anthony well, and he did not, as I recall, take a very active part in editorship.'

Alastair MacDonald distinctly remembers being introduced to both Redgrave and Fedden by Blunt, and articles by him and his friends appear in every one of the six issues of the magazine. The late John Lehmann, a Trinity friend of Blunt's and a fellow contributor to *The Venture*, stated, moreover, that Redgrave and Blunt were 'very close'.

The first issue of *The Venture* appeared in Bowes & Bowes and the other Cambridge bookstalls in September 1928, at the start of Blunt's third undergraduate year. In later life Blunt poured scorn on the magazine he helped found and edit. He called it 'short-lived' and 'jejune', hinting perhaps that editorial differences had caused Redgrave to remove his name from the masthead. Nevertheless, Blunt continued to contribute articles to *The Venture* until it folded in 1930, when Redgrave succeeded John Lehmann as editor of the semi-official *Cambridge Review*.

Anthony Blunt's articles did, however, stake out his claim to fame as Cambridge's premier undergraduate art critic. With topics ranging from Flemish art to Cubism, from Gothic architecture to the baroque, his writings are as impressive for their diversity as for their forcefully expressed opinions. The pieces also have more in common with his spirited schoolboy dogmatism than with the frosty rationality and dry dissection of minutiae that became the hallmark of his later writings as an art historian.

The article that made the biggest impression on the Cambridge mind was based on a trip to Bavaria and Austria during the 1928 Easter vacation with Michael Robertson and John Hilton. Robertson recalled that Blunt was already 'hooked' on the baroque. 'I was very much the pupil,' Robertson said. 'Anthony just told me what to think about all that fascinating baroque stuff in those churches.'

Hilton recalls the trip, which, he says, was made before Blunt's 'aesthetics were overlain by politics,' and whose 'fitting climax was fabulous Melk, whose photographs we had pored over in the close confines of our studies at Marlborough. From the hotel window Anthony preached a sermon to the empty moonlit street.' Blunt's enthusiasm for the opulent decoration and the 'sacred theater' of the churches of southern Germany had first been aroused by his father's strong disapproval during a family tour seven years earlier. The 'fantastic atmosphere' of baroque churches became Blunt's lifelong passion.

Blunt's love of the baroque suggests that he was essentially a Stoic who was fascinated by the discovery that he too was not immune to the powerful emotional appeal of the art and architecture of the Counter-Reformation. The austerity of his writing reveals a deep-rooted belief that only by putting aside passion and indulgence can an individual reach true wisdom and insight. Yet while one side of his scholarly temperament pulled him toward becoming the supreme historian of the rationality of Poussin and French classicism, his other half wrestled with coming to terms with the emotionalism of the baroque period.

Again and again throughout his career we find Blunt, like an addict in search of a fix, making pilgrimages to southern Europe, in his quest for the architecture that, he conceded, 'to a northerner, often influenced, though perhaps unconsciously, by the traditions of Puritanism, may seem vulgar, even irreligious.' Blunt justified his addiction for baroque by insisting that it was 'entirely wrong to suppose that, because this rhetorical art made a direct appeal to the emotions and even to the senses, the artists who produced it were not intellectual.'

It is significant that even at university, Blunt's articles appear carefully timed to further his career. They certainly succeeded in capturing the satiric attention of his contemporaries. 'Is Anthony Blunt?' asked *The Trinity Review*. It quipped: 'We wish we could have seen Mr Anthony Blunt wheeling Daan Hubrecht round the Italian pictures in a bath chair.' Hubrecht, a former Marlburian who was also at Trinity, accompanied Anthony to the exhibition at Burlington House during the 1929 Easter vacation. Blunt's critique appeared in the summer issue of *The Venture*, where he asserted that 'Michelangelo marks the summit of Renaissance painting'.

Blunt, it seems, had now come full circle from his adolescent rejection of the High Renaissance. Despite his later suggestions to the contrary, it is clear that *The Venture* made his Cambridge reputation by promoting his utterances on art. But more important, during his second undergraduate year, Blunt became a member of the exclusive literary and artistic circle orbiting around the stars of the older Bloomsbury generation. He gained access to this charmed circle of dons and intellectually minded undergraduates partly by cultivating a friendship with John Lehmann.

Lehmann was a Trinity contemporary who had also aimed high only to swoop dangerously low academically during his first year. An Eton College classics exhibitioner, Lehmann switched subjects after failing to get a first. Again like Blunt, Lehmann had discovered his homosexuality at school. He later claimed 'no bitter regret at having turned out to be a lover of my own sex.' Yet both young men faced 'the guilty feeling of being a misfit' and 'the danger of being pursued by the law and being branded as a criminal'. And both become Marxists. Lehmann's conversion came after a 1934 trip to Russia. Interrupting his career as a writer and left-wing editor with the Woolfs' Hogarth Press, Lehmann went to Vienna where he cooperated with the Communist underground as a courier at the same time as Kim Philby.

It is a matter for speculation whether an intrinsic homosexuality contributed to Blunt's or Lehmann's decision to become a Communist. But finely chiseled features and a yearning to be taken seriously as a poet were certainly no drawbacks when Lehmann aspired to join the salons of Bloomsbury-on-Cam. His sister Rosamond, whose first novel had made her an instant literary celebrity in 1927, facilitated his entrée. She had dedicated her best-selling book to her friend George Rylands, a golden-haired young fellow of King's, who was known to his friends as 'Dadie'. Out of friendship for Rosamond Lehmann, he became her brother John's literary mentor. John Lehmann was one of those who introduced Blunt to Rylands and brought him into his circle of influential friends.

Networking – or the technique of making friends and influencing people – was the key to Blunt's success during this year. The most influential and elitist network at Cambridge was that of the Society of the Apostles – and Rylands was one of the prominent senior members. The 'Cambridge Conversazione Society' was a century-old intellectual brotherhood founded in 1820 by twelve evangelical-Christian undergraduates who had taken to referring to themselves as Apostles. Kingsmen dominated the Society throughout the 1920s, so Rylands' support counted during the vetting of the 'embryos', as potential Apostles were known to other members.

Blunt's friendship with Rylands was certainly a factor that helped him find a 'father' to sponsor his election to Cambridge's most elite secret society. The membership lists compiled by a distinguished senior member of the society from the secretary's records, known as the Ark, show that Blunt was elected on 5 May 1928. This was rather late in his second year. Since embryos were usually invited to join after proving themselves first-class intellects in their freshman tripos papers, it suggests that Blunt received his invitation after some considerable lobbying by his supporters. If he did, his eventual election was a tribute to his subtlety. Embryos who reached above themselves were quickly disposed of as 'unapostolic'. Anthony, however, had already proved that he had a sixth sense when it came to ingratiating himself with the right sponsors.

That Blunt was an Apostle, and so was Guy Burgess, together with at least three other Cambridge graduates suspected of spying for Moscow, has led to the popular belief that the society was the only forum for Soviet recruiting at Cambridge. This myth has been encouraged by the traditional apostolic fetish for secrecy. Understandably this has brought embarrassment for a super-elitist fraternity that traditionally restricted new elections to an average of one or two of the best and brightest of each undergraduate year. Among the society's select membership of over a century and a half are many eminent intellects. The best known of the Apostles of the nineteenth century are Poet Laureate Alfred Lord Tennyson, physicist James Clerk Maxwell, historian Thomas Babington Macaulay, and philosopher Bertrand Russell. Twentieth-century luminaries include economist John Maynard Keynes, writer E. M. Forster, poet Rupert Brooke, philosopher Lugwig Wittgenstein, Nobel Laureate Sir Alan Hodgkin, and the contemporary author, theater director, TV personality and polymath Jonathan Miller.

Blunt openly declared in 1973 that he was a member of the

Apostles, insisting that it was 'no longer indecent' to refer to the society in public. But most of his surviving contemporaries are still too outraged at his betrayal to discuss him. George Rylands (elected in 1922) has repeatedly declined invitations to comment, although he could have shed some light on Blunt's election over more obviously qualified embryos. Richard Bevan Braithwaite, the outstanding mathematician and moral scientist of his generation at Cambridge (elected in 1921), did agree to discuss his contemporaries. But the then eighty-four-year-old professor abruptly terminated the interview when asked about the Apostles, whose affairs, he reminded me, were strictly confidential.

Fortunately for history, some of the more junior members of the society have adopted a more liberal interpretation of the fearsome oath of apostolic confidentiality. According to a recent paper on the history of the society, secrecy was considered necessary by the Victorian Apostles who played a leading role in opposing the doctrinaire authority of the Church of England. Members adopted a quasi-religious ritual, referring to themselves as 'brethren' and outsiders as 'phenomena'. Graduate Apostles who had 'taken wings' and become 'angels' were released from the obligation to attend every meeting. Ritual secrecy continued even when the aggressive logical humanism of the 1890s replaced liberal Christianity.

The philosophers James MacTaggart, George Edward Moore and Bertrand Russell ensured that the Apostles became the intellectual nursery for the Bloomsbury generation. At the Saturday evening meetings the chosen member took to the 'hearthrug' to deliver a discourse while the assembled brethren feasted on 'whales', as the Apostles referred to their quasi-sacramental sardines-on-toast, which were served in lieu of the original anchovies. By this time the society, according to a paper on its history read to the members in 1985, was 'agnostic in religion and liberal in politics'. The society had already become something of a sanctuary for homosexual discussion after Oscar Wilde's trial and conviction for sodomy in 1895. That was the year in which Goldsworthy Lowes Dickinson, a leading exponent of 'romantic friendship' between older and younger men, became an Apostle. Goldie, as he was known to E. M. Forster and other admirers, was an inspiring Hellenist who subscribed to Socrates' teaching 'that the love for men is of a higher kind than that for women.' This contrasted oddly with his desire for humiliation by young men wearing boots. Not surprisingly his romantic affairs with a succession of undergraduates invariably ended in anguish.

A distinct change had overtaken the society by the turn of the century; the members no longer discussed politics but became 'obsessed by homosexuality', which was 'discussed in terms of Moore's criterion that good states of mind involved the contemplation of art or of the beloved object.' It was Lytton Strachey who persuaded the brethren that it was silly and affected to talk of a love that dared not speak its name. Breaking with Dickinson's idea of romantic love, Strachey and his homosexual confrere Keynes pursued what they called 'the higher sodomy'.

Keynes, who would later dismay homosexual brethren by marrying the Russian ballerina Lydia Lopokova, conceded that his generation of Apostles had repudiated 'customary conventions and traditional wisdom' to become 'in the strict sense of the term immoralists'. He and Strachey regarded the Apostles as their special preserve for the pursuit of that 'true combination of passion and intellect'. Male beauty and homosexual inclination became a qualification for embryos, as Strachey and Keynes competed for the election – and seduction – of their 'adorables'. Squabbles over apostolic boyfriends inevitably led to friction. Keynes' philandering led Strachey to describe his friend spitefully as a 'safety-bicycle with genitals'. Ludwig Wittgenstein, the ascetic Viennese philosopher who was Russell's protégé, was elected in 1912, then walked out, protesting that the Apostles 'had not yet learned their toilets, a process which though necessary, was indecent to observe.'

Virginia Woolf took such amorous apostolic love spats in her stride. 'They were men who tended to be devoid of female company,' she noted, subscribing to the Bloomsbury view that homosexual relationships were a necessary demonstration of individual freedom. She tartly referred to them as 'the society of equals enjoying each other's foibles'.

World War I saw a decline in the society's preoccupation with homosexuality as an essential qualification for election, but another overtly homosexual Apostle was Dennis Robertson, who later received a knighthood as one of Britain's leading economists. He was elected to the society in 1926 and, as a Trinity don, would have encouraged the election of Blunt, whose own homosexuality and lean boyish good looks were certainly no drawback to ensuring his own election two years later.

By the late twenties, when Blunt entered the society, the idealism and pacifism engendered by World War I had begun to fade, so the predominance of King's and the society's preoccupation with sociology make it all the more surprising that Blunt, a Trinity College aesthete and failed mathematician, was ever elected member 273. In his university generation he was preceded by his first-year mathematical classmate Alister Watson and classicist Philip Dennis Proctor, both of whom obtained firsts as freshmen and were King's College scholars. They were elected in January and October 1927. Since it was traditionally the role of the junior Apostles to vet the embryos, there is some significance that Blunt's immediate predecessors – Watson and Proctor – were both in later years suspected of and investigated for spying for the Soviets.

No matter who engineered it, Blunt's apostolic elevation was reassuring recognition of his intellectual superiority, and it wiped out the stigma of his first-year academic stumble. 'I really felt I had reached the pinnacles of Cambridge intellectualism' was how Julian Bell felt when he became the next member six months after Blunt. There could never have been doubt that Virginia Woolf's nephew, then in his second year at King's, would be elected. But it is ironic that it fell to Blunt, as the most junior Apostle and the sixty-seventh secretary of the society, to arrange for the election of the son of Clive Bell, the art critic who had been a major formative influence over him at Marlborough.

'Bloomsbury *un peu passé*,' was how Julian Bell described the

Apostles' philosophical anarchism 'in the mode of Blake and Dostoievsky'. According to Bell, 'Practical politics were beneath discussion.' He observed that the aesthetic discussions in which Blunt, who delivered no fewer than eleven papers, played a leading part assumed 'a classic post-impressionist view of the arts'. Rather surprisingly, in view of the eleven occasions he took to the hearthrug, Blunt later insisted that 'on the whole my own activities lay very largely outside' the society. He sourly insisted that the Apostles 'were never primarily interested in art.'

Despite Blunt's disparaging attitude, these were heady times to be a young Apostle. Fry and his friends Keynes and Forster were then at the height of their fame. Membership in the society opened doors to one of the inner sanctums of Bloomsbury. Blunt had finally realized his schoolboy dream. Bloomsbury led to future connections, which he would exploit in both his public and secret careers. The society played an especially important role by introducing ambitious undergraduates to the twin clans of the Trinity and King's dons who constituted a dominant force in Cambridge. Dadie Rylands, for example, was close friends with Andrew Gow, a Trinity don and a member of 'The Family', a dining club of Jacobite origin, whose members included the master of Trinity, J. J. Thompson, and A. E. Housman, the celebrated poet and university professor of Latin. Rylands also shared Gow's enthusiasm for bridge, and Blunt, who played a polished hand of cards, quickly became Rylands' regular partner. But it was art and not cards that was Blunt's principal reason for cultivating Gow.

Aloofly austere, this Trinity classics don nursed a deep feeling for art, especially Renaissance painting. A fine connoisseur, Gow inherited his eye from his father, a clergyman headmaster who was a member of the Royal Society of British Artists. His mother was also the daughter of a noted Victorian painter. Gow's keen interest was fostered by an uncle, who was keeper of the Royal Academy.

A lifelong friendship between Blunt and Gow arose, not from a Marxist conspiracy as it has been misinterpreted but from a shared intellectual passion for the arts. In a rare public statement in 1978, Blunt persuaded *The Times* to print his personal embellishment to Gow's formal obituary. He declared that even though Gow's influence 'only spread to a small circle of undergraduates, it had a vitally important effect on them and through them on others in Cambridge and eventually elsewhere.' This unusual tribute prompted Brian Sewell, Blunt's friend in later life, to conclude that Gow – who once spoke of his influence over Blunt – was the *éminence grise* and original recruiter of the Soviets' Cambridge espionage network. But interviews with Sewell and those who knew Gow, along with investigation of his papers, have failed to reveal anything more sinister than his dominant influence over Blunt's aesthetic development.

Gow's political views – in so far as he held any – appear to have been those of a 'rock-ribbed conservative' according to those who knew him. Blunt's obituary makes it clear that his esteem for Gow was because 'he did more than anyone to foster a real understanding of the arts in a Cambridge that had very little feeling for them.' He went on to describe him as 'almost the only don to take a positive interest in the art of the past and his rooms were one of the few places where one could find good library books about the Italian Renaissance, a fine collection of photographs of paintings and above all stimulating conversation about the arts in general.' Gow assumed the role of Blunt's artistic guide at a critical juncture in the young man's development. Blunt's reference to his mentor's enthusiasm for the Renaissance is most significant in the light of his own rejection at Marlborough of Italian painters of the sixteenth and seventeenth centuries. It was Gow who opened his eyes to the importance of the Renaissance and 'was willing to discuss the ideas of even the most heterodox student, *and often helped him clarify his thought*' – apparently a direct reference to his own artistic education.

'Granny Gow,' as he was known for his bespectacled gaze and legendary fastidiousness, could be scornful to the point of derision with those he considered slipshod or pretentious. Because Blunt was conscious that his intellectual relationship with his natural father had been lacking, his devotion to his Cambridge mentor was strong and enduring. Hilton says that Blunt always spoke of Gow 'in tones of reverence, as though he were the embodiment of all wisdom.'

Some of Blunt's friends suspected that there was a homosexual element to Gow's special fondness for Blunt. Gow was widely regarded as one of Cambridge's 'bachelor dons', who made no secret of his enjoyment of the company of intelligent and attractive undergraduates. 'He spent most of his time in his room in Neville's Court and was very hospitable, if you happened to be a member of a certain sort of circle,' Michael Robertson told me archly. He reluctantly added that aesthetes, such as his friend Blunt, received a warmer welcome at Gow's Saturday evening sherry parties than rugby players like himself.

Gow's homosexuality appears to have been more sublimated than predatory. He was the typical product of an Edwardian generation of Cambridge graduates raised on the precious Victorian homoerotic poetry and the so-called Uranian writers who spoke largely in code. His friend Housman's love for an Oxford undergraduate named Moses Jackson inspired 'A Shropshire Lad'. The surprising popularity of this poem, which gave acceptable expression to the yearnings of upper-class intellectual homosexuals for blond English youth, inspired Forster to write *Maurice*. It also promoted a national cult of homoerotic patriotism. By the outbreak of World War I this peculiarly British obsession extended far beyond the Bloomsbury group's worship of Rupert Brooke to reach the corridors of power in Whitehall, and even into the Cabinet.

The all-male Oxford and Cambridge colleges have been described as a 'homosexual' environment because of the high proportion of bachelor dons ministering to a majority of undergraduates fresh from the homoerotic subculture of their public schools. The educational system of the British elite was steeped in the Socratic Greek tradition of an older teacher sharing his cultural heritage with budding male intellects. Discussing the so-called romantic friendships of Hellenist dons such as Gow, the former provost of

King's College and noted Cambridge historian Lord Annan states in his unpublished essay 'The Cult of Homosexuality' that 'it can safely be said of these bachelors that they were never guilty of any homosexual act that went further than the chaste kiss or caress.'

Annan concedes, however, that dons like A. E. Housman who would never have attempted to seduce an undergraduate of their own social class 'probably made love with soldiers or working class boys'. He also cites the Victorian poet Leslie Barford who wrote under the 'Platonic pseudonym of Philebus': 'Boys of rough trade and the laddies of leisure/All give me equal and infinite pleasure.'

Most of the homosexual dons, Annan believes, sublimated their passion. Some, like the left-wing economist from King's, Arthur Pigou, enjoyed taking handsome undergraduates mountaineering. Others haunted the bathing sheds on the Cam where male members of the university swam in the buff. According to Annan, Gow favored the university library as 'a convenient place to cultivate new friendships'. Annan believes that the overt homosexuality of such dons as the Trinity economist fed on the social reaction to World War I.

'The homosexuals of the nineties treasured their secret passwords,' he observes, 'but the homosexuals of the twenties came out of the closet into the drawing room.' While a minority wrote manifestos, or boasted publicly of their criminal conduct, many made no attempt to conceal their differences. 'One no longer had to admire chi-chi or pose lily in hand or court choirboys. Homosexuality became a way of jolting respectable opinion and mocking the establishment that had "made" the war.' In support of his contention, Annan points out that for Blunt's generation homosexuality 'had all the thrill of being illicit (as taking drugs has today) and all the pleasure of being certain to outrage the older generation.'

Annan's view is confirmed by John Lehmann who wrote, 'It was definitely considered bad form, in fact ridiculous to show embarrassment or guilt.' He observed that 'this was to some extent due to the liberating influence of Bloomsbury with which

King's was permeated at the time.' Lehmann's friends 'made no bones about preferring their own sex.' They talked 'openly of their romantic attachments to choristers, telegraph boys and young beauties of their own generation.' Another Cambridge fellow, the international literary critic George Steiner, pointed out in a *New Yorker* essay on Blunt that proper account has not begun to be taken by historians, sociologists and psychologists of 'the vast theme of homosexuality in western culture since the late nineteenth century.'

Investigation for this book has shown that historians have not begun to explore the importance of homosexual networking. The existence of extensive lines of personal influence and favors goes a long way toward explaining the power that Blunt attained – power he was to manipulate for the Soviets, as well as for his own ends. The homosexual network reached out like a cobweb across the pinnacles of the British Establishment, with connections in Whitehall ministries, the universities, the foreign service, the church and the armed services. Its communicating filaments were powerful strings of hidden influence, so fine that they were not easily detectable.

What does become obvious, however, is that several of the lines of this web of influence were spun by homosexual Apostles who, by the twenties, had anchored themselves firmly in the upper reaches of Whitehall. Although Keynes was without doubt the society's most prominent influence, the leading behind-the-scenes string-puller in the interwar years was Edward Marsh. He was longtime personal secretary to Winston Churchill, to whom 'dear Eddie' would attach himself like a faithful hound whenever Churchill had a ministry. When his master was out of office – an increasingly frequent occurrence in the thirties – Marsh was always at hand to polish the statesman's prose, happily performing the unsung role of editor and literary critic.

Given the importance of the apostolic connection that Blunt certainly was aware of, it is surprising to find that he spoke so dismissively of the society. Julian Bell, by contrast, wrote that the society 'played a more important part in my life than any other institution.' Since Bell's frank correspondence with his mother documents his homosexual affair with Blunt, it appears that the Apostles *must* also have played a central part in Blunt's undergraduate career.

Julian Bell's letter to his mother, dated 14 March 1929, announces that his 'great news is about Anthony'. Couched in the matter-of-fact terms that might be expected of the eldest son of Virginia Woolf's sister, he informed Vanessa: 'I feel certain you won't be upset or shocked at my telling you we sleep together – to use the Cambridge euphemism.' There is good reason to believe that this affair was Bell's first full-blown sexual encounter with either man or woman. Blunt, on the other hand, did not seem exhilarated by the relationship. The two men shared little in common but their membership in the Apostles and a passion for France. Julian Bell – described by Strachey as 'fat and rather plain – socialistic, I fancy' – was hardly the ideal partner for the handsome Adonis of MacNeice's letters. Perhaps pedigree and Bloomsbury connections compensated for Bell's lack of physical attraction?

Julian Bell's infectious enthusiasm and his fondness for debating were more than a match for Blunt's intellect. But, it appears, he had already learned how to compartmentalize his life. 'It's a great mercy thinking that you aren't a moral and disapproving parent,' Julian wrote to his mother. 'Still, don't let it go any further, or it might get round to Virginia [Woolf] and then one might as well put a notice in *The Times*.' Bell made his plea for confidentiality to protect Blunt! He explained to Vanessa that since 'Anthony's parents were strict and proper clergymen of the Church of England, and a number of his friends highly shockable athletes, we have to take our precautions.'

Certainly Blunt always took the greatest care to hide his homosexuality from his mother. One example of Blunt's preoccupation with his public image was his captaincy that spring of a scratch Cambridge hockey team, for which he recruited a member of the university rugger team. In the event, Blunt's team easily beat a side of Oxford aesthetes captained by a young poet, Stephen

Spender, who managed to score a goal against his own side. At the celebratory tea party the guest of honor was E. M. Forster, who disappointed the Oxford visitors because he 'talked solely to the rugger blue'.

The out-of-character excursion on to the games field succeeded in camouflaging Blunt's homosexual affair with Bell from most of their friends. But it did not fool the knowing Forster – or Keynes, who delighted in incestuous apostolic dalliances. Keynes appears, however, to have taken a dislike to Anthony. He wrote to Vanessa Bell in May 1929, wondering 'whether Anthony Blunt (with whom he's completely and helplessly infatuated) is quite all that Julian thinks him.' Vanessa, to whom Julian was deeply attached, wanted to believe her confidant. Writing in 1937 after her son's death in Spain, where he was driving an ambulance for the Loyalists in the Civil War, she consoled herself that her son's 'first love affair with A.B. [Anthony Blunt] was not a very real one.'

Real or not, the affair continued for six months. Blunt was a guest of the Bell family at their home in Charleston in Sussex. 'Please God I say these delightful & divine people don't come and make me concentrate again all in my face & brain,' neighbor Virginia Woolf confided to her diary on 21 September 1929. She was spared that visit – and a month later Julian admitted to Vanessa that, 'Anthony and I being about equally bored with each other,' he intended to 'make the acquaintance of more young women.' That summer he had begun his first serious relationship with an undergraduate at Girton, the first of a series of affairs with women that, as Lehmann noted, led to a 'succession of mistresses'.

Blunt's six-month homosexual affair with Bell must have exposed him to Julian's left-wing political enthusiasms. Under the influence of his uncle Leonard Woolf, Bell had become a socialist at the age of fifteen. Bell never espoused the Communist cause either openly or secretly, as Blunt was to do. But he was a Marxist in all but name by the time he went off to Spain 'to throw overboard all weak charity-mongering idealism and get down to guts and brawn.' Blunt, however, would never have agreed with Bell's conviction that 'what is sauce for the proletarian goose is surely sauce for the intellectual gander.' He preferred covert plotting and manipulation to 'guts and brawn'.

John Lehmann recorded that the 'atmosphere of intellectual Cambridge at the time was strongly pacifist since there were many younger dons who had been through the war or who had some of their dearest friends killed.' This mood had fueled the fires of Bell's socialism and Lehmann's own disillusion led to his dalliance with Marx. George Steiner, who has written about Blunt's intellectual psyche, believes that he was not immune to the political forces that deeply affected his friends and contemporaries.

'It is thought likely,' Steiner asserts in his provocative essay 'The Cleric of Treason', 'that Blunt became actively interested in and sympathetic to Communism as an undergraduate at Trinity College, Cambridge between 1926 and 1929.' When I put it to Steiner that Blunt had stressed, 'the sense of detachment' at Cambridge in the twenties, he smiled knowingly. This he did not believe to be so. Steiner advised me to examine the primary sources.

Subsequent research exposed the mirage of another of Blunt's myths. The Cambridge Union minute books, college magazines, letters of dons and records of undergraduate societies show that university life was anything but 'detached' during Blunt's undergraduate years.

Still more intriguing are British records uncovered in Washington that show MI5 knew that the Soviets had targeted Cambridge for penetration long before Blunt was recruited as one of Stalin's Englishmen.

6 'A World Doomed to Destruction'

Cambridge was becoming increasingly politicized leftward by the end of the twenties. The Labour Club membership had risen to over two hundred, and there was even a vocal Communist society of thirty. While this does not prove that Blunt was a Marxist during his undergraduate years, it does indicate a far more power-ful left-wing political undercurrent among his contemporaries than he ever admitted.

This was especially true for scientists like Alister Watson, who later joined the Cambridge Communist party. Only after Blunt's secret confession in 1963 was Watson interrogated by MI5 on suspicion that he too had been recruited by the Soviets. No confession was extracted, but this did not lay to rest the strong suspicion that Watson, a scientist who later worked on top-secret submarine-detection systems, had become another of the Soviet network during his Cambridge years.

In disentangling the intellectual clues that may have led both Watson and Blunt to Marx, a common factor is their under-graduate interest in the prophetic philosophy of William Blake. Watson, it turns out, wrote the *lead* article of the first issue of *The Venture* on 'The Wisdom of Blake'. England's eighteenth-century iconoclast painter/poet was praised for being 'the passionate enemy of the traditional ideas of the judgment of human actions and affairs by ethical and moral philosophies'. According to Watson's interpretation, which Blunt later reflected in his own published study, Blake put the study of Science 'beside the exercise of Art as one of the greatest objects of human life'.

In the *Venture* article, which presumably Blunt endorsed by giving it such prominence, Watson pointed out that Blake had been pilloried 'by the skeptical and leisured gentlemen of his time', whose definition of reason 'did not apply to scientific investigation but to moral thought – and it is still there.' This statement clearly expresses the author's strong personal conviction that even in the twentieth century the reactionary British Establishment was still prejudiced against men of science and vision.

Mutual identification with Blake as a symbol of the predicament of budding intellectuals in Britain appears to be the first expression of a shared resentment. It led the two apostolic confreres to conclude that the future belonged to the more 'scientific' organization of society reflected in Marx's vision. They were not alone. Such views were common enough among Watson's fellow scientists, who resented the traditional lack of political recognition and respect the British accorded to those who were dedicated to pushing back the frontiers of human knowledge.

This atmosphere in the world's most advanced research centre made Cambridge rather than Oxford the focus for Soviet intelligence and propaganda efforts, and Cambridge was to pay the price. In time Britain's second-oldest university gained an unenviable reputation as the alma mater of spies and traitors. Yet research shows that British authorities for some reason chose to ignore the mounting evidence that Cambridge's scientific reputation had made the university a special target for Moscow's intelligence and subversion. Declassified papers in Cambridge scientific archives, as well as MI5 and Special Branch police files, indicate that although the threat was perceived, neither its magnitude nor its danger was appreciated.

After the lessons learned from fighting Germany in World War I, the British government had no excuse for ignoring the role of science in contributing to the advancement of the peacetime economy. Although much of the Cambridge effort was concentrated in the area of 'pure science', bequests from industrial foundations such as that set up by Lord Melchett, founder of the giant Imperial Chemical Industries, provided much of the special funding for nuclear research at the Cavendish Laboratory. Under Rutherford's direction, the team led by John Cockcroft and E. T. S. Walton was making steady progress toward the first actual splitting of the atom. A crucial contribution to Cavendish research was made by the Russian physicist Peter Kapitza.

Just how important his efforts were is evident in the recently released Cockcroft papers. His enthusiastic report to Rutherford, dated 16 April 1930, discloses that in less than four years after Kapitza's appointment as assistant director of the Magnetic Laboratory funded by the Department of Scientific and Industrial Research, it had developed the equipment to produce enormously powerful magnetic fields 'of over 300,000 gauss' which 'proved that a wide field of research was open which take several men's lifetime to cover.' In less than a year Kapitza's experimental genius had perfected 'a very efficient liquid hydrogen plant which we made ourselves,' enabling them to extend their work 'to the region of 14 degrees absolute. I think that, without exaggeration,' Cockcroft wrote to Rutherford, 'our magnetic laboratory possesses unique facilities for further investigation of a new region in modern physics.'

The significance of Kapitza's low-temperature and magnetic work was recognized by the British scientific establishment within six months. Although he had only become a fellow of Britain's prestigious Royal Society a year before, in November 1930 he was made its Messel Professor and awarded a £15,000 grant to establish a permanent magnetic and cryogenic laboratory.

British recognition of Kapitza's achievements came less than a month after his return from a trip to Leningrad. He had begun making these annual trips in 1926, when his appointment as assistant director of the Cavendish brought an invitation and promise of a safe return to England from Leon Trotsky. But in 1929, Lev Kamenev, Trotsky's successor as president of the Collegium of the High Council of the People's Economy Board of Science and Technology, put Kapitza on a retainer as a consultant for the establishment of a new Technical Institute at Kharkov. According to Kapitza's wife, Anna, Kamenev had warned Kapitza that he would be expected to return to complete his important work in the Soviet Union as soon as suitable laboratories were built.

Two other leading Russian scientists, physicist Lev D. Landau and mathematician George Gamow, also appear to have been part of the same long-term Soviet technical espionage operation. Both graduated from the University of Leningrad before working in the Institute of Theoretical Physics at Copenhagen University, where Nobel Laureate Niels Bohr developed the relation between the quantum theory and nuclear structure that paved the way to the splitting of the uranium atom. Both Landau and Gamow worked for a time alongside Kapitza at Cambridge. Landau returned to play a leading role in the Soviet atomic bomb project and was elected in 1946 to the Academy of Sciences. Gamow went back to Leningrad in 1931 and was denied an exit visa for two years. Kapitza's retainer as an adviser for the Kharkov project was a clear indication that the Soviets retarded him as essential to their scientific effort. Another indication was the visit to Cambridge in 1931 by Nikolai Bukharin, then president of the Soviet Academy of Sciences. Following Stalin's personal instructions, his mission was to persuade Kapitza to return permanently to the Soviet Union. Kapitza demurred and continued to return to Cambridge after his annual visits to Leningrad until the summer of 1934, when his exit visa was denied.

Significantly, this was a year *after* his new Mond Laboratory, lavishly equipped for low-temperature and magnetic research, had been completed. Despite Rutherford's lobbying of the British government and protests by the international scientific establishment, Moscow refused to relent, claiming that Kapitza was 'a citizen of the USSR, educated and trained as a scientist at the expense of his country' who 'was sent to England to continue his studies and research work' and had 'stayed in England rather longer than he should have done.'

Kapitza at first protested against his forced detention and

refused to continue his research. Or that was the story that was believed by his former colleagues in Cambridge. Whether he was a witting or unwitting tool of Soviet scientific espionage can never be known for sure. The Stalin regime certainly made their prodigal son comfortable with a spacious new home, cars and a dacha. Most important of all, Moscow succeeded in persuading the British government to sell them, at knockdown prices, the entire contents of the Mond Laboratory. These were carefully packed up under the supervision of Kapitza's erstwhile colleague John Cockcroft and shipped to the Moscow Physics Problems laboratory in 1935.

The scheme to purloin Western technology had been hatched a decade earlier by Mikhail Abramovich Trilisser of the OGPU Foreign Department and later the Comintern in collaboration with Russian Military Intelligence. The plan, ironically, appears to have been inspired by the Grand Tours young eighteenth-century English gentlemen of substance made to acquire aesthetic knowledge, as well as European paintings and sculpture to bedeck their country houses. The Soviet Union sent its most brilliant young physicists abroad in the twenties and recalled them in the early thirties with a priceless haul of technical data and equipment.

The Soviet scientific espionage plan succeeded in part because after World War I it had become a matter of faith to many researchers that science had transcended political creeds and national boundaries. This was especially true in the field of theoretical physics, where investigations into the structure of matter depended on the free interchange of technical information. The Soviet Collegium assiduously fostered this belief.

The importance of Cambridge to the Soviet technical espionage operation in the early thirties has been confirmed by a former senior US counterintelligence official, who was told by the British that MI5 had uncovered evidence that the GRU had actually stationed one of their undercover officers there to manage the operation. The real payoff came twenty years later, when the scientific foundation laid by physicists like Kapitza, Landau and

Gomow played its part in the Soviets' crash program to develop their own atomic bomb. Kapitza always denied playing any personal role in this work, but in the opinion of US analysts his work made an important contribution to the Soviet scientific effort.

On evidence currently available it is impossible to give credence to the claim, recently revived, that Kapitza fathered the Soviet hydrogen bomb with secrets stolen from Cambridge. His research at the Cavendish was not directly connected to atomic fission. But it is interesting to note that Kapitza's annual trips back to Leningrad began only in 1926, *after* his own magnetic-research program started to produce significant results. Obviously his masters in the Kremlin wanted him to keep his former colleagues in the Leningrad Institute abreast of the groundbreaking work at the Cavendish Laboratory. However long a leash Kapitza had been given, he could not have been unaware of his obligations to Moscow. Soviet intelligence agencies would have known that Kapitza moved in a remarkable circle at Cambridge. He counted as his associates and friends some of the most brilliant physicists and mathematicians in Europe.

'The inexhaustible resources and the diversity of matter are becoming clearer every day,' noted an intriguingly explicit *Pravda* report less than a year after Kapitza's return. Commenting on the work being done at Cambridge, a Soviet scientist named Lapirov-Skobolo noted: 'Research into the nature of the atom is in its turn calling into existence new methods of producing a vacuum, new methods of super-high voltage techniques.' The article, noting the 'leftward' tendencies among the new generation of Cambridge scientists, called on them to 'break with a world doomed to destruction'.

Was it therefore beyond the flight of fancy of a scientific commissar in the Kremlin to divine the ultimate significance of the work being done at the Cavendish Laboratory? A simple equation of basic physics revealed that by splitting the atom energy could be released. Whether this was practical in the laboratory was still a matter of theoretical debate in the mid-twenties, even among Cambridge scientists. But Russian researchers took it as an article of political faith that Lenin had decreed that 'Communism equals electrification plus Soviet Power.' Kapitza's experiments with harnessing electricity to generate powerful magnetic fields encouraged some scientists in Leningrad to discuss the feasibility – as early as 1932 – of experiments to produce 'controlled thermonuclear reaction'.

Achieving nuclear *fusion* – the basis of the hydrogen bomb – was not achieved for more than twenty-five years, and then only by nuclear explosion. What is surely significant is that some Russian scientists and their Kremlin masters were seriously contemplating fusion at a time when the team at Cambridge was still two years away from the first step toward nuclear *fission* – the splitting of the atom.

Dr Arnold Kramish, a distinguished nuclear physicist who was a member of the American Manhattan Project and historian of the Soviet Union's nuclear research effort, believes Bukharin's remarks to be significant. 'The Russians, through Kapitza and Gamow, had opened the window into the technical advances being made in the Cavendish Laboratories,' Kramish said. 'It is not impossible that an exceptional scientific mind like Bukharin's could guess that the work being done by Cambridge physicists would eventually turn the key to releasing the energy of the atom.'

Cockcroft, one of the Kapitza Club's founding members, later acknowledged the role these lively intellectual brainstorming sessions played in helping fuse together the theoretical and experimental scientific effort that resulted in his success, along with Walton, another club member, in splitting the atom in 1932.

Alister Watson was a junior member of Kapitza's famous club. Here the political views of Blunt's fellow Apostle and devotee of Blake were subject to the influence of more mature Cambridge scientists who had already openly embraced the Marxist philosophy. Chemist J. D. Bernal, a pioneer of X-ray crystallography, was a beetle-browed Irishman who followed an extreme socialist ideology fired by his Jesuitical education. His enthusiasm for dialectical materialism was inspired by his belief – later dubbed 'Bernalism' by an Oxford scientist – that the duty of science was to improve the welfare of society and that pursuit of knowledge for its own sake was as irrelevant to social progress as the solution of crossword puzzles. Bernal did not hesitate to apply the torch of Marxism to scorch the political nonbelievers and fire the left-wing enthusiasm of P. M. S. Blackett, another physicist in Kapitza's influential Club.

The Cambridge scientific establishment held the essentially Marxist view that science was an ideology like religion, philosophy, law, literature and art. Under capitalism, science was made to serve the interest of the ruling classes. Only in the supposedly classless Soviet Union, where the abolition of capitalism had also abolished the distinction between 'pure' and 'applied' research, could science truly serve the needs of the community.

The Cambridge physicists and biochemists who were thrusting back the frontiers of science were those most influenced by proto-Marxist philosophy. Brilliance combined with powerful egocentric personalities led men such as Bernal to adopt radical philosophies and nonconformist life-styles. This was certainly true of J. B. S. Haldane, the idiosyncratic biochemistry professor whose extramarital relations offended the staid Trinity dons as much as his habit of bringing bottles of urine to the college's high table. The radicalism of J. B. S. Haldane and Joseph Needham, who succeeded him as professor, was stimulated by Sir Frederick Gowland Hopkins, the director of the Institute of Biochemistry, whose greatest interest after biochemistry was socialism.

In 1928 Haldane followed Maurice Dobb in making the Cambridge left-wing intellectual's obligatory pilgrimage to Moscow to observe the new scientific state at first hand. But unlike Keynes and Russell, whose innate liberal humanism had been affronted by their encounters with Stalin's emerging police state, Haldane and his second wife, Charlotte, an American journalist, returned as ardent champions of the supposedly scientific foundations of the Soviet Union.

No less egocentric, and dedicated to the same brand of scientific left-wing idealism – although he never joined the Communist party – was Dr Joseph Needham, a biologist who believed in the unique blend of socialism and Social Gospel of the Reverend Conrad Noel, the so-called Red Vicar of Thaxted. A prewar Cambridge graduate and friend of composer Gustav Holst, he was an Anglo-Catholic who preached that Christ was a 'militant revolutionist' and placed the Red Flag and a Sinn Fein banner alongside the Cross of St George in his church.

Needham and his left-wing Cambridge colleagues were among the influential voices who called throughout the thirties on the need for scientists to be given a more responsible role in the British social and political process. One of the leaders in this movement was Julian Huxley, the radical Oxford biologist and president of the Union of Scientific Workers – an organization that already had an influential cell of Communists in its Cambridge branch, including Maurice Dobb.

Needham, Huxley, Bernal and many others echoed the theme of the Soviet scientific delegation who had made a dramatic arrival in London by air at the end of June 1931. Bukharin contrasted the economic crisis of the capitalist world with the 'entirely new phenomenon' of scientific Marxism and the collective organization of scientific research on a vast scale in the Soviet Union. According to Bukharin, this 'new type of intellectual culture which dominates the mental activity of millions of workers is becoming the greatest force of the present day.'

'I can say that the inspiration for my own work and that of many others in science,' Bernal later wrote, 'can be definitely traced to the visit of Marxist scientists to the History of Science Congress in 1931.' Even those less ideologically committed than Bernal felt the impact of their first exposure to dialectical materialism. They were impressed with the status and importance the Soviets apparently accorded to their scientists. Here was an example to be emulated.

The Congress and its potential impact did not go unnoticed by Special Branch, which obtained copies of Bukharin's papers and intercepted a Tass telegram to Moscow reporting on the proceedings. The Soviets had been 'impressed' by the younger delegates.

152 Mask of Treachery

Singled out for special mention was the Cambridge group, led by Needham, who 'called themselves mechanists', not because they opposed dialectical materialism but because they had as yet 'unheeded it'.

Special Branch reports on the revolutionary leader's visit indicate how by 1931 the MI5 Registry contained some bulky files on Cambridge scientists who were potential targets of, and sympathizers with, the Soviet Union. The records that have come to light show that elaborate measures were in place to monitor the activities of Needham and his cohorts, especially Maurice Dobb, who had been identified as a longtime member of the Communist faction of the Union of Scientific Workers. Dobb was already the university's leading spokesman for the new vision of the classless, scientifically run society that was to hypnotize the third wave of Cambridge undergraduate recruits to Marxism in the years to come.

Until the end of his life, Maurice Dobb steadfastly played communism's John the Baptist, preaching the Decline of Capitalism to successive generations of undergraduates. In 1965, when I attended his classes, he was white-haired and weary after nearly half a century in his self-appointed role. But he still mustered the persuasive enthusiasm of the true convert who was also an inspiring teacher. Unlike some of his younger colleagues in the Economics Faculty, whose ferociously statistical arguments were virtually impossible to follow, let alone take notes on, Dobb's twice-weekly classes were a breath of common sense to a confused newcomer to the Economics Tripos.

Dobb was a patient teacher and this made him a highly effective spokesman for Marxism. After reading one of the 1925 Home Office reports on Communist subversion, King George V wrote to the chancellor of Cambridge demanding to know why such a well-known Marxist was permitted to indoctrinate undergraduates.

Dobb was not a simple ideologue, propagandist, or undercover agent. He studiously avoided activities that could have led to his prosecution or being turned out of his Cambridge teaching position. Although he was often suspected of being a Soviet agent, he was always able to defend himself by pointing to the openness of his communism. Given the intellectual environment in which he operated, his unswerving loyalty to Moscow, and the scores of committee positions he held in such front organizations as the Union of Scientific Workers and the Society for Cultural Relations, Maurice Dobb was one of the Comintern's most influential assets in Britain.

Dobb's activities had not escaped the notice of MI5 and the Special Branch officers responsible for monitoring Soviet subversive activities. In one of the files reporting on the Society for Cultural Relations, which has turned up in the US Archives, Dobb is noted as 'the Cambridge economist, a well known Communist and a prominent member of the SCR.' The file contains a 1929 letter from a Comintern official to a London subordinate, in which Dobb is characterized as 'one of the staunchest friends of Soviet Russia in England, and in view of his position at Cambridge, he can do much for cultural rapprochement.'

Cultural rapprochement was, as this report makes plain, only a euphemism. The Society for Cultural Relations was one of a number of front organizations that mushroomed in the late twenties as a cover for Moscow's increasingly sophisticated subversion. The SCR had been formed in 1924 with the support of many leading members of Britain's progressive intelligentsia, while the Friends of Soviet Russia was set up to appeal to the masses. Both organizations were identified as 'component parts of the vast machinery of propaganda directed from Moscow.' Most of the early meetings were devoted to 'enthusiastic accounts of conditions in Russia' by returning travelers, almost all of whom were 'of strong Left Wing or Communist sympathies'.

Reflecting Soviet interests, the SCR's 'cultural' orientations became increasingly 'scientific'. The Soviets made special efforts to develop the Cambridge branch of the SCR. While researching at the London School of Economics after graduating from Cambridge in 1922, Dobb became a founding participant in the 'nucleus membership' of the original Communist cell of the National Union of Scientific Workers.

Counterintelligence officers were keeping a close watch on Dobb and his Cambridge associates. Monitoring by MI5 and Special Branch revealed a more sinister 'cultural rapprochement', according to the evidence in the Home Office records. One area of particular concern, as we can now see, was Soviet film propaganda.

The Special Branch file titled 'The Cambridge Film Society' provides a tantalizing glimpse of the extent of surveillance mounted on one specific area of the Cambridge Communist network's activities. The Scotland Yard files reveal that neither Special Branch nor MI5 had dropped its guard after the expulsion of the Arcos mission and the Soviet delegation to Britain. In fact, surveillance and monitoring of mail to organizations like SCR and individuals such as Dobb had uncovered a new area of Comintern propaganda activity.

Just six months after the Arcos raid, Special Branch intercepted a 'Yours fraternally' letter from German Comintern activist Willi Münzenberg inviting the Honorable Ivor Montagu (a 1925 Cambridge graduate and the socialist son of a Liberal peer) to a November conference in Berlin to organize the production and distribution of 'proletarian films and letting them out of bourgeois film-theaters'.

Lenin himself had decided that 'of all the arts, for us the cinema is the most important.' Western governments also appreciated the propaganda power of the Soviet cinema, and Britain attempted to ban the import and public showing of these movies. But Münzenberg devised a scheme to use the front organizations he was operating from Berlin, under the banner of the International Workers Relief, to arrange for the clandestine distribution of films.

A Special Branch report, obviously based on intercepted mail, indicated that Montagu had invoked the aid of the Russian Trade Delegation and a number of leading British Communists to beat the Home Secretary's proscribed list of Soviet films which included Eisentein's *The Armoured Cruiser Potemkin*, which the

British Board of Film Censors refused to certificate in 1926 on the ground that 'it dealt with mutiny against properly constituted authority' and 'depicted scenes showing the armed forces firing on the civil population'.

Customs officers had been alerted to look out for the banned Soviet films, and police warrants for the seizure of fourteen titles had been issued. Captain Guy Liddell, acting on information MI5 passed on of a Soviet scheme to flood Britain with Soviet films smuggled into the country from the Irish Free State, asked the police to extend 'existing arrangements' to west-coast ports.

'That they are of high technical merit is undoubted,' noted a critically attuned British Home Office official, 'but that is not the only criterion. The films are *clearly propagandist* in character and if publicly exhibited are *quite likely to lead to disorder*.' The secret Special Branch reports, however, reveal that the concern was not so much with the supposedly inflammatory nature of the films, as with the widening Soviet infiltration and subversion of which these two films were only the most prominent examples.

Intercepted mail to the London office of the Friends of Soviet Russia exposed the extent of the scheme cooked up by Münzenberg (who was described in the report as 'the notorious Communist, who presides in Berlin on behalf of Moscow over the doings of the League against Imperialism and the Friends of Soviet Russia'). Not until November in 1929 did MI5 issue a report on the latest move in the Comintern's cinema offensive: the setting up of the Federation of Workers Film Society British branch. As with all Moscow's front organizations, its ample council included eight 'professed communists'. Among the party stalwarts were Maurice Dobb, Emil Burns, Harry Pollitt and Willie Gallacher. The report noted 'the great majority of the remainder being active in almost the same sense'.

Some idea of the extent of MI5 interest and Special Branch surveillance of leading British academic Communists in the late twenties – particularly of those at Cambridge – emerges in the Special Branch reports on the showing of Russian films in the university that same year. Letters intercepted before delivery to

Montagu alerted MI5 and Special Branch that an undergraduate named G. Moxon and a left-wing fellow of St John's College, Dennis Arundell, had set up a Film Society based in King's in November 1928 to 'show film privately in a local cinema on Sundays'. The local Cambridge police were 'discreetly' instructed to investigate. Calculating that the home secretary would be reluctant to obtain a warrant to stop a genuinely private viewing, Special Branch efforts to thwart Dobb and his friends came to naught. They waited until 23 March before alerting the chief constable of Cambridge, advising of the need to 'be careful to hide the source of our information'.

The Special Branch reluctance to prejudice its sources of information, even in this relatively minor operation, is a pointer to the extent of the efforts then under way against the Comintern and its agents.

This Special Branch file, which must be representative of other more weighty operations, is an important indicator of the true extent of British counterintelligence operations. It reveals not only that the mail of known British Communists was being regularly intercepted but also that particular attention was being paid to the Cambridge circuit of Comintern sympathizers. This explodes the myth perpetrated by Blunt and others that Soviet recruitment at Cambridge did not start in earnest until the mid-thirties. It has even been asserted that MI5 and Special Branch were slow in following up the evidence of a growing network of supporters of the Comintern among university dons. But those MI5 reports and Special Branch memoranda that have now come to light do not justify this view. For example, a Cambridge graduate named Philip Spratt had been arrested at Meerut in 1929 and charged with leading a conspiracy of Communists in India. As a result, throughout the thirties MI5 sent the Indian police the Special Branch dossiers on Oxford and Cambridge graduates with Communist associations who went out to the Far East.

The records of secret liaison meetings between Special Branch officers and their contacts at the US embassy in London just do not support the promoted view that the British intelligence services turned a blind eye to Comintern agents operating in Cambridge – or elsewhere in Britain – during Anthony Blunt's undergraduate years.

Reports from MI5 still bearing their old secret classification show that, following the raid on Arcos, the security service, far from ignoring Soviet subversion in England, increased its nationwide surveillance. The expulsion of Soviet diplomats in 1927 had been a setback for the Comintern's British operations, but the British authorities did not drop their guard.

Countering Russian subversion had certainly become more difficult after MI5 and Special Branch lost the advantage of eavesdropping on Moscow's communications with the Soviet embassy. But the Russian Trade Delegation, much reduced in numbers, continued to maintain a small presence in London. Within months the diplomats who had been expelled from London began to reappear in various Western European capitals.

Berlin became the site of a growing number of Soviet facilities. These included centers for the fabrication of documents and altering of passports. Large printing establishments were set up, as well as safe houses for agent training and commercial companies used as fronts. To control the Berlin center and coordinate its extensive non-German activities, Moscow gave increased decision-making authority to its local representatives. Berlin was soon the communications center not only for OGPU but also for Comintern-front activity.

Propaganda and subversion after 1927 were directed through a system of sympathizers and couriers recruited by mushrooming front organizations. The League Against Imperialism and International Workers Relief were based in Berlin. So were the Russian Red Cross, the Friends of the Soviet Union and the Society for Cultural Relations.

Wrapping political subversion and propaganda in the trappings of cultural or humanitarian objectives proved a favourite strategy of the Kremlin. Many British public figures, not just established left-wing intellectuals, became unwitting allies of the Comintern. By agreeing to lend their names as members of worthy committees, they endowed an organization like the Society for Cultural Relations with a cloak of respectability and authenticity. It is now clear that it was a nine-page Secret British report of 1929 that alerted the Americans to the central subversive role of VOKS, the Russian acronym for the Society for the Promotion of Cultural Relations abroad, that is, SCR. The nominal head of the British SCR was Margaret Llewelyn Davies, a radical matriarch of one of Cambridge's leading academic families. Through her efforts distinguished visitors such as John Maynard Keynes, H. G. Wells and Bernard Shaw were persuaded to make the trip to the Soviet Union, the 'bait' of VIP reception with free travel and accommodation.

Just as in Britain, when Arcos had been the nerve center for much of Moscow's clandestine activity, so the Berlin trade mission called Westorg assumed a new importance in 1927. The trade representatives launched an aggressive recruitment program among the foreign embassies, telephoning low-paid clerks and messengers and asking them out to dinner. Those from the US embassy who accepted the invitation usually were met by a 'Mr Poull', who proceeded to offer the clerk a monthly salary of $300 with an extra $100 for expenses. In exchange for these payments – a princely sum in Germany at the time – the clerk provided access to the contents of the US embassy's diplomatic pouch for a brief time prior to its dispatch. Germany was also the field headquarters for the massive Soviet maritime operation, which had infiltrated crews of all nationalities. Thus Moscow's center in Berlin had an extensive network of couriers and agents who were able to move easily from port to port and country to country under cover of their seamen's papers.

To meet the increased threat from the Soviets, the British made more and more requests for confidential American assistance in tracking down suspected Comintern and OGPU operatives. The British complained that English-speaking agents acting under cover of Amtorg, the Soviet-American trading company, entered the United States with 'false passports prepared and issued in Moscow'. The US State Department rejected this charge. Amtorg visas were subjected to special scrutiny; but State did concede 'the possibility of Soviet agents (not posing as Amtorg representatives) fraudulently securing quota visas.' The extent of the Soviet illegal operation was uncovered the following year when a naturalized US citizen, Jacob Kreitz, was arrested, ostensibly on a watch-smuggling charge. Customs officials found he was carrying a leather-bound book containing the names of sixty-five Soviet agents operating in the United States, China and Japan. He also had a supply of signed American baptismal certificates, birth certificates, passport applications and other documents.

The records reveal that the US embassy in London was being provided, on a regular basis, with copies of telegrams in both plaintext and cipher, which MI5 had intercepted between Comintern headquarters in Moscow and the New York secretariat. In one instance the British, by mistake, actually passed on a photostat of the front page of a telegraph company's file copy of a 12 February 1929, message from 'LCO Wolfe' in New York to 'LUX' in Moscow. 'You will notice that this cable was sent on the northern route,' the US embassy pointed out in a cover memo to Washington, drawing attention to the implication that US traffic was also being similarly intercepted. The memorandum pointed out that 'no doubt Washington would be interested to know that there is a [British] Government peace-time censorship on certain cable lines from America to Europe.'

Interception of telegrams and mail was still MI5's most reliable source of information on the Comintern. The northern route, which relayed transatlantic cable traffic through Britain to Europe, was especially useful in monitoring communications to and from the Netherlands. The Hague had become another center of Soviet efforts to infiltrate Soviet intelligence agents into Britain. These were principally 'illegals' who used forged passports and identities to pose as residents. Confirmation of The Hague's strategic importance was later provided by Walter Krivitsky, a high-level Soviet intelligence official who defected through France in 1937. In the late twenties and early thirties Krivitsky was a rising young officer with the Third Section of Soviet Military Intelligence, which worked alongside the OGPU with the European 'illegals and with the Communist international'.

Krivitsky may not have been, as he proclaimed himself, the chief of Soviet Military Intelligence for Western Europe, but he was one of the most highly placed Soviets ever to defect. Too highly placed, it seems, for the comfort of Stalin. On 10 February 1941, he was found by the chambermaid in the bedroom of a seedy Washington hotel. Three apparent suicide notes on the bedside table, plus a lack of suspects, led the DC police department to conclude that Krivitsky had taken his own life. But there is now reason to suspect that Stalin's emissaries were responsible for eliminating Krivitsky.

In 1939, when Krivitsky was interviewed by British intelligence, he charged that Moscow had managed to infiltrate the Foreign Office. Unfortunately, most of his information was intriguingly imprecise, gathered from documents he remembered seeing in Moscow many years earlier. These referred to a Soviet agent 'from a good family' in the British diplomatic service: it was eleven years before this Soviet spy was identified as Donald Maclean. So much has been made of this *ex post facto* discovery that the significance of other concrete evidence Krivitsky provided has been overlooked. The former Soviet spymaster also identified two low-level Foreign Office spies who had been recruited long before Donald Maclean. They were both cipher clerks. John Herbert King was quickly identified, and in 1939 secretly tried and convicted. The other spy could not be brought to justice. He had been dead for six years. The official verdict at the time was suicide, but now it appears he, too, was a victim of the sinister skills of the OGPU's Operations Division. The British have *never* officially identified this second Soviet spy, but the evidence shows he was Ernest Holloway Oldham. Disgruntled over his failure to obtain a pay raise in 1929, Oldham had gone to the Soviet embassy in Paris to offer information on British codes.

Oldham provided a double bonus for Moscow when he persuaded his colleague Captain King to join his treachery.

King proved to be the more damaging long-term agent. The pressure of spying soon weighed too heavily on Oldham. He broke off his communications with the Russians after resigning from his Foreign Office post in September 1932. Twelve months later, he was found unconscious in the gas-filled kitchen of his Pembroke Gardens flat and pronounced dead on arrival at nearby St Mary Abbot's hospital. Oldham's convenient death bought Soviet intelligence seven additional years of King's tapping of Foreign Office code and traffic.

The coroner's verdict was that Oldham had taken his life by 'coal gas suffocation' while of 'unsound mind'. But a favorite OGPU saying in the thirties was: 'Anyone can commit murder but it takes an artist to commit a suicide.' This seems especially appropriate in the Oldham case, a fact that had never been officially admitted by the British government. Not until 1945 did the British learn, from the Dutch intelligence service, that Oldham had been run by Hans Gallieni, an OGPU illegal, who operated from Holland. The information came from an associate on the same underground circuit, Hans Pieck, who defected after World War II. Pieck had been introduced to the Oldhams in the thirties by Gallieni and MI5 arranged in October 1945 that he should come over to London to help Mrs Oldham identify Gallieni. The day before the meeting was due to take place, she was suddenly taken ill and died before identification could be made.

Oldham and the other Soviet spies in the Foreign Office code room were run by an OGPU illegal operating from Europe and not by the British Comintern chief. After Arcos, the Soviet intelligence services were having to be far more careful of the threat posed by MI5 and Special Branch. The resident Comintern agent in Britain until 1929 was a bulbous-nosed Ukrainian with protruding ears. His name was A. D. Pestrovsky, but he used the English alias A. J. Bennet. He had married Rose Cohen, an English Communist, and his mission was not to recruit agents but to bring the Communist party of Great Britain under Moscow's full control. This required 'cleansing the party of all right wing and conciliating tendencies' and engineering the removal of the independent-minded Andrew Rothstein from the party's central committee. Pestrovsky then secured the authority of Moscow loyalists Clemens Palme Dutt and Harry Pollitt over the CPGB. These *apparatchiky* remained in control of the British party for the next twenty years.

Pestrovsky demonstrated no less acumen in infiltrating the Conservative party, helped by an equally unscrupulous manipulator named Arthur Maundy Gregory. A homosexual wheeler-dealer, Gregory had made a fortune on commissions from brokering the sale of dukedoms, peerages and honors to replenish Liberal party coffers during Lloyd George's postwar coalition administration. He remained untouched by a scandal in 1922 that resulted in changes in the law making it illegal to purchase titles by contributing to party funds.

A mere act of Parliament, however, was no obstacle to Maundy Gregory. This Oxford-educated son of a Southampton clergyman impressed the honors-hungry rich with an elaborate charade of extensive establishment connections. As publisher of the *Westminster Gazette* and proprietor of London's fashionably plush Ambassadors' Club, Gregory had both the façade and the facilities for continuing his profitable role as a middleman for the buying and selling of knighthoods or baronetcies. Nor was Sir John Davidson, the Conservative party chairman, above turning a blind eye to the law when it came to arranging substantial donations to Conservative party coffers.

The potential for an explosive scandal increased, however, when Gregory began hiking his already steep commissions. His greed, evidently, finally persuaded the Prime Minister to act. Baldwin did not turn to the police or to the Secret Service but to Davidson, his trusted party chairman and adviser on the security services. Their strategy was simple and effective. A spy was infiltrated into Gregory's organization to obtain a list of his clients, all of whom were then excluded from the honors list.

According to a cryptic footnote in Davidson's official biography, the 'task of penetrating the Gregory organization was undertaken by A. J. Bennett.' The Tory MP for Nottingham, Albert James Bennett, was appointed assistant treasurer of the Conservative party in 1927. But Davidson's confidential papers reveal that in addition to A. J. Bennett, Davidson had enlisted the aid of Pestrovsky (Bennet) in his secret schemes. Evidence that Pestrovsky became a part of Davidson's plot to rid the Conservative party of the tiresome Maundy Gregory appears in Davidson's memorandum of 28 November 1929. In it he emphasizes: 'For his eyes only spell out the informant as either A. J. Bennett or A. J. Bennet, *taking great care to get the spelling of the surname correct* according to which one of the two it refers.' Davidson, as Tory party chairman, took this decision because 'it would be less likely to arouse comment than the use of any code name.' That Bennet was indeed Pestrovsky is evident because the note states 'the same method of reference is currently being used in communications with Balfour, Remnant and Bogovout-Kolomitzev in Paris.'

It was Bogovout-Kolomitzev, an emigré Russian wheeler-dealer, who accompanied the British Industry Delegation to Moscow in 1929 (a trip made with the approval of Prime Minister Baldwin and his adviser J. C. C. Davidson) to discuss possible investment in a wide range of big industrial deals including oil drilling, construction of canals and the building of the Moscow subway project. But none of the promised Soviet construction contracts materialized. Although the French police, who were tipped off to his extensive Soviet connections, after the expulsion of the Arcos trade delegation from London, Bogovout-Kolomitzev became one of the go-betweens through whom Moscow sought to reestablish direct links with British industrialists willing to trade with the Soviet Union.

Among the prominent Tory businessmen who courted the assistance of Bogovout in the belief that they could trust a White Russian were Major Hugh Kindersly (later a director of the Bank of England), Sir Arthur Balfour and the industrialist Ernest Remnant. Confidential information obtained from a Swiss source by author Richard Deacon suggests that a subsidiary role was played in these back-channel dealings with Moscow by Sir Arthur Pigou. This left-wing Cambridge economist had maintained his links with prewar Russian revolutionary contacts in Geneva.

Bessedovsky, the acting Soviet chargé d'affaires in Paris, played a central role in the secret commercial negotiations with the British before his headline-making leap to freedom over the embassy wall in 1929. Although he provided valuable information to the British and French, he later cast his lot back with the Soviets by becoming Bogovout's business partner.

It was the role that Pestrovsky played as contact man with Bessedovsky and the secret commercial wheeling and dealing that proved an unexpected ticket of admission into the skeleton-packed closets of the Tory party.

Why did the Conservative chairman, of all people, turn to Moscow's man in London to help rid the party of Maundy Gregory's predations? Evidently Pestrovsky already possessed the information on the honors racket that Davidson and Bennett needed because Soviet intelligence had been keeping tabs on Gregory ever since his leadership of the Free Ukraine campaign began in the early 1920s. Pestrovsky had succeeded in penetrating Maundy Gregory's organization and in learning of his homosexual connections in the political and Whitehall establishment. Among them were the intimate friends of Eddie Marsh and a number of leading Tory MPs. The potential for an explosive sexual scandal appears to be why Davidson sought Pestrovsky's aid to neutralize Maundy Gregory. Moscow also saw the chance to kill two birds with a single stone. Not only did Soviet intelligence acquire useful blackmail information on the homosexual network, but with Maundy Gregory out of business, funding for the Free Ukraine campaign would dry up.

Yet the best efforts of Pestrovsky and Davidson did not quite succeed. Maundy Gregory persisted until 1933, when he was charged with trying to sell an honor to a naval officer. Even then, Davidson 'brought pressure to bear on the authorities' to enable Gregory to plead guilty and retire to France on a comfortable pension after serving a brief prison sentence. Such plea-bargaining was unprecedented under English law. But Tories feared that Maundy Gregory would carry out his threats to implicate highly placed homosexuals. In addition, there was the danger that a prolonged trial might reveal the role played in the affair by Soviet intelligence. In fact, that appears to have been the greater concern. It seems no coincidence that Maundy Gregory was not brought to book until four years after Bessedovsky's defection resulted in Pestrovsky's hurried return to Moscow at the end of 1929.

These clandestine channels of Soviet influence and disinformation to the Tory party, the sworn enemy of Bolshevism, survived the political crisis of 1929, when Baldwin and the Tories were defeated in a June election. The incoming minority Labour government formed by Ramsay MacDonald with Liberal acquiescence also brought the Soviets a bonus. Britain's second Labour Cabinet voted to restore Anglo-Soviet diplomatic relations in October 1929, the very same month that Wall Street stock prices crashed.

This dramatic harbinger of the Great Depression was portrayed by Comintern propagandists as the beginning of the final collapse of capitalism as prophesied by Marx. To the Communist party of Great Britain and its Marxist sympathizers, the financial shock waves were taken as a sure sign that capitalism was collapsing and that the new decade would usher in the long-awaited communist millennium. The Comintern issued instructions to step up propaganda and infiltration in British army camps and naval bases.

British security officials knew they were now facing a much greater threat. Even before the first members of the new Soviet delegation arrived in London to reopen the shuttered embassy in Chesham Place, both MI5 and the Metropolitan Police Special Branch faced the challenge of increased Soviet subversion. Unfortunately, their separately controlled organizations were short of manpower and resources.

'Communist efforts to tamper with HM Forces have increased and are still increasing,' MI5 reported in February 1930, warning that these efforts, 'if allowed to spread unchecked, will, in the long run, prove disastrous to the Forces as a whole.' These fears came dangerously close to materializing the following year, when the unity of the Labour Cabinet crumbled in the face of a severe fiscal crisis. Prime Minister Ramsay MacDonald and two ministers who supported his demand for massive cuts in government and service expenditures joined the Conservatives and Liberals to form an emergency national government. One of their first steps was to cut servicemen's pay. News of these cuts was met by a wave of protest among the sailors of some warships of the Atlantic Fleet based on the west coast of Scotland.

INVERGORDON MUTINY was how the newspapers headlined what was in reality a minor and quickly suppressed revolt. But it rocked the Royal Navy. For the first time there was real alarm about the political threat to the empire's front line of defense. The right-wing press and parliamentarians reacted with a 'Red Scare' outcry. The CPGB and the few Communists among the mutineers were slow off the mark and restricted to a belated agitation after the handful of ringleaders had been arrested. More important, the mutiny panicked foreign bankers.

After there had been a crippling run on the pound, the British government did what it had vowed never to do: abandon the gold standard. The economy reeled from the double blow. Exploiting a mood of high crisis, Ramsay MacDonald, with Baldwin as his deputy, appealed to the electorate to support the national government. The national government won a landslide majority in the October 1931 election, flooding the House with Tory supporters. The Labour party, deserted by its former prime minister, was cut back to a parliamentary rump. Despairing socialists began paying attention to the siren song of Communist propaganda.

In the wake of the Invergordon Mutiny, the Conservative-dominated national government resolved to combine fiscal expediency with the need to increase internal security. The task of monitoring civil and military subversion was once and for all united, and MI5 was given responsibility for investigations 'dealing with the Communist and foreign revolutionary movements'. Captain Liddell and his Central Registry files came under new management. Scotland Yard's Special Branch continued to carry out the actual investigations on MI5's behalf, only now the Yard was directed by a unified organization, which, for the first time, could properly be described as Britain's 'security service'.

General Kell's newly united forces did not underestimate the dimension of the new tactics of subversion being launched by Moscow. They knew from Bessedovsky and other defectors that the OGPU had grown to be a vast empire within the Soviet state. It controlled the military forces guarding the Soviet Union's frontiers, plus the extensive prison system and labor camps. The Fifth Section of the OGPU Intelligence Division ran intelligence gathering and counterintelligence with the assistance of the Foreign Division. 'Moscow Center', as it became known, controlled one of the most important organs of power and control in the Soviet Union. The twenty-five hundred OGPU officers at Moscow headquarters occupied 'the whole district between the Lubianka and Srietenka'. This was an area of several square blocks centering on the notorious prison complex in the heart of the Soviet capital.

No one in the relatively tiny MI5 Cromwell Road headquarters, Britain's front-line command post in the secret war, can have underestimated the magnitude of the threat posed by the Soviet Union or the Communist virus developing within Oxford and Cambridge, the universities charged with grooming future proconsuls of the British Empire. What they did not know was that the Soviets had developed an ambitious long-range plan to infiltrate Britain's governing classes by recruiting high-flying undergraduate Communist sympathizers as moles who would burrow their way up into the Establishment. A scheme that must rank with the Trojan horse as one of the most devious and successful stratagems of intelligence history.

The origins of this strategy were rooted in the important organizational change in the Communist intelligence apparatus that occurred after the 1927 Arcos raid. The Soviets had learned that the exposure of one spy ring must never again lead to their embassy. Safety measures were introduced by Mikhail Trilisser, the OGPU Foreign Division's founder and chief until 1930, who ordered his agents to build up an illegal *rezidentura*. The OGPU officers sent abroad to build up these secret networks no longer enjoyed diplomatic immunity. Armed with false passports, they concealed their Russian nationality by assuming the identity of a national in an occupation that could justify lengthy periods of residence in their assigned country of operation. These illegals were ordered to remain independent of the local embassy and Communist party. They established their own channels of communication with Moscow through mail drops, cutouts, and trusted couriers who were entirely separate from Comintern activities and the official diplomats.

The *rezident* director of the Soviet underground in a foreign country ran his network of sources with the aid of two or more assistants, each of whom was an experienced staff officer from Moscow headquarters. They were the hard core of the illegal network or *apparat*, 'close mouthed and on constant guard with almost everyone else'. They operated through assistants who controlled two to five group leaders, most of whom were trained and trusted former members of the national Communist party. Their job was to maintain contact with the informants, known as 'sources'.

The principal mission of the *apparat* was to recruit both high- and low-level government employees who were in a position to learn state secrets or otherwise aid the Soviet cause. Sources were rated according to three ascending categories. The *stukach*, or lower grade of informers, were usually low-level government officials who provided information for pay. The *agenty vliyaniya* (agents of influence) were reliable sources in foreign governments, business, the media or academic institutions who did not spy for money. They were usually Communists or Marxist sympathizers who saw it as their duty to provide assistance to further the goals of the great socialist revolution. The *agenty vliyaniya* have often been categorized as 'fellow travelers', who declined official party membership to protect their careers or because they were not committed Communists. In the context of Cambridge, the *agenty vliyaniya* could include either open Communists like Maurice Dobb or ardent secret sympathizers like Arthur Pigou. In the American context, they were US State Department officials in the Far East section who facilitated the growth of communism in Asia after World War II. *Agenty vliyaniya* are regarded as being so pro-Soviet that their files in Moscow headquarters carry the stamp *nash* – literally 'ours' – a term Soviet intelligence usually reserved for full-fledged agents.

The infiltration, or penetration, agents like Oldham and King, Blunt and Philby, were recruited under discipline and controlled by a Soviet intelligence service officer who was either an embassy legal or an illegal *rezident*. After the mid-twenties it was the exception for Comintern officials to be involved in running the agents, who, according to one Soviet defector consulted, were known as *proniknoveniye*.

Trotsky's expulsion from the Soviet Union in 1929 provided the OGPU Foreign Division with an additional reason to expand the underground tentacles of its overseas networks: Stalin increasingly relied on the OGPU to monitor the exile, who remained a potential focus of opposition. Until he was confident enough to order the elimination of his erstwhile rival, Stalin's suspicion fired his determination to be master of his own intelligence network.

Distrustful of the judgement of his subordinates, Stalin repeatedly warned his intelligence chiefs against 'equations with many unknowns'. He constantly urged them to acquire as many informants as possible to provide him with secrets obtained from locked dispatch boxes, ciphered communications and the classified files of foreign governments. Stalin's obsession imposed a special mind-set on the KGB. Unlike Western intelligence operations, which sift important intelligence data from the mass of information legitimately available in newspapers, scientific journals and records of parliamentary debates, the Soviets subscribe to the theory that *razvedka* – true intelligence – can be obtained only surreptitiously. OGPU's Foreign Division was therefore devoted to acquiring secret informants, undercover agents and stolen documentation, while the Special Division intercepted and deciphered foreign codes and ciphers in addition to guarding the security of Soviet communications systems.

The sharpest insider description of Soviet intelligence during the early Stalin era was provided by Leon Feldbin, who used the name General Alexander Orlov when he defected to the United States in 1938. During the five years he served in the uppermost ranks of Soviet counterintelligence in Moscow, Orlov was involved in preparing intelligence training manuals and drafting top-level briefs for Stalin. Hungry for stolen secrets about foes domestic and foreign, the Soviet dictator insisted on having personal access to raw data. 'An intelligence hypothesis may become your hobbyhorse on which you will ride straight into a trap,' Orlov records Stalin as saying. As one of the heads of Soviet intelligence, Orlov recalled Stalin's penchant for dismissing as 'dangerous guesswork' the estimates of his intelligence chiefs. 'Don't tell me what you think,' Stalin would interject. 'Give me the facts and the source.'

Stalin's lust for obtaining secret intelligence endowed OGPU and its 'organs' with unrivaled power, and he stepped up the pressure to expand the penetration of foreign governments. The primary target was Britain – the main adversary, in Stalin's eyes – where after a decade of effort, the number of Soviet spies infiltrated into the government was still too small to produce truly important secrets. The Foreign Office secrets and ciphers supplied by Oldham and King had been valuable, to be sure, but Moscow knew that these code clerks had no prospects of ever rising to the upper echelons of the British government. The OGPU tried to help its low-level infiltrators attain promotions, but as Orlov recorded 'the results were spotty and far from satisfactory.' What the Soviets needed was a way of inserting trusted agents into the highest echelons of Western governments. These agents would have to have the right social and professional qualifications to make their way in the British ruling establishment. Once they were in place, their rise could be facilitated by dispensing good advice, covering their expenses for off-hours entertainment of colleagues, and even exercising the influence on trusted *agent vliyaniya* informants.

Not until 'the early 1930s' – according to Orlov's account – did one of his fellow chiefs in Soviet intelligence 'hit upon an idea which solved this most difficult problem as if by magic.' He succeeded, we learn from Orlov, 'because he approached the problem not only as an intelligence man, but as a sociologist.' The 'magic' plan was based on 'the fact that in capitalistic countries lucrative appointments and quick promotion are usually assured to young men who belong to the upper class.' The obvious targets for Soviet recruitment were therefore the 'sons of political leaders, high government officials, influential members of Parliament'. In Britain as in most European societies, privileges often brought promotion, and as Orlov noted, 'it does not surprise anyone if a young man of this background, fresh from college, passes the civil service examinations with the greatest of ease and is suddenly appointed private secretary to a cabinet member and in a few short years assistant to a member of the government'.

Orlov was and is regarded by the Americans as a highly authoritative source on Soviet intelligence operations. While there seems no reason to doubt Orlov's assertion that the OGPU was the architect of the scheme, it has been pointed out that the Soviet Foreign Ministry officials at the time included Litvinov, Rothstein and Ivan Maisky, the polished counselor to the Soviet diplomatic mission in London who returned there as ambassador in 1932. These men certainly would have made their contributions to the scheme. They would have endorsed the feasibility of the strategy and confirmed that the network of educational privilege in Britain focused on Oxford and Cambridge.

The Soviet blueprint for penetrating British government institutions also owes something to the patience inherent in the Russian national character. Years would pass before the young British penetration agents recruited at university proved themselves. The Soviets would also have recognized the need to allow for spillage and corkage of their university vintage. For each Blunt or Philby, there were many more undergraduates who were approached, only to fall by the political wayside or fail to meet the career goals set by Moscow. But as Orlov pointed out, there was no shortage of potential recruits. The increasingly disaffected political climate of the thirties encouraged the acceptance by the younger generation of what he termed 'libertarian theories'.

According to Orlov, the plan was put into operation 'in the early 1930s'. The OGPU ordered their *rezidentura* to look for undergraduates who were 'tired of tedious life in the stifling atmosphere of their privileged class' and who were responsive to a libertarian appeal 'to make the world safe from Fascism and abolish the exploitation of man by man.' The undergraduates spotted and cultivated as penetration agents were also discouraged from joining the Communist party. They were advised they could be much more useful as members of a revolutionary underground.

'The idea of joining a "secret society" held a strong appeal for the young people who dreamed of a better world and of heroic deeds,' Orlov wrote. 'These young men hardly regarded themselves as spies or intelligence agents.' Nor was solicitation couched as a brash demand to work for communism or the Soviet Union. It was something far more subtle and seductive. Anthony Blunt characterized his own recruitment as an invitation to join an 'International Movement'. The appeal of participating in global power was also a powerful inducement to Kim Philby. 'It is a matter of great pride to me,' he wrote, 'that I was invited, at so early an age, to play my infinitesimal part in building up that power.'

The secret of the Soviet strategy, as Orlov recognized, was the 'sublime idea of making the world safe from the menace of Fascism.' This proved a powerful lure to young intellectuals adrift in the cynical political wasteland of the interwar years. 'By their mental makeup and outlook,' they reminded Orlov of the anti-tsarist Decembrists of the nineteenth century. He complimented them on restoring to the Soviet intelligence service something of the 'true fervor of converts and the idealism which their intelligence chiefs had lost long ago.' Such was the fervor and dedication of this new breed of *proniknoveniye* that Moscow Center no longer worried about financial inducements for their new recruits. These 'came automatically,' as Orlov noted.

Orlov makes it clear that the Soviets were also quick to appreciate the advantages of tapping into homosexual networks, whose fraternities guaranteed both secrecy and multiple recruiting opportunities. He also indicates how the lines were cast into other European universities, but conditions at 'Oxbridge' were especially favourable for the Soviets. And although Tom Driberg, as we shall see, was not the only Communist agent to emerge from Oxford, Soviet intelligence had a stronger presence at Cambridge. Thanks to the Comintern, they had in place a network of senior members, of whom Dobb was the most active. The GRU had its own line into the Cavendish, and Moscow had the sympathetic attention and interest of many Cambridge scientist. The seeds of Marxism were beginning to sprout in the Society of the Apostles, helping foster a Marxist attitude among the elite undergraduate intellectuals.

Cambridge was therefore the obvious place for the Soviets to start selection of the first ideological recruits for their novel program of deep-cover penetration agents – the so-called moles.

7 'We Talk Endlessly in the Society About Communism'

Anthony Blunt confused the trail that should have led to the heart of the enigma: it was when the Apostles became adherents of dialectical materialism, which they equated with Marxism.

'I became a Communist and more particularly a Marxist in, let us say, 1935–36,' Blunt said with remarkable imprecision when confronted with that pertinent question at the opening of his press conference in November 1979. His choice of words was a deliberate attempt to fudge, because, as a professional historian, he appreciated the importance of precise dates when making attributions on paintings. Blunt, moreover, gave an excuse for becoming a Communist that was equally vague. Conveying the impression that he was an elderly gentleman more sinned against than sinning, he insisted that by 1934 'all my friends – that is, an enormous amount of my friends and almost all the bright young undergraduates who had come up to Cambridge – had suddenly become Marxists under the impact of Hitler coming to power.' This was a carefully rehearsed alibi.

'Cambridge had literally been transformed overnight by the wave of Marxism,' Blunt had in 1972 told his Courtauld students. He claimed that 'the undergraduates and graduate students were swept away by Marxism' and that 'during the next three or four years almost every intelligent undergraduate who came up to Cambridge joined the Communist party some time during his first year.'

That Blunt's alibi was accepted at face value by the media is surprising: that it has remained largely unquestioned over the years is extraordinary. Still more incredible is Peter Wright's revelation that Blunt's assertions about Marxism in Cambridge were not followed up (or seemingly even challenged) by MI5 investigators in 1963 when he gave his hollow excuse for becoming a Communist in his secret confession to the intelligence service.

The credibility of Blunt's assertions that he did not come under Marxist influence until five years after his graduation was, however, questioned by George Steiner. In 'The Cleric of Treason', a penetrating analysis published in *The New Yorker* a year after Blunt's press conference, Professor Steiner concluded that it was likely Blunt 'became actively interested in and sympathetic to Communism as an undergraduate at Trinity college.' A longtime Fellow of Churchill College at Cambridge, Steiner explained that he came to his conclusion after a great deal of thought and that his reasoning had nothing to do with simple politics.

'Political logic,' Steiner explained to me, 'is not the most reliable guide to explain why certain intellectuals in the thirties allied themselves to the Communist cause.' But Steiner's contention that Blunt must have become a Marxist many years earlier than the 'official' version claimed caused a minor storm at the Cambridge high tables. The obvious inference – though Steiner was too scrupulous to say so himself – was that some dons found his rationale politically embarrassing. Why? Because they too had been youthful experimenters with the Marxist dialectic.

Steiner's conclusion that communism was embraced by Blunt and his circle of Apostles while they were still undergraduates in the late 1920s rests on the presumption that a fastidious intellectual such as Blunt could not have come either lightly or quickly to embrace the dogmatic precepts of Marxism–Leninism. One of Steiner's preoccupations was to try to rationalize the process by which someone with Blunt's highly tuned academic mind could become an 'out-rider to Stalinism'. There had to be a more convincing explanation for such 'radical duplicity, the seeming schizophrenia, of the scholar-teacher of impeccable integrity and the professional deceiver and betrayer.'

Another Cambridge academic who questioned Blunt's veracity

was Lord Annan, an authority on Britain's 'intellectual aristocracy' – a phrase he coined in a seminal essay on the subject. Blunt's excuse that he became a Marxist only because 'almost all the intelligent and bright undergraduates' were Communists between 1933 and 1937 was dismissed by Lord Annan as 'arrogant rubbish'. Annan emphasized that he was among the vast majority of undergraduates who never felt any inclination to join the party – even though he had arrived at King's in 1935, the year that marked the crest of the Marxist tide. Not only did Annan reject Blunt's assertion that Cambridge intellectuals 'suddenly became Marxists under the impact of Hitler's rise of power,' but he also pointed out that the actual percentage of card-carrying Communists in his undergraduate generation was 'very small'.

Blunt's cover story was believed only by those who did not know any better, who accepted the popular myth about the Marxist takeover of Cambridge. Investigators from MI5, such as Peter Wright, had less excuse than the journalists for being taken in by Blunt's mythmaking. They, after all, had access to the secret Registry records of the surveillance of Cambridge Communists. Their suspicions should also have been aroused by Blunt's claim that Marxism hit Cambridge in 1933 as an overnight phenomenon. From the MI5 reports in the US National Archives, it is evident that Special Branch must have been monitoring the academic Marxists for more than a decade!

While Blunt was not an overt revolutionary activist, he was associated with dons like Roy Pascal, who were members of the university Communist cell. It is difficult to accept that inherently suspicious counterintelligence officers really accepted Blunt's assertion that he was a political innocent merely because he disdained vulgar proletarian protest. Blunt's brand of Marxism may have been far removed from such revolutionary activity as joining street demonstrations, selling *The Daily Worker*, or hissing the national anthem in the town cinemas, but this did not make him any the less a Marxist. He was first and foremost an academic who, like many dons, regarded himself as a member of the high priesthood of the intelligentsia. For many of these people

Marxism's appeal was its aura of scientific rationality. This offered the opportunity for conceptual dissection, an essentially intellectual exercise that could be used to show superior knowledge and insight. The need to demonstrate his intellectual superiority over lesser mortals was important to Anthony Blunt.

'Blunt was someone who loved achieving power over people and institutions,' Annan told me. His conclusion, formed of Blunt before the war, was confirmed in the early sixties when he was a member of the London University selection board who rejected Blunt's chosen candidate for the chair of Fine Arts and Architecture. Blunt's conversation was a 'mixture of charm, mischief making, subtle denigration, and a way of inferring that individuals act from base self-interest or class-inspired motives,' said Annan. He also recalled the intractable director of the Courtauld with whom he dealt as provost of University College, London. Annan now believes that Blunt's espousal of Marxism was intimately linked to his need for personal power and influence – and suggests that it was this quest that ultimately led Blunt into espionage.

The first step in his career of treachery was the successful effort of Blunt and his allies in the Apostles to exploit 'investigative Marxism' to capture the society. Annan, as a historian member of Cambridge's secret brotherhood, spoke frankly of the need to lay to rest the myths that have grown up around the much-maligned society. Annan's own investigation has shown that despite the society's preoccupation with the 'higher sodomy' before World War I, by the thirties only a minority were homosexual. The majority, by contrast, 'rather prided themselves on their successes with the girls at Newnham and Girton.'

During our conversations, Annan registered his greatest surprise when I told him about a 1933 letter written to Keynes by Lord Victor Rothschild, who was elected to the Apostles at the end of 1932.

'We talk endlessly in the Society about Communism which is rather dull,' Rothschild complained to Keynes. 'We need your presence.' The hitherto accepted view that politics was never discussed in the society can now be rejected. Rothschild's letter makes it plain that by late 1933, when this letter was written, Marxism had become a staple preoccupation of the Saturday evening meeting.

The discovery of this letter and a comparison with the full membership rolls as reconstructed from the surviving Apostles' minute book enables the role the society played to be properly understood. Since the Apostles *did* discuss Martxism in 1933, their discussions of dialectical materialism must have commenced several years earlier. In fact, it is now possible to chart the Society's leftward turn as starting in the late twenties. It was then, despite the better judgement of Keynes, that the Apostles were lured by the intellectual pursuit of Marxism. Observing that the tendency toward communism was particularly strong among those whose intellectual ability marked them out for potential membership, Keynes – according to his official biographer – 'attributed it to a recrudescence of the strain of Puritanism in our blood, the zest to adopt a painful solution because of its painfulness.'

Annan confirms that Keynes was indeed powerless to prevent the 'marxisant brethren', as he categorized those who 'had been influenced by a Marxist vision of the world', from capturing the society. Reconstructed membership records provide evidence that the radical faction began infiltrating the membership the year before Blunt's election in the late spring of 1928 – and this infiltration continued until his departure from Cambridge in 1937. Just as good looks and intelligence were prerequisites for the birth of new members in the decade before 1914, Annan believes that being a 'marxisant' became a qualification – although not an exclusive one – for election in the decade between 1927 and 1937.

Analysis of the twenty-six Apostles elected between 1927 and 1937 (see chart below) shows that no fewer than twenty of these Apostles, or 75 per cent of them, are identifiable as left-wing socialists, Marxist sympathizers, Marxists or committed Communists. Fourteen of them (or more than half of all the new elections in this decade) fit into the broad category that Annan defines as marxisants. Of these, nearly a third became open or secret Communists. This, in a student body that was no more than a fraction of one per cent Marxist, is most significant.

The Cambridge Apostles 1919-1939

No.	Name	Papers	Elected	College	Politics*
259	Penrose, A. P. D.	4	29/11/19	King's	
260	Spicer, R. H. S.	3	6/3/20	King's	
261	Sprott, W. J. H. (62 Secretary)	?	30/11/20	Clare	
262	Penrose, L. S.	9	30/11/20	St John's	
263	Braithwaite, R. B.	18	26/2/21	King's	Left Wing
264	Ramsey, F. R.	10	22/10/21	Trinity	
265	Rylands, G. H. W.	7	25/2/22	King's	
266	*Thompson, G. D. (63S)*	*13*	*10/11/23*	*King's*	*Communist*
267	Harmer, F. E. (64S)	7	24/1/25	King's	
268	Watkins, A. R. D.	5	24/10/25	King's	Left Wing
269	Lucas, D. W. (65S)	11	7/11/25	King's	
270	Robertson, D. H.	1	15/5/26	Trinity	
271	*Watson, A. G. D. (66&68S)*	*19*	*29/1/27*	*King's*	*Communist Int. MI5†*
272	*Proctor, P. D.*	*3*	*22/10/27*	*King's*	*Socialist Int. MI5*
273	*Blunt, A. F. B. (67S)*	*11*	*5/5/28*	*Trinity*	*Communist Confessed Spy*
274	Bell, J. H.	13	17/11/28	King's	Marxisant
275	Crusoe, F. J. A.	1	3/6/29	King's	
276	Lintott, H. J. B.	3	30/11/29	King's	Socialist
277	Champernowne, A. G.	?	30/11/29	Trinity	
278	*Cohen, A. B. (69S)*	*?*	*8/11/30*	*Trinity*	*Marxisant*
279	Sykes-Davies, H.	6	16/1/32	St John's	Communist
280	Llewelyn-Davies, R. (70S)	4	30/4/32	Trinity	Marxist Int. MI5†
281	*Burgess, G. de. M. (71S)*	*?*	*12/11/32*	*Trinity*	*Communist Confessed Spy*
282	Rothschild, Lord (72S)	2	12/11/32	Trinity	Socialist
283	Walter, W. Grey (73S)	2	25/11/33	King's	Marxisant
284	Collio, H. O. J.	2	26/10/34	King's	
285	Champernowne, D. G. (74S)	2	30/11/34	King's	
286	Hodgkin, A.	1	22/2/35	Trinity	
287	*Straight, M. S. (75S)*		*8/3/36*	*Trinity*	*Communist Soviet Recruit*
288	Humphrey, J. H.	0	6/3/87	Trinity	Marxisant
289	Waterlow, J. (76S)	?	6/3/37	Trinity	Marxisant
290	Croadsell, G. B.	0	6/3/37	Pembroke	Marxisant
291	*Long, L. H.*	*2*	*15/5/37*	*Trinity*	*Communist Confessed Spy*
292	*Astbury, J. P.*	*?*	*5/6/37*	*Christ's*	*Communist Int. MI5†*
293	Bosanquet, R. G. (77S)	?	16/10/37	King's	
294	Hodgart, M. (79S)	4	16/10/37	Pembroke	Marxisant
295	Rawdon-Smith, A. F.	1	7/11/37	Peterhouse	Socialist

No.	Name	Papers	Elected	College	Politics*
296	Kisch, O. C.	2	13/11/37	Trinity	
297	Prince, P. D. V.	2	22/10/38	King's	
298	Mayor, A.	1	1/11/38	Trinity	Socialist
299	Luce, J. M.	1	10/2/39	King's	
300	Noyce, C. W. F.	0	2/5/39	King's	
301	Hobsbawn, E. (78S)	1	11/11/39	King's	Marxisant
302	Wallich, W.	0	11/11/39	King's	

*As far as can be determined from contemporaries and documented sources
†Based on MI5 Investigations
? Unknown how many papers delivered

For Marxism to have become such a potent force in the Apostles, it must have put down strong roots in the 1920s. A prime mover of Marxism in the Apostles emerges from the membership lists, and the subsequent record of his professional career, as being a contemporary of Blunt's from King's College: Alister Douglas Watson. And he was aided and abetted by a senior Apostle who was his mentor: George Derwent Thomson. A classical scholar in 1922, who became an Apostle in 1924 and a fellow of King's in 1927, Thomson nursed a 'hatred of capitalism' and later wrote *Marxism and Poetry*. He left Cambridge in 1937 to be professor of Greek at Birmingham University – where he was the organizer for the Communist party for many years. (Significantly, Birmingham, a center for industrial and scientific research, emerges from later MI5 reports as being second only to Cambridge as a haven for academic communism.)

From the time of his election to the society in 1923, Thomson's passionate support for the Sinn Feiners had been at the heart of his radical influence on his fellow Apostles, and especially Watson who had first become acquainted with Blunt in their first-year maths lectures. Unlike Blunt, he took firsts in 1929 for both parts of the Mathematical Tripos. After winning a succession of graduate studentships, he was elected in 1933 to a King's fellowship. His fellowship expired at the same time that World War II started and he joined the Admiralty as a temporary scientific officer. The brilliance of his work on radar and engineering designs led to his postwar promotion as senior scientific officer and an appointment in 1953 to the Admiralty's Submarine Dectection Research Establishment.

Watson's research contributed to the development of low-frequency sonar that was of vital strategic importance to NATO's ability to track Russian submarines. His work continued through 1967. Then, four years after Blunt's secret confession, MI5 investigators dug into Watson's background and learned that not only had his Cambridge Marxism led to a lifelong secret commitment to the Communist party, but surveillance showed him currently making contacts with KGB agents in London. Intensive interrogations and offers of an immunity deal similar to Blunt's failed to produce a confession. His interrogators were convinced that he had been a long-term Soviet agent. But since there was no evidence on which to bring an espionage charge, Watson was quietly shunted to nonsecret work at the National Institute of Oceanography until he retired in 1972. Ten years later he died of a stroke, taking his secrets to the grave.

For all Watson's brilliance as a mathematician, he appears never to have overcome his schoolboy resentment and his rebellious political enthusiasm for an independent Ireland. This was reinforced by Thomson and his friendship with the Llewelyn-Davieses, a Cambridge family with connections to the university's 'intellectual aristocracy' and supporters of the Irish Nationalists. (Margaret Llewelyn-Davies was also the national chairman of the Society of Cultural Relations.)

Just as Blunt's adolescent obsession with modern art appears to have embodied his early revolt against established authority, so Watson's adoption of the Sinn Fein cause appears to have been a convenient flag of youthful rebellion. His restless intellect was increasingly focused on the works of Karl Marx. Under the guise of 'investigative Marxism', Watson quickly became the most articulate proselytizer of Marxist faith among the Apostles. Watson wrote an incisive defense of the Marxist approach in the 1934 *Cambridge Review* which boldly praised 'the tactics of

Lenin, which have converted Marxism into the "official philosophy" so much hated and scorned . . .'

'I learned my Marxist theory at Alister's feet,' Blunt admitted to MI5 investigator Peter Wright in 1966. Under Watson's tutelage, Blunt seems to have concluded that Marxism offered a scientific justification for a much broader assault on the social, political and aesthetic underpinnings of British society. Blunt had already become imbued with the intensely rationalist philosophy current in France, and it should not be overlooked that in the thirties Gide and other French writers proclaimed the continuity of a European intellectual tradition that descended from Descartes via Diderot to Marx.

Watson supplied the radical political theories, Blunt exercised his talent for manipulative intrigue, and the pair of them set about restructuring the Apostles. They raised the banner of Marxism in defiance of a tired, self-indulgent Bloomsbury liberalism of the past. They enlisted the support of Julian Bell to seize control of the society through the traditional authority of the junior Apostle to vet embryos. Their object – at least initially – seems to have been to overturn the authority of the older members of the society. Marxism became the convenient vehicle of intellectual rebellion against the powerful hold that Keynes and his Bloomsbury friends still exercised.

The first of the new Trinity Apostles was Andrew Benjamin Cohen, who became a member in 1930. Cohen was a historian and scholar from Malvern School, whose father was a former economic supervisor of Palestine and whose mother was the principal of Newnham College. Considered an energetic socialist by his contemporaries, Cohen later made his career in the Colonial Office. After wartime service that included helping organize supplies for Malta, he became a leading proponent in Whitehall for African nationalism. The Labour government appointed him governor of Uganda in 1949, and he was knighted in 1952. Following Blunt's secret confession twelve years later, Sir Andrew was questioned by MI5 on his radical record and his Cambridge friends. Suspicion also clouded the final years of his, distinguished career, but he had made no admission by the time of his death from a heart attack in 1968.

The pattern of apostolic elections, averaging two or three a year, suggests that two of Cohen's contemporaries, Hugh Sykes Davies and Richard Llewelyn-Davies, might well have been elected with him in 1930 – if there had not been objections from senior members. Since no apostolic elections took place in 1931 – a characteristic symptom of 'birthing' difficulties, according to Annan – Keynes and his friends may well have tried to block the efforts of Blunt and Watson to recruit the left-wing faction. If so, their resistance collapsed in the spring and summer terms of 1932, which saw the election of Hugh Sykes Davies and Llewelyn-Davies. Both had by then graduated, and both were considered marxisants by their contemporaries. Davies became a member of the Communist party in 1937. A poet and writer associated with Empson's *Experiment* magazine, he later became a fellow of St John's College. Shortly before his death fifty years later, he confirmed to author Richard Deacon: 'It was Anthony Blunt who persuaded me to join the Apostles.'

Hugh Sykes Davies confirmed that he and Andrew Cohen were 'always in each other's rooms', making up what he termed 'the inner circle of younger Apostles' who were 'in constant contact with Llewelyn-Davies, Blunt and Watson'. The society's membership roster (pp. 179–80) confirms the critical role played by this inner circle.

Another influential left-wing Apostle was Dennis Proctor. He was elected the year before Blunt, three years after he came up from Harrow to King's. Proctor earned a first-class degree in economics and became one of the highest-flying civil servants of his generation. He started his career in Whitehall's corridors of power in 1929. The following year, he was made private secretary to Stanley Baldwin, the Conservative prime minister. Baldwin's son recalled that Proctor was on the 'extreme left' but that proved to be no obstacle to his rapid rise in the civil service. Proctor served in the Ministry of Health, and was a senior Treasury official when he abruptly resigned in 1951 shortly after the defection of Burgess and Maclean. After three years in Copenhagen with a Danish shipping company, he returned to London, resumed his career, and became a permanent secretary in the Ministry of Power. After receiving a knighthood, Proctor retired to become honorary Fellow of King's College.

Following Blunt's confession in 1963, Proctor was investigated by MI5. He denied that he had ever been a party member or that the curious disruption of his Whitehall career had anything to do with the defection of Burgess and Maclean. Available evidence indicates that Proctor was almost certainly marxisant, but that his involvement in the spy ring was probably peripheral.

New evidence has come to light that Roy Pascal, a Cambridge Fellow and not a member of the society, may have played a crucial role in effecting Blunt's transition to Communism. Pascal was second only to his mentor, Maurice Dobb, in promoting the Communist cause at Cambridge. In particular, he was responsible for converting George Derwent Thomson from Marxist to zealous Communist upon his return from Galway University to King's in 1934. Pascal had also been a friend and influence on Blunt since 1929, when they were both graduates in the Modern Languages Faculty and carrying out part-time teaching to supplement their research grants.

Pascal had taken a first-class degree in modern languages from Pembroke College in 1927, and then won a Tiarks research scholarship. This enabled him to spend two years in Germany, working on his doctoral dissertation on Martin Luther and the social basis of the Reformation. The scholarship also unwittingly financed Pascal's deeper appreciation of Marxism. During his time in Munich and Berlin he saw at first hand the increasingly turbulent political struggle between the Nazis and Communists. By the time he returned to Cambridge, Pascal was a fervent Communist. His vigorously expressed politics alarmed some of the Pembroke dons, who argued that he was an unsuitable candidate for a fellowship. But he was elected despite their objections to join Dobb as a privileged senior member of the college. By now he was also a lodger at Dobb's small house in Chesterton Lane.

Known as 'Red House', it was the epicenter of Comintern activity at Cambridge. Here Dobb worked as a tireless propagandist of the Communist cause. He was a founding member and Cambridge organizer of the Society for Cultural Relations and the League Against Imperialism but he maintained links with the Marxist scientists at the Cavendish Laboratory. The 'Red House', as we now know, had been under frequent surveillance by MI5 since the mid-twenties.

Pascal's pivotal role in the Cambridge Communist network owed much to his marriage to Feiga 'Fanya' Polianovska as it did to his association with Dobb. This darkly attractive Russian Jew had met Pascal at Berlin University, where she was taking a doctoral course in philosophy. 'Fanya' was a dedicated Marxist whose revolutionary ardor was born of her experience of pogroms. Her 'darkened childhood' in the Ukraine had been 'branded by the anti-semitism of Tsarist Russia'. That the Soviets granted her an exit visa to study in Berlin raises the presumption that her postgraduate work was not confined to philosophy.

Fanya's marriage to Pascal also coincided with the founding of the first Communist cell at Cambridge in 1931. Pascal and Dobb were the prime movers. Communist party headquarters detailed Clemens Palme Dutt, the Cambridge-educated botanist brother of the CPGB leader Rajani Palme Dutt, to become one of its eight founding members. A graduate of Queen's College, Dutt was 'an expert on work among students', according to Dobb, who welcomed the participation of such 'an able and persuasive propagandist'. Among the other founding members of this cell were D. H. Stott, a psychologist, and an ex-miner Trinity undergraduate named Jim Lees, who became a friend of both Burgess and Philby.

The Pascals assumed a pivotal role in the proselytizing activities of the Cambridge cell. Pascal spread the Marxist gospel in the Modern Languages Faculty and canvassed support from the left-wing members of the History Faculty for a series of Marxist histories under his own editorship. The project never came to fruition, but as the author of studies on the ideology of Marx and

Engels, Pascal was the standard-bearer of a fervent brand of intellectual communism that he took with him to Birmingham University in 1939 on his appointment as professor of German.

Pascal was an 'intellectual snob' and his wife 'a very demanding and dogmatic woman, the type of central European who always took the view that England was very "inferior",' according to Professor Henry Ferns, who came to Birmingham as professor of political science after the war and became an academic friend of Pascal's. Ferns, a Canadian who had become a Communist at Cambridge in the mid-thirties, told me that Fanya was the iron in her husband's political soul. She also had all the right qualifications for a full-fledged Comintern agent, as evidenced by her activities at Cambridge. Fanya became an activist with the Cambridge branch of the Anglo-Soviet Society, and was soon elected to the committee of an organization that was one of the principal links betwen the university and the Comintern in Moscow.

Professor Fern's most startling revelation was that just six weeks before Pascal's death in 1977, 'Roy told me he had once been approached by Soviet intelligence, not to work for them but to recommend young people they might approach.' Pascal assured Ferns he had demurred. 'In such a serious matter as treason,' he had declared, 'individuals must decide for themselves.'

Yet Ferns did not fully accept that this would have been the response of Pascal, whose 'special enlightenment through Marxism' made him superior. 'I don't doubt the truth of what he said,' Ferns told me, 'but somehow I found it hard to imagine Roy saying no to anyone as plainly as he suggested he had done to the Soviets.'

Whether or not Pascal actually became one of the Soviet's Cambridge talent scouts, the significance of the approach is that it shows the high degree of trust and confidence Pascal enjoyed. Although Pascal did not specify the year when the approach was made, Ferns agrees that by virtue of university and party seniority, it took place after 1931 and before 1935 – the year Blunt, by his own admission, became their Cambridge recruiter.

That Pascal, a Communist with a direct Comintern connection, was closely associated with Blunt before 1930 and was also responsible for converting Thomson, another senior Apostle, to communism is highly significant for two reasons:

First, it shatters the myth that Guy Burgess was the primary Marxist influence in the Cambridge Apostles.

Second, the approach to Pascal to become a Soviet recruiter himself is a clear indication that Moscow's blueprint for subverting undergraduates was already in operation earlier than the mid-thirties, as has previously been supposed.

The efforts of Dobb, Pascal and the others in the Cambridge cell went well from the very beginning. They found a ready audience for their ideas, politics and propaganda among an increasing number of undergraduates disillusioned by a capitalism that seemed to be crumbling under the weight of the worldwide depression. The far left, with its dreams of a Sovietized Britain, was particularly attractive to those who were angry at the Labour party's campaign failures and its cooperation with the Conservatives.

Kim Philby had come up to Cambridge in 1929 – three years after Anthony Blunt; Burgess came up the following year and Maclean in 1931. While many student radicals took to the barricades and became open Communists – among them James Klugmann and David Haden-Guest – Philby, Burgess and Maclean remained for the most part in the background. So did Blunt.

The man who became the best known of the Cambridge spies, Harold Adrian Russell Philby – nicknamed Kim, after the young hero of the Kipling novel – never joined the Communist party during his undergraduate career at Trinity.

Philby was the son of a Trinity-educated father who began his career in the Indian Civil Service. In 1917 he was transferred to Transjordan as an emissary and adviser to King Ibn Saud. According to a secret report given to the State Department in 1945 by the British, he was 'soon at loggerheads with the Colonial Office' about pay and policy. He was dismissed in 1924 after he had 'several times acted in deliberate violation of official policy'. Turning his back on the British Empire, he settled in Jidda, becoming a Moslem and a member of Ibn Saud's Privy Council, where he was often able to influence the king in direct 'opposition to British policy'. With more historical justification than his one-time friend and fellow Arabist T. E. Lawrence, Harry St John Philby really can lay claim to having played a leading role in laying the foundations for the modern state of Saudi Arabia.

Kim grew up in the shadow of his often-absent father, whom he worshiped at a distance. At a very early age young Philby echoed his father's disgust for the British Establishment by declaring himself a Labour party supporter at school. He was remembered at Westminster as a stocky, taciturn youth with a pronounced stammer and a reputation as a hard worker. At school Kim did little to distinguish himself, but his academic ability proved impressive enough for him to win one of Westminster's three closed 'exhibitions', or scholarships, to Trinity College. There, he recorded, 'one of my first acts was to join the Cambridge University Socialist Society (CUSS).' But his ideological commitment appears to have been lukewarm. He said his stammer prevented him from making public speeches. Philby's plodding political dependability was rewarded in 1932 when he was appointed treasurer of CUSS. But there were already signs that what one Westminster friend referred to as 'Kim's vaguely socialist ideas' were shifting farther leftward.

Disillusioned with a dismal third class in Part I of the History Tripos, Philby switched to economics, a field of study that reinforced his radicalism. And he first met Guy Burgess under the aegis of Trinity's economics supervisor, Dennis Robertson, an old college associate of his father's and a homosexual confrere of both Burgess and Blunt. When Burgess and Philby met in Robertson's rooms in the fall of 1931, Burgess immediately fell for the contemplative, pipe-smoking youth. Philby was not homosexual, but if Burgess is to be believed, Philby's initial resistance crumbled before his overwhelming charm and persuasiveness. But even if Philby did succumb to Burgess's predations, it appears to have been a once-only encounter that made more impression on the sherry-time gossip of the Trinity homosexual clique than on Philby.

The encounter was also too early in the Marxist enlightenment of Burgess to have had any serious political repercussions. Philby's own account describes how his political awakening, like that of so many of his generation, was the collapse of Ramsay MacDonald's government in 1931. After campaigning hard for Labour in Cambridge with John Midgely, a CUSS associate, Philby said he took the victory of the national government personally. 'It seemed incredible that the [Labour] party should be so helpless against the reserve of strength which reaction could mobilize in times of crisis,' Philby wrote.

By contrast, Guy Burgess was not at this point deeply involved in the politics of the left. One of the myths that has grown up around this larger-than-life character is that he came to Cambridge from Eton as a revolutionary Marxist. At least, that is the way the Burgess-like character in the film *Another Country* is portrayed.

But the Cambridge record shows that Burgess did not become an active Communist until late in his final year as an undergraduate. He spent most of his first year with Etonian friends as a member of the reactionary Pitt Club, where a daily bottle of hock did not interfere with his ability to get a first in Part I of the History Tripos.

Burgess was a shameless exploiter of his boyish good looks. He made himself a sexual guide and erotic compendium for a regiment of contemporaries as well as male pickups from waiters to sales clerks. He was a witty libertine whose endless talk of his outrageous exploits offered a catharsis for those who indulged their homosexuality more furtively, fearing they could be clapped in jail for their inclinations. Guy's cheery devil-may-care self-assurance, his vitality and his superficial maturity enabled him to provide convincing justifications for his actions and attitudes. He took particular delight in explaining how his aversion to women was the result of the trauma he suffered extricating his hysterical mother from under his father who, he claimed, expired in the act of copulation.

Most of Burgess's close friends dismissed his dramatic story as a typical piece of Burgess embellishment, although his father, a retired Royal Navy commander, did die of a heart ailment in 1925 when Guy was barely thirteen. His mother, Evelyn Burgess, soon remarried a retired army colonel, John Retallack Basset, who made gifts of cash to curry favor with his already overindulged stepson. Defective eyesight had already liberated young Burgess from the harsh regime of the Britannia Royal Naval College, and he returned to Eton.

Guy Francis de Moncy, as he had been named as a tribute to his French Huguenot ancestors (Burgess was the English corruption of de Bourgeois) joined his younger brother Nigel at Eton. His schoolmasters later recalled him as a well-read, precocious pupil who had 'something to say about most things from Vermeer to Meredith'. Yet for all his charm and briliance Burgess never made 'Pop', the self-electing prefectorial elite of Etonian swells. The taint of homosexuality denied Burgess the prestige he felt he deserved and kindled a flame of personal rebellion that was fanned when his close friend David Hedley became school captain. Their friendship nevertheless endured, and Burgess's influence on Hedley continued at Cambridge, where neither disguised their shared sexual preference any more than their eventual ardent embrace of communism.

Burgess was indeed a 'kind of Figaro figure, ever resourceful in the service of others in order to manipulate them to his own ends.' This was the judgement of his Oxford contemporary and close friend Goronwy Rees, who suspected that Burgess's 'power of manipulating his friends' came because they were chosen 'precisely because they were willing victims'. Although not himself homosexual, Rees asserted that Burgess was usually the aggressive partner and 'gross and even brutal in his treatment of his lovers'. This insight was supported by their mutual friend Maurice Bowra, the eminent Oxford classicist and dean of Wadham College who was one of Burgess's many 'victims'. Bowra himself observed – not without a certain relish – that Burgess had 'shit behind his finger-nails and cock-cheese behind the ears.' This was in keeping with Burgess's prescription that sex with the working-class males, whom he referred to as 'rough trade', was the ultimate remedy for releasing bourgeois homosexuals from their inhibitions.

Burgess's interest in socialism developed during his second year, prompted, he said, by his study of nineteenth-century European history. But it is now apparent that his political education was also affected by his more left-wing associates in the Trinity Historical Society. One was J. P. 'Jimmy' Lees, the ex-miner who was a founding member of the Cambridge Red Cell in 1931. (Lees was studying at Trinity on a trade-union scholarship.) Burgess was elected to the Historical Society committee in November 1931 – at the same meeting where Maurice Dobb addressed the members on communism, a talk followed by what the minute book recorded as an 'animated discussion'. Also attending that lively evening was Victor G. Kiernan, then a first-year Trinity historian who was to become one of the members of the Communist cell in Trinity, both as an undergraduate and a don.

The Trinity Historical Society, a heretofore uninvestigated forum, appears to have played an important formative role in inspiring Marxism in its members. The minute books reveal an increasing preoccupation with contemporary political issues. Through Lees, Burgess got to know David Haden-Guest, the son of a Labour MP and fellow Trinity undergraduate, who became his guide to dialectical materialism. Haden-Guest was a socialist when he abandoned his study of philosophy under Wittgenstein early in 1932 to spend two terms at the University of Goettingen. When he returned from Germany that autumn, after a spell of imprisonment for taking part in demonstrations against the Nazi party, Haden-Guest was a militant Communist. Burgess was sufficiently impressed by such personal dedication to spend much of his second year reconciling his own historical theories to the dialectical materialism in Haden-Guest's copy of Lenin's *The State and Revolution*. Burgess insisted that his conversion was 'intellectual and theoretical' rather than an emotional issue of faith. His Marxism was not of the 'Damascus Road' intensity that inspired Haden-Guest's willingness to die for his political beliefs on the Ebro front in the Spanish Civil War.

Among the undergraduate Communists whom Burgess met through Haden-Guest was James Klugmann, who had come up to Trinity on a modern-languages scholarship, as had his friend Donald Maclean, both from Gresham's School, in Norfolk. Gresham's, founded in the sixteenth century, was not a conventional public school. Its teams did not play other schools, and discipline was enforced primarily through an honor code that called for students voluntarily to report any transgressions. Among Klugmann's and Maclean's near contemporaries at school were the poet W. H. Auden, composer Benjamin Britten, and Sir Alan Hodgkin, a Nobel Prize-winning geneticist.

At Gresham's, Klugmann was a short, stout boy who considered himself 'one of Nature's rebels'. Like many Jewish boys in Britain's public schools, he was regarded as 'a clever oddity' with the brains to win all the scholastic prizes, but denied respect and authority by a prejudiced society. Klugmann decided to take revenge on the snobs in his final year by calling himself a Communist to annoy the authorities.

'I hadn't any clear idea, to begin with, what a good Communist really stood for,' he recalled, 'but having a very inquisitive mind, I soon remedied that.' So he became his own Marxist mentor and the inspiration and guide for his friends. Maclean, anticipating strong parental disapproval, took care never to mention Klugmann or introduce him at home during vacations. Instead, the two met frequently to share Marxist politics in London pubs and cinemas during vacations.

Klugmann was introduced to Burgess by Haden-Guest. The two became close friends, most likely toward the middle of 1933 when Burgess became an active member of the Communist circle. Through Burgess, Klugmann got to know Blunt socially, although the latter would also have supervised him in French. Klugmann was also responsible for introducing Burgess to his old school friend Maclean. Burgess was much taken with the tall freshman Marxist from adjoining Trinity Hall. With his customary predatory panache he was soon boasting that Maclean had been added to his list of conquests.

Burgess's later protests, that he was nauseated by the very idea of Maclean's 'large, flabby, white whale-like body', do not jibe with contemporary recollections that they were often seen together, or that Maclean was a tall, athletically built undergraduate whose playful cowlick of dark hair accentuated his youthful good looks. As a college cricketer he was not regarded as homosexual. But there was nonetheless an effeminate quality to Maclean, whose diffidence hinted at sexual ambivalence.

After Maclean's father, the Cabinet minister, died of a heart attack in the summer of 1932, Klugmann remembers that he saw a good deal of Maclean, who 'was cheerfully open now about his unreserved allegiance to the Communist cause.'

Maclean, however, was not a participant in a meeting of university Communist party representatives that Klugmann hosted at his parents' Hampstead home during the 1932 Easter vacation. Delegates from the London School of Economics, University College, London, as well as Oxford and Cambridge, gathered to hear Douglas Springhall, the national organizer of the CPGB, address the need for increased action. Some writers have made Springhall out to be the sinister mastermind behind the Cambridge spies, but he was too identifiable a Comintern figure for the OGPU. Springhall was an inspiring leader for the open Communists. 'We simply *knew*, all of us, that the revolution was at hand,' said Klugmann, recalling his heady emotion of the time. 'If anyone had suggested that it wouldn't happen in Britain, for say thirty years, I'd have laughed myself sick.'

Among those who were intellectually sympathetic but not fully committed to communism at this time were Philby and Burgess. 'It was a slow and brain-racking process,' Philby wrote. 'My transition from a Socialist viewpoint to a Communist one took two years.' According to him, it was not until the summer of 1933 – with Dobb's encouragement – that he finally decided his life 'must be dedicated to communism'. To seal his faith he recalled how he spent his college prize money on the collected works of Karl Marx and set off on his motorbike for Europe to witness the struggle of Marxism against Fascism at first hand.

Burgess also became a Communist in 1933, his final year as an undergraduate, and for a time threw himself wholeheartedly into revolutionary activities. He helped the Communist party foment a threatened strike by Trinity College waiters, addressed the Majlis Society of nationalist Indian undergraduates, and even booed the chancellor of the exchequer, Neville Chamberlain, at the annual Trinity Founder's Day Feast. Burgess also invited John Strachey to address the Trinity Historical Society in May 1933 on his forthcoming book *The Menace of Fascism*. This meeting, devoted to discussing communism as a historical alternative, attracted Philby and his fellow Marxist Apostle Richard Llewelyn-Davies as visiting participants.

Burgess devoured sex as he did alcohol – an overindulgence that suggests he was drowning a deep sense of sexual inadequacy. Uninhibited, outrageous, and articulate, Burgess was a blue-eyed schemer, whose good looks and irrepressible lasciviousness had caught the attention of two of Trinity's homosexual predators, Robertson and Blunt. Burgess's talent for biting caricature is plain to see in a drawing of a sardonic don in one of his surviving sketchbooks. Intimate friends believe this is Blunt, suggesting that it dates from the time he and Burgess had a homosexual love affair.

Blunt was certainly intensely fond of Burgess, and his personal loyalty never wavered. Although he allowed that Burgess was 'perverse in many ways' in his debauched later years, Blunt insisted he was always 'a terrific intellectual stimulus'.

Blunt was nothing if not precise, but many appear to have misinterpreted the essential stimulus Burgess provided him in their long relationship. Burgess and Blunt did *not* share a lifelong sexual passion for each other, according to other bedmates. This is another myth that owes more to journalistic license and the demands of television producers than to the facts. Such evidence as there is confirms that their intimacy quickly outgrew the bedroom. This was in keeping with the character of Burgess and his insatiable sexual appetite. Burgess would not have acquired his reputation as the most notorious *homme fatal* of his generation if he had remained Blunt's bosom companion for long. Burgess had a peculiar talent for transforming his former lovers into close friends. To many of them, including Blunt, he became both father confessor and pimp who could be relied on to procure partners.

For Burgess, communism was a call to arms against what he perceived as Britain's economic, political and social injustices. His politicization was that of a disillusioned undergraduate of the thirties who yearned for revolutionary action. Blunt's communism, by contrast, was more esoteric, evolving as it had in the late twenties from a philosophic Marxist apostolic rebellion against the dominance of Keynes and the 'milk-tea' liberalism of Bloomsbury. For Blunt, communism was not so much a political battering ram as a personal vehicle for fulfilling his quest for intellectual authority and secret power.

In contrast to Blunt's and Pascal's, the Marxism that was embraced by the undergraduate generation of the turbulent thirties, such as Burgess, had been crystallized by the shock of external political events. The lengthening dole queues and the spreading poverty of the Depression sharpened the political awareness of the new generation of Oxbridge students. So did firsthand accounts by contemporaries of the repercussions of Hitler's rise to power in Germany. But it was the decimation of the Labour party at the polls in October 1931 that raised the specter of a similar threat to social democracy in Britain.

By 1932 the dream of achieving socialism in Britain through parliamentary democracy appeared so bleak as to be hopeless. As the Depression bit even deeper, it put into ever-sharper relief the glaring social inequality of British society. No single group was more deeply affected by left-wing sympathies than the disaffected and increasingly radical undergraduates of the privileged classes. Many were swayed by the persuasive Marxist sophistry of John

Strachey, whose book *The Coming Struggle for Power*, published in 1932, was followed by *The Menace of Fascism*. The Oxford-educated son of St Loe Strachey, the editor of *The Spectator* magazine, had once quipped that he had become a Communist as a result of 'chagrin at not getting into the Eton cricket XI.' Now he issued a rallying call to 'the best intelligences' in Britain to join 'the essential work of clearing the ground for the new order'.

Strachey's revolutionary rhetoric echoed that of the Communist party and the futility of attempting to introduce socialism through parliamentary democracy. Marxism had acquired a fresh and urgent appeal to undergraduates such as David Haden-Guest, a Trinity contemporary of Burgess who had experienced the clash between Nazism and Communism at first hand. His arrest and imprisonment in Germany for taking part in an anti-Nazi rally endowed him with a reputation for action that made him the leading Communist proselytizer of the generation that came up in 1930. Among those Haden-Guest helped convert to communism were Burgess and his Eton friend David Hedley, Dennis H. Stott of Clare College, and a postgraduate Trinity student named Maurice Cornforth.

Haden-Guest also brought into the Dobb/Pascal Communist cell William Jackson 'Bugsy' Wolfe, a Downing undergraduate biologist from a Jewish family in London's East End. Another scientist of Haden-Guest's generation with Communist sympathies was Allan Nunn May. He was a shy and introspective Trinity Hall undergraduate, who 'managed to convey the distant impression of always being spiritually in the laboratory.' His first class natural-sciences degree led to a career in nuclear physics. In the Communist-led Association of Scientific Workers, Nunn May became a leading activist and promoter of the Comintern's belief in the universality of science.

Burgess was fired politically in a way that Blunt never was: he blamed the British government for the country's economic and political decline. But Burgess's erratic character and openly unconventional life make it most unlikely that Soviet intelligence would have chosen him as the mastermind of the spy ring they wanted to build at Cambridge. In 1932, the year in which it is most likely that the OGPU began its Cambridge recruiting in earnest, Burgess was not even a full-fledged Marxist. Charles Madge, a Communist acquaintance from Magdalene College, has confirmed that Burgess 'cut me dead in King's Parade' in 1932 after Madge had joined the university Communist party. This is convincing corroboration of Burgess's contention that he did not become a party activist until the following year, although Burgess's Eton master Robert Birley, who visited his rooms during the summer term of 1932, was shocked at finding 'a number of Marxist tracts and textbooks' along with 'extremely unpleasant pornographic literature' on his bookshelf.

In November 1932, when Burgess became an Apostle, he was therefore a Marxist but not yet a Communist. Yet Blunt and others have successfully promoted the view that it was Burgess who converted them and the society to communism. A clearer reading of the facts and of the chronology leads to the obvious conclusion: it was the marxisant clique of Apostles – Blunt, Watson, Thomson and the rest – who converted Burgess *after* he joined the society. This conclusion is reinforced by the letter that a then junior Apostle Victor Rothschild wrote to Lord Keynes. The head of the famous banking family complained that Blunt and the other Apostles talked 'vehemently and endlessly' about 'communism', which was 'the all pervading topic'.

Victor Rothschild had been elected to the Apostles at the same time as Burgess, in November 1932. He had come up to Trinity from Harrow School that October, shortly before his twenty-first birthday, when he inherited a £2.5 million trust fund, a house in Piccadilly and a Bedfordshire mansion, Tring Park. Rothschild had inherited his uncle's fascination with zoology, but his overbearing cleverness made him many enemies at Harrow. 'Being intellectually precocious, no doubt unpleasantly so, I was frequently punished,' Rothschild wrote, recalling that he was frequently beaten for being cheeky. When one of the senior boys threatened to report him for 'lip' unless Rothschild agreed 'to have a homosexual relationship' with him, he responded to the blackmail by reporting the boy to the housemaster.

Rothschild won a scholarship to Trinity in 1930, but in deference to an appeal from his mother he gave up his studies at Trinity in 1931 to help manage the family bank through the financial crisis. But the young man quickly discovered he did not like banking and, after six months, returned to Cambridge to make his career as an academic in 'a relaxed and perhaps somewhat unworldly atmosphere'. At Cambridge his reputation for arrogance and a biting tongue had preceded him. But his darkly romantic good looks and willingness to charm led to his marriage in 1933 to Barbara Hutchinson, who moved with the Bloomsbury set. He shared with his friends generous hospitality, his love of fast sports cars, and his talent as a jazz pianist. Among the most loyal, he noted, was 'a clever, dissolute young man called Guy Burgess with whom my mother got on very well.'

Through Burgess, Anthony Blunt also became one of Rothschild's close friends. 'I first got to know Blunt a year after I went up,' Rothschild wrote. An 'excellent conversationalist and partygoer', Blunt was a welcome and frequent weekend houseguest at Tring Park. There he was able to impress his host with his insights into the Rothschild art collection. In fact, it was his rich friend's generosity that made it possible for Blunt to purchase a Poussin painting, *Eliezer and Rebecca at the Well*, in the spring of 1933. He had spotted the genuine hand of the master beneath the badly darkened surface varnish of a dingy painting on sale for £300 by a local art dealer. He had to ask Rothschild for the loan of a hundred pounds: he was given it outright. A MacNeice letter makes it clear the coveted Poussin was in his hands by April.

The Poussin was Blunt's pride and joy. He told Alister Macdonald that to get it he had to ring up Lord Rothschild and tell him that he had found a 'very interesting investment'. Blunt told him what it was and how much it cost.

'Well, Anthony, you're not really talking about an investment,' Blunt said, imitating Rothschild's booming voice. 'What you mean is that you want me to buy it for you.'

When recalling the Apostles in 1977, Rothschild said that he 'rarely attended meetings' and did 'not remember any emphasis on Marxism'. Rothschild's complaint to Keynes about the society's discussions suggests something different and demolishes the myth promoted by Blunt and others that Burgess was the Man in the budding Soviet spy ring at Cambridge.

Yet it is hardly surprising that Burgess emerges from a cast of gray dons with his role inflated into the central figure in the Cambridge spy ring. Journalists, writers, historians – even MI5 officers such as Peter Wright – appear to have succumbed to the myth that this Rabelaisian intriguer must have been the chorus master of the so-called Cambridge spy ring. But from what is now known of the priorities of Soviet intelligence in the early thirties, it is impossible to make a convincing case that the staid and calculating case officers at Moscow Center would have rated Burgess a potential leader. The OGPU would not have regarded Burgess's dirty fingernails, liquor-laden breath and wild homosexual antics as sensible camouflage for an undercover agent. Even Burgess's instinctive grasp of Marxist dialectic, which was attested to by his many friends, could not have offset his drawbacks since Moscow was not looking for openly declared Communists. And his larger-than-life reputation was not the best qualification for an agent whose mission was to insinuate himself unobtrusively into the upper reaches of Britain's starchy Establishment.

Then there is the failure of Burgess to make the required grade for a Foreign Office or academic career. Although he was a senior scholar with a Part I first, his enthusiasm for communism in his final year left him unprepared for his Part II exam, which he flunked. An unspecified 'illness' was the official reason for awarding Burgess a consolation *aegrotat* or pass degree in the summer of 1933. He abandoned his thesis on the English bourgeois revolution in favor of a Marxist interpretation of the Indian Mutiny, and after little more than eighteen months of postgraduate studies, Burgess gave up all efforts to become a don.

Burgess's lack of persistence was confirmation of his deep-seated self-destructive impulses. Soviet intelligence was looking for recruits of sterner mettle. Moscow Center analysts were already applying the principles of psychology in their search for suitable spies. They knew that recruits to their secret world of undercover operations had to live under a state of psychological tension not dissimilar to schizophrenia. There is a dual reality for spies, who must function in the ordinary world without betraying their secret lives. Switching back and forth between these two worlds demands a cool character and prodigious mental power.

Even the most superficial personality assessment would have found Burgess wanting in several respects, in contrast to the coolly analytical Blunt. The role playing implicit in a spy's life was an important stimulant to Blunt, whose intimate friends repeatedly spoke of the powerful charge he derived from covert activity. This charge has been compared to the sexual stimulation experienced by the married man who takes a secret lover and has to resort to the same elaborate subterfuges as a spy – clandestine rendezvous, camouflaged communications and elaborate alibis.

In contrast to Burgess, who made passes at every man and delighted in astonishing his friends with graphic descriptions of his lechery, Blunt went to great lengths to conceal his homosexual activities from his mother and all but the most intimate of his Cambridge friends. One of the interesting discoveries about Blunt at Cambridge is that he seems to have delighted in encouraging ambivalent romantic relations with eligible young women at the same time as he pursued active relationships with members of his own sex. Of the several surviving women whose names Cambridge contemporaries gave as romantically linked with Blunt, only one was prepared to talk about her relationship with him.

'I was attracted to Anthony by his gentleness – he was one of the most gentle men I have ever known,' Lady Mary Dunn said with a wistful smile as she recalled what it was that drew her to Blunt. Now a petite and perky widow in her late seventies, she is still elegantly attractive. When Blunt first met her in the summer of 1930, she was Lady Mary St Clair-Erskine – the daughter of the Earl of Rosslyn – just out of her teens, with the boyish looks and enthusiasm that appealed to him. They became acquainted at a weekend house party at Tring Park. She was immediately attracted by the sharp intellect and keen sense of humor of the tall, thin young man who arrived from Cambridge in the company of the irrepressible Guy Burgess. There was much amusing talk over the dinner table and during the lazy afternoons beside the tennis courts. Both Rothschild and Blunt were good tennis players and she enjoyed partnering either of them in mixed doubles.

Although she and Blunt flirted with each other, Lady Mary recalled kissing him only once. She was far too naïve, she said, to suspect he might be homosexual, and she put his reticence down to gentlemanly insistence on correct behavior. Lady Mary Dunn admitted she was 'deeply fond' of Blunt, but was not certain how serious his attentions were until he invited her to accompany him to the Wimbledon Ladies' Final. After watching Helen Moody easily defeat Elizabeth Ryan, Blunt took Lady Mary to meet his mother at her cottage on Ham Common. He was very proud, she said, of the family's royal connections, but Hilda Blunt's home was 'frugal and Victorian and certainly not the sort of house to entertain the queen to tea.'

The spartan discomfort of his mother's home had been a constant trial to Wilfrid, who complained of its drafts, hard chairs, prehistoric mattresses, barely glowing gas fires and lamps dimmed to save electricity. According to Lady Mary, Anthony was not in the least embarrassed by his frugal home. He seemed devoted to his mother, whom she found a 'little woman, friendly and middle class in the sense she was determined to do everything *correctly*.' At the same time Lady Mary felt that she was being vetted over the tea cups as a potential bride, and Hilda Blunt made no secret of her displeasure at finding that Lady Mary was a Roman Catholic.

At Cambridge, Blunt was often seen in the company of Jean Stewart, the daughter of the university reader in French studies. She was also a teacher in the Modern Languages Faculty.

A number of Cambridge contemporaries have emphasized that while they now have no doubt that Blunt was a member of the Trinity homosexual circle, he enjoyed the attentions of intellectual women. Apart from Jean Stewart, the daughter of the Trinity dean, there was a certain undergraduate from Girton who boasted of her successful seduction of the gangling, aloof young don. Blunt, it seems, took special pleasure in carrying off the ultimate double bluff. His glacial self-possession would have impressed his Soviet assessors as much as his talent for organizing and manipulating his peers. He fitted the Soviet intelligence profile of the high-flying intellectual with a grudge against the British system and sufficient belief in the superiority of Marxist dialectic to betray his own society for the glory of contributing to the historic Communist experiment.

Moscow's plan to infiltrate the British Establishment depended on spotting potential recruits, particularly those who had demonstrated their ability to achieve rapid advancement. By October 1932, when Blunt was elected to a fellowship of Trinity College, he met many of the most important criteria that Soviet intelligence had set for its long-term Cambridge recruiter.

Blunt's teaching placed him in a good position to further the Soviet objective of penetrating the British Foreign Service. A good languages degree was an essential requirement for graduates hoping to do well in the Foreign Office examinations. As the Trinity don who supervised undergraduates studying French, Blunt could monitor the progress of the star candidates for the Modern Languages Tripos. Through the Marxist group in the Apostles and his friendship with Roy Pascal, who provided indirect contact with the university Communist party, Anthony could keep tabs on potentially successful undergraduates who were sympathetic to communism.

The testimony of General Orlov makes it very clear that Soviet intelligence wanted to avoid Comintern-type Communists. At Cambridge, then, the Marxist Apostles were an obvious target from which to select potential recruits. The secrecy of the society provided a perfect cover, while the elitism of the society ensured the patronage of highly placed senior members in the civil service, virtually guaranteeing graduating members good jobs.

Orlov and other Soviet defectors explained to American intelligence officers how, by the thirties, recruiting foreign nationals was very carefully monitored, with a rigorous procedure that followed a lengthy schedule before anyone was signed on as a Soviet agent.

The induction process was organized in four distinct phrases: Selection, Evaluation, Development and Recruitment. The four stages could take a year or more to complete. Therefore, it can be stated with some certainty that Blunt was selected as a potential agent no later than 1932. This is based on the fact that we know he was acting as a Soviet-intelligence talent scout by 1935, exercising a supervisory role over his American recruit Michael Straight in 1937: it was most unlikely that Straight would have been assigned to a foreign recruiter of less than a year's proven reliability and experience.

Blunt's initial recommendation may well have come to the OGPU *rezident* at Cambridge from one of the trusted *agenty vliyaniya* in the university cell. Though the OGPU had a healthy disrespect for Comintern members as espionage agents, it nonetheless tapped them for such information as a list of dons who were Marxist sympathizers.

Discreet 'tire-kicking' sessions, as former CIA analyst Crowley calls them, would have been conducted in the course of normal social encounters. A review of potential character strengths and weaknesses was essential to deciding whether the prospect exhibited the self-control and discipline necessary to become a secret servant of Moscow. In accordance with standard Soviet practice, the preliminary assessment was written up and passed on along the underground *apparat* to the Control Commission, which was usually the senior OGPU officer in the Soviet embassy.

Only if the candidate met with formal endorsement would the next stage in the review process begin. This involved sustained observation over a period of months by a second Soviet officer after a face-to-face encounter designed to conceal any links to other OGPU officers.

In Blunt's case, it seems likely that the Soviets would have exploited his interest in art to elicit an article, critique or essay for publication. A token payment would have been presented as certifying regard for his ability, but it was common practice to get a signed receipt both to establish the professional nature of a relationship and to provide incriminating documentary evidence to remind the candidate of his commitment.

'Flattery and status building were essential techniques of inflating the prospect's self-esteem and securing an ongoing relationship,' according to Crowley. The sustained 'playing' of a candidate always followed a set pattern, adjusted according to the personality of the prospect. As Crowley put it: 'The Soviet intelligence officers always need to keep uppermost in their minds the possibility of having to extricate themselves quickly and cleanly if their solicitations are reported to the authorities.'

If the candidate passed all the tests, recommendation was passed on to Moscow Center. There, every piece of the accumulated biographical data was checked with the extensive files maintained in the central registry at Soviet intelligence headquarters. Contacts and family connections were reviewed for leads that might provide clues to the potential usefulness of the candidate. The Soviets placed great reliance on data they could double-check. Moreover, in Blunt's case it is now clear that Moscow records must have turned up what the OGPU reviewers would have regarded as two highly significant hits: the family association with the British royals and the Scawen Blunt connection.

We know that Blunt made no secret of his aunt's friendship with Queen Mary and of his own aristocratic Trinity friends, such as Prince Chula Chakrabongse of Siam, so there is every reason to suppose that this would have been picked up by the Soviets. An even more important family credential would have been provided by Theodore Rothstein, who was then a ranking member of the Soviet Foreign Affairs Commissariat but who in 1907 had been a representative of the Bolshevik revolutionaries in Britain. His cover role was London correspondent for the *Egyptian Standard*, and Rothstein had been in league with Wilfred Scawen Blunt, Anthony's black-sheep cousin, who was a vociferous campaigner for the independence of both Egypt and Ireland.

The impression would have been reinforced by their attitude to Blunt's homosexuality. His carefully camouflaged appetite for male sexual partners would have been regarded as a valuable potential asset. Thanks to Petrovsky's involvement in the Maundy Gregory affair, Moscow Center would have an extensive file listing the homosexual contacts in the British Establishment. Blunt, as an Apostle with links to Eddie Marsh, would have been identified as a junior member of the homosexual network that extended into the very highest reaches of Whitehall.

General Orlov testified to the 'considerable success' that OGPU agents had achieved extracting information from foreign diplomats 'tainted with homosexual perversions'. Soviet intelligence had concluded that 'the biggest concentration of homosexuals can be found in the diplomatic services of Western countries.' Blackmail offered a convenient mechanism for effecting control over homosexual informants who were instructed to approach their friends in the diplomatic corps. 'The Soviet intelligence officers were amazed,' Orlov declared, 'at the sense of mutual consideration and true loyalty among homosexuals.' The loyalty was ensured by the very fact that homosexual activity was a criminal offense. As British counterintelligence officers discovered to their cost too late, even those homosexual diplomats and government officials who refused inducements to treachery were still too fearful of exposing their illegal sexual habits to denounce those who made the approach.

The final stages of Blunt's recruitment would have involved a series of carefully staged practice 'meets' designed to discover his appetite for clandestine operations as well as measuring a repertoire of psychological attractions necessary to bring him under control. The Soviets also watched for evidence of hostile counterintelligence officers whose presence would be taken as a clear sign of betrayal by the candidate.

'The Soviets have a reputation for playing very sophisticated games to test recruits,' Crowley explained. 'But the missions were important only as elaborate tests of a candidate's ability to accept and carry out a mission spiced with a strong flavor of criminality.' Performances were closely observed, and the reports on those prospects who passed a series of such tests sent on to Moscow headquarters for review by a team that included psychologists as well as case officers with experience in the British field. 'Orlov made it very clear,' Crowley stressed, 'that the penetration plan developed by Soviet intelligence in the early thirties depended on a degree of expertise and professionalism that the Western intelligence services did not begin to match until after World War II.'

8 'I Saw Myself as a Spy'

At his carefully staged press conference in 1979, Blunt appeared before the television cameras in a rumpled tweed jacket. On the only occasion when he was called to account for his treachery before the bar of British public opinion, the silver-haired old English gentleman offered the nation an offhand apology for what he admitted was his 'appalling mistake'.

The cool condescension with which Blunt answered the reporters made their questions seem impertinent. And there was little evidence of penitence behind Blunt's mask of professional reticence. His invocation of the Official Secrets Act constraints was his excuse for being conveniently vague, particularly regarding the events that had overtaken him over forty years earlier when he had shortsightedly succumbed to appeals from his best friend: 'to try to help anti-Fascism which was obviously the issue of the moment.'

'I think he is only telling the truth as far as his own conscience will allow him,' Andrew Boyle told reporters afterward. As the author of *The Climate of Treason* (published in the United States as *The Fourth Man*), the book that had finally forced the government to disclose Blunt's treachery, Boyle was one of the few not taken in by Blunt's claim that he had not become a Marxist until the mid-thirties.

Boyle told me that he had always known that the true story was very different. By nature a careful and diligent man, Boyle is a veteran radio journalist and prize-winning biographer of such British notables as Brendan Bracken, Churchill's press chief. Boyle earned the respect of highly placed sources as he painstakingly followed the elusive trail that led to Blunt.

'Various people had been dropping hints to me for some time,' Boyle explained, 'but I did not know precisely who did what until the summer of 1976.' That August, he told me, marked his first meeting with a former senior officer of the British security services. 'I told him that it was an amusing coincidence that my initials "A.B." happened to coincide with the name of the man at the center of my suspicions and inquiries,' Boyle recalled. 'My source didn't like my hint. He was clearly very disturbed. But he did warn me I would have to be very, very careful.'

From that reaction Boyle knew that his investigations were on the right track. But it was not until the following spring that he obtained confirmation from Goronwy Rees of Blunt's early involvement in the conspiracy. It was Rees who provided the name Boyle was looking for after a rendezvous in The Strand on the Green, a public house near Rees's home in the Thameside suburb of Turnham Green.

While crossing the road to Chiswick Common, Boyle recalled, he had been surprised when Rees drew him close and whispered, 'Anthony Blunt'. Rees made it clear that he knew Blunt was a Communist when he first met him in the early thirties. Rees told Boyle how he had lived to regret bitterly his encounter with 'the man who had cast a long shadow over my life'.

Rees, one of the most brilliant Oxford undergraduates of his generation, had arrived at New College in 1928, a year after Blunt went up to Trinity. A ruggedly handsome Welshman, Rees was also blessed with a mental agility that enabled him to overcome the lack of a public-school education. His reputation as a scholar was secured by a first in modern greats, as the politics, philosophy and economics course was known at Oxford. He then went on to win a coveted prize fellowship at All Souls in 1931. As an undergraduate, Rees had become a 'socialist and Marxist', in revolt against the very system of values from which he benefited.

In the twenties, Oxford undergraduate politics had yet to assume the dominating part it would play in the life of both the older universities in the following decade. A. L. Rowse, the literary historian, recalled coming up as a state-school scholar to the snobbish Christ Church in 1922 to find that there were only two other socialists in his college. When he became a fellow of All Souls three years later, Labour Club membership had increased to ten thanks to his proselytizing.

A. J. P. Taylor, one of the twentieth century's most prolific historians, was already a committed socialist when he came up in 1924. He was soon enrolled as a Communist, although he 'did not attach any importance to it' and remained a member of the Independent Labour party. In 1925 he visited Russia, which 'still seemed full of revolutionary enthusiasm'. Taylor recalls holding monthly Communist party meetings in Tom Driberg's rooms; curtains drawn and candles lit, with 'Tom shuffling round the room in his dressing gown to the sound of a jazz record.'

Driberg brought a dandyesque quality to the Oxford Communist party. By combining homosexuality with communism, Driberg also contrived a double affront to social and political morality and a cover for the improbable role he contrived for himself. As the *Daily Express*'s successful society columnist under the nom de plume William Hickey, he used his openly declared Marxist views as camouflage for hiring himself out as double agent for both the Soviets and the British security services, eventually becoming a long-serving member of Parliament and a Labour peer.

Rees graduated from Oxford in 1930, *before* the major political upheavals of the decade. His communism and Blunt's therefore had nothing to do with saving democracy from Fascism. The motives that impelled Rees toward Marxist philosophy, as in Blunt's case, appear to have had more in common with intellectual snobbery than with direct political action. Both discovered in Marxism the attraction of a secret shrine of individual rebellion. Neither went about publicly declaiming his left-wing political beliefs and sympathy for the masses. Their inspiration seems to have been more opportunistic – the need to ensure their membership among the intellectual elite by becoming the clandestine outriders of the Communist revolution.

'I saw myself as a spy,' Rees wrote – with perhaps more than intended significance – 'dispatched on some desperate mission abroad whose success depended above all on disguising his identity by a process of protective coloration and on the thoroughness with which he adopted the manners and the customs of the country to which he had been assigned.'

Rees's strictly intellectual approach to communism bore many similarities to that of the Marxist Apostles like Blunt and Watson. This peculiar brand of late-twenties Oxbridge Marxism was founded on the assumption that it shared with liberalism the same humane and enlightened purpose: the only issue was the question of methods. It was to become even more closely identified as Rees became close friends with both Burgess and Blunt.

Burgess already enjoyed the reputation of being a brilliant Cambridge undergraduate when Rees first met him in Oxford in the summer of 1933. The occasion was a dinner party at which Burgess was the guest of Maurice Bowra, who was at that time infatuated with him. Burgess animated the dinner conversation that evening at the table of Felix Frankfurter, then a visiting professor from Harvard, who went on to become an associate justice of the US Supreme Court.

Later that night, as Rees and Burgess continued their discussion over whisky in a deserted All Souls common room, Rees experienced Burgess's aggressive homosexuality. After deflecting his 'tentative amorous advances', Rees decided that Burgess regarded sex as a game 'which it was almost a duty to practice.' Four years later, in 1936, during another whisky-drinking session, Burgess came to his point. Choosing his moment carefully, and with a challenging look, he asked: 'I want you to work with me, to help me.' In response to Rees's question 'Does anyone else know about this?' Burgess said he would give him one name only, that of Anthony Blunt. In *A Chapter of Accidents* Rees could not name Blunt for legal reasons. 'I both liked and respected him, and with him I would gladly have joined in any enterprise,' he wrote of this anonymous person. 'I don't suppose he could have carried more weight with me.' Since 1932, when he had met Blunt through Burgess, Rees had been close friends with the Trinity don. Burgess swore him to secrecy because it was 'essential in this kind of work, that as few people as possible should know who is involved.'

Rees's account has been seen by many as confirmation that Burgess was indeed the principal recruiter of the Cambridge spy ring. To American counter-intelligence experts it proves the direct opposite. Burgess violated all the established rules by making such a direct approach and then revealing Blunt's name.

Whether or not Rees succumbed to the blandishments of his friends is still a matter of debate. Although he admitted that he 'was accidentally caught up in it,' Rees – according to Boyle – denied 'to the very end that he ever became a communist agent.' But we now know that MI5 interrogators shared the doubts expressed to me by Rosamond Lehmann. After Rees told her about Burgess's approach, she asked the obvious question: 'Did you agree to join him?' In response Rees only blustered and tried to confuse the issue. Her conviction that Rees was lying was reinforced when he threatened 'to strangle her' if she told anyone. He had already abandoned his All Souls' fellowship to make a career as a journalist and if he did join the conspiracy, it seems that Stalin's show trials shattered his convictions about the Soviet Union and that he had withdrawn his commitment by the time of the 1939 Nazi-Soviet pact. Rees served in British military intelligence in World War II and briefly in MI6 in Germany afterward. After the war, he never fully lived up to his early academic promise, although he was successively estates bursar of All Souls College at Oxford, and principal of the University College of Wales at Aberystwyth. In 1956, after Burgess and Maclean 'reappeared' in Moscow, Rees authored a series of anonymous articles for *The Sunday People* that made thinly veiled allegations about Burgess and Blunt. The charges that blackmail and homosexuality had contributed to extensive Marxist penetration of the British security services caused a sensation.

'The explosion detonated by these articles was atomic,' Lord Annan observed, 'but the blast walls of the Establishment are so cunningly constructed that the person most hideously wounded was Rees.' His friends deserted and condemned him for attempting to start a McCarthy-type witch hunt in Britain. Rees was eventually forced by what he claimed to be the 'priest-and-professor-ridden' Aberystwyth to resign his principalship and turn to making his living as a novelist and free-lance writer. Fifteen years passed before he attempted a more detailed justification of his charges to Andrew Boyle in 1977.

'At the time of our original meeting Guy was already an open Communist,' Rees told Boyle shortly before his death from cancer in 1979. 'Blunt – no matter what he says now – was by then also a covert member of the party and, as a young don, a kind of Grey Eminence behind Burgess and other disciples, most of whom belonged to the Apostles.'

The picture of Blunt that emerged from Rees's deathbed confession was of a Volpone who exquisitely manipulated his friends through the agency of the Mosca-like Burgess. Rees did not realize the web of conspiracy he was entering in the summer of 1933. At that time, Blunt was already making a name for himself as the *Spectator*'s delightfully waspish art critic.

Common enthusiasm for the efficacy of Marxist theory was a handy tool for criticizing British bourgeois art as well as social institutions. The Oxford Union had voted in the celebrated debate a fortnight earlier 'That This House Would Not Fight for King and Country.' The British press and public were shocked. Antiwar councils sprang up and mounted exhibitions at the universities. In November 1933 this success encouraged the Socialist Society to join with the Student Christian Movement to carry a wreath in the Poppy Day or Armistice Day parade inscribed 'To the victims of the Great War, from those who are determined to prevent similar crimes of imperialism.' Even though the police insisted on the removal of the words 'of imperialism', the hundreds of left-wing undergraduates who joined the parade on Saturday 11 November came under constant attack from the hearties determined to prevent them from laying the wreath at the Cambridge War Memorial. The police made repeated baton charges to break up the fighting between the rival groups of jeering and shoving undergraduates. Julian Bell drove his Morris-Cowley with its bullnose draped with a mattress and Guy Burgess navigating. The mobile battering ram was pelted with tomatoes but kept moving forward.

The wreath was laid and the Cambridge left posted notice of its triumph in the *New Statesman and Nation* with Bell's article declaring that politics was 'the only subject of discussion' and that 'a very large majority of the more intelligent undergraduates are Communists, or almost Communists.' The sons of Britain's leisured and educated classes, he claimed, had found that communism answered their need for 'the moral equivalent of war'. Bell ignored his own warnings about the need to beware 'neurotic salvationism in our brand of Communism' by announcing to the world, 'We are all Marxists now', a hyperbole inspired by the determination of the older activists not to be left behind by the new generation of undergraduates. A growing percentage of freshmen from the public schools had arrived at Cambridge station that October with heroic visions of leading the first charge in the Communist revolution in Britain.

John Cornford was the outstanding left-wing leader of the 1933 freshman intake. He was the son of Francis Cornford, a Trinity classics don whose wife was a granddaughter of Charles Darwin, and his dark piercing eyes, square jaw and swarthy handsome features were the raw material from which heroes were carved. Cornford's arrival galvanized the older generation of Marxists such as Burgess and Maclean. Maclean was a very visible political figure at the Poppy Day demonstrations, according to Robert Cecil, who was then in his second year at Caius College. Cecil had become friendly in 1933 with Maclean and others who spent long hours discussing Marxism. One evening, after a prominent member of the Trinity cell made some arguments that seemed particularly persuasive, Cecil recalls coming to the conclusion that communism did indeed provide all the answers. But his conviction faded with his morning hangover, and as he put it, 'nobody came to see me the next day on a follow-up mission.' But Cecil continued his association with his left-wing friends including Maclean, with whom he walked for a short distance on a Hunger March in February 1934. It was shortly after this that he discovered for the first time that Maclean really was a Communist.

'I went to Donald's room in Trinity a week or so later and was surprised when he told me he had spent the whole morning arguing with a Moral Re-Armer,' Cecil said.

'Why you?' he asked Maclean.

'Because I'm a Communist and it would be a great feather in their cap if they signed me up!'

Shortly after this, however, Cecil noticed that Maclean became less active in undergraduate politics. He appeared to be devoting himself to working for a first in his finals and his passion for cricket occupied any spare time in the summer term. His open Communist activities ceased. Some of his friends suggested that this was in response to the increasingly frequent visits of Lady Gwendolen Maclean, who was determined that her eldest son should finish his Cambridge career in a blaze of glory.

Cecil now believes that his Cambridge friend's sudden abandonment of communism was because Maclean was already coming under instruction from his Soviet recruiter. He cites a recollection of how Maclean's mother asked Donald if he was attending some political demonstration in London. Lady Maclean was immensely relieved when he told her: 'Well, you must take me for a bit of a weathercock, but I've given all that up.'

Maclean also dropped his long-talked-about plans to go to the Soviet Union to do his bit for the revolution by driving a tractor or teaching English to Russian peasants. Instead, he concentrated on preparing for a career in the diplomatic service. Since this demanded he put his name down a year in advance for the Foreign Service examination and sign up with a crammer, Cecil – who would follow the same route the following year – is persuaded that Maclean must have come under some form of Soviet control during the summer of 1934.

Maclean had excellent prospects of achieving one of the OGPU's primary goals: the penetration at a high level of Britain's

Foreign Office. Maclean's family connections and first-class degree considerably enhanced his chances of eventually becoming an ambassador. Soviet hopes were not disappointed the following year when Maclean was placed in the top six of those who took the highly competitive Foreign Service examination. Later, before the interview board, Maclean brazenly fielded a question about his undergraduate Communist activities with the admission: 'I did have such views – and I haven't entirely shaken them off.'

The Soviet determination to press their Cambridge moles into British government service offers an explanation of why Philby, a year earlier, had told his Trinity tutor that he was intending to sit for the Home Civil Service exams. He was patently unqualified because his degree, an upper second in economics and a third in history, would not have impressed a selection board looking for only the best Cambridge had to offer.

That Philby would even consider a Whitehall career *after* deciding to become a Communist suggests that he too had come under cultivation by the Soviets before he left Cambridge. Philby claimed in a 1988 interview in Moscow that he had already been 'spotted' that summer by Maurice Dobb, who passed him on to a Communist group in Paris. This accords with Soviet practice and is further evidence of his actual recruitment the following year, after playing his small supporting role in what British Foreign Secretary Sir John Simon called 'the mad little civil war', which erupted in Vienna during the winter of 1934.

Philby claims he was sent by Dobb to the Paris Communists to Vienna, a haven for European socialists. He made the journey on a motorbike bought with a graduation gift from his father. In Vienna he met Alice Kohlman Friedman, an engaging divorcée known as Litzi, who was a militant Communist in the Red underground movement that was cynically manipulating the Social Democrats who controlled the city. Tensions rose as the Austrian government coalition under Chancellor Engelbert Doll-fus sought to establish its authority.

Confirmation that Philby was a 'convinced Communist' in Vienna was provided by George Gedye, *The Daily Telegraph*'s

Central European correspondent. When fighting broke out between the Social Democrats and the Austrian government troops in February 1934, Gedye discovered that Philby was a member of the Red underground unit known as the Kirov Brigade. Philby had appealed for his help in smuggling his fellow Communists out through the sewers to escape heavy government artillery fire. Kim married Litzi, and they made good their escape on his motorbike, their joint safety assured by Philby's British passport.

Philby visited Cambridge shortly after his return from Vienna. Supposedly his trip was for the purpose of rallying the Socialist Society to help the Viennese left, the collection for their families actually being organized by Burgess. Philby claims that it was only after he returned to England that he was approached by a man who 'was not a Russian, although working for the Russians,' and asked if he would like to join Soviet intelligence. Significantly it was only *after* this visit that he dropped all his connections with the left. He then took a job as an assistant editor of the *Review of Reviews*, a struggling liberal periodical. This post now appears to have been the first stage in an elaborate exercise to camouflage his communism in the cloak of respectable liberalism.

In his autobiography Philby states that at this time he was already under Soviet control, although not yet able to provide them with any useful information. He described himself during 1934 as 'a sort of intelligence probationer' who wondered at 'the infinite patience' of Moscow and that of his control officer, who made his weekly rendezvous in 'one or other of the remoter spaces in London'. His account suggests that despite his despondency, this period was a crucial part of the process of his education as an agent, since his unnamed control officer was free with 'painstaking advice, admonition and encouragement'.

Both Maclean and Philby appear to have been spotted and taken through the evaluation and development stages of the Soviet-intelligence recruitment process during their final year at Cambridge. But they do not appear to have been brought under discipline and control until sometime after graduation. This supports the contention of American intelligence officers that the actual signing on of Soviet penetration agents in the thirties was conducted outside the country.

Such was the thoroughness of the Soviet vetting procedure and manipulation that it was very rare indeed for any candidate who made it to the final stage to withdraw. The new agent recruit was then invited to sign documents attesting to a willingness to act in subordination to Soviet authority, and the impression was given that any transgression would quickly be reported through a vast network of hidden informants. By exaggerating the extent of their underground networks, the Soviets also reassured their recruits that they belonged to a vast secret army.

Philby's account reveals just how successful was the spotting, evaluation and development of the Cambridge recruits. 'I did not hesitate,' Philby wrote of his own recruitment in the preface to *My Silent War*: 'One does not look twice at an offer of enrollment in an elite force.'

'How, when and where I became a member of the Soviet intelligence service is a matter for myself and my comrades,' Kim Philby wrote in 1968. Eleven years later, Professor Blunt took his cue from his Cambridge contemporary's self-serving autobiography.

All that Blunt would admit to questioning journalists was that 'anti-Fascism' prompted him to serve for two years as a Soviet 'talent spotter' with no other duties. Guy Burgess was responsible for his enrollment to 'help him with his work for the Russians'. Blunt's memory was apparently not precise enough to say when this was, but he did 'think it was just before the Spanish Civil War'. When asked if he could recall the specific year, he was painfully equivocal.

'No,' Blunt replied, strangely unable to pinpoint one of the most important decisions of his life. 'I could only say that I should think late 1935, early 1936.'

That this was the same alibi Blunt had given sixteen years before to MI5 is clear from details Peter Wright supplied in his best-selling book *Spycatcher*. His other interrogators have confirmed that Blunt stuck to his guns and did not provide significantly more information about his actual recruitment than had already become public. They agree that Wright is correct in asserting 'there was nothing like the wealth of detail we expected.'

Given Blunt's reticence, one surprising revelation to come out of Wright's memoir is the degree to which MI5 went along with Blunt's story that Burgess was the primary Communist recruiter of the Soviet agents in Cambridge. The acceptance of this alibi underscores both Wright's lack of experience as a counter-intelligence officer (he was trained in electronic surveillance) and the failure of MI5 as a counterintelligence organization. On the evidence we now have, it is clear that MI5 either never grasped the dimension, or chose not to reveal the fundamental mechanics, of the Soviet infiltration plan. Critics who have maintained healthy suspicion of the credibility of Blunt's confession have had their worst fears confirmed by reading *Spycatcher*. Wright's book suggests, however, that MI5 and the uninformed public believed in the overnight recruitment of Cambridge spies by a mysterious brotherhood.

Based on their extensive research and analysis, however, the Americans' knowledge of the history and mechanics of the covert operations of the KGB and its predecessors leads them to believe the Cambridge network could not have been masterminded simply by the Comintern. Washington's analysis indicates that it was the Soviet intelligence service, not the Comintern – of whom Stalin was inordinately suspicious in the early thirties – that recruited, directed and controlled Blunt and his associates.

The CIA, like the KGB, has always recognized the importance of research and analysis. In the area of counterintelligence operations, both maintain highly trained analysts dedicated to this task. But the evidence in *Spycatcher* gives no indication that Wright – or anyone else in MI5 – exercised this critical function with anything like the skills and experience marshaled by the Soviets. Indeed, there is a somewhat amateur element in MI5's attempt to run down the Soviet moles by relying heavily on the collective wisdom of senior female staff in the MI5 Registry and the research department.

At least one former MI5 officer involved in the great mole hunt has told me Wright 'cocked up' his two-hundred-hour-long effort to pry the truth out of Blunt. Wright's inside account, he said, reflects the faulty procedures of MI5 in permitting a relatively untrained officer to assume the burden for a major internal-security audit that failed miserably for want of professional research and analysis. (As we know now, MI5 did not do a thorough research and analysis of the Blunt case until 1971.)

That Blunt lied repeatedly becomes very clear from the significant differences between two public accounts he gave purporting to explain how and when he became a Communist.

In 1979 Blunt declared that he had 'a sabbatical year's leave from Cambridge in 1933–34 and when I came back in October 1934, I found that all my friends ... had suddenly become Marxist.' In an earlier 1973 article, 'From Bloomsbury to Marxism', based on an 'informal talk' to his Courtauld students, he wrote that his conversion occurred 'quite suddenly in the autumn term of 1933'.

The year's difference must raise major questions about Blunt's truthfulness and underlying motives for giving conflicting accounts of when and how he became a Communist. But the actual record of Blunt's peregrinations between 1933 and 1934 can be pieced together from the surviving MacNeice-Blunt correspondence and Blunt's *Spectator* art reviews. The *Spectator* articles indicate that Blunt remained in England without a major break until late August 1933. Then after traveling to Paris and Rome by way of Monte Carlo he returned to London in January 1934 to review the Winter Exhibition at Burlington House. Mac-Neice's letters and subsequent gallery reviews show that Blunt remained in London until late spring. Then he traveled to Munich; in June he went up through the Black Forest to the medieval university town of Freiburg, where he stayed with Dr Walter Friedlander, a leading authority on Poussin. By September he was back at Cambridge.

The record shows that Blunt's sabbatical did not take him out of the country for a twelve-month stretch. His earlier account about being absent from Cambridge only for the first term of the academic year is therefore the more accurate version.

Another major flaw in both of Blunt's accounts was his naming of James Klugmann, John Cornford and Guy Burgess as the principals who influenced his decision to become a Communist. They were the 'very powerful' and 'very remarkable group of Communist intellectuals' and the 'individuals who dominated the movement'. In fact, the record shows that Burgess *never* was one of the leaders of the Cambridge Communists. He was never accepted into the inner councils of the undergraduate Communist movement, even though he played a leading role with Julian Bell in the Armistice Day demonstrations.

Blunt also went out of his way to praise Klugmann. He described him as 'an extremely good political theorist', who 'ran the administration of the Party with great skill and energy and it was primarily he who decided what organizations and societies in Cambridge were worth penetrating.'

How did Blunt know this if he was not deeply implicated in the cell?

Blunt's statement reveals a familiarity with the inside workings of the Cambridge Communist party that is significant. To know how decisions were taken about penetration suggests that he and Klugmann must have been on very close terms.

When and for what reason could he have come to know James Klugmann, who was seven years his junior, not a Apostle, and by all accounts not especially interested in art? Blunt may have been his French supervisor, but the requirements of Klugmann's tripos studies hardly required passing on the secret decisions and planning of the university cell.

Did Blunt know this because it was Klugmann's job to keep him briefed, and did he – through Klugmann – exercise a sinister influence on the Communist cell?

What prompted Blunt to reveal his inside knowledge of the Cambridge Communist party just six years before he was publicly exposed as a Soviet spy? Blunt was still a senior member of the staff at Buckingham Palace and presumably anxious to avoid any tarnishing of his public reputation: why then even reveal that he was once a Marxist?

Blunt's decision to risk publicly admitting a limited flirtation with Marxism can only be explained by the pressing need to deny a larger guilt. The clue to what prompted his extraordinary action can be found in the statement made to me by British author Nigel West: that it followed an internal MI5 reappraisal of the Blunt case which had reached very disturbing conclusions.

In 1971 – a surprisingly late date, considering the secret confession made in return for immunity eight years earlier – Anne Orr-Ewing (one of the leading forces of K7, the section investigating Soviet penetration) carried out the first in-house review of Blunt's secret confessions.

According to another reliable informant, Orr-Ewing's report was unequivocal in declaring that Blunt had *never* told the truth – either in his 1964 confession or in his many lengthy debriefing sessions with Wright. Surprisingly MI5 took no further action after the Orr-Ewing report. The obvious course would have been to begin a new round of tough interrogations to expose the inconsistencies and tax Blunt with his failure to tell the truth. Significantly, Wright – who retired in 1976 – does not mention the Orr-Ewing report in *Spycatcher*. So either he was not told of its conclusions – which seems unlikely in view of his long and close association with the report's author – or, more likely, he chose not to reveal his own failures in his interrogations of Blunt.

The overwhelming need to keep the Blunt case under wraps appears to have influenced the decision to take no action on the Orr-Ewing report. Fear that forcing Blunt to recant might prompt him to 'go public' might have been MI5's overriding concern. The damage that his revelations could do to any British government – not to mention to the already tarnished reputation of Britain's security services – apparently outweighed any information that might be gained.

Since Wright continued to call on Blunt until he left the service in 1976, he may, inadvertently or by design, have given some hint to Blunt of trouble ahead – either pressing certain questions too closely or increasing the frequency of visits.

This would have tipped Blunt off that the 'office' entertained fresh doubts about his story. On the eve of an illustrious retirement, he would have been especially anxious to remind the British government of the gentlemen's agreement that guaranteed his continued status as Sir Anthony and a Buckingham Palace courtier. What better way to make his point than a specific public reference to his involvement with the Cambridge Communists? That he chose to do so in a lecture and then allow publication in a magazine article must have made very plain his lack of concern about putting his youthful Communist indiscretions on the public record. Blunt, it should be noted, also engineered his remarks to bolster the story he had already given Wright in his secret MI5 debriefings.

In 1979 Blunt reinforced the view that Guy Burgess was a kingpin of the Cambridge Communists by adding almost a year to the date when he claimed he had become a Marxist. This conveniently gave the impression that Blunt himself could not have become a Communist until autumn 1934, *after* Burgess returned from his trip to Russia with Oxford Communist and fellow homosexual Derek Blaikie. According to Goronwy Rees's sensational articles in *People*, Burgess's recruitment had occurred that summer after 'a long secret interview with Nikolai Bukharin, one of the most famous leaders of the Communist International.'

Rees's questionable assertion had made it possible for both Blunt and the British government to promote the legend that Burgess really was the First Man of the Cambridge ring. This myth has gained credence over the years even though it does not jibe either with historical facts or with what is now known about Soviet recruiting methods. Bukharin could *not* have recruited Burgess in Moscow because by 1934 he held no official position in the Comintern; he had just been dismissed from the editorship of *Izvestia* and his authority was sliding fatally towards his purge in 1938. (Tom Driberg's 'official' biography of him in 1956, actually denied that he had even met Bukharin.) But even if, as Rees told Andrew Boyle, Burgess had also talked of meeting Ossip Piatnitsky, head of the Comintern Liaison Section, the Comintern, as has been seen, was unlikely to have been trusted by Stalin to recruit agents in Cambridge.

If for no other reason than Burgess's collapse in a drunken stupor in the Moscow Park of Rest and Culture, his visit could have done nothing to impress Soviet intelligence that he was a suitable candidate to become one of their Cambridge penetration agents. But the trip to Moscow was by 1979 a convenient protest for Blunt to claim that Burgess returned from the Soviet Union as the First Man in the Cambridge network. Both Blunt and MI5 had good reason to reinforce that impression. Blunt wanted to dispel any suspicion that his own treachery could possibly have predated that of the now deceased Burgess. The British security services wanted to cover up from the government the investigative failures that were being revealed by the highly secret Orr-Ewing report.

Nor should it be forgotten that Moscow's agents also appear to have closed the recruitment of Kim Philby and Donald Maclean during the first half of 1934. So Blunt therefore may have had additional reason to say that he was out of the country at the very time when two of the most notorious Cambridge spies were inducted into the OGPU network.

Since the Apostles were already Marxist by 1932, Blunt's assertion that he did not become a Communist until 1934 appears nothing more than a Machiavellian charade. His correspondence with Louis MacNeice offers additional evidence. There is a suspicious gap in the volume of letters from MacNeice between 1930 and 1931. This suggests a 'weeding' of their correspondence by Blunt. (For the letters that have survived do so only *by courtesy of Blunt*, who deposited them in the King's College archives in 1969 – ten years before his public exposure.) The period covers the critical two years during which Blunt and Alister Watson were masterminding the marxisant take-over of the Apostles. Blunt did not destroy another letter that gives a clue to the motivation and chronology for his life as a spy: his rejection in 1934 despite a set of glowing testimonials to Birmingham University from Gow and his influential friends for the professor of fine arts.

Blunt was not even short-listed for the post. 'The bloody old sots are, I fear, not going to have you,' MacNeice wrote in November 1934, breaking the news that to Birmingham's 'everlasting shame' the selection board considered his friend too young and inexperienced, despite their being 'especially impressed by your testimonials'. The Barber professorship eventually went to the director of the Dublin Gallery of Fine Art. To a Marxist determined to become one of the new wave of 'scientific' art historians, such a snub would have been taken not only as a personal slight but also as an irrational insult from the fuddy-duddies who ran the British Establishment.

MacNeice also provided another clue that dates his friend's Marxist conversion – and one Anthony was powerless to erase. In 1933 MacNeice published a biting short poem, 'To a Communist', which likened the transitory appeal of intellectual Marxism to a pristine snow. 'But before you proclaim the millennium, my dear,/consult the barometer.' He does not name the person – clearly an intimate friend – for whom he intended this curious poem. But since MacNeice often used 'My dear' as a form of address to Blunt in his letters, Blunt was the most obvious candidate for this highly personal meteorological admonishment.

Although it will never be possible to establish precisely when Blunt was brought under Soviet control, all the circumstantial clues point to late 1933 or the first half of 1934. This would tie in with Soviet intelligence's lengthy evaluation process and a probationary trial before fulfilling his role as a Cambridge talent spotter in the recruitment of Michael Straight in 1936. Since the consensus of American intelligence opinion is that Blunt's 'signing on' would have taken place outside England, it is likely to have occurred in the spring of 1934, when Blunt was traveling through France and Austria en route to Italy.

Also, Blunt's artistic interests may well have played an instrumental role in setting up his relationship with the Soviets. Blunt implied direct access to 'the highest circles in the Kremlin' as a recruiter and was sufficiently self-important to defy orders to defect in 1951. Blunt's inflated view of his status in Moscow could have come about if he believed he had volunteered himself for service with Soviet intelligence or that his induction was so arranged that it led Blunt to believe that he, not the Soviets, had initiated the process. Although it is possible that he could have simply been a 'walk-in' like the Foreign Office clerk Oldham, it is more likely that it was his artistic pursuits that led Blunt to make an initial approach to a Soviet embassy, which the Russians later turned to their own advantage.

Such a scenario, given Blunt's art and the sophistication of the Soviet recruiting techniques, is probable because the early thirties saw the publication of the first catalog of the paintings looted in the Revolution from the palaces of tsarist nobles and merchant princes. Anatoli Lunacharsky, people's commissar of enlightenment and culture, had for years been battling against the policy instituted by Stalin and the Commissariat of Foreign Trade of secretly selling off parts of this priceless heritage of European old masters to raise hard currency. Lunacharsky, playwright and critic, was the official sponsor of the book *Selected Works of Art from the Fine Arts Museums of the USSR*, which listed the principal old masters hung for the public in state museums.

There were a great many Poussins in the Soviet collections. So, publication of Lunacharsky's catalog in 1930 could have prompted Blunt, ambitious to establish his reputation as a 'Poussiniste', to ask the Soviets for permission to study the paintings which had previously hung in the private houses of Russian nobles and merchants and thus had not been readily accessible to scholars.

Such a request for visitation rights denied other scholars since the Revolution would have brought Blunt to the attention of Soviet intelligence. If he was already targeted or under evaluation, it would have reinforced their interest in him. In addition, the prospect of special access to the Poussins would have provided OGPU case officers with a hook for Blunt while leaving him with the impression that he was in control.

Christopher Wright, a former pupil of Blunt's and himself an authority on Poussin, confirms that even today dealing with Soviet museums is usually effected on a quid-pro-quo basis. 'If I request photographs of paintings in their collection, I always anticipate being able to offer something in return,' he told me. Wright also agreed that it was entirely possible that Blunt's early thesis studies brought him into contact with the Soviets, since the Leningrad Poussins represented the second largest body of the artist's work outside the Louvre.

'It would have been impossible for Blunt to complete his thesis without access to this collection' is Wright's considered opinion. Blunt did indeed get to see the collection on his summer trip to the Soviet Union in 1935. This was a year before he was due to submit his thesis, by which time he had already embarked on a far broader study: an analysis of the artistic theories in the paintings of the Italian Renaissance. Significantly, Blunt never accounted for switching away from Poussin to a more general focus, merely acknowledging that his studies 'spread backwards into the sixteenth century.'

Blunt himself provided another clue as to why he put aside his projected thesis: Poussin was a less suitable subject for Marxist analysis than the Renaissance. The pointer to this can be found in the revised version of his fellowship thesis that was finally published in 1940 as 'Artistic Theory in Italy'. In the Preface Blunt paid tribute to Friedrich Antal for 'instruction in a method, which has, I fear, been applied in an only too slipshod manner in this book and for many ideas on individual points.'

The 'method', which Blunt was evidently reluctant to identify, was the Marxist analysis of art. Antal was a leading exponent of the application of the principles of dialectical materialism to the study of art. He had arrived in London as an exile from Germany in 1934, and although he 'had not at that time written much,' he tutored Blunt 'at great length verbally.' Blunt also late admitted to being a devotee of the articles on the 'general application of the Marxist theory to the arts' authored by Klingender, another German émigré.

Marxism required Blunt to make 'a complete reversal' of his aesthetic canon. 'Art for Art's sake, Pure Form, went by the board totally,' he would later recall. The Marxist theory of art derived from the 'scientific' rationalization that because works of art were created by men who were the products of the society in which they lived, their artistic achievements must be determined by social and ultimately economic conditions.

Naturalism and Realism were the determinants of the Marxist aesthetic canon. Even the Impressionists fell under the critical logic of the true Marxist believers for falling into the trap of 'optical effects', and Cézanne was condemned for 'dehumanizing' art. Cubism had drifted away from contact with human life, and Surrealism was lost in a purely private maze of abstraction.

Anthony Blunt's conversion to Marxism is apparent as early as 1933, when his weekly *Spectator* column on art began to echo his extreme socialist interpretation. Blunt's early art pieces crackle with a provocative fire that makes his later academic writings appear desiccated. His criticism was always incisive, sometimes witty and often waspish, but always reflecting a dogmatism, increasingly Marxist in tone.

Rather than merely analysing a painting through the technical achievements of the artist, Blunt saw it as his Marxist duty to 'define the historical position of the artist, saying what influences went to form him, what kind of society produced him, and what other artists were influenced by him.'

Assembling the snippets of dialectic from Blunt's *Spectator* reviews reveals his progress toward an uncritical acceptance of full-blown Marxism, which holds that social and economic revolution chart the course of artistic development.

By 1935 Blunt was firm in his belief that contemporary artistic movements were subject to revolutionary process. In times of social upheaval, he argued, the artist has a duty to reach beyond abstraction so as to give explicit expression to his ideals, making art 'openly propagandist'. Although he was careful not to label himself a Communist, his beliefs were increasingly implicit in such assertions as 'Art is only valuable when it corresponds to the needs of society of its time.'

Professor George Steiner, who has made a study of the influence of communism on European intellectuals, suggests that the frustrations that afflicted Blunt were not uncommmon in those years. Before the truth about Stalin's regime became known, wishful thinking and propaganda led many academics to a distant envy of the 'philosopher priests' of the Soviet Union, who supposedly exercised their right to rule the masses by virtue of their special insight into the 'scientific' principles of Marxism. This was no less true in the art world.

'Blunt had arrived early at the conviction,' Steiner concludes, 'that great art, to which he ascribed preeminent value in human consciousness and society, could not survive the fragmented and anarchic and always modish government or private patronage and mass media trivialization.'

Most of the British intellectual and artistic community held in particular scorn the rise in popular culture after World War I. They saw the United States, especially through the impact of Hollywood films, as debasing English values and bringing about a society overly concerned with material gain. The crass American media tycoon bent on exploiting the mindless English-speaking masses became a common theme in the novels of Evelyn Waugh, plays and literary criticism of the period.

The anti-Americanism that Blunt shared with many of his academic contemporaries was more than just the traditional British snobbism toward the colonials. The intellectuals were reacting to the worldwide ascendancy of the United States and Britain's concurrent economic decline and loss of prestige. The academic community – especially the dons at Oxford and Cambridge – saw it as their duty to stand guard over Britian's unique cultural heritage.

Anti-Americanism was a theme Blunt returned to time and time again in his *Spectator* articles. In 1935 he lamented that Britain had 'become the inexhaustible storehouses upon which American wealth and lack of discretion have for decades been drawing.' Forty years later he was vehemently outspoken about the need to halt the flow of artworks to the United States. As a member of the Reviewing Committee on the Export of Works of Art, Blunt wrote to *The Times* in 1971 to condemn the selling of artworks from major British collections as a 'sign of cultural barbarism.'

Blunt's early views on American cultural barbarity were colored by Maurice Dobb's reports of how the Soviet system venerated and promoted the arts. 'Museums and galleries have been thrown open and increased in number,' Dobb recorded of the 'cultural revolution' he witnessed in Moscow. Artists' exhibitions toured the provinces and 'at least half the tickets at theaters, operas and concerts are supplied at half price to the trades unions and factories'.

The supposed openness, accessibility and importance of art in Soviet society contrasted favorably with the situation under capitalism, where governments were powerless to prevent American millionaires from buying up Western Europe's old masters to lock them away as investments in bank vaults, or to display them in private behind their mansion gates. This rosy view of the Soviet cultural utopia could have been a persuasive argument to a budding art historian whose career depended on gaining access to these works of art. Nor is it difficult to comprehend how an intellectual Marxist like Blunt needed little persuasion to believe that the best hope of preserving a common European heritage from what Steiner terms 'prostitution in the money market' was by allying himself with a Communist system that not only promised but ostensibly did make public all private art collections – under the supervision of the intellectuals, of course.

'If western painting, sculpture and architecture were to regain classic stature, they must do so under the control of an enlightened, educative and historically purposeful state' is how Steiner rationalizes the way Blunt might have come to believe in a central authority over the arts. The precedent for an elitist cultural authority owes as much to Plato's 'guardians' as it does to Karl Marx. But in his belief that great art is of too universal a significance to be traded like stock certificates in a capitalist system, Blunt was evidently persuaded that the Leninist commissariat for art and the revolutionary ministry of culture in Mexico met the need for a modern-day equivalent of the Florentine Medicis.

Steiner contends that the belief that 'great art is not, cannot be, private property' played a crucial part in crystallizing Blunt's 'contemptuous loathing for capitalism'. It precipitated his slide from undergraduate and salon Marxism into the practicalities of treason. Blunt's pact with Stalin's emissaries owed something to a common affliction among scholars that Steiner terms 'odium philogicum', the yearning of the academic mind for power and authority in the real world.

Yet, as Steiner emphasized, many British academics in the thirties became Communists, but only a very few committed treason in the name of Marx. Blunt was one of them. What may have begun as a misguided belief that a Communist regime held out the best hope for the survival of Europe's heritage eventually translated 'into clandestine performance, into covert mendacity and, possibly, murder (the men and women Blunt tagged for Soviet vengeance in Eastern Europe).'

As a Trinity don, Blunt may have concealed his role as a talent scout for Soviet Intelligence. But he seems to have made no effort to conceal his Marxism. There was really no need to; at Cambridge communism was acceptable, in some circles fashionable. Members of the undergraduate socialist movement remember the reverential tones in which Anthony's name was mentioned as one of the Communist dons.

'Blunt was well known in left-wing circles,' recalled Leonard Miall, who was then a leading undergraduate politician reading law in St John's. As a 'right-wing socialist', Miall became president of the Union and chairman of the Cambridge Union Socialist Society Club in 1936. 'Not everyone on the left was brave or foolhardy enough to become a card-carrying Communist,' he noted. But as a *Spectator* reader, the future BBC foreign correspondent knew all about the Trinity don's Marxist views long before he first met him at an undergraduate party in 1935. Miall recalls the solicitude shown by Blunt, who warned him of the disastrous consequences of mixing gin and sherry.

'Blunt was the sort of don you met regularly at undergraduate parties,' according to Miall. He was frequently in the company of Burgess. Miall regarded it as somewhat unusual for a fellow of Trinity to mix so freely with undergraduates. 'Except for King's, where fraternizing was normal, the dons tended to keep themselves apart socially,' said Miall. Not until 1979 did he reflect that this unusually gregarious behavior was essential to Blunt's role as a Soviet talent scout.

'While Blunt was not an active Communist,' Leo Long said, 'he was known to us in the Trinity cell as one of the senior members who were theoretical Marxists'. A London secondary-school boy, the son of an unemployed carpenter, Long regarded himself as a Communist before he won the scholarship in modern languages that brought him up to Trinity in 1935.

'My name had been passed to James Klugmann even before Blunt became my supervisor,' Long insisted, explaining that his decision to join the college cell in his first year had nothing to do with Blunt's tutoring him in French. 'I was a Marxist because I was against the inequities of society,' Long said. To a solitary working-class youth, the social and political egalitarianism of the Trinity cell offered a unique opportunity to make contact with 'Hons and Rebels' from the public schools, who might otherwise have considered themselves socially superior to a carpenter's son from Hackney.

Two prominent Cambridge 'Hons' who came up to Cambridge in 1934 and were 'sucked into the prevailing Marxist vortex for a time' were the Hovell-Thurlow-Cumming-Bruce brothers. As the sons of a baron they managed to combine their membership in the Communist cell with foxhunting. Their brief flirtation with communism did not affect their careers. James, after studying law in Magdalene, rose to become a lord chief justice of appeal. His brother Francis, 'reputed to sing the "Red Flag" even in his bath' at Trinity, became Lord Thurlow after a distinguished career in the diplomatic service. Francis 'admired and was rather awed' by Blunt's erudition but conceded that he 'didn't like him much'.

A young man who turned out to be one of the most important figures in Blunt's life, an American named Michael Straight, came up to Trinity in 1934. Straight became a member of the college's Communist cell early in 1935, but he remained ignorant that the 'very pale, very slender, very tall' don in Trinity was a Marxist. In retrospect, Straight is now convinced that from the day he first passed through the Trinity Great Gate, his politics and family ties had already marked him out as one of Blunt's future recruits.

As the younger son of the late Willard Straight, a partner of the Morgan Bank who founded *The New Republic* magazine, and Dorothy Whitney, the heiress of one of America's great industrial fortunes, Straight represented potentially important connections and influence. His education in New York and England left him with schizophrenic loyalties that reinforced the powerful radicalism absorbed from his mother, a former suffragette who had campaigned for the rights of American labor unions. After Willard Straight's death she had married a penniless Englishman named Leonard Elmhirst and founded Dartington Hall, an experimental school in South Devon where Michael and his elder brother, Whitney, completed their education.

Dartington's 'progressive' education, which put Freud above algebra, had stamped Michael with a fiercely impatient intellect. An intense dark-haired young man, he arrived at Cambridge with two novels and two volumes of poetry, all unpublished, determined, as he put it, to 'gate-crash eternity' by making his reputation as a poet, not a Wall Street banker. Harold Laski was a family friend and arranged that before Cambridge Michael would study for a year at the London School of Economics where the socialist economist was the principal. Travel in India, participation in a Pittsburgh steel strike, and dancing with a ballet company sponsored by his mother, had further nurtured his restlessly impetuous temperament.

He was preceded at Cambridge by his older brother, whose passion for racing cars had made him a playboy celebrity. Whitney introduced Michael to the Pitt Club, where he encountered Guy Burgess. Michael quickly dismissed Guy as 'an alcoholic adventurer, a name dropper and a gypsy'. A month after his arrival at Cambridge, Straight was courted by a different circle from that found around the Pitt's bar.

'My name had obviously been passed down to the Trinity cell by the Communists at the LSE, where I had been regarded as a "C" prospect,' Straight said, explaining that potential Communist converts were graded on the amount of political persuasion needed to secure their loyalty. 'I was a C contact, which meant that I had lots of unanswered questions and they would have to work on me.

'One had a birdlike head and manner; his name was James Klugmann,' Straight recalled. The other was John Cornford, whose 'dark, deep-set eyes' fixed Michael: 'His entire body was taut; his whole being seemed to be concentrated on his immediate purpose.' Their objective, Straight explained, was to recruit him for CUSC. He readily agreed. CUSC was dominated by a Marxist core, and he guessed that it served as an 'antechamber' to the party itself. About one in four of its two hundred members belonged to Communist cells. But he knew that the 1935 meeting of the Seventh World Congress of the Communist International had revised the attitude to other socialist parties and had called for a Popular Front to fight Fascism.

The Socialist Society became Straight's point of entry into the Trinity Communist cell. He became a member 'early in 1935', attending its weekly Thursday meetings, having fallen under the personal spell of John Cornford whose idealism he intensely admired, both as a poet and political thinker. Later Straight was to discover that the Communist leaders in Cambridge took their orders directly from the London CPGB headquarters in King Street. Even though he 'got along well with Harry Pollitt, the working-class leader of the British Communist party to whom, at James's urging, I gave as much money as I could without feeling the pinch,' Straight insisted that he felt 'no sense of loyalty to the party as such.'

Straight considered himself a 'casual member' of Cambridge's best-led radical student movement, but he believed that his actions were directed 'by my own free will'. Notwithstanding, he drew a distinction between himself and those whom he regarded as the hard core of dedicated Communists. In contrast with his fellow comrades, who put party above self, he considered his commitment more an intellectual than a political creed.

Straight took his cue from Victor Kiernan, whom Klugmann and Cornford had persuaded to become a Communist in 1934. To Kiernan, who became a graduate student in history and then a Trinity research fellow, Marxism was more than a political creed because it supplied the 'right answers' and provided a philosophical base for his historical studies. He believed that Marxism 'could lift us to a plane far above the Cambridge level.'

Kiernan, like Blunt, was an influence behind the scenes. It is evident from the minute books of the Trinity Historical Society that he was, with Burgess, important in giving a powerful leftward tilt to the group. 'Harry' Ferns, another historian, recalls Kiernan as one of the two leading lights in what was 'very much a Marxist debating ground with its emphasis on the economic interpretation of history.'

There was a more shadowy tier to the Communist organization at the university. Soon after Michael Straight joined the cell on 18 March 1935, he noticed that Egerton Herbert Norman – who twenty-two years later mysteriously committed suicide in Egypt, where he was Canada's ambassador – ceased to appear among the dozen or so students at the regular Tuesday evening meetings. Klugmann explained that Norman would be working with the Indian students and 'in our terminology became a mole'. The word *mole* had yet to acquire its popular association with espionage. For 'reasons of security' Norman had gone underground: as an open Communist working among the Indian students he would be sure to draw the attention of the Colonial Office. The Indian Security Police were receiving regular reports from MI5 on the activities of the Cambridge Marxists. Kiernan also became a mole when he took over the Indian work the following year, after Norman returned to Canada.

According to Straight, other moles included the Italian Marxist economist Piero Sraffa, whom Keynes had brought over to Cambridge and who was in danger of deportation if his party affiliation was revealed, and John Cairncross, who was aiming for the civil service and could not therefore afford to be labeled as an open party member. A Union friend of Straight's at Pembroke had already stopped coming to meetings when he decided to make his career as a barrister.

Blunt was never himself mentioned as one of the moles by any member of the Trinity Communist cell. Dons were not supposed to involve themselves in undergraduate political activities. Maurice Dobb had nearly lost his fellowship over the issue of proselytizing. But Straight insists that this injunction did not cut Dobb's Communist activities, because he also encountered Dobb at meetings of the town cell. All Communist undergraduates had to join under party rules intended to prevent the Cambridge intellectuals from considering themselves an elite and to maintain contact with the lumpenproletariat.

Straight was certain that Anthony Blunt had no outward political commitments to either the Trinity or the town cell – or any overt relationship with Klugmann. Blunt's insistence that Burgess was the third member who dominated the Cambridge Communists, Straight finds 'absurd'. Burgess was 'certainly not in any organized continuing way' considered by the Trinity-cell members to be one of the leaders.

Clues that suggest Blunt may indeed have been acting as a secret Communist functionary in 1935 also appear in the political sympathies he expressed in veiled terms in *Spectator* articles that year under the pseudonym of 'Your Cambridge Correspondent'. In them, Blunt's cheering on of the Cambridge Communists from the sidelines of the *Spectator* became noticeably more strident after his return in 1935 from a summer trip to the Soviet Union. The organizers were Charles Rycroft of Trinity and John Madge, brother of the Communist poet Charles, who obtained free passage for himself by rounding up five others willing to pay the fifteen-pound Intourist fare for passage by steamer to Leningrad and back.

'Anthony and I were making the journey in search of pictures and architecture,' Wilfrid Blunt recalled. But since the group was 'for the most part left-wing pilgrims to the promised land', according to his unsophisticated judgment, it attracted the special attention of MI5.

On the same trip were Michael Straight and Brian Simon, another member of the Communist cell. Simon was to make a career as a leading educator and became a member of the Central Committee of the CPGB. Also on board was Charles Fletcher-Cooke, another Trinity man, a rising Union radical who later became a Tory MP. He knew Blunt through their mutual friend Victor Rothschild. Also on the trip was Michael Young, a sociologist from London University, a Dartington school friend of Straight. Two Oxford undergraduates were also in the group. Christopher Mayhew, a future Labour minister and lord, who was a former pupil of Wilfrid Blunt's at Haileybury, came with his friend Derek Nenk. The party sailed for Leningrad from the Pool of London on 10 August 1935.

'Freedom at last,' one of the party exclaimed when they landed at Leningrad. There was no one at the landing stage to meet them, for their Intourist guide was still asleep. 'We tried not to see the poverty, the squalor, the primitiveness that surrounded us wherever we went,' Straight wrote. 'We huddled inside our illusions, responding as Intourist intended we should to a dozen carefully staged interviews.' From Leningrad they traveled by train to Moscow 'hard class'. Photographs of the Kremlin were forbidden, but the future Lord Mayhew remembers how he enlisted Blunt's aid to violate Soviet regulations: Blunt held his legs so that he could lean out of their room in the Moscova Nova at the corner of Red Square.

According to Straight's recollections of what he termed 'the summer pilgrimage', Blunt was mysteriously and repeatedly absent. Neither did Blunt join the group on a grueling two-day rail trip south to Kharkov and Kiev. Straight was shaken by witnessing the Red Guards firing their rifles to drive half-starved children from the tracks.

In his autobiography Wilfrid makes no reference to his younger brother's mysterious disappearance. Nor is it clear from his account whether he was with Anthony all the time. But he does provide confirmation that his brother must have obtained special privileges because, apart from a token visit to a Moscow shoe factory, the Blunts 'managed to escape the organized tours of factories and the other wonders of the Soviet regime.'

Did Blunt spend all his time absent from the main party studying the Poussins in the Hermitage and the Pushkin Museum in Moscow, as Wilfrid maintained? Or it is more probable that the extended absences so distinctly remembered by Straight provided the opportunity for Blunt to slip away from his brother and meet with officers of Soviet intelligence?

Straight also told the FBI in 1963 that Blunt left the ship for one day. He remembers taking a picture of Blunt and Fletcher-Cooke being lowered over the side in a boat to go ashore. The purpose was to visit a German medieval town on the Baltic coast. Straight told me that this was later confirmed by one of the MI5 officers who debriefed him in 1965.

Blunt's return to London abroad the merchant vessel *Smolny* on 12 September was duly noted by MI5 – as the American records show the passenger manifest was scrutinized carefully by MI5. Particular attention would have paid to this group because Harry Pollitt was aboard for the return trip. Straight's name was reported to the US embassy, so Blunt's must also have been added to MI5 registry files.

Questioned at the 1979 press conference about whether he had ever visited Russia, Blunt said he had made a 'holiday' trip in either 1935 or 1936. He could not recall which year. 'It was one of the ordinary Intourist visits,' he said, implying that visiting the Soviet Union during the Stalin years was a common excursion for British tourists.

'It was not . . .' Blunt then hesitated – perhaps as he thought better of denying that there was any sinister purpose to the trip – and then concluded with: 'I went with a group of enthusiastic left-wingers, mainly Communists, mainly undergraduates.'

Spectator readers had the benefits of Blunt's enthusiastic report of this trip a few weeks after his return in 1935. 'The best blocks of living houses in Moscow are extremely impressive,' Blunt wrote, though he found that the rising Palace of the Soviets 'threatens to look more like a giant Selfridge's wedding cake than a worthy monument to the October revolution.'

When it came to the revolutionary contribution to painting Blunt did not find the result particularly attractive, but he approved of the rejection of abstraction in favor of realism. He predicted that 'the greatest achievements of Socialist art would be in decorative painting on a large scale – as was the case when painting was last a communal art in the middle ages.'

Marxism rather than Blunt's aesthetic sense had obviously influenced his judgement about the merits of Communist realism. Within a month of his return from Moscow he was telling *Spectator* readers that 'art has been on the wrong track since Impressionism and that the steady recession of art from nature and life has led to its reaching complete futility in the last abstractions of the Cubists and the intimate meanderings of the Surrealists.' Blunt saw the work of Salvador Dali and Max Ernst as the 'phase during which art under capitalism gradually destroys itself as the contradictions in the social system become more acute.' Blunt thought that the proletariat needed heavy doses of socialist realist art of the kind produced by Diego Rivera and José Clemente Orozco. Their highly animated and vividly executed murals dramatized the political and social aims of the 1910 Mexican Revolution. 'In a century or two communism may have produced its Raphael,' Blunt declared, calling for 'an art dealing with social problems of the day, an art more closely connected with life than any since medieval times.'

Blunt also made no secret of his Marxism in Cambridge intellectual circles. 'I knew perfectly well what his views were,'

Professor G. F. Wickens of Toronto University assured me. A Trinity freshman from a London high school, who came up in the 1935–36 academic year, Wickens read modern languages. Blunt supervised him in French while Pascal tutored his German. Wickens vividly remembers arriving for his first supervision and finding a lethargic-looking Blunt lounging on a sofa in a silk dressing gown. He quickly came to know from the way they both conducted their classes that they were Communists. 'Pascal had a very clear intellectual grasp of Marxism,' Wickens said. 'Blunt didn't. He used to talk in catchphrases and was rather a light-weight when it came to Marxist theory.'

'It was not so much intellectual snobbery, as social snobbery,' Wickens recalled. 'He made me feel I was a hardworking, grubby little bastard.' Wickens did not rate a place in Blunt's web of intrigue. Blunt's concern was not with recruiting the under-graduate foot soldiers for the party, but with spotting, cultivating and passing on to Soviet intelligence those left-wing students most likely to succeed in making their mark on the governing establishment.

Michael Straight was a prime candidate. Blunt came to know him on their summer pilgrimage to Russia. As one of only four to get a first in Part I of the Economics Tripos in his freshman year, Straight was an academic high-flyer who had both wealth and social position.

Although Straight was unaware of it, he was also under scrutiny for the Apostles by David Champernowne, a graduate left-wing economist of King's, after he defended a paper on Karl Marx's theory that Champernowne presented at a meeting of the Political Economy Club that October. Keynes responded to their dialectical efforts by saying that he had 'read Marx, as if it were a detective story, trying to find a clue and never succeeding.' Straight was taken aback.

'It was the only instance that I had heard of a leading intel-lectual at the university challenging the new orthodoxy,' Straight recalled. 'I was shaken, but my political allegiance was unchanged.'

Straight's confidence was restored in November at a dinner with Anthony Blunt and Guy Burgess, arranged by James Klugmann. Straight was so 'enthralled' and 'flattered' by the 'worldly brilliance' of Burgess and Blunt that when he returned to his rooms at half past eleven he had to put pen to paper. Writing to his mother, he confessed that he had 'learned to love the Communist students, even if I don't love Communism itself'; he burned with 'unreasonable and inexplicable' commitment as he tried to 'describe the terrible significance of it all.'

The vision Blunt and Burgess held out was that the world was at the dawn of a New Age. The old age was dying – disintegrating economically and socially. 'Anthony and Guy made it appear that they had leapt from one age to the other,' Straight said. 'They were no longer representatives of a dying culture, but spokesmen for an emerging culture.'

'Looking back,' Straight said, 'this was plainly the targeting of a potential recruit from the student Communist cell who was being turned over for inspection and cultivation by Blunt.' He began receiving frequent invitations to the informal gatherings that Blunt held in his fine set of rooms above the cloistered colonnades of Trinity's New Court, in the shadow of the imposing Wren Library. Straight met Blunt's close circle of friends, among whom were Victor Rothschild and his lively first wife, Barbara.

As Lord Annan has pointed out, a Marxist orientation was a prerequisite for election to the Apostles at this time, so it appears no coincidence that Straight was soon invited to become an Apostle. Straight learned that Blunt, Burgess and Rothschild were among the active younger members, along with his sponsor, Champernowne.

At his induction meeting in Keynes's rooms on 8 March 1935, Staight was obliged to take 'a fearful oath, praying that my soul would writhe in unendurable pain for the rest of eternity if I so much as breathed a word about the society to anyone who was not a member.' As the only Apostle elected from his year, he assumed the traditional duties of the youngest member as secretary, keeper of the 'Ark', and arranger of meetings.

Communist rhetoric that had brought sweat to the forehead of the junior Apostles three years earlier, and which Keynes, with fatherly indulgence, attributed to a youthful 'zest to adopt a painful solution because of its painfulness,' had subsided by 1936.

'No Communist views were expressed in my presence, at least at society meetings,' Straight insisted. Burgess made a point of traveling to Cambridge for the Saturday meetings because 'he derived an almost sensual pleasure from the discussion of ideas.'

Blunt seldom appeared, even at Saturday meetings. When he did speak, usually on artistic themes, he held forth at length. But Straight soon became aware that Blunt was trying to bring him under his influence. 'He went out of his way to make himself a protector of mine and to make me indebted to him,' Straight said, recalling how Blunt claimed to have intervened on his behalf in a row with the College Council in May 1936.

Straight had been the first to sign a petition protesting that the Trinity servants received less than a living wage from the college. Called upon to explain himself to the fellows, he made the rounds of painful interviews amid rumors in the Senior Combination Room about his possible expulsion. The waiters eventually got their wage raise and Straight stayed. Blunt made a special point of dramatizing the role he had played in persuading the other fellows that Straight had been foolish rather than malign.

The whole affair was typical of what Straight called 'Blunt's love of conspiracy and maneuver'. What he did not know was that Blunt's attempt to set him up appears to have been another devious move in Blunt's long-standing feud with Keynes.

A feud that backfired in 1936, when Blunt told the King's electors that a Harris Fellowship would provide him with the opportunity to turn his dissertation on 'The Pictorial History of Painting' into a book. He claimed that he had already completed more than half of this project and would also carry out more research in southern Italy for his intended second book about baroque architecture.

Blunt, it seems, made a very great effort to obtain the King's

Fellowship, but Keynes was openly hostile. He dismissed Blunt's work as 'a lot of Marxist nonsense'. Blunt was rejected. This was a bitter blow, the third time that Blunt had failed to meet the grade set by his fellow academics.

A few weeks later Blunt went off with Louis MacNeice on an Easter trip to Spain. The two old friends were both nursing wounded egos. MacNeice's wife had run off with an American from Oxford, 'life was bloody', and he was so deeply in debt that Blunt had to pay for his steamship passage to Gibraltar.

In Spain the Fascists and the rightist Falange party were openly protesting against the election of a Popular Front government of liberals, socialists and Communists. MacNeice advised Blunt to tell their friends that they were going 'to look at the churches before it is all burnt down'. The civil war did not break out for three more months, but the political mood in Spain that March was as ugly as the weather: it rained continuously. 'The Hammer and Sickle was scrawled all over Spain that Easter,' MacNeice wrote. Blunt could barely contain his delight. 'If Spain goes communist,' he declared, 'France is bound to follow. And then Britain, and then there'll be jam for all.'

During the two-week trip, as they toured churches and art galleries, Blunt talked enthusiastically of the death of easel painting, with town halls and factories blooming with murals and bas-reliefs in concrete. Blunt's sanctimonious Marxism – preaching the 'Categorical Imperative' – bore heavily on his more imaginative and free-thinking friend.

'The great danger of Marxist doctrine is that it allows and even encourages opportunism,' MacNeice observed when he came to write about the trip with Blunt. 'After a bit the Marxist, who is only human, finds such fun practicing strategy – i.e., hypocrisy, lying, graft, political pimping, tergiversation, allegedly necessary murder – that he forgets the end in the means, the evil of the means drowns the good of the end, power corrupts, the living gospel withers, Siberia fills with ghosts.' Did Blunt make an all-out effort on the trip to persuade his old schoolmate to become a Communist? If so MacNeice resisted the overtures to join the

Gadarene stampede that had sucked in Blunt and now beckoned his fellow left-wing Oxford poets Stephen Spender and W. H. Auden.

'You always were so handy with the intellectual spanner,' MacNeice wrote to Blunt shortly after their return from Spain. As a poet, MacNeice was not born for dogma, and, as he wrote, 'You can't feed Marx to an artist as you feed grass to a cow.' After their return from Spain, he made one last effort to salvage his friendship with Blunt. Loading a sculpture made by a Birmingham friend, Gordon Herrick, into his car, MacNeice drove to Cambridge on 5 May believing that Blunt would help him sell the semi-abstract piece to Victor Rothschild.

The highly polished stone *Cyclamen* was set up in Blunt's 'coquettishly chaste room with white panelling and Annunciation lilies'. Blunt protested that his Marxist convictions made it impossible for him to push the sale of a work that was primarily abstract. 'Couldn't you get old VR to buy it to reduce his weight if nothing else?' Louis pleaded. 'I didn't think that it's merely a decorative work anyway.'

MacNeice soon abandoned the effort to raise money for his friend's artistic effort. 'Cambridge was still full of Peter Pans, but all the Peter Pans were now talking Marx,' he observed disparagingly after an evening with Blunt's Trinity coterie. MacNeice was too much of a romantic to be a Communist revolutionary. The next morning, while Blunt was teaching, he decided to take his own revenge on Marx and 'drank myself blind before lunch; it seemed an exquisite outrage to the room and also to Dialectical Materialism'.

'You see I am really much happier when drunk,' MacNeice wrote to Blunt after driving back to Birmingham. He had given a lift to Guy Burgess and John Cornford, the latter to stand trial for causing an obstruction by distributing Communist pamphlets in the city center. 'There is still hope for the human race,' he wrote of Cornford, congratulating Cambridge for producing 'the one chap of the whole damn lot of you who is going to be a great man.' He told Blunt that Burgess, even though he 'thought all the young men in the streets of Birmingham were queer,' was 'quite the nicest of your pals.'

Two months later, when MacNeice was in Iceland with W. H. Auden on a travel-book project, Blunt received a spoof postcard of a local boy with the suggestive message: 'A donor who prefers to remain anonymous is sending a very pretty piece to King's this October. Impey's the name.' Later that year Auden and Mac-Neice published a celebrated joint poem full of cryptic references to leading political figures and their friends, couched as a 'Last Will and Testament'. MacNeice had bequeathed Blunt 'A copy of Marx and £1000 a Year/And the picture of Love Locked Out by Holman Hunt.'

This very public flagging of Blunt's Marxism may have been the final straw for him. There are no more letters after 31 October 1936, and MacNeice makes no mention of Blunt after that date. But the poem's biting anti-Marxist cynicism about 'the Comrades . . . who wanted to be at home with Stalin' suggests MacNeice's long friendship with Blunt foundered at this point.

The Spanish Civil War had erupted in July with the revolt of the generals in Morocco led by Franco. To the intellectuals of all shades of left-wing opinion the issue was clear: Britain had a moral duty to help save the democratically elected Popular Front government from a rebellion engineered by the Fascist generals. It was left to the Soviet Union to send arms and technicians to help the government in Madrid. The war in Spain became the subject of bitter debate; the wedge between the left and right in Britain was driven deeper and deeper. 'The Spanish Civil War was felt to be a war of light against darkness' was how Oxford poet Stephen Spender described its impact on his friends.

John Cornford was the first Cambridge Communist to demonstrate that he was ready to lay down his life for his political beliefs. To his contemporaries this was in itself enough to transform the tousled Communist into a romantic hero.

Julian Bell, David Haden-Guest, Tom Wintringham, Stephen Spender, and briefly Auden himself, made the journey to the front line of what they believed was the pivotal battle between the forces of democracy and fascism. Within a year, as Russian troops arrived to enforce Moscow's own Communist goals, the International Brigade was subordinated to Soviet generals. Democracy was not on the political agenda that Stalin had drawn up for the reeling Popular Front government. The executions and intrigues in Spain and the relentless trials in Moscow as Stalin systematically purged the remaining opposition to his dictatorship took a heavy toll on the idealism of British intellectuals like George Orwell, Auden and Spender. The anti-Fascist front of the left shattered over what Spender described as 'a refusal on behalf of all but the most convinced ideologists to tell the lies required by the Stalinist communists.'

Anthony Blunt, immersed in the unemotional world of Poussin's painting and secure in his aseptically white intellectual aerie in Trinity, continued with his detached promotion of the Marxist theory of art.

Since the Marxist canon demanded that art had to be socially useful, it also had to be realistic enough to convey a political message. Picasso, according to Blunt, failed to meet the criterion by running off into abstraction and 'ingenious but empty cleverness'. Blunt's respect for the most important artist of the twentieth century was irrevocably shattered when he saw *Guernica*, which dominated the Spanish Pavilion at the International Exhibition in Paris in August 1937. The huge, nearly monochrome canvas with its jagged and screeching images of horror had instantly become one of the most celebrated visual statements of its time. Inspired by the artist's outrage at the destruction wrought by the civil war in his native land, Picasso had dedicated *Guernica* to the Spanish people. It memorialized the small Basque town that was reduced to rubble by the bombs of the Condor Legion sent by Hitler to hasten Franco's victory.

Blunt's immediate reaction to *Guernica* was a mixture of cynical disgust and dialectical disparagement. His words spoke no less eloquently about his own essential cold-bloodedness. With the chilling delusion of a Stalinist, he dismissed as 'disillusioning' the one work that stands today, as it did in 1937, a testament to the inhumanity of war. 'It is not an act of public mourning,' Blunt wrote, 'but the expression of a private brain storm which gives no evidence that Picasso has realized the political significance of *Guernica.*'

Over his lifetime Anthony Blunt admitted making a few errors. But this was one of his greatest. And he was forced to acknowledge it again and again. His shallow Marxist diatribe against Picasso left a blot on his reputation as a judge of art that lasted for years. Many years later Blunt tried to justify himself by asserting that he 'was very much moved by it' but 'horrified by it from a theoretical point of view.' Although many years later he admitted the integrity and artistic significance of Picasso's best-known work, Blunt could never completely live down the accusations he made in the *Spectator* under the heading 'Picasso Unfrocked'.

'Picasso should have seen more than the mere horror of the Civil War,' Blunt railed on with the dogmatic indignation of a *Pravda* editorialist. The struggle in Spain was only 'a tragic part of a great forward movement'. The Revolution demanded optimism; Picasso had once been a 'giant', but now, for Blunt 'in a harsher glare, and up against more exacting standards, he appears a pygmy.'

Rees, then assistant editor of *The Spectator*, was openly skeptical, going so far as to suggest that Stalin's bloody purge of his opponents was 'historically necessary'. Blunt, through his expanding network, was proving his sinister capacity to serve Moscow's interest in ways that could not have been foreseen when he became one of the first of 'Stalin's Englishmen'. And he went so far as to give a clear indication of the ultimate reward he anticipated for this loyal service, in a January 1937 review of an exhibition of 'masterpieces lost in the attics of our large and older feudal residences'.

'What a field day the Minister of Fine Arts will have,' Blunt proclaimed, 'when, after the Revolution, the State takes over all privately owned paintings and collects the best in a central museum!'

Blunt, it seems, was already casting himself as the Commissar of Art and Culture. As a Marxist propagandist and a secret recruiter for Soviet intelligence, Blunt apparently intended to ensure that by aiding the Revolution he also advanced his own career as a cultural overlord.

9 'Many a Fickle Makes a Fuckle'

The news that Cornford had been killed in action on 28 December 1936 a day after his twenty-first birthday made him Cambridge's most heroic figure since Rupert Brooke.

Blunt's portrayal of Cornford in his 1973 article 'From Bloomsbury to Marxism' as a 'glamorous figure' and a 'vehement orator' was a 'travesty' to Michael Straight. He regards it as highly significant that Blunt chose to describe Cornford as 'a highly emotional character' who 'might have gone back on his Marxist doctrine.' The gratuitous assertion that it was 'appropriate' that he 'should have gone to Spain to get killed' because Cornford was 'the stuff of what martyrs are made of' was most revealing of all. 'An incredible statement,' Straight observed: 'Only a hardened Communist functionary could have made a statement like that.' Michael Straight had taken it upon himself to break the tragic news to Cornford's family and his lover, Margot Heineman. He also arranged for the care of Cornford's estranged girlfriend, Ray Peters, and her infant son, James. That the Party made Cornford a propaganda symbol was no shock to Straight, but he was quite unprepared for the way that Blunt exploited his friend's death two weeks later, when he received a summons to Blunt's elegant rooms.

'I assumed that he wanted to talk to me about the Apostles, or about Victor Rothschild's unhappy wife,' recalled Straight. 'Instead, he asked me what I planned to do when I graduated from Cambridge.' Blunt listened to his hopes for becoming a British citizen and member of Parliament.

'Some of your friends have other ideas for you,' Blunt coolly told him. Then, with calculated reasonableness, he went on to explain that Straight's political activities might make it difficult for him to obtain naturalization. Since Britain was a declining nation, he suggested that Straight's talents would be better applied in the United States, which was destined to play a far larger role in world affairs. He should use his family connections in J. P. Morgan to make his future career in international banking.

'Our friends have given a great deal of thought to it,' said Blunt. 'They have instructed me to tell you that is what you must do.' Straight recalled his surprise when Blunt identified the 'friends' as 'the Communist International'. The implication was that Moscow had decided his mission was to provide them with inside information about Wall Street's plans to dominate the global economy. Blunt said he was under instructions to help Straight prepare for this assignment by breaking all his political ties with the left. He was to use his grief at Cornford's death as a pretext for cutting himself off from the Cambridge Communists.

Straight remembered how he sank deeper into Anthony's gray sofa as he tried to protest. It would mean abandoning his friends in the university Socialist Society and giving up the presidency of the Union that his recent election as secretary guaranteed. But Blunt undermined his resistance with an air of compassionate understanding and an obvious effort to sympathize with a predicament that required personal sacrifices to serve the cause. By implying that he was only acting for a mutual friend who wanted Straight to know he 'regrets very much that he is not permitted to identify himself,' Blunt gave Straight the impression that Burgess was Moscow's shadowy eminence. Straight weakened and agreed to the plan. But the very next evening he was back in Blunt's rooms, pleading for reconsideration. Blunt was sympathetic and promised to intercede with the 'friend'.

A week later Blunt told Straight that Moscow had rejected his appeal. There was no choice but for him to return to the United States and go underground, even if he refused to become a banker. Straight says that he protested more strongly. Blunt never once raised his voice or lost his air of friendly authority. He simply assured Straight that he would make yet another plea on his behalf: this time it 'would be considered in the highest circles of the Kremlin.' Blunt thereby implied that he himself would use a direct line of communication and that his appeal would reach Stalin himself. However, there was one condition. Straight had to stage his 'breakdown' without further delay and cut his ties with the Communist movement. No more time could elapse if Straight's political retreat from the Party was to be convincingly attributed to an emotional reaction to Cornford's death.

'That was the bargain that was offered to me,' said Straight. 'I accepted it.' He claimed that in his emotional state he simply lacked the will to stand up to Blunt's strong manipulative personality. 'I did not subject Blunt's proposal to any rational analysis,' Straight insisted. But by striking the bargain, he later recognized that whatever Moscow's reaction, he had lost the fight to determine his own future. Blunt's asssault on his insecurity had exposed his own submissiveness. Had Blunt been didactic or doctrinaire, Straight admits that he might have found it easier to resist.

'Anthony was, on the contrary, compassionate; he seemed as unnerved as I was by the sadness of the situation in which we found ourselves,' Straight recalled, admitting that in the weeks following Cornford's death his defenses were down. 'I wanted to be a martyr' was how Straight rationalized his capitulation, 'I needed to sacrifice myself, as John had done.'

Straight's personal agonizing made it easier for him to stage a convincing charade of his breakdown. Under Blunt's tutelage he abandoned lectures and work and quarreled with the members of Trinity cell. He alienated his socialist supporters by advising them to vote for a Conservative candidate in the Union because he was not planning to return to Cambridge the following autumn. Only one of his friends, Leslie Humphrey, guessed what was happening. He came around one evening to confide that Blunt had approached him too. Blunt later told Straight that Humphrey did not possess the dedication to communism sufficiently strong enough to survive going underground.

The full appreciation of his predicament made Straight fiercely determined not to let any of his other friends get snared in the same web. When the Girton undergraduate Teresa (Tess) Mayor – who later became Victor Rothschild's second wife – was being pressured to join the student Communist movement that spring, he exercised his veto, as chairman of the Socialist Society, against her enrollment. 'I already had the veil lifted from my eyes by Anthony and I was determined not to let Tess get sucked in,' Straight told me.

By the end of the Easter term, Straight's personal crisis and the strain of faking a breakdown had reached the point where he could not stay on for the finals. Straight's mother was upset and pleaded that he reconsider. Blunt, Burgess and Simon drove down to Dartington in April to offer their support. Blunt promised Straight's concerned parent that he would watch over her son. For his part Burgess drank too much whisky, and infuriated Blunt by giving the clenched-fist socialist salute as they drove off from Dartington Hall.

Shortly afterward Straight sailed for America with his step-father. Aboard ship he began to have second thoughts. He wrote to Blunt in desperation, offering to make over all his wealth to the party if he could escape from his commitment. Once back in Washington, Straight resolved to return to Cambridge after all. Blunt helpfully arranged with the Trinity bursar for Straight to have rooms in New Court near his own. Straight isolated himself from all his former friends in a desperate attempt to catch up with his economics studies for the finals. But if he intended to defy what he believed were Moscow's orders, he found Blunt prepared to exercise an additional psychological hold over him.

'My plea to be released had been reviewed by Stalin, so Anthony told me when I returned to Cambridge,' Straight wrote in his autobiography *After Long Silence*. In his talks with me Straight said he had been able only to hint at Blunt's Machiavellian manipulation while the old spy was still alive. But after

Blunt's death Straight could be franker. He explained that the web in which he was snared by Blunt was not woven simply around loyalty to Cornford's memory, but was also a cynical manipulation of a young man's emotional life and subtle sexual blackmail.

A year before Cornford's death, Straight had fallen for Tess Mayor. In his own words, he was 'stricken' with the 'unearthly beauty' of Tess, who 'had the gaunt nobility of Yeats's beloved Maud Gonne, and some of Maud Gonne's cold fire.' He tried to press his affections on Tess in his rooms at Whewell's Court, but despite the sound of Mozart's concertos on the gramophone and the reading of plaintive verses of Yeats's poetry, their love did not take fire, because, Straight concluded, 'there was a knot within her that I could not untie.'

Frustrated, Straight turned to the ever-solicitous Blunt for advice on his affection for Belinda Crompton, an American girl who was to become his first wife. The extent to which the Trinity don was already a master at putting people in his debt was evident from the solution he proposed: Straight should enter into a romantic liaison with the wife of one of his best friends, whose marriage was on the rocks. Not surprisingly, Straight was reluctant. But Blunt engineered a meeting between the two at one of his social gatherings. To Straight's surprise, the woman embraced him as they walked through the darkened cloisters of New Court and proposed they begin their affair right away. He rejected her advances, knowing that her husband was both possessive and jealous. But the woman did not take no for an answer. With Blunt acting as their go-between, she continued to pursue him as long as he was at Cambridge. Straight insists that Blunt repeatedly tried to push him into the affair although he knew Straight was involved with a German ballet dancer and his now serious courtship of Belinda.

'I regarded Anthony as a confidant. Now I realize he was only putting me deeper in his debt,' Straight said. 'He placed himself between me and the Crompton family and between me and ___ ___.' Straight thereby appears to have made his emotional life a hostage to Blunt, who used this leverage to insist that Straight continue seeing his friend's disconsolate wife.

'She was desperate, genuinely in love with me, and I felt I had to be kind to her,' Straight explained. He survived an attempted seduction under a blanket after a champagne picnic beside the Cam one May evening. But her husband's jealous rage on his return that night to find her reading Donne's poems by candlelight made Straight reluctant to see her again. Once more, Blunt prevailed. He said she was becoming suicidal. So Straight agreed to another meeting – but only in a London restaurant. Looking back, Straight cannot understand why Blunt went to such lengths to risk the wrath of her jealous husband. He speculates that not only did Blunt use the liaison to consolidate his hold over him, Blunt may also have been calculating enough to arrange an adulterous liaison for the husband to facilitate an eventual divorce, so putting another person in his debt.

Blunt's manipulation of Straight also had another dimension. During his last two terms at Cambridge Straight rendered a further service to Blunt by 'fathering' the 'birth' election of a record intake of five new Apostles. In 1937 the society's active membership had shrunk disastrously. Apart from Straight, the only other undergraduate member was Alan Hodgkin, a non-Marxist scientist who later was awarded a Nobel prize for biophysics.

Straight confirmed that in February, before he renounced his left-wing views, as secretary of the society he was told by Keynes to summon all fourteen senior members for a meeting to discuss the urgent need for new undergraduate elections. As the youngest Apostle it fell to Straight to make recommendations. He recalled that he was so overcome by other matters that he simply put forward names of Marxist friends whom he considered apostolic. From among the circle who used to chant the 'Internationale' and 'Arise Ye Prisoners of Starvation' at his drinking parties, he selected John H. Humphrey and John Waterlow, both of Trinity, and Gerald Croadsell, who became a president of the Union. Within two weeks they were all members of the society.

'The ones I picked,' Straight told me, 'were people I knew, almost without exception, as active members of the student Communist movement.' Keynes's resistance had evidently waned, because he considered the undergraduates 'amateur Communists' who would grow out of their revolutionary ardour. But he had not calculated how skillfully the Soviet intelligence service, through Blunt, might exploit their ideological commitment. This was the case with Leo Long, an active Communist from Trinity. His recruitment was actively canvassed by Blunt and John Peter Astbury of Christ's, who was elected at the same time in the summer of 1937 as a result of Straight's recommendation. Astbury's brother confirmed that John Astbury was indeed an ardent Communist at Cambridge – a fact established by the records of the Cambridge Union, which show that he spoke on the losing side in favour of the triumph of the 'dictatorship of the proletariat' and the 'victory of the working class over Capitalism . . . according to the principles of the Parties affiliated to the Communist International.'

The records of subsequent elections reveal that the Apostles Straight fathered represented the high tide of apostolic communism. Since this group inevitably influenced the new elections, they ensured that the current of Marxism continued in the society right up until the outbreak of World War II, but after Blunt left Cambridge in 1937, the degree of emphasis on communism began to subside. However, Blunt used the Apostles in his own way, recruiting Leo Long, for one, into his wartime espionage network. And Blunt, according to Straight, approached at least one other member of this group, an indication that Blunt regarded these Apostles as being in some way preselected when it came to recruiting potential Soviet agents.

Straight drew my attention to the fact that four of his five fellow Communist Apostles appear with him in the historic photograph commemorating Haile Selassie's visit to the Cambridge Union at the end of May.

Michael Straight's Union speech of welcome, translated into impeccable French by Anthony Blunt, was punctuated by the red glow of bursting rockets flickering through the Gothic windows onto the rows of undergraduates packing the Victorian debating chamber's leather benches.

The fireworks came from Victor Rothschild's house on the other side of the river, where a lavish farewell party for Michael Straight and his Union friends was already in full swing. Still in the white tie and tails customarily worn by Union officers, Straight headed off for the party. Union ex-president Leonard Miall remembers piling into Straight's Railton sports car and roaring over Magdalene bridge toward Merton Hall, the Rothschild residence.

'When we arrived, a vodka and caviar supper was being served on the terrace,' Miall recalled. There was a Hungarian band in the floodlit garden, and Victor Rothschild was playing duets with the jazz pianist Cab Calloway. Straight recalls that he stayed only forty minutes, even though he was the guest of honour. Feeling tired and desperate, he left early to escape from Blunt's married friend.

According to Miall the free-flowing liquor and the sylvan setting of the warm May night aroused Blunt's romantic passions. On a stroll with Charles Fletcher-Cooke, Miall recalls coming upon Blunt lying on a garden seat deep in the embrace of a male, an undergraduate from Pembroke.

'I wasn't surprised at all, because Trinity men had that reputation,' Miall said. 'Quite some time later I happened to take another walk, and there in exactly the same position was Anthony Blunt, this time embracing the wife of a don from Jesus.'

This surprised and amused Miall. Later, Blunt appeared looking rather drunk in search of another vodka.

'Aren't you being a little fickle this evening?' Miall jokingly asked him.

'Many a fickle makes a fuckle,' Blunt said, tapping his nose with his forefinger.

Blunt applauded the culmination of a term when the Union, the bellwether of undergraduate opinion, had rejected rearmament, condemned British imperialism, and elected Haile Selassie its honorary member. 'All of which shows that its heart is in the right place and rather solidly fixed there,' Blunt wrote with unmistakable emphasis.

The swan song on which Blunt parted with Cambridge was a very public declaration of his Marxism in his contribution to 'Art under Capitalism and Socialism', published that June in Cecil Day Lewis's book *The Mind in Chains*. Blunt's contribution to this strident collection of Marxist cultural essays was to proclaim that 'in the present state of capitalism the position of the artist is hopeless' and to call on artists to 'collaborate by arousing the proletariat to political consciousness and organizing it for the struggle.' He quoted Lenin's axiom that 'socialist culture will take over all that is good in *bourgeois* culture and turn it to its own ends.' He anticipated the disappearance of paintings 'as a unique private possession', and predicted the development of mural paintings in 'communal buildings devoted to culture and recreation of the workers.' Art was an offensive activity, Blunt contended, quoting Lenin's declaration: 'Every artist . . . has a right to create freely according to his ideals, independent of anything. Only, of course, we communists cannot stand with our hands folded and let chaos develop in any direction it may. We must guide this process according to a plan to form its results.'

With the publication of this astonishing declaration, Blunt had unmistakably and very publicly unfurled the red banner of his communism. There was also an element of spite in this parting shot fired at the university that had once again rejected him. Blunt's failure to attain a permanent Cambridge fellowship meant that, like Straight, he was reluctantly preparing to leave the ancient college that had been his home for eight years.

When Straight came to Blunt's rooms for the last time, he received the first indicator of the impositions that might be made on him as a result of his commitment to Moscow. Blunt arranged for them to meet in London a few days later. It was with a sense of foreboding that he picked up Blunt as arranged on a sweltering June morning in Oxford Street. The meeting in busy traffic shows that Blunt was taking precautions about being followed. Straight took his directions on a circuitous drive to what he described as a roadhouse on the Great West Road, somewhere near where Heathrow Airport is now located.

They made their way to the crowded swimming pool, where Blunt introduced Straight to a thick-set, dark-haired man that Straight remembered only as a 'beefy Russian'. Over a cigarette and a beer Moscow's emissary showed very little interest in the new recruit. Between plunges into the pool, the Russian reminded him to observe the rule about using the public telephone to avoid detection. 'He was more like the agent of a small-time smuggling operation than the representative of a new international order' was the impression that Straight took away from this first meeting with a member of the Soviet intelligence *apparat*.

When I asked Straight why he had not at this point abandoned his involvement, he reminded me of the influence that Blunt had established over him. Blunt reassured him this Russian was merely a 'slab of beef' and the meeting an administrative detail. The Soviet, he said, was only part of a much grander and more elaborate scheme.

Blunt briefed Straight to be prepared to be on his own for some time when he returned to the United States. A new contact would be arranged as quickly as possible. He then asked Straight for a personal document. Straight took a drawing he had in his pocket, done in blue ink by his girlfriend, Belinda Crompton. Blunt tore it into two pieces and handed one back. The Soviet agent who made contact with him in New York would produce the other section, Blunt advised.

'I pretended to myself that the trap that I was in was merely an illusion,' Straight said. He recalled how he tried to shut out all thoughts of Blunt during his voyage back to America. 'I told myself that the ragged piece of the drawing that had been taken from me would never be thrust back into my hand.'

Blunt's use of the torn document and the meeting with the mysterious Russian after months of manipulating Michael

Straight gives every indication that, by the spring of 1937, Blunt was acting as a supervisory agent of the Soviet intelligence service.

Yet at his press conference forty-two years later, Blunt brazenly invoked the Official Secrets Act to deflect a question about whether or not he had had direct dealings with the Soviets.

'There was not a man, an agent, no letter drops or anything like that?' asked one of the three handpicked reporters present. The reporter found it difficult to believe that Blunt had no direct contact with the Russians.

'I was eventually in touch myself,' Blunt admitted. 'I don't know with whom; I have no idea what his name was.' When pressed, he said he was 'trying to get his memory straight', but he supposed this might have been during the war. On how he communicated with the Soviets he replied: 'I am afraid I cannot say.'

There was no challenge to these statements because his meeting at the swimming pool to present Michael Straight to the Russians was not then public knowledge.

Straight was correct in thinking that the 'beefy Russian' was not an important agent; he was too unsophisticated to have been Blunt's case officer, since his presence at an introductory meet with a prospect did not fit the pattern of security the Soviets usually imposed on their important controllers. Most likely he was a relatively lowly 'legal' officer from the embassy detailed to carry out a preliminary inspection on the instructions from Blunt's control. And this leads to the all-important question: who was Blunt's control? Who was his Soviet case officer?

At his press conference, Blunt insisted that the identity of this Soviet officer, along with the names of his other recruits such as Straight, was 'an official secret'. Whoever he was, and we'll discuss his identity later, he had to have been a sophisticated, learned character.

Although Philby denied he was ever a member of 'a Comintern cell', much has been made by the Cambridge spies, and by other writers, of their assertion that they were members of, or were run by members of, the Comintern. This is significant. Initially the Comintern had no intelligence function aside from the collection of data relating to local political and security considerations. But early in the twenties, the Cheka's counterintelligence chief, Mikhail Trilisser, began infiltrating his secret police into all levels of the Comintern. As a result, the direction and control of its covert mission began to change. Foreign members of the Comintern could carry out espionage and sabotage for Moscow much more easily than the Soviets could for themselves. Under the guise of Marxist education, the Comintern became an important pool of agent recruits for the Soviet intelligence and security organs.

The concept of an international organization devoted to the radical alteration of the world's ailing economic, social and political structures – with the aim of elevating the status of mankind – had a broad appeal to many people in a way that communism did not. From the perspective of Soviet intelligence, however, the Comintern provided an appealing 'false flag' for recruiting suitable prospects into the Soviet service. Once the recruits were in, they were in for life, like it or not.

After the Arcos raid, Soviet intelligence for many years relied on the so-called illegals – undercover agents with false passports and 'legends' – to run their networks in Britain. This continued until the mid-1930s. Many of these agents were formerly Comintern members, but it was now the organs of Soviet intelligence, and not the Communist International, who ran them.

The OGPU had taken over effective control of the Comintern in 1932. Two years later Stalin reconstituted the OGPU as the NKVD – the Russian acronym for the People's Commissariat for Internal Affairs – what is today the KGB. In the period from 1934 through 1937, as Stalin's purges decimated the upper ranks of Soviet intelligence, the Comintern officers assumed a major role in foreign-intelligence operations. The clues given by Blunt during his interrogations all point to the recruitment of the Cambridge network by a member of Dzerzhinski's old guard when, by the thirties, these Comintern ideologues were all operating under NKVD control. By not making this distinction Blunt perpetuated a misleading myth and confusion as to who should be credited with originally recruiting and running the Cambridge agents. Until Blunt's confession became publicly known, there were two prime candidates for controller of the Cambridge agents: Samuel Cahan, Moscow Center's *rezident* in London, who was operating under diplomatic cover as first secretary of the embassy; and the longtime Tass representative in Britain, Semyon Rostovsky, who wrote under the name Ernst Henri.

The argument against either Cahan or Rostovsky as the Cambridge recruiter was their 'legal' status as Soviet citizens with diplomatic positions. In the decade after the Arcos debacle, Moscow generally avoided using such people to run spy rings. Any exposure of their role in the chain of command would have jeopardized not only their official status but also Moscow's hard-won restoration of Anglo-Soviet diplomatic relations. Moscow Center would also have reasoned – correctly, as we now know from MI5 reports – that Soviet officials in London were subject to intense scrutiny by British counterintelligence. And Soviet intelligence would not have risked exposing one of its most important underground operations to such close surveillance.

'We were recruited individually and we operated individually,' Philby has declared. But all the evidence points to his recruitment and control of the Cambridge agents by the same highly sophisticated illegal. Blunt admitted as much when he told MI5 that his recruitment by Burgess was orchestrated by a middle-class Eastern European whom he knew only as 'Otto'. Blunt described him as being 'short with no neck and swept back straight hair'. But despite being shown volume after volume from the extensive MI5 Registry of photographs of Soviet agents and suspects, Blunt never matched a face and name to this individual he vaguely recalled as being Czech.

'For some reason, we were never able to identify "Otto",' Peter Wright of MI5 wrote, disclosing that two other members of the Cambridge ring, Philby and Cairncross, had told MI5 about their contacts with the mysterious 'Otto' also without knowing or revealing his real name. During his 'confession' to MI5 officer

Nicholas Elliott in Beirut shortly before his defection in 1963, Philby said that 'Otto' was a Comintern agent he had met in Vienna.

Wright concedes he was never able to identify 'Otto'. Nor did anyone else in MI5 discover why Blunt and the other surviving members of the Cambridge network were so determined to preserve the identity of the mysterious Eastern European who between 1939 and 1940 was their mentor and link with Moscow.

What Blunt was doing to MI5 is what the fox does to the hounds: double back on his own trail and watch the pack rush by. First Blunt insists that he had to have been recruited by Burgess in 1936, which we now know to be untrue. Blunt also says that a man named Theodore Maly had recruited Philby, Maclean and Burgess. Then Blunt denies ever meeting Maly because he had been recalled from England in '1936–37', so he had to be recruited by the mysterious 'Otto'. It is here that the fox doubles back on his trail, because there *is* evidence that Maly was in England after the date that Blunt gave. Furthermore, Maly was engaged in other espionage activities besides recruiting the Cambridge spy ring. The Registry file on Maly must have been thick and complex because he operated under a series of aliases, including the names of Paul Hardt and Peters. Maly also appears to have been the principal NKVD *illegal* operating in England from 1932 through 1937.

Maly also fits exactly with Philby's assertion that the recruiter was 'not a Russian but working for the Russians.' One of the most remarkable non-Russian Comintern agents who ever served as undercover Soviet intelligence officers, Maly was a newly ordained Hungarian priest, who became a regimental chaplain with the Austro-Hungarian army when World War I broke out. Captured by the tsar's army on the Carpathian front, he was horrified by the starvation and disease in the prisoner of war camps.

'I lost my faith in God, and when the revolution broke out I joined the Bolsheviks,' Maly once told a friend, explaining how service with the Cheka and Red Army during the brutal civil war against the Whites had hardened him. Like many of the foreign Communists who served Dzerzhinski, Maly played a key role in the burgeoning Soviet intelligence apparatus in the twenties. But Mikhail Trilisser recognized that Maly's real value to the *apparat* sprang from his passionate pride and his intellect and charm. Maly's ability to pass himself off as a cultivated European intellectual made it easy for him to recruit young left-wing Oxbridge intellectuals for the Soviets' secret global crusade.

Early in 1932, using the alias of Paul Hardt, Maly arrived in London as an illegal resident with the immediate assignment of running King and Oldham, the spies in the Foreign Office. When King was finally arrested in 1940, the payments made to his bank account led back to one of the key subsidiary operatives in Maly's network, Bernard Davidovich Gadar, another illegal Soviet agent. Moscow had established him in an appropriately nondescript company, a rag business in London's seedy East End, which served as a front. Gadar acted both as paymaster and communication point, while Maly assumed the role of a business representative who traveled extensively in search of waste linen.

According to a friend who knew him in Moscow before he left for London, Maly was 'a handsome, tall Hungarian with blue eyes and the charming smile of the naturally shy.' By a strange quirk of fate, Maly's younger brother was making his career as a pianist and he attended one of his brother's concerts in London, but shrank from making contact with his dead past. Theodore was an articulate idealist in his mid-forties, and his dedication to his Communist beliefs was so complete that he willingly returned to Moscow in 1937 at the height of Stalin's purges, even though he knew he was going to his death. 'They betray their own people,' Maly explained to his Comintern friend Elizabeth Poretsky before leaving England. 'They will enjoy killing a Communist.'

It is not difficult to conceive how Maly's inspirational faith made such a powerful impression on young Cambridge minds in search of a new God. Blunt told Peter Wright that Maly's 'students worshipped him.' Although Blunt claimed that his recruitment came too late for him to hear the message for himself from the blue-eyed Theo, Blunt later told Wright 'on many occasions' that he would not have joined the cause if the appeal had been made to him by a Russian.

Blunt's glowing and supposedly secondhand testimonial for Maly's abilities contrasts oddly with his inability to recall anything more about the mysterious 'Otto' than his thick neck and swept-back hair. There is other evidence that Maly must have been the principal recruiter of the Cambridge ring.

First, there is general agreement that Maly recruited Philby and Maclean. So if Blunt was recruited anytime between 1934 and 1937, then Maly had to have been the one to bring him in.

Second, from what is now known about Maly's career, he possessed the intellectual resourcefulness, engaging personality and social sophistication that was needed to win Blunt's respect. It must have taken a person of extreme subtlety to mold, motivate and direct Blunt's orientation to serve Moscow. His recruiter and initial controller confronted a formidable challenge as Noël Annan's assessment of Blunt makes plain. Blunt, he wrote, was a 'fascinator', who baited his conversation with 'inside gossip' and had 'too much hauteur to be a charmer'. But Blunt was more than fascinating. 'He was a manipulator. He wanted more than most people in academic life to have his own way, appoint his own protégés and rule the roost.' Blunt may never have responded to the spiritual appeal of communism, but Maly, a former priest who had served both the old and new gods, would have generated seductive echoes that rang deeply in the empty well left by Blunt's rejection of his religious upbringing. Maly would also have played upon Blunt's vanity by inflating the importance of the role that he could play in the grand international design for world communism.

Since Michael Straight's testimony shows that Blunt was acting as a Soviet agent in the spring of 1937, he could only have been operating at Maly's direction. We have only Blunt's word that he was not recruited by Maly, because the fact is that Blunt was lying about when Maly left London. Telling proof that Maly was still fully operational as late as April 1937 comes from the evidence of his involvement in the celebrated Woolwich Arsenal case. The rounding up of a Soviet spy ring in the all-important government-run armaments factory just down the River Thames from historic Greenwich Palace, has always been portrayed as one of MI5's most successful operations.

This was thanks to Maxwell Knight, a former merchant-navy officer who joined MI5 in 1925 and who applied the field craft he had learned as a poacher in the salmon rivers of south Devon to his counterintelligence operations. The successes of Olga Gray, a bright thirty-year-old secretary, in penetrating the headquarters of Britain's Communist party came with her employment at Party headquarters. For the next three years Gray reported to Maxwell Knight from the heart of the King Street headquarters of the CPGB.

In February 1937, Percy Glading, a Moscow trained British Communist, asked Gray to set up a safe house that could serve as a photographic workshop for copying documents from the Royal Arsenal at Woolwich. In April she met the handsome 'Mr Peters', who she was told was an Austrian who had served as a captain in the Russian cavalry after spending some time in a monastery. From Gray's description of Peters, Knight had little difficulty identifying him as Theodore Maly.

Gray did not see 'Peters' again. He was briefly replaced by someone she described as a 'rather bumptious man', and, in August, Glading brought 'Mr and Mrs Stevens' to the flat and told Gray that she would receive a five-pounds-a-week pay raise to act as their assistant. Checking Gray's description of the 'Stevenses' against Registry records, Knight was able to establish that they were a Romanian-born Jewish couple, Willy and Mary Brandes.

Recently recovered after gathering dust for nearly half a century, MI5 reports in the American archives reveal that the British knew from their port records that the passports issued to the Brandeses had been 'unlawfully obtained'. The Brandeses were identified as Soviet NKVD illegals who had arrived in Britain in

January 1937. At that time Willy Brandes was using the cover of a traveling salesman for the Phantome Red Cosmetics Company of New York and an agent for the Charak Furniture Company. Both these companies were controlled by Americans of Russian descent whom the FBI suspected of being Russian agents.

Olga Gray reported to Knight that when the Brandeses used the photographic equipment they instructed her to remain in the bedroom. But on 21 October she managed to obtain blueprint numbers from some photographic plates hung up to dry. Woolwich Arsenal records confirmed that these were top-secret plans for a new 14-inch naval gun. MI5 officers took up watch and tailed Mary Brandes to Hyde Park, where she passed a bundle to a gray-haired man later identified as George Whomack, an engineering foreman in the naval department at the arsenal.

The trap had been sprung, and the British knew that they had two key NKVD agents in the bag. But no arrests were made! On 2 November, Glading told Gray that the 'Stevenses' were leaving for Moscow because their daughter was ill. He said they would 'probably never return' and that there would be no work for her until Christmas. The Brandeses left for Paris on 6 November.

What is so puzzling about the Woolwich Arsenal case is that MI5 did not move in promptly to roll up the spy ring before the two Soviet agents most deeply involved left the country. Instead, MI5 waited more than a month before moving in.

At 8:15 on the morning of 21 January, Glading went down into the lavatory at Charing Cross Station. There he handed over a parcel to Albert Williams, a Woolwich Arsenal carpenter. The police swooped and arrested them both as they made their way up the stairs to the station platform. Special Branch officers picked up Charles Munday and George Whomack a few hours later; and all were charged at Bow Street police station with offenses under the Official Secrets Act.

The trial of the Woolwich Arsenal spies made headlines in the first week of February 1938. The jury found Glading and all but one of his fellow conspirators, against whom charges were dropped, guilty. The judge handed out stiff prison sentences and praised the 'extraordinary courage' of the patriotic blonde who was publicly identified for her own protection only as 'Miss X'. Olga Gray observed with bitter amusement how the popular press transformed her into a glamorously seductive counterspy, an overnight sensation. Max Knight was promoted to take charge of his own department, which mounted clandestine operations from an independent base in Dolphin Square, a block of luxury flats overlooking the River Thames.

Fifty years later, American records show the Woolwich Arsenal was far from the sensational counterintelligence coup it was made out to be at the time. MI5 may have succeeded in knocking out an important Comintern espionage operation, but only the British end of the ring ended up in jail. Not just one, but three principal Soviet agents implicated in the ring managed to escape arrest. Some might argue that there was insufficient evidence in April to arrest Theo Maly for espionage. But at the very least he could have been taken into custody as he tried to leave Britain on his false passport. Moreover, six months later, when the time was ripe for MI5 to move against his successors, the Brandeses were also permitted to escape, even though we can now see that MI5 had clear proof that they were involved in espionage.

Why were the Brandeses permitted to leave the country five days after MI5 received the warning that these top Soviet operatives were about to depart for Moscow? The hitherto accepted version is that MI5 watchers looked on helplessly on 6 November 1937, as 'Mr and Mrs Stevens' loaded their luggage into a taxi at Fonset House in the Edgware Road and drove to Victoria Station. This revelation comes from Nigel West, a British writer and authority on intelligence. West told me that there was a 'debate', presumably between the senior MI5 officers involved, Guy Liddell and Knight, about the 'advisability of allowing two Soviet agents to leave the country.' But West – on good authority – says, 'Eventually it was decided that, since they both could claim diplomatic immunity if arrested, there was little to gain by taking them into custody.'

If this information reflects MI5's 'official' justification for letting the Soviet agents slip away, it is made nonsense of by the recent discovery of the contemporary reports on the Brandeses' false Canadian papers. These show that MI5 cannot have been under any illusion that the couple had diplomatic immunity. The British knew by November that the Brandeses were Soviet *illegals* operating under the name of Stevens – a false 'legend' unlawfully obtained in Canada.

Yet MI5 was left to round up the small fry after a high-level decision allowed the big fish to slip through the net.

Why the Soviet spymasters were allowed to escape now becomes the important question: chance, miscalculation, or deliberate tipoffs are the only possible explanations.

Chance or miscalculation may well have played a part. But to paraphrase one of Oscar Wilde's more abrasive aphorisms: to lose one spy may be regarded as a misfortune, but to lose both looks like carelessness. If MI5's failure was the result of carelessness or miscalculation, the very fact of its repetition – first Maly, then the Brandeses – suggests negligence, bungling – or worse. Was there another leak in MI5 as there appeared to have been at the time of the Arcos raid? The possibility that some senior MI5 officer had tipped off the Soviets was as unthinkable in 1927 as it was in 1937. But after Blunt, Maclean, Burgess, Philby et al., it is surely not farfetched to consider the possibility that in the Woolwich Arsenal case the Soviets were tipped off, not once, but twice, that their principal London agent had been unmasked.

The fact remains that the British let Maly and the Brandeses slip through their fingers. The evidence that Maly was instrumental in the foundation and running of the Cambridge network may also explain why Blunt and Philby both went to great lengths to camouflage the fact that his role as their controller continued until his recall in the early summer of 1937. The invocation of the mysterious 'Otto' has, according to a consensus of American intelligence officers, all the appearances of a classic disinformation ruse. The Soviets always provided their agents with a well-rehearsed cover story based on information likely to be in the possession of their interrogator. Only when additional incriminating information has been disclosed will an agent under interrogation construct a new story based on what he has learned. And any new admission is designed to produce a sense of victory in the mind of the interrogator.

Another tantalizing clue about Otto appears in Peter Wright's *Spycatcher* with reference to documents which Blunt removed from the Registry. No information is given about the documents, but the implication is plain.

Even though the MI5 Registry data were supposed to be inviolable, other cases of the removal and destruction of files has emerged. In 1941 Max Knight personally removed reports on the disruptive personal behaviour of a Royal Marine officer he wanted to bring into MI5. Any Soviet-directed cleanup carried out by Blunt and Philby – both of whom had access to the Registry files during the war years – would not have been limited to settling private scores. The extent to which they were able to doctor the records by removing or altering incriminating documents can only be guessed at.

This may be one reason why tracking down the truth about Blunt's network proved so difficult. But, as Nigel West has revealed to me, the 'sanitizing' of the Cambridge network files was not simply a matter of unauthorized deletions. 'The MI5 files on Burgess and Maclean were all rewritten after 1951,' West said, assuring me that his sources for this information were 'absolutely reliable'.

'The first time that an MI5 file was altered, so far as I have been able to establish, was the Fuchs file,' West said. In 1946, the Registry records on atom spy Klaus Fuchs contained sufficient indications that the nuclear scientist might be a security risk. But nothing was done. To cover up the failure, MI5 records were doctored after the FBI produced the evidence that led to Fuchs's confession in 1950.

The Burgess and Maclean files as they now exist in MI5 – presumably the ones Wright relied on in 1963 – were, according to West, 'manufactured' to remove any evidence of negligence.

Under the direction of Deputy Director General Guy Liddell, the files were completely reconstructed with the object of demonstrating that there had been no MI5 foul-up. West said that one of the purposes of the changes was to show that Burgess *had been under investigation* at the time of his defection. This simply was not true, according to West's source. This alleged investigation was also mentioned in the 1955 White Paper issued by the British government on the missing diplomats.

The 'reconstituted' Burgess–Maclean file was presented as a peace offering to the FBI in an effort to 'prove' that MI5's record was clear. But it was 'all garbage', as West put it. He explained how Sir Percy Sillitoe, the then Director General, and investigator Arthur Martin were sent to Washington in June 1951 with the doctored files. The FBI, however, had been mounting its own intensive investigation, and was not taken in. When William C. Sullivan, J. Edgar Hoover's deputy director for domestic intelligence, read the offering, he exploded with indignation. He dismissed the MI5 report as 'horseshit!' And an embarrassed Arthur Martin could only offer an uncomfortable smile.

There is another twist to the story: what Arthur Martin and MI5 didn't know was that the FBI already had evidence pointing to Burgess's involvement in a high-level homosexual ring with disturbing Communist connections.

10 'Assisting Lord Rothschild'

The FBI files on Burgess and Maclean reveal why the Americans were furious.

The day after the news broke in the press about the disappearance of the British diplomats, the MI6 and MI5 liaison officers stationed at the British embassy in Washington went downtown to a meeting at FBI headquarters. Kim Philby and Geoffrey Paterson called on Robert J. Lamphere. The thirty-two-year-old Lamphere, a native of Idaho, was then the bureau's deputy chief of counterintelligence, and he recalls that it was an uncomfortable meeting.

'My discussion with Philby and Paterson went nowhere,' Lamphere says. He was angered because he was convinced that MI5 had been keeping the results of its own investigations into Maclean from the FBI.

Lamphere had every reason to be suspicious. In 1949 he had received firm evidence from signals intelligence sources in the US Army showing that Moscow had a highly placed spy inside the British embassy in Washington in 1944. But the British seemed to drag their feet in investigating the matter.

'We decided that the British were holding out on us, and we decided to go after everyone we could find who knew anything about Burgess and Maclean.' That was how Lamphere explained the massive FBI investigation that got under way *after* the FBI learned of the diplomats' defection at the end of May 1951. A secretary at the British embassy, who had worked for Burgess, was questioned and reluctantly disclosed that she remembered Burgess had been in touch several times with the writer Christopher Isherwood.

On 16 July, orders went out by telegraph to the Los Angeles

Bureau of the FBI. The following day one of its best field agents headed toward the Pacific Palisades to track down the expatriate British writer. Best known as the author of *Goodbye to Berlin*, the novel that inspired the musical *Cabaret*, Isherwood had come to America as a refugee from England in 1939 with the poet W. H. Auden. Brushing off the accusations of moral and physical cowardice made by their contemporaries who stayed to fight Hitler, these literary giants made no attempt in their new homeland to conceal their left-wing opinions or their homosexuality.

'It was Christopher Isherwood who really opened up the whole can of worms,' says Lamphere. With the sharp, cameralike focus with which he had limned the denizens of the Berlin underworld, Isherwood now portrayed for the FBI the decadence of prewar London's homosexual literary scene. Burgess, he explained, was pathetically desperate to be 'in on everything significant'. He also identified more than a dozen contacts who were under Burgess's influence or close friends of his.

'The names of well-known writers like Auden and Spender leaped off the page when I read the report from Los Angeles,' Lamphere recalls. The names are blacked out, however, in the copies released under the Freedom of Information Act. The bureau, it seems, is still bound by the secret Anglo-American intelligence agreement dating back to World War I that requires compliance with a formal request by the British authorities to withhold intelligence about British citizens. But the FBI reports in the Presidential Libraries are more complete, and sufficient textual clues survive, plus the tops and bottoms of letters missed by the censor, to make it possible to reconstruct the list of people that the FBI knew were close associates of Burgess.

'What we dug up alarmed and astonished us,' Lamphere says. 'We could not believe that the British would have allowed such people access to their diplomatic and security services.'

Deciphering these reports nearly four decades later, it is not hard to appreciate the sinking feeling they must have caused in FBI headquarters in July 1951. It would have been especially true in connection with one name that, surprisingly, survived the sanitizer's pen. Isherwood revealed that Lord Inverchapel was associated with Burgess in 1936. He was the British ambassador to Washington from 1947 to 1949, on whose staff Maclean served. More intriguing still is the discovery that Isherwood told the FBI that Burgess's closest friend was 'a person named Tony'. Not until his second interview did Isherwood recall that the mysterious Tony's surname was Blunt.

'We did not at the time realize the full implications of all the names – or the Cambridge connection,' Lamphere conceded after reviewing the FBI reports I showed him, the originals of which he had puzzled over thirty-seven years earlier. 'We could not figure out how Inverchapel or Blunt fitted into the puzzle, or even Philby's connection to Burgess and Maclean. But we concluded that Philby had somehow been involved in their disappearance.'

The FBI then sent out agents to track down leads about anyone who might have been only remotely associated with Burgess and Maclean in the United States. The scale of the operation, judging from the pile of interview reports it produced, puts to shame the genteel and restricted investigation that was alleged to have been carried out simultaneously by MI5 in Britain. Had the British extended their sweep to include gas station attendants, restaurant waitresses, secretaries and university friends who had contact with the missing diplomats as did the Americans, it must have exposed Blunt immediately.

By July 1951, as Lamphere confirms, even though the FBI did not have all the pieces of the puzzle, the agency knew that Burgess had associated with German Communists in a homosexual network whose connection reached into the highest echelons of the Foreign Office and Britain's security services.

Lamphere had the daunting job of preparing the briefings of this information for J. Edgar Hoover. Defaced though these briefings are by the censor's deletions, a clear pattern emerges. At the height of Senator Joseph McCarthy's campaign against Communists in the US government, the reek of sexual misconduct and left-wing chicanery on the part of Burgess and his Foreign Office friends must have fired Hoover's puritanical fury. The FBI could do little more than speculate about the Cambridge network: it did not matter that they suspected that MI5 was deliberately keeping them in the dark. The FBI played it straight. It methodically passed on what it had learned from Isherwood and the others to the MI5 liaison officer in the British embassy. These reports, for some obscure historical reason, were addressed to the British embassy using the code name SMOTH.

'I suppose you could call us naïve – and in those days we were rather green about such matters,' says Lamphere. But as he explained, Hoover had little choice but to put on a show of cooperation with the British intelligence services, whom he disliked and distrusted only marginally less than his new rivals in the CIA. But the FBI now had the hard evidence to prove that MI5 had made a determined effort to pull the wool over their eyes about the true significance of the defections of Burgess and Maclean.

Within two months of Burgess's defection, Lamphere, with the help of his FBI colleagues in the Los Angeles office, had identified the key members of the prewar circle around Burgess and Blunt. They learned how the group frequented the Café Royal, the gilt and plush London restaurant that had been a favorite watering hole for Oscar Wilde fifty years earlier. Isherwood said that he pitied Burgess, who drank too much and was 'a confirmed social climber and pretty obvious in his tactics.'

Isherwood also told the FBI that high-ranking members of Parliament and diplomats were among Burgess's favorite targets. His allusions to 'close friendships' left little doubt that a powerful undercurrent of homosexuality explained Burgess's association with Harold Nicolson and senior members of the Foreign Office such as Lord Inverchapel.

For the Americans, the most worrying of Isherwood's revelations was that Burgess had been a close associate of Lord Inverchapel. A Scot with florid features and a large nose, Archibald Clark Kerr was an eccentric in a career where eccentricity was usually a hindrance. But he had risen to the top despite his preference for bagpipes over bridge and the relaxing company of personable young left-wing intellects rather than diplomatic receptions. His peerage came with his appointment as Britain's envoy to Moscow in 1942. Five years later, when he arrived in Washington, his eccentricity caused unhappiness in the State Department and his Russian valet caused extreme discomfort to the director of the FBI.

Robert Cecil, who came to know Inverchapel well, described him as a lonely but nonetheless genial superior. He had first met Clark Kerr in the Baghdad embassy before the war and later served under him in Washington. Like other senior members of the embassy staff, Cecil knew about his bedroom eccentricities.

'There was no doubt in my mind that he was bisexual,' Cecil says. Inverchapel had taken a petite blonde Chilean woman as his wife, only to divorce her for desertion and then remarry her on his appointment to Washington. His Lordship's private secretary in Moscow had told Cecil that the ambassador's attitude to sex was: 'If it moves, go for it!'

Cecil doubts that Inverchapel could have been a witting traitor. He did not have the right psychological makeup for a spy: 'He was too sentimentally stupid about the Russians and too bluff to have been a mole like Philby.' But Cecil concedes that Inverchapel's strong left-wing sympathies and cozy wartime relationship with Stalin would have made the British ambassador a very useful agent of influence.

New evidence has come to light, however, that suggests that Inverchapel's naïve enthusiasm for the Soviet Union may have been more sinister than Cecil or the Foreign Office suspected.

In 1933, after the newly knighted Sir Archibald Clark Kerr arrived in Sweden, it is now known that he became an intimate friend of Stig Wennestrom. This Swedish air-force officer, although grounded by his lack of competence as a pilot, had taken on an astonishing career of espionage. When he was eventually unmasked in 1963, Wennestrom admitted he was a deep-penetration agent for Moscow and had secretly held the rank of major general in the KGB. Nor was Wennestrom the only known Soviet agent whom Inverchapel befriended in his career.

While ambassador to China in the late thirties, Clark Kerr had become an enthusiastic admirer of Mao Tse-tung and the Chinese Communists. He also maintained suspiciously close personal links to the Soviet military attaché, who, according to a former member of Britain's legation, was a frequent late-night visitor to the ambassador's residence.

'Archie', as he was known to his friends, sponsored Günther Stein, a German journalist with Comintern connections, in a successful application for British naturalization papers. He also recommended him for journalistic assignments that enabled him to travel all over the Far East on the eve of World War II. US Army Intelligence learned during its postwar investigation of Richard Sorge's spy ring that Stein had been a key member of the Red Army's Far Eastern GRU network.

The amiable pipe-smoking ambassador never made a secret of his sympathy for the Soviet Union. He was given to lecturing his Foreign Office colleagues on this favorite topic and they tolerated his 'steady passion for the Soviet Union,' regarding it, like his bisexuality, as just another harmless eccentricity in a veteran diplomat.

Yet even if Inverchapel was not a 'spy' in the strict sense of the word, the evidence suggests that the Foreign Office blundered in its failure to appreciate that his sexual peccadilloes, and his favorable view of Russia, made him a major security risk. Whether the ambassador's passion for the Soviet Union was a clever camouflage for a more sinister purpose may never be known. But during wartime visits to London, he held parties for English intellectuals sympathetic to Russian writers. Soviet diplomats were guests at those receptions, as was Blunt's school friend Louis MacNeice and former Communist Stephen Spender. Inverchapel did not restrict himself merely to improving cultural relations. In 1944, he was a leading advocate in pressing the Foreign Office to accede to Stalin's demand for the forcible repatriation of all Soviet citizens.

The rapport that Inverchapel established with the Soviet dictator cannot be attributed simply to a mutually shared devotion to pipe-smoking or to huddling together in the Kremlin shelter during German air raids on Moscow. The ambassador was so cozy with the Soviet dictator that he secured the release from prison of a Red Army deserter whose sister was on the British embassy staff. Instead of facing a firing squad, Yevgeny Yost found himself presented – like some medieval serf – as a valet to Inverchapel when he left Moscow and returned to London at the end of 1944.

It was the presence of the Soviet valet, when Inverchapel arrived in Washington two years later, that raised eyebrows of State Department officials – and the hackles of J. Edgar Hoover at the FBI. Well past retirement age, Inverchapel owed his posting to his left-wing sympathies, which appealed to Labour Foreign Secretary Ernest Bevin.

'Inverchapel was no stuffed shirt, but he was a dead loss as our ambassador to the United States at this critical time in the Cold War,' Cecil declares. The ambassador dodged the press corps, avoided official receptions, and upset the State Department. But it now appears that it was Hoover's concern about his valet, Yost – who had to be sent back to England – and the ambassador's high regard for Stalin that were instrumental in effecting Inverchapel's departure in 1948 on the diplomatic pretext of 'ill health'.

Two years later, Inverchapel's former first secretary, Donald Maclean, defected. The FBI's suspicions about the ex-ambassador were then given a further dimension after Isherwood's revelation about his intimate friendship with Burgess, whose homosexual coterie had included a German expatriate named Rudolph Katz. 'Rolf', as Isherwood referred to him, was an old friend from his days in Berlin in 1931.

On 28 June 1951, the FBI had tracked down Katz in New York. He was staying at the St Regis Hotel on what he claimed was a business trip. Yes, he admitted he had known Burgess between 1936 and 1938, at which time they had fallen out, although he admitted receiving 'infrequent letters' from Burgess afterward. Katz was careful to insist that he had no reason 'to suspect that Burgess had been a member of a Russian espionage ring.'

Katz was evasive about why he had left Britain in 1940. Inquiries to London revealed that Katz had been 'ordered out of England due to homosexual contacts with British naval personnel.' While his sexual predations may have gotten him into trouble with the British police, it was believed that Katz really crossed the Atlantic to Argentina to escape an internment camp for enemy aliens. In Buenos Aires he became the editor of a successful economic journal.

We can now see, however, that what Katz told the FBI about how he had first met Burgess provided an important and hitherto missing link in the complex web of intrigue surrounding Blunt and his Cambridge spies. As reported to Hoover in the approved bureaucratic style: 'Rudolph Katz advised that he met Burgess in England in 1936 when he was assisting Lord Rothschild. Burgess was a social acquaintance of the Rothschild family.'

Heavy black ink erases the details of precisely what assistance a German Communist could have been providing the Rothschilds. But despite Katz's protestations that his relationship with Burgess had been 'purely social', Isherwood had already told the FBI that 'Burgess worked with Katz for a while in 1936–37 or 1937–38 in the publication of a magazine which devoted itself to surveys of economic and political matters.' Since Katz had later run a successful investment and stock magazine in Buenos Aires, his association with Burgess in 1936 provides a clue to explaining why the Rothschilds regarded Burgess as a budding financial analyst – one of the most enigmatic of the myths at the heart of the Blunt affair.

Michael Straight has always been puzzled, ever since Burgess revealed himself as a dedicated Marxist in the fall of 1935, exactly how Burgess's communism allowed him to accept the hundred pounds a month he supposedly received to act as investment counselor to Mrs Charles Rothschild. This amount was four or five times more than Burgess's contemporaries might have anticipated earning. Thanks to Rudolph Katz, the myth of Burgess as a financial wizard now takes a different twist. It was Katz who did the real work that allowed Burgess to claim that he was acting as an investment adviser. *The Daily Express*, on 14 June 1951, the first newspaper to break the story of the disappearing diplomats, Burgess and Maclean, mentioned Burgess's friendship with 'Rolf Katz, a chunky man in his fifties,' who was 'an important Comintern agent'.

When the FBI interviewed Isherwood he was apprehensive. The McCarthy 'hysteria' in 1951 encouraged him to play down Katz's Communist connections. He conceded that his old Berlin friend was 'undoubtedly leftist' and might once have been involved in publishing a Comintern newspaper in Berlin. While Katz 'at one time had probably adhered to the Communist party' Isherwood said that he believed him to be a 'sort of real old classical Marxist'.

The FBI had little difficulty penetrating Isherwood's smoke-screen. They discovered that Katz was already an active Communist when he knew Burgess in London in 1936. German police and Gestapo records captured during the war confirmed that Katz, an economist, had joined the KPD (Kommunistische Partei Deutschlands) in 1921. His credentials also included his time as a correspondent for *Imprecor*, the journal of the Comintern. The KPD, which had received six million votes in the 1932 elections to the Reichstag, had been the third largest political party in Germany. But Moscow's orders forbidding its joining in a united front with the socialists emasculated the KPD in its bid to prevent the Nazis from taking over control of the German parliament the following year.

Like most of the leading KPD activists, Rudolph Katz fled from Germany. He went to France in 1933. This was after Hitler had charged the Communists with setting the fire that gutted the Berlin Reichstag building on the last night of February. When the KPD leaders, Walter Ulbricht and Wilhelm Pieck, who became the postwar bosses of East Germany, arrived in Moscow, Stalin changed policies and called on all Communist parties to join in a united front against Fascism.

The Comintern leader who brilliantly succeeded in translating Moscow's Popular Front policy into a political and propaganda reality was Willi Münzenberg, a bearlike man who was the organizational genius of the KPD. MI5 records show that Guy Liddell had been tracking Münzenberg ever since the early twenties when he emerged as the force behind the Workers International Relief. The success of this organization, known in party slang as 'The Münzenberg Trust', spawned The League Against Imperialism whose headquarters were quickly reestablished in Paris. By May 1933, MI5 was warning the Americans that Münzenberg was back in business. This time Münzenberg's masterstroke was the creation of The World Committee for the Relief of the Victims of German Fascism. It launched an international juridical commission to investigate the Reichstag fire. These hearings at the Law Society in London, under Sir Stafford Cripps, a prominent Labour-party lawyer, exposed the Nazis' plan to make the Communists the scapegoats for the blaze.

British agents were successful in penetrating Münzenberg's outfit because the following year, they were able to alert the Americans that Münzenberg and his aide, Louis Gibarti, were en route to New York to address rallies in an attempt to establish a US branch of the anti-Fascist front. It was a classic Münzenberg creation, skillfully window-dressed with an international committee of worthy non-Communist liberal and socialist figureheads. When the Spanish Civil War broke out, the front threw its support to the Republicans.

Münzenberg had the popular reputation of being a 'Red Millionaire', not in terms of money but in the remarkable power he wielded in his organizations. He was 'the grey eminence and invisible organizer of the anti-Fascist world crusade,' according to the writer Arthur Koestler, who worked for the French publisher of the so-called Brown Books that documented the 'Hitler Terror'. The actual author was Münzenberg's chief lieutenant, a Czech named Otto Katz (no relation to Rolf). This former avantgarde Berlin theater director had been a friend in Prague of the author Franz Kafka and had attended one of the Comintern schools in Moscow. By 1929, when he had earned Münzenberg's confidence, Otto was already a trained agent of the NKVD under orders to monitor Münzenberg.

Otto Katz was a 'smooth slick operator', a dark and handsome man who possessed what Koestler called a 'seedy charm'. Otto's literary skills and facility with half a dozen languages made him indispensable to Münzenberg's proliferating organizations. Posing as 'Ludwig Breda', an Austrian journalist, or as a French writer by the name of 'André Simone', Otto travelled widely and stealthily as a contact man and fixer in European capitals. He helped Münzenberg organize the Reichstag countertrial, promoted the Republican cause in Spain and the 1937 International Writers Conference in Paris. This literary circus, which E. M. Forster attended, demonstrated the solidarity of intellectuals in the Popular Front against Fascism and Nazism.

The purges that had begun with the Moscow show trials of Zinoviev and Kamenev in 1936 eroded the intellectual unity of the Popular Front. Münzenberg, too, was soon purged from his Comintern propaganda empire, a fall from grace that began with a dispute with Ulbricht and expulsion from the KPD in October 1937. The following year he broke with Stalin and on Moscow's orders, Otto Katz had obediently attacked Münzenberg.

MI5 concluded by 1938 that Münzenberg's expulsion from the Comintern was no ruse, because the charges of Trotskyite contacts were 'equivalent to political liquidation in the Stalinist movement'. Undaunted, Münzenberg continued his anti-Nazi campaign through 1939, now with the support of the French government through a network of secret broadcasting stations. But macabre confirmation of Liddell's judgement call was to come in 1940, when Münzenberg's decomposed corpse was found with wire around its neck, under an oak tree in the forest of Caugnet a hundred miles southeast of Lyons.

State Department records seem to rule out Otto Katz's direct complicity in Münzenberg's murder, but he was implicated in the 1948 murder of the non-Communist Czechoslovak foreign minister, Jan Mazaryk, shortly after the Communists took control of the Czech government. The Byzantine settling of old scores did not come until 1952, when he was hanged in a Prague prison yard on 3 December 1952, after confessing to being a 'Trotskyist,

Titoist traitor and enemy of the Czech people in the service of American imperialism.'

Yet Otto Katz appears to have played a useful decoy role from the grave, since Philby and Blunt's references to a mysterious controller named 'Otto' are clearly an identikit description of Otto Katz. An even more enigmatic turn to the Münzenberg–Otto Katz saga was provided by Ellen Wilkinson, the feisty red-headed ex-Communist and longtime Labour MP from Jarrow. Before her death in 1947, Wilkinson confided that Münzenberg had once informed her that both he and Koestler, who escaped to England in 1938, had an enemy in the British counter-intelligence service.

The suggestion that some ranking MI5 officer might already have been working silently for Moscow as early as 1938 deserves attention. The MI5 records reveal that Otto Katz was known to be a key figure in the Comintern fronts and his Communist namesake, Rudolph – with whom Otto has often been confused – was permitted to reside in London until 1940. The ease with which the two Katzes and many of their German KPD associates were able to operate in Britain must raise questions about the quality of MI5's surveillance. What is particularly puzzling is the revelation that in 1933 the British Cabinet *was* alerted to the danger of subversion by the Communist activities among the German refugees fleeing to England. No less an authority than the minister responsible for MI5, Home Secretary Sir John Gilmour, advised the British Cabinet of 'a risk that the influx of refugees from Germany may include a certain number of Communists.'

It was not just the two Katzes; there was another German Communist party member in London, a Jew of Polish extraction named Jürgen Kuczynski, who even managed to obtain a government post as a statistician. One of his contacts was Klaus Fuchs, who came to England to continue his physics studies at Bristol University. Fuchs was eventually granted citizenship and given a top-security clearance to work on the British atomic-bomb project, although it has been claimed that in 1934, MI5 opened a file on him because of his KPD associations.

So it is unlikely that Rudolph Katz could have remained in London without coming to MI5's attention. Piecing together what the FBI learned from Isherwood, it is clear that Burgess's association with the expatriate Rudolph Katz provided him with the convenient claim to have been a financial adviser to the Rothschilds. It is a matter of record that Katz's weekly financial newsletter failed through inaccurate forecasts and lack of subscribers. Even Rothschild's astute sister, Miriam, has admitted that she very much doubts that Burgess's advice can possibly have been worth his large fee because she recalls that he was 'out of his depth' in financial matters, and that his role as her mother's 'financial adviser' might have been a convenient cover. The question therefore arises, if Katz was the financial analyst, what service was Burgess providing?

An important clue is provided by Rudolph Katz himself: he told the FBI that Burgess 'was helping a group of individuals who were acting as consultants to Winston Churchill, and that Burgess's field was Russia and India.' One of the single most bizarre elements in the quixotic career of Guy Burgess is that while he was a secret Marxist, and a salaried consultant to the Rothschilds, he also became a member of the pro-Hitler right wing of the Tory party. And when he failed to obtain a post in the Conservative central office, through his friendship with Harold Nicolson, with his many connections in the Establishment homosexual network, Burgess succeeded in infiltrating himself as the secretary and personal assistant to a newly elected, right-wing Conservative MP. Captain John Robert Macnamara was a thirty-year-old ex-guards officer who had won the plum seat of Chelmsford for the Tories in the November General Election of 1935. He shared Burgess's sexual tastes, and the latter, acting the role of the servant who is really the master, served as his political counselor and procurer. Through 'Captain Jack', Burgess met Macnamara's financial sponsor, the Venerable J. H. Sharp, the homosexual heir to a Dundee jute-mill fortune who had taken holy orders, and who was then the Church of England's archdeacon in southeastern Europe.

In the spring of 1936, the trio set off for the Rhineland,
accompanied by Macnamara's friend Tom Wylie, a young official
in the War Office. Ostensibly they were escorting a group of
pro-Fascist schoolboys to a Hitler Youth camp. But from Burgess's uproariously bawdy account of how his companions discovered that the *Hitlerjugend* satisfied their sexual and political
passions, the trip would have shocked their sponsors – the
Foreign Relations Council of the Church of England.

Macnamara was not, however, simply just another member of
the post-World War I generation of Cambridge homosexuals like
Christopher Isherwood and John Lehmann, for example, for
whom the muscular blondness of the Nordic males had a powerful erotic appeal. Captain Jack was an outspoken advocate of
improving relations with Hitler. He was one of the parliamentary
members of the Anglo-German Fellowship. He was also a member of the Link, a less reputable pro-Nazi fringe organization that
had been founded by Admiral Sir Barry Domvile when he retired
as director of Naval Intelligence in 1930.

The Anglo-German Fellowship was not, like the Link, simply a
refuge for the extremist fringe, although many of its members,
such as Captain Archibald Maule Ramsay, the MP for Peebles,
belonged to both groups. The Fellowship was an influential and
well-organized pressure group with direct connections to powerful men in the British press, banking, church and government.
Sponsored and financed by a group of leading Conservative businessmen, it boasted the support of three directors of the Bank of
England and the backing of fifty members from both houses of
Parliament. Its well-heeled members enjoyed lavish receptions at
the German embassy and at banquets bedecked with swastikas in
the fashionable Mayfair Hotel.

The Anglo-German Fellowship attracted members of the
Prince of Wales's set. The future Edward VIII was known to have
strong pro-German sympathies. Not since the balmy days before
World War I had so many of the leading names in the *Almanach
de Gotha* appeared together at the London dinner tables. The
Duchess of Brunswick, the daughter of the exiled Kaiser, the

Prince and Princess von Bismarck, and a slew of counts and barons sipped champagne with the emissaries from Berlin. The Nazi leaders were quick to seize the initiative and exploit the fascination of London society for aristocratic Fascism. They responded quickly to the call from one Conservative MP 'to advertise the merits of Germany's internal and foreign policy'. Trips to Germany to take in a Nazi rally at Nuremberg or attend the 1936 Olympic Games in Berlin became a fashionable pastime for the smart set of London. They entrained for Germany with the same excited enthusiasm with which their undergraduate sons were making their uncomfortable pilgrimages to Moscow and Leningrad.

One new recruit to the Anglo-German Fellowship who did not go to Germany was Kim Philby. He had joined the Fellowship in 1936, but not because of admiration for Hitler. He became a dutiful supporter of Anglo-German reconciliation at the direction of his Soviet masters. His new role was to obtain information and hide even deeper his Communist past. With the assistance of Burgess, who as Macnamara's aide was a familiar figure in the Fellowship offices, Philby was introduced to Lord Mount Temple and Lord Redesdale, for whom he was soon ghosting speeches and articles. The glamorous banquets he attended while editing the Fellowship's magazine were a strange environment for the four-pound-a-week subeditor of a foundering Liberal monthly. But his friends, amazed that his political allegiances should have careened so far to the right, were fobbed off by Philby's explanation that he was doing it for money. His marriage with Litzi was on the rocks; so it was no surprise to those who knew him that within a year he would take off for Spain to cover the civil war from the Nationalist side.

Ironically, most of the leading Conservatives and businessmen Philby encountered in the Fellowship had joined because they feared communism. While their children paid tribute to the struggle against Fascism being waged by the Soviet Union and the Spanish Loyalists, their fathers saw Hitler and Nazi Germany as a bulwark against the spread of the Red Revolution from the East.

In much the same way as the Society for Cultural Relations with the USSR served as a front for furthering Stalin's objectives with the younger generation, the Anglo-German Fellowship helped shape their parents' appeasement of Hitler.

This generational schizophrenia was very much to the taste of Guy Burgess. To former left-wing Cambridge friends who expressed surprise at his newfound enthusiasm for the Nazis, Burgess shrugged off his interest with the evasive comment that 'one may as well see whether there is anything in it.'

Goronwy Rees, who renewed his own friendship with Burgess after returning from a spell in Vienna and Berlin in 1935, was not fooled. He assumed there was some deeper reason for Burgess's turnabout. In one respect, however, Burgess remained unchanged. His quick ear for gossip and adaptive mind were useful attributes for a mole. But it was Burgess's special charm and taste for homosexual philandering that propelled him, in a matter of months, into the unsuspecting arms and confidences of some of the principal pro-German members of Parliament.

So successful was Burgess at penetrating the Anglo-German Fellowship that it has always been assumed he could have been acting only under the direct orders of Moscow. This is an accusation that, interestingly enough, Burgess himself rejected. He denied that he went to Germany in 1936 as a Communist agent or that he was under Communist direction. He asserted – through Driberg – that such a suggestion was 'particularly wide of the mark'.

Burgess had many reasons to lie about many things. But this denial – made some twenty years later, from Moscow – has a ring of truth about it. The Soviets had already planted Philby, a controlled and disciplined agent, deep into the Anglo-German Fellowship movement. So it makes sense that Burgess may have been dropping a very broad hint that in 1936 he was operating in the same right-wing milieu as Philby, but under the direction of someone else.

If the Soviet NKVD did not recruit and direct Burgess to become a mole in the right wing of the Conservative party, who did?

*

The evidence pointing to the identity of Burgess's sponsor begins with two clues. The first was provided by Rudolph Katz when he told the FBI in 1951 that he met Burgess while 'assisting Lord Rothschild'. The second appeared in the biographical apologia written by Burgess's friend Tom Driberg, which derived from extensive interviews with Burgess in Moscow. In *Guy Burgess: A Portrait with Background*, there is a reference to how: 'the house of Rothschild had been deeply disturbed by Hitler's accession to power.' In truth, the Jewish banking dynasty could not fail to be sensitive to the growing Nazi threat in the 1930s. But it was the growth of pro-Germans among the city's merchant bankers and business interests, who worked together with right-wing Tories for a rapprochement with Hitler, that was most alarming to the Rothschilds.

As a potential bulwark against Bolshevism, Hitler was one thing. The increasingly hysterical anti-Semitism of the Nazis was something else. The Rothschild family shared, with other leading members of the Jewish establishment in England, the hope that subtle persuasion in Whitehall would win Jews the right to settle in Palestine.

The Rothschilds were also concerned that their hard-won social status, as accepted members of Britain's ruling class, might be endangered if they openly backed the Zionist call for an independent state of Israel. Their influential friends were quietly working to get the British government to accept Palestine as a homeland for Jewish refugees fleeing Nazi persecution. And they knew they were tiptoeing on a slippery high wire spanning the chasm between national loyalties and political compromise. Their fears increased when the Anglo-German Fellowship proclaimed the 'immense potential significance' of the growing ties between the Conservatives and Hitler. Consequently, countering the spread of Nazism became as important for the Rothschild interests, and their London Bank in New Court, as it was to dispossessed Jewish members of the Comintern like Rudolph Katz.

The Rothschilds were no strangers to the necessity for a private intelligence network. They had been using such a sophisticated operation for more than a century. The founding father of Britain's Rothschild dynasty, Nathan Mayer Rothschild, had ensured his financial success by organizing a faster and more extensive spy service than the British government's. In 1815, his couriers followed Wellington's armies – which his loans helped finance. The Rothschild agents also spied on all the fractious European courts. Their mission was to collect and transmit to their employer timely intelligence reports regardless of the expense. He also established a courier pigeon-post to and from the Continent. Nathan Rothschild was therefore the first in London to receive news of Napoleon's defeat at Waterloo, and this information enabled the House of Rothschild to make a killing on a jittery London Stock Exchange awash with rumors of a French victory.

Since private intelligence was an essential element of the Rothschild business operation, what better cover could they give their latest recruit in 1935 than to characterize Burgess as an investment counselor and dispatch him as their private spy to monitor the Anglo-German Fellowship? Information about threats to the House of Rothschild resulting from secret deals between British sympathizers and the Third Reich would more than justify the hundred guineas a month paid to Guy Burgess.

Victor Rothschild had implicit faith in his Cambridge friend because he, like Blunt, knew of Burgess's true loyalties. But Burgess's volatile enthusiasms would help persuade his right-wing friends that he had recanted his earlier Marxism. His homosexual appetite would prove an exploitable talent when it came to sharing the bed of a pro-German Tory well placed to pull strings and advance an ambitious young man's career. Nor should it be forgotten that Rudolph Katz, with his own extensive network of homosexual and Comintern contacts, also contributed to Rothschild's private intelligence network that, at the time, shared with Stalin a common enemy: Hitler.

Blunt, who was as close a friend of Rothschild as Burgess, may well have had a hand in staging and scripting the game that Burgess had embarked upon. Blunt was 'the clever young English historian who had a kind of pupil-and-master relationship with Guy, from whom he imbibed the principles of the economic interpretation of history.' This was the thin disguise that Rees, fearing a libel suit, gave Blunt in his autobiographical recollection of the odd coterie who used to meet of an evening in the flat Burgess rented in Belgravia.

The eye-popping red, white and blue decor of Burgess's rooms overlooking the plane trees of Chester Square anticipated Pop Art. But it was not for artistic or patriotic reasons that Burgess chose the patriotic colors that he said were the only ones 'any reasonable man could live with'. It struck Rees forcibly that it had been a 'very strange collection' of men who had gathered in a room often submerged by the debris of the previous night's drinking bout and stinking from the saucepans of congealed garlic-flavored porridge on which Burgess sustained himself at home. They were all, he said – not excepting himself – 'to some degree infected with Marxism.'

Kim Philby, about whom Burgess 'always spoke in terms of admiration so excessive that I found it difficult to understand on what objective virtue it was based,' was, according to Rees, also a visitor. But it is likely that Philby was not a frequent presence. To associate too often and too closely with other members of a spy ring would break the rules of security that Soviet intelligence instilled in its disciplined agents.

Philby justified his 1936 association with Burgess because of their shared participation in the Anglo-German Fellowship. But such meetings were impossible after February 1937, when Philby left for Spain to report on the war from the Nationalist side. This was the first test of his cover story and the right-wing contacts he made among the Fellowship. MI5, when it was investigating him, blundered by assuming that his trip was sponsored by the *Times*. The record shows that he did not become an accredited correspondent until May 1937 and a simple check of his bank records would have shown that he did not have the means for 'gallivanting around Spain' for any length of time.

Philby proudly admitted that 'the enterprise had been

suggested to me, and financed by, the Soviet service.' His assignment was to use his cover as a journalist to provide intelligence from the Nationalist side, and he carried his code on a tiny piece of edible paper. For two and a half years Philby carried out his mission, supplying his Soviet contacts in France with military and political information and keeping the *Times* readers informed about the war. His fellow correspondents believed that his dispatches often unfairly promoted the Nationalist cause. None of them guessed that he was zealously following Moscow's orders. His career as a Soviet agent was almost terminated on New Year's Eve, 1937, when a shell from a Russian cannon hit a car full of journalists. Two of his companions died, but Philby, although wounded, survived to be decorated personally by Franco with the Red Cross of Military Merit.

To recuperate from wounds to his head and arm, Philby was ordered to France for a brief rest. It was on a visit to Paris early in 1937 that he met up with Burgess who had also – according to Philby – helped replenish his funds.

When Philby went to Spain, by a curious coincidence, Donald Maclean was attached to the Spanish desk of the Western Department of the Foreign Office. Although Maclean lived less than a mile from Chester Square in a small flat in Chelsea on Oakley Street, there is no record that he ever visited Burgess. Rees, however, does recall that he met Maclean on a yachting weekend on Southampton Water. He had heard Burgess talk admiringly of Maclean, whom he had seduced at Cambridge. But Rees disliked the young man, whom he found 'rather superior'.

Another member of the circle was a 'working-class ex-chorus boy', whom Rees called Jimmy. In reality, his name was Jack Hewit. Jackie, as he was known to the group, was the son of a Tyneside tinsmith. A tubby boy with glasses, Hewit was teasingly called 'Porky Suet' by his schoolmates. His overprotective mother died when he was twelve and his father intended to apprentice him to a plumber. In 1932, at the age of fifteen, he left home to come to London to fulfill his boyhood ambition to become a dancer. After a succession of jobs as a hotel page boy he managed in 1936 to get into the chorus line of *No No Nanette*.

Hewit saw Burgess one night outside the stage door and the incongruity of his first meeting at a party in the War Office still amuses him.

'What on earth is all this,' Hewit recalls asking himself as he was introduced to a smoke-filled room of twenty men who were all drinking and 'my dearing' each other, talking a kind of upper-class shorthand like a Noël Coward sketch. Hewit knew at once he had stumbled into the upper reaches of London's homosexual demimonde. The nineteen-year-old working-class lad was so overwhelmed by it all, he quite forgot his initial dismay that there was nothing to eat with the liquor flowing as freely as the outrageous conversation.

Burgess he recognized and found even 'more attractive' than the night he had seen him outside the South London theater. To Hewit's relief and delight, Burgess came to his rescue when a fat man began to paw him and make himself objectionable. 'A big fat man, an enormous lump' was how Hewit described the German who had introduced himself in heavily accented English as Rolf Katz. Burgess offered to drive Hewit home, but instead took him to the Chester Square flat that he was to share with Burgess for the next four years.

'Guy was a very amusing companion. He was not ashamed to take his boyfriends everywhere,' Hewit said. 'He had this fixation about working people and he wore them like some men wear badges.' Hewit did his best to keep up appearances, tidying up the flat, making sure Burgess bathed, cleaned his fingernails and put on clean shirts, but despite these efforts, he said, 'Guy always looked like an unmade bed.'

In return, Burgess, who called Hewit 'Mop', tried his best to waken his literary tastes, encouraging him to delve into Jane Austen and Mrs Gaskell. These Hewit recalls enjoying, but he rejected Burgess's attempts to educate him politically. He told Burgess that Thomas Paine's *The Rights of Man* was rubbish and that he couldn't afford to be a socialist. 'We never talked politics again.' Their domestic arrangements were never easy. Burgess was an insomniac who regularly took Nembutal sleeping tablets at night and Benzedrine pills to wake up in the morning.

Burgess, according to Hewit, was 'promiscuous to a degree'. His infidelity was the cause of 'very, very frequent rows', which often sent Hewit over to Blunt's bed-sit in Palace Gate for consolation. 'I'd arrive saying I was going to kill Guy,' Hewit recalled, explaining how Blunt would always calm him down. Blunt and Burgess were extremely close and together they always managed to patch things up with Hewit. He found Blunt kind and considerate and admired his wicked sense of humor.

Hewit does not recall exactly when he moved in with Burgess but thinks it was sometime in late 1937. He recalls meeting at the flat on several occasions with the anti-Nazi diplomat from the German embassy whom Rees wrote about as being a frequent visitor to the Chester Square menagerie and another key player in the conspiratorial group.

This was Baron Wolfgang von und zu Putlitz. A member of Ambassador Leopold von Hoesch's staff at Carleton House Terrace since 1934, Putlitz was the son of a Junker and heir to an ancient Prussian lineage. He was a career diplomat in the German Foreign Service and took an immediate dislike to the Nazi regime when Hitler came to power in 1933. By his own admission he began passing information to the British in 'the autumn of 1937'.

Records in the State Department archives confirm his value to the British Foreign Office. They suggest, however, that Putlitz might have become a mole even earlier. And there is now every reason to believe that he served both London *and* Moscow as a double agent.

Putlitz wrote a carefully constructed memoir with the approval of the KGB some twenty years later. In it he claims that only after Ribbentrop arrived as German ambassador to London in 1936 did he begin furnishing confidential reports to Sir Robert Vansittart, the permanent head of the Foreign Office. He remained one of the key sources for what became known in the Foreign Office as 'Vansittart's Private Detective Agency' after he was posted as a counselor to the 1938 German legation at The Hague.

Putlitz's cover was blown by the Germans during the Phoney War after they had penetrated British intelligence in the Netherlands. In November 1939, they learned about Putlitz when they kidnapped the senior MI6 officer, Major Richard Stevens, and his undercover British associate Captain Sigismund Payne Best, after luring them to a rendezvous on the road to Venlo near the German border. Fortunately for Putlitz, his ambassador entrusted him with the task of decoding an eyes-only cable from Berlin that was intended to seal Putlitz's fate. With his manservant Willi Schneider, Putlitz 'disappeared'. Using a secret radio transmitter to call for a rescue plane, they flew to England before the Gestapo caught them.

Shortly after Dunkirk, in June 1940, Vansittart tried to arrange American visas for the baron and his companion to prevent their being confined in one of the internment camps set up for enemy aliens during that summer's invasion scare. An unusual plea was made to the American ambassador, Joseph Kennedy, that Putlitz 'had rendered him [Vansittart] invaluable services.' But the State Department refused to grant the visas because the Gestapo had not taken the usual reprisals against Putlitz's family in Germany and this raised suspicions that he might be a Nazi undercover agent.

A ten-day landing permit in New York for Putlitz and his manservant, en route to Jamaica, was all they were permitted. The State Department also instructed the FBI to conduct round-the-clock surveillance as soon as the two exiled Germans landed. Hoover's men reported that instead of trying to meet known German agents, Putlitz and his companion spent their time making contacts of a rather different nature while 'patronizing places frequented by homosexuals'.

State Department records confirm that Putlitz *was* part of an extensive network of informants that Vansittart had built up to keep the Foreign Office informed about developments in Germany – intelligence that he shared with a select circle outside the government, including Winston Churchill. Confidential information supplied by Dutch diplomats shows that they knew that

Putlitz was 'collaborating with British intelligence' by using his 'so-called servant to maintain the risky contacts and pass on the information.'

American suspicions about Putlitz were aggravated by Hoover's undisguised aversion to homosexuals. So despite appeals to Vansittart from Putlitz's American friends, he was never permitted to reenter the United States. Obliged by 'financial misery' to remain in a Jamaican internment center for three years, Putlitz finally received official permission to return to England in January 1944. After working under close surveillance for the Political Warfare Executive, preparing anti-Nazi broadcasts, in 1946 the baron was finally allowed to return home to Kiel as a translator in the British occupation zone. With his family estates in the East under Soviet control, he was penniless. He taxed Vansittart about his penurious condition in a letter complaining that his fellow Germans regarded him as a traitor. Worse, he warned his 'old friend' of the dangers in store for the 'alien' and misguided British occupation.

'Things are drifitng into a state which will be fatal not only to me but also to you,' Putlitz wrote to Vansittart, without explaining his cryptic warning. Vansittart failed to come to the rescue of his now-discarded agent. With no hope of an influential position in the new Federal Republic of Germany, Putlitz turned to his other masters and the Soviets finally let the baron come in from the cold.

On a snowy January day in 1952 Putlitz finally exposed his true Communist colors and took the one-way ride on the S-Bahn from West Berlin to settle in East Germany. It was just six months after the defection of Burgess and Maclean. Suspicions about his true loyalties, and his links to the Cambridge moles, were clarified five years later when he published his memoirs. They contained an effusive tribute to Burgess, who had by then reappeared in Moscow, saluting him for his courageous defection, which showed his disgust with Britain's 'final and total dependency on the United States'. Burgess, he claimed, was 'one of the first young Englishmen I had ever met who seemed really to have made a study of Marx.'

More surprising was Putlitz's unexplained tribute to 'Mr Anthony Blunt, whose kindness and understanding I will never forget.' At the time of his book's publication, this slighting reference to the surveyor of the Queen's pictures, who had just been knighted, must have mystified everyone but Blunt himself. What MI5 made of it is still an official secret. But it seems that the KGB intended to remind Sir Anthony that his primary loyalty was to the occupants of the Kremlin rather than to the reigning monarch in Buckingham Palace.

It was not the first time that Putlitz had been involved in sending a 'valentine'. What is now clear is that he was a crucial, if minor, player in the events that led to the abdication of King Edward VIII.

Over the years, the Soviets had maintained a discreet line to Prime Minister Baldwin's right-hand aide, J. C. C. Davidson, via Anatoli Baykolov, or Baikaloff, as he was known to MI5. Supposedly a 'mild liberal' White Russian, this foxy London journalist made himself an expert on Soviet affairs. In this capacity he acted as an adviser to the General Council of the British Trades Union Congress. But Baykolov's true mission was to maintain a close liaison with prominent right-wing Tories. He proved to be a powerful influence on Kitty Atholl, the Scottish Conservative. She moved so far to the left in her campaign against the government's nonintervention policy in Spain that she became known as the 'Red Duchess'.

Yet as early as 1933, a warning had been sent to MI5 by the Russian émigrés in Paris that Baykolov was working for the Soviets. MI5 ignored these warnings and continued to use him as a clandestine channel of communication. Liddell, according to recently discovered letters to Vansittart, remained in contact with Baykolov until 1951, believing him to be a reliable source of information. Whether Liddell ever suspected that Baykolov was a double agent whose primary loyalty was to Moscow – or if Liddell knew and concealed it – remains unclear. But his long association with Baykolov adds yet another question mark against one of MI5's veteran counterintelligence officers.

Meanwhile, new evidence has come to light that Moscow did not hesitate to activate the Baykolov back channel when it believed Moscow's interests could be served.

This appears to have been the case on 30 January 1936, the day King George V died. There was a widespread concern about the pro-German sympathies of the new king, Edward VIII, and members of his entourage such as Lady Cunard. It was feared that Edward's coronation would accelerate a rapprochement between London and Berlin. There is evidence that the Soviets activated the Baykolov connection to pass word of this danger, which was already worrying Britain's Prime Minister. The Soviets were getting their information from inside the German embassy via their mole Putlitz and it seems they tipped Baykolov to alert Davidson that Wallis Simpson was a putative German agent.

MI5 must have known that the new king's mistress, Mrs Ernest Simpson (she was not yet divorced), was a frequent visitor to the receptions at the German embassy, thrown for the Anglo-German Fellowship by Ambassador von Hoesch. And it was through the Baykolov back channel that Davidson learned just how friendly Mrs Simpson was with the German ambassador. Davidson's source was, after all, the same one through which he had obtained the damning information that helped sink Maundy Gregory's honors racket.

Davidson's personal, unpublished papers reveal the reasons for his concern. The king had been consorting with Ernest Simpson's wife at the same time he had sponsored Simpson's membership in the Masons. To ensure Simpson's election, the king had stated that he was not involved with Mrs Simpson, a lie, and Simpson was apparently going to take action against the king on the grounds that the king was breaking his Masonic vows by having an adulterous affair with Wallis Simpson. There was the added complication that the king intended to marry Mrs Simpson, which would make for an impossible situation.

*

In a most-secret memorandum dated 14 February 1936, Davidson wrote: 'I am quite convinced that Blackmail sticks out at every stage. H[is] M[ajesty] had already paid large sums to Mrs S[impson] & given valuable presents. I advocate Most Drastic steps if it is true that S. is an American but if he isn't the situation is very difficult. The Mason vow is very clear. The P of W got S. in on a lie & is now living in open breach of the Masonic law of Chastity because of this lie he first told. So Mrs S. who is obviously a golddigger has obviously got him on toast . . .' The most important line in Davidson's memo, however, is the last, which sets forth the real problem: 'Mrs S. is very close to Hoesch and has, if she likes to read them, access to all Secret & Cabinet papers!!!!'

This latter problem, together with the King's pro-German sympathies, can only have hardened Baldwin's attitude to Edward from the outset of the abdication crisis. It must therefore have been no little relief that on Good Friday Ambassador Hoesch was found dead on his bathroom floor.

Rumors ascribed his sudden death from a weak heart to execution by the Gestapo. His valet believed that Hoesch had committed suicide with a drug overdose. But his death now appears to have been suspiciously coincidental with Davidson's terse recommendation that 'Most Drastic steps' be taken in the Simpson affair. Both the British and the Soviet governments had pressing motives for removing Hoesch: this raises the intriguing possibility that the back-channel liaison with the Soviets could have resulted in a contract with the NKVD on Hoesch.

All such speculation aside, it is established fact that Blunt, Putlitz and Katz were all involved intimately with Burgess while he was in Rothschild's pay.

What puzzles intelligence experts is the unusual evolution of the Cambridge Soviet agents who flouted all the rules of good security by keeping such close company with one another. Only in Burgess's case is it explicable since in 1936 he would have been acting for the Rothschilds and was not yet a full-fledged Soviet agent.

It seems that Blunt was running Burgess as a subsidiary agent in much the same way that Blunt had involved Michael Straight. This would have advanced Blunt's standing with his Soviet masters, and it would provide Moscow with the information that Burgess was obtaining from the Anglo-German Fellowship at no additional effort or risk to its own operation. It also appears to have compromised Victor Rothschild, who became the unwitting sponsor of an extension of an NKVD network.

11 'It Was All a Bit of a Lark'

Evidence now available leads one to the conclusion that Burgess did not come under the direct control of Moscow Center until 1939, years later than had previously been accepted.

Soviet intelligence exercised extreme care in picking its foreign penetration agents, and quite apart from his lack of career qualifications, Burgess was an undisciplined dilettante compared with Kim Philby. Before being sent to Spain, Philby managed to work his way into a position of influence in the Anglo-German Fellowship hierarchy, but Burgess never achieved an office in the Fellowship. On the contrary, Burgess's contacts were personal: as the 'secretary' to an eccentric homosexual right-wing MP. Moreover, by the spring of 1936, when Philby was still beavering away, writing the Fellowship's pro-German press releases and speeches, Burgess abruptly left the organization to try out as a journalist with *The Times* of London.

The reason Burgess gave Goronwy Rees for leaving Captain Macnamara's employ was: 'He really was *too* absurd.' This contradicts the popular myth that Burgess was already a Soviet agent, as does his blunder of making a direct recruiting approach to Rees. Worse, by revealing Blunt to be a Comintern agent, Burgess was breaking a fundamental tenet of Soviet undercover operations and is a further indication Burgess had not yet been brought under discipline or NKVD control.

The characterization Burgess gave to Rees of Blunt as an *éminence grise* is evidence, moreover, that Blunt was running Burgess as a subsidiary free-lancer. This explains many of the discrepancies in the case. It suggests how Burgess's usefulness was brought to the attention of the Soviets. With Blunt serving as the channel of access for the gossip that Burgess picked up, Moscow Center used the intelligence he provided while remaining safely insulated from any debacles that might result from his volatile enthusiasms.

Much of Burgess's intelligence came from the secretive homosexual network that maintained its 'special' friendships with politicians and bureaucrats in the French capital. Edouard Pfeiffer was one of those contacts – and he proved to be one of the most valuable sources Burgess met while working for Macnamara.

Pfeiffer was a former secretary general of France's right-leaning Radical-Socialist party. Pfeiffer was an arch-intriguer 'who would not normally respond to anything except the grossest kind of appeal to self-interest.' Surprisingly, he became an ardent supporter of appeasement, and, as one of Edouard Daladier's *hommes de confiance*, he served as the principal secret negotiator with the French right.

As a connoisseur of homosexual decadence, Pfeiffer had few equals, even in Paris. An officer of the French boy-scout movement, his private life was devoted to the seduction of youth. Burgess discovered all this when he first visited Pfeiffer's apartment in Paris and found a group of men in full evening dress watching Pfeiffer play table tennis with a naked young man serving as the net. While Pfeiffer deftly flicked ping-pong balls over the youth's athletic thighs, he explained to Burgess that the young man was a professional cyclist, who just happened to be a member of Jacques Doriot's pro-Hitler Popular party.

Burgess found Pfeiffer's combination of conspiratorial politics and homosexuality irresistible. They became intimates, and Pfeiffer often turned up at Burgess's flat in Chester Square whenever he was in London. Rees recalled how he often encountered a 'peculiarly detestable Frenchman who seemed to me to smell of every kind of corruption.'

Thanks to Pfeiffer's inside gossip, Burgess was soon better informed than the Foreign Office about the Machiavellian maneuvering of the French government. Burgess was to find himself uniquely well placed to exploit his private line into the

French Cabinet because, in October 1936, he landed a job with the BBC. He was always suspiciously vague about how he pulled off this coup, especially after having failed to get on to the *Times* staff. Earlier writers have believed that Burgess moved as a response to Moscow's orders to find a job in one of Britain's major communications institutions. But this does not fit in with his other desperate, and simultaneous, attempt to become a correspondent for a right-wing French newspaper financed by Otto Abetz, a German who later was appointed as the Nazi regime's ambassador to occupied France. Burgess's journalistic ambitions led to a month's trial in May 1936 as a *Times* subeditor. But it took less than four weeks for Burgess and the *Times* newsroom to realize that they were ill-suited. During his probationary work with the newspaper, Burgess made the acquaintance of Roger Fulford, a member of the newspaper's editorial staff.

Fulford was another member of London's literary homosexual circuit. During the war Fulford would become an MI5 officer, recruited, significantly, by Roger Hollis, the future MI5 director who was later suspected of being the Soviet's most senior mole in Britain's intelligence services. Hollis had just returned from China and was also trying to become a *Times* journalist that November 1936.

Hollis, like Burgess, was also turned down by *The Times*. Within a year, however, Hollis managed to get into MI5. Fulford not only kept in touch with Hollis, whom he had known from their days at Worcester College, Oxford, in the late twenties but, in 1940, was himself recruited into MI5 by Hollis, who was then a rising member of F Division, responsible for monitoring the activities of the Communist party in Britain. Fulford therefore represents a link between Burgess and Hollis.

Curiously, Wright makes no mention of Fulford. He also appears to have overlooked another clue linking Burgess to Fulford, who was later knighted for political services to the Liberal party. The archives of the BBC reveal Roger Fulford as a prewar friend of Burgess. Furthermore, Fulford made frequent BBC broadcasts after Burgess had become a 'Talks' producer.

It will not be possible to establish precisely how Burgess arrived at the BBC until the Confidential Staff Archives are opened to researchers after being sealed for seventy-five years. But from other files, it appears likely that he prevailed on his friend Harold Nicolson for a strong recommendation. Nicolson had already established his reputation as an accomplished broadcaster, and through his Foreign Office connections, he had influential contacts in the BBC. But the person actually responsible for appointing Burgess was George Barnes, the deputy director of Talks.

Barnes, like Burgess, was another Cambridge man. He joined the BBC in 1935 from the Cambridge University Press. Like Burgess, he also had been a Dartmouth cadet and had graduated from King's in 1925. He then taught at the Royal Naval College before returning to Cambridge as assistant secretary of the university press. Barnes, moreover, must have known all about Burgess's communism since Burgess had lodged in his house.

'George Barnes was greatly impressed with Burgess as being a young man bursting with ideas,' says Lord Annan. Cambridge gossip was that Barnes was one of the few men who successfully kept a boyfriend and a mistress at the same time. This could have given Burgess a secret hold over Barnes. It also allowed Burgess to share Barnes's circle of friends, Cambridge radicals who included John Hilton, the unconventional professor of industrial relations. Hilton was also one of Britain's first national radio celebrities, whose success began in 1933 with a series of talks on industrial relations. He was a natural broadcaster. His *This & That* series, based on his talks to the unemployed clubs, ranged from tips on pensions to international affairs. His left-wing appeal derived not merely from his firsthand experience of trade unions and proletarian life but from his tireless efforts to establish social clubs to help the unemployed. Later, during the war, Burgess would become one of Hilton's producers.

The surviving internal BBC correspondence between Barnes and Burgess confirms that they both shared Hilton's views. Unlike Burgess and Blunt – whom it is clear from BBC records that Barnes also knew – Barnes was never openly a Marxist, either at Cambridge or during his long career at the BBC (for which he received a knighthood for the part he played in televising the coronation of Queen Elizabeth II). Broadcasting one's political views was forbidden, but the records of the Talks Department confirm that Barnes invariably took Burgess's point of view whenever politics intruded. He not only monitored his protégés progress during the three months that Burgess spent at the BBC staff training school but quickly promoted him to be a producer in the Talks Department.

If Barnes was the alter ego of Burgess as a broadcaster, one of the beneficiaries of the relationship was Anthony Blunt. He was one of the first speakers Burgess brought before the microphone in June 1937 after the completion of his training. The exchanges between Blunt and Barnes about his proposed broadcast on the Sistine Chapel suggest that the deputy director of Talks and Blunt were already on familiar terms. Blunt would later broadcast for Burgess on many occasions, thereby adding to his reputation as a wide-ranging authority on art.

Listeners were unaware that the supposedly spontaneous talks and discussions broadcast by the BBC were then carefully scripted and approved by the government. Despite the BBC's jealously guarded tradition of impartiality, the corporation's records reveal that the government exercised tight control over the producers. The Foreign Office exercised vetting rights over all scripts referring to international affairs. They could censor, request changes and ban discussion on sensitive topics – even veto certain broadcasters.

The Spanish Civil War was a specially sensitive area for the British government. Burgess and Blunt would have congratulated themselves on their small triumph in broadcasting derogatory references to Franco and the Fascist victors. The ability of Burgess subtly to influence and color BBC broadcasts become more apparent in 1938, a year that saw Europe teetering on the brink of war when Hitler annexed Austria and then demanded the return of the German-speaking Czechoslovakian territories. Unnerved and divided, the British and French governments retreated in a policy of appeasement as they tried to dignify their position at the bargaining table at Munich in September 1938.

Burgess – thanks to his French homosexual connections – found the key that would admit him into the British intelligence service via the back door: it was Pfeiffer who became the ace in Burgess's hand.

Burgess has always been taken at his word when he claimed his coup occurred in 1936, but the record indicates that it was really 1938, when Pfeiffer obtained the details of the French Cabinet's Munich deliberations directly from Edouard Daladier.

Daladier was *not* a member of the French government in March 1936. The French records *do* show, however, that on 11 March *1938*, as minister of national defense and war in Premier Camille Chautemps's Cabinet, Daladier *did* argue strenuously for military action against the Anschluss – provided the British agreed to participate. The following month Daladier came back into power as premier in the Cabinet reshuffle precipitated by the Austrian crisis.

This greatly increased the value of the connection Burgess maintained with Pfeiffer. On his return to London he passed it on to 'a friend' who was 'a distinguished novelist, who happened to work for the Secret Service.' A few days later Burgess effectively became an MI6 agent when that same friend paid him a sum of money 'sufficient to cover his Paris expenses'.

Burgess admitted that the Pfeiffer connection opened the door for him to become an MI6 informant and Guy's 'giveaway' reference makes it possible to identify his MI6 friend as David Footman, already an accomplished writer of fiction.

A mousy, scholarly man with a very dry sense of humor, Footman was – like Blunt – the Marlborough-educated son of a Church of England cleric. After graduating from Oxford and winning a Military Cross in World War I, he obtained a post with the Levant Consular Service. In 1935, he transferred to Section I of MI6, the Secret Intelligence Service, the political division. He became a Russian expert. His intense study of the Soviet Union surfaced in a series of books on communism and Russian history that were published in the postwar decade before he retired to pursue his interests as an Oxford don.

Just how Burgess became acquainted with Footman is unclear but the initial contact could have been made through mutual friends in the left-wing London literary scene. Once the introduction was made, however, Footman became one of Burgess's most valuable contacts and he was instrumental in getting both Burgess and later Philby into MI6. Philby deliberately alludes to Footman as being 'a strong ally' at the time of his 1944 coup to take over the Counterintelligence Section.

'I don't think Footman was ever given a completely clean bill of health,' a wartime member of the Foreign Office told me. He said that after Blunt's exposure, he had asked Sir Dick White whether he ever knew where he stood with Footman. 'No, I wish I had,' the former director of MI5 and MI6 ruefully admitted.

In the spring of 1938 Burgess was regularly passing on to Footman intelligence obtained from the French Cabinet via Pfeiffer, and by May, Burgess became a subcontractor for MI6. One of the assignments was Konrad Henlein. A former gymnastics teacher and leader of the Sudeten German party, Henlein provided Hitler with the excuse for making his bid to occupy the northern part of Czechoslovakia. He came to London in May with instructions on how to hoodwink the British government with his demand for independence and denial that he was 'acting on instructions from Berlin'.

Burgess told his boyfriend Hewit all about Henlein. Because of his switchboard experience, Hewit was to substitute for the telephone operator at the Goring Hotel, where the leader of the Sudeten Germans was lodging.

'It was all a bit of a lark,' Hewit told me, recalling how he monitored all of Henlein's calls. After 'work,' he said he then met with Burgess and David Footman at a pub in Westminster near the St James's underground station that served the Broadway Buildings that were MI6's headquarters. Hewit said that he felt 'used' by Burgess, who had pressured him into becoming an unofficial secret agent. Their relationship had already cooled because of Burgess's generosity in 'lending him out' to friends who were in need of a lover. Burgess then added insult to injury by returning from a holiday trip to Cannes with his mother and a 'very attractive seventeen-year-old boy named Peter Pollock in tow'. The *ménage* left Hewit feeling neglected. In August 1938 he packed his bags and went off to Belgium with Christopher Isherwood.

The British Cabinet may have been hoodwinked by Henlein, but Burgess was not. In his capacity as a BBC radio producer he hoped to alert the country to the danger of failing to face up to Hitler over Czechoslovakia. He planned a series of talks on 'Aggression in the Mediterranean'.

The Prime Minister, who distrusted the hard-line anti-Fascist Vansittart, preferred to negotiate his deal for Mediterranean appeasement through his confidant, Sir Horace Wilson, who had opened up a private channel to Rome. This was done via Sir Joseph Ball, the Conservative party's research director who, thanks to his pro-Fascist friends in the Anglo-German Fellowship, had already established his own direct lines to Count Grandi, the Italian ambassador.

Into this Machiavellian web of diplomatic intrigue the homosexually inclined Ball introduced his protégé, Guy Burgess. Burgess knew how to cultivate such a confidant. He later revealed that he, too, was acting for 'an unofficial intelligence organization which supplied information not only to Neville Chamberlain but to Sir Horace Wilson, head of the Civil Service and Chamberlain's *éminence grise.*' Burgess was now in his element in these furtive maneuverings, working for no fewer than three masters. He acted as the go-between for Chamberlain and Daladier as they plotted their appeasement of Hitler. Their communiqués about how to secure peace at any price were written in the third person and signed by subordinates. Burgess disgustedly referred to their letters as 'the communications of a confused and panic-stricken patriot to an ignorant provincial ironmonger.' He was fully aware of their contents because he fed the correspondence to a third party. This was MI6. They monitored the secret traffic between the British and French premiers for Sir Robert Vansittart, the watchful head of the Foreign Office.

Burgess, although he was careful not to brag about it, also must have been passing this information about the secret British and French exchanges to the Soviets. The question is: did he pass the information through Blunt? Or by 1938 was he also a trusted, disciplined NKVD agent – and, if so, how was he controlled?

Here again, it is interesting to find that Blunt seems to have done his best to confuse the picture. According to Wright's account, Blunt insisted that in 1938 their espionage ring was supposedly 'out of touch and apparently abandoned' following the recall of their controller 'Otto' to Moscow. This, as has been shown, does not square with the MI5 records that indicate that 'Otto' was a nonexistent control, a fabrication for disguising the fact that Theodore Maly, the original founder-controller of the Cambridge ring, had not left Britain until the summer of 1937 – a year after his supposed recall by Moscow.

Furthermore, Blunt told Wright that it was Burgess and Philby who reestablished contact with the Soviets through Litzi Friedman. The first Mrs Philby, supposedly a 'longtime European Comintern agent', he claimed had passed messages through Edith Tudor Hart (the wife of Dr Tudor Hart, a prominent member of the Communist party) via 'Bob Stewart, the CPGB official responsible for liaison with the Russian embassy.' But Blunt's explanation does not hold water because: (a) Philby's own account demonstrates that he was in direct contact with the NKVD in Paris from the spring of 1937 onward and (b) MI5 had already penetrated the headquarters of the British Communist party.

Wright reports that Blunt later confessed that it 'had always puzzled him that the Cambridge ring was not detected at this point.' Now that we have the documentation on the Woolwich Arsenal case, showing the extent to which Olga Gray and Maxwell Knight's other MI5 agents had burrowed into the inner sanctums of the CPGB, it becomes apparent that Blunt's contrived

Exporting the Revolution: Cambridge undergraduate "special constables" (above) volunteered to fight the general strike in 1926. The Metropolitan Police (below left) guard the Arcos offices on May 12, 1927, during the raid on the nerve center of the Soviet Union's subversive operations in Britain that was masterminded until his death in 1926 by Feliks Dzerzhinski (below right) who founded the Cheka, the predecessor of the KGB.

Aesthetic Rebel: Clifford Canning (above left) was the principal mentor of Anthony Blunt at Marlborough College. In Blunt's farewell portrait given to his friends, the school prefect (above right) chose an unconventional but characteristically authoritative pose. The studied aesthete (below) posing in a very unmilitary "wopsical" sun hat during OTC (Officer Training Corps) camp.

Image Making: Blunt forged his successful "Anonymous Society" with Louis MacNeice and John Hilton (above left), together with the handsome rugby-playing "hearty" Michael Robertson (in striped tie, above right with Hilton). Blunt's artistic efforts (below left) won him no accolades for painting, but his mathematical ability was rewarded with a scholarship to Trinity and prize books shared (below right) with classmate John Hilton.

"Bloomsbury un peu passé": Rosamond Leh[mann] and her brother, John (left), with Lytton St[rachey] at Ham Spray. Blunt with fellow Apostles D[ouglas] Lucas and Julian Bell (below). Jean Stewa[rt,] daughter of the dean of Trinity, and her [sister] were frequent female companions to cam[ouflage] Blunt's 1929 homosexual affair with Bell. [Michael] Ramsay's celebrated photograph of the ma[le] Apostles (bottom) celebrating their "captu[re" of] the society shows (left to right) Richard Lle[wellyn] Davies, Hugh Sykes Davies, Alister Watso[n, An]thony Blunt, Julian Bell, Andrew Cohen.

THE ESTATE OF JOHN LEHMANN

"University is really rather amusing": So Louis MacNeice, the Oxford Aesthete (top right) wrote. Cambridge boasted the flamboyant homosexual John Tresidder Sheppard of King's "performing" (top left) with Lydia Lopokova, the ballerina wife of John Maynard Keynes. Andrew Gow of Trinity (above left) cultivated Blunt's artistic sensibilities, while Anthony flirted with Lady Mary St. Clair Erskine (center). Peter Kapitza, (above right) the brilliant Soviet physicist, was another prominent Trinity don who enrolled Blunt's fellow Apostle Alister Watson in his famous scientific discussion group.

Cambridge Contemporaries: Blunt, as a Trinity
don caricatured by Burgess (right). Active Communist party dons Maurice Dobb and Roy Pascal
(opposite, top left and center) were "spotters" for
the Comintern. Their task was facilitated by liberal
Bloomsbury intellectuals opposed to Fascism such
as E. M. Forster (opposite top right). The prime
targets for moles were disaffected undergraduate
Marxists such as Donald Maclean, Guy Burgess,
and Peter J. Astbury (opposite, middle), not charismatic revolutionaries like John Cornford (opposite, bottom left), who recruited Michael
Straight (opposite, bottom center) into the Trinity
Communist cell. Straight, however, talked Teresa
Mayor (opposite, bottom right) out of joining the
party; she later became the second wife of Blunt's
Apostle friend Victor Rothschild (below).

Popular Fronts: Edouard Pfeiffer (above left), the Machiavellian French politician and homosexual contact of Burgess, intrigued with the Communist "fronts" in Paris promoted by Willi Münzenberg (above center) and his one-time aide, Otto Katz (above left). The Popular Front of the late thirties forged an alliance of socialists and liberals against advocates of Fascism like Sir Oswald Mosley (below right) and aristocratic supporters of Hitler such as Prince Philip of Hesse, shown (below left) with Princess Mafalda, daughter of King Umberto of Italy, Mussolini's supporter.

The Royal Connection: Blunt knew Prince George, Duke of Kent (above left) on the London homosexual network. But it was on his secret mission to Germany in 1945 for King George VI that he discovered the true extent of the intrigues involving the Duke and Duchess of Windsor, who met Hitler at Berchtesgaden in 1937 (above right). Noël Annan (below left), who served in 1945 with the British Control Commission in Germany, suspected Leo Long (below right), whom Blunt had run as a subagent for the Russians. Goronwy Rees (below center) also served with army intelligence but always denied passing information to Blunt.

The American Connection: FBI investigations launched before the end of World War II exposed the pattern of Communist infiltration in the United States. Testimony of penetration in Washington was provided by Elizabeth Bentley and Hede Massing (above left) and Whittaker Chambers (above right). It is now clear that decrypted Soviet cipher traffic played a critical part in extracting a confession from physicist Klaus Fuchs (below left) in 1949. The same source also helped expose the atomic espionage network operated by Ethel and Julius Rosenberg (below right with fellow accused Morton Sobel), but the FBI was not allowed to introduce the Venona decrypts at their controversial trial and subsequent execution.   NATIONAL ARCHIVES

KEYSTONE

MRS. KEMBALL JOHNSTON

The "Missing British Diplomats": Anglo-American relations were soured and Foreign Secretary Herbert Morrison (above left with Ambassador John Foster Dulles) was embarrassed by the defection of Burgess and Maclean. The weekend before they left, Burgess had visited his old Trinity and wartime MI5 friend Kemball Johnston (left) and reminded him of his Marxist sympathies with a sketch of Stalin (below left). Philby (below right) brazened his way through his 1951 interrogations to be completely exonerated in 1955.

I wonder what Kemball is thinking? *G.B.*

MRS. KEMBALL JOHNSTON

KEYSTONE

"The Uninvestigated Mole in MI5": Guy Liddell (above left) was a gifted child cellist, whose musical career was terminated by army service in World War I (center), after which he joined Special Branch and became the longtime head of MI5 counterintelligence (above right). Maurice Oldfield (below center) told American contacts shortly before his retirement as head of MI6 that Liddell was his prime suspect and should have been thoroughly investigated. Analysis of the prewar MI5 records supports that suspicion. But MI5 investigators — including Peter Wright (below right) — considered that the former deputy director-general had to be blameless of any complicity, conceding only his "unfortunate" friendship with Blunt (below left).

puzzlement was a highly sophisticated double-bluff to persuade MI5 to begin revising its previously rock-solid conclusions.

Apparently the trickery worked. Wright stated that MI5 'had always assumed the Ring had been kept entirely separate from the CPGB apparatus,' but now 'it appeared that we had missed the greatest CPGB secret of them all.' As we can see, however, the claim that the ring was run through British Communists until 1940 does not fit the facts.

The BBC's records reveal that Blunt and Burgess often arranged to be in Paris together in 1937. While this is, of course, no proof that either communicated with the Soviets while in the French capital, it seems to be no coincidence that Blunt stayed at the Hôtel Récamier on the Place Saint-Sulpice. This discreet left-bank pension happened to be a short walk from the tightly shut gates of 79 Rue de Grenelle, which a brass plate engraved with a hammer and sickle discreetly identified as being the Soviet embassy.

Paris, as MI5 records and Philby's account confirm, was the principal European base of operations for Soviet intelligence during the Spanish Civil War. Surveillance of the Russian embassy by the French secret service was complicated. The embassy was located (in or near) the warren of narrow back streets of the Latin Quarter. The French capital boasted a far larger number of both *legal* and *illegal* Soviet agents on the ground than did London. This arrondissement included both the Soviet embassy and the Sorbonne university, plus the Café de Flore and the Deux Magots, which were the best known of the artists' cafés serving as meeting grounds for a whole generation of young French intellectuals under the spell of André Malraux and his followers. Malraux, the dominant Communist philosopher, polemicist and passionate champion of the Spanish Loyalists, was credited with converting more young people to communism than Marx ever had.

When Donald Maclean arrived in Paris toward the end of 1938, he too moved into a left-bank apartment and became an habitué of the two famous cafés in the shadow of the Romanesque tower of Saint-Germain-des-Près. By day the formally attired young diplomat diligently waded through official paperwork in the British embassy across the river. By night he shunned his fellow diplomats to join the Bohemian crowd that gathered at the marble-topped St Germain café tables.

The Left Bank was also home to Münzenberg's shadowy empire of Communist-front publishing houses, propaganda factories and workers' relief organizations. The myriad of safe houses tucked away in the Parisian student quarter, where all-night comings and goings attracted little attention, enabled NKVD officers to move in and out of the nearby Soviet embassy to clandestine meets and recruiting operations.

Moscow Center would have had no difficulty running the Cambridge agents from Paris after Maly's recall from London in the summer of 1937. That was, after all, where Philby implies that he was controlled from while in Spain. With Maclean also in the French capital in 1938, and with Blunt and Burgess making frequent trips across the Channel to Paris, it would have made security sense for the Soviets to administer the British agents from Paris.

Without the French police records that disappeared during World War II, it is not possible to identify the recruiter, or establish precisely when it was that Burgess might have signed on with the NKVD. Conversations with American intelligence officers with extensive contacts in the DST, the French counter-intelligence bureau, produce a scenario that has to take into account the extreme selectivity and caution of the NKVD between 1937 and 1938 (when Stalin's minion Yezhov was purging the organ of its old Comintern agents). Burgess, they believe, was managed by trusted NKVD officers in the Soviet embassy in Paris, who cultivated him as a 'source' rather than as an agent. They would have encouraged him to think he was nominally under Blunt's direction – until such time as Moscow Center had established his access to vital information and his willingness to submit to their discipline and control.

This would not have precluded the Soviets from using Burgess for missions of the kind Philby revealed that he ran in 1937, to 'replenish my funds'. This was the probable destination for the 'bundles of bank notes' that Goronwy Rees 'caught sight of stuffed away in the indescribably untidy cupboards' of Burgess's flat in Chester Square. One of these 'replenishment' runs for Philby may have coincided with the trip that Burgess made to Paris in the early summer of 1937 when he accompanied Rees to a conference of the Writers' International. His eagerness to participate in the 'impassioned revolutionary oratory' of the Writers' International also brought him into contact with Münzenberg's operatives. Senior MI5 officials have been credited with believing that Burgess must 'have learnt a lot' from these contacts because they were 'tremendously good operators'.

When Britain's seventy-year-old prime minister was preparing to bargain with Hitler at Munich in 1938, Burgess made his own move. Thanks to his clandestine trips he already knew what the outcome of this search for 'peace with honour' would be. So he tried to use his position as a BBC producer to turn public opinion against Chamberlain's appeasement policy. He had an effective weapon at his disposal, a BBC series entitled *This Week*.

The topical current-affairs program had proved an enormous success. Ambitious members of Parliament wined and dined Burgess for the privilege of receiving an invitation to appear on his shows. It was to his friend Harold Nicholson that Burgess turned as the member of Parliament most qualified to provide what were the only topical commentaries broadcast by the BBC at the time of Munich.

Egged on by Burgess, Nicolson tried to condemn Hitler's blackmailing diplomacy. But the Foreign Office demanded that the proposed script be heavily censored.

Ten days later, Chamberlain returned to Heston aerodrome. Before a swarm of reporters, the smiling but gaunt prime minister, clutching his umbrella, triumphantly waved Hitler's signature on the ruinous scrap of paper that he declared guaranteed 'peace in our time'.

Burgess knew better than most of his countrymen that

Chamberlain had brought neither peace, nor honor, back from his sell-out to Hitler. Burgess later told his BBC colleagues how he had telephoned the Soviet ambassador for his advice at the height of the Munich crisis. Ivan Maisky, he claimed, had urged him to go and see Churchill 'to call on him in the name of the Youth of Great Britain, to intervene.' Whether it was the Soviet ambassador or his own whim that prompted him to drive down to Kent, Burgess *did* visit Churchill at his country home in Chartwell to persuade him to make an anti-appeasement broadcast.

It was a Saturday morning and Burgess picturesquely claims that 'like Balbus' he found the gruff elder statesman, trowel in hand, building his famous orchard wall. Evidently impressed by the eloquence of the young BBC producer's conviction of the ominous inevitability of war, Churchill declined to speak but presented Burgess with a leather-bound copy of his speeches, *Arms and the Covenant*. He inscribed the volume: 'To Guy Burgess, from Winston S. Churchill, to confirm his admirable sentiments. September 1938.'

Churchill's book became a cherished possession of Burgess. One of his 'party pieces' was to relate a highly embellished account of his close and warm relationship with Britain's wartime leader. 'If I ever return to a position of responsibility and power and you wish to help me just bring the book along,' Burgess would claim Churchill said when bidding him farewell, adding the assurance: 'I shall never forget.'

These statements may have been more imagined than real, just as Burgess claimed that he was fired from the BBC a short time afterwards. He also claimed that after leaving the BBC he received an invitation to join Section IX of MI6 after serving the organization on a free-lance basis. But the truth, as it has recently come to light, is that he was invited to become a producer for a highly secret clandestine broadcasting operation, which the government conjured into being at the end of 1938 to wage a secret radio war against Hitler. No comprehensive records of the innocuously named Joint Broadcasting Committee exist in the British archives. The JBC had grown from the determination of the Foreign Office that a British prime minister's conciliatory words could counter the bellicose speeches of Hitler.

The belief that Hitler could be influenced by the German population led the Foreign Office to look for alternative ways to expand clandestine broadcasting operations. The JBC came under the aegis of Major-General Laurence Douglas Grand. He liked to describe himself as Director of Fortifications and Works at the War Office. Grand was a tall, mustachioed man, whose already dashing impression was accentuated by the red carnation he always wore in his buttonhole. He had been appointed in March 1938 to head up MI6's Section D. The designation of his new outfit was officially derived from 'D for Destruction'. It might more accurately have stood for 'Dirty Tricks', since the unit's assignment was to prepare ways for 'attacking potential enemies by means other than operations of military force.' The caveat imposed on D Section was that none of its operations were officially sanctioned to go into operation until war broke out.

In the aftermath of Munich, however, Grand's masters in the Foreign Office decided that they did not have to wait until the balloon went up to start clandestine propaganda broadcasts into Germany in defiance of the International Broadcasting Convention. Grand selected Burgess for this task – on the recommendation of Harold Nicolson and his MI6 friend David Footman.

Since the clandestine operations of the JBC are still considered so sensitive that its records are virtually nonexistent, it is not clear precisely how these broadcasts were put out. What is known is that at least some of Burgess's programs, recorded on large shellac discs, were taken by couriers to European commercial stations such as Radio Luxembourg. But there is a tantalizing reference in one Foreign Office docket about a prerecorded message of the Prime Minister's that was to be prepared 'for smuggling into Germany' for broadcasting from one of the 'mobile units inside Germany'. Just how Grand and MI6 managed to organize such facilities under the noses of the Gestapo is still a closely guarded secret.

The operation was modeled on – and may even have utilized –

the existing facilities of the underground anti-Nazi broadcasting networks operated by Hitler's old party comrade Otto Strasser and Willi Münzenberg's 'Freedom Station' that was beaming anti-Nazi propaganda into German under the secret sponsorship of the French government. So sensitive was the job that Burgess did for MI6 in the JBC between 1939 and 1941 that any reference to it has been excised from the FBI files in Washington at the request of the British government. The cloak of official secrecy still shrouds details of operations that Burgess must have betrayed to the Soviets. But there is little doubt that his JBC role in MI6 had also made him a potentially valuable agent to Moscow. With an 'official' excuse to travel all over Europe, he demonstrated his usefulness on courier and liaison duties. During the early months of 1939, while Franco's forces were winning Barcelona and recognition from the British government, Burgess headed south from Paris to the French border town of Saint-Jean-de-Luz, where he met the war-weary Kim Philby.

The Soviets were already cutting their losses and abandoning the Spanish Loyalists. Philby, however, had been told by Moscow to remain in his reporter's job. He stayed in Spain until July 1939, doggedly reporting the tide of Fascist military victories for the readers of *The Times*, with little to console him but the affections of his attractive mistress, Bunny.

Burgess was able to offer little more than encouragement to Philby, who must have been heartened – and not a little envious – to learn from him how he was rapidly advancing his career in the British secret service. That this meeting took place during the critical months of 1939 suggests that it must have been held at the direction of Soviet intelligence. As a member of MI6, Burgess would now have been regarded as a very valuable asset by Moscow Center. It is probable that it moved very rapidly after Burgess joined the JBC in 1939 to convert him from a regular 'source' to a controlled agent.

The critical transition in Burgess's relationship with the NKVD could well have taken place during the visit to Philby. The latter seems to have always been fully aware of the status of his fellow Cambridge agent's links with Soviet intelligence. For despite what Blunt told Wright, it is clear that both he and Burgess were under direct NKVD control in the months leading up to World War II. This is plain from Blunt's admission to Nigel West in the year before his death that, at the end of 1938, he had tried to obtain a commission in the Officers' Emergency Reserve. This move, he explained, was his response to the instructions of his Soviet controllers to position himself to infiltrate either the military or civilian intelligence organizations should war break out.

Since Christopher Blunt had already enrolled as a member of this particular reserve branch of Britain's part-time Territorial Army, Anthony asked his younger brother, who was then working in the City, for help. Anthony's embarrassment that he had involved his brother in a recommendation to the War Office was enormous when his application was flatly rejected.

Blunt's repeated statements that it was Burgess who was the organizing genius of the Cambridge network now appear to have been intended to throw MI5 off the scent. What is obvious is that his own failure to get into the Territorial Army in 1938 reveals that someone in the War Office was fully cognizant of his background.

Yet less than a year later, Blunt was enlisted in the army's intelligence section.

Blunt and Burgess were in the south of France on a motor tour
when the newspaper headlines of 23 August 1939, caught their
attention. The news from Moscow was that Hitler and Stalin had
signed a nonaggression treaty. The two men cut short their tour
and hurried home.

For the diplomats in London and Paris this alliance came as a
devastating blow. Britain had joined France on 31 March that
same year in unilaterally guaranteeing Poland's sovereignty. Two
weeks later, newly promoted Soviet Foreign Minister Vyacheslav
Molotov formally proposed a triple alliance against a German
attack. British and French diplomats had been shuttling to and
from Moscow ever since to hammer out the terms of an acceptable
treaty. But suspicions of Moscow's motives, and a deep aversion
to any alliance with communism, snarled the negotiations. Meanwhile, Stalin was no less suspicious of his potential Western allies
and had begun making secret overtures to Berlin.

The clamor of Hitler's saber rattling presented the British and
French governments with 'brutal truths'. That is what Churchill
called them in a House of Commons debate on the stalled Russian
alliance. 'Without an effective "Eastern front", he declared,
'there can be no satisfactory defense in the West, and without
Russia there can be no effective Eastern front.'

Chamberlain and Daladier fumbled disastrously and Stalin
struck one of the most cynical diplomatic bargains in history. In
return for a ten-year nonaggression treaty, he and Hitler agreed in
a secret protocol to carve up Poland and the Baltic states. The
treaty was seen as a devil's pact by many British people, and it

caused real consternation on the left. The trauma was especially severe for those in the Communist party and their sympathizers. Goronwy Rees was typical of those Marxists who broke immediately with the Communists over what he saw as 'the treachery of the Soviet Union'. He wrote that he noticed how even the normally unshakable Burgess was in 'a state of considerable excitement' and appeared 'frightened' when he arrived back in London. But when Robert Cecil asked Blunt during an interview in 1981 whether they were all shaken by the Nazi-Soviet pact, Blunt burst out with laughter.

'Guy and I were not at all upset because it was just what we thought was going to happen,' Blunt said with assurance. He and Burgess taking their cue from Moscow asserted that Daladier and Chamberlain had been trying to push the Russians into war with Germany and the pact had been Stalin's only way out. 'We argued that it was simply a tactical necessity for Russian to gain time,' Blunt said, echoing the standard Stalinist platitude that 'it gave them time to rearm and to get stronger to resist.' But he did concede that when they heard the news they turned the car around and headed back for England without a moment's hesitation.

'We came back immediately to London because we knew that war was about to break out,' Blunt told Cecil. Then he admitted that the person who was most upset was Rees. That Burgess had abandoned his car at Calais – 'one of the possessions which he values most in the world' – suggests that Blunt and Burgess had rushed back to England to prevent Rees from defecting, but he proved recalcitrant. He believed that 'one might as well entrust the interests of the working class to a rattlesnake.'

'I never want to have anything to do with the Comintern for the rest of my life,' Rees told Burgess, adding: 'Or with you, if you really are one of their agents.' If Rees had been a part of their conspiracy up to that point – as Rosamond Lehmann and others firmly believe – Blunt and Burgess henceforth ceased to regard him as trustworthy.

Cecil found it strangely significant that Blunt chose to

dramatize the issue by asking him to go into the bathroom at this point, proceeding to turn on all the taps.

'I think that other room is bugged,' Blunt breathed to Cecil over the rush of water. 'I want to tell you that Rees was one of us and this was the time he quit.'

Cecil said the whole performance was most odd. It puzzled him why Blunt should be so concerned about making the admission. Not until Cecil read *Spycatcher* some six years later did he appreciate that Blunt had not made this admission during any of his interrogations with Peter Wright. Confirmation that Rees was more deeply involved in the conspiracy than he had ever admitted is apparent from his statement that Burgess pressured him 'to forget about the whole thing'. Burgess refused to be satisfied until Rees assured him that he would 'never mention it again'. A short time later, Rees donned his Territorial Army uniform and reported for duty on the London docks when, as Blunt and Burgess had so confidently predicted, Hitler launched an attack on Poland.

On 3 September 1939, Chamberlain, his reedy voice cracking with emotion, announced on the BBC that Great Britain would honor its commitment to defend Poland and 'we are now at war with Germany.' The Prime Minister's declaration created a tricky dilemma for Blunt and the other members of the Cambridge network. Communists who had previously been antagonistic to appeasement were now obliged to adopt what MI5 described as 'a policy of mild opposition to what they termed "Britain's Imperialist war".' This discredited the party in the eyes of many of the left. The security services therefore wisely decided not to 'molest the Communists at present'.

From the day war broke out until the Soviets became Britain's allies two years later, in July 1941, Blunt and his fellow conspirators in the Cambridge network were guilty of double treason. But as soon as the fighting broke out, Blunt resumed his efforts to get into intelligence. He was clearly responding to orders from Moscow to find a position in which he could best serve its interests. Since his lack of army service and previous rejection by the War Office precluded a direct entry into Military Intelligence, he took an alternative route.

The BBC issued an appeal for linguists to volunteer for a special wing of the Corps of Military police. Blunt responded promptly, volunteering because of his fluency in French and German. He filed multiple applications to different departments calculating that the War Office would be too inundated by emergency paperwork to run more than the most cursory checks with MI5. Blunt would claim later that because of a bureaucratic foul-up he was both 'accepted and rejected by the same post.'

Blunt simply tore up the letter of rejection, kept the one of acceptance, and on 23 September 1939 he reported to Minley Manor. This, and the neighbouring Mytchett Barracks, near Aldershot, were the headquarters of the Corps of Military Police and its offshoot, the Field Security Police. There he submitted to the indignities of basic military training that he had despised at school: relentless drill, kit inspection and scrubbing the floors of the uncompromisingly bare barrack huts.

This diversity of talent was 'fairly routine material' to Brigadier John Shearer, who commanded the basic-training establishment. His recruits received only the most rudimentary lectures in gathering field intelligence. The program presupposed the current campaign would be fought under the same conditions as the Western front of World War I. There was no discussion of military secrets: the recruits were told only what MI5 and MI6 stood for, not how they operated. Yet it is significant that someone in the War Office now decided that Blunt's background of Marxism made him a potential security risk for even this minimal indoctrination in intelligence.

Three days after Blunt arrived at Minley Manor, Brigadier Shearer summoned him to inform him that the War Office had ordered him out of the training course because of 'a rather adverse report'. At breakfast that morning Shearer explained to other staff officers that Blunt was being withdrawn because he had been a Communist at Cambridge.

Blunt reported as ordered to the War Office. There he faced

questions from Major Kevin Martin, the deputy director of Military Intelligence. According to Blunt, MI5 had come up with a 'trace' against him in its Registry records. Martin told Blunt that there were 'two items on his file', Cecil said. The first was his trip to Russia. Blunt explained this away by pointing out that he had gone to study paintings in the company of Fletcher-Cooke and his brother, for whom there were no MI5 traces. The second trace referred to the three articles he had written for the Communist-leaning *Left Review*. These he fobbed off, doubtless relieved that his Marxist essay in *The Mind in Chains* had been overlooked.

Fortunately for Blunt, Major Martin was not very astute. He could not hide what he had written but there was no thorough vetting.

'Major Martin had no use for MI5 and was very happy to send me back to Minley Manor,' Blunt told Cecil with a wry smile. Martin was also confronted by a self-possessed young man whose aloof prefectorial authority was the essence of the 'officer-and-gentleman' quality that the British army regarded as essential for leading men into battle. As Cecil emphasized, the decisive factor was that the army had found itself desperately short of French-speaking officers at exactly the moment when General Gort's 158,000-strong British Expeditionary Force was being dispatched to northern France.

Burgess had been correct. He had predicted the year before that the war would give Blunt his break, and Blunt went straight from the War Office to Burgess's apartment to celebrate achieving the first step in becoming a part of the British intelligence apparatus.

Promoted to captain, Blunt was assigned command of the 18th Section of the Field Security Police. One of his lance corporals, Alan Berends, recalled how he appeared one day '"fully armed from the brow of Zeus" and looking very military with his swagger stick.' On 9 December the unit embarked for France to assume the policing of the Boulogne sub area of the British Expeditionary Force command. Their unit was armed with rifles and equipped with thirteen motorcycles. Blunt was issued a revolver and a small Austin to serve as his staff car, driven by his batman, Private Hunt.

'I worked with him more closely than the rest of the section back in Boulogne who spent most of their time censoring the mail of leave-bound troops,' Berends said. He told me how one of the captain's duties involved the local prostitute population, which mushroomed overnight when many of the cafés installed a girl in the back room to supplement the overextended services of the one municipally licensed brothel in Boulogne. Concern about the medical and security risks involved Blunt in a plan to open a second official facility. But despite his command of the French language, he was unable to overcome obstruction from the town councilors and the café proprietors.

As Berends explained it, the command did not exactly overtax the military skills of either the tall, austere captain or his men. 'There was really no intelligence work at all,' Berends stated emphatically. Their time was spent preventing the troops from taking uncensored letters on leave to England, or liaising with the four different French police forces, whose protocols and rival sensitivities Blunt appeared to understand very well. The most dramatic incidents were preventing friction with the local populace and filing the once-weekly report to BEF HQ in Arras.

Blunt spent five months of the Phoney War in France, carrying out the most mundane duties, increasing his chance for a really important intelligence posting once Hitler attacked France and the shooting war began.

Lord Rothschild had also volunteered for military service. He was not posted, however, to a humdrum unit of the Field Security Police. Rothschild's brains, financial contacts and scientific talents had been quickly snapped up by MI5. His task was to prepare a series of secret reports on 'German Espionage Under Cover of Commerce'.

Rothschild was attached to B Division of MI5. Its deputy director, since 1931, had been Captain Guy Liddell. From an organization report prepared for the Americans in August 1940, it is clear that Liddell, even before his promotion that May as head of the Counter-Espionage Investigation Division, exercised more authority, more continuously and with more detailed knowledge of Communist activities, than any other officer of MI5.

According to this document, Liddell had responsibility for many key areas: 'Counter-Espionage, Enemy and Neutral. Commercial Espionage, Sabotage. Communications, Censorship Liaison. Leakage of information and Examination of aliens arriving in the UK.' His responsibilities overreached and overlapped with those of others, including F Division's. This was the Subversive Activities Section that monitored 'Internal Security in HM Forces and Government Establishments, Left and Right Wing Movements, Pacifists & New Politics and Social Movements'. It was F Division that Roger Hollis joined in 1938. He was assigned to the unit that monitored subversive Communist activities.

The MI5 records show that Liddell had acquired the most intimate picture of Communist subversion in Britain since the early twenties. More often than not, it is his signature that appears on the reports about Communist activities and individuals; he often carried them personally to trusted officers of the US embassy in London. And it was to Captain Guy Liddell at the secret MI5 mailing address – Box 500, Parliament Street P.O., London SW1 – that the State Department sent data and answers to queries from FBI records.

In March 1938, Liddell embarked on the *Queen Mary* to make his second visit to the United States to discuss 'matters of mutual interest'.

What is clear from American and British records is that Liddell's trip to the United States had a specific purpose: his mission was to persuade America to reconsider its earlier rejection of the British suggestion that there be an official exchange of information on Nazi and Fascist problems. The exchange would be similar to that 'in force on Comintern affairs'. The State Department had objected because of 'practical difficulties'.

Liddell reported to London that these 'practical difficulties' were 'obviously' bureaucratic. The American armed forces had been 'clamouring for years for the necessary funds to set up a counter-espionage organization.' Moreover, the FBI was definitely 'anxious to establish a liaison with us, which could cover not only Soviet, German and Italian activities, but also those of the Japanese.' So he advised shifting the liaison program on espionage matters to the British military attaché in Washington and to the FBI because of the 'very close contact' he had established with 'Mr Hoover's organization' in Washington and New York.

On 5 September 1939, two days after the outbreak of war in Europe, a strongly worded protest by James C. Dunn, State's Adviser on Political Relations, touchily expressed his concerns about the 'delicacy and gravity of the present international situation'. He 'desired' therefore that MI5 be advised that 'information should continue in the regular channels established many years ago.' Dunn, who jealously believed himself to be the State Department's 'Mr Intelligence', had won the first round. (Eventually he would lose this bureaucratic battle with Military Intelligence and the FBI for exclusive control of this vitally important information.)

It was ironic, therefore, that it was State Department bureaucracy that blocked Dunn's trading a US residency permit for information from one of the most knowledgeable Soviet intelligence officers ever to defect to the West. Samuel Ginsberg, better known as Walter Krivitsky, had begun his career in the GRU prior to transferring to Soviet Intelligence. Before defecting in 1937 Krivitsky had been the principal NKVD underground *rezident* in Holland.

An intense, intellectual and quiet-spoken man, Krivitsky had been posing as an Austrian bookseller in The Hague. It was a perfect cover for his clandestine job as 'chief of the Soviet Military Intelligence for Western Europe', as he explained it. He was the possessor of many of the most closely held secrets about the Soviet networks and penetration agents in Britain and the United States. Marked for assassination by the NKVD, he had received police protection from the French in return for information. But he had no guard when he reached New York in December 1938, and he found that he was shadowed by members of the local Soviet consulate whom he knew well as former colleagues.

Krivitsky made a number of visits to the State Department, but he failed to secure legal immigrant status. Facing penury and deportation, Krivitsky took the advice of fellow Russian exiles, including the journalist Isaac Don Levine. He contracted to write for *The Saturday Evening Post* a series of articles at $5,000 per article in an attempt to alert America to the menace of 'Stalin's Secret Service'. A month after war broke out in Europe, Krivitsky agreed to testify before the House Committee on Un-American Activities in return for a halt in the threatened deportation proceedings. He exposed the Soviet Trade Mission, Amtorg, as one of the principal cover organizations of the NKVD, and claimed that it had 'agents planted in all institutions, governmental and industrial' in the United States (including the armed services). But he was still disappointingly unspecific. He explained that he would withhold total exposure until the State Department granted him resident status. The committee supported his claim, and he went into seclusion to await the fulfillment of his request.

Krivitsky may have withheld much information from his articles and testimony, but he had confided some vital nuggets relating to Soviet agents in key positions in the British government. With Britain fighting Hitler, who was now Stalin's ally, Isaac Don Levine, like many Jewish Americans, believed it his duty to pass on the information to the British. Krivitsky had identified to the British Ambassador in Washington one agent as being 'a code clerk in the secretariat of the Cabinet', a man named King. He did not know the name of the other, but described him as being 'a member of the Council of Imperial Defense'. He also referred to another traitor in the Foreign Office 'whose name was Scottish and whose habits were Bohemian'.

Lothian's ciphered telegram bearing Krivitsky's news reached the desk of the permanent head of the Foreign Office the following morning. 'Very unpleasant' was how Sir Alexander Cadogan noted it in his confidential diary, 'which seems to fix us a line on the 'leaks' of the past few years.'

Cadogan's comment is revealing. It shows that the Foreign Office had been aware of serious leaks but had been unable to track them down. Now MI5 moved swiftly. Although there were no code clerks in the Cabinet office with that name, one of Krivitsky's suspects was quickly identified as being Captain John H. King of the Foreign Office. On 15 September Cadogan's diary reveals that the counterintelligence chiefs of MI5 and MI6 were putting King and another suspect, whose initials were 'O.K.' through a 'Third Degree' examination. Robert Cecil points out that the involvement of rival counterintelligence organizations indicated the extreme seriousness of the situation. 'The Foreign Office regarded MI5 officers as little better than policemen in big boots,' he told me. 'They were always unhappy whenever they were involved in internal investigations. Cadogan had to keep the dirty laundry in-house, if possible.'

'Looks pretty black against King,' a worried Cadogan wrote in his diary. 'Very disturbing; shall have swift and discreet action at the right moment.'

The suspects had been suspended from their duties and sent on sick leave. King's apartment and that of his girlfriend, Helen Wilkie, were searched and their bank accounts investigated. King had already confessed to receiving money over the past six years from a Dutch agent of the Soviets: Henri Pieck. Whatever an MI5 'Third Degree' interrogation involved, it produced the desired result. On the evening of 25 September Cadogan reports receiving the news that MI5 has decided 'to jug him' that night. 'There is no doubt he is guilty – curse him – but there is no absolute proof,' Cadogan noted, adding cryptically, 'They are on the track of Mrs (. . .)' This appears to be a reference to King's girlfriend. Sure enough, a safe-deposit box in Helen Wilkie's bank in Chancery Lane held a stash of large-denomination notes (£5 and £10 notes were large denominations in prewar England). The records of their serial numbers at the Bank of England showed that some had been issued to the Moscow Narodny Bank in London. Another £500 was traced to Bernard Davidovich Gadar.

Confronted with this evidence, King confessed. But he claimed he had never handed over Foreign Office code books. On the strength of his admission of guilt, he was quickly tried and convicted *in camera* before Mr Justice Hilbery in No. 1 Court, Old Bailey, on 18 October 1939. Wartime regulations permitted the government to impose a publicity blackout on King's trial and his ten-year prison sentence.

Since no details of the case were published, for the next seventeen years the Foreign Office denied there had been any internal spies. Not until 1956, when Isaac Don Levine testified before the US Senate, did the truth begin to emerge. Levine's claim that Krivitsky's evidence had resulted in King's execution led to questions in Parliament. To avoid embarrassment, the British government issued only a brief statement on the case. Yes, a low-grade code clerk had been caught spying for Moscow. But Captain King had not been executed as Levine claimed; he was still living in England. The affair was played down. There was no discussion of how long King had been a spy, or what information he might have passed to the Soviets.

MI5 was so determined to keep the significance of Krivitsky's revelations secret that it also hushed up the involvement of the second spy and possibly a third suspect at work in the Communications Department. These startling facts emerge from the unpublished secret passages in Cadogan's diaries. They indicate that MI5 also investigated two other (unidentifiable) officials. There was not enough evidence to make them stand trial, but Cadogan records that they were nevertheless sacked for 'irregularities'. The damage was so great that Cadogan decided the Foreign Office had no option but to try to rebuild the security of its Communications Department from the ground up – starting with an entirely fresh cipher staff.

The Cadogan diaries do not reveal, nor has the Foreign Office ever admitted, that this monumental breach of security actually began ten years earlier, when King's fellow code clerk E. H.

Oldham walked into the Soviet embassy in Paris.

The reluctance to explain the anomalies arising from the King case is one of the more puzzling skeletons in the MI5 closet. Surprisingly, not a single reference to King or Krivitsky surfaces among the secret communications exchanged between Liddell and the US embassy in London. Nor is Oldham mentioned. And there are no fresh clues provided by Nigel West whose book *MI5* relies on inside sources, and states: 'None of Krivitsky's revelations were relevant to Burgess, Maclean, Philby or Blunt.'

Yet as Krivitsky had been vindicated over King, it is astonishing that Krivitsky's reference to 'a young man in the Foreign Office of good family' was too vague to have enabled MI5 to uncover Donald Maclean in 1940.

Gladwyn Jebb, as a rising young diplomat, was in 1939 private secretary to Sir Alexander Cadogan. It was in this capacity that he met Krivitsky early in 1940. Yet when I interviewed him in 1982, he was carefully vague about why Krivitsky was believed to be so valuable an informant that the British government offered to send a destroyer, or submarine, to bring him to England for a full debriefing by MI5. By mid-December, however, he agreed to make the voyage and he arrived in London on 19 January 1940.

The responsibility for Krivitsky's interrogation lay with Brigadier A. W. A. Harker's B Division of MI5, which had authority over counterespionage investigations. Harker was, by all accounts, a military figurehead rather than a leader. One colleague recalled him as being 'a sort of highly polished barrel which, if tapped, would sound hollow (because it was).' But it was his experienced deputy, Guy Liddell, who had charge of the day-to-day operations. Gladwyn Jebb, who sat in on some of the discussions and saw the final MI5 reports on Krivitsky, recalled that Liddell was 'intelligent and introspective'. These were precisely the qualities needed to deal with the jumpy NKVD defector, who knew how deeply Moscow had tapped into the Whitehall machine.

Liddell assigned Jane Sissmore, a former barrister and one of MI5's most sympathetic officers, to the delicate task of debriefing

Krivitsky. Their conversations continued for three weeks. Sissmore was already well versed in the makeup of Soviet espionage networks. Her former colleagues credit her with doing a superlative job of extracting a mass of information from a not always cooperative subject. Nigel West suggests, however, that beyond showing that Soviet intelligence had 'well established agents in a position to transmit the contents of all Foreign Office documents,' Sissmore's report, 'Summary of Interviews with General Walter Krivitsky,' dated January 1940, was *not* especially informative.

Other writers disagree. Seven years before West began his 'revelatory' investigations, Brook Shepherd of the *Daily Telegraph* had quietly and systematically interviewed intelligence officers on both sides of the Atlantic. He asserted that in three weeks of 'skilled and systematic debriefing', Krivitsky had identified ninety-three agents around the world of whom 'no fewer than sixty-one were named by him as operating in the United Kingdom itself, or directly against British interests elsewhere'.

Krivitsky was also able to confirm names of the principal secret illegals who had operated in London, including Pestrovsky, Maly and his subagent, Gadar. They were among the twenty-six whom Krivitsky named as being members of the NKVD *apparat*. Six were legal spymasters in the Soviet embassy or trade mission, and twenty were illegals working under varying nationalities, backgrounds and professions. Their job was to run the thirty-five agents who were actively engaged in espionage against Britain. Of the sixteen British nationals Krivitsky named in this menacing category, eight were active in left-wing politics and the trade-union movement, six were civil servants and two were journalists.

According to Brook Shepherd's inside source, only half of these names were new to MI5. Immediate steps were taken to 'neutralize' them, but none were ever prosecuted or their identities revealed. What then was the extent of MI5's knowledge of Soviet penetration in 1940?

From the wealth of reports passed to the State Department

about American Communist activists studying in British universities, it is clear that MI5 and Special Branch had not overlooked the academics. Cambridge had long been a focus for Special Branch surveillance. The reports in the US archives can be only the tip of a large iceberg of MI5 surveillance documentation. From the considerable volume of British reports filed under the 800 'B' (for Bolshevik)] classification, many bearing Guy Liddell's signature, it does *not* appear that MI5 was neglecting the potential Communist subversives at home.

But even Krivitsky's warnings did not prompt MI5 to investigate whether Oxbridge Communists were in the Whitehall machine. For among the Cambridge graduates who divided loyalties in varying degrees with Moscow, we now know that Andrew Cohen was then in the Colonial Office, Dennis Proctor was in the Treasury, and John Cairncross and Donald Maclean in the Foreign Office. Although they had gone underground and the identity of many of their sympathizers remains concealed to this day, at least one other Oxford graduate, Jenifer Fischer Williams, had admitted to being a secret party member when she joined the Home Office in 1938.

Until the British government releases the MI5 reports, it will be impossible to know with certainty whether Liddell investigated, ignored, or dismissed these warnings that Communists were rising to influential positions in Whitehall.

Philby further muddled what is publicly known about Krivitsky's evidence by alluding in his Soviet-approved autobiography to a 'nasty little sentence', presumably in Sissmore's January 1940 report, which said that 'Soviet intelligence had sent a young English journalist to Spain during the Spanish Civil War.' He also 'recalled the statements of Krivitsky' which mentioned a Foreign Office recruit 'of good family who had been to Eton and Oxford', whom the Soviets recruited in Europe in the 'mid-thirties' and who was 'an idealist working without payment'.

Again this clue did not lead directly to Maclean. He had neither attended Eton nor been to Oxford. But Philby acknowledged that when he was in Washington in 1949, a Foreign Office investigation that matched known leaks against Krivitsky's shadowy candidates produced a list of 'perhaps six names', including Maclean's.

A year after Krivitsky went to London for his interrogation he was discovered by a chambermaid in a seedy Washington, DC, hotel with a bullet in his head. His 'suicide' could not have come at a more convenient moment. The next day the Soviet defector had been scheduled to resume his testimony on Capitol Hill.

The secrets that Krivitsky took to his grave with his 'suicide' on 10 February 1941 have yet to be admitted by the British, who are evidently acutely aware of the potential for embarrassment they could still cause. Perhaps this explains why the self-appointed 'official' historians of British intelligence continue to dismiss Krivitsky's significance.

According to Peter Wright, when he checked the still very secret file on people named by Krivitsky, he was quickly able to pinpoint a Captain Charles Howard Ellis as having given information to both the Germans and the Soviets via the émigré connections of his White Russian wife. What had sparked Wright's interest was that Philby had been through the files before Wright, at a time when Philby was the head of Section IX, the Soviet section of MI6.

'Who is this man Ellis? NFA (no further action)' was what Philby had written in the margin on the file. This puzzled Wright because, at the time, Philby's office in 1945 was just down the corridor from the one occupied by the same Ellis. Not only had Ellis apparently given the Germans the MI6 order of battle at the outbreak of the war, he had also warned the Germans that the British had tapped into the private conversations between Ambassador von Ribbentrop and Hitler's office in Berlin. Another treasonable act attributable to Ellis' leaks was that he was responsible for the Venlo incident of November 1939, mentioned earlier, when the Germans captured two high-ranking British intelligence officers near a Dutch border town. Even more worrisome was the fact that, during the war, Ellis had been the deputy of Sir William 'Intrepid' Stephenson's operation in New York.

It was the conclusion of Wright and the Fluency Committee, set up in 1964 by MI5 and MI6 to investigate Soviet penetration, that Ellis could well have been an undercover agent for thirty years: first with the GRU before the war and later, after Philby saw his file, blackmailed by Philby into spying for the KGB. The case is all the more astonishing because of (1) the apparent ease with which Philby was able to cut off any investigation into Ellis, and (2) the fact that Wright had obtained a partial confession from Ellis. But Ellis suffered from heart trouble, and Maurice Oldfield, the new head of MI6, preferred to give Ellis the benefit of the doubt because it 'was all long ago and best forgotten'.

After all, one is talking about going back to when the intelligence organization was leaderless. At the time of the Venlo incident, Admiral 'Quex' Sinclair, who had been head of MI6 since 1923, had just died of cancer. His chosen successor, Colonel Steward Menzies (pronounced Mengies), had been the head of Section II (military) and had been deputizing for Sinclair during his illness. Menzies, however, was not formally appointed as the new 'C' by the Prime Minister until November, two weeks after the Venlo incident.

A forty-nine-year-old ex-Etonian and Life Guards officer, Menzies had an aristocratic wife and mother and was a London clubland figure who hunted with the Duke of Beaufort's pack near his country home in Wiltshire. One colleague recalled Menzies's 'maniacal fondness for security', sorely needed, as 1940 opened with revelations of fresh disasters in the Foreign Office.

On 26 January a report was made to Cadogan that 'secret documents' had leaked to the German government from the Central department of the Foreign Office. This is the only reference to what must surely have been another major breach of British security. Cadogan confessed bitterly in his diary entry 26 January 1940: 'I can trust *no-one*.'

The fresh alarm did, however, convince him that security was a major priority. Ten days later the Foreign Office named its first security officer, a retired diplomat named William Codrington. But he had no salary or assistant, and the post had little real impact until a fully staffed Security Department was established after the war.

As the start of one of the most crucial years in Britian's history, the Foreign Office was in turmoil because of spies and leaks. This contrasts oddly with a glowing presentation prepared for the Americans barely six months later. Labeled STRICTLY CONFIDENT-IAL, the report emphasized the success of British efforts 'to ferret out and counteract the purposes and activities' of subversive groups. The report was transmitted to the State Department in August 1940 with the 'wholehearted co-operation' of MI5, and the thirty-page report, which was recently uncovered in the US National Archives Regional Center at Suitland, Maryland, is a masterpiece of bureaucratic wishful thinking. It sets out the full extent of British secret-service operations, though in a way that has never been officially acknowledged.

This report owes its genesis to the new prime minister, Winston Churchill, who recognized that the Battle of Britain in the air was only a preliminary round in a desperate struggle. His rhetoric in the House of Commons had rallied the nation. But it was not enough to hurl back the threatened German invasion. His three-month-old coalition government had to woo from the Roosevelt administration the military, economic and political support that was being withheld by a resolutely isolationist Congress.

Churchill was so anxious to secure the means with which to keep on fighting Hitler that in return for fifty overage destroyers, he was offering more than just British territory to be used for US naval bases. The files suggest that by offering a blueprint of the British security service, Churchill may also have intended a larger trade-off of secret intelligence.

'The English have done a very smart thing in connection with counter-espionage, which might well be copied by the United States,' was how the US embassy in London reported the offer to Washington. 'Unknown to the British public, unknown to the newspapers, and unknown even to most of the Government officials,' the report continued, 'there has been in existence for 31 years an elaborate organization for the detection and prevention of the activities of foreign governments.' It went on to reveal that the security service had grown from four officers and half a dozen clerks in 1914 to 'between 250 and 300 people now in the Service, of whom more than 100 are official [sic].'

According to the US report on MI5: 'The scope of the organization can be seen from the fact it now embraces 300 Chiefs of Police – 250 from Great Britain and Northern Ireland and 50 from the Empire.' Senior officers of the British security service declared 'that no British newspaperman has ever discovered the true scope of their organization,' noting that MI5 was the 'only counterespionage activity which is ever mentioned in the newspapers.' Furthermore, the report confirmed that neither the British people, nor German intelligence, had 'any inkling' of the extent of the security service: 'Apparently the public is completely unaware of the existence of the super machine of which MI5 is only one cog.'

The 'super machine' that was the British security service relied on a 'centralized control' that embraced the army and navy intelligence services and MI5, plus links that reached out through the police chiefs into the network of constables all over the British Isles and the police forces of the empire. The reach was therefore truly global. It supplied information for the 'central index of suspicious persons', which was one of the 'major activities' of the security service. The Registry index by 1940 contained 'the name of every person ever suspected in any part of the world of anti-British activity – a total of 4,500,000 names.'

This window dressing may have seemed essential to impress the Americans about Britain's vaunted security apparatus. But the truth was something different. The super machine, which Churchill hoped to export to the United States, was already breaking down. Blunt and Philby were about to be recruited into the British intelligence apparatus because of inadequate vetting – or preexisting high-level penetration by the Soviets. As the summer months of 1940 were to prove, the super machine of British security was as futile a defense for England as was France's vaunted Maginot Line.

13 'Keep That Man
Out of the Office'

On 10 May 1940, the German assault on the West promptly disposed of the Maginot Line. On the same day Winston Churchill began his 'walk with destiny' as Britain's pugnacious wartime prime minister. (A month earlier the German invasion of Denmark and Norway had ended the Phoney War, and Chamberlain's ineffective leadership collapsed.) But within five days of taking office, the new prime minister found himself facing military disaster.

Resistance in bombed and battered Holland collapsed. Queen Wilhelmina and her government escaped to England in a destroyer. Then the French army broke on the Sedan salient on 14 May and an avalanche of German armored might burst out onto the plains of northern France. Three panzer divisions raced for the French coast to isolate the retreating British Expeditionary Force that was withdrawing from Belgium to reinforce the battered French army now falling back on Paris. Covering the retreat for *The Times* was Kim Philby, who was evacuated through Blunt's sector in Boulogne.

Captain Blunt received the alarming news that the Germans had broken out and were heading for Boulogne. The equanimity with which he received the message astonished the men of his platoon. 'In April 1940, we had been disarmed to equip the troops in the Norway campaign,' Alan Berends explained. Except for a single rifle and Blunt's revolver, the 18th Field Security Section had no weapons to defend themselves.

In truth, the commanding officer of the 18th Field Security Section was fast asleep in his billet when the Germans arrived on the outskirts of Boulogne on 25 May. 'It was only when we got a call from someone in the navy back in Dover telling us to get out fast that we decided to do so,' Lance-Corporal Curry recalled, adding how he had 'to go and dig Blunt out of his billet.' Six of the platoon elected to make their escape via Dunkirk, but Blunt and the other six men managed to find a lone boat packed with explosives intended for the demolition of harbor installations. 'The ship didn't have time to unload before we got away,' Curry observed wryly. Their precarious position atop all the high explosives, while German planes bombed and strafed all around them, was relished by Blunt. His sangfroid left an indelible impression on his men.

Yet Curry believed there was something unnaturally calculated about Blunt's glacial coolness under fire. His demeanor appeared to have had more to do with a cold-blooded intellect bent on testing itself to the limit than with bravery in the accepted sense.

That summer, the dogfights of the Battle of Britain etched their surrealistic patterns in the skies over southern England. In the House of Commons, and over the BBC, Churchill's bulldog rhetoric rallied the nation with his call to fight the expected German invaders on the beaches, streets and hills – and never surrender.

In the lecture room of the Warburg Institute, appropriately attired in his army uniform, Dr Blunt resumed lecturing as the avenues of his beloved Paris echoed to the goose-stepping Nazi victory parades. The determination to combine art with his military duties, gave Blunt's war effort a schizophrenic quality. On the one hand, he was preparing his Cambridge thesis, 'The Artistic Theory in Italy', for publication. (It bore a surprising dedication to Guy Burgess in acknowledgment of 'the stimulation of constant discussion and suggestions on all the more basic points at issue'.) On the other hand, he was heeding Moscow's instructions to find himself a post in the British intelligence services.

Since the outbreak of war, both MI5 and MI6 had expanded rapidly by recruiting some of the best intellects from Oxford and

Cambridge as well as the legal professions. Friends of Blunt's now in the service could be relied on to put in a good word for him on the old-boy network.

One of the most prominent was Lord Rothschild who had joined MI5 shortly after the war began in 1939. His claim to have merely given up his Trinity fellowship and biophysical research into the fertilization of frog eggs to concentrate on counter-sabotage does not do justice to his remarkably versatile career as an intelligence officer.

A July 1940 report, newly discovered in the US Archives and signed by Rothschild, shows that he was originally brought into MI5 as an investigating officer in the Commercial Espionage unit of Division B. (Only later did he transfer to the countersabotage section, where he won the George Medal in 1944 for dismantling a German time-bomb device concealed in a box of Spanish onions.)

Just how Rothschild came into MI5 has never been revealed, but his sponsor appears to have been Guy Liddell, who was then B Division's deputy director. A recommendation from Burgess (then working in Section D of MI6) may also have persuaded the B's director of the need to tap into the Rothschilds' network.

Access to extensive commercial intelligence data helped Rothschild make a unique contribution to MI5's efforts to counter German espionage operations in Britain.

The magnitude of the danger facing Britain from commercial espionage early in the war appears in the detailed analysis Rothschild made of one of the most important sectors of British industry: machine tools. He found this to be heavily dependent on German suppliers and their agents, who had infiltrated the business. The only prudent solution was for the Ministry of Supply to transfer its business to American machine-tool manufacturers.

Rothschild's report must have made a great impression with Liddell, because he sent Rothschild himself to the US embassy to alert the Americans. This suggests not only his regard for Rothschild, but the authority he exercised as the head of B Division after Churchill's shakeup of MI5 in May 1940 put him in charge of counterespionage.

Rothschild had both Liddell's respect and access to him and thus could easily draw his attention to Blunt's abilities. Blunt admitted at his 1979 press conference that his recruitment, 'like all of that kind' was 'done simply' on the basis of personal recommendation. 'Someone who was in MI5 recommended me,' he stated. 'I was recommended.' What is more, he confirmed that his referee on the old-boy network was well aware of his open Communist convictions.

Ever since, the fear of libel action has obliged writers to make careful allusions to an anonymous MI5 officer who recommended Blunt. This despite Blunt's 1981 interviews with Robert Cecil, at which he admitted embarrassment at using his close friend Rothschild to write the necessary letter of recommendation.

'That Rothschild had become acutely sensitive about his relationship with Blunt is understandable because he had originally recommended Blunt for recruitment into the Security Service and had introduced him to Guy Liddell' was the assertion made by Nigel West in *Molehunt*. 'This was a matter of record within MI5 and was known to a great many of his former colleagues, some of whom had mixed feelings about Rothschild.'

Lord Rothschild did not press West with his threatened libel suit. But Rothschild's friends still protest that he has 'been wrongly accused of being responsible for bringing Blunt into MI5.' Indeed Rothschild has let it be known that he 'now has proof that MI5 has no letter showing that he introduced Blunt into MI5.'

After such vigorous denials, I asked *Molehunt*'s author whether he still stands by his assertion that Rothschild was instrumental in getting Blunt into MI5. Now a Conservative member of Parliament, Rupert Allason, who writes under the pen name of Nigel West, confirms 'absolutely' his original account. Like Robert Cecil, he is one of the few people outside Britain's security service to have interviewed Blunt before his death. Furthermore 'West' explained that he does not make his case on what Blunt said, but on his own face-to-face talk with Rothschild in January 1987.

'I am not denying that I introduced Blunt to Guy Liddell,' Rothschild told West. 'In fact, I'll tell you a funny story about it.'

He then related how Liddell, his B Division boss, had asked him to arrange a meeting with Blunt 'to look him over'. That tête-à-tête took place, shortly after Blunt's escape from France, at the three-floor London maisonette that Rothschild and his first wife, Barbara, then occupied on Bentinck Street. (Liddell insisted that he be introduced as Captain Black.) Liddell was a keen amateur art collector and got on famously with Blunt. Halfway through the evening it became apparent that Blunt's appointment with MI5 was a foregone conclusion because, as Rothschild told West, Liddell dropped the charade and identified himself, much to the amusement of all present.

According to West, after this personal introduction, subsequent vetting was a mere formality. The right school and college were an almost automatic guarantee of acceptance during MI5's rapid expansion to meet the demands of war. By the end of 1939, its dramatic growth necessitated moving out to Wormwood Scrubs, a forbidding-looking Victorian prison in West London. The four-foot-thick walls may have provided adequate physical protection for the secrets of the extensive Registry files until an incendiary bomb forced their evacuation to Blenheim Palace near Oxford in September 1940. Vetting admitted some startlingly indiscreet new members to the premises.

'You know anyone could come into the Scrubs and put up a sign saying he's starting a new section to cover this and that,' Liddell had joked in 1939. Anyone, that is, who had been to the right public school and Oxbridge college. Little attention seems to have been paid to the political reliability of these new recruits. Vetting was so lax, for example, that shortly after Blunt's admission, the notorious aesthete Brian Howard was engaged to report on Fascist sympathizers among the upper-class London nightclub set. The 'beautiful Peter Pollock', the boyfriend Burgess had picked up in Cannes, was also living it up in the Dorchester on an MI5 expense account. His mission was to 'keep an eye on aliens – particularly Hungarians.'

Blunt, however, was seriously determined to make an efficient secret-service officer – even if he was serving two masters – when he joined D Division in the late summer of 1940. For the first two months, Blunt served Brigadier H. I. Allen in that part of the division that an organizational chart designates as being concerned with 'General Military Security Problems'. Although D Division was somewhat remote from the real center of MI5 operations, this was a logical appointment, given Blunt's previous army experience in the Field Security Police. But his desk job was in the section that handled the security of Britain's armaments factories, ports, and armed services. For Soviet intelligence, there was an additional bonus in having Blunt work for Brigadier Allen. The wartime organization chart reveals that Allen was also responsible for supervising the work of C Division. This was the outfit that carried out security vetting, euphemistically described as the 'Examination of Credentials' of civilians and military personnel in 'key positions'.

Although Blunt would complain about routine paper-pushing during his first two months in MI5, he had access to valuable data to pass on to his Soviet controller. He had a legendary photographic memory, so had no need to copy documents or make notes that would make him vulnerable to any security searches. On the one occasion when he did take secret papers out of the office, he was stopped by the police who, much to his relief, failed to spot the incriminating documents. This close call was a salutary lesson. Blunt never again removed papers. He thenceforth relied on his memory to carry information to his Soviet control officer.

At his 1979 press conference, Blunt took care to be evasive about the identity of his Soviet control officers and how they communicated. His excuse was that 'these are things which ought not to be discussed.' But when pressed, he conceded that he had been in touch with a member of the staff of the Soviet embassy in London after joining MI5 in 1940. In subsequent private conversations with Nigel West, Blunt was less reticent. He said his first wartime controller used the code name 'George'. In 1940, he was replaced by a Soviet embassy official named 'Henry'. MI5 never succeeded in identifying 'George's' diplomatic cover, but during interrogations in 1964 Blunt did identify 'Henry'. From visa photographs of the wartime Soviet legations, he picked out Anatoli Gorski, who served as a first secretary and who arrived in London in 1940 and left four years later for Washington. Gorski, who was also known as Anatoli Gromov in the United States, is therefore the most likely candidate for the wartime control officer of Blunt and the other leading Cambridge moles.

In resorting to its old practice of employing legals in the Soviet embassy to run its foreign agents in the wartime emergency, the NKVD had to offset the advantage of exercising more direct control against the increased risk of more direct surveillance. Operatives who passed themselves off as diplomats were already known to the 'watchers' whose job it was to tail them for MI5. This required elaborate precautions by both the agent and the control officer in establishing their meets.

Blunt told West that 'Henry' and he never had any problems, even though they used to rendezvous on a regular basis. Blunt gave the impression that he met his control every week, more often than not in the smoke-filled saloon bars of public houses. Golders Green and East End bars were particular favorites of the Soviets. The long journey to these outer London suburbs required trips by underground and bus, which simplified the roundabout routes and doubling back required to shake off any tail. Blunt's military uniform made him inconspicuous among so many others in the packed wartime bars, and the blackout made it easy for them to slip away into the night undetected.

After a couple of months 'Johnson', as Blunt was code-named by Moscow Center, received instructions from 'Henry' to seek a position closer to the heart of MI5 operations. Liddell was 'terribly susceptible to flattery', according to one of his wartime officers, and he was carefully cultivated by Blunt. The two men toured the wartime London salerooms with Blunt advising Liddell which pictures to buy. Before long Blunt was made Liddell's personal assistant in the B Division directorate.

Blunt's diligence and attention to detail impressed Liddell. He gave Blunt the task of reporting on the efficiency of the watchers who tailed MI5 suspects. This enabled Blunt to go through all the reports and warn the Soviet embassy how best to avoid the surveillance of its diplomats. Unfortunately for Moscow, its agent 'Johnson' proved too diligent. Blunt's growing influence over the director of B Division, who increasingly deferred to him, ignited the resentment of Margo Huggins, Liddell's longtime secretary.

A straightlaced woman, Huggins objected to the smooth-talking intruder not because she suspected his motives but because she found her own influence with Liddell threatened. She sought an ally in Dick Goldsmith White, the deputy director of B Division. The former Oxford scholarship student and Common-wealth fellow was himself interested in art and confessed to having enjoyed Blunt's polished conversation and civilized camar-aderie. But he could not help but notice how his Cambridge contemporary went out of his way to single him out in the canteen for a chat. Blunt, he recalled 'made a general assault on key people to see that they liked him.'

White resented the way that Blunt 'cultivated Liddell as a way of protecting himself.' But White did not suspect his colleague of treachery. Nor was White any stranger to intellectual superiority, since the members of his own Oxford college irritated members of lesser foundations by parading their arrogance and referring to Christ Church snootily as 'The House'.

White was neither an intellectual, political nor social snob. A mild-mannered, studious undergraduate, he had no taste for the revolutionary politics that afflicted so many of his contem-poraries. Nor was he less intellectual than his peers, as is con-firmed by his exhibition in history to Christ Church, followed by postgraduate studies at the universities of Michigan and Cali-fornia. As a result of his firsthand experiences in the United States, White had begun his career as a public-school master possessed with a pro-American sympathy and understanding that was unusual for most Englishmen. He regarded the decline of Britain's power and the steady rise of the United States – which caused resentment in so many of his contemporaries – as part of the historical process.

Despite his ramrod bearing, White's patient understanding and quizzical eyes are more evocative of the musty classrooms where he began his career. Even Philby paid him the grudging compliment of admitting White's 'gifts for chairmanship.' He was groomed and ready to move into the post of deputy director when Liddell was promoted to head B Division in May 1940. His fundamental good sense and knack of avoiding departmental fights were the qualities that would eventually lead Sir Dick Goldsmith White, KCMG, KBE, to the top of both MI5 and MI6.

White's skill at soothing ruffled feathers restored tranquility in Liddell's office. After his spell with the Watchers, Blunt was transferred to B(1)b (maintaining surveillance on the foreign embassies in London).

The redoubtable Miss Huggins, however, did not assert her authority over the director fast enough to save the life of a Russian mole whom the British had run for seven years on the Politburo staff in Moscow. He was a school friend of an MI6 officer named Harold 'Gibby' Gibson, who had been educated in prerevolutionary Russia. While Gibson was in Moscow he had been able to persuade his friend, who was then working in the private office of Anastas Mikoyan, that his disenchantment with Stalin could be repaid by espionage. Shortly after Blunt's arrival in B Division in the fall of 1940, this valuable inside source in Moscow dried up.

Charged by Wright with silencing 'Gibby's spy' during his interrogation twenty-five years later, Blunt made no effort to deny his responsibility. 'He was a spy,' he snapped back with icy disdain: 'He knew the game; he knew the risks.' For a brief instant Blunt dropped his mask, and Wright glimpsed the ruthless professional agent who had proved his worth to the NKVD.

But Blunt was not the only Cambridge mole to start paying rich intelligence dividends by mid-1940. Donald Maclean was reestablished at the Foreign Office in London after a hair-raising escape from France with his wife. He had hurriedly married Melinda Marling, his American student girlfriend.

When Maclean reported for duty at the Foreign Office, he was not assigned, like the rest of the embassy officials, to the French Department. Instead he was put into a newly formed General Department. This section dealt with economic warfare, handling issues such as shipping, contraband, and the international repercussions of Britain's decision to impose a naval blockage of German seaborne trade. Maclean's more ambitious colleagues considered such concerns very low-grade duties. But such technical data was of immense value to the Soviets.

Meanwhile, Burgess was also feeding 'Henry' information from MI6, plus the nuggets he gleaned from his MI5 friends. Burgess was now a vital player in the NKVD game plan. His shadowy activities in the Phoney War as producer for the Joint Broadcasting Committee proved a convenient cover for pursuing an independent liaison with members of the European Communist underground. This was not so much on account of the value of the intelligence he was supplying, but because he was uniquely placed as a gatekeeper to ease the admission of Philby and other agents into the British intelligence services.

After war broke out Grand's attention switched from propaganda to the sabotage operations. Burgess championed a plan for starving the Germans into defeat by setting the wheat fields of Central Europe ablaze with incendiary-carrying balloons. After the fall of France cut Burgess off from his European radio network, he became one of the principal ideas men in Grand's Section D. The very sprawling nature of the empire that Grand had built enabled Burgess to exploit its inconsistencies and confusion to recommend his friends for jobs. His first success was to get Kim Philby into Section D by skillful lobbying with Grand and other War Office and MI6 contacts. He even contrived to attend Philby's second and final vetting interview, which took place with Marjorie Maxe at the St Ermin's Hotel. Afterward, Philby reported for duty to Burgess's office, having handed in his resignation to *The Times*.

It was not, as Philby admitted, 'the ideal starting point for what

I had in mind.' His first objective had been to join the Government Code and Cypher School. This was the top-secret code-breaking center at Bletchley Park, where a team of brilliant Cambridge mathematicians turned cryptanalysts were already beginning to penetrate the mysteries of the German Enigma codes. But to Philby's fury – and the dismay of his Soviet controller – he was turned down. According to Philby, this was because Birch 'could not offer me enough money to make it worth my while'. But it is more probable he was rejected because his father, St John Philby, was then regarded as a pro-Nazi sympathizer.

According to Philby, there was 'Nothing Recorded Against' his name in the MI5 Registry. So when Burgess recommended him for a job in Section D, only the most cursory check was made into his background credentials. But once admitted to MI6, he was soon able to pass on to 'Henry' the important administrative details of MI6. He also convinced Grand that what his outfit needed to become really effective was a school for civilian saboteurs. Burgess took the credit, but it was Philby who in July 1940 turned his friend's 'riot of ideas' into a series of cogently argued memoranda that resulted in official approval for establishing a training school for saboteurs in the secluded Brickendonbury Hall estate in Hertfordshire north of London.

Philby and Burgess were appointed members of the staff of what they jokingly called 'Guy Fawkes College' which was set up in July 1940. Burgess, meanwhile, hatched a plot too Machiavellian to ascribe to any Soviet control officer. He proposed to Harold Nicolson, now the parliamentary secretary to Alfred Duff Cooper, the minister of information, that Burgess and his Oxford friend, Isaiah Berlin – a fellow of New College and a fluent Russian speaker – were uniquely qualified to be the press attachés to Sir Stafford Cripps, the ascetic left-wing Labour MP whose appointment as ambassador to the Kremlin had just been announced.

Nicolson's recommendation, coupled with a convenient bureaucratic silence from the Foreign Office and some fast talking by Burgess, enabled him to set off with Berlin for the United

States at the end of June. Their plan was to travel by way of San Francisco across the Pacific to Vladivostok and on to Moscow. But it came unstuck when they reached Washington. A cable arrived from the Foreign Office making it very plain that Cripps had most strenuously objected to the pair.

Burgess had suffered a setback, but he was infinitely resourceful and made the best of his time in Washington by renewing contact with Michael Straight.

Straight had recently married his Cambridge sweetheart, Belinda Crompton. They were living in a rented home across the Potomac in Alexandria, Virginia. According to Straight, Burgess was the least welcome of his British visitors. During their lunch at the Little Garden Tea House, Burgess went out of his way to remind his fellow Apostle of the pact that he had made before leaving Cambridge. 'I am completely out of touch with my friends,' Burgess said. 'Could you put me in touch?'

Straight says that Burgess was sounding him out to see 'whether he was still cooperating' with the Soviet intelligence service. But Straight did not tell Burgess that he had had contact with a Soviet agent. Nor did he rise to the bait that evening, after Burgess had invited himself to supper at the Straight residence. The topic came up after Burgess had insisted on cataloguing his sordid excursions with Pfeiffer to the male brothels of Paris.

When Straight disclosed the details of Burgess's 1940 visit to FBI investigators (twenty-three years later, in June 1963), he admitted that he had felt unable to report either this meeting, or the contacts he had been having with agents of the Soviet intelligence service that began in December 1937.

The first contact had been made by telephone when the caller identified himself as Michael Green and conveyed greetings 'from your friends in Cambridge University'. Straight told the FBI that he 'sensed immediately it had originated with Anthony Blunt.' He was then living at his mother's apartment on Park Avenue in New York City. He had approached Edward Stettinius of United States Steel while 'looking around for a job'. This was after he and a friend from Cambridge, John Simmonds, had spent most of the summer and fall chauffeuring Roger Baldwin, the head of the American Civil Liberties Union, on a speaking tour of the United States.

The call from Green, Straight said, he had been apprehensively hoping would never come ever since he left Cambridge. Nevertheless, he 'made arrangements with Green for a personal meeting which was consummated.'

Michael Green shook his hand warmly with a firm grip. Although he apologized for having 'mislaid' his half of the torn blue-ink drawing of Belinda that Blunt had retained a year before, he introduced himself by using the 'verbal parole' (passwords) Straight had been given.

Straight later told the FBI that Green was in his early thirties, a dark-haired 'chunky' man with a flattened pugilist's nose. They had 'a couple of meetings' in New York. Straight remembered they had walked through Central Park and visited the zoo. He said that Green made no demands 'but endeavoured to study and appraise him and appeared to have prepared topics and lines of conversation to test his thoughts and points of view and to shape his mind.' He said that he was 'usually witty and given to making puns'.

Green was obviously Russian, although Straight was impressed that he spoke English fluently. From his 'inexpensive' American-cut suit – which was a half size too small – and bureaucratic manner, Straight assumed he was posing as an American businessman. From FBI photographic records he 'immediately and positively' identified Green as William Grienke.

Declassified FBI files characterize Grienke as Straight's 'Soviet Intelligence Service (SIS) handler'. Straight himself stated that he did not believe Green trusted him and did not regard him as a 'dedicated Communist'. This he felt may have been because he insisted on maintaining his friendship with Roger Baldwin and his sister's pro-tsarist drama teacher, which caused Green/Grienke annoyance and displeasure.

Straight had moved to Washington in the spring of 1938 and through his connection with Eleanor Roosevelt, the president's wife, was given an unsalaried assignment under Herbert Feis, who was then an economic adviser to the State Department. He told the FBI he 'was sure' he had told Green of his plans, which perhaps explains why the Soviet intelligence-service officer phoned him. They had 'three or four meetings' in Washington 'at intervals of approximately one a month' at Washington restaurants during which they 'discussed topics of current interest'. In his autobiographical memoir, Straight said that Green suggested he could assist him by taking 'interesting' documents home from the State Department 'to study'.

According to the FBI records, Straight admitted that he furnished Green with a memorandum on 'Economic Consequences of European Rearmament', which he had prepared for the secretary of state. He also conceded that on one occasion he met Green by car and passed over 'two official State Department documents' that he had not prepared. Straight insisted these were 'not highly classified', although he admitted they were 'not for public consumption and may have borne the classification Confidential.' He recalled how on this occasion he had dropped his Russian handler off in the vicinity of the Soviet embassy 'so he could have copies made', and then picked him up later.

Straight also told the FBI that during the period when Green was out of touch with him, he had been contacted by a Solomon Adler in the summer of 1938. Adler turned out to be an associate of Solomon Lichinsky, the man whom Elizabeth Bentley was to link in 1948 to the Soviet espionage ring in the State Department. Adler told Straight to 'lie low', that he would be recontacted,and that he had been referred to him as 'a Communist in the Department of State' by a radical co-worker named Donald Stephens, who had been a friend of Straight's mother.

Green eventually reappeared and continued to contact Straight after he had left the State Department early in 1939. Straight told the FBI that Green was 'dissatisfied with his departure from government service but 'mollified' when he 'invented' the possibility that he was hoping to get a job at the War Department. Straight's decision to turn down a permanent position in the

Office of the Economic Adviser to work for the Department of the Interior, Straight says, was influenced by his resistance to Green's continuing pressure to hand over more classified government documents to the Soviets.

Tommy 'The Cork' Corcoran and his associate, Benjamin U. Cohen, counsel for the National Power Policy Committee, were two of Roosevelt's New Deal cronies. With Europe heading for war, Straight jumped at the opportunity to write speeches for the president, the Cabinet and the liberal leaders of Congress. The speeches were 'non-classified', so Straight felt less constrained in handing over to Green his anti-Stalinist attack on the Nazi-Soviet pact, together with 'four or five other commentaries' prepared for the Department of the Interior. But his main job was speech-writing. He hoped that his words might make some contribution to a shift in America's stance from neutrality toward an active participation in the struggle against Hitler.

This put Straight, on matters of policy, at loggerheads with the official Moscow position of supporting Hitler. The 1940 appearance of Burgess in Washington therefore only increased Straight's discomfort. So, after driving Burgess back to Washington that night, Straight told his wife that he had been having contacts with an emissary of the Soviet Union. In response to her understandable concern, he says he promised to break off contact with Green. And it was in response to her appeals that Straight left the Department of the Interior soon after to get away from Washington and spend time with his family in Wyoming. When he returned in August and obtained a position as assistant to James Dunn, the chief of the State Department's European Division, he was careful – as he told the FBI – not to let Green know about his new post. His Soviet handler, as a result, did not attempt to contact him again until after he had left the State Department, in May 1941.

Burgess, it seems, had overplayed his hand, not only with Straight but with Whitehall. After returning to London, his brainchild, the 'Guy Fawkes College', was closed down and merged with the Special Operations Executive (SOE). Burgess was transferred with Philby to SOE headquarters at 64 Baker Street. With Grand no longer his sponsor, the undisciplined Burgess soon found himself without a job. He fell 'victim to bureaucratic intrigue', as he explained his sacking in November to Philby – who anticipated the same fate. But to Philby's surprise he was appointed to SO1 (radio and propaganda operations) as an instructor. His field, propaganda techniques, eventually became the Political Warfare Executive at Woburn Abbey, where the future Labour party leaders Richard Crossman and Hugh Gaitskell worked with Sefton Delmer and his team of German expatriates (later to include Baron von und zu Putlitz), waging the 'black propaganda' war of leaflets and radio broadcasts against the Nazis. It was part of Philby's job to liaise with Woburn, but he spent the first part of 1941 languishing – as far as his secret mission for Moscow was concerned – in Hampshire at SOE's Beaulieu training establishment.

Philby was eventually rescued from the SOE backwater to which bureaucracy had assigned him by Tomas Harris, who emerges as one of the most enigmatic characters in the whole Blunt network. He was a friend of Burgess, and either on his own or on Philby's urging, Burgess had persuaded Grand to appoint him to the staff of Brickendonbury Hall as 'a sort of glorified housekeeper, because he and his wife Hilda were inspired cooks.'

Harris was a year younger than Blunt and had a devotion to the arts that was both passionate, practical and profound. Unlike his Cambridge friend, however, Harris was a gifted artist, sculptor, engraver and ceramicist. (His talents had secured him a scholarship to the Slade School of Art at the age of fifteen.) His striking Mediterranean features were accentuated by his swept-back hair, beaky nose and intense dark eyes. Evidently Blunt had made his acquaintance, when he was a fellow of Trinity, through his father, Lionel Harris, whose Spanish Art Gallery in Mayfair dealt in the Works of Velásquez and Goya. Harris had been one of the first dealers to recognize the importance of El Greco at a time when few in England appreciated his masterpieces. Lionel's gifted son Tomas was brought up amid considerable family wealth and educated in Spain – where his mother was born – which accounted for the idiosyncratic spelling of his first name.

A gregarious and brilliant man, Harris was known to his friends simply as Tommy, and believed by at least one of his wartime colleagues to have been bisexual. Harris was unusual in that someone who was such a close personal friend of Blunt and Burgess also struck a chord with Philby. It is surprising that Philby, whom his wartime colleague Malcolm Muggeridge described as having an 'allergy to nearly all things intellectual and spiritual', was to write of his 'close and highly prized friendship' with the 'brilliantly intuitive' Harris. Effusive tributes from two self-confessed Soviet spies give good reason to believe that Harris was deeply involved in their web of conspiracy, the more so since they were written some years *after* his death, when their own part in the plot was known to the authorities. Blunt later engineered and wrote a glowing entry for his friend in the *Dictionary of National Biography* – the bibliographic equivalent of a memorial plaque in Westminster Abbey.

Circumstantial evidence as well as new documents suggest that Harris was another Soviet mole whom the Cambridge ring conspired to infiltrate into the security service by the back door. The most specific charge was made by a former member of a Soviet network in Switzerland that Harris's recruiter was an underground Italian Communist, who was also an art dealer. Spain became Harris's most profitable hunting ground and perhaps it was not coincidental that he was traveling extensively and buying up Spanish art during the civil war at a time when the Soviet 'advisers' to the Loyalists masterminded the systematic stripping of monasteries, churches and castles of their art treasures.

Stalin's orders were that the Spanish comrades on the Loyalist side had to pay for the 'fraternal aid' received from Moscow. Besides carting off all the gold bullion held by the Spanish National Bank, Soviet intelligence was using unsuspecting art dealers in Paris and Brussels to sell off the looted Spanish paintings. One of these was alleged to be Alexander Zelinski, the White Russian father-in-law of Charles Howard Ellis, the MI6 officer who later confessed to passing information to the Abwehr. Soviet defector Georgi Agabekov was employed by one of these White Russian art syndicates, which in the summer of 1937 arranged for him to be sent to France to help suppress the shipping of the looted Spanish treasures across the Pyrenees border.

Harris, it seems, was part of the same network of French and Belgian dealers who were raking in handsome profits as middlemen selling the Spanish artworks looted by Soviet agents. He was seen by a friend of Ellen Wilkinson, the British Labour MP, at one of the high-mountain inns in the Pyrenees in July 1937 talking with Agabekov. Shortly afterward, Agabekov disappeared on one of the mountain trails, the presumed victim of an NKVD retribution murder.

Twenty-seven years later, Harris was himself to die in curious circumstances. On 27 January 1964, his new Citroën DS suddenly left the road and hit a tree while taking a gentle bend on the road east of Palma, Majorca. No apparent cause was ever found to explain the accident. It appeared inexplicable to his wife, who survived the crash, and to the local Civil Guard. It was midafternoon, the road was dry and her husband was neither drunk nor speeding on the route they both knew well.

That Harris was held in such high regard by both Blunt and Philby – whose eldest son's education he paid for – inevitably raised questions about the wealthy art dealer's real loyalties. It appeared doubly suspicious that Harris died so soon after Philby's defection and Blunt's confession. The publication of *Spycatcher* in 1987, however, revealed that Peter Wright never got around to interrogating Harris before his untimely death. The 'official' verdict of his former MI5 colleagues gave Harris the benefit of the doubt. But this convenient decision to let him rest in peace appears to owe a good deal to an official unwillingness to admit another major Soviet penetration.

Flora Solomon, who had known (since 1937) that her longtime friend Philby was an underground Communist, remained convinced to her dying day that Harris was another Soviet agent. She also believed that her 1962 confession to MI5, which finally exposed Philby's treachery to the authorities, also contributed to the chain of events that caused Harris's death.

The Solomon story provides another connective thread in the tapestry of treachery woven by Blunt and Philby. Flora was the daughter of a banker named Grigori Benenson, whose wealth enabled him to surmount the stigma of being Jewish in Czarist Russia. He was one of the backers of Alexander Kerensky, whose government was overthrown by the Bolsheviks in 1917. After fleeing to England in 1917, Flora married Colonel Harold Solomon, whose family was prominent in the Jewish community in London. During the thirties she was an active promoter of Zionism, a cause that involved her with many prominent British socialist leaders.

During a trip to Palestine in 1923, she met the eleven-year-old Kim Philby and his father at her parents' house in Jerusalem. She encountered Philby again, eleven years later, on his return from Vienna with his vivacious Jewish bride. From her Viennese housekeeper, Solomon learned about Litzi Friedman's communism, but this did not concern someone as passionately anti-Nazi as Solomon, who was a sympathizer and friend of left-wing intellectuals. John Strachey and the Stafford Crippses patronized her salon. For a time she employed Auden to tutor her son and he, or Philby, often brought Burgess to her large house in Addison Road.

Solomon carefully avoided giving the impression in her autobiography that she had gone out of her way to cultivate Philby. But Arthur Martin, who was later to debrief her for MI5, suspected that the widow Solomon – her husband had died in 1930 – had developed an intense romantic attachment for Philby. Given her 'hard left' sympathies and strong Zionist allegiance, her claim that she did not know about his pro-Nazi sympathies and involvement with the Anglo-German Fellowship seems incredible.

Solomon's own account hints at a maternal attraction to the 'gentle charm' of the well-mannered Philby, who 'mingled easily' with her socialist friends. She found Philby's stutter attractive, and a strong bond developed between them. But, according to Philby, she was also 'hard left' and she mothered the dedicated young Communist twenty years her junior. That much is clear from her admission that just before he set off for Spain in the spring of 1937, Philby revealed to her that he was secretly working for the Comintern. He would not have confided in her, or asked her to join him in 'important work for peace', if he – and his controller Theodore Maly – had not been supremely confident that Solomon would not betray him.

Solomon says she declined the invitation not because of her Russian capitalist background but because she was too busy saving the persecuted Jews of Europe. The following year, during one of his trips home from Spain, Philby evidently tried again to recruit her. This time he appealed to her maternal instincts by revealing that he was in 'great danger'. She, for her part, was left in no doubt that he 'was still associated with the Communist Party.'

On this visit Philby, then estranged from his Litzi, met the woman who became his second wife, Aileen Furze. Solomon was then a staff director of Marks & Spencer, the department-store chain run by her Zionist friends Simon Marks and Israel (later Lord) Sieff who had given their blessing to bringing Jewish refugees into the organization. Philby felt an instant attraction to Aileen, who was one of Solomon's principal assistant managers. When he returned to London from France in May 1940, he moved into a flat with Aileen, where they lived together as man and wife.

Flora Solomon saw a good deal of Philby when he was in SOE. Its London headquarters was two floors above the corporate offices of Marks & Spencer in Baker Street. In 1945, when Philby finally married Aileen, Flora Solomon was one of the witnesses at their wedding at the Chelsea Registry Office. The best man was Tomas Harris. But Solomon did not come forward to reveal what she knew about Philby's Communist past when he came under public suspicion after Burgess and Maclean's defection. She might have done so if she had known that Philby had written to

Burgess, telling him that in desperate straits he could go to Solomon for help, because she knew all about his secret life. Blunt later admitted he had discovered and pocketed this incriminating letter while he was 'assisting' MI5 in its search of Burgess's London flat in 1951.

Fear of setting off a McCarthy-type 'witch hunt' was what Solomon said had restrained her from exposing Philby in 1956, when his loyalty was at the center of the 'Third Man' parliamentary row. But the death of her old assistant, Aileen, whom Philby abandoned with his children when he went as a journalist to Beirut, and the strident Arab bias of his *Observer* articles, finally killed her remaining affection for him. Her love for Israel proved greater than her old socialist loyalties.

'The thought occurred to me that Philby had, after all, remained a Communist,' Solomon wrote, ingenuously, of her mounting distress at the pro-Soviet tone of his dispatches. In August 1962, during a reception at the Weizmann Institute, she told Lord Rothschild of her concerns. Rothschild had close connections with Mossad, the Israeli intelligence service, and she knew that Philby had been a wartime colleague of Rothschild's in the British intelligence service because they had worked together in Paris.

'How is it that *The Observer* uses a man like Kim?' Solomon demanded of Rothschild. 'Don't they know he's a Communist?' She insisted that he 'must do something about it'. Rothschild appeared startled, but said he would 'think about it'.

When Solomon returned to London, she received a call from Rothschild asking her to meet him at his London house along with a member of the security services. She was hesitant, but eventually agreed. The interview took place at Rothschild's London house.

Flora Solomon was a 'strange, rather untrustworthy woman', according to Wright, who monitored the interview conducted by Arthur Martin with a hidden microphone at Rothschild's house. He said they were both convinced that Solomon 'never told the truth' about her relations with Philby, even though she 'clearly had a grudge against him'. The implication was that she was much more deeply involved and knew more than she had admitted. Why else had she not come forward to tell the authorities all she knew six years earlier?

The two MI5 officers interpreted Solomon's curious behaviour as implying that she had shielded Philby because of some deep loyalty; possibly, they reasoned, he had once been her lover.

There may have been a more sinister explanation.

As Wright reveals, Solomon flatly rejected Martin's suggestion that she appear as a witness if Philby was brought home to stand trial. She said she feared what the Russians might do to her family. MI5 suspicions that Solomon was more deeply implicated than she cared to admit increased when she named Harris as a co-conspirator of Philby's. She would give no evidence for this, only insisting cryptically that 'those two were so close as to give me an intuitive feeling that Harris was more than a friend.'

Solomon could not have known that it was Harris who had been instrumental in rescuing Philby from operational oblivion in SOE. But it was Harris who made a point of inviting Philby to the receptions at his home in Chesterfield Gardens so that he could meet Dick Brooman-White, the head of the Iberian unit of MI5's B Division. In September 1941, when Brooman-White was transferred to set up an Iberian unit in Section V of MI5 (Counter-intelligence), Harris – who was promoted to B(1)g in MI5 – lobbied on the old-boy network for Philby's appointment to this new section. The move to Section V proved to be the breakthrough in Philby's career. Within a decade this secret Soviet agent was being tipped as the future director of Britain's foreign-intelligence service.

Just how Harris himself managed to jump to MI5 has never been properly accounted for. Burgess, who was responsible for obtaining Harris's semi-official MI6 status, had no direct office contact with Liddell. Yet while Burgess's hoped-for appointment to MI5 was blackballed by the personal animosity of the director, Liddell approved Harris – an unqualified and noncommissioned member of SOE – for a direct transfer right into B(1)g, the heart of MI5's principal operational division.

Harris could not have made the change without the approval of B Division's director. It is significant that not only was Harris a close friend of Blunt's, but his move was made while Blunt was working as Liddell's personal assistant.

Blunt and Harris would have found it easy to cultivate the artist *manqué* in Liddell. Throughout the war, he was a frequent guest at the Harris home. The Mayfair mansion that served as his father's gallery was a veritable museum. Velásquez paintings and Goya drawings competed for attention with tapestries and furniture as fine and rich as those of any castle in Spain. Guy Liddell and other senior members of the secret intelligence fraternities were frequent guests at lavish parties thrown by hosts who were able to ignore the normal frugalities of wartime rationing.

In the cliquish British intelligence service, the 'Chesterfield Garden Mafia' represented a powerful network that continued long after the war with Liddell's attendance at the Harrises' Garden House salons. Harris, who worked in the Iberian unit under Dick Brooman-White, easily found a niche in MI5 for his sister, Violetta, as a Spanish-speaking officer in Section B(1)a. Harris's friends were a remarkable group of young, Oxbridge-educated secret-service talent. Blunt and Rothschild, along with Liddell's brother, David, and his immediate superior, Brooman-White, were from MI5. And Philby's Westminster friend Tim Milne, and Peter Wilson, the future chairman of Sotheby's, provided the connections into MI6.

The Harris 'Mafia' enabled Blunt to introduce new recruits into the security service on a social basis. Nor were they all brought in as potential moles. His old Marlborough friends John Hilton and Alastair MacDonald, both of whom transferred to MI6, served with loyalty and distinction. But Guy Burgess, whom Blunt tried his best to get Liddell to accept as a full member of the service after his rejection by SOE in November 1940, was flatly rejected. Impressed though Liddell was with Blunt, he was fastidious when it came to MI5 and he had been unfavourably impressed by

Burgess's unsavory reputation and light-fingered intelligence free-lancing.

'Liddell thought that Burgess was a disgraceful figure,' Dick White confirmed. 'He did not approve of the goings-on that were associated with Burgess. He told everyone in MI5 that no one was to have anything to do with Burgess.'

When it became clear to Burgess that he would not find an official welcome in the bosom of MI5 as Harris had, he rejoined the BBC as a Talks producer. But, as Blunt's closest friend, he proved impossible to keep out of MI5's corridors. His brother, Nigel, and his wife had also been taken into the 'office'. Nigel Burgess, after service with an antiaircraft battery, joined F Division under Roger Hollis, where he worked with Blunt's left-wing Cambridge friend, Kemball Johnston, monitoring the activities of the Communist party. So although Burgess was officially persona non grata, Christopher Harmer, another wartime recruit to B Division, remembers how he 'was always in and out of the "office".' He had the impression that Burgess was 'a great friend of Liddell,' who, he says, was 'indiscreet' and 'talked a lot out of school.'

Liddell must have relaxed his ban on Burgess because it is now known that MI5 continued to exploit his talents as a homosexual intriguer to tap sources in the various London embassies. One of those contacts was a homosexual Communist diplomat from Switzerland, 'Orange'. Sir Dick White has conceded that MI5 *did* receive useful information from agent 'Orange' through Burgess. However, White insisted that Blunt 'never ran GB [Guy Burgess] as an agent.' It seems logical, then, that Liddell must have authorized the use of Burgess as an MI5 free-lance agent.

'Intellectual spiv' and adept charmer though Burgess was, he could not have bulldozed himself back into the good graces of B Division's director without the help of his many friends. Blunt and Harris were his most influential advocates, but it was another friend, Victor Rothschild, who permitted Burgess to install himself in the London maisonette in Bentinck Street, which was conveniently close to his job at the nearby BBC Broad-casting House.

So much sensationalism had grown up about the ménage that coalesced around Burgess and Blunt that their wartime living quarters have become synonymous with a homosexual bordello serving as a viperous nest for Soviet spies. The truth, as far as it can be established from eyewitnesses, suggests that, like all scandals, this one has been exaggerated in the telling.

Lord Rothschild leased the three-story maisonette at 5 Bentinck Street. It had been constructed in the mid-thirties above the ground floor offices of *The Practitioner*, a doctors' magazine. When the London Blitz began in September, Rothschild and his pregnant wife, Barbara, decided to retreat to the country. Although the Rothschild lease ran out at the end of 1940, the flat was convenient and had an excellent bomb shelter in the basement. So he offered it to Anthony Blunt and their mutual friends Teresa Mayor and Patricia Rawdon-Smith, who had just been bombed out of their Gower Street flat. The lease was too expensive for three of them to manage on their own, so Blunt suggested Burgess share it. *The Practitioner* said that having four people's names on the lease was like 'signing up a football team', so it was Mayor who took on the responsibility.

In 1941, Mayor began working for Rothschild at MI5 as his secretary/personal assistant, and she was to marry him after his first marriage to Lady Barbara ended in divorce in 1946. Patricia Rawdon-Smith née Parry was estranged from her husband. After her divorce she would marry Richard Llewelyn-Davies, a close friend of Blunt and a fellow left-wing Apostle of her former husband's.

Blunt, with his knack of taking care of details, managed the accounts. The quartet sorted out their living arrangements to share the kitchen and sitting room on the first level for general entertaining. Blunt took the bedroom and dressing room on the second floor, sharing the bathroom with Burgess, who had the other bedroom down the corridor. The two girls shared the top floor. An Irish maid, Bridie, came in to clean and cook for whoever was in that evening. The bomb shelter was a great attraction for visiting friends and many of them stayed overnight.

'Everyone at Bentinck Street was a friend of Lord Rothschild,' Jackie Hewit told me. He said that Mayor and Parry knew that Blunt was sleeping with Hewit and that Burgess and some of his friends were bringing boys back to the flat. Burgess also used to partner Parry at the big dances around London; Mayor helped Blunt prepare the manuscript for his book on François Mansart.

According to Hewit and others, Rothschild was a visitor to Bentinck Street. He could not have been unaware of its homosexual ménage, since he knew that Blunt had moved Hewit into his dressing room on the second floor as a permanent resident in the autumn of 1940. He remained as a part of the Bentinck Street household, pooling his wartime ration book for the mutual benefit of the entourage until late 1944, when his army unit was posted to the Continent after the liberation of France.

Hewit had attached himself to Blunt rather than to his old lover Burgess because he was, in any case, never sure who would be found in Burgess's bed. 'If Guy fancied someone, he'd go up to him in the street and proposition him,' Hewit explained. 'His theory was that any man between the ages of seventeen and seventy-five was haveable.' During all the time he lived in Bentinck Street, he can remember that Blunt had only one person ever stay with him: his friend from Cambridge, Peter Montgomery.

'Anthony was always much closer physically to Peter than to Guy. I suppose you could describe them as long-term lovers,' Hewit said, insisting that the very idea that Blunt and Burgess had any physical relationship was 'absolute rubbish'. Despite what others have speculated, Hewit asserts that in all other respects but the sexual, Burgess and Blunt were 'Mutt and Jeff'. His statement carries the conviction of someone with intimate experience of both men.

'Guy achieved the excitement in his life that Anthony would have liked to have if he had been as liberated. I could see that he got a great deal of vicarious satisfaction listening to Guy's endless sexual talk,' Hewit observed. 'And how Guy would talk, he had no hang-ups about himself or other people.'

Burgess used to meet him regularly at his 'haunt' – the Reform Club – and then they would go to the Gargoyle or Le Boeuf sur le Tôit, a risqué bar in Orange Street: 'Where you see the aristocracy drinking itself to death/With the lesser lights of democracy who never draw a sober breath.' Blunt found the atmosphere 'altogether too camp', according to Hewit, who accompanied him one night to the bar that was rumored to be one of the best spots in town to pick up lonely GIs on a London furlough.

Yet for all Burgess's one-night stands and homosexual banter, Hewit says indignantly, far too much has been made of Goronwy Rees's spiteful charge that the Bentinck Street flat had 'the air of a high-class disorderly house, in which one could not distinguish between the staff, the management, and the clients.' If there has been an exaggeration in people's recollections concerning sexual revelry, there can be no doubt that the political hue of this exotic wartime salon was deepest red. John Strachey was for a time a resident before he joined the RAF. According to Hewit, Burgess said that Richard Llewelyn-Davies, another marxisant Apostle, whose wartime duty as an architect was with the LMS railway company, was like the-man-who-came-to-dinner. He was a regular visitor who finally moved into the top-floor flat in 1943 when he married Patricia Rawdon-Smith. Rothschild lent them a stable flat at Tring, where they lived after 1945 when their daughter was born.

Another frequent animator of the Bentinck Street salon, especially when it came to arguing (after Hitler's attack on Russia) that the bomber offensive should be ditched in favour of opening a second front, was J. D. Bernal. A wartime scientist with Lord Mountbatten's Combined Operations, the Communist sage of prewar Camberidge was, as Hewit personally noted, a 'great friend of Tess and Anthony'. It was his presence that so forcibly struck Malcolm Muggeridge. After his one and only visit to what he described as 'this millionaire's nest' in Bentinck Street, Muggeridge – then a junior member of MI6 – felt himself 'morally afflicted'. A heavy air raid going on contributed to his discomfort at finding himself sheltering in 'so distinguished a company – Cabinet Minister-to-be, honored Guru of the Extreme Left-to-be, Connoisseur Extraordinary-to-be, and other notabilities all grouped round Burgess, Etonian mudlark and sick toast of a sick society.'

On occasion, Maclean was a wartime guest. And Philby dropped in whenever he was in London. Rosamond Lehmann recalls meeting him during her one visit. Another member of the inner circle, according to Hewit, was Tommy Harris, whom he described as 'very macho, an absolute sweetie, very close with Anthony and Guy.' Other members of MI5, including Patrick Day, who worked alongside Blunt in B(1)b, and Geoffrey Wethered, were familiar faces in Bentinck Street. This may well have been because their chief, Guy Liddell, was one of the most frequent and welcome guests.

Liddell's seemingly close involvement with the exotic coterie at Bentinck Street would later raise serious suspicions over whether or not he had also been sucked into Blunt's conspiracy. These are strengthened by Hewit's admission that the 'quiet and gentle' head of B Division was 'definitely not a partygoer'. This suggests that the company revolving around the homosexuality and Marxism of Blunt and Burgess must have had a strong personal attraction for Liddell, who was now leading the private life of a reclusive bachelor. It has been suggested that it was the former rather than latter that attracted him, and that the breakup of his marriage had left him lonely and vulnerable after his wife left him to go to the United States in 1936.

'If anything Liddell was a "voyeur",' Hewit says, 'not in the strictly sexual sense, but he enjoyed the company of homosexuals like Guy and Anthony. He was amused by the repartee and reveled in the interplay of personalities.' The plain fact that one of the most important directors in the British secret service had been drawn into the heart of Blunt's coterie must have given cause for some self-congratulation at NKVD headquarters in Moscow.

More astonishing is that Liddell could have been so unsuspecting of the dangers of compromising his status. He must have been aware that the flagrant homosexuality of the Bentinck Street ménage exposed its male participants to serious criminal charges – even in wartime. Yet the head of B Division appears to have had no reservations about spending much of his off-duty time with Blunt, Burgess and their male friends. It seems that Liddell's dislike of Burgess was a smokescreen directed mainly to impressing his deputy Dick White and his colleagues at the Office. Off duty, he liked nothing better than to let his hair down in Burgess's outrageous milieu. Hewit says Liddell shared his passionate enthusiasm for the music hall. He would join them to the Metropolitan in Edgware Road one week, and Chelsea Palace of Varieties the next, on a regular basis. Blunt rarely accompanied them. His preference was for more serious pursuits.

Liddell, as Hewit told me, also knew that Hewit was being used as a free-lance agent for B Division. 'In a sense, I was working for Anthony, even though I was not officially attached to MI5,' Hewit said, explaining how in 1940 he had found himself transferred to the War Office from the Royal Artillery regiment in Essex to which he had been posted. Thanks to Blunt and Liddell, Hewit was reassigned just in time to prevent him from being sent overseas to North Africa.

When asked precisely what he did do for Blunt, he became coyly evasive. The assignments he was sent on for MI5 are still official secrets. 'I suppose you could say that I was a decoy,' Hewit added enigmatically, although he admitted that he played a part in helping Burgess and Blunt arrange for 'Orange', the Swiss diplomat, Eric Kessler, to become an MI5 informant. Blunt would assign him certain 'targets', who, it appears, were probably homosexual foreign diplomats. He was, he said with a knowing smile, 'a sort of middleman', who occasionally accompanied Blunt whenever he took the night express from King's Cross to Newcastle or Edinburgh. This was to do with providing a military escort for the couriers of the foreign embassies in

London as they shuttled their diplomatic pouches to and from the sea- and airports in the north of England.

It was Robert Cecil who shed light on these missions. In the spring of 1941, Cecil's diplomatic career led to his appointment as assistant private secretary to Sir Alexander Cadogan. He arrived in the Foreign Office early one morning during the darkest days of World War II and came face to face with Blunt, whom he had last seen six years earlier in Trinity Great Court. So complete was Blunt's transformation, Cecil did not immediately identify the smartly turned-out army officer with the aloof Trinity don he knew at Cambridge.

'I came into the anteroom to Cadogan's office to find a distinguished-looking military officer enthusiastically engaged in an animated conversation with Peter Lockersley,' Cecil recalled. 'Who the devil was that?' he asked after the strangely familiar figure had left the office. His colleague, Cadogan's other assistant, explained that it was Major Anthony Blunt from MI5. He had just 'had an incident with one of the foreign governments' diplomatic bags.' Cecil could not have been more astonished.

'Anthony was effervescing over this absolutely hair-raising incident he had just been through,' Cecil vividly recalled. 'But what struck me forcefully was that at the same time he was as cool as a cucumber and obviously immensely enjoying the whole business.'

The tricky business was gaining covert access to the contents of the diplomatic bags of various Allied governments-in-exile. These included Poland, Holland and Denmark, as well as the neutral countries of Spain, Switzerland and Sweden.

'It was not an easy job, and it required iron nerve and split-second timing.' Blunt acted as the commander of the military escort that accompanied foreign couriers during their journeys to and from ports and airfields where ships and planes could still make the trip in relative safety to the other non-Axis countries.

To gain the trust of the couriers, decoys plied them with alcohol, or even arranged for appropriate sexual consolation during the long journeys that were made in locked compartments on blacked-out trains. When the couriers had been distracted or lulled into a drunken stupor, Blunt supervised the discreet removal of the diplomatic pouches. They then were passed to a specially trained assistant in another sealed-off compartment. He carefully slit open the stitches. The papers were taken out and photographed. The pouches were then skillfully stitched up again with identical threads and, with their official seals still intact, were slipped back into the courier's compartment.

The timing of these intricate operations did not always go smoothly. In the event of a slip up, it fell to Blunt to try to persuade the courier that the diplomatic pouch had not been tampered with. It was his job to use blackmail, or any other means at his disposal, to persuade an alarmed dupe not to make a formal report. Blunt could be extremely persuasive and was usually successful. But MI5 was under order to alert Cadogan's office on any of these close calls so that the Foreign Office was ready to issue the appropriate denials. That was what Blunt had been reporting to Lockersley that morning when Cecil barged in.

'I was impressed by the effervescence and the incredible sangfroid of the man,' Cecil told me. 'Although I never witnessed him chatting up the Queen, I knew from my own experience what a consummate act he could put on.' Other sources say that is why the Queen 'would not hear an ill word spoken about him until his public exposure.' Blunt's sheer nerve and ability as an actor is why, Cecil said, 'MI5 and the Foreign Office believed for so long in his integrity.'

Yet during the war, in Cadogan's office, Cecil also observed the ruthless side of Blunt's character that he described as 'ice cold'. It left him wondering what sort of man could be so inhuman as to have betrayed so many lives – not to mention sovereign nations – to the Soviets. Blunt's extensive contacts with his Warburg patrons, such as Saxl and Wittkower and the other émigré European art historians, ought to have aroused his compassion for those who had been forced to flee from Hitler. His rifling of the diplomatic secrets of wartime refugee governments of countries like Poland, Estonia, Latvia and Czechoslovakia would have enabled him to pass the names of those opposed to Moscow on to the Soviets.

'Anthony showed not a shred of sympathy for the refugees from the occupied Baltic states and Eastern Europe,' Cecil told me. With all the bitterness of a betrayed colleague, he added: 'We now know that he either exploited their misery in order to make them work for the Russians, or if they would not, then he was bloody well ensuring that Stalin knew who was on his side and who was not.'

This information was invaluable when the Soviets rang down the Iron Curtain on Eastern Europe. Speaking from his unique vantage point as the assistant private secretary to the Foreign Office's permanent under secretary, Cecil attaches special importance to the note of 23 December 1943, in Cadogan's diary that says: '4 (pm) Blunt.' This, Cecil says, is a telling indication of just how high Blunt had risen in the intelligence hierarchy. 'No other representatives of MI5 were received by Cadogan while I was in his office,' Cecil assured me, 'except the director general, Sir David Petrie, and his deputy, Guy Liddell.'

14 Thwarting a 'Need to Know'

The night of 10 May 1941 saw the most savage German air raid of the war. That night the Luftwaffe tore into the heart of London, and incendiary bombs ignited more than two thousand fires. Three thousand Londoners died or were wounded. It was days before the Fire Brigade brought the fires under control.

Jackie Hewit has vivid memories of that awful night. He was driving home with Burgess and Blunt when a police roadblock stopped them on the road that crosses Hampstead Heath on the outskirts of the city. From this high vantage point, five miles northwest of St Paul's Cathedral, they had a grandstand view of the raid, with the dome of the cathedral rising above a spreading sea of flames.

The shells fired by the antiaircraft batteries that surrounded London added to the shriek of falling bombs and the clanging bells of distant fire engines. Overhead, golden mushrooms of flak burst in a dark sky crisscrossed by icy-white searchlight beams. There was terrifying awesomeness to the devastation, but Blunt remained detached. It was as if he were in some Olympian gallery studying the details of one of the demonic *Last Judgments* painted by Hieronymus Bosch.

'The worst attack was the last,' Churchill wrote later. The bombing was particularly hurtful for the Prime Minister because incendiary bombs had consumed his beloved House of Commons.

The up side was that the air-raid sirens in Britain's beleaguered capital did not wail again for months to come. This was a blessed relief to Hewit and the other residents of Bentinck

Street who prayed for temporary relief. But Blunt possessed secret knowledge that the blitz had ended. He already knew that Hitler had ordered the Luftwaffe's bombers to airfields in the east of Germany and Poland.

There was only one interpretation to put on this information: the Soviet Union was about to be attacked by Germany. The sources from which the Joint Intelligence Committee had assembled its estimates ranged from diplomatic rumors circulating in the U.S. and other friendly embassies, to MI6 sources, including a reliable Abwehr mole named Paul Thümmel. But it was the code breakers at the GC&CS establishment at Bletchley Park who provided the definitive evidence.

'Hitler has made up his mind to have done with Soviet obstruction and intends to attack her,' Britain's Joint Intelligence Committee advised when it met to weigh up the intelligence picture on 12 June 1941. 'It remains our opinion that matters are likely to come to a head during the second half of June.' The next day Churchill approved Foreign Secretary Anthony Eden's decision to tell the Soviet ambassador of the British estimates of the imminent German offensive – with the offer to send a military mission to Moscow.

That is why the recently published volume of the official history of British intelligence in World War II asserts with finality that there is 'no truth in the much-publicized claim that the British authorities made use of the "Lucy" ring, a Soviet espionage organization, which operated in Switzerland, to forward intelligence to Moscow.'

Moscow should not have been taken by surprise when the invasion began shortly before dawn on 22 June 1941, with a cataclysmic artillery barrage along the 1,800-mile front. Despite all the official and unofficial warnings Stalin received, he was powerless to prevent the mechanized German tidal wave from engulfing the Red Army in European Russia. But this was no fault of Anthony Blunt and the other members of the so-called Cambridge spy network, who had systematically conspired to betray Britain's most valuable strategic intelligence asset: Ultra.

Admission to the 'Ultra secret' – as the wartime Enigma signals intelligence or SIGINT has become known – was jealously guarded and controlled by the MI6 director, Stewart Menzies. The overall direction of the code-breaking operation at the Government Code and Cypher School was under C's fiat. His authority derived from the Foreign Office's responsibility for the 'Golf Club & Chess Society', as the Bletchley recruits irreverently referred to their establishment.

Menzies, who had a fetish for code names, had originally ascribed this 'absolutely reliable' source of intelligence to a notional Germany agent code-named 'Boniface'. Later it became 'CX' until the Admiralty replaced its 'Hydro' with 'Ultra' in June 1941. This had a certain ring of authority that stuck. Soon it was used extensively to apply to all Axis SIGINT. Despite its changing nomenclature, an immutable security governed Ultra. Theoretically, only C had full access to all the decrypts. These he circulated in condensed and paraphrased form to the Prime Minister, plus about thirty others in Whitehall who were involved with the higher direction of the war and intelligence effort.

Dick White has confirmed that he and his chief, Guy Liddell, were fully aware of Ultra. Blunt was never officially a member of the exclusive circle. But he had no need to be because, from 1941 on, he was working in a unit of B Division that devoted itself to making assessments of enemy military intelligence and therefore received and examined many key Ultra reports. This was B(1)b, whose head was a distinguished barrister, who later became a high-court judge, Helenus 'Buster' Milmo. He was a Trinity College contemporary of Blunt's; so was another Cambridge barrister, who became a lord justice of appeal, Edward B. Stamp. Two left-wing Oxonians, the lawyer Patrick Day and the philosopher Herbert Hart from New College, completed the formidable analytical brainpower available to the section.

Herbert Hart, who had 'unlimited access' to all Ultra derived from decrypts of the Abwehr traffic, married Jenifer Fischer Williams in 1941. A quarter century later, she would admit to MI5 investigators that she had been an underground member of the Communist Party while working in the Home Office. She claimed that she gave up her Communist affiliation before her marriage, and that the loyalty of her husband, who later became professor of jurisprudence at Oxford, was beyond reproach. Jenifer Hart was another Bentinck Street regular. So was Patrick Day, who Blunt in 1945 had invited to take over Tess Mayor's share in the maisonette.

Evidence that the Soviets had also recruited a separate spy network from left-wing Oxford intellectuals emerged from interrogations of Mrs Hart. Wright strongly suspected that it overlapped Blunt's Cambridge agents. At any rate, B(1)b, as the clearing house for Ultra German intelligence-service reports, would have been of intense interest to the Soviets. According to Christopher Harmer, then a junior officer in B Division, it was Professor Hart's task to analyse all those decrypts coming in from Bletchley.

There is now general agreement among wartime MI5 veterans that Ultra was an open secret to Blunt because of the ever-increasing volume of raw intelligence data that flowed through the office he shared with Hart. So until the end of 1941, Blunt fed 'Henry' material culled from these decrypted Abwehr ciphers. And at Bletchley, Oliver Strachey digested the raw intelligence into summaries. Which, with a panache worthy of his deceased brother Lytton, he designated 'ISOS' – Intelligence Source Oliver Strachey.

Blunt must therefore have seen ISOSes, realized their importance, and alerted Moscow that Bletchley had broken the cipher keys unlocking the Abwehr and Security Police Enigmas. This breakthrough enabled the British to monitor the communications of the German military-intelligence service, and it produced a flood of data ranging from the reports of secret agents to military-intelligence assessments. ISOS Ultra proved especially important for Moscow because the traffic contained reports from Abwehr units attached to the German armies invading the Soviet Union.

Ultra ISK, so designated to honor former King's fellow Dillwyn 'Dilly' Knox, who had broken the Abwehr Enigma, also

368 Mask of Treachery

provided the British intelligence services with the opportunity to develop what became one of the most successful and secret counterintelligence operations of the whole war. What evolved into the Double-Cross operation had begun shortly after Dunkirk when the Germans took alternative measures to obtain intelligence for Operation Sealion, their projected invasion of Britain. They tried to infiltrate agents: dropping them by parachute, or landing them from submarines, or introducing them from neutral countries, such as Spain.

'Either we could have treated it as a simple security problem and apprehended and executed every agent that we could lay our hands on,' noted one of the British organizers, 'or we could have turned round some at least of the agents we caught, let the Germans think that they were still at large and working for Germany.' A nine-page draft report on 'controlled enemy agents' in Yale University was written by a senior MI5 officer and also helps reinforce the contention that Dick White was responsible for the original idea of turning captured German spies into double agents. Between the autumn of 1940 and the end of 1941, the report discloses that some twenty-five double agents were recruited after they were captured.

'Very slowly we came to the conclusion we did, in fact, control virtually the whole of the German system in this country,' declared the British report. The program went into high gear in January 1941 when the 'Twenty' Committee – so-called from the pun on the XX symbol for a Double-Cross – was established under the 'Wireless Board'. It brought together representatives of the two intelligence services, the navy, army and air force under J. C. Masterman, an Oxford don with extensive personal knowledge of Germany. The choice of this self-deprecating historian was influenced by Dick White, whom Masterman had tutored at Christ Church twenty years before. A tall, finely chiseled figure who had been an outstanding undergraduate athlete, Masterman ran the Double-Cross Committee with the finesse of an Oxford tutorial. He combined a rigorous intellectual authority with tea and buns at the committee's weekly meetings.

Of the six key objectives that Masterman set for the Double-Cross, the most important was to control the German intelligence system in Britain. As the Yale report makes plain, by feeding the Germans 'a good deal of true information', they kept the Abwehr satisfied and the Germans sent 'less and less spies over'. At the same time the British 'did at least know what information the Germans had and what they did not'.

Apart from the revelations about the 'personalities and methods' of the Abwehr, and providing a channel for deception, Double-Cross also produced valuable intelligence of the Germans' operational intentions.

While Masterman's committee set guidelines and monitored the information that was fed to the Germans by their turned agents as 'chicken-feed', MI5 officers under the direction of the head of B(1)a conducted the actual running of the spies. Its head was Colonel T. A. 'Tar' Robertson, a clever graduate of Sandhurst military academy, who had abandoned his army career for counterintelligence work and had been a partner with Liddell in B Division since 1933. Eventually Robertson's group turned some 120 operatives into Double-Cross agents.

One of the MI5 officers who demonstrated a supreme ability when it came to handling his double agents was Tomas Harris. He was responsible for managing 'Garbo', a Spanish hotel manager named Juan Pujol García, whose fictitious British network helped fool the Germans about the D-Day landings in what turned out to be one of the most important deceptions of the war.

The bizarre names assigned by the British to their Double-Cross agents, such as 'Bronx', 'Giraffe', 'Scruffy' and 'Treasure', reflected the equally bizarre range of occupations – in these cases: diplomat's wife, French army officer, Belgian seaman and émigré Russian vamp – from which the Abwehr recruited its would-be spies. One of the most notorious was 'Tricycle', a Yugoslav adventurer by the name of Dusko Popov, who was ordered by the Abwehr in 1941 to spy on Pearl Harbor, and who has became the center of a popular myth, largely as a result of his own writings.

Blunt worked closely with Tar Robertson's case officers running the double agents. So he knew all the secrets of the Double-Cross operation. Another of Blunt's Cambridge friends associated indirectly with Double-Cross was Lord Rothschild, who was running a small section known as B(1)c to counter German sabotage operations. Many of these involved bombs that originated from the same Abwehr operatives who dispatched undercover agents to England from the Iberian peninsula.

According to Hewit, Blunt made frequent trips down to MI5's interrogation center at Wandsworth in the early part of the war. His analytical abilities and languages made Blunt a valued assistant at the debriefing of potential German agents and in deciding who could be turned. During these sessions Blunt also found the opportunity to provide some direct assistance to these Soviet agents. Unfortunately, only after the war was it realized – in both London and Washington – that some key German agents in the Double-Cross operation were really Soviet-run Triple-Cross agents.

One of the 'triples' was Natalie Sergueiev. Lily, as she preferred to be known, was a striking auburn-haired French girl whose father was a Russian. Only after the war was it realized that she had been inducted into the Soviet network by her uncle, Nicolay V. Skoblin, aide to her other uncle, former czarist General Yevgeny Miller. Skoblin was a turncoat in the Paris-based White Russian veterans' organization. According to Natalie Grant Wraga, Skoblin's wife, the singer Nadezhda Plevitskaya, was responsible for his becoming an NKVD agent in the network that she bankrolled in the 1937 assassination of General Miller. Skoblin, it seems, also 'doubled' as an undercover informer for the Sicherheitsdienst, the German Secret Police, and his SD connections enabled Lily to get herself recruited by the 'Abwehr under the code name 'Tramp'. She distinguished herself as the only female spy in German service during World War II who was trained and trusted to operate a clandestine radio.

It was under the code name of 'Treasure', however, that Sergueiev achieved her great wartime success, recruited into MI5's double-agent operation by Tomas Harris. Not until long afterward did American intelligence sources discover that 'Treasure' was really of value to the Soviets, to whom she passed 'detailed plans of American–British operations in the closing stages of the war'. It is obvious now that the detailed knowledge Blunt obtained of Double-Cross could have helped Soviet intelligence infiltrate other triples like Sergueiev into the operation. Postwar CIA investigations of other British wartime anti-Nazi agents recruited from émigré communities in Europe revealed many who had been working for the Soviets.

Undoubtedly the most valuable function Blunt performed during the early part of the war was to keep Moscow posted – through his control officer at the Soviet embassy – about the eavesdropping on the German intelligence services. He was also in the unusual position of being able to update and check this information with British assessments of the German Order of Battle.

This information was passed along through Leo Long, who now occupied a key position in military intelligence. Long, a fellow Communist Apostle, had been cultivated by Blunt at Trinity. He had spent a year, after graduating in 1938, teaching in Frankfurt. In the wartime call-up he enlisted in the Oxford and Bucks Light Infantry, and when the chance came to use his languages to obtain a posting with military intelligence, Long jumped at it. He said that the army was so desperate for German linguists that no one bothered to ask about his politics. It was 'purely accidental', Long assured me, that he obtained a commission as a second lieutenant in the army intelligence corps.

Long was also insistent that it was an 'equally accidental thing' that he was posted to MI14 in December 1940. He claimed that Blunt did not know that he was working in this sensitive section because he had 'lost touch with him when I was called up.' So, when they happened to meet in the bombproof basement at the War Office, where the staff of MI14 worked analysing the steady stream of SIGINT that came in on the chattering banks of teleprinters, Long says that 'it was a genuine surprise' to Blunt.

'This was not a preplanned thing, that was an accident,' Long stressed. The encounter, he agreed, had taken place in 1941 when Blunt arrived on 'lawful business'. Just what brought an MI5 officer primarily concerned with foreign diplomatic missions into the army-intelligence office that made the detailed analysis of Oberkommando Wehrmacht dispositions, Long could not say. Nor was he able to recall precisely when this 'chance' confrontation with Blunt took place. Yet it was obviously a critical moment in his life, since Blunt 'took up where we left off before', proposing that Long pass on to Blunt top-secret German intelligence.

'I can't remember, it was around that time,' Long said, pausing for a long time when I asked whether Blunt approached him before the German invasion of Russia. His deliberately evasive answer suggested that this was not the first time that he had been asked to clarify this crucial point. Blunt was always careful to insist that he had not passed anything of value to the Soviets *before* Churchill announced his offer of an alliance to Stalin in the mutual fight against Hitler on 21 June 1941.

'Any man, or state, who fights on against Nazidom will have our aid,' the Prime Minister promised. He had no idea how reassuring this BBC broadcast was for Blunt and his network. They now regarded themselves as 'double patriots', conveniently forgetting that up until that day they had been 'double traitors'. Instead of betraying their country to Stalin, who also happened to be Hitler's ally, they now saw themselves as fighting Hitler for King and Country *and* as proxies of the Soviet Revolution.

Long dismissed the issue of when he betrayed official military secrets to Blunt as a 'meaningless question'. Surprisingly, it did not appear to concern him whether the Soviet Union was an ally or not. Blunt, he said, was aware of his political sympathies when he asked him for 'every piece of information that could be useful to the Russians.'

Long was so defensive about recalling whether he had begun passing information to Blunt before 22 June 1941, that he gave the clear impression that his treachery predated Britain's alliance with the Soviet Union. He had, it seemed, been similarly elusive when interrogated by MI5 after Blunt had exposed him in 1963. Peter Wright thought that he lacked the class of the other Apostles. He found Long an 'officious, fussy man with a face like a motor mechanic's,' whose 'superior' take-it-or-leave-it account did not tally with Blunt's.

It is not known precisely what Blunt told MI5 about the information he received from his tame subagent in MI14. But according to Long, they met on a weekly basis, usually at lunchtime to avoid suspicion, in a pub in Portman Square, or at a snack bar called Rainer's on the corner of Jermyn Street, which was conveniently midway between the War Office and the MI5 offices in St James's. He would pass under the table a handwritten report that he described as a 'sort of boiled-down version of the weekly departmental appreciation'.

It incorporated *all* the intelligence sources available to MI14. But Long was adamant that he did not give Blunt notes of the raw Ultra. His claim that he was 'too concerned about protecting the security of the source' sits oddly with his willingness to trust Blunt with some of the most sensitive military intelligence in the whole of the War Office. His repeated assertion that he did not pass on Ultra intelligence because it was 'too hazardous' seems to confirm that he began feeding his weekly summary to Blunt in the spring of 1941 when there was justification for fearing that Stalin might leak it to Hitler.

'I was not one of those officers who said 'Oh God! we cannot give away our secrets to anyone', Long said, recalling, in an attempt to justify his actions, what he called the 'long debate about how much information should be given to the Russians.' His wartime colleague in military intelligence, Noël Annan, recalled that Long could be 'very dismissive' about anything that did not coincide with his views. This was the same arrogance that he shared with Blunt and other Communists, a belief that their cause justified putting the survival of Britain at risk. Annan has no sympathy with the argument that Long and Blunt were justified in taking matters into their own hands to provide the intelligence that saved the Soviet Union. This was a governmental function Annan contends. He regards their actions as 'monstrous' because, if the Germans had captured information revealing the Ultra secret, history shows that it could have cost the Allies the war.

Nor was Leo Long the only member of the Cambridge network who kept Moscow supplied with intelligence from the code breakers at GCHQ. Under interrogation in 1963, Blunt named John Cairncross, who had left the Treasury in 1940 to join the strong Cambridge contingent at Bletchley.

Like Long's, his intellectual communism had fused with his working-class background. Cairncross had left Britain after falling under MI5 suspicion in 1951 as a result of papers containing Treasury information that were found in Burgess's flat and identified by his Trinity College contemporary Sir John Colville. But it was not until 1964, when Arthur Martin confronted him with Blunt's accusation, that Cairncross finally confessed to his wartime spying at GCHQ's Bletchley Park establishment, Station X.

Cairncross was originally assigned to the section where most of the Luftwaffe Red Traffic was assessed. But because this Enigma contained much army information, Cairncross had access to the more than 250 translators, analysts and filing clerks who worked in shifts around the clock, processing the Wehrmacht intercepts in a sprawling group of buildings known collectively as Hut 6. (Bletchley Park had collected so many of the best Cambridge brains – including eleven fellows of King's College, Cambridge – that 'Little King's' was the nickname they gave to the wartime establishment.)

Cairncross may not have been a brilliant mathematician like Hugh Alexander, Gordon Welchman of Sidney Sussex, or Alan Turing. But his Trinity College credentials and first-class degree in modern languages were a laissez-passer among the analysts, who included the pick of the prewar crop of the university's classicists, linguists, historians and mathematicians. Nor did he have direct access to Hut 3 where Alan Turing perfected the electromechanical computers known as *Bombes* which spluttered and sparked through thousands of numerical calculations a minute to speed up dramatically the processing of the Enigma intercepts. Wartime members of the Bletchley team insist that Cairncross was never seen in Hut 3 and that tight security would have kept the Soviets from learning the secrets of the *Bombes*. Yet by his own admissions, Cairncross was able to pass on to Moscow much valuable intelligence he gleaned at Station X. Once inside GCHQ, Cairncross confessed to Arthur Martin, he had copied and passed on Ultra documents and data over a period of nearly four years. However, the details of his confession remain locked away in MI5's most secret files.

What we do know is that the Russians considered Cairncross important enough to provide him with the money to purchase a small car. This made it easier for him to make his weekend meetings with 'Henry' in London on a regular basis. A car would also serve as a convenient and mobile safe house for debriefing and passing data. So pleased was Moscow Center with the intelligence received from Cairncross that after the decisive battle of Kursk in the spring of 1943, 'Henry' relayed a special commendation for the contribution Cairncross had made to the Red Army's decisive victory. Cairncross also admitted supplying the Enigma decrypts that contained the Luftwaffe dispositions. He also told Peter Wright and Arthur Martin in 1964 in Paris and Rome that he was congratulated on supplying the information that enabled the Red Army to destroy hundreds of German planes on the ground.

These incomplete glimpses of Soviet gratitude that Cairncross chose to provide are a measure of the importance and quantity of the intelligence to which he had access between 1940 and 1944. That he occupied a key position of trust in the Ultra operation for such a long period must make Cairncross one of the most important of all the Cambridge spies. Nor, by his own admission, was he the only mole in GCHQ. During meetings with Martin and Wright, Cairncross 'burned' four other agents. Their names have not been disclosed because they are still alive. Three turned out, on investigation by MI5, to be suspects, but there was not enough evidence to proceed against them. The fourth, according to Wright, was cleared.

Wright was convinced that Cairncross remains a committed Communist and was fully aware that he was immune from prosecution on the Continent where his debriefing took place. So it is unlikely that he revealed any more than he – and the Soviets – considered necessary to provide a cover story after Blunt had named him in his confession. Given the methodical thoroughness of Soviet intelligence operations, it is certain that Moscow Center had other moles in place at Bletchley Park, on whom they could rely for Ultra data. Otherwise Cairncross would not have been permitted to transfer to section V of MI6 in 1944.

After working briefly on German counterintelligence, Cairncross moved to the Balkans Division. There he capped his golden career as a Soviet mole by reinforcing the efforts of his Cambridge contemporary, James Klugmann, in helping the Communist takeover of Yugoslavia. Despite his open association with the Communist party, Klugmann had managed to join SOE on the strength of his Serbo-Croatian languages. He was assigned to the Balkans Division headquarters in Cairo. His responsibility for communications with the Yugoslav partisans enabled him to help undermine the anti-Communist General Mihailovich and promote the cause of Tito – Josip Broz – as the eventual leader of the resistance to the Germans.

The extent of Cairncross's treachery shocked Arthur Martin. But Cairncross insisted that it was not Blunt who had recruited him as a spy and introduced him to the Soviets, but Klugmann. He confirmed that his principal control officer while he was at GCHQ was Anatoli Gorski, the same Soviet embassy official (codename Henry) who ran Blunt, Burgess, Philby and Maclean.

Blunt was assigned by 'Henry' to run Long as a subagent and Long told me that he had dealt only with Blunt and never met directly with any Russians. Obviously Moscow Center placed a great trust in Blunt, who, it is now clear, also managed for a time both Burgess and Straight. That Blunt jealously guarded this authority is clear from what he told MI5 about another Cambridge man whom he discovered making an attempt to recruit Long. He had even made an unsuccessful effort in 1946 to arrange for Long's transfer into MI5, writing a recommendation and canvassing Dick White's support!

Apart from Long and Cairncross, Blunt named five other contemporaries who could have been spies. But as Wright lamented, Blunt 'always pointed at those who were either dead, long since retired, or else comfortably out of secret access and danger.' In the vernacular of espionage, Blunt succeeded in the classic tactic of offering up sacrificial small fry who had long since become 'burnt-out cases'.

Blunt himself nearly fell victim to 'burning' by the inadvertence of his Soviet masters in 1941. Even since he had joined B(1)b in late 1940, one of his standing instructions from 'Henry' was to help identify the MI5 moles in Britain's Communist party. He spotted one, code-named 'M8' in a routine report on the CPGB that he probably saw in Liddell's office. From a reference to a book that had been written by 'M8' Blunt deduced and passed on to his controller that this particular informant was Tom Driberg, then a *Daily Express* journalist.

Driberg was one of MI5's most reliable sources inside the CPGB. He had been run for years by Captain Maxwell Knight, who was conducting countersubversion operations from his headquarters in Dolphin Square. It was his female infiltration agents who had rooted out the Communist spy ring in Woolwich Arsenal in 1937, and obtained the conviction in 1940 of Tyler Kent, an American embassy code clerk, for passing copies of Churchill's secret telegrams to a pro-Hitler group of Russian émigrés.

Knight became suspicious that it had been someone in MI5 who had leaked that Driberg was a secret informer after Driberg had been perfunctorily informed by a Fleet Street 'comrade' that he was 'no longer a member of the Party'. Blunt was even angrier than Driberg. He protested to his Soviet controller over the clumsy handling of the affair that had jeopardized his own position.

There might have been more serious trouble for Blunt if Knight's standing in MI5 at the time had not been so low because of the imprisonment of Benjamin Greene, the former private secretary of Ramsay MacDonald. Greene was released after becoming the focus of a public storm over the misuse of the 18b Defense of the Realm regulation that had enabled the government to lock him up with Nazi sympathizers such as Sir Oswald Mosley. The affair had damaged Knight's credibility within the security service and his reports on Communist infiltration went largely unheeded by Liddell.

'I am sure M never suspected Blunt,' Joan Miller, Knight's assistant, confirmed. She wrote nonetheless that it was 'rather odd really as he had several protégés at Cambridge before the war and certainly knew all about the Apostles.' Could Knight have been as well informed about the Cambridge Comintern as Miller asserted? Given what is now known about Special Branch monitoring of the university Communists in the twenties, it is not impossible.

'Max didn't like Blunt – and he didn't want to work with him,' recalled Knight's deputy, John Bingham, later Lord Clanmorris. 'He used to say that he wouldn't have that "bugger" round the section.' Liddell's reaction was not so much a recognition of Blunt as a potential spy, but a distrust that too close an association might expose his own vulnerability. And other wartime MI5 officers have confirmed that Blunt always paid close attention to Knight and the infiltration activities he ran semi-independently from B Division: Blunt had a remarkable sense for nosing out and blocking those who threatened him.

Yet despite Blunt's warnings, the CPGB it seems failed to appreciate the scale of MI5's surveillance operation. Knight's agents were instrumental in trapping Douglas Springhall, a veteran of the Spanish Civil War and a longtime member of the CPGB Central Committee. In April 1943, MI5 watchers tailed Springhall to a meeting with his source, who turned out to be Ormond Uren, yet another Communist graduate. A Hungarian speaker, Uren had transferred as a temporary captain from the Highland Light Infantry to the Hungarian section of SOE in May 1942. At his in camera trial, Uren denied having any direct links with the Soviets. But he confessed to passing details of SOE communications and policy for Eastern Europe to Springhall to demonstrate that he was a 'sincere believer in Communism'. Uren received a seven-year jail term. Springhall, who was also charged with trying to steal the secret of the newly developed jet engine, was also tried in camera and sentenced to seven years' imprisonment. He then suffered the ultimate indignity of expulsion from the Communist party.

Once again Moscow Center had burned its fingers by hooking its espionage operations too closely to the Communist party. Blunt could only have been wryly amused at the self-congratulatory mood within B Division after the successful convictions of Uren and Springhall. There must have been a certain grim satisfaction in knowing that MI5 had eliminated only one of the minor moles.

Of all the agents in place when the Japanese attacked Pearl Harbor on 7 December 1941, not even Blunt was to advance to a position of such trust and influence as Kim Philby. Reflecting on Philby's astonishing accomplishments during his debriefing with Peter Wright, Blunt attributed his comrade's success to their different outlooks on life: 'He only ever had one ambition in life – to be a spy.'

After languishing in SOE's backwater for more than a year, Philby jumped at the opportunity to join MI6 to 'get away from the Rhododendrons of Beaulieu.' As previously argued, there is good reason for believing that Tomas Harris had sinister objectives in canvassing so hard for Philby on the old-boy network. And it is ironic that it was the resolution of a dispute between MI5 and MI6 that gave Philby his chance to insinuate himself into the heart of the latter.

MI5 complained that Menzies and his lieutenants treated their opposite numbers like poor relations: they jealously restricted the flow of intelligence. A particular target of Liddell's was Felix Cowgill, who in January 1941 had succeeded Colonel Valentine Vivian as head of Section V – the MI6 counterespionage operation. The result was a deep internal division among the professionals in MI6 and the wartime intake of academic amateurs. This gave rise to a good deal of cynical amusement among these younger officers, who included the writers Malcolm Muggeridge and Graham Greene, and their Oxonian academic friends in MI5, Stuart Hampshire and Hugh Trevor-Roper.

The prewar professionals 'sometimes regarded the war as a dangerous interruption of the Service' was how Trevor-Roper, Oxford's future regius professor of history, scathingly wrote of his painful wartime experiences in MI6. 'There were the metropolitan young gentlemen whose education had been expensive rather than profound, and who were recruited at the bars of White's and Boodle's by Colonel Dansey,' the future Lord Dacre complained. They were frequently at odds with 'the Indian policemen who were recruited, through the Central Intelligence Bureau in New Delhi, by Colonel Vivian.'

Only through the tactful intervention of Dick White, Liddell's diplomatic deputy, was a resolution reached in the bitter territorial dispute between MI5 and MI6. A deal was struck in which Brooman-White transferred from MI5's Spanish desk to head a separate Iberian group in Section V. His role was to liaise with Tomas Harris, his former deputy, who became his opposite number in B Division. Harris then worked assiduously to get Philby into MI6.

Cowgill confirmed to me that Philby was first recommended for a post in the Iberian group 'via Harris and Brooman-White'. He said Harris claimed to have known Philby in Spain. Since Section V was given a 'No Trace' background slip from the MI5 Registry files, an approving chat with Vivian, who had known Philby's father in India, was sufficient to get him the job.

Cowgill first encountered Philby when he arrived at Section V's wartime headquarters at Glenalmond, one of a pair of neighboring country houses on Lord Verulam's estate near St Albans, twenty miles north of London. His first impressions of Philby were favorable. The new recruit was efficient and effective. He did not complain about putting in long hours. But Cowgill was a stickler for enforcing the 'need to know' principle. He suspects that by working late, Philby was able to flout office security rules by familiarizing himself – and his Soviet controller – with the contents of the Central Registry files of MI6, which were located in offices adjacent to those of Section V, in the house known as Praewood.

Philby later paid a backhanded tribute to Cowgill's 'fiendish capacity for work'. Cowgill was also an authoritarian who despised the office politics and intrigues that were a daily fact of life in the fractious MI6. On the other hand, Philby, the *apparatchik*, loved them and cunningly exploited the conflicting rivalries. He picked his sides carefully, no doubt aware that some of his Oxbridge contemporaries knew too much about his undergraduate communism. Many years later, Trevor-Roper would acknowledge that he 'knew of Philby's Communist past'. But he insisted that it 'never occurred to me, at that time, to hold it against him' because 'our superiors were lunatic in their anti-Communism.' That Trevor-Roper did not expose Philby owes as much to his own hostility to MI6 as an institution as to his failure to discern from Philby's 'congenial' conversation that he adhered to a quietly fanatical brand of communism.

While Philby was playing up to Cowgill, he smugly admitted he had also 'cultivated MI5 assiduously'. His own account leaves no doubt that he succeeded in charming his principal target: Guy Liddell. In contrast to his scathing remarks about Cowgill, Philby praised the 'subtle and reflective mind' of the head of B Division, but Philby had good reason to gloat. Once he had won the confidence and trust of the director of counterintelligence, both MI5 and MI6 were wide open to Soviet infiltration. Hewit's testimony has made it plain that Liddell was not merely a casual guest in the eclectic social circle that treated Bentinck Street and Chesterfield Gardens as a saloon bar for off-duty intelligence officers. Liddell's weekly forays to Chelsea and to the London music halls in the company of Hewit and Burgess – whom he had supposedly banned from the office – suggest that he derived emotional as well as intellectual stimulation from the 'homosocial' entourage.

Liddell's former security-service colleagues to a man – and a woman – fiercely reject any suggestion that Liddell might have been trapped by homosexual tendencies into becoming a traitor. What cannot be denied, however, is that he made himself very vulnerable by seeking solace in the male companionship to be found at Bentinck Street. The fact is that Liddell was suffering deep emotional scars caused by the desertion before the war, by his wife Calypso, for her American half brother. The ensuing battle for custody of their children, which resulted in the dissolution of their marriage in 1943, is enough to give pause to a professional counterintelligence officer.

For the soon-to-be-divorced head of an operational division of the British secret service to mix even socially with a homosexual coterie was not only curious, it ran serious risk of misinterpretation. That Liddell sought the company of Burgess and Hewit on a weekly basis for several years gives ground for suspecting that something more than a 'love of the music hall' motivated his choice of off-duty companions. The valid suspicion remains that Liddell placed himself in a situation in which he could be compromised.

The Liddell case has an unsatisfactory conclusion for the historian. There are no documents available showing what Liddell's response was when it became known in 1951 that Burgess and Maclean were Soviet agents. All we have for the record are statements by Liddell's faithful colleagues that his failings were those of 'incautious' friendship and 'unfortunate' wartime association with homosexuals. But the logic of the situation, as the historian charts it, leads to the conclusion that Liddell's associates could say nothing else. To do so would have put their own actions and decisions at risk. Was this logic sound?

I flew to Washington in 1987 with the documents I had discovered on the matter to consult with a former senior member of American counterintelligence, who was personally aware of the events related above. I put my question to him. He paused in deep reflection before he answered. 'I'd prefer not to comment on this,' he said. 'I know what I know, and I see no point in opening old wounds that would only benefit the KGB and hurt my friends.'

As the year 1942 drew to a close, the tides of war were changing in favor of the Allied cause. The American navy had won the crucial battle for the control of the Pacific at Midway in June. The British Eighth Army soundly defeated Rommel that October in the battle of El Alamein and, with the help of the newly arrived Americans, was forcing the Germans to begin their retreat from North Africa. In November, the Red Army launched its counteroffensive against Stalingrad, marking the beginning of the end for Germany's hopes to win the war.

While the average allied infantryman fighting from hill to hill might not have had an appreciation of the new direction the war was taking, the political leaders in the capitals of the world were aware of it. So were Blunt, Philby and Burgess. It was time to start planning for the future, for what would happen after the war ended.

In his spare time, when he was not engaged in his program of opening courier bags, Anthony Blunt was working in his chosen field. Already a London University reader in the history of art, he had been made deputy director of the Courtauld Institute and was preparing the first catalog of the drawings in the royal collection at Windsor Castle.

Guy Burgess was back at the BBC as a successful talk-show producer, and was trying to work his way upward in the monopoly that controlled all broadcasting in Great Britain.

Kim Philby was to stay on doing what he did best: intelligence. With Liddell neutralized, Philby had already enhanced his reputation as an effective administrator by establishing a close liaison with MI5 while serving as head of the section running the Iberian operations at MI6. Philby's ability to elicit the confidence of his superiors, his mastery of detail and the cool skill he displayed at interdepartmental meetings impressed not only Cowgill but Valentine Vivian, C's vice-chief, and Menzies himself.

Philby prided himself on his ability 'to sniff the breezes of office politics' and play on the conflicting personalities and rivalries within MI6. He maneuvred against Cowgill in 1943 by discreetly mobilizing the Section V staff in favor of moving back to London from their irksome isolation in St Albans. Their new headquarters would be in Ryder Street, just two minutes from MI5, thereby achieving the 'propinquity' between the two operations so long desired by Sir David Petrie and politely resisted by Cowgill and Menzies.

Section V's return to London also made it more convenient for direct access to Blunt who was still running the operation that rifled the diplomatic pouches leaving London. Philby's connection with this highly successful operation is evident from his revelation that the Soviet embassy was the only foreign government immune to the activities of Blunt's team. This was not simply because Russian paranoia led to the employment of two couriers to guard their diplomatic pouches, but because of a rumor – perhaps put about by Blunt himself – that the diplomatic bags of the Kremlin were booby-trapped with 'bombs designed to obliterate the inquisitive'.

What Philby does not admit is that the move of Section V back to London, done against the better judgment of Cowgill, enabled Philby to meet with his Soviet controller more easily. Just as he was anxious to impress his superiors in MI6, Philby was even more concerned to prove to Moscow Center his ability as an agent. The amount of sensitive intelligence to which he had access was steadily increasing; all was relayed rapidly to Moscow via 'Henry'.

To serve two masters Philby had to work long hours. This willingness to burn the midnight oil impressed Cowgill as much as the efficient management Philby brought to running the counterintelligence activities of the Iberian unit. Philby had come to the attention of Menzies by reporting to the Joint Intelligence Committee, in June 1942, the clues he unearthed in the Abwehr Ultra that revealed a German scheme to monitor the Strait of Gibraltar with undersea sonar devices. Thanks to Philby, the potential threat to Operation Torch was thwarted before the November Anglo-American landings in North Africa. As a result, his responsibilities were extended to include counterintelligence activities in North Africa and Italy.

When Cowgill visited the United States a short time later, he assigned Philby to deputize for him. This was a sign to Philby's colleagues that he was on the ladder for rapid promotion. So too was his membership in the Athenaeum, the club preferred by bishops and the upper echelon of Whitehall civil servants. His rise in the MI6 hierarchy enabled Philby to be more than a simple conduit of information for the Soviets. He was now also able to act as an 'agent of influence', swaying decisions that worked in favour of Moscow rather than the other Allies. In the summer of 1943, for instance, he used his authority to block the circulation of a report that argued, from clues in the Abwehr Ultra, that some German army officers were preparing to put peace feelers to Churchill and Roosevelt. It was not in the interests of the Soviet Union to encourage a separate peace that would leave Russia at the mercy of Hitler.

Philby's rise in MI6, fortuitously for the Soviets, coincided with the arrival in London of the first echelons of American intelligence officers. These were the men in General William O. 'Wild Bill' Donovan's Office of Strategic Services (OSS). Philby was presented with the opportunity he was waiting for: to secure his reputation with Washington. At the end of 1943, he succeded by staking his reputation on the judgement of Allen Dulles, the future CIA chief, who in 1943 was the OSS representative in Switzerland. This put him into conflict with C's pompous deputy, Claude Dansey, who had dismissed as too obvious a plant the suitcase full of documents that Dulles said had come from the Foreign Ministry in Berlin. After Dansey's haughty rejection, Philby checked the documents with the cryptanalysts at Bletchley who compared them to the intercepted messages sent by the German military attaché in Tokyo. They quickly and enthusiastically confirmed the authenticity of the Dulles haul – much to the chagrin of Dansey who had regarded the Americans as amateurs poaching on his Swiss preserve.

Since June 1942, when the OSS established its X-2 counterintelligence operation under James R. 'Jimmy' Murphy, Donovan's former assistant, the Americans had been trying to negotiate an exchange of information and personnel with MI6 and MI5. The British – especially Liddell, Dansey and Menzies – resisted. They feared that the Americans would commandeer their Ultra-based empire, so they stalled by suggesting that the admission of untutored and unsuitable OSS amateurs would risk upsetting the security of counterintelligence operations.

The British went out of their way to impress the Americans with how MI5 and MI6 handpicked their officers by a ritual steeped in the social mystique of England's old-boy network. According to a contemporary report prepared for the OSS, the process had more in common with raising thoroughbred racehorses than with clandestine operations.

The Americans were told that His Majesty's Secret Service could not risk the wrong kind of chap making an application. Suitable candidates had to be 'initially recommended to the service by friends already in the service or by particular alumni of the service designated for this purpose because of their experience in the types required and because of their appropriate situation in life.' This was the job of former MI6 and MI5 officers who acted as talent scouts 'in the British universities'. In practice the dominance of Oxford and Cambridge produced 'young men with unusual qualifications of language and travel'.

Further evidence of the degree to which Britain's ruling establishment deluded itself, even at the height of the war, that family connections and the old-school tie guaranteed national security emerged in a confidential report by the War Cabinet's panel that investigated staff 'Engaged on Secret Work'. Established civil servants were 'rarely put under any sort of scrutiny'. Nor should

they be submitted to such indignities. Only if they were 'transferred to appointments involving MOST SECRET work' was a
vetting necessary, and then the due weight would be given to
'personal recommendations from persons whose judgment can be
relied on and who have close acquaintance with the candidate.'

Liddell passed these War Cabinet recommendations to the
American embassy in June 1942.

There is a bitter irony that the Soviet intelligence service had
already exploited the old-boy network in which the British placed
so much trust. The MI6 objections, moreover, that the OSS
lacked the system they considered so essential to ensuring the
security of a secret service, were also unfounded. The majority of
the senior officers in the OSS were self-selecting Ivy Leaguers like
Donovan. A large number were graduates of Yale, whose collegiate system had traditionally maintained close links with Cambridge, while Harvard men considered themselves spiritually
closer to Oxford.

The soft-spoken X-2 chief, Murphy, did not hail from either
Yale or Harvard. But he was instrumental – after some high-level
lobbying on Downing Street by Donovan – in negotiating a joint
operating agreement with MI6 in May 1943. It took six more
months before the OSS reached a similar arrangement with MI5.
A quarter of a century later, Philby, writing under the disparaging eye of the KGB in Moscow, described the American
arrivals as a 'notably bewildered group'. Somewhat to Philby's
surprise, Cowgill continued to hold back information from the
professionals in the FBI, even though Section V indoctrinated the
OSS officers, who were, in the words of one of them, 'a bunch of
ignorant bums' compared with Hoover's men. The quip was
ascribed to Norman Holmes Pearson, one of the four OSS men
assigned to MI6. The remark would have been delivered with the
engaging good humour of this poet and English-literature lecturer
from Yale who would also make a joke about belonging to an
organization with an 'Oh So Social' acronym.

Whatever sour twist Philby found it convenient to give Pearson
in his book, the X-2 wartime reports show that Pearson quickly

struck up a close working relationship with Cowgill. Section V issued new red stamps marked TOP SECRET to replace the MOST SECRET British classification. Full access was given to Pearson's liaison team, who were working on the MI6 agent operations, and ISOS and ISK Ultra material.

'I was always able to talk to you easily and directly, without the flourishes of a gavotte which other tunes demanded' was how Pearson paid tribute to the 'mutual respect' that developed into close friendship between the Yale academic and the former Indian policeman. During our discussions, Cowgill recalled for me the twinkling eyes and warm manner of the 'professor', whose somewhat birdlike appearance was accentuated by a limp caused by tuberculosis of the hip. While not himself a Rhodes scholar, though many of his British colleagues took it for granted that he had been one, Pearson had studied at Oxford. So even when promoted to head up the X-2 organization in London, with the code name 'Saint', Pearson carefully underplayed his role as the affable Yankee intruder. His diary suggests that the chefs at Prunier's and the Connaught, whose virtuosity with meager wartime rationing only an American officer's pay could afford, helped Pearson win over the senior officers of MI6 and MI5.

Pearson was also admitted to the innermost secrets of Double-Cross as an ex-officio member of the Twenty Committee. Masterman also accorded the head of X-2 the unusual privilege of a desk in his office in MI5 headquarters on St James's. Pearson's hip ailment precluded him from making the two-minute bicycle ride to Ryder Street, where his office, 22-A, was just down the corridor from Philby's.

The OSS obtained the priceless 'fruits of many decades of counterespionage experience,' Pearson would report later. 'Furthermore, the British offered to train American personnel in the techniques essential to the proper use of all categories of their records.' Within two years, the OSS 'gained full access to the experience and extensive files of both the internal and external experience of the British counter-espionage services' and was 'treated as an independent equal'.

Pearson could take much credit for that success, but it was one of Pearson's former students at Yale who joined the X-2 team at Ryder Street. He became the leading theorist of American counter-intelligence strategy. James Angleton, an English-literature graduate of Yale and an accomplished poet, had been drafted into the army from Harvard Law School in the spring of 1942. Looking for a military career that would stimulate his intellect, he volunteered for the OSS, where his outstanding performance at the OSS schools and training course impressed Murphy. He assigned Angleton the Italian desk in his Washington headquarters on the strength of the young man's experience of Italy, where his father had been vice-president of the National Cash Register (NCR) subsidiary in Rome. He joined the X-2 team in MI6 after the agreement on full cooperation with the British in 1943.

Pearson put the rake-thin young American in charge of Italian affairs for X-2. A brooding theoretician, Angleton had already become intrigued by the problems of counterespionage and security. He amazed his British colleagues by moving an army cot into his Ryder Street office, the better to concentrate on developing his belief that counterintelligence could be made into a science. The key, he concluded from close analysis of Ultra's application in MI6 operations, was penetration – a conviction reinforced by his future experiences on the ground as OSS chief in Italy.

It became a central axiom of Angleton's theory that penetration was essential to achieve the manipulation necessary to deceive an enemy by forcing him into an unreal world. When Angleton became the CIA's chief of the counterintelligence staff in 1954, he finally had the chance to test his theories of deception and penetration in a global contest with the KGB at the height of the Cold War. He was fully cognizant that obsessive suspicion was one of the dangers inherent in his theories. The constant testing and analysis necessary to guard against enemy infiltration of false information, or suborning, could lead the contestants, as Angleton himself once graphically acknowledged, into 'a wilderness of mirrors'.

We can see from the X-2 reports how Angleton's analysis of counterintelligence, based on Britain's Double-Cross operations against the Germans, shaped his perceptions of the Soviets. A recently discovered X-2 report on the 'Theory of Counter Espionage', which reflects Angleton's thinking if he was not the author, declared that the 'ideal situation had come close to being achieved' by the wartime British secret service. The 'incalcuable benefits' of the 'Most Secret Source material' – principally Ultra – had been the key 'to the innermost recesses of the enemy's espionage system [that] enabled the British (and later the Americans who shared the secret) not only to obtain a constant and increasing flow of up-to-date information on the organization of German intelligence and its officials, but also to keep track of agent activities in the United Kingdom, western Europe, and to some extent, indeed throughout the world.'

His experience in wartime Britain taught him how vulnerable even the most supposedly secure counterintelligence service is to clandestine penetration.

That was the lesson Angleton would draw from the British failure to realize that their own secret service might be subject to penetration. He found this especially ironic, given the British achievement in completely taking over and controlling the Abwehr's network in England. The trap into which the British had fallen was overconfidence at their own success. A contributory factor was the concentration of all counterintelligence resources on defeating the Axis, and the assumption that the Soviet threat had been eliminated by the fifty-year Anglo-Soviet treaty of friendship and alliance in which both nations had pledged not to interfere in the other's internal affairs.

It can be argued that Liddell, as director of MI5's counter-espionage division, ought, given his experience, to have been more skeptical. He should have known that it would take more than a scrap of paper to turn the devious old Bolshevik enemy into a trustworthy ally. But Liddell was also making frequent appearances at Bentinck Street, as well as spending weekly nights out with the persuasive Burgess, who never concealed his admiration for the Soviet Union.

Burgess had been among the first of the BBC producers to

submit proposals for shows on Russian themes. Shortly after the German invasion, the BBC and the Foreign Office were still debating whether it was safe to broadcast the 'Internationale'. But Burgess put in a full raft of suggested topics.

The BBC archives reveal that after consulting John Strachey and Professor Bernal, Burgess presented his suggestions, 'put down hastily, as the problem is urgent,' he reminded his superiors. He bubbled over with ideas that displayed the depth of his knowledge of Russian literature, from 'Lenin's favorite passage' in *War and Peace* to Ilya Ehrenberg and the satires of Zoshchenko. He urged the BBC to reverse the broadcast ban on Professor Haldane so that he could talk about Soviet science. He proposed Christopher Hill, a Marxist who was a fellow of All Souls, as the 'best authority in England' to give talks on Russian history.

When it came to speaking about art, Burgess put forward the names of Dr Klingender and Dr Blunt. 'Neither is a Communist,' he emphasized for the benefit of the head of Talks. This was knowingly disingenuous. Klingender was the émigré German art historian whose theories had shaped Blunt's own Marxist aesthetic interpretations. But Burgess knew that before anyone could sit before a BBC microphone during the war, he had to receive MI5 clearance.

That such an open Oxford Marxist as Christopher Hill, albeit a distinguished Oxford historian, could be recruited for secret government work, first in SOE then in the Northern Department of the Foreign Office, where he had access to sensitive papers on relations with the Soviet Union where he was obviously in a position to influence crucial policy decisions, was a serious lapse by MI5. That Burgess regarded Hill as a Communist in 1941 suggests that MI5 must also have known, otherwise Burgess would not have alerted the BBC. Nor would he have put Hill's name forward to the BBC Talks Department if he had had any doubt that clearance could be easily arranged through his MI5 contact. The Oxbridge Communist network had, it appears, a direct line to someone inside MI5 other than Blunt (who, by

1941, was no longer in C Division) able to deal with vetting Registry files.

A clue to where the other moles might have tunneled in the apparatus emerges in the dismissive treatment of Max Knight's memorandum on the Comintern's future threat. Knight was one of the few members of B Division who had not dropped his guard. He continued to warn of undiminished Soviet subversion. But his voice was often drowned out by comments from F Division, where Roger Hollis relied on two assistants whose own Marxism meant that they may have been far from disinterested parties.

One was Roger Fulford, Hollis's longtime college friend, who had also been associated with the London 'homintern' network of which Burgess was a member. Another was Kemball Johnston, a Trinity contemporary of Blunt's. According to his eldest son Johnston hated the Establishment throughout his life. 'You could not get much further left than Father,' he said. Like Goronwy Rees and many other Marxist sympathizers, Johnston joined the Territorial Army as a personal commitment against the British government's deal with Hitler at Munich in 1938. But illness kept him from being sent to France when war broke out, and he missed Dunkirk. He became an assistant to Hollis in F Division, and grew close to Burgess and Blunt, who became godfathers to Johnston's second son: Guy Anthony. It may be that Blunt and Burgess obtained information from him unwittingly. In the light of the suspicions of disloyalty that were later to surround Roger Hollis, it is significant that other MI5 officers have confirmed to me that Johnston was not the only member of F Division who was known to have Marxist sympathies long before the Soviet Union became Britain's ally.

This surprising MI5 tolerance of Marxists had its limits, however. The risk of being caught and charged with espionage was greatest to anyone who had direct links to the Communist party. That was because Knight was as ardent a pursuer of Communist subversion as of German fifth columnists.

The Uren/Springhall espionage case in June 1943 provided a

warning jolt. Menzies was sufficiently concerned to order Vivian, his assistant chief and adviser on security, to conduct an investigation to see if anyone else in MI6 had party connections. His report was sufficiently unsettling to send Menzies hurrying in to see the permanent under secretary of the Foreign Office.

Friday, 13 August 1943, was not a good day for Sir Alexander Cadogan, according to his terse diary entry: ' "C" about Communists in his organization.' The line, which was carefully excised from the edited version of the diaries approved by the Cabinet Office in 1971, confirms that even as the marriage with the American OSS was being consummated, Menzies knew of Communist penetration.

In the absence of Vivian's report, which is still classified Secret, it is impossible to be certain about the extent of the damage Vivian discovered. However, Air Vice-Marshal Sir James Easton, who succeeded Vivian as C's assistant in 1949, but who was not in MI6 at the time, believes that David Footman became a prime suspect. That not even the slightest whisper of suspicion was raised toward Philby leads Cowgill to suppose that C must have been referring to a relatively low-level inquiry that led to the dismissal of a secretary in Section V. The Uren/Springhall case should have reminded the directors of both MI5 and MI6 of the continuing threat of subversion. If the 1943 investigation put Philby and Blunt on their guard, it also bolstered their confidence. Vivian's failure to identify any major penetration would only have served to reinforce Menzies's conviction that the old-boy network had once again proved its value by keeping Communists out of the officer ranks of MI5 and MI6.

Yet a very different attitude prevailed when it came to foreigners. Distrust and suspicion were the reflexive responses of the British security-service office. In April 1943, the Prime Minister learned that members of the French National Committee, some of them known to be Communists, were on their way to England to work with the Allies on intelligence preparations for the landing in the south of France. An urgent telegram was fired off from Downing Street to the British representative in Algiers.

'I suppose you realize that we are weeding remorselessly every single known Communist from our secret organizations,' the Prime Minister curtly told Duff Cooper. 'We did this after having to sentence two quite high-grade people to long terms of penal servitude for their betrayal, in accordance with the Communist faith, of important military secrets. If therefore the French Committee or any representatives sent here are infected with Communism, they will certainly not be made party to any British or, I expect, American secrets.'

The Prime Minister, like his security-service directors, was blissfully unaware that Soviet agents were already deeply involved in the secret Overlord strategy. Dozens of British counter-intelligence officers obtained secondments to Eisenhower's staff to play leading roles in planning and overseeing the elaborate security and deception operations at Supreme Headquarters Allied Expeditionary Force (SHAEF). Eisenhower's headquarters was at Norfolk House, a red-brick office block in St James's Square, conveniently close to both Section V of MI6 in Ryder Street and MI5 headquarters at the top of St James's Street, and the gentlemen's clubs of Pall Mall.

One young lieutenant colonel who found a plum appointment at SHAEF headquarters was Christopher Blunt. The US Army files reveal that he became one of the principal officers in the censorship office. This came under the Counter-Intelligence Division of G-2, where Colonel Dick White, Liddell's deputy in MI5's B Division, was deputy to Colonel Sheen of the US Army. Many of Anthony Blunt's other acquaintances from MI5 and MI6 had moved into Norfolk House.

One of the potentially disastrous results of this jobs-for-the-boys approach was to let Anthony Blunt – and therefore Moscow – into another of the greatest secrets of the war. This negated all the elaborate security precautions intended to keep the Soviets from learning in advance the actual invasion date and the target beachheads for the Allied invasion of Normandy. While it was not in the Soviet interest to prejudice the invasion, Churchill had good reason not to communicate the date and real targets to

Stalin: the code breakers at Bletchley had ample evidence from the German Ultra intercepts that the Germans had broken some of the Soviet military-cipher systems.

Despite all precautions, the secret of D-Day was leaked to the Kremlin. Philby knew it; so did Blunt. According to William Cavendish-Bentinck, both men knew a secret considered so vital that Allied officers – even in MI5 – had to receive special clearance for D-Day planning material stamped BIGOT. As the wartime chairman of the Joint Intelligence Committee that provided the analyses and forecasts on which Churchill and the British Chiefs of Staff based all their decisions, Bentinck remembers that Blunt attended several of his meetings. 'He struck me as being rather a dull dog,' Bentinck recalled. He insisted that he never once suspected Blunt or Philby – who also sometimes attended the JIC sessions. Blunt told Robert Cecil that he had gone to 'one or two' JIC meetings 'while he was working for SHAEF'.

Yet Blunt was never officially part of the SHAEF intelligence establishment. This comes from Sir Dick White, who was himself one of the senior officers in the setup. A search of all the recently declassified G-2 and G-3 SHAEF records confirmed the authority of his statement. While there are many documents identifying Colonel Christopher Blunt and his activities in the censorship division, there is not a single memorandum, assignment, or telephone number for Major Anthony Blunt.

How then did Blunt get into SHAEF and act as a representative at the Joint Intelligence Committee? This had puzzled Cecil. He pressed Blunt on this point during his interviews with him. The answer he was given fits the facts, because on 24 April 1944, in order to impose the maximum security precautions, all diplomatic mail was subject to search and censorship.

'Anthony said that he found himself out of a job at the end of April. The suggestion was made, he could not remember by whom, that he should help out with the D-Day deception scheme,' Cecil told me. 'Since he was already a uniformed member of MI5, which was heavily involved through the Double-Cross operation, he was "lent" to SHAEF. It was in this capacity that he attended one or possibly two JIC meetings.'

Blunt talked so enthusiastically about his work for SHAEF that Cecil concluded he must have hugely enjoyed his part in the deception. The plan was to persuade the German High Command that the main target of the D-Day landings was the Pas de Calais area rather than the Normandy coast of France. Code-named Fortitude South, the elaborate and minutely constructed deception operation had been under way since the beginning of the year. Dummy landing craft were assembling in the ports of the Thames estuary and the region was spouting inflatable tanks, canvas trucks and wooden guns. Radio traffic was rerouted to convey the impression that the First US Army Group (FUSAG), under General George C. Patton, supported by Canadian and British divisions, was assembling and training in the fields of Kent and Sussex for an assault over the shortest cross-Channel route. While this phantom invasion force grew in the east, the real concentration of Allied military might was gathering in Hampshire, Dorset and the West Country ports for the actual invasion two hundred miles down the French coastline from the Pas de Calais.

The most sensitive component in the Fortitude plan was the use of controlled enemy agents to feed misleading information about Patton's forces in southeast England.

In the early summer of 1944, the ISOS intelligence provided by Bletchley confirmed that the Abwehr believed that the double-cross agents known as 'Garbo' (Juan Pujol) and 'Brutus' (Garby-Czerniawiski) were their most reliable sources in England. 'Garbo' was run by Blunt's close friend Tomas Harris, while 'Brutus' was run by the Honorable Hugh Astor, a friend of Christopher Blunt's. So it is not surprising to find that Blunt arrived at SHAEF to collaborate with Harris and Astor.

According to what Blunt told Cecil, his special responsibility was to play commander of the 4th Canadian Armored Division. Using the elaborate Fortitude South plan as his guide, he worked out of the Ops B war room at SHAEF headquarters with its large map of the dispositions of Patton's phantom FUSAG forces. By advancing the flags representing the Canadian tanks and men from their notional training camp at East Grinstead in Sussex to concentration at their embarkation port of Dover during May, he devised credible sightings for the reports that Harris and Astor had their agents relay to the Germans.

Blunt's work at SHAEF headquarters lasted only from the end of April through June 1944. But he told Cecil that he was very proud of his contribution to the masterpiece of deception that guaranteed the success of D-Day. Blunt seems to have been paying himself an indirect compliment when he paid tribute in the *Dictionary of National Biography* to the 'extraordinary imaginative power' of Tomas Harris, who was 'one of the principal organizers of "Operation Garbo".'

No one disputes that deception was Blunt's forte. There is no surprise among those who knew him that he probably derived as much pleasure from helping deceive the Nazis as he did from passing on the secrets of D-Day to his Soviet controller. In this context, it is significant to note that Anatoli Gorski, the case officer for the leading members of the Cambridge ring since 1940, did *not* transfer to the Soviet embassy in Washington until July 1944. It has always been assumed that Gorski – otherwise known as Gromov, who later became head of the KGB's First Directorate dealing with Anglo-American territories in the fifties – followed Donald Maclean across the Atlantic when he was promoted in March 1944 to become the first secretary of the British embassy in Washington.

An explanation for Gorski's four-month delay in following Maclean to the United States was the importance that Moscow attached to monitoring the D-Day operation. The Soviets were reluctant to risk disturbing the direct channels of communications with Blunt as long as he remained at SHAEF headquarters. Gorski's departure from England in July also happened to coincide with the end of Blunt's stint with the Fortitude team at Norfolk House. It was then that Boris Krotov, another Soviet embassy official, replaced Gorski as the high-level agent runner in London.

Blunt evidently did not get on warmly with Krotov, his new controller. During his interrogations with Wright, Blunt portrayed Krotov as a technocrat, in contrast to his more individualistic prewar controllers. This was a reflection of the methodical professionalism demanded of agents by Lavrenti Pavlovich Beria, who succeeded his chief, Yezhov, as director of the NKVD in December 1939. A Georgian, like Stalin, Beria ruled for fifteen years with a unique combination of ruthlessness and administrative efficiency that restored order and coherence to Soviet intelligence operations after the disruptions caused by the purges.

The cold dedication of Beria's new breed of Soviet technocrat agent did not impress Blunt. Minutely detailed demands relayed from Moscow contrasted with the urbane relationship the Cambridge spies had once enjoyed with Theodore Maly and 'Henry'. By the summer of 1944, Soviet operations in London were being run with ruthless mechanical efficiency to gather quality intelligence from Stalin's Englishmen. Expectations were raised. Beria knew that his Cambridge agents were now rising high enough in the British government apparatus to satisfy Stalin's demands for secret intelligence.

While Maclean was en route to the United States, and Blunt and Philby were passing on the secrets from SHAEF, Burgess too was in the process of moving to a more productive position. On 4 June 1944, Burgess resigned his post of Talks producer at Broadcasting House to take up an appointment in the press department of the Foreign Office. It was a far more rewarding monitoring post for picking up the high-level government intelligence that Krotov wanted. But the most cheering news that summer for Beria's Foreign Department chief in Moscow was not that the NKVD now had another of its British undercover agents inserted into the Foreign Office, nor the opening of a second front against the Nazis. It was Krotov's report that Philby, as its chief penetration agent, was in line to head MI6's renewed assault on communism in postwar Europe.

According to Felix Cowgill, the SIS files on Communists had 'been on ice' since he completed sorting them in August 1939. 'It was C's idea that the anti-Soviet operations would be run by Section IX, which would absorb the staff of my Section V after the dissolution of its wartime establishment' was how Cowgill explained the proposed reorganization. Felix Cowgill was originally designated as the commander to lead Britain's battle against postwar Communist subversion in Europe by drawing on Section V (v)'s experience. Unknown to Cowgill, his most dangerous rival was his seemingly dutiful and hardworking deputy: Philby began conspiring against his unsuspecting chief as soon as he realized that MI5 transfer Jack Curry, who was deaf and near retirement age, was only a stopgap head of Section IX.

'For the next few weeks, virtually all my discussions with my Soviet contact concerned the future of Section IX' was how Philby recounted working out his strategy with Krotov. Moscow Center was intimately involved in ensuring that its man in MI6 undermined Cowgill's authority. Krotov directed Philby that he 'must do everything, but *everything*' to ensure his becoming head of Section IX. Philby followed Moscow's orders to the letter. He subtly played on the enmity between Vivian and Cowgill with 'the greatest care'.

There were plenty of opportunities for Philby to work his plan because Cowgill had put him in charge of Section V when he himself went to the United States in June 1944. As a result of his position as acting head of Section V, Philby had access to the full dimension of Allied counterintelligence secrets in the critical weeks leading up to D-Day.

Ironically, Philby appeared more reticent about briefing his boss than the Soviets when Cowgill returned to London just three days before the Allied troops went ashore in France. When Philby arrived that evening at their flat for a late briefing, Mrs Cowgill suspected that something was up.

'Philby was hedging, and his stutter, which he put on when he was in trouble, was worse than usual,' Mrs Cowgill recalled. 'I remember saying to Felix after Kim left, "That man is after your job".'

Mrs Cowgill's intuition proved correct. Philby was already

preparing to walk over her husband to get his job. By early September 1944, while Cowgill was on a trip to Belgium, arranging for Section V's Special Counter-Intelligence units to operate behind the lines of Montgomery's advancing 21st Army Group, Vivian's report on Section IX landed on Menzies's walnut-inlaid desk. It came out strongly against Cowgill as head of the anti-Soviet operations of MI6, and recommended that Philby should be Curry's successor in Section IX. Menzies moved without waiting for Cowgill to return. He summoned Philby and told him he was to take over Section IX immediately. For the first time he called him Kim. Then C even gave him Vivian's memorandum – which Philby had already seen but nevertheless pretended to read. Insidiously using his 'I-hope-I-am-not-speaking-out-of-turn-sir' approach, Philby then asked for – and quickly obtained – written approval of Philby's appointment by the MI5 chief, Sir David Petrie, plus Petrie's promise of full cooperation.

When Cowgill returned from Brussels early in October, he was confronted by a fait accompli. Realizing that Philby's appointment to Section IX had effectively cut him out of a job he believed he was better qualified to take on, Cowgill resigned after a stormy confrontation with Menzies. Philby's friend Tim Milne, who had succeeded Philby as head of the Iberian desk in Section V, assumed responsibility for the whole section.

'I never saw Philby again,' Cowgill said. The residual bitterness about the whole episode was evident in the deliberate way Cowgill told me how he 'handed over' to Milne on 18 January 1945, before taking up an assignment with the British Control Commission in Germany. He took some comfort in the letter of consolation he received from Norman Holmes Pearson. The head of the OSS X-2 mission in London wrote of his 'numbness at the pit of the stomach' upon officially learning that his friend was no longer in charge of Section V which was 'in all truth your creation'. He told Cowgill he was speaking for his boss, James Murphy, in assuring him that 'American counterespionage owe[s] its maturity to your education.'

Philby, meanwhile, had impatiently assumed command of

Section IX by drafting a charter of operations, for C to sign, giving his outfit the responsibility for 'the collection and interpretation of information on Soviet and communist espionage and subversion in all parts of the world outside British territory.' Menzies himself, Philby noted with pointed satisfaction, added the rider that 'he was on no account to have any dealings with any of the United States services.'

Philby's mischievous assertion appears to be yet another reflection of the Soviet strategy to drive a wedge between the wartime allies. But as he assumed the burden of his new anti-Communist duties, Philby was increasingly confronted with having to deal with American interests. MI6 and the OSS jointly operated the Special Counter-Intelligence units that were operating in the rear of the Allied advance through France and the Low Countries. They were uncovering, and deploying, as double agents a growing number of German stay-behinds to act as CEAs and feed false information to the retreating forces of the Wehrmacht. Some of the best of these agents were later discovered to have been originally infiltrated into the Abwehr by the Soviet intelligence services – a fact that Philby must have known as he made frequent trips to SHAEF counterintelligence headquarters in Paris in October 1944.

Malcolm Muggeridge, then an MI6 agent attached to De Gaulle's Services Speciales, recalls how on one visit, Philby took him to an expensive dinner in a Left Bank restaurant and then, as he talked about his new responsibilities, insisted on walking up the Boulevard Saint-Germain to the Rue de Grenelle.

'I realized without any particular amazement, that we were making for the Soviet embassy,' Muggeridge recalled, vividly describing the bizarre scene that took place in front of the large stone building with its impassively tall blue wooden gates and shuttered windows. 'How are we going to get in there?' Philby kept saying as he shook his fists and regaled his astonished junior colleague with the difficulties of penetrating the Soviet embassy.

In the sober light of the next morning, Muggeridge concluded that too much wine and cognac had ignited the bizarre display that Philby had staged for his benefit. Although Muggeridge enjoyed Philby's company, he described him as 'one of nature's *farouches*', and a 'wild man'. The histrionics in front of the Soviet embassy were not the only unsettling incident that had occurred during Philby's October visit to Paris. Muggeridge had arrived with Lord Rothschild shortly after the liberation of the city, when the priceless ornaments, French furniture, and art treasures of the gilt- and marble-encrusted mansion were being brought up from the basement, where they had survived the German occupation.

'Hitlers may come and go but Rothschilds go on for ever,' the ancient concierge philosophically remarked as he organized the mansion as Rothschild's billet. Records in the US Army files – some of which were withheld at the request of the British government – conform that 'Col. Ld. Rothschild' operated from the Rue Petrach offices of 105 Special Counter-Intelligence attached to SHAEF advanced headquarters.

When Philby came to Paris he, too, was put up at the Rothschild mansion on the Avenue de Marigny. Over dinner one evening, a bitter argument broke out among them about the Soviets' right to have full access to Allied intelligence. It was Rothschild, Muggeridge recalled, who led off the discussion of whether Moscow had been supplied with everything that SHAEF knew from Ultra about the German order of battle. Rothschild knew how extensive this intelligence was because he had access to it on a day-to-day basis as it came into SHAEF headquarters.

Muggeridge reminded his host that some caution was legitimate because, in 1940, Stalin had been passing intelligence to Hitler. The British and Americans had to be on their guard against treachery. The debate grew heated. Philby joined in. 'He spluttered and shouted that we were duty bound to do everything in our power, whatever it might be, to support the Red Army,' Muggeridge said, recalling that he insisted that this included risking the security of the Ultra secret.

Rothschild became highly indignant that the Russians were not getting all the information, and, as a dedicated opponent of communism and a loyal MI6 officer, Muggeridge remembers, he suddenly found himself like a skeleton at a feast. He would later conclude, incorrectly, that Philby's treachery began during his trip to Paris.

Philby, as Muggeridge reminded me, was not the only member of the Cambridge ring to use the Rothschild mansion as a high-class billet in the months after the liberation of Paris. Both Burgess and Blunt came and stayed shortly afterward. When Rothschild's former personal assistant from MI5 arrived for a week's visit, she found it highly amusing that the two notorious residents of the Bentinck Street flat had already been guests in the Avenue de Marigny mansion.

Kitty Muggeridge still enjoys chuckling over how her cousin Tess Mayor, the future Lady Rothschild, had wickedly quipped to Malcolm: 'How nice to have the buggers in the house again!'

What exactly Anthony Blunt did in Paris that September 1944, and for the remaining months of the war, has been the subject of considerable speculation. His MI5 superior Sir Dick White, who was then deputy head of SHAEF counterintelligence, has stated that Blunt was 'not really' with *his* outfit. At the same time, White acknowledges that Blunt did not come to Paris 'purely as an art historian', who had been 'brought in by the fine arts people in London after the invasion to come over to Europe to try to find some of the works of art stolen by the Nazis.'

It is curious that Blunt's name appears nowhere in the records of the special Monuments and Fine Arts section (MAFA) of SHAEF that was established in May 1944. With the rank of lieutenant colonel, Leonard Woolley, the archaeologist who had won international renown as the excavator of the cradle of Western civilization at Ur in Mesopotomia, had taken the responsibility for recruiting the British contingent. He brought together many of the country's leading art historians, including Blunt's school friend and lifelong professional associate Ellis Waterhouse. Their mission was to follow the Allied armies and survey the state of Europe's ravaged cultural heritage.

Woolley wanted Blunt's help. 'The officer I would prefer and could most strongly recommend as a capable man, a first rate German speaker and out of the top drawer as an art historian, is Major Anthony Blunt, now serving with MI5,' Woolley wrote the SHAEF MAFA German Section. He had 'spoken to Major Blunt, who promised to make strong representations to his CO but did not hold much hope that he would be released.' Woolley pleaded with Colonel Bridge to do 'anything you can to help us get the services of this officer.' Despite the high regard of the art world for Blunt's professional abilities, Woolley could not get him released from MI5.

The inference to be drawn from Woolley's communication is that MI5 considered Blunt too valuable to release as head of SHAEF's German art mission. Blunt spent the final months of the war on some other jobs of special intelligence so sensitive that no official records exist.

In unraveling the mysteries behind Blunt's immunity deal, it is now possible to see exactly how these missions provided him with a gilt-edged 'insurance policy' that later would protect him from prosecution should it be learned he was a Soviet agent. To use the word *blackmail* may be melodramatic, but it seems obvious that what Blunt knew – secrets that caused Prime Minister Churchill and Buckingham Palace to exert all their powers to keep them hidden – were the trump cards in Anthony's deadly game of espionage.

So highly classified were Blunt's actions at the end of the war, claims Peter Wright in *Spycatcher*, that even MI5 was forbidden to pry into its details thirty years later. This Wright discovered when he assumed responsibility for interrogating Blunt in 1965. He discovered, to his surprise, that Buckingham Palace was already aware that there was a confessed Soviet spy in its midst. Michael Adeane, the sovereign's private secretary, assured him 'in the detached manner of someone who wishes not to know very much more about the matter,' that the Queen 'has been fully informed about Sir Anthony, and is quite content for him to be dealt with in any way which gets at the truth.'

One matter, however, the Queen absolutely did not wish discussed – even within the British security service. This was 'an assignment he [Blunt] undertook on behalf of the Palace – a visit to Germany' that he had made at the end of the war.

'I never did learn the secret of his mission at the end of the war,' Wright said, observing foxily that the Palace had become adept in the 'difficult art of scandal burying' over several centuries, whereas 'MI5 have only been in the business since 1909.'

Wright's statement in 1987 provides the first authoritative confirmation from an MI5 source that Blunt spent the last months of his wartime service on some highly secret personal mission for the King. Professor Hugh Trevor-Roper had dropped the same hints a few days after Blunt's exposure in 1979. The former regius professor of history was seconded in 1945 by Dick White to his counterintelligence group at SHAEF and his familiarity with captured German records enabled him to write the first major postwar study of Adolf Hitler. Trevor-Roper was therefore regarded as speaking authoritatively – if somewhat indiscreetly – when he told a reporter from the *Sunday Times* how he ran into Blunt at the St James's MI5 headquarters as Blunt was reporting to Guy Liddell on his mission.

Trevor-Roger gathered that Blunt had been sent to Germany on the orders of King George VI to retrieve documents that were believed to be in the hands of the royal family's many German relations. According to Trevor-Roper, the main objective had been the long and intimate correspondence that Queen Victoria maintained with her eldest daughter, 'Vicky', who in 1858 married Frederick III of Prussia and became the mother of Kaiser Wilhelm II. The King, and particularly his mother, Queen Mary, who had corresponded with her German relatives and been a frequent visitor in her youth to the Hesse castles that were now in the US Army's zone of occupation in the Frankfurt area, were fearful that the intimate secrets of Britain's royal family could fall into unscrupulous hands – even making headlines in the American press.

According to Blunt, his mission had been successful. Trevor-Roper recalled that Blunt made a special point of telling him that among the massive collection of royal letters he had discovered one from a court official who had called on Karl Marx. So it was obvious that Blunt had made himself familiar with the contents of whatever papers he collected. Blunt also told Trevor-Roper how he dined one evening in grand style at a German castle that appeared untouched by the privations of war. Twenty people had sat down to a magnificent six-course meal served by liveried footmen behind every chair.

The *Sunday Times* reporters had difficulty persuading the reluctant eighty-three-year-old Prince Wolfgang of Hesse to talk with them. But when they did, he confirmed that Sir Owen Morshead, then the royal librarian from Windsor Castle, and Anthony Blunt, had driven up one day in the spring of 1945 in a military truck. He was not precise about the date, but it was sometime after the troops of General George S. Patton's Third Army had arrived in the village of Kronberg in the last week of March 1945.

It must have been late April or early May 1945, since Prince Wolfgang mentioned that their massive nineteenth-century palace was already functioning as a GI rest camp. The British party had first been to Schloss Friedrichshof, five kilometers away, only to be redirected to the townhouse in the shadow of the old Kronberg castle to which the Hesse family had been unceremoniously evacuated by the Americans.

The royal librarian produced a letter signed by King George VI requesting his distant cousin's permission to remove sensitive royal papers to Britain for safekeeping. But this was technically a matter for the Landgrave of Hessen, the titular head of the family – Wolfgang's twin brother, Prince Philip. The former Nazi state president of Hessen and lieutenant general in the Storm Troops had fallen out of favor with Hitler after Mussolini's capitulation, when he was sent to Flossenbürg concentration camp. His wife, Princess Mafalda, had died in Buchenwald in an American air raid. Prince Philip survived the camps, only to face another period of captivity as one of the wanted Nazi leaders.

A hurried family conclave concluded that the princes' seventy-two-year-old mother, Princess Margaret, would give her written approval for the removal of what Prince Wolfgang claimed were over a thousand documents. They were part of the family archives stored in packing cases in the attic of the schloss. Armed with this information, Blunt and Morshead returned to their army truck and drove up the five miles of winding road that went through the Hesse estate.

The dark tower of the Friedrichshof that broods over the wooded slopes of the Taunus Mountains above Kronberg bears an uncanny resemblance to Queen Victoria's beloved Balmoral castle in Scotland. The castle that Princess Victoria built for herself reflects her mother's taste for the wooden-beamed Scottish baronial style with its entrance hall and corridors cluttered with paintings of her English royal relations. Now restored, it is run by the business-minded Hesse family as the Schloss Hotel. Guests who can afford $1,100 a night can stay in the Royal Suite used by Queen Victoria when she visited the Friedrichshof to stay with her 'Dearest child' on 26 April 1895.

In one of those strange congruences of date, it was half a century later – probably to the week – when Blunt and Morshead drove their two-ton army truck up to the stone portico emblazoned with Tudor roses. They entered bearing the warrant signed by Queen Victoria's great-grandson, George VI, and endorsed by her granddaughter, the Princess of Hesse. But their unique authority, according to Prince Wolfgang, did not impress Captain Kathleen Nash of the US Women's Army Corps. She was in command of the rest camp. She did not have the authority, she said, to relinquish control over papers that were now the property of the US Army.

With characteristic verve, Blunt resorted to subterfuge. While Morshead and the soldiers accompanying them headed up to the attic to locate the two packing cases of documents described by Prince Wolfgang, Blunt took on the intractable Captain Nash. After considerable argument he persuaded her to telephone US Army headquarters in Frankfurt. Meanwhile the crates had been brought down and loaded onto the waiting lorry. The irate WAC captain emerged from her office too late to stop Blunt and Morshead from driving off with their haul.

The successful execution of this mission for the House of Windsor created an unexpected setback for their royal cousins. Prince Wolfgang remained convinced to his dying day that the episode led directly to what *The New York Times* was to call 'the greatest gem theft in modern times'.

Until the emissaries of the King of England arrived on her preserve, the WAC captain was as oblivious as any other wartime volunteer from the rural heartland of Wisconsin might be to the significance of the Hesse-Kassel family in the intermarried tree of European royalty. But Nash's friend Colonel Jack Durant, an army flyer, was a savvy graduate of Georgetown Law School. Together they reasoned that the schloss might contain more royal documents that might fetch a high price from American newspaper editors. A tip from one of the German bartenders led them to a bricked-up subcellar. Inside they found the cache of fifteen hundred bottles of wines of ancient vintage and, buried beneath the stone floor, a lead-lined wooden box containing the Hesse family jewels. The chest also contained engraved silver items, a Bible with royal signatures, and nine volumes of original letters to the queen-empress from her daughters. The collective value of the diamonds, emeralds, rubies and pearls in the tiaras, necklaces, bracelets and rings was, in 1946, conservatively estimated at over $3 million.

'We first decided we would turn them in,' Captain Nash stated in her confession. 'Then we thought we could take only a few pieces and then we decided we would take the lot.' She and her friend Durant pried the jewels from their irreplaceable antique settings to smuggle them back to the United States with the aid of a US Army major and a corporal, who joined the conspiracy for a 25 per cent split of the loot. The Hesses did not discover that their priceless heirlooms had been stolen until April 1946 when they tried to retrieve their jewels on the eve of the marriage of Princess Sophie, the sister of Prince Philip of Greece, who the next year became the husband of the future Queen of England. As fate would have it, Durant and Nash, now in the United States and honorably discharged from the army, were planning their own nuptials.

On 28 May Kathleen Nash and Jack Durant became man and wife in Chicago. Their wedding added a romantic twist to the

'Kronberg Heist' headlines when the story broke after their arrest by military police a week later. The bulk of the Hesse treasure was recovered from a luggage locker at the railroad terminal. The glitter of huge canary-yellow diamonds and flawless green emeralds on the baize tables in the Pentagon hearing room added sparkle to the discomfiture of the US Army, which had recalled the newlyweds to active duty to face court-martial for looting. They were both found guilty under the Eightieth Article of War and were sentenced to jail.

The headlines added to the embarrassment of the House of Hesse-Kassel and its royal English Windsor cousins because the US Army arrested Prince Philip of Hesse on 29 April 1945, after liberating him from Dachau concentration camp. The SHAEF intelligence records indicate that, as target number 53 in the Nazi hierarchy, the former president of Hessen-Nassau had a high priority in the Ashcan operation that rounded up several thousand alleged German war criminals for interrogation. Although he did not face trial at Nuremberg, Philip of Hesse was only one of the ex-kaiser's relations to have fallen under Hitler's spell. He was an SA general and, until 1943, one of the most sycophantically Nazi of the German princes. His wife was the daughter of King Umberto of Italy. For this reason Hitler used him as a special mediator with Mussolini at the time of the Austrian Anschluss, and again during the Czechoslovak crisis. His success as an intermediary, and the Führer's belief in the importance of blood ties, made Prince Philip the obvious choice to mediate with the Duke of Windsor, with whom he shared the distinction of being a great-grandson of Queen Victoria.

This revelation was made by Prince Wolfgang to the *Sunday Times* in 1979. While he hesitated to confirm that Prince Philip of Hesse had been an intermediary for Hitler, he described the role as 'unofficial' mediation. This he said was 'not proper mediation in the true sense of the word' but discussions conducted with King Edward VIII through his youngest brother, George, Duke of Kent. When Edward came to the throne in 1936, Hitler concluded that the time was ripe to attempt a rapprochement with the British through their new and impressionable monarch. Like his youngest brother and closest confidant, Edward had a great affinity for Germany. Despite his popular image as a champion of the unemployed, Edward was a fierce anti-Communist. He believed that the Nazis had saved Germany from the Revolution. 'Every drop of blood in my veins is German,' he once said, reflecting his love for the homeland of his royal predecessors.

A Germanophile and an authoritarian at heart, Edward admired Hitler's leadership, which he contrasted with the inability of his own ineffectual ministers to resolve Britain's economic woes. So Hitler had no difficulty maintaining a private channel of communication to Edward, both while he was King and later, after he abdicated, as Duke of Windsor, through his royal cousins Philip of Hesse and Karl Edward, duke of Saxe-Coburg-Gotha.

Coburg, who was a schoolfellow of Edward's, was rewarded for his devotion to the Führer with an appointment as a senior officer in the Sturmabteilung. It was no accident that this ranking officer of the notorious Nazi stormtroopers was a frequent visitor to London. He was actually closeted with the new King during the first critical hours of Edward's reign in January 1936, when the German army was in the final stages of its preparations to move into the Rhineland. It must have been a great relief for Hitler to learn from his royal emissary that he could defy the Versailles treaty. There would be no risk of military intervention from the British government because of the new King's 'sincere resolve to bring England and Germany together'.

King Edward, it now appears, was intent on developing a 'nonofficial' British foreign policy toward Germany. He intended to orchestrate it personally with the Führer via his cousin, and Coburg said on his return to Berlin that Edward requested that he 'visit him frequently in order that confidential matters might be more speedily clarified in this way.' Edward appeared ready to overstep constitutional restraint if necessary. 'Who is King here, Baldwin or I?' he testily reminded Coburg. 'I wish to talk to Hitler, and will do so here or in Germany. Tell him that please.'

The immediate clash with Baldwin came not from Edward's determination to engineer a rapprochement with Nazi Germany but from his affair with the twice-divorced Wallis Warfield Simpson over which he went down to defeat in a constitutional battle with Prime Minister Baldwin that summer. This was a setback to Hitler's grand design for making Britain his ally. Hitler had regarded the King as 'a man after his own heart and one who understood the *Führerprinzip*, and was ready to introduce it into his own country.' There were still, however, plenty of arrows in Hitler's quiver. One of them was Mrs Simpson herself.

The ambitious and chic Mrs Simpson had been courted by the Anglo-German Fellowship and Hitler's ambassador to London. After the abdication, when King George VI denied her the title of Her Royal Highness, the scene was set for a long and bitter feud. Hitler promptly turned it to his advantage by inviting the Windsors to visit Germany. 'The duke accepted the invitation because he wanted to compensate the duchess by giving her the experience of a state visit,' Sir Dudley Forwood told me, recalling how the King had told him he wanted 'every possible step' taken to dissuade his brother from making the trip.

The private visit, billed as the first leg of an international tour to study labor conditions, caused consternation in Britain when Nazi propagandists made it a triumphal two-week showcase of royal approval. To the astonishment of his erstwhile subjects, their former King was photographed with Goering and Goebbels – even giving what appeared to be his version of the stiff-arm Nazi salute. The Duke of Coburg orchestrated the attentions of party bigwigs and the duchess was treated royally by the cheering crowds and addressed as Her Royal Highness at banquets.

The high point of the Windsors' visit was the Führer's invitation to his Berchtesgaden hideaway in the Bavarian Alps. Hitler insisted on using his personal translator Paul Schmidt. This irritated the duke, according to Sir Dudley, who recalled that the duke repeatedly spoke in fluent German. But both ex-King and Führer were careful to avoid promises in the informal talks in which Windsor stressed his understanding of the Germans as a result of his family and blood ties. But even this took on a sinister significance. 'The duke was never able to forget that he was abdicated royalty and of no importance compared to what he had been,' Sir Dudley said. 'I think he may have thought that his wise counsel might sway the Führer from confrontation with England.' As *The New York Times* commented, the duke's tour 'demonstrated adequately that the Abdication did rob Germany of a firm friend, if not indeed a devoted admirer, on the British throne.'

The duke was too loyally pro-British to be compromised, according to Sir Dudley, but *The New York Times* pointed out that he had been 'very critical of English politics as he sees them and is reported as declaring British ministers of today and their possible successors are no match for the German and Italian Dictators.' Sir Dudley also concedes that the duke had fallen prey to 'manipulators' like Charles Bedaux, the American-born 'time-and-motion' millionaire who had lent the Windsors his château at Candé for their wedding and had become part of their entourage. Bedaux had engineered the German visit through Nazi connections that became known in 1942 after his arrest in North Africa. He died in mysterious circumstances in a Miami detention center after his arrest as a Vichy undercover agent. The British had confiscated an attaché case of documents in which Bedaux was alleged to be carrying a US Army intelligence file whose contents might have shed light on the shadowy intrigue that so compromised the embittered ex-King.

Sir Dudley Forwood is in no doubt that the Windsors became the center of a German plot because of the attempt to suborn him. 'The outcome of this war is probably clear to you,' Bedaux conspiratorially told Forwood over dinner at Claridge's a day after hostilities erupted in September 1939. 'I can assure you that when the result does take place, I will look after you and see you get a good post.' Forwood left the duke's staff, but he agrees that Bedaux was a 'clever manipulator' and the Windsors had 'no idea what a four-letter man he was.' They were easy prey for a conspiracy. The private diary kept by Windsor's faithful equerry,

Major Edward Metcalfe, reveals the degree to which Bedaux was an intimate member of the Windsor entourage during the Phoney War. 'Fruity,' as the faithful but pedestrian retainer was known, did not put as much trust in Bedaux as his royal master did. 'He knows too much,' Metcalfe wrote suspiciously. 'He hinted at Berlin being one of those places,' Metcalfe observed just a month after war broke out – adding, as if to reassure himself, 'He beats me, but he is my pal!!!'

What is now clear is that Bedaux was close to Ribbentrop and his emissary, Otto Abetz, whom the French police expelled from Paris in 1939. (Abetz returned to settle old scores as Germany's much-despised ambassador.) Captured documents reveal that Bedaux's mysterious peregrinations were an integral part of the web of shadowy 'peace maneuvering' that preoccupied the Berlin Foreign Ministry – and the secret services – of Britain, France, Italy and Germany during the Phoney War. The evidence that Bedaux was a channel of communication between Windsor and Hitler appears in the January 1940 communication to Germany's undersecretary for foreign affairs, Baron Ernst von Weizsäcker, from the German ambassador in The Hague.

'Through personal relationships I might have the opportunity to establish certain lines leading to the Duke of Windsor,' Count Julius von Zech-Burkesroda reported, explaining that the duke was not 'entirely satisfied' with the role he had been given as a member of the British Military Mission. 'Also there seems to be something of a *Fronde* forming around W[indsor) which for the moment of course still has nothing to say, but which at some time under favorable circumstances might acquire a certain significance.' Windsor's significance, it seems, was already appreciated by Hitler.

Because he was a trusted major-general on the staff of the British Military Mission, with access to the most senior officers in General Maurice Gamelin's headquarters, Windsor had comprehensive and detailed intelligence on the Allied order of battle, plus the French defensive dispositions. He also demonstrated a sound grasp of the alarming military deficiencies of the western front as shown by two still-classified, highly critical reports that he prepared for the British staff. To prepare these assessments, the duke had to have knowledge of Plan D. This plan required the British Expeditionary Force (BEF) to advance northward in the event of a German invasion of Belgium – a move that both Windsor and the German High Command foresaw would expose a catastrophic weakness in the Ardennes sector north of the Maginot Line.

The Ardennes was precisely the sector where General Guderian's XIX Panzer Group burst through on 10 May, when Hitler unleashed his offensive in the West. This fact raises the possibility of a connection between the Duke of Windsor's activities at Allied GHQ and the German decision of February 1940 to scrap their original attack plan in favor of a bold drive through the Ardennes to the Belgian coast so as to cut off the British forces. The connection becomes clearer now that we know that when the duke was not at the front rallying the troops, and bracing himself with frequent halts for 'kettly' (his infantile jargon-word for fresh-brewed tea), he was back in Paris dining in the best restaurants with an entourage that often included Charles Bedaux.

Published accounts and diaries of the Windsor circle report that the duke was an opinionated, compulsive and indiscreet talker at the dinner tables of the Ritz. His hefty tabs were usually left to Bedaux to settle. If, as now seems indisputable, Bedaux was in the pay of the Germans, their investment paid off. The connection is reinforced because, throughout the Phoney War, Bedaux made frequent trips to his office in Holland – and it was the German ambassador in The Hague who identified the duke in his reports to Berlin as being the source of important military intelligence.

On 19 February, Zech-Burkesroda cited the 'D. of Windsor' as the origin of detailed information on how the British and French planned to deal with a German invasion of Belgium from the 'exhaustive discussion at its last meeting' of the Allied War Council. By comparing Allied and German records, it is now possible to develop a convincing case that an intelligence leak leading back to the Duke of Windsor may well have played a significant part in prompting Hitler to order his generals to change their battle plan. The revised strategy was one the German High Command considered risky. But the Führer was vindicated when it succeeded five months later, cutting off the BEF at Dunkirk and starting the snowballing rout of General Gamelin's traumatized French army.

Whether Windsor contributed wittingly or unwittingly to the disasters that led to the fall of France, the evidence of captured German Foreign Office documents suggests that he played another, more knowing role in the subsequent plot to use him as a pawn in Hitler's bid to bluff Britain into suing for peace. Even the British Foreign Office acknowledged 'the backwash of Nazi intrigue which seeks now that the greater part of the continent is in enemy hands, to make trouble about W[indsor).' But not until after the war, when the German records fell into Allied hands, was it appreciated just how deeply Windsor and his wife were involved in the intrigue. The remarkable collection of telegrams in the German Foreign Office Windsor file shows that the plot began in earnest on 23 June, two days after the Windsors arrived in Madrid after fleeing France. For the next seven weeks, German emissaries assiduously courted the duke, first in Madrid and then in Lisbon. The operation was masterminded by one of Reinhard Heydrich's ranking SD agents, Walter Schellenberg, who told Windsor to 'hold himself in readiness' for a starring role in Hitler's master plan. 'Germany,' the Windsors were told, 'is determined to compel England to make peace by the use of all methods and would be prepared in such an event to pave the way to the granting of any wish expressed by the Duke and Duchess, in particular with respect to ascension of the English Throne by the Duke and Duchess.'

The cables reveal that the Germans had high hopes when the Windsors went to Portugal, after British pressure to do so, that the presence in Lisbon of the Duke of Kent for the jubilee celebration would prove a decisive factor. 'The Duke is toying with the idea of dissociating himself from present tendency of British public policy by a public declaration and breaking from his brother [King George VI],' Eberhard von Stohrer, German ambassador to Spain, advised Berlin on 23 July. The Germans continued their unrelenting and subtle pressure on the Windsors. Emissaries who ranged from businessmen to housemaids arrived with warnings of intrigues against them by Britain's secret service agents, and hints of changes in the British constitution about which 'the Duchess in particular became very thoughtful'. They also tried persuading the duke and duchess to return to Madrid under German protection, and Schellenberg made elaborate plans to stage a 'kidnap' of the duke and duchess during a hunting expedition.

'The Duke hesitated right up until the last moment,' Stohrer reported to Berlin. An ocean liner was held for him in Lisbon until 1 August.

Only after Churchill's emissaries, led by the Windsors' former solicitor, Sir Walter Monckton, persuaded the duke to accept a less-than-glamorous wartime role as governor-general of the Bahamas was the episode closed. According to the German reports, 'his legal adviser was once again able to exert his influence.' He convinced the Duke that the 'possibility of peace did not exist at the moment.' If Windsor acted contrary to the British government's directions, as the duke explained it to the emissary of Berlin, he would 'let loose upon himself the propaganda of his British enemies which would rob him of all prestige for the moment of possible intervention.'

Shortly before embarking on the American steamship *Excalibur* for Bermuda en route to the Bahamas on 1 August, the duke and duchess attended a farewell reception. It was given by their Portuguese host Dr Ricardo Espiritu Santo e Silva, a banker who was reported to be friendly with the Germans and whom the duke assured of his 'deepest sincerity and expressed admiration and sympathy for the Führer'. Moreover, Windsor said, 'he could, if necessary, intervene from the Bahamas,' and 'promised to remain in constant contact' with 'a code phrase on receipt of which he would immediately return'.

Germany's ambassador to Spain had played a key role in the

month-long drama. He confirmed that Schellenberg had 'reached certain agreements which are to facilitate a resumption of relations with the Duke.' This the duke put into effect as soon as he reached Bermuda on 15 August, when he telegraphed Silva 'asking him to let him know as soon as action is necessary on his part.'

When these telegrams came to light five years later, they caused consternation at Buckingham Palace. 'King fussed about Duke of Windsor file & captured German documents,' Cadogan recorded in his diary on 25 October 1945. But that was not the reaction of the British army officer who had tumbled on this most confidential material in the German Foreign Office records five months earlier.

'Drinks all round!' is the penciled congratulation that appears at the end of Lieutenant Colonel Robert Currie Thompson's report on how he tracked down thirty boxes of microfilms buried in the grounds of a Schloss in the Thuringian Mountains. They included 'the most top secret German Foreign Ministry papers containing a complete account of Germany's foreign policy and doings from 1933 to 1944, and including correspondence and records of conversations between Hitler and Ribbentrop on the one side and Mussolini, Franco, Laval, Molotov and Japanese and other personalities on the other, also reports by ambassadors and ministers on the most secret matters.

Among the thousands of page-images in those thirty rolls of microfilm was an extensive collection of papers covering 'German-British Relations', including a thick dossier on the Duke and Duchess of Windsor.

The potential dynamite in these documents quickly reached the ears of General Eisenhower. He later described how he 'had them thoroughly examined by Ambassador Winant and by my own Intelligence Staff.' Under the terms of the inter-Allied agreement *all* captured German records were technically held as joint property of the British, Americans, French and Russians. Eisenhower, however, decided he had to make an exception in the case of the Windsor file. Later, he sought to justify his decision to hand the papers over to the British, saying his advisers had conveniently concluded that 'there was no possible value in them, that they were obviously concocted with some idea of promoting German propaganda and weakening the Western resistance, and that they were totally unfair to the Duke.'

When Prime Minister Clement Attlee received the file he concurred. The documents had 'little or no credence'. Their publication 'might do the greatest possible harm,' he advised former Prime Minister Churchill, who was given the sensitive file for his comments.

'I earnestly trust it may be possible to destroy all traces of these German intrigues,' Churchill urged. He had been one of Edward's most outspoken parliamentary supporters in the abdication crisis nine years earlier and, despite the events of 1940, still had great affection for the king he had lost.

Despite this high-level conspiracy to 'edit' the documents, Ribbentrop's microfilms had a charmed existence. They survived intact this second order for their destruction and became available to the Allied historians responsible for compiling the German Foreign Office documents. An objective assessment of the Windsor papers' true significance came when the historians decided to include that part of the file dealing with the exchanges of the German ambassadors in Spain and Portugal. Publication was scheduled for 1954.

The German papers on Windsor therefore resurfaced to haunt Churchill at a most inconvenient moment: he was back in harness at Downing Street at the head of a new Conservative government. A month before the June 1953 coronation of Queen Elizabeth II, there was every reason for concern. He intervened directly and sent a 'Secret and Personal' letter to President Eisenhower, urging 'My dear Friend' to 'exert your power to prevent their publication'. The episode was of 'negligible historical importance' in Churchill's view. Inclusion of the telegrams in an official publication would 'leave the impression that the Duke was in close touch with German agents and was listening to suggestions that were disloyal.' Eisenhower replied, promising he would investigate but 'I do not know exactly what it is possible for me to do.' Churchill was recovering from a slight stroke and 'Ike' sent his 'earnest prayers' for his old friend's 'early return to full and vigorous health'.

When neither the American president nor the French government appeared willing to bury the past, Churchill appealed to the Cabinet. He disclosed that the late King George VI had seen the file and insisted that if 'publication could not be avoided,' his brother the duke be given 'timely warning'. But Churchill's Top Secret memorandum of August 1953 that circulated to the Cabinet reveals that the Nobel Prize-winning chronicler of the war was thwarted by the historians.

The British editor in chief, the Honorable Margaret Lambert, threatened to resign if there was any government interference with the Anglo-American agreement of June 1946 guaranteeing its historians the right to 'select and edit' the documents they desired and to publish them 'on the basis of the highest scholarly objectivity'. Churchill was partially successful in his fallback position: to delay publication for possibly 'ten to twenty years on the grounds that these papers, tendentious and unreliable as they should undoubtedly be regarded, would give pain to the Duke of Windsor and leave an impression on the minds of those who read them entirely disproportionate to their historical value.' The volume of German documents containing the Windsor telegrams did not appear until 1957. Then it included the caveat about its being a 'necessarily much tainted source' and the assertion that the Duke of Windsor 'never wavered in his loyalty to the British cause.'

One of the Allied historians who had no doubt about the historical veracity or value of the German Foreign Office material was Donald Cameron Watt, now Stevenson Professor of International History at the University of London. He confirmed that by 1948 more than four hundred tons of documents had arrived from the Allied Documents Center in Berlin for analysis under the more secure conditions of the Rothschild mansion at Waddesdon Manor in Buckinghamshire. Watt believes he was the first historian to see the Windsor section of the German Foreign Ministry files, including all the exchanges that took place in Spain and Portugal in 1940.

'Everything was there which we thought should have been there, with one exception,' Watt observed. The exception, he said, was the record of the Windsors' meeting with Hitler at Berchtesgaden. This struck him, and the other historians, as being particularly odd because the two groups of Duke of Windsor material and the file on Edward as king had been kept in the same file record. Yet even without the Berchtesgaden record, the documentary evidence makes it difficult to avoid the conclusion that the duke was not as unwilling a participant in the German intrigue as Churchill and his other defenders have tried to make out.

An objective reading leaves an uncomfortably wide margin for suspicion that the duke really was wavering in his loyalty. The Windsors were embittered royal exiles. They were isolated by what they believed to be continuing rebuffs from Buckingham Palace and Downing Street. But they were too easily persuaded to enter into negotiations – if nothing more – with the emissaries of Hitler. Their justification may have been a misguided belief that by helping to make peace, Windsor was freeing Germany to deal with the Soviet Union. The duke undoubtedly believed he was helping save the empire – and the world – from being overrun by the Communist menace. Nor was he alone among his countrymen in believing that despite its totalitarian unpleasantness, Nazi Germany was Britain's natural ally.

Under Britain's ancient law, treating with the king's enemy in the hour of Britain's mortal peril must surely have been high treason. But for his unique royal status and Churchill's indulgence, it seems that the duke came perilously close to committing this most serious crime. Further evidence to reinforce this charge comes from American intelligence agents who monitored the Windsors' activities in the Bahamas during the war. These reports confirm that the duke made good on his promise to Hitler to 'remain in constant contact' while the Windsors struggled to come to terms with the 'rust and discomfort' of the governor's mansion overlooking the tranquil emerald waters of Nassau Bay.

Suspicion continued to hover over the Windsors in their palm-fringed backwater. This explains the surprising number of FBI and US Navy intelligence 'enemy agent' category reports filed under 'Windsor, Duke and Duchess of' that document their suspicious activities and those of their Bahamas coterie. The prime suspect was Axel Wenner-Gren, the Swedish millionaire blacklisted by the British and American governments for trading with the Axis. He arrived in Nassau harbor in his magnificently appointed yacht *The Southern Cross* shortly after the Windsors.

Most British historians with whom I have discussed this documentary evidence still loyally take the view that the duke and duchess were more sinned against than sinning. But John Loftus, a trial attorney who worked in the US Department of Justice, has assured me that the Windsor FBI documents so far declassified represent only part of an even more substantial file on the Windsors. As the special investigator who coordinated the search for Nazi war criminals living in the United States, he was armed with a security clearance that enabled him to see classified material still held by the FBI and CIA. Loftus spent more than two years combing thousands of still-secret files and interviewing agents involved in wartime counterintelligence against the Nazis.

'Purely by accident I came across an "Eyes Only Attorney General" file on the Windsors,' said Loftus, who is an Irish Catholic graduate of Boston Latin School. He served as an army officer before simultaneously obtaining a master's degree in public administration and a law doctorate, then joining the Office of Special Investigations in 1979. His systematic search of all the Top Secret files pertaining to American knowledge of Nazis had taken him up to the sixth floor of the Justice Department building on Pennsylvania Avenue in Washington DC, where there is a locked vault containing the most confidential records.

Loftus explained that because he had the proper security clearance, it was only necessary for him to add his signature to the others on the cardboard cover sheets to obtain the *still* unclass-ified complete FBI dossier on the Windsors.

'It contained a bureau precis of the British and American intelligence reports on the duke and duchess,' said Loftus. He was surprised to read J. Edgar Hoover's report that surveillance confirmed the Windsors were indeed considered a major threat to Allied security. Hoover recommended their internment for the duration of the war. Although the US Government did not take this drastic step – presumably in deference to Churchill and to avoid embarrassment to the British royal family – the files reveal that Hoover brushed aside demands from the duchess herself to stop censoring her mail and telephone communications.

Loftus also recalls seeing in this highly secret Windsor file a report that while Edward was still on the throne, he had been in the process of setting out the basis of a deal with Hitler. The origin of the intelligence was obscure, but considered reliable by the US State Department. As part of the 'nonofficial' foreign policy that the King was promising, he would see to it that the British government turned a blind eye on German intentions to annex Austria and Czechoslovakia and move into the Balkans against French interest, in return for Hitler's protection of British interests in Poland. Without the documentation itself and without checking the reliability of the source, there is, of course, no way of judging the degree to which Edward's 1936 signal to Berlin of his 'sincere resolve to bring England and Germany together' might have encouraged Hitler on the road to Munich.

The final verdict of history is not yet in on the role played by Windsor. Churchill's unprecedented action in 1945, and then again in 1953, to suppress part of the German Windsor File, and Buckingham Palace's injunction to Peter Wright in 1967 against questioning Blunt about his mission to Germany, all suggest an extraordinary and continuing effort to keep a skeleton of substan-tial dimensions nailed up in the Round Tower of Windsor Castle, where the Royal Archives are kept.

Whatever bones of the Windsor/Hitler intrigue are still secreted in the Royal Archives, there can be no doubt that King

George VI personally charged Anthony Blunt in 1945 with the delicate task of gathering up those remaining in the various castles of his royal German cousins. That it was an extensive operation lasting several years is now evident from revealing correspondence from the royal librarian. A memorandum of 1947 from Owen Morshead, which turned up in an obscure Foreign Office file on captured German records, finally provides the documented confirmation of their secret mission to collect the Hesse documents from Schloss Friedrichshof.

The file describes how Blunt and Morshead were still on their royal magpie mission in August 1947. This time they flew to The Hague. Their hunt was prompted by a still-classified memorandum from John Wheeler-Bennett, later official biographer of George VI but then editor in chief of the captured archives of the German Foreign Office. It seems he came across a reference in these files to the role played in the Windsor saga by Kaiser Wilhelm II, whose son Friedrich Wilhelm and his wife, Cecilie, were both used by Hitler as royal intermediaries. The old Kaiser had died in 1941, but Haus Doorn in the Netherlands, where he spent his exile, still contained his private papers and possessions.

Morshead's report on their return to the King's private secretary, Sir Alan Lascelles, specifically notes that 'no documentary material was found'. But they did locate the Kaiser's Garter insignia, and Blunt did spot a Cosway painting of the Duke of Clarence, whose 'proper home is in the Royal library at Windsor'. Blunt suggested the King make a personal request for Queen Wilhelmina 'to quitely' [sic] permit the transfer of certain items to England. A month later, Morshead noted the King's delight that the British ambassador in The Hague had quietly retrieved the Garter and picture. The memorandum concludes with a revealing paragraph that not only alludes to the Kronberg mission, but suggests that even the King had doubts about the legality of possessing the Hesse papers that were now securely locked away in the Round tower of Windsor Castle. Morshead wrote:

'The King expressly told me that we only hold them on the same footing as we hold the things which I brought back from

Frankfurt, i.e. if the German Family in the future want them back . . . well, we have no title to them; we hold them in security for them, over here in England till things are settled.'

Morshead does not specify what it was that he brought back from Frankfurt. But the reference to the mission to Schloss Friedrichshof in the spring of 1945 is clear. Since it is a matter of public record that Captain Nash and her boyfriend discovered the hidden gems and the bound volumes of Queen Victoria's letters, the Doorn memorandum reinforces the conclusion that the papers Morshead and Blunt collected had even greater importance and more contemporary significance. Prince Wolfgang confirmed that before she died in 1954, Princess Margaret of Hesse requested, and received from Windsor, her mother's correspondence and 'other papers'. Prince Wolfgang and the surviving members of the family have kept discreetly silent about whether Philip of Hesse's papers were among those returned – and if so, whether they contained the records of his role as an intermediary for Hitler with the Duke of Windsor and his brother the Duke of Kent.

Indirect corroboration that the Hesse archives *did* contain documents relating to the Duke of Windsor's communications with Hitler also comes from the former Justice Department investigator John Loftus. He told me that it was after he had read the Top Secret FBI Windsor file 'late in '79 or early '80' that he interviewed two former US military intelligence officers from the SHAEF T-groups attached to Patton's forces. His interest now fired up by the potentially high-level British–Nazi connection, Loftus inquired whether they had come across any documentary evidence. One of the officers confirmed that he had indeed seen references to communications between the Duke of Windsor and Hitler. He had discovered them in what he described as a 'villa that was owned by a close relative of the duke which was occupied as an American officers' club.'

My own research confirms that the relative mentioned by Loftus's source must have been Hesse. The prohibitive expense of occupying the Schloss Friedrichshof full time had obliged

Princess Margaret and her sons to live since 1925 in the expansive villas they had built in the wooded glades north of the main courtyard of the castle. This officer also told Loftus that shortly after he had reported his discovery, the British arrived to collect the highly embarrassing papers. The record shows that the Allied T-group officers in Operation Goldcup reported directly to SHAEF main headquarters.

The organizational charts show that Lieutenant Colonel Dick White was deputy head of counterintelligence in the G-2 organization, which was heavily staffed with MI5 officers. Another future MI5 director, Major Martin Furnival Jones, was in charge of Evaluation and Dissemination under White. Thus, it is obvious that any discovery of the Hesse-Windsor documents would have resulted in the relaying of the news by the most secure channels to King George VI and the Prime Minister. They would have recognized the need to act swiftly and secretly to prevent these documents – and any others like them – from falling into American hands. Deciding their fate presented less of a problem than effecting their retrieval from under the noses of inquisitive US Army intelligence officers. Since they were private papers and not government documents, according to Professor Cameron Watt, they were justifiably removed to the security of the Royal Archives, because they were not covered by the inter-Allied agreement.

The involvement of the royal archivist was a prerequisite. But Owen Morshead, although he had served with distinction in World War I, was well into his fifties and needed the assistance of an experienced intelligence officer. With his proven finesse for removing documents from diplomatic pouches, plus the confidence of his MI5 colleagues at SHAEF HQ and lack of official attachment, Blunt was the obvious man for the job. He was already an internationally recognized art authority and the OSS Art Looting Investigation Unit established in late 1944 by Norman Holmes Pearson's X-2 OSS counterintelligence group provided him with a ready-made cover for the secret royal mission.

Dick White's reference to Blunt's post-D-Day involvement

with looted art appears to corroborate that looted art was the convenient cover for the secret operation to scoop the royal documents. Nor, it seems, was Kronberg the only target of Blunt's mission. Prince Wolfgang was adamant that the six-course dinner Blunt recalled for Trevor-Roper could not have taken place at the Friedrichshof, which was already a US officers' club. But even allowing for exaggeration, it is conceivable that such an elaborate affair was laid on for the royal emissaries of King George by the Hesse-Kassel cousins at one of their residences at Darmstadt or Wolfsgarten. Ellis Waterhouse recalls Blunt joking about returning to Windsor Castle and having to keep Queen Charlotte's crown in a chamber pot overnight. If Waterhouse remembered the item correctly, then Blunt must have retrieved this diadem at some royal residence other than Kronberg. For when Blunt went to Kronberg, the Hesse jewelry was still safely stowed in a lead box buried in the wine cellar of the Friedrichshof.

Still unanswered is the enigma of what Blunt was doing between August 1944 and April 1945, the earliest date at which he could have been in Kronberg. How many months did he spend on other missions before he went to Germany to retrieve royal letters and jewelry? He was always adamant that he was not made surveyor of the king's pictures as a quid pro quo for his secret mission. Even if we take Blunt at his word, it is significant that the *Times* announcement that appeared on 27 April 1945 *backdates* his appointment to the first of the month. In a curious blunder that must have given both Blunt and Soviet intelligence some cause for wry amusement, one London paper reported that Blunt "works on the British newspaper published in Russia".

While the Soviets preferred that Blunt continue to serve their interests by remaining in the British intelligence services, his appointment to the Court was the first indication that he was determined to resume his artistic career. One of the most astonishing features of Blunt's schizophrenic life is that he had allowed neither his wartime duties, nor his spying for the Russians, to interfere with his relentless pursuit of his artistic aims. As the deputy director of the Courtauld, he continued lecturing and writing throughout the war whenever his MI5 duties permitted – even though the strain of two jobs plus his undercover work had taken its toll.

Blunt's iron constitution flagged in 1942. Mental exhaustion and physical illness forced him to retreat on medical leave to the Northern Ireland home of his Cambridge friend Peter Montgomery. But after a few weeks of rest, Blunt returned to London to resume his punishing schedule. And he still found time to produce learned commentaries for *The Journal of the Warburg* and *The Burlington Magazine* at an average rate of four a year, ranging from a discourse on Blake's pictorial imagination to the landscapes of Nicolas Poussin.

Since 1943 Blunt had been devoting much of his off-duty time to Windsor Castle. In the reverent silence that reigns behind the mullioned windows of the Royal Library, he spent hour upon hour peering through his magnifying glass cataloguing old-master drawings. Even before his scholarly book on five hundred French drawings was published two years later, to universal academic acclaim, his painstaking study had brought him to the attention of the royal household as an obvious candidate for surveyor of the king's pictures.

The post, created by Charles I, the greatest of Britain's royal art patrons, involved maintaining and cataloguing the huge collection of more than five thousand pictures and hundreds of pieces of furniture and porcelain that the Crown had acquired for its palaces from Tudor times. Since 1934, the appointment had been reluctantly held by the director of the National Gallery, Sir Kenneth Clark. The Oxford-educated millionaire's son, whose reputation as an art historian was built on his stylish writing, had been dragooned into the job by King George V, who was known to be more interested in his stamp collection than in paintings.

Clark claimed he was 'too obstinately committed to aesthetic values to give up my time to second-rate limners of royalty.' Yet following the accession of George VI in 1937, he struck up a rapport with Queen Elizabeth, later the Queen Mother, who became an attentive pupil, admirer and lifelong friend. With

Benedict Nicolson, the son of Harold Nicolson, as his deputy, Clark had supervised the packing and removal of the royal treasures for safe storage at the outbreak of the war.

Clark, an urbane connoisseur, got on surprisingly well with Blunt, whose bent was to dissect art mathematically. They had both served on the same exhibitions committee of the Royal Academy before the war, and it seems both believed in an aesthetic responsibility towards the common man that meant the inevitability of socialism. The return of the collection from the safety of the mountain caves in Wales raised the need for a cataloguing and restoration program that Clark had neither the time nor the inclination to oversee.

The task was tailor made for Blunt. He saw, and grasped, the chance to profit from his reputation as Britain's most promising young academic art historian; by producing the first comprehensive catalog of the royal drawings at Windsor, he marked himself for preferment.

Apart from Blunt's professional qualifications, there were the ties of blood, family and school on which he could advance himself with influential members of the royal household. Most important was Blunt's distant kinship with Queen Elizabeth (he was her third cousin). He patiently deferred to her untutored interests in painting and Her Majesty delighted in deflating Blunt by having him perform the role of a giraffe in after-dinner charades.

One of Blunt's strong supporters was the royal librarian, Sir Owen Morshead. He was also an old Marlburian and pre-World War I Cambridge graduate, as well as a confidant of Queen Mary. As the matriarch of the House of Windsor, she not only knew the Blunt family but avidly read books about art, and regarded herself as something of an expert on the vast artistic collection.

'Queen Mary was an enthusiastic collector, though her taste was for objets d'art rather than paintings,' Blunt would later acknowledge. Until Queen Mary's death in 1952, Blunt took great care to defer to and remain on good terms with her. She returned the compliment by slipping into the Courtauld from time to time to hear him lecture on her favorite painters.

Blunt's royal patron subscribed to *The Burlington Magazine* and counted herself among his most devoted students. When he wrote of a Venetian painting 'lost' to the royal collection, she triumphantly remembered it had been hanging all the time in a dingy corridor of Holyrood Palace. The affectionate regard in which Queen Mary held Blunt made an indelible impression on Jackie Hewit. He said that each Christmas a small personal gift would arrive for Blunt from Marlborough House. When she sent a 'reticule' that she hoped 'Dear Anthony' would find 'useful', it became an enormous joke among his homosexual friends – the Queen Mother had given the regal Blunt what appeared to be a handbag.

Although Queen Mary's 'reticule' was an unintentional blunder, it was certainly known at the Palace that Blunt was a homosexual. His fellow art historian, Ellis Waterhouse, insisted that 'everyone knew about Anthony's personal habits' by 1947, when Oliver Millar, Blunt's eventual successor as surveyor, was appointed to be his assistant. According to a former British SOE officer who frequented Windsor Castle, even the guardroom used to crack jokes about the need for 'backs to the wall' if Blunt was about.

Homosexuality was not a drawback when Blunt started to work his way into royal favor. Membership in the royal household has traditionally provided homosexuals with the same comfortable security as the cloistered enclaves of an Oxbridge college. This applies not just to the courtiers upstairs, but also to many members of the male staffs in the royal palaces.

It was the present queen's cousin, the late Lord Mountbatten, who tartly dismissed criticism that his naval servant was homosexual: 'Of course – all the best valets are.' As one distinguished royal biographer pointed out: 'Many of the footmen and butlers are homosexual because they have to put in long hours for relatively low reward.' This source also assured me that older members of the royal family even preferred the attentiveness shown them by homosexual courtiers like Blunt. Their lack of family commitments, willingness to partake in the whimsical royal after-dinner parlor games, and their biting gossip about the upper crust of British society made them sought-after companions.

The rule is to 'know but not openly acknowledge' the important role that homosexuals have always played as royal retainers. Yet while the amorous adventures and marital infidelities of the junior members of the House of Windsor make newspaper headlines, there is still a strict taboo on gossiping about the homosexual networking that operated in the prewar royal London circle. Those in the know claim that it revolved around Edward, the Prince of Wales, his younger brother, George, the Duke of Kent, the Queen's brother, David Bowes Lyon, and their cousin Lord Louis Mountbatten. The principal players are dead and cannot deny stories that they were observed making discreet visits to the London pubs where guardsmen were for rent. But some of those who knew them are still alive. Before and during the war, they have assured me, a pub called the Pakenham was the favorite haunt of Blunt and the royal set in pursuit of illicit male sex.

'I want to be like the boys at the Pakenham and go about whackin' 'em and stickin' my jack in 'em.' According to Robert Harbinson these were the first lines of a bawdy ballad that celebrated the notorious pub in Knightsbridge that was conveniently close to Whitehall, Buckingham Palace and the barracks occupied by the Household Cavalry and the Guards. This unashamedly bisexual author, who writes under the name Robin Bryans, recalled his own visits to the Pakenham as one of Blunt's intimate circle, which he joined after Guy Burgess picked him up at Oxford early in 1944.

'You see, Anthony was very, very proud of his royal connections,' Harbinson contends. He talked frankly about his personal experiences, producing letters and family trees that mapped out the web of interlocking friendships that connected Noël Coward, and London's theatrical homosexuals, to the Foreign Office network that included Burgess's friend Harold Nicolson, to the country-house homosexual circuit into which

Blunt was introduced by Peter Montgomery. In turn, this enabled Blunt to plug in to the special friendships associated with the royal set.

Harbinson was insistent that it was important to take into account Blunt's prewar association with the Duke of Kent, the black sheep of the royal family, who was killed in an RAF crash in 1942. Even Palace biographers have acknowledged that the tall, fair-haired duke had what, today, would be called a drug problem – not to mention a series of amorous entanglements until he was persuaded to settle down and marry Princess Marina of Greece in 1934. The Duke of Kent's handsomeness attracted partners of both sexes. He had a long-standing affair with Noël Coward, according to Harbinson, who says he possesses letters that reveal how Lady Bridget Parsons broke off her liaison with Prince George after discovering he was sleeping with a male relative.

Much of what Harbinson told me appears to be gossip that can never be properly substantiated. But it does contain some hard facts. It is recorded that Blunt met the Duke of Kent, who was five years his senior, through his Trinity College contemporary Prince Chula Chakrabongse. Blunt was anxious to make his reputation as an art historian, and Prince George had inherited his mother's interests and established himself as a discriminating connoisseur who spent lavishly on paintings. Whether Blunt was ever amorously involved with Queen Mary's wayward youngest son, as several of Blunt's intimates believe, there is now no way of proving.

Bizarre though some of Harbinson's theories may be, those that could be checked mesh with the established record. When I made inquiries, I discovered that many of Harbinson's more exotic assertions about the degrees of homosexuality in the Palace network were discreetly confirmed by reputable authorities who knew of the matters through their official positions or personal contacts. They, too, are of the opinion that Blunt would not have hesitated to exploit his personal connections, or knowledge, in preparing his way to become a trusted member of the royal household.

Blunt's appointment as surveyor of the King's pictures was also, on the face of it, a curious career move for an intensely ambitious art historian. While it brought prestige and responsibility, it was a job that Kenneth Clark said involved too many pointless duties and was excessively demanding in terms of time. Ellis Waterhouse recalled how he 'thought it was an insane thing for Anthony to do.' His attitude prompted Blunt to admit to him after his exposure thirty-three years later: 'You know, Ellis, the only time I thought you might ever suspect me was when I became surveyor.'

Now it is clear that Blunt's acceptance of the post was not, as Waterhouse thought, simply because he thought the prestige would enhance the Courtauld. Blunt's main objective seems to have been that he needed to persuade his Soviet masters that he could withdraw from MI5 and continue serving them by resuming his career as an art historian. To have been able to do this was a unique achievement because those who joined Stalin's underground service were expected to make a commitment to serving Moscow for life. But Blunt shrewdly realized that, as a member of the Court, he could position himself as able to serve as an informant for Moscow from an even loftier position in the British establishment.

The British sovereign, by virtue of constitutional authority, has the right to – and does – read *all* the most important state papers and consults with Cabinet ministers on a weekly basis. History shows that dictators like Hitler, on the basis of their own Byzantine court intrigues, misinterpreted the real influence and power of the British monarchy and aristocracy. This misunderstanding applied with even greater force to Stalin and his intelligence chief, Beria. Neither had any conception of the mechanisms of constitutional democracy, and their Soviet regime was run with a despotic absolutism that few of the tsars could equal.

'From 1945 I ceased to pass information to the Russians,' Blunt declared publicly in 1979. The reason he gave was his loss of conviction that the Soviet regime 'was following the true principles of Marxism'. However, a curious slip suggests he did not finally decide that the Kremlin was no longer the repository of the true faith until *six years* after his supposed break with Moscow. For he added: 'By 1951, anyhow, I realized that this was totally false.' Blunt also tried to give the impression that handing in his notice to the Soviets was no more complicated than resigning from an ordinary job. 'It just happened,' Blunt told the reporters. 'They realized I was no longer interested.'

Blunt's assertions are dismissed as disingenuous by the American intelligence community. They know from their experience in debriefing other KGB defectors that such a mutually agreed unilateral withdrawal is so unusual as to make Blunt the unique exception to the rule in the history of Soviet intelligence operations.

Blunt's departure from the security service at the end of the war cannot be viewed as an act of spontaneity on his part. Breaking with Moscow is never easy, and is usually effected only if the agent defects or confesses: there is no evidence that Blunt did either. In his case, the Soviets had too many coercive levers that could have been used to force him to continue. Blunt was allowed to leave MI5 to take up the Palace appointment only *after* it had been examined with great care both by his Soviet controller and his senior officers in Moscow Center.

The Soviets did permit Blunt to leave MI5. This leads to the presumption that they already had another agent in place in the British security service. While American and British intelligence officers differ on some aspects of the Blunt case, the consensus of those I have consulted is that Moscow Center would have sanctioned Blunt's 1945 move from MI5 only if two conditions were satisfied:

(1) Moscow already had in MI5 another agent – or agents – of equivalent seniority and access.

(2) Blunt convinced Moscow that he would continue providing high-level intelligence about the British government.

Leaving for later analysis the contentious issue of who took over from Blunt as the principal mole in MI5, Blunt would have had no difficulty satisfying his Soviet controller as to the second condition.

'Blunt had good connections at Court and no doubt he exaggerated what he could make of these,' Robert Cecil emphasized. 'Without concluding that he had any link with the homosexual royal circle, it seems clear that his ability to chat up people and relay their gossip would have enormously impressed his controller and his bosses in the Kremlin.'

Even before Blunt accepted the post of surveyor, his access to the Palace and SHAEF headquarters would have made him aware of the cover-up of the Windsor affair. This information would have been an additional bonus for the Soviets, to whom he certainly disclosed the contents of the Hesse files, plus the contents of any other incriminating documents that he scooped up on his secret missions to Germany. While it may be true that the royal appointment was offered to Blunt *before* he set off with Morshead for Kronberg, the end of April announcement, which backdated his appointment to the first, may reflect the refusal of his Soviet masters to agree until *after* he returned with the incriminating Hesse documents.

Once Blunt gained knowledge of the explosive royal secret, it became his gold-plated insurance policy. Even if his espionage was uncovered, Blunt would argue, his crime paled before the enormity of Windsor's wartime activities. And given the lengths to which the British government was willing to go to cover up these activities, Blunt would have been able to make a convincing case that he had a cast-iron guarantee against ever being publicly exposed. The Kremlin must also have appreciated that, in the Palace, Blunt could also provide a safety net for the other Cambridge agents. No one Blunt had recruited could ever be brought to public trial in Britain without implicating Blunt. Again, to expose Blunt would threaten the Windsor secret. Eighteen years later, when the royal insurance policy had to be cashed in because Michael Straight burned Blunt with the authorities, the policy proved to be pure gold. It protected Blunt and his subsidiary agents from public disgrace for another sixteen years.

So Blunt's insistence that he did 'absolutely nothing' for the Soviets after 1945 can now be rejected as 'totally untrue'. By his very presence in Buckingham Palace, Blunt assisted Moscow's schemes. So were his assertions about working for MI5 merely 'tying up loose ends'.

In 1945 Blunt was highly respected. And it was not only the Soviet intelligence service that was anxious for him to find a way of staying on. His position of trust at the Palace enhanced rather than hindered his continuing close association with his former friends in MI5. Blunt admitted that he met 'one or two of them socially, over a drink' including Dick White and Guy Liddell. 'By that time I was also going to the Travellers' Club, and he [Liddell] was a member so I used to go and meet him there,' Blunt said.

Blunt's claim to have broken formally with both MI5 and Soviet intelligence is also disputed by Leo Long. In 1946 Blunt unexpectedly dropped in on Long at 21st Army Group head-quarters, forty miles southwest of Hanover at Bad Oeynhausen. Long was then serving with the British Control Commission, a job he said he took rather than return to intelligence work in London for MI4 following his hospitalization. He had been injured when his jeep overturned near Le Havre during the Normandy landings. Long told me he had come to Germany to get away from what he called 'the spying business'. But if this was so, then he ended up in the wrong job. Long was on the staff of the organization that included Felix Cowgill. Their job was rounding up Nazis and weeding out Communist subversives to set the stage for returning the British zone of occupation back on the road to political normalcy.

'I was under the impression Blunt was on some hush-hush mission from MI5 headquarters in London,' Long said. 'As direc-tor of operations in intelligence, I was the obvious man for him to contact.' He recalls driving Blunt to 'some castle'. But Long does not know much more about the mission. Nor, he insisted, did Blunt put any pressure on him to provide secret information, although, he admitted, he 'had access to most Allied intelligence reports'.

One of the inconsistencies in Long's story is that he admits that Blunt persuaded him to apply for a post in MI5. When he was later interrogated by Peter Wright, Long said Blunt had written out his recommendation. Although his candidature was rejected, Blunt had canvassed and obtained the backing of Dick White – a letter of recommendation that later caused the future director of MI5 and MI6 considerable discomfiture. Long then moved to Düsseldorf to continue his intelligence work for the Control Commission. He ducked behind the Official Secrets Act when I asked him precisely what he had been doing there. But he insisted it had nothing to do with the Russians. Wright, who was privy to the details of Long's job, did not believe him. He says that Long's repeated denials of contact with Blunt, or any other Soviet agents, was 'rubbish'.

Noël Annan, who was then serving in Germany as a colonel in the Political Division of the Control Commission, also has his doubts. Annan says he found Long was suspiciously 'opposed to anything which helped the Christian Democrats,' whose leader, Konrad Adenauer, was prepared to accept the political division of Germany.

According to Nigel West's MI6 sources, the real function of Long's job was to infiltrate agents behind the Iron Curtain, but 'his efforts were largely nullified by his then undiscovered dual role as a Soviet spy.'

More evidence is coming to light from the US Archives that suggests that the full story has yet to be told. It appears that Long was a link in a major Cold War plot to infiltrate Soviet agents into the US intelligence services with the connivance of their other moles in MI5 and MI6. This conspiracy, for which we now have the first documentary evidence, was so immense that its dimensions were not fully appreciated for another twenty years.

17 'An Enormous Amount of Influence'

The defeat of Hitler was only a matter of months away on 4 February 1945, when the Big Three leaders arrived at Yalta for a summit meeting in the imperial splendor of the Livadia summer palace. The British and American leaders faced a dilemma: how to prevent a resurrection of German power without leaving the Soviet Union dominant in Europe.

The Yalta Conference for the first time brought Winston Churchill face to face with the painful reality of the new superpower politics. Britain no longer commanded top-dog status at the conference table. The prime minister found Roosevelt deaf to his entreaties about the need for military guarantees to prevent communism from rolling over Poland and Eastern Europe. 'Britain fondly imagined she had won the war. She had not,' declares historian Noël Annan. 'America and Russia had won the war. Britain had merely, in her finest hour, not lost it.' When and where the Iron Curtain would descend on postwar Europe was going to be determined by the Soviet Union and the United States.

By the end of World War II the British government had also ceased to be the primary target for Soviet penetration. The United States became the major objective of Soviet clandestine assault.

'An Iron Curtain is drawn down upon their front,' Churchill warned Harry Truman, the new American president, on 10 May 1945, barely forty-eight hours after the official celebration of victory over Germany. Could Stalin be trusted to keep his word now the Red Army held a line from the Baltic to the Adriatic that occupied half of Europe? Before the question could be answered, Churchill was swept from office by a landslide Labour victory. So he was unable to influence the resolution of these concerns at the Allied conference in Potsdam that July.

We can now see that Churchill's fears about what could happen behind the Iron Curtain were tragically ironic. At the very moment when the dropping of two atomic bombs on Japan brought the global conflict to its shattering climax in August 1945, a veritable brood of Soviet moles were roaming undetected in the corridors of Whitehall – and, as we shall see, also in Washington. Three of the original Cambridge recruits had done credit to their alma mater by rising to positions in the British governing elite. Blunt was untouchably ensconced behind the throne of the British monarch (with Guy Liddell, now deputy director of MI5, effectively compromised and in his pocket); Philby was in charge of anti-Soviet operations in MI6 and grooming himself for C's office; and Donald Maclean was the first secretary of the British embassy in Washington.

Stalin's Englishmen could now ensure the Kremlin an inside track on Anglo-American foreign policy. This access was doubly secured by Donald Maclean and Guy Burgess, who, in 1945, managed to satisfy a selection board that he should be taken into the permanent establishment of the Foreign Office. When Clement Attlee's Labour government took office, Burgess became personal assistant to Hector McNeil, a young Scottish socialist MP and journalist friend from BBC days. McNeil was an aide to His Majesty's minister of state for foreign affairs. While Ernest Bevin approached Moscow with the rugged skepticism of a tough trade-union leader who had successfully fought Communist infiltration, the fact that Burgess was in his outer office gave Stalin the advantage.

According to Filip Vasilievich Kislitsyn, who at the time was a cipher clerk in the Soviet embassy in London, Burgess was one of the most productive spies the Soviets were running. Ten years later, when Kislitsyn was with the Soviet legation in Canberra, he told Vladimir Petrov, his senior MVD officer, how 'Burgess was bringing out briefcases full of Foreign Office documents, which were photographed in the Soviet embassy and returned to him.'

When Petrov sought asylum in Australia in 1954, he provided a sworn affidavit about this for the American embassy. It explains how well Kislitsyn knew the London embassy case officer responsible for Burgess. He 'used to return with muddy clothes after his meetings, which evidently took place at some obscure country rendezvous.' Kislitsyn, who was in London from 1945 through 1948, recalled how he used to encipher 'the more urgent information and cable it to Moscow'. The rest he prepared for dispatch by courier in the diplomatic bag. Back in Moscow in 1949, Kislitsyn specialized in English until his appointment to the KGB's First Directorate and the responsibility for 'a special one-man section' of top-secret archives.

'This section was devoted solely to the great quantity of material supplied by Maclean and Burgess,' Kislitsyn told Petrov. 'Much of it had not even been translated or distributed to the ministries concerned, but Kislitsyn used to show particular files and documents to high-ranking officials who visited his section for the purpose.'

Apart from his role as Soviet spy, the garlic-chewing Burgess was also an 'agent of influence'. Despite the slovenly dress that infuriated the exacting Foreign Office mandarins, his position papers – invariably coffee stained and embellished with doodled cartoons – were persuasive, skillfully argued and subtly designed to manipulate the outcome of policy issues in a way that favored Moscow. Burgess, however, was by no means the only agent of influence among his Cambridge contemporaries.

These agents were just the tip of the Soviet penetration effort to come to fruition from prewar recruiting. (Only in the KGB archive in Moscow are the complete files that could tell us for certain how many spies, agents of influence and sympathizers the Soviet intelligence services had infiltrated into government on both sides of the Atlantic by the end of World War II.)

What we know now is that in Whitehall, in the Colonial Office, a fellow Apostle, Andrew Cohen, began to play a critical role in molding the views that set the stage for the dismantling of Britain's empire in Africa. In the Treasury there was Dennis Proctor, and in the Admiralty, Alister Watson, also a member of the society, worked on top-secret devices for submarine detection. Allan Nunn May, the nuclear physicist then working in Canada on the Manhattan Project, was providing Soviet agents in Canada with samples of enriched uranium used in the Hiroshima bomb. Another Communist of the same Cambridge vintage, the Canadian-born Egerton Herbert Norman, was a rising diplomat in Canada's External Affairs Ministry attached to the staff of General Douglas MacArthur in Tokyo.

In the spring of 1940, Norman returned to complete his doctoral thesis on 'Japan's Emergence as a Modern State'. After completing his Harvard doctorate in May, Norman returned to the Canadian External Affairs Ministry. His career as a diplomat began with a posting to Japan in 1940 as third secretary of the Tokyo embassy. Eyewitness testimony indicates that these two former members of the Trinity cell were also enmeshed in the circle of Communists and their close sympathizers who were involved in far-eastern affairs.

Professor Karl Wittfogel testified that he knew Norman in 1937–38 as being a member of 'a small Communist study group' of Columbia academics. Norman also had contacts with Chi Ch'ao-ting, a Moscow-trained Comintern agent associated with the American Friends of the Chinese People. Dr Chi, who went to Chungking in 1941 as an economist in Chiang Kai-shek's Ministry of Finance, was a secret protégé of Chou En-lai under whom he served as a high official in Mao Tse-tung's Communist regime.

Philip Jaffe, a Communist and a businessman who made his fortune in greeting cards, would also testify later that Herbert Norman was 'certainly a very close fellow traveler' to whom he had been first introduced in 1935 by Chi Ch'ao-ting. According to Jaffe, Dr Chi acted as 'the leader of the Far East Group of Communists operating on the East Coast of the United States' who 'corrected our ideological mistakes'.

According to Jaffe, another 'intimate friend' of Chi's was Frank

Coe, also a Canadian, who gravitated to the US Treasury Department. Another member of the Harvard circle suspected of being a Communist was Far East faculty member Dr John K. Fairbank. A wartime OSS adviser and future Harvard professor, Fairbank denied the accusation.

Records of the Senate Judiciary Committee show that Jaffe had been 'confidentially assisting the Internal Security Subcommittee since approximately 1951'. He corroborated testimony that Norman was in the Communist network cell at the Institute of Pacific Relations, an organization that the executive of the Communist Party of the USA regarded as being 'the Little Red Schoolhouse for teaching certain people in Washington how to think with the Soviet Union in the Far East.'

The Institute for Pacific Relations, headquartered at 125 East Fifty-second Street in New York, was an international group established in 1925 to promote public and governmental awareness of the economic, political and cultural affairs of the nations of the Pacific rim. Ostensibly representing the liberal left, its organization was that of a classic Münzenberg Communist front. An international secretariat made up of prominent Asian scholars, politicians and businessmen acted for branches that contained Communists and their sympathizers. There was a section in Moscow. One of the representatives of the British branch was Günther Stein, the Shanghai journalist with NKVD connections and links to Mao Tse-tung's American eulogist, Agnes Smedley.

'The IPR itself was like a specialized political flypaper in its attractive power for Communists' was the conclusion of a US Senate investigating committee, which in 1952 reported that 'a remarkably large number of Communists and pro-Communists showed up in the publications, conferences, offices, institutions of the IPR, or in letters and homes of the IPR family.' In the words of the majority report, the 'effective leadership' of the institute had diverted that organization's 'prestige to promote the interests of the Soviet Union in the United States'.

Another name to be linked with the IPR was that of Michael Straight, who had broken away from the Soviet network by quitting his State Department job in May 1941 to become Washington editor of *The New Republic*. He also involved himself with liberal causes, including the American Peace Mobilization and the North American Spanish Relief Committee. Because of his close friendship with John Cornford, the war in Spain held emotional ties for Straight, whose sister-in-law had married Gustavo Durán, a pianist and composer, who had been a Loyalist officer in the Spanish Civil War.

Straight's involvement with what the FBI regarded as 'a number of organizations of varying degrees of Communist and non-Communist sympathies' prompted J. Edgar Hoover to authorize 'extremely discreet inquiries' into his activities and those of *The New Republic*.

That an American capitalist fortune should fund left-wing propaganda evidently galled J. Edgar Hoover. His vexation intensified at the end of 1941 when the Straight family lent money and support to the promotion of the Free World Association. Its declared objective was 'to promote the cause of justice, democracy and human freedom in the USA and throughout the world.' The Free World Association attracted the support of many distinguished liberals, politicians and internationalists. But it had all the trappings of a Communist front. Although the FBI detected 'no known members of the CPUSA' in the organization, careful monitoring of its meetings and publications led to the conclusion that its 'general tenor' was pro-Communist.

The FBI had good reason for its suspicion because Louis Dolivet played a central role in the Association and its related publication, *World*. Dolivet has always denied these suspicions, but FBI, State Department and Military Intelligence records support congressional testimony that he was a former associate of Willi Münzenberg.

Straight introduced Dolivet to his sister, Beatrice. Notwithstanding that the charismatic Hungarian looked like Beethoven and, according to FBI records, was living with an Irish-American movie director's daughter, he wooed and married Beatrice in Des Moines, Iowa, in November 1941, taking care to initial his signature in the wedding register 'L. B.' (his real name was Ludwig Brecher). Fired by Dolivet's Free World philosophy and the January 1942 signing by the Allies of the Declaration of the United Nations, Straight began writing and speaking on his vision of the postwar world organization.

'The New Deal is more dynamic than Fascism and more revolutionary than communism,' Straight declared in March 1942 at a dinner that marked the tenth year of the Roosevelt administration. The significance of that statement did not escape conservative newspaper columnists. They pointed out that Straight's radical pronouncement followed hard on *The New Republic*'s assertion: 'Known Communist sympathizers are again finding it relatively easy to get Government jobs.' The following month, *The New Republic* carried Straight's attack on the FBI for 'still hounding union leaders, while, on the New York waterfront, Axis agents have no trouble signing on as stevedores.'

Hoover could not ignore this affront to the integrity of the bureau. FBI records show that in February 1942 its investigation of Straight was given a more sinister designation: 'Internal Security-R[ussian]'. Straight's ardent championship of a radical New Deal philosophy encouraged the Soviets to make a fresh effort to reclaim his services. After an interval of two years, in the late summer of 1942 when he was back at the family's Old Westbury estate, Straight received a telephone call from 'Michael Green' (Walter Grienke). Twenty-one years later, Straight would tell the FBI how he took the Long Island Railroad from Westbury to Jamaica Station. While driving around the suburbs of Queens for 'an hour or more', Straight renewed his acquaintance with the Russian described in the bureau records as his 'Soviet handler'. Straight could not recall any 'requests or discussions', but said only that it was a general conversation about what he was now doing.

Straight also told the FBI that he had at least one other meeting with Michael Green at a New York restaurant called Longchamps. Straight's FBI file notes that either at this or an earlier meeting, 'at the request of Michael Green', Straight had supplied letters of accreditation for a Swedish woman journalist and for Mark Julius Gayn. (The journalist was later identified by a defector as a Soviet agent, and Gayn, a Chinese expert with IPR affiliations, was arrested in the *Amerasia* case.)

The FBI was particularly anxious to fix the date for Straight's final meeting with Michael Green. He agreed that it must have occurred after 24 November 1942, because that was the day Straight registered for service with the US Army Air Corps. This decision, Straight said, was prompted both by Michael Green's renewed attention and by the birth of his son that October. He reiterated to the FBI his hope that military service would enable him to 'avoid subsequent contacts' with the Soviets.

The FBI records also disclose that in December 1942 Straight attended an Institute of Pacific Relations conference held at the Canadian resort of Mont Tremblant in Quebec. Since one of those invited was Egerton Herbert Norman (he returned from Japan in August 1941 aboard the liner *Gripsholm* with other repatriated Allied diplomats), the conference brought together two former members of the Trinity Communist cell. Straight, however, cannot recall whether he met Norman at Mont Tremblant.

Although the Communist parties were playing down their commitment to violent revolution, the FBI provided the US attorney general with a list of proscribed organizations, including Communist fronts, membership in which made applicants unsuitable for government work. The IPR was not yet on the list but was soon to be implicated in raising support for Mao Tse-tung's struggle to overthrow the government of Chiang Kai-shek.

Central to this strategy was persuading Roosevelt and the American people that Mao Tse-tung's Russian-backed-and-equipped People's Army and its leaders were not really Soviet-style Communists. Wallace's diary reveals that Currie and Fairbank had successfully convinced the vice-president that the Chinese Communists 'were agrarian reformers'. Even Soviet Foreign Minister Vyacheslav Molotov joined in the 'window dressing' by scornfully calling the Chinese 'margarine Communists', saying they had 'no relation whatever to communism'. The popular press in America quickly echoed the new theme.

'For the foreign reader it is somewhat confusing that this Chinese agrarian reform movement is called 'Communism', *The Saturday Evening Post* told its audience. 'Communism in China is a watered-down thing today.' In the State Department, John Stewart Service, another of the 'pro-Chinese liberals' with IPR connections, wrote of Mao's New Democracy, contrasting his rosy view of the Yenan regime with the corrupt and intractable Nationalists. With sympathizers in the Roosevelt administration and a supporting chorus of popular propaganda from pro-Communist writers such as Agnes Smedley and Günther Stein, Mao began preparations for the final leg of the Long March that would take the Communists to power.

The expulsion of the Nationalists from mainland China four years later ended with a search for scapegoats in Washington. The notion that infiltration of the Roosevelt and Truman administrations could have been responsible for what right-wing Republicans portrayed as the 'loss of China' fueled the flames of the anti-Communist outcry. Historians still furiously debate what portion of the blame – if any – lies with Washington as opposed to the inherent corruption and military incapacity of the Nationalists. The Senate committee that investigated the Institute of Pacific Relations in 1952 concluded, however, that the institute and its alumni in the administration were the 'vehicle used by the Communists to orientate American far eastern policies toward Communist objectives.'

The orientation, it is now clear, also involved what can be called espionage. *Amerasia* was an 'obscure little magazine' linked to but published independently by the institute which printed an article on the Nationalist Chinese army that was a virtual paraphrase of a secret OSS report only two months old.

An investigation led, on the night of 11 March 1945, to an OSS surveillance team picking the lock on the *Amerasia* office door. They found the premises 'literally strewn with Confidential government documents'. The case was now turned over to J. Edgar Hoover. Armed with a warrant, the FBI raided *Amerasia* and seized some one thousand clearly classified government documents, including papers from the State Department, Naval Intelligence, OSS and British Intelligence. The FBI arrested six suspects, among them Philip Jaffe, the editor; Mark Gayn, a liberal journalist; Andrew Roth, a lieutenant in the Office of Naval Intelligence; and his State Department liaison officers: John Stewart Service and Emmanuel Larsen.

Conspiracy to violate the espionage act was the charge against the *Amerasia* group. There was an immediate outcry. Newspapers portrayed the raid as a flagrant attempt by the FBI to curtail freedom of the press. The Roosevelt administration backpedaled furiously to avoid an explosive political issue. For security reasons, the contents of the Navy and State Department documents were not disclosed to the grand jury, which refused to indict three of the defendants, including Service. The government dropped espionage charges against the others, who then faced lesser counts of 'conspiracy to embezzle, steal and purloin' government property. No mention was made of communism in the *Amerasia* case and Jaffe's defense was that he had 'transgressed the law' only 'from an excess of journalistic zeal'. This plea did not prevent his conviction and fine.

The reluctance to prosecute Roth and the other State Department employees became a club for Senator McCarthy five years later when he belabored the Truman administration for burying the *Amerasia* affair to cover up the Communist infiltration of a Democratic administration. But recently declassified records of FBI phone taps on New Deal influence peddler Tommy Corcoran show that he worked the coverup. As one of Chiang Kai-shek's American lobbyists, Corcoran had Truman's blessing to try to 'fix' the *Amerasia* affair to avert 'a Dreyfus case'. The fear was that the disclosure of Chiang's corruption might arouse Congressional opinion against the Chinese Nationalists.

The *Amerasia* case, nonetheless, exposed the depth of suspected infiltration in the Roosevelt administration.

Declassified FBI records dating from the autumn of 1945 reveal an extensive network of Communists in government. The files identify twenty-seven officials suspected of involvement with the Soviet espionage network in Washington. The list covered some half-dozen departments and agencies. It named seven from State, including Assistant Secretary Alger Hiss; eight Treasury officials, including Assistant Secretary Harry Dexter White; three officers from the Pentagon; more than two OSS officers; and a Justice Department official.

More than a hundred names were given to the FBI by Elizabeth Terrill Bentley when she began telling of her eleven-year career as a Communist and underground Soviet agent on 8 November 1945. A plump and rather dowdy graduate of Vassar College, then in her forties, Bentley had joined the CPUSA in 1935 while studying for a master's degree in Italian at Columbia. She said she was motivated by her revulsion against Fascism when she accepted orders to go underground in 1938 and take directions from Jacob Golos, her Russian-born control officer. He operated using the cover of World Tourist Inc, an Amtorg-related corporate front in New York. When Bentley's involvement with Golos blossomed into a full-blown romance, she learned that as a member of the Control Commission of the CPUSA, he was one of the ranking Soviet intelligence agents in America.

Bentley used the code name 'Helen' while she worked for Golos as a courier between him and underground Communist networks in the government. Bentley sometimes had more than forty rolls of filmed documents to bring back in the knitting bag she carried on her fortnightly train trips to Washington.

Bentley obviously possessed considerable authority in the Soviet underground *apparat*, and after Golos suddenly died of a heart attack in 1943, she took his place. For almost a year she directed both the Gregory Silvermaster group in the US Treasury, and a second network established by Victor Perlo in the War Production Board. But in the fall of 1944, she received instructions to hand over both to the direct control of a Soviet officer. Bentley claimed to the FBI that there was a third network in the State Department. She said that her Soviet contact had also alluded to the existence of a fourth group, but she learned no more than this.

The significance of Bentley's testimony was that it corroborated and illuminated many details another defector from the same GRU network had omitted. This was David Whittaker Chambers, who three years earlier confessed to the authorities.

A dropout from Columbia Law School, Chambers had abandoned the law to become a Communist journalist. He joined the CPUSA in 1925 as editor of *New Masses*, when he was recruited for 'underground work'. He served as courier and manager of a GRU-linked Washington Communist network until 1937, when Stalin's purges aroused in him 'a profound upheaval of spirit'. He broke with the party in 1938. Fear of reprisals prevented Chambers from coming forward until 1939, but with the encouragement of Kurilsky's lawyer Isaac Don Levine, Chambers gave Assistant Secretary of State Adolf Berle a list of his Communist contacts within the administration.

Berle's memorandum on the 'Underground Espionage Agent', which contained an outline of Chambers's allegations of his involvement in a Communist network of New Dealers, arrived on President Roosevelt's desk at a most inopportune moment. Its potential for destroying Roosevelt's unprecedented bid for a third term – at the very moment he was stretching the Constitution to bring America into the war against Hitler – prompted Berle to bury the report and not to send it to the FBI for another four years.

When Hoover obtained Berle's report in 1942, the FBI questioned Chambers, but did nothing more about him until 1945. They did not act on the information Chambers provided because he was, by turns, furtive and revealing. No doubt mindful of the twenty-year jail term under the Espionage Act, he did not reveal until 1948 – five years later at the hearings of the House Un-American Activities Committee – that he had evidence in the form of filmed State Department documents and a handwritten memorandum from Harry Dexter White, which he had secreted, as an insurance policy, in the shaft of a dumbwaiter at his wife's sister's home in Brooklyn. Aided by his fellow Communist Nathan Silvermaster, then an economist with the Railroad Retirement Board, Chambers obtained from the Treasury briefcases full of official documents for photographing. A principal source was Harry Dexter White, assistant secretary to Harry Morgenthau at Treasury. He was the architect, along with John Maynard Keynes, of America's postwar fiscal policy and the International Monetary Fund. White may not have been a member of the party, according to Chambers, but he was a 'fellow traveller' who 'enjoyed being of the Communist Party but not in the party and not subject to its discipline.' So far as Assistant Secretary of State Alger Hiss was concerned, Chambers testified under oath that Hiss was a member of the Communist cell established in Washington by Harold Ware.

Hiss's East Coast establishment family was comparable to the privileged background of the Cambridge Communists. The Depression had encouraged Hiss, like his British counterparts, to a certain sympathy with the intellectual adherents of Marx. He made the most of the war and established himself as a wunderkind, rising fast and high to become one of the youngest assistant secretaries in the State Department. His grasp of how policy was made enabled him to play a prominent role at the Yalta summit. As acting secretary general of the 1945 meeting of the UN in San Francisco, Hiss seemed destined – because of strong Soviet support – to become, at the age of forty-one, its first permanent head.

But when it came to Communists in strategic positions in the government, Bentley attested that it was Harry Dexter White and Lauchlin Currie, of the State Department Far East section, who were 'two of our best ones' in the administration. She portrayed these two as having 'an immense amount of influence. They knew people and their word would be accepted when they recommended someone.' On one occasion, Bentley said, Currie had sent word to Moscow via White that the United States was about to break the Soviet codes.

Bentley dutifully relayed this warning to Golos, whose own superior in the NKVD *apparat* was Gaik Badalovich Ovakimian, the *resident* in the New York Amtorg office. In partnership with Vassili Zubilin, the second secretary of the Washington embassy, Ovakimian, it was later established, had directed Soviet intelligence activity in North America since the early thirties. Ovakimian, known to the FBI as 'the wily Armenian', was arrested in May 1941 on charges under the Smith Act, which required agents of a foreign government to register with the attorney general.

When Zubilin returned to Moscow in July 1944, his replacement directed Bentley to hand over control of the Silvermaster and Perlo networks to two Soviet intelligence officers. She knew one of them as 'Al'. From FBI photographs Bentley established 'Al' to be Anatoli Gromov, who had used the cover name 'Henry' when he controlled the Cambridge agents in London. Gromov's decision to strip Bentley of her authority contributed to her decision to defect: in August 1945 she first reported to the FBI office at New Haven in her home state of Connecticut.

In a series of debriefings that ran through November, Bentley had no difficulty identifying 'Al'. Bentley's account was given more credence when she turned over to the Bureau the $2,000 obtained from her meeting with 'Al' (Gromov) on 17 October 1945. She subsequently arranged another meeting with the Russian, this time under FBI surveillance, on 21 November. But Hoover's hopes of using his tame defector as a double agent evaporated when she received no instructions from 'Al'. Gromov, it seems, had become suspicious. A few weeks later he returned to Moscow.

Bentley had failed to trap a top Soviet spymaster, but she had named more than a hundred individuals with connections to Soviet espionage, of whom twenty-seven were government employees. She also stated that she learned from Golos that he was running an English agent in New York with the code name 'Benjamin', an officer with William 'Intrepid' Stephenson's British Security Co-Ordination from 1941 to 1943, who allegedly passed to the Russians a manual on Scotland Yard surveillance techniques and other papers.

The FBI was primarily interested in Bentley's Washington contacts. Of those she named, the FBI decided that fifty-one individuals were of 'sufficient importance to warrant investigative attention by the Bureau.' The fact that only four of Bentley's names had appeared in the information supplied up to then by Chambers, confirmed that he had provided the FBI with a very incomplete account.

Bentley had no hard evidence to support her staggering story. But documents confirming the extensive reach of the Soviet networks in North America soon came from an unimpeachable source: a defecting GRU cipher clerk at the Soviet embassy in Ottawa.

Igor Gouzenko had been responsible for encrypting most of the confidential traffic of both Ambassador Georgy Zarubin and the military attaché, Colonel Nikolai Zabotkin, who was head of the GRU networks in Canada. When Gouzenko defected on 5 September 1945, he walked out of the embassy with a carefully selected sheaf of secret cables and pages from Zabotkin's handwritten diary. These Russian files provided the most conclusive proof yet obtained in the West of the extent to which the Soviets had breached the security of Canada, Great Britain and the United States.

The Royal Canadian Mounted Police carried out Gouzenko's debriefing; officers from the FBI eventually assisted them. The Bureau discovered at first hand that Zabotkin's network extended beyond Canada. It was a cable ordering Zabotkin to 'take measures to organize the acquisition of documentary materials on the atomic bomb' that caused the most alarm in Washington. The instructions were intended for one of four scientists whom Zabotkin controlled. The physicist's code name was 'Alek'. Zabotkin's cable of 31 July 1945 alerted Moscow that he had 'worked out conditions of a meeting with Alek in London' because the scientist had been recalled to fly to England in September to take up an appointment at King's College.

This information enabled MI5 to identify 'Alek' as the Cambridge scientist Dr Allan Nunn May. Although Nunn May had never joined the party, he had made no particular secret of his Communist leanings. Nothwithstanding his obvious sympathies, MI5 cleared Nunn May in April 1942 to join the Cambridge team working on the top-secret Tube Alloys atomic-bomb project. In January 1943, Nunn May again received MI5 clearance when he went to Montreal to work at the Atomic Energy Division of the Canadian National Research Council. Nunn May had access to the Chalk River heavy-water facility and the Chicago Metallurgical Laboratory, plus other facilities of the Manhattan Engineering District, where the atomic bomb was being assembled by the US Army Corps of Engineers.

One of the most worrying of the Zabotkin cables brought by Gouzenko revealed that 'Alek' had supplied him with a sample of uranium 235 on platinum foil. Alarm about the extent of the breach that the Soviets had made into the Manhattan Project brought Canadian Prime Minister Mackenzie King hurrying to Washington for a top-level meeting on 30 September with President Truman and Secretary of State Dean Acheson. Anatoli Yakolev, the Soviet vice-consul in New York, was identified as the focus of atomic espionage in the United States. But Truman – at the request of Prime Minister Attlee – cautioned against premature action until full investigations had been conducted.

'I was expecting something like this,' Nunn May said when he was taken into custody and charged on 4 March 1946. His arrest came a few days after thirteen Canadians were detained by the Royal Canadian Mounted Police on charges of espionage. Nunn May pleaded guilty and received a ten-year prison sentence.

One of the thirteen Canadians arrested as a result of Gouzenko's revelations was Israel Halperin, a mathematics professor at Queen's University, Kingston, Ontario. Although subsequently acquitted of conspiracy charges. Halperin's notebook contained several references to Herbert Norman. The FBI began inquiries at Harvard about the ex-Cambridge Canadian, who was then a liaison officer on MacArthur's staff in Tokyo, with the rank of minister.

The FBI found of greater importance the information supplied by Gouzenko that appeared to confirm the accusations of Chambers and Bentley about Alger Hiss. Gouzenko claimed that Zabotkin's deputy, Lieutenant Kulakov, had told him in May 1945 that the Soviets had an agent 'who was assistant to the then Secretary of State, Edward R. Stettinius.'

This startling statement was appended to the report that Hoover sent to the White House on 25 November 1945. It set out in much greater detail the preliminary warning he had given on 8 November that 'a number of persons employed in the Government . . . have been furnishing data and information to persons outside the Federal Government, who are in turn transmitting this information to espionage agents of the Soviet government.'

The FBI already had put the twenty-seven individuals named in Hoover's report under surveillance, including phone taps where authorized. But of all the names, those of Harry Dexter White and Alger Hiss gave President Truman the most cause for worry. The other senior White House official Bentley named – Lauchlin Currie – was not on the list because he had left government service. Roosevelt had died in April 1945, and a month after moving into the White House, Truman let it be known that he was 'very much against building up a Gestapo' in the FBI. Now Hoover was telling him that two of his senior officials might be Soviet agents. Truman, who came to the presidency with no knowledge of Communist conspiracies, was skeptical. He chose to take no immediate action. Truman allowed White's nomination as executive director of the International Monetary Fund to go ahead for Senate approval.

Hiss, then the director of Special Political Affairs, found a fierce defender of his integrity in the secretary of state, a fellow graduate of Harvard Law School. Dean Acheson, a product in the same idealistic New Deal liberal mold as Hiss – like his government contemporaries in Britain – just could not believe that Communist traitors could bloom in their carefully groomed elite plot.

'They just plain did not want to believe us,' as Robert Lamphere, a Midwesterner who at the time was a Soviet espionage officer in the FBI told me with characteristic bluntness. 'They,' he said, were the White House and Justice Department officials who pointed out that there was little except Bentley's allegations on which to base a prosecution. He also believed that Hoover's reports to Truman, despite their top-secret status, were quickly leaked to suspects.

The bureau soon learned that the Soviets were alerting their Washington networks. This information surfaces in the FBI records released to Michael Straight. The transcript of a 1975 interview of Straight reveals that he learned how Bentley had, in 'late 1945', identified Straight's Soviet contact Michael Green as Grienke, and that by 'early 1946' the Soviets began warning their contacts of the danger and 'advising them of what action to take to avoid being implicated.'

Lamphere told me he remembered that the New York field office received 'definite playback' from reliable informants 'within a month or two' that the Soviets were passing the warning around their networks. They were instructed to take precautions by breaking off their contacts and keeping their mouths shut.

'I still believe that if we had been allowed to move in right away we could have got the corroborating testimony that would have enabled us to get a successful prosecution against White and many of the others on that list Hoover sent to the White House on 25 November,' Lamphere told me. He recalls the exasperation felt by him and his fellow agents that an opportunity was slipping away. He also acknowledged that he was 'second-guessing' the decisions made by many of his old friends, principally Bill Harvey, the FBI's resident counterintelligence expert.

'Experience in later espionage cases suggests that with as many suspects as we had in 1945 we could have found one or two who might have broken ranks under close interrogation to give us the confessions we needed to implicate the rest,' Lamphere asserts. He points out that the secret of successful interrogation is to move in, 'right bang', taking the subject by surprise 'when he is not ready for what's coming'. The time to have moved in, he contends, was immediately after Gouzenko's defection, when the Soviet intelligence apparatus in North America was in a state of shock and no one on the other side knew how much the FBI had learned from Gouzenko and other defectors.

Lamphere said that by 1947 the suspects knew the FBI did not know that much. So when the Justice Department finally put Bentley before a federal grand jury in 1947, it was a signal to the subpoenaed witnesses, such as Harry Dexter White, that the FBI had no hard evidence against them.

Forewarned and forearmed that they faced only Bentley's unsupported allegations, the defense attorneys confidently attacked her as a liar. As a result, no indictments were returned against any of those named by Bentley. Instead, the grand jury shifted its focus and, in July 1948, returned twelve indictments against the leaders of the CPUSA for alleged violations of the 1940 Smith Act. Within weeks, the public was reading about the sensational revelations of the 'Red Spy Queen'. Following Bentley's testimony on Capitol Hill, the Communist takeover of the Czechoslovakian government and the Soviet blockade of Berlin set the stage for another Red Scare of the type that had spread across the United States in 1920.

Michael Straight knew personally that some of those whom Bentley and Chambers testified about were members of the Washington underground Communist network. Why, FBI officers asked Straight in 1963, had he not contacted them in 1948 instead of waiting another fifteen years to volunteer his story? He replied that he had 'considered doing so on many occasions but was afraid.' Straight said that he 'could not bear the publicity of the hearings and trials, with the resultant injury to his wife and children.'

Straight was also agonizing over his old Cambridge loyalties. His FBI records confirm that this conflict came to a head when he traveled to England 'on personal business' in 1946, shortly after leaving the US Army Air Force. On this trip – which in his book written twenty years later he sets in 1949 – he said he saw Burgess for the first time since the summer of 1940. He attended the annual dinner of the Apostles in a private dining room of the Royal Automobile Club. Straight recalls in his book that he became embroiled in a row over Czechoslovakia with Eric Hobsbawm, a rising Marxist historian. Blunt, who witnessed the dispute from the far end of the room, came up when the dinner was breaking.

'Guy and I would like to talk to you,' Blunt announced in his courteous but clipped manner. 'We'll meet you here tomorrow morning.'

The next day their discussion became bitter when Straight accused the Soviet government of endangering the peace over the issue of the atomic bomb. Burgess questioned the motives of the American government. Straight 'told both of them that he had grown up and was completely disillusioned with the communist movement.' This made them 'hostile and tense'. Blunt, who up until this moment had been silent, suddenly intervened.

'The question is, are we capable of intellectual growth?'

'Exactly,' Straight replied, getting up to leave. Burgess looked at him intently and asked: 'Are you still with us?' Straight said he was not. In answer to the question of whether he was 'unfriendly', he replied: 'If I were, why would I be here?'

Straight admits that he still had to come to terms with his past and gave 'a weak evasive answer' of the sort he 'habitually gave' when he 'faced a confrontation of any kind'. Blunt appears to have known only too well how to manipulate Straight's complex psychological predicament. Despite what he described to the FBI as a 'confrontation' with his Cambridge recruiter, his continuing silence was all but guaranteed by the apostolic oath. As articulated by E. M. Forster, it put loyalty to friends before country. In his often misquoted statement, he said: 'If I had to choose between betraying my country and my friend, I hope I should have the guts to betray my country.'

After another meeting with Straight the following year, which included lunch at the Savoy in London, Burgess would have been able to reassure Blunt and Yuri Modin, their new Soviet controller, that their secrets were still safe. If Straight was not 'with them' he was certainly not 'against them' either.

The first test of Straight's commitment to the bond of apostolic secrecy came with the 1948 House Un-American Activities Committee hearings. He was torn between his journalistic commitment to the truth, his family duty and his loyalty to old friends. The result was an agonizing compromise. As editor of *The New Republic*, he decided that even if he could not go to the FBI about his peripheral involvement with the Communist underground in Washington, he had a commitment to his readers to support – if not explain – the truth.

'In general we believe that the outline of Elizabeth Bentley's story is largely accurate,' Straight declared in a signed editorial. It cost him the disdain of many of his New Deal liberal friends.

The House Un-American Activities Committee (HUAAC), the permanent successor in 1946 of the Dies Committee, which had investigated internal Nazi and Communist subversion before the war, was already warming up for its self-appointed mission to purge the federal bureaucracy of Communists. It planned well-publicized hearings aimed at weeding out 'Reds' in the Hollywood film industry. Encouraged by carefully orchestrated leaks to legislators from J. Edgar Hoover, Richard Milhouse Nixon and the Republican politicians on the committee sought to remedy the failure of the judiciary to deal effectively with the reality of Soviet penetration. On 31 July 1948 Bentley sat at the witness table. A packed committee room heard her tell, for the first time in public, a staggering tale of infiltration and subversion.

The star turn came when Whittaker Chambers sat in the spotlight to corroborate Bentley's account. Characterized by Nixon as the 'reluctant witness', this self-confessed ex-member of the Communist underground was led through a penetrating cross-examination to implicate Hiss and White in the conspiracy.

When White came to the stand, he parried Nixon's questions skillfully. Although he was recovering from a heart attack, he issued a steady stream of denials and eloquent appeals to the 'American creed' of free speech. Three days after he appeared before the committee, on 16 August 1948, White died of a second and fatal heart attack.

When Alger Hiss appeared at the witness table he was dignified and suavely confident as president of the Carnegie Endowment for International Peace. Hiss appeared before the committee two days after Chambers finished his testimony. He firmly denied all Chambers's allegations. He conceded only that he dimly remembered Chambers when Chambers was using the alias of George Crosley to 'soft touch' him for a loan for a secondhand car. The polished, self-confident ex-diplomat then threw down the gauntlet by daring the man he had called a 'deadbeat' journalist to repeat his charges outside the privileged sanctuary of the hearings.

Chambers promptly did so on a radio show. And when Hiss sued for libel, Chambers led FBI investigators to the dumbwaiter in Brooklyn and the yellow foolscap pages in White's handwriting. From the hollowed-out center of a pumpkin on the pumpkin patch on his Maryland farm, he retrieved a film he said he had kept for ten years as a 'life preserver' against possible revenge by the Communist underground. The film contained notes of the confidential State Department reports. Chambers alleged Hiss had produced these for him on his Woodstock typewriter. The documentary evidence that Chambers had withheld so long from the FBI transformed the case, although the delay led some to doubt its credibility.

Since Hiss had denied under oath that he gave any government information to Chambers, he was called to account for perjury. A grand jury returned an indictment on two perjury counts in December 1948. The first trial ended in an eight-to-four hung jury in July 1949.

At the second trial in January 1950 a former Soviet spy runner, Hede Massing, a GRU/NKVD undercover agent in the Soviet-American *apparat*, gave her eyewitness testimony describing a confrontation she had with Hiss in 1935 over cell member Noel Field (who had vanished behind the Iron Curtain in 1949) which made a strong impression on the jury. Hiss was convicted of perjuring himself as to whether he had known Chambers, not over whether he had lied about passing on government information. His stiff five-year prison term (he continued to protest his innocence after his trials) roused the liberal press to fury.

Then on 23 September 1949 the president stunned the nation with the announcement that the Soviets had exploded an atomic bomb. The news that the United States had lost its military supremacy, which most Americans took for granted as their stipend from World War II, was compounded the following month when Mao Tse-tung proclaimed final victory in the Communist takeover of China. Seven months later, the Cold War turned into a hot one in Korea.

The Communist infiltration became the convenient collective scapegoat for these foreign-policy disasters and was given demagogic volume by Senator Joseph McCarthy. Even before US troops went into action under the UN flag to drive the North Korean army back across the 38th parallel, this obscure and undistinguished junior senator from Wisconsin had launched a crusade against domestic communism. In a fiery speech he charged that the State Department harbored over fifty Soviet agents.

At a time when GIs were being killed by Communist bullets, the reprise of the testimony of Elizabeth Bentley and Whittaker Chambers helped spark what was later described as a 'tawdry reign of terror'.

The hearings polluted the political debate and served as a smoke screen to cover Soviet intentions. Counterintelligence officers like Lamphere and his colleagues in the Soviet Espionage section of the FBI deplored Senator McCarthy's 'witch-hunting' approach as fervently as those who proclaimed themselves champions of constitutional rights. 'It turned many liberals against legitimate efforts to curtail Communist activities in the United States, particularly in regard to government employment of known Communists.'

In weighing the historical record of those times the historian must not forget that 'McCarthyism' is a political epithet not a valid rubric for dismissing a vast body of corroborative testimony that confirms the known blueprint of Soviet-directed subversion. When evaluating the recently released congressional investigatory records, and the testimony of scores of witnesses in both public and private executive sessions, historical judgements must ultimately be made by weighing the balance of probabilities. While giving due consideration to the dangers of relying on 'guilt by association', the political associates and beliefs of an individual cannot be ignored. Even at the height of the furor over McCarthy, it is significant that *The Nation* – the magazine that had championed the American intellectual left through the Depression – was not insisting on evidence that could sustain the rigorous 'test of guilt' that would be applied in criminal courts: 'Impartial observers should ask themselves whether sufficient *credible evidence* has been presented to lead reasonable men to conclude that the accused individuals were spies for a foreign power.'

Historians and writers continue to take opposing sides in the debate. But of one central factor in the equation there can be no doubt: Moscow *did* target the US administration for penetration. The historical argument therefore becomes one of evaluating the degree of its success.

Moreover, as Lamphere and other intelligence officers have emphasized, US Army code breakers provided the key to checking the accuracy of at least part of Bentley's evidence. The breaking of the wartime US–Moscow cables, the so-called Venona traffic, gave positive corroboration that the Soviets were indeed receiving information from the American agents who were inside, and outside, the US government. The Venona intercepts are still yielding information, so none of the intercepted signals has been officially released.

'I began to receive this confirmation of Bentley's testimony sometime after 1948,' Lamphere told me. But he was never permitted to use it as corroborative evidence – even in the highly contentious case of Ethel Rosenberg, who was also identified in a Venona decrypt. The decrypts were – and still are – a highly classified military-intelligence secret.

What is now known about the corroboration that Venona gave to Bentley's original testimony must add authority to the 1953 report of the Senate Judiciary Committee's subcommittee that investigated 'Interlocking Subversion in Government Departments'. After a new round of hearings, its report catalogued the awesome extent of the Soviet penetration operation.

The report detailed how the prewar target for Communist penetration had been the New Deal agencies managing the economic-recovery programs. During the war the target had shifted to 'such wartime agencies as the Board of Economic Warfare, the Federal Economic Administration, the Office of Strategic Services and the like.' Then, toward the end of the war, the infiltrators were 'operating in the foreign policy field', and after 1945 'gravitating towards the international agencies'.

The Senate Judiciary Committee (*not* McCarthy's Committee) established that the modus operandi of the Communist networks in the US government was not simply espionage but also acting as classic agents of influence:

They colonized key Committees in Congress. They helped write laws, conduct congressional hearings, and write congressional reports. They advised Cabinet members, wrote speeches for them, and represented them at intergovernmental conferences. They staffed interdepartmental committees which prepared basic American and world policy. They traveled to every continent as emissaries and representatives of the American people. They attended virtually every international conference where statesmen met to shape the future.

Noting that 'almost all the persons exposed by the evidence had some connection which could be documented with at least one – and generally several – other exposed persons', the committee stressed its findings of an 'interlacing combination' was evidence of '4 Soviet espionage rings operating within our Government.' The committee cautioned that 'only 2 of these have been exposed.' It found, too, that there was a characteristic common to all those who had been exposed: 'Virtually all were graduates of American universities. Many had doctorates or similar ratings of academic and intellectual distinction.'

The Senate Judiciary report in essence confirms that Soviet intelligence turned the same deep-penetration strategy against the

United States as it had used against Britain. Both penetrations depended on the recruitment of ideologically committed members of the university-educated elite. The number of Harvard graduates in the American communist networks paralleled the dominance of Cambridge graduates in Britain. There was, moreover, a transatlantic crossover between the two networks in at least two known cases: Norman and Straight.

In contrast to their operations in Britain, where the vigilance of MI5 and Special Branch ruled out the exploitation of the CPGB by the NKVD after 1927, Soviet infiltration and control of its moles in the US government was facilitated by the openness of American society and the CPUSA. Until Bentley defected from the *apparat*, the FBI, it is clear, underestimated both the scale and objectives of the Soviet assault.

Since the confidential State Department records prove that MI5 had been supplying the Americans with top-secret reports on Soviet subversion since the early 1920s, this leads to a crucial question: why was the FBI so taken by surprise when it learned that the United States government had become the prime target for Soviet penetration?

Two possible answers are immediately self-evident. First, in 1945 the various American intelligence services were involved in a battle for turf. The OSS was being shut down; the CIA had not appeared on the scene. British information on Communist subversion was no longer being channeled via the State Department for dissemination to all the intelligence agencies in Washington. Instead, it was coming to Hoover from his good friend Guy Liddell of MI5. And Hoover was trying to preempt the postwar counterintelligence scene for the FBI. This theory is substantiated by an OSS report from London to Washington that discussed Liddell's trip in early 1946 to the United States.

'It should be pointed out that Captain Liddell has been for years a close friend and great admirer of the FBI, and during this trip spent most of his time in Washington with FBI officials,' the senior OSS representative in London cabled headquarters. Liddell, in his new capacity of deputy director of MI5, had 'spent a great deal of time with Mr Hoover and Mr Ladd of the FBI.'

The second answer is that the Americans really shouldn't have been surprised by the extent of the Soviet penetration into the American government. British counterintelligence, which had been keeping track of Soviet subversion inside England until the war, was also being made to look foolish – even to the point of having Soviet infiltrators moving up to positions to run British counterintelligence. Here was Guy Liddell advising J. Edgar Hoover about Soviet penetrations, and Liddell did not know what was going on in his own shop. Or did he?

'It has given me great pleasure to be able to pass the names of
every MI5 officer to the Russians.' Anthony Blunt made this
off-the-cuff comment during a preretirement chat with Colonel
T. A. Robertson in November 1945.

'It was an electrifying remark,' recalled Robertson, a bluff man
with piercing blue eyes who is not given to overstatement. 'I
couldn't keep it under my hat. I must have told Guy Liddell.'

While Blunt had reputation for cynical humor, Robertson's
account makes it plain that he *did not* take the astonishing statement simply as a mischievous jest. The very nature of the remark
appears to have been deliberately contrived so that Robertson, an
ex-army officer and stickler for security, was forced to relay it in
confidence and verbally to his chief. That Blunt should risk such
a statement indicates that he could rely on a personal defense
from Liddell, the head of B Division. Other counterintelligence
experts view the remark as being a deliberate 'testing of the
circuit' by Blunt before he retired from full-time service with
MI5.

Liddell never took any formal action as a result of Robertson's
report, so Blunt had reassuring proof that his friend really was a
trustworthy protector. This asset would become immensely valuable in later years.

Had it not been for the Labour government and its suspicions
about MI5 dating back to the notorious Zinoviev letter, Liddell
would probably have become its director general. But Prime
Minister Attlee, distrusting an internal appointee, brought in
Percy Sillitoe, former chief of the Kent Constabulary. As an

outsider, he never settled in comfortably as director general at Leconfield House, the postwar headquarters overlooking South Audley Street, a block away from Hyde Park. The former police chief never fathomed the subtleties of the network of school and college loyalties that bound MI5 together. And during Sillitoe's tenure, it was silently acknowledged that the deputy director, Liddell, was the indispensible power behind the throne. As Director of B Division, he had built an empire within the heart of the organization. It was Liddell who had forged close personal ties with the mighty J. Edgar Hoover and the American intelligence community. Above all, Liddell possessed another attribute that Sillitoe lacked: a personal network that reached through the clubs of Pall Mall and St James's, providing the MI5 directorate with the informal contacts with the civil service that were essential for the smooth functioning of the security service.

When Sillitoe moved into Leconfield House on 30 April 1946, Blunt was moving out. In the six months since his formal retirement, Blunt had been popping in and out of the office, handing over his various projects. And for the next five years, his mournful face was never absent for very long from the inner sanctum of the deputy director. Blunt was never too busy lecturing at the Courtauld, or with his duties at the Palace, to give advice or carry out free-lance missions for Guy Liddell.

Just how many of these private missions had to do with art and how many with intelligence is impossible to judge. But Liddell, according to Sir Dick White and others, was a passionate collector of paintings. With his friend's lofty position at the Palace, Liddell now had even more opportunities to indulge in his hobby.

Blunt saw to it that he was on the VIP guest list for all the Royal Academy functions such as the Royal Academy's winter exhibition that opened in October 1946. One of the first admiring visitors was Queen Mary. She recorded in her diary: 'The pictures looked lovely and were well hung by Mr Blunt and the Committee, all the rooms were filled.'

Liddell also regarded Blunt as an adviser for his own picture collecting. While this may help explain the power that Blunt continued to hold over his wartime MI5 chief, it appears that he brought Liddell something considerably more valuable than intellectual companionship. In February 1944, Christie's auctioned an unattributed painting of two heads from the collection of the Earls of Carlisle. Shortly afterward, the painting passed into the Liddell family collection. But now its value was dramatically increased because Blunt had identified it as a fragment of a long-lost Poussin painting of the *Adoration of the Golden Calf*. Its authenticity, however, came to be hotly disputed, except by Blunt, as the result of X-ray analysis conducted in the Courtauld laboratories by Professor Stephen Rees-Jones. 'He would only accept my findings if it suited him,' Rees-Jones allowed, recalling that when Blunt became the institute's director in 1947, 'he ruled it like a medieval court.'

As surveyor of the king's pictures, however, Blunt played the role of deferential courtier in Buckingham Palace. But at the Courtauld, he was an autocrat. He moved himself – and his succession of male lovers – into the director's two-bedroom flat. From atop the elegant Robert Adam house, overlooking the leafy oasis of Portman Square north of the bustling shops of Oxford Street, for the next twenty-five years Blunt invoked his undisputed authority over staff and students. Former students still recall the deferential hush that overtook the corridors of the institute whenever the footfalls on the magnificent marble spiral staircase announced the descent of the director, his academic gown billowing out over a formal gray-flannel suit.

Blunt treated the Courtauld staff as his household retainers. This came as a surprise to the long-serving librarian of the institute, Lillian Gurry, who was one of those who 'thought it a joke for a Communist to get a royal appointment.' But the director quickly earned recognition for the Courtauld and for himself by his prodigious output of articles, books and lectures stressing the historical and social context of art, and he gave up the Marxist clichés – along with the red ties that Gurry had remembered him wearing before the war.

As a full-fledged professor of London University, Blunt was

not content. He determined to transform the Courtauld into *the* center for artistic studies in Britain. When he became director, the institute's reputation was that of a genteel and undemanding finishing school for the sons and daughters of the wealthy, or for those going into the antiques trade. This he quickly changed. Under Blunt's directorship a rigorous teaching curriculum and a carefully managed admissions policy turned the Courtauld into a postgraduate center with an international reputation. By the time he retired twenty-five years later, Blunt could pride himself on having nurtured a host of graduate students who, by the time of his death, were gravitating into the top directorships and plum curatorial positions of Britain's leading art galleries, museums and auction houses.

In a grand design to propagate his view of art history, Blunt took a leaf out of the Soviet book. Just as the momentum of his privileged education and contacts had carried him into the upper reaches of the British *governing* establishment, Blunt set about using the institute to groom ideological devotees of his artistic theories whom he intended, eventually to take control of the British *art* establishment.

To achieve his ambition of stamping the art world with the imprimatur of his scholarship, and building an unparalleled network of influence, it was vital that Blunt preserve the secret of his clandestine allegiance to Moscow. Ironically, during his last months as a full-time MI5 officer, Blunt discovered that a couple of defecting Soviet intelligence officers stood between his potentially illustrious career and a very long prison sentence.

Here was an unpleasant reminder of just how fragile the cover of the Cambridge moles really was. Unlike most Soviet spies, they had not operated through a series of insulated cells. The principal members of Blunt's network were not only known by their wartime associates in MI5 and MI6 to be friends, but each member's treachery was known to the others. Each realized that exposure of one would immediately cast suspicion on the rest, a risk enhanced by Burgess's bizarre behaviour.

The first threat to Blunt was Konstantin Volkov's attempted

defection in August 1945. This Soviet intelligence officer did not make it clear whether he was KGB or GRU when he first walked into the British consulate in Istanbul, and provided John Reed, a British Foreign Office official, with a 'shopping list' typed in Russian. Volkov insisted that his request to defect not be communicated to London by telegram, because, he said, a number of the British diplomatic ciphers had been broken.

Reed's rough-and-ready translation of the shopping list in part read: '. . . files and documents concerning very important Soviet agents in important establishments in London. Judging by the cryptonyms [the code names in secret cables between London and Moscow] there are, at present, seven such agents, five in British Intelligence and two in the Foreign Office. I know, for instance, that one of these agents is fulfilling the duties of Head of a Department of British Counter Intelligence.'

Unfortunately for Volkov, although Reed's report reached London a week later by diplomatic pouch, Sir Stewart Menzies regarded the matter as one of 'such delicacy' that he summoned Kim Philby and insisted that he handle it himself. As Head of Section IX, which had by now swallowed up Section V and controlled all the Soviet counterintelligence operations in MI6, Philby read the report from Istanbul and immediately recognized the danger it posed to himself and the other members of the Cambridge agents.

'I stared at the papers rather longer than necessary to compose my thoughts,' Philby would write later. 'The only course was to put a bold face on it.' Philby managed to persuade C to let him handle the matter by flying to Turkey, as we have seen. Meanwhile Philby alerted his Soviet controller, Boris Krotov, who had taken over the running of the high-grade agents from Anatoli Gromov, who was now in Washington.

To give Moscow time to arrange for the 'repatriation' of its would-be defector, Philby delayed his flight to Turkey. By the time he reached Istanbul, nearly two weeks later, the Turks reported that Volkov and his wife had been flown to Moscow strapped to stretchers.

Philby returned empty handed to London. Menzies accepted Philby's inadequate report and the specious rationalization that Volkov's nervousness must have betrayed him during the three weeks it took MI6 to respond to his offer. Philby was then permitted to keep Volkov's shopping list in his own safe. Thus he kept it away from the Registry and from those who might have considered it worthy of more objective analysis.

Volkov's report was not examined again for six years – until suspicion fell on Philby after the Burgess and Maclean defection in 1951. Then it seemed that Philby was the obvious suspect fingered by Volkov as the man who was 'fulfilling the duties of Head of a Department of British Counter Intelligence' because, in October 1944, Philby had only recently become head of Section IX of MI6.

In 1965, however, a retranslation of Volkov's original Russian list was made at the request of mole-hunter Peter Wright. This was done by Geoffrey Sudbury, a fluent speaker of Russian, from GCHQ. This translation revealed that Reed had mistakenly omitted the words *otdela* ('section') and *upravleniya* ('directorate') from his original translation. What Volkov had actually tried to tell the British, according to this interpretation, was that 'one of the agents is fulfilling the duties of head of a *section* of the British Counterintelligence *Directorate.*'

The new translation made it unlikely that Volkov was pointing to Philby, because 'Counterintelligence Directorate' was how the Soviets customarily referred to MI5; Philby was in MI6. The correctness of this new evaluation was confirmed by three more Soviet defectors: Igor Gouzenko, Vladimir Petrov and Anatoli Golitsyn.

If Volkov's mole was not Philby – or any section head in MI6 – who was he?

The term 'fulfilling the duties' suggested to Sudbury and Wright that, whoever he was, he must have been 'acting head' of some section in MI5. Wright considers the obvious candidate to be Roger Hollis. As head of F Division, which monitored political parties, Hollis held the rank of assistant director until early 1947 when he took over C Division, which made him a full member of the MI5 directorate. But if Volkov's information was a year old and related back to 1943, the identification could equally well apply to Roger Fulford, the deputy head of F, who assumed the responsibilities whenever Hollis was absent recuperating from his recurrent bouts of tuberculosis.

However, if by 'fulfilling the duties' Volkov meant that Moscow's agent was *simply doing the job* of a division chief, which made him ex officio a member of the MI5 directorate, then it could have been any one of the five directors – including Guy Liddell.

Philby's personal response in 1945 was commensurate with his belief that Volkov was pointing at him. But he may have known better by the time he wrote his KGB-sponsored account in 1968. Significantly he devoted a whole chapter to the Volkov affair, reinforcing the impression that he was the Soviet agent identified by Volkov.

What is so striking about the Volkov list, and the information supplied a month later by the defection of the GRU cipher clerk in Ottawa, is that both cases produced such seemingly clear indications of massive Soviet infiltrations into MI5 and MI6. Yet both cases seemed to be quickly buried with no action taken. In MI6, Philby, who was in control of all counterintelligence operations, stifled any further investigation by locking the Volkov file in his personal safe. But MI5 handled the case of Igor Gouzenko. That *neither* service made any serious attempt in 1945 to respond to the evidence of Soviet penetration is astonishing. Either the 'mental equipment' of Sir Stewart Menzies – and of his opposite number in MI5 – was as truly 'unimpressive' as Philby claimed – or the Soviets had a stronger grip on the British intelligence apparatus than anyone appreciated at the time.

The failure to respond to similar items of evidence was so dilatory that it can be argued that the Soviets not only controlled the counterintelligence chief of MI6, but also a ranking officer in MI5. More importantly, this officer was *not* Anthony Blunt, because the evidence about another Soviet agent in MI5 came from an impeccable GRU source: Igor Gouzenko. The stocky, twenty-six year-old Red Army cipher clerk had smuggled out the GRU cables that led to the arrest of the atomic spy Allan Nunn May, exposed Soviet espionage rings in Canada and the United States, and provided MI5 with some startling information about cipher traffic he had seen two years earlier in Moscow.

When Gouzenko gave his secret testimony in February 1946 before the Royal Canadian Commission, he recalled that the GRU ran two agents who had the similar cryptonym of 'Elli'. (American intelligence sources confirm that this was not an unusual Soviet practice.) Since they operated on different sides of the Atlantic, there was little room for confusion.

One of the cryptograms had appeared in a telegram from Moscow on 24 August 1945. This castigated Gouzenko's chief, Colonel Zabotkin, for giving Ambassador Zarubin a 'report on financial credits' which 'had uncovered the identity of our source on the objective ELLI.' Gouzenko identified this female 'Elli' as Kay Willsher. She confessed later to the Royal Canadian Mounted Police that she had indeed supplied information to the Soviets while working in the office of Malcolm MacDonald, Britain's high commissioner in Ottawa.

'There is some agent under the same name in Great Britain,' Gouzenko said; but he did not know who it was. Unlike the female 'Elli' – whom the RCMP designated 'Ellie' to avoid confusion – Gouzenko could not produce any documentation on the use of the male cryptonym. Nor is it clear from the Gouzenko files that have been declassified to date just how much detail he gave the commission about the male 'Elli'. But seven years later in a 6 May 1952 memorandum to the head of the RCMP's Special Branch, Gouzenko insisted that he 'was not told by somebody, *but saw the telegram myself* [his italics] concerning the person' (the male 'Elli').

Gouzenko recalled that in 'the latter part of 1942, or the beginning of 1943' he had been working the night shift at the cipher branch of the GRU headquarters in Moscow. He was sharing a worktable with Lieutenant Lubimov, a former student friend of his from the Moscow Architectural Institute, which they had both attended before joining the Red Army. Gouzenko explained how they 'quite often showed each other interesting telegrams.' On this particular night, what aroused their interest was a cable referring to a GRU agent named 'Elli' who was 'one of five of MI'. He was obviously a very important source, because 'personal contact with this man was avoided'. The telegram referred to arrangements for collecting information supplied from him at a *dubok* (the Soviet intelligence nomenclature for a dead drop) in a graveyard 'in a split between the stones of a particular tomb'.

This particular cable struck Gouzenko and his friend as being so 'unusual' they had a 'short talk about it'. Lubimov told Gouzenko that he had seen previous telegrams about the same agent, from which he had learned: 'This man has something Russian in his background.' Another cable from Moscow that Gouzenko recalled translating two years earlier in Canada reinforced his belief that this male 'Elli', who apparently was contacted only by *dubok*, and only every one or two months by the GRU in Britain, must be a very high-ranking MI5 officer.

The second message was a warning to the Canadian-based Zabotkin to take extra care because 'representatives of British "Greens" [counterintelligence] were due to arrive in Ottawa with the purpose of working with the local "Greens" [RCMP].' According to Wright's investigations, this cable appears to have coincided with Guy Liddell's secret visit to North America in 1944, providing additional corroboration that the leak must have been coming from a highly placed Soviet source in MI5.

No exhaustive attempt was made to uncover the identity of the Soviet agent in 'five of MI' until 1965. The Wright investigation then uncovered the cables about Gouzenko's revelations that were sent to London by Peter Dwyer. Dwyer was the MI6 representative in Washington who had flown to Ottawa to help in debriefing Gouzenko. The cable containing the information about a spy code-named 'Elli' was dated 18–19 September 1945. According to Wright, it was the only one of the entire series of telegrams that had four folds dirtied along the edges as if it had been stuffed into a pocket. Philby had also initialed and dated it – but *two days after* it had come into his office.

Analysis of the cable-traffic logs of the Soviet embassy in London revealed a dramatic increase during the week that ended on 22 September. One of these undeciphered cables sent to Moscow on 19–20 September stood out. It had been sent with the most urgent priority. Moreover, the GCHQ cryptanalysts found that a count of its number groups corresponded to the approximate length of the verbatim telegram with the grimy folds about the male 'Elli'. Since it had been sent by the Soviet intelligence section, it was obviously the message that alerted Moscow to the news of 'Elli' that Philby had received the day before from Canada. A search for high-priority messages going the other way yielded only one that could be Moscow's reply.

Wright says that by late 1965, a 'determined attack on this message' finally succeeded in breaking out the plaintext:

Consent has been obtained from the Chiefs to consult with the neighbors about STANLEY's material about their affairs in Canada. STANLEY's data is correct.

Wright recalls that at first he thought there was a mistake. 'Stanley' was clearly Philby's cryptonym. But why, he wondered, did Moscow Center's reply suggest that it doubted the warning passed on by its senior mole in MI6? The answer soon became obvious: Beria's MGB (the KGB's immediate predecessor) truly did not know about the GRU spy in MI5 code-named 'Elli'. Therefore the 'Chiefs' – the Soviet Politburo – authorized consultation with the 'neighbors' – the GRU. The subsequent flurry of cables on the London to Moscow circuit was commensurate with urgent instructions to step up security.

The 1945 Soviet signal traffic initiated that Gouzenko's revelations about the mole in MI5 caused a major flap in Moscow Center. But this was not confirmed until Wright's investigation in 1965 because twenty years earlier, neither MI5 nor MI6 had the key to break the Soviet cable traffic. Air Commodore James Easton, whom Menzies brought into MI6 as the successor to his assistant chief of staff, Colonel Claude Dansey, confirmed that C *did* know about Gouzenko's male 'Elli' in 1945. 'He told me about it at our first meeting and raised it with me regularly afterwards,' Easton has stated. 'Since Colonel Vivian was the chief of internal security, I raised 'Elli' with him, and Vivian responded that "he had his best man on it".'

The best man was Philby.

When Easton summoned the head of Section IX to his office, Philby said '*he* had *his* best man on the job.' This was Tim Milne, whom Easton described as Philby's 'closest friend and deputy in counterespionage'. Milne was 'fairly consistent in the view that the suspect was not in SIS [MI6] at all but in the Security Service [MI5].'

According to Easton, C thought David Footman was the only possible suspect in MI6, and he naturally preferred to believe Gouzenko's assertion that the spy was in MI5. Milne also shared that view. C told Easton that 'there were a number of politically doubtful characters in MI5, including the head of the counterespionage division, Guy Liddell, who had some very rum friends.'

This disparaging reference to Liddell by C could be of significance. But then again it might simply have reflected the bad blood between MI5 and MI6 rather than any serious suspicions. After all, it was C who agreed to Philby's proposal that instead of sending him to Canada to interview Gouzenko about 'Elli', MI5 should undertake the mission.

Moscow Center evidently regarded Gouzenko as a far more serious threat than Volkov had presented a month before. This time, Krotov evidently instructed Philby to remain in London where he could monitor the progress of the investigation. So instead of making the trip to Canada himself, Philby persuaded C to get MI5 to send Roger Hollis, whom Philby described as his 'opposite number' in charge of the 'section investigating Soviet and Communist affairs'. This was not completely true. Hollis appears to have been a somewhat surprising selection for a mission that would have been more appropriate for a senior member of MI5's B Division, which handled counterintelligence, or C Division, which handled security. Hollis had spent most of the war monitoring political subversion and was hardly an experienced counterintelligence officer.

The justification Philby gave in his book was that he and Hollis 'never failed to work out an agreed approach . . .' when they served on the Joint Intelligence Subcommittee dealing with Communist affairs. Another plausible explanation for choosing Hollis was that Philby's Soviet control wanted it arranged so that the MI5 officer who went to Canada would not dig too deeply into Gouzenko's allegations.

Hollis's surprisingly shallow 'Elli' investigation was later taken as further evidence that he was the Soviet agent in MI5. He was also 'violently anti-American', according to Sir William Stephenson, whom Hollis saw when he reached New York. Stephenson's biographer goes so far as to say that 'Intrepid' so distrusted Hollis that he wired London: 'Sending your man back by next available transport.'

The records show, nonetheless, that Hollis did go to Ottawa, where he and Peter Dwyer attended high-level briefings with the Canadian external affairs minister on Nunn May. The diary of Mackenzie King contains a 23 September entry noting Hollis as saying: 'The Russians have got a lot of information on the atomic bomb.' Also as early as 1946, Hollis made a second trip to Ottawa and personally questioned Gouzenko. According to Gouzenko's account, his three-minute session with 'the gentleman from England' was so brief that there was not even time for them to sit down.

Wright confirms that Gouzenko's information was given very little credibility in Hollis's 1946 dispatch from Ottawa – or in his later report. If 'Elli' existed at all, Hollis apparently suggested that he might have been a member of the Double-Cross Committee. When Gouzenko was shown the Hollis report on him in 1972, he described it as an 'old gray mare', charging that it was so full of lies and distortions that it was deliberately faked to destroy his credibility.

'If the report was written by Hollis, then there was no doubt he was a spy,' Gouzenko insisted. 'I suspect Hollis himself was 'Elli'.'

Gouzenko's story was convincing, and while not final proof, it persuaded Wright in 1965 that he had pinpointed the identity of the mole in MI5. Further evidence seeming to point to Hollis came from another Soviet defector, a lieutenant colonel named Yuri Rastvorov who fled from the Soviet embassy in Tokyo in 1953. He told the CIA how Lieutenant Skripkin, a former friend of his, had tried to defect to the British in the Far East in 1946, but his plan was blown. On a trip back to Moscow to collect his wife, Skripkin betrayed himself to MGB officers posing as MI6 contacts, was tried and shot. An examination of the Skripkin records revealed that *Hollis* had handled the case in F Division and that he had ordered the files buried away in the Registry without taking any investigative action. But when they were first examined in 1954, following Rastvorov's report to the CIA, it was thought that *Philby* was the culprit.

What is truly astonishing is that MI5 appears to have taken no steps before 1965 to mount any far-reaching investigations into the evidence of high-level Soviet penetration. This is curious because Wright disclosed that the office diary of Liddell – code-named 'Wallflowers' by Wright, who countermanded an order for the diary's destruction by Hollis – *did* take note of the Hollis and Dwyer reports on Gouzenko to the extent of recording his thoughts on who the spy 'in five of MI' might be. That Liddell relied on the disparagement of Gouzenko by Hollis (who was a long way from being the best-qualified counterintelligence officer to make such a dismissive judgement), is still more intriguing, given that he seems to have done nothing about looking into the affair.

It must be suspicious that Liddell, the head of counter-intelligence, on the eve of his promotion to deputy director of MI5, failed to order a full investigation into prima facie evidence of high-level Soviet penetrations of British Intelligence. He, after all, knew more than anyone else in MI5 about Soviet intelligence objectives and penetration operations. His failure to act when the alarm bells were sounded by Gouzenko evidently surprised Anne Last, one of MI5's most dedicated research officers. After the Burgess and Maclean defection in 1951, Last set to work with Evelyn McBarnett to compile a handwritten book on all the cases that pointed to evidence of systematic Soviet penetration of MI5. They discovered that Maxwell Knight had minuted warnings throughout the war that he was sure a Soviet spy was operating in the upper reaches of the service, but no action had been taken. They also discovered that Gouzenko's allegations had been filed away to gather dust.

'People didn't believe him,' McBarnett assured Wright when, in 1963, she showed him Gouzenko's allegations in Last's secret analysis book. 'They said he [Knight] had got it wrong. There couldn't be a spy inside MI5,' McBarnett told Wright.

Menzies evidently shared the same belief about MI6. In his postwar reorganization, Philby became head of a newly designated R5 anti-Soviet counterintelligence section. C also put him down for a 'gong' for his wartime work. Philby became a member of the Order of the British Empire in the 1946 New Year's Honours List. But it has emerged there were already some vague American suspicions of him: the unofficial OSS representative on the Double-Cross Committee, Norman Holmes Pearson, learned from John Masterman that he should be circumspect in his dealings with Philby.

Philby's phenomenal run of luck finally ran sour over his marital affairs that same year. After living with Aileen Furze for six years as man and wife, Philby, as one of the rising stars of MI6, realized, in 1946, that his marital irregularity could be a stumbling block to his career. So he made a clean breast of it to Colonel Vivian, the head of MI6 security. He also revealed that he was divorcing his first wife, Litzi Friedman, who had left him in 1938, to marry Aileen. The private ceremony took place in September at the Chelsea Registrar's office. Philby invited only his two intimate friends, Flora Solomon and Tomas Harris, as their witnesses.

The price Philby paid came when Vivian ordered a routine check on his first wife. The Registry files revealed that Litzi Friedman had been living with an Austrian Communist, a suspected Soviet agent named George Honigmann, who in 1945 had moved to Berlin. As a matter of course, Menzies learned of Philby's transgression. Normally a stickler about these matters, such was the esteem that Menzies held for Philby's talents that he did not think it necessary to order a follow-up on why Philby's former wife had run off with a Communist. But Philby's false declaration about Aileen Furze could be a potential embarrassment – so they decided to post Philby out of the country as the MI6 station chief in Turkey.

'Philby must have had rather a pleasant, interesting and extended holiday, for we did not use Istanbul much while he was there,' Easton observed. This is the impression that Philby himself conveyed in his book, suggesting that he spent much of his time on expeditions to Mount Ararat as cover for running agents across the Soviet frontier. But it is now clear that Philby also rendered more valuable service to the Soviets than tipping them off about British operations and the contacts of Ismail Akhmedov, a GRU officer who had defected to Turkey.

The full extent of the damage done by Philby in his two years in Turkey will never be known, but since MI6 had no grounds for suspicion, Menzies believed Philby was now ready for one of the most important assignments in MI6: liaison with the United States.

After receiving a telegram from headquarters in August 1949, Philby records that it took him 'less than half an hour' to make up his mind to accept the Washington post. The final decision was not his to make, although he says he accepted it 'without waiting for confirmation from my Soviet colleagues.' But it did not need second-guessing on his part to realize that Moscow Center would share his view about the 'irresistible' lure of the American job.

'At one stroke,' Philby wrote, his appointment as liaison officer to both the FBI and CIA 'would take me right back into the middle of intelligence policy making and would give me a close-up view of the American intelligence operations.' His statement that the Washington-based intelligence organizations 'were already of greater importance' than those in London was a 'tongue-in-cheek' affirmation that the Soviets must have sustained their high-level penetrations of MI5 and MI6 *despite* Philby's overseas posting.

The timing was highly opportune for the Soviets. In late summer, 1947, Congress had passed the National Security Act, which established the Central Intelligence Agency under the National Security Council 'to advise the President with respect to the integration of domestic, foreign and military policies.' The new agency absorbed its precursor, the Central Intelligence Group. This was an uneasy stepchild of the Departments of State, War and Navy that the Truman administration had established by executive order the previous year to inherit the functions of the disbanded OSS. But J. Edgar Hoover had not succeeded in making the FBI the principal US counterintelligence authority. He did, however, connive with Truman to ensure that the former OSS chief William Donovan did not become head of the CIA. That post went to a compromise candidate, Roscoe H. Hillenkoetter, an amiable admiral who authorized the CIA's first covert operations against the Soviet Union: a radio transmitter for broadcasting to the Soviet bloc and a fleet of balloons for showering Eastern Europe with propaganda leaflets.

Amateurish though these first operations were, the Cold War was heating up. By 1949, the rapidly expanding CIA posed a growing threat to the Soviet Union. The 'unlimited potentialities' open to Philby in Washington enabled him not only to act as a monitor for the Soviet intelligence service but also to assist with the infiltration of the CIA's European operations. This became clear when Easton briefed Philby on his Washington assignment, which was to redress the balance of British cooperation in favor of the CIA and away from the FBI. Easton insists there were no grounds to doubt Philby's loyalty when he departed for Washington in September 1949.

Philby anticipated problems with Hoover. But of far graver

anxiety was his briefing with the 'formidable' Maurice Oldfield, as Philby describes the counterintelligence officer who had taken over his old post as head of R5, as the anti-Soviet section of MI6 was now designated. Oldfield indoctrinated Philby for the first time into the top-secret Anglo-American investigation then under way to track down the person who had been leaking to the Soviets information from the British embassy between 1944 and 1948 and the atomic bomb data from Los Alamos.

It did not tax Philby's ingenuity to guess that the British embassy spy was his old Cambridge contemporary Donald Maclean. More significant was the fact that Philby knew within two days, from his Soviet controller in London, that Moscow also knew about the FBI investigation. This Soviet contact was later identified as Yuri Modin, an embassy official who succeeded Boris Krotov. He was also in touch with Burgess and Blunt. Philby records that he had 'been nagged for months' by his Soviet control officer in Istanbul to find out what the British were doing about the Washington embassy investigation. It seems that Moscow had already learned of the new danger to their deep-cover moles, and is yet more evidence that 'Elli' 'in five of MI' was keeping Moscow fully posted.

What Philby learned from Oldfield was that the alarm bells for this high-level penetration had not been sounded by a Soviet defector who could be so easily disparaged. They came from the most reliable source of all, SIGINT, the proverbial horse's mouth.

The 1943 Britain/USA agreement, which provided for 'a full exchange of the cryptographic systems, crypt-analytical techniques, direction-finding, radio interception and other technical communications matters,' had been extended, in 1947, by a secret pact still unacknowledged by either government and known by its acronym UKUSA (United Kingdom–United States Security Agreement). This continued the wartime arrangement for pooling SIGINT gathering and the resultant cryptanalysis of Soviet cipher traffic. When this most secret of all agreements was made, no one in the United States suspected that the Soviets had in

Philby a direct line into the British intelligence service. As one American intelligence officer put it, the UKUSA agreement was 'like opening up a party line to Moscow Center'.

The worldwide collection of Soviet traffic by the United States, Britain, Canada and Australia had the cover name Operation Bride. But it was the US Army who made the first significant breaks in the traffic that the British and Americans code-named Venona.

When Robert Lamphere arrived at FBI headquarters in 1947 to establish a counterintelligence office covering the Soviet satellite countries, he found locked in a safe in the espionage division a few pieces of paper with fragmentary decrypts from the MGB messages sent in 1944–45 by the Soviet consulate in New York to Moscow Center. Gouzenko's knowledge of how the GRU encrypted and used its 'one-time pads' provided a valuable insight into how the MGB used its similar system. The messages were first encrypted from a code book into five-digit groups. Low-priority cables were sometimes sent out in this form, but most important messages went through a second encryption process in which their five-digit groups were added (by 'false addition') to a random sequence of five-digit groups used only for that message – hence the description 'one-time pad'.

Theoretically, the enciphered message was decodable only with access to an identical cipher pad. Use of a separate additive sheet for each message endowed the one-time pad with a near-impregnable security. But cipher clerks were fallible; so was Russian bureaucracy. Sometimes a careless code clerk enciphered two messages with the same pad.

The code breakers of the US Army Security Agency (ASA) had been given a head start because in November 1944 OSS chief Donovan had purchased from the Finns some 1,500 pages from a partially charred MGB code book that had been recovered on a battlefield. In a dubious and misguided display of international probity, Secretary of State Edward Stettinius had insisted on returning the originals to the Soviets in 1945. Fortunately, Donovan had defied orders and copied them. Meredith Gardener, a cryptanalyst and linguist with ASA, used the old code book to tackle some duplicates of the cables sent by the Soviet consulate in New York.

Lamphere began making his fortnightly trips to Gardener's office at ASA headquarters across the Potomac in Arlington. Progress at first was painfully slow. 'We started with very, very fragmentary information,' Lamphere told me, 'trying to read between the lines while the code breakers worked on the messages.' The major breakthrough came after the FBI's New York field office answered Lamphere's request for help by sending him a large bundle of documents. The material dated back to a carefully executed break-in the FBI had mounted on the New York offices of the Soviet Purchasing Commission.

'When I got the material it was mostly in Russian, and it was like searching for a needle in a haystack,' Lamphere explained. 'I had no idea that it would turn out to be a gold mine.' The FBI haul included plaintext messages of the enciphered cables already intercepted by the Americans. Most valuable of all was the discovery that the trade mission had received a set of one-time code pad additives that duplicated those sent to the MGB agents in New York – the result of a bureaucratic foul-up in Moscow. With three parts of the cryptographic puzzle in his possession, Gardener hit the jackpot: he had been able to re-create the plaintexts of several enciphered messages.

From the time of this breakthrough in the spring of 1948, Lamphere began to acquire a steady stream of fully and partially decrypted Soviet reports of their intelligence networks in the United States. Working with the FBI case file for 1944, and drawing on his own knowledge of the Russian émigré community in the United States, Lamphere was able to fill in some of the gaps and develop leads that led to surveillance and arrests of Soviet operatives including Judith Coplon, a political analyst in the Foreign Agents Registration section of the Justice Department, and her contact, Valentin Alekseevich Guibitchev, a Russian attached to the Soviet UN Mission. The first clue that would later tie the Rosenbergs in to the notorious atomic espionage case emerged from a single reference in a Soviet cable to a woman with the forename of Ethel. Another lead came from a fragmentary series of decrypts that indicated someone in the British embassy in Washington had been providing the Soviets in New York with copies of high-level cable traffic between the United States and the United Kingdom.

Lamphere obtained copies of telegrams exchanged in the late spring of 1945 between Churchill and Truman. From them Gardener established a word for word translation of some of the Soviet messages – even down to the British identifying cable numbers and dates.

In the fall of 1948 Lamphere told the Washington representatives of MI5 and MI6, Peter Dwyer and Dick Thistlethwaite, about these developments. As it happened, this was shortly after the source of those leaks – Donald Maclean – had departed for a new posting at the British embassy in Cairo. Since October 1944 he had been a model of diplomatic efficiency as the first secretary in Washington, and this had led to his appointment a year later as acting head of chancellery – which included access to the code room.

In 1948 neither Lamphere, nor the British, had any reason to suspect Maclean. But the decrypts revealed that someone in the embassy was leaking very high-grade information to the Soviets. According to Lamphere, both Dwyer and Thistlethwaite were 'startled by this revelation, as well they should have been, and agreed to provide a list of possible suspects. The security damage implied by several of the Soviet cables was so serious that Lamphere expected immediate action. But when nothing happened for a week, then a month, he became concerned.

'I just couldn't believe it,' Lamphere recalled. 'I tended to say to myself: "What the hell's the matter with them that they are not getting anywhere!" His frustration with MI5 lack of progress became so intense at one point that he considered unilaterally asking the State Department to help in trying to get such an investigation going. Lamphere contends that if the situation had been reversed, with a spy in the American embassy in London, the FBI would have been working around the clock to establish, from a roster of embassy staff and the records, who could have seen the cables and what their movements were. Yet to his amazement, months passed, and his British opposite numbers had still not produced a list of suspects.

'Every month or so, when I inquired about it, I would be told that there was no new information, but that MI5 and MI6 were still working on finding that possible spy,' Lamphere recalled. When Philby arrived in Washington in October 1949 to take over as the MI6 liaison officer, Philby's immediate 'lack of friendliness' struck him forcefully. When Lamphere asked why there were no leads about the identity of the embassy spy, Philby said it was not the direct responsibility of MI6.

Lamphere did not realize of course that Philby knew who the spy had been. Nor did Lamphere know that Michael Straight's wife had tried to alert the embassy, via her psychiatrist, Dr Jennie Welderhall. But for reasons of professional etiquette, Welderhall decided not to pass on the information that Guy Burgess was a Soviet agent. Had the message been relayed, the Cambridge connection would have been an obvious pointer to Donald Maclean as the spy in the British embassy.

Yet in his book, Philby goes out of his way to heap scorn on the FBI, which, he says, 'was in sorry shape when I reached Washington.' He blames its 'conspicuous' record of failure for not catching Maclean or Burgess: but Lamphere is adamant that he never stopped reminding the British about the case. And the evidence now available certainly confirms that London's failure to identify Maclean – and consequently to implicate Burgess and Philby in the same Soviet network – before May 1951 was not because of any failure on the American end. The real culprit could only have been the Soviet mole in MI5 who ensured that the investigation crawled forward at a snail's pace.

The MI5 file on the investigation into the spy in the British embassy remains, after nearly forty years, officially secret. But Lamphere is not the only American counterintelligence expert to have assured me that there is really no excuse for the incompetent way in which MI5 handled the case. The information may have been incomplete, but as Lamphere points out, by 1949 the clues that should have made Maclean the obvious suspect had piled up. The clincher was his weekly train trips via New York to Massachusetts where his wife Melinda was staying at her mother's. These weekly trips coincided with the dates of the Soviet cables transmitting the Anglo-American conversations to Moscow.

'MI5 was not a very efficient outfit,' Lamphere told me. 'One of our criticisms of it was that there were too many case officers sitting at desks who had no real experiences of field investigations.' Another factor was the 'bad faith' of the British, an issue that still disturbs Lamphere because he knew that Paterson and Philby had lied to him about there being 'no progress' in the investigations in London. It is a curious, but nevertheless consequential, fact that the failure to conduct a speedy investigation – and therefore the responsibility for organizing the coverup over Maclean – can only be attributed to B Division, whose head was none other than Guy Liddell. Moreover, there is good reason to believe that nothing would ever have been done about the embassy spy case had it not been for another code-break. Again, this was the result of Lamphere's and Gardener's efforts and it revealed that Dr Klaus Fuchs had supplied most of the secrets of the atomic bomb to Moscow agents.

This was an explosive discovery, causing Lamphere's investigation into the possible leakages of atomic secrets after the Soviets on September 23, 1949, had exploded an atomic bomb of their own. The stunning news that the Russians had nuclear weapons a good five to ten years earlier than the best military intelligence estimates prompted J. Edgar Hoover to take action. He ordered Lish Whitson, the head of the FBI Espionage Section, to investigate whether leaks from the Manhattan Project had been penetrated in the United States. It was already known that the Cambridge scientist Allan Nunn May had breached the Canadian end of the project. Gardener had already provided Lamphere with a newly deciphered 1944 MGB decrypt containing references to the gaseous-diffusion process of uranium enrichment.

Lamphere dropped everything to work on this message. With the help of a friend in the Atomic Energy Commission, he located the original paper of which the message was a summary. The second part of the decrypt dealt with the agent, or messenger, who had provided the information, and the two parts together, according to Lamphere, confirmed beyond any reasonable doubt that the MGB in New York City 'had had an agent within the British mission to the Manhattan Project.'

The prime suspects were: Rudolf Peierls, another scientist whom Lamphere declined to name, and Dr Klaus Fuchs, the author of the paper on gaseous diffusion. A search of the files produced derogatory information only on Fuchs. The first was from a Gestapo file from 1933, which identified Fuchs as a Communist: the Germans had considered him dangerous enough to issue a warrant for his arrest. The second derived from Fuchs's name in the notebooks of Israel Halperin. The Canadian scientist had been charged – but not convicted – of acting as a GRU agent on evidence supplied by Igor Gouzenko four years earlier.

Lamphere could not be absolutely certain of the identity of the Soviet agent in the Manhattan Project, but he was so sure it must be Fuchs that he set out his reasoning, along with the evidence, in a top-secret letter addressed to SMOTH at the British embassy.

This time the British responded within a few weeks. They too considered Fuchs to be the prime suspect. But since there could be no question of ever revealing the Venona decrypts in court, the only way to get the evidence to convict him of espionage was to coax a confession from Fuchs. William Skardon was the best interrogator in MI5. His first interview with Fuchs took place on 21 December at Harwell, which the nuclear scientist had joined in 1946 as head of the Theoretical Physics Section. With patient but wearing questioning, Skardon, a deferential but infinitely persistent former policeman, gradually wore down the physicist, whose high forehead made him a living caricature of the egghead scientist. On 24 January 1950 Fuchs confessed to his espionage and to his double life, which he described as being in a state of 'controlled schizophrenia'. Six months later Fuchs pleaded guilty at the

Old Bailey to a four-count indictment under the Official Secrets Act. The brief thirty-minute trial ended with the judge sentencing him to a fourteen-year prison term.

Fuchs's admission of guilt spared the British government from trying to obtain a conviction when not even an 'in camera' jury could be allowed to learn of the political and intelligence secrets implicit in the Fuchs Venona traffic. That was the problem confronting the FBI when Lamphere followed up a lead given by Fuchs that finally uncovered the identity of the mysterious 'Ethel'.

After Fuchs had identified a Philadelphia chemist named Harry Gold as one of the contact men with the Soviets, Gold led FBI investigators to David Greenglass, a US Army machinist who had worked on the atomic-bomb casing at Los Alamos. In turn, Greenglass incriminated his brother-in-law, Julius Rosenberg, as one of the principals in the Soviet spy ring in New York. Rosenberg denied he was in the service of the Soviets, but other Venona decrypts tied him to two of his former Communist college friends, Max Elitcher and Joel Barr, whom the cables had revealed as feeding technical information to the Soviets.

Julius and Ethel Rosenberg, and the rest of their group, were arrested in 1950. Indictments followed for their conspiracy to transmit classified military information to the Soviet Union. But none of the clinching circumstantial evidence contained in the Soviet cable traffic could be revealed by the prosecution at the lengthy and controversial trials that ended in stiff jail terms for their associates and the death penalty for the Rosenbergs. No presidential pardon saved the Rosenbergs from the electric chair in 1953. They went to the execution chamber still protesting their innocence. In the minds of many Americans they are still martyrs and sacrificial victims to McCarthyism.

Klaus Fuchs, the scientist who supplied the Rosenberg network with the secrets of the atomic bomb, emerged from a British prison in 1959. He returned to nuclear research in East Germany, a national hero and a member of the Communist Party Central Committee.

Arguably, MI5's failure to pick up the blatant trail of clues about his treachery ranked alongside the treason of both the Rosenbergs and Fuchs. 'Traitor by courtesy of incompetence' is how *The Times* of London headlined Dr Fuchs's obituary notice on 29 January 1988. The degree of incompetence shown by MI5 in the Fuchs case was so devastating as to be criminal. There is now a mass of evidence showing that after Fuchs had fled Germany in 1934, he had maintained his connections with the exiled KPD Communists in England.

Even more astonishing was why MI5 gave Fuchs clearance for top-secret work in 1941, when Fuchs had made no secret of his Communist activities in support of the exiled German KPD run by his friend Jürgen Kuczynski. Fuchs's communism was apparent to those who knew him before the war at Edinburgh University, where he worked in Max Born's laboratory. Nor did Fuchs make any secret of his beliefs during his 1940 stay in an internment camp on the Isle of Man and later in Canada.

Yet a year later Fuchs was brought back to England. Cleared by MI5, he joined the team at Birmingham University led by Otto Frisch and Rudolf Peierls, who were working on the top-secret Tube Alloys atomic-bomb research.

Nor was there any MI5 objection the following year when Fuchs achieved British naturalization. It is difficult to believe that MI5, who we know had closely monitored the student Communists at Cambridge, was not by then aware that the GRU had also made Birmingham University another of its prime targets because of its extensive scientific and engineering research. The faculty and student body at Birmingham hosted a strong Communist organization and even before the war had become the refuge for many of the Cambridge Communist activists, including Professor Derwent Thomson, Blunt's friend Roy Pascal and his militant Marxist wife, Fanya.

It was also MI5 that gave Fuchs his clean bill of health to transfer to the Manhattan Project at the end of 1943 and the US Army and FBI received assurances from MI5 that it had thoroughly vetted all the members of the British mission.

Therefore there was no suspicion of his trustworthiness when, in August 1944, at the personal request of Professor Rudolph Peierls, Fuchs transferred to the heart of the Manhattan Project – the assembly and design laboratory at Los Alamos. After attending the early conferences that laid the theoretical groundwork for the hydrogen bomb, and working on preparations for the atomic-bomb test at Bikini Atoll in 1946, Fuchs returned to England in July of that year.

Even though Nunn May had admitted by then he was a Soviet spy, MI5 evidently did not see fit to check either its own, or the captured Gestapo files, when Fuchs became head of the Theoretical Physics Section and deputy scientific director of Harwell in 1940. This burgeoning, top-secret government research station near Oxford was supposedly dedicated to the peaceful development of nuclear reactors. In reality, Britain had assembled its own team of scientists and engineers clandestinely to develop its own atomic bomb after being cut off from US atomic secrets when Congress passed the McMahon Act in 1946.

Had it not been for Venona and the FBI, Fuchs's career as a physicist might have continued until, like Blunt, he was rewarded with a knighthood. It is significant that Venona information had been used to extract from Fuchs a full confession *without any offer of immunity*. He admitted that since 1941 he had been in touch with a Russian he knew as 'Alexander' – otherwise Simon Davidovitch Kremer, secretary to Moscow's military attaché in London and a senior GRU agent runner. In the autumn of 1942, 'Alexander' passed Fuchs on to a new control officer he claimed he knew only as 'Sonja'. This was Ruth Kuczynski, the sister of Jürgen, who, in preparation for her deep-cover mission in England, had married a Briton named Len Beurton. Sonja had come from Switzerland in 1940 to set up the family home in Summertown near Oxford.

A GRU major, Sonja ran a stable of spies from her cottage, which was not far from MI5's wartime outpost at Blenheim Palace. For over a year she met with Fuchs – usually at Banbury, the nursery-rhyme market town midway between Birmingham and Oxford. She transmitted his written reports to Moscow in cipher via her radio with its aerial strung out in her loft. The ever-resourceful Sonja had smuggled the radio set into Britain with some of its key components concealed in her children's teddy bears. Complex mathematical equations that she could not encode went to Kremer at the embassy for transmission by the diplomatic pouch.

A damaging indictment of the failure of the wartime counter-intelligence effort mounted by MI5 against Soviet infiltration is Peter Wright's revelation – from his inside knowledge of the case file – that Sonja's importance did not become clear *until 1972*. Only at that late date did a sophisticated computer analysis break open a large batch of GRU messages code-named HASP. These had been transmitted by the Soviets from Britain during the war and intercepted by the Swedes, who passed them to the British in 1959. These decrypts yielded literally dozens of cryptonyms of British scientists and journalists who fed intelligence of military value to the Soviets during the war. Among them were the Cambridge-educated cinema specialist Ivor Montagu and J. B. S. Haldane, the biochemist who, during the war, worked on secret projects for the Admiralty. Most revealing of all was the series of messages relayed by Kremer, the GRU *rezident*, describing his meetings with Sonja.

Wright says: 'Kremer's messages utterly destroyed the established beliefs.' The conventional wisdom in MI5, based on the authority of Alexander Foote, who defected back to the British in 1947, was that Sonja had given up her spying when she left Switzerland. But the traffic emanating from the Soviet embassy in 1941 proved beyond doubt that Sonja was running a bevy of agents *before* she began handling Fuchs. The Hasp traffic contained not only details of the payments Sonja made, but the times and durations of her own radio broadcasts.

The sheer volume of those messages suggests that even such a careful clandestine transmitter as Sonja's would have been picked up by the MI5 department known as the Radio Security Service (RSS). Its mission was to scan the broadcasting frequencies to monitor and track down any illegal radio transmission. Churchill, after 1941 when Stalin became an ally, had embargoed any attempt to eavesdrop on the Soviet embassy. But a rash prime ministerial injunction would never have been applied to the illegal transmissions of undercover agents of Moscow.

If so, who in MI5 failed to authorize action against this most active of Soviet spies? Still more curious is Sonja's failure to leave England for sanctuary in East Germany in 1947 when, after Foote's defection, two MI5 investigators arrived on her doorstep to interview her. One was the ace interrogator William Skardon. Yet even after Sonja's cover had been blown, she still did not depart for East Germany until 1950. This was *after* Fuchs made his full confession, in which he named *Sonja* as his Soviet controller!

Even more curious is that Sonja was never, at any time, put under surveillance by MI5, either during or after the war. Yet Soviet defector Walter Krivitsky had, according to a reliable source, tipped off the British in 1940 that Kremer was the GRU *rezident* and the presumption was that any sustained tailing of him must have revealed his contacts with Sonja.

Either the redoubtable Sonja was unbelievably lucky, or MI5 was incredibly incompetent – or this key GRU agent had an invisible GRU ally *inside* MI5 who was senior enough to quash both the wartime investigation of the radio messages and any postwar investigation. None of Blunt's wartime work for MI5 could have provided him with the access, or the authority, to bury RSS reports or stop investigations of such obvious leads. Nor was he in a position to arrange Fuchs's clean bill of health for top-secret atomic work, or to provide the protection that it seems Sonja received until 1950.

Ironically, the Russians, thanks to Fuchs, probably knew more about Britain's top-secret race to build its own atomic bomb than did the Americans. It was not until May 1948 that a member of the US Atomic Energy Commission on a visit to Harwell discovered that the research reactors he saw there had been designed to produce plutonium and *not* power!

Another curious twist to the Fuchs–Sonja case is contained in Professor Robert Chadwell Williams's carefully documented study of the Fuchs case, which cites evidence from a former MI6 officer that suggests that the atomic spy *did* meet Sonja again in 1947. If this source is reliable – and the British government is covering up another skeleton – it raises the possibility that from 1947 onward, the authorities *knew* that Fuchs was a Soviet spy. Did the deep-cover Soviet mole 'Elli' have a hand in protecting Fuchs from exposure? An equally plausible explanation is that any espionage Fuchs carried out was believed to be less important than harnessing his considerable talents as a physicist in Britain's secret race to build her own bomb. In the eyes of Prime Minister Attlee, and the half-dozen Labour Cabinet members who had secretly authorized the £100 million atomic-bomb project without parliamentary approval, the possession of nuclear weapons was Britain's ticket to retaining her status as one of the Big Three powers. There is now good reason for believing that if the FBI had not intervened and presented the incontrovertible evidence of their so-called Foocase files, MI5 would never have moved against Fuchs.

The same deduction of either criminal negligence, or complicity by officers of MI5, can be drawn from the case of Bruno Pontecorvo, the Italian nuclear physicist who had worked in the Paris laboratories of the unashamedly Communist scientist Pierre Joliot-Curie in 1940. After the fall of France, Pontecorvo headed for the United States. In 1943 he joined the British atomic-research team in Canada, eventually working on heavy-water research alongside Nunn May at the Chalk River facilities in Ontario. The RCMP relied on assurances of a British security screening of Pontecorvo that had never taken place! Nor did any derogatory information surface from his Communist past when he transferred to Harwell in 1949 and was granted British citizenship. He underwent security clearances no fewer than six times by UKAEA officials who relied on data supplied by MI5.

Pontecorvo had originally hoped to work on nuclear energy in the United States. But the FBI, suspicious of his past, had arranged for a discreet search of his American home and found incriminating Communist documents. This information was passed in 1949 to the MI6 officer in Washington: Kim Philby. He suppressed the file, but alerted his Soviet controller. Pontecorvo was then tipped off by the Soviet underground network in Britain and induced to defect. As one of the few scientists with an intimate working knowledge of the reactor technology necessary to produce lithium deuteride, Pontecorvo was a valuable asset for the Soviets' H-bomb project. His damning FBI report did not come to light until after Pontecorvo ended up in Moscow.

The news that Pontecorvo was behind the Iron Curtain did not break for over a year, but his 'assumed defection' had occurred barely six months after the trial of Klaus Fuchs. To the FBI it was another security disaster for the British. Whether it was another success for 'Elli' was not clear. But because of the remarkable similarities to the Fuchs case, an immediate investigation by MI5 into the adequacy of its vetting procedures would have been in order. But there is no evidence that Liddell, who in his capacity as deputy director bore the ultimate administrative responsibility, ever considered ordering a full investigation. What is even odder is that Liddell, despite his long track record in counterespionage, did not order a major review, or internal investigation, into security-service vetting procedures.

The chronic incompetence of the British secret services did not contaminate the FBI alone. The CIA was soon to suffer similar symptoms that could be attributed only to an astonishing run of bad luck – or to infection from too close an association with MI6.

The first American organization afflicted was the Office of Policy Coordination (OPC). Though it sheltered under the umbrella of the CIA, OPC was not yet an integral part of the agency. The OPC was a euphemism for all covert action programs, i.e. psychological, international organizations, paramilitary, political and economic activities and propaganda. It was set up in 1948 to run anti-Soviet subversion operations on a worldwide basis under the direction of the Department of Defense. The OPC head was Frank Wisner, a prematurely balding, self-important forty-three-year-old who had acquired a taste and talent for covert activity while serving in the OSS with distinction in Istanbul and the Balkans. His aim was to take a leaf from the Comintern book and turn the weapons of subversion and infiltration against the Soviets and their satellite regimes. This was nothing new.

Turning the tables on the Bolsheviks was a dream that had preoccupied British intelligence in the immediate aftermath of the Russian Revolution. But the revolutionaries in Moscow had proved to be more devious and cunning than anticipated. MI6 had been badly burned in the early twenties when its agents, including Sidney Reilly and Robert Bruce Lockhart, had been trapped by the cleverly contrived plots of 'The Trust', one of the more deadly brainchildren of Dzerzhinski's fertile scheming.

Stewart Menzies, then a rising star of MI6 in the thirties, had covertly channeled British funds and support to anti-Bolshevik organizations that included General Aleksandr Pavlovich Kutepov's Combat Organization to act as an irritant to the Soviets. Many groups of dispossessed and disaffected Byeloruss-ians – who adopted exotic code-names such as the Prometheus Network, the Intermarium Program and the Abramtchik Faction – were already penetrated by the Soviets before World War II broke out, when the Abwehr recruited the leaders and members in 1939 to the German cause. Two years later when Germany invaded Russia, many Ukrainian nationalists rallied under Stefan Bandera, the head of the 'Organization of Ukrainian Nationalists' (OUN) which later formed links to Hitler's SD. Many of the leaders of the so-called anti-Bolshevik factions became avowed Nazis and Hitler's puppets in the German occupation of Byelorussia and the Ukraine.

In 1945, when these shadowy organizations were once again pushed toward the West by the tides of Soviet victory, Menzies's dream was revived. Despite their Nazi records, C believed that their supposed anti-Communist zeal, inflamed by the Soviet takeover of Eastern Europe, would make them ideal mercenaries for launching an underground war against the Communist bloc.

Many of the surviving members of Intermarium, Prometheus and the Abramtchik, along with an ill-assorted band of Caucasian separatists, Albanian monarchists and anti-Tito Yugoslavs, were secretly funded and reemployed by MI6. A united front known as the Anti-Bolshevik Bloc of Nations (ABN) was formed by the merger of three constituent groups: the Organization of Ukrainian Nationalists (OUN) from the Ukraine and Polish Galicia, the Prometheus League representing Poland and White Russia, and the Intermarium Confederation, which claimed to represent the old Catholic states of the Austro–Hungarian Empire. The Americans were also separately rallying Soviet-bloc exiles into a Committee for a Free Europe, nominally a privately funded operation that included Allen Dulles, who would later become head of the CIA, and Dwight D. Eisenhower.

How best to employ the combined resources of the ABN, funded primarily by the British, became a matter of secret debate inside MI6 and the Foreign Office. In 1948, a Russian Committee, under Gladwyn Jebb, was set up with the declared objective 'to liberate the countries within the Soviet orbit by any means short of war.' With the shining example of Anglo-American successes with 'Double-Cross' German agents in mind, counter-intelligence officers in Britain and the United States seized on the idea that there was an underground army of émigré East European nationalists ripe for recruitment and infiltration into the Soviet bloc to foment revolution and unrest.

President Tito's break with Stalin in 1948 encouraged the British and Americans to believe that an opportunity for successful covert operations existed in the Balkans. The target selected was not Yugoslavia, but the mountainous country to the south, Albania. The Americans accepted the Foreign Office's Russian Committee proposal for a plan 'to detach Albania from the Soviet orbit'.

When Philby arrived in Washington – where his duties included liaising with Frank Wisner at OPC – he participated in the strategy meetings for the Anglo-American covert operation to use Albanian émigrés to overthrow the Communist government there. Malta would be the forward base for an operation for which the Americans supplied the finances and logistical support from their Libyan air-force bases. 'Kim was the one who made all the operational decisions,' recalled George Jellicoe, a member of the British planning team. Alluding to the bitter wrangling that went on between the British and Americans, Philby archly states it was 'perhaps surprising that the operation ever got off the ground.'

Lives and Anglo-American goodwill would have been saved if Philby had *not* applied his talents to pulling the disparate operation together. But by alerting the Soviets to every one of its operational details, he ensured the failure of the entire operation – from the first night in October 1949 when the initial boatloads of British-trained agents landed on the rugged Albanian coastline. In what Philby vaingloriously characterized as a rehearsal for the CIA's Bay of Pigs operation twenty years later against Cuba, the British and Americans continued to send infiltrators across the border and parachute their agents into Albania to certain capture and execution until November 1950.

Philby encouraged laying the blame for the Albanian debacle – with some justification – on inadequate security at the émigré training bases in the Mediterranean. But others besides the perennially suspicious Hoover were beginning to wonder if there were more sinister reasons than sheer bad luck to explain why every operation against the Soviets involving the British had turned sour. The suspicion began to grow in the months after the termination of the Albanian adventure, especially after another Venona code-break gave the FBI an additional important clue to the source of the 1944 leak at the British embassy. By late November or early December 1994, Lamphere knew that the spy's code-name was 'Homer' and that he had made weekly trips to New York throughout 1944 to meet his Soviet contact.

'This information should have dramatically shortened the list of possible suspects,' Lamphere contends. 'Yet when I pressed Geoff Paterson [the MI5 liaison officer] to come up with such a list, he'd report back that London said there was "nothing new" on the investigation.'

Whoever was sitting on the investigation in MI5 must have realized that the latest 'Homer' information from Washington had narrowed down the choices. The FBI could not be stalled much longer. Hoover's concern was growing that MI5 was paralysed by incompetence. If the Americans discovered the identity of 'Homer', it would be more difficult to contain the damage and would start a hunt for the MI5 officer responsible for two years of inactivity.

The 'Homer' development arrived at the Foreign Office just at the time that Patrick (later Sir Patrick) Reilly assumed responsibility for intelligence and security and the chairmanship of the Joint Intelligence Committee. He is on the public record as stating that it was this information, received 'at a fairly late stage', that enabled him to cut down the list of suspected officials, ranging from code clerks to first secretaries, from thirty-five to nine.

'The investigation of these people,' Reilly explained, 'was a long and tedious job, and so it was not surprising that for a long time MI5 had nothing to report.' But Lamphere nonetheless finds it difficult to believe that it took Reilly and MI5 another year to winnow down the short list of nine candidates to pinpoint Maclean. Lamphere says 'Homer's' frequent train trips to upstate New York would have been a simple matter to check and connect to Maclean, who made weekly visits to his wife, Melinda, at the Dunbar family farm. Then there was Moscow's incautious congratulation on the birth of a child. Lamphere believes that the FBI could have tracked him down if MI5 had only seen fit to provide either the long list of thirty-five or the short list of nine. To this day, Lamphere still cannot understand why the British kept the FBI totally in the dark about the investigation.

Sir Patrick Reilly, a former senior Foreign Office official, begs to differ. He is on record as insisting that it is 'pure fabrication' and 'totally untrue that the Foreign Office told MI5 not to inform the FBI that Maclean had been identified.' Furthermore, Reilly contends, Sir Percy Sillitoe had 'kept Hoover informed with special messages which were sent over for special security through MI6 and therefore, of course, through Philby.'

'I was in charge of the American FBI investigation in the "Homer"-Maclean matter, and I would be glad to swear to this in a court of inquiry, or court of law, that we in the FBI were never informed of the identification of Maclean until after his flight,' Lamphere wrote to me after reading Reilly's assurances given in a 1986 letter to British historian Dr Anthony Glees. 'I was also told by Arthur Martin that it was Foreign Office pressure and the sensitivity of the investigation which caused MI5 to hold out on us.'

Even if the Foreign Office prevented the FBI from learning that the hunt for 'Homer' was narrowing down, 'Elli', the mole in MI5, and Philby both knew all about it, as did Moscow Center. The Soviets might well have considered it prudent to have Maclean's control officer in Cairo alert him. This would explain why his behaviour in Cairo suddenly became increasingly erratic in the early spring of 1950. Maclean's bouts of drinking worsened in their violence and frequency. On 8 May 1950 he broke into the apartment of a woman who worked at the American embassy, drank her whiskey, and smashed up the furniture. The American ambassador lodged a formal complaint. The Foreign Office recalled Maclean to London on sick leave and urged him to seek psychiatric counseling.

Surprisingly, George Carey Foster, who was then Foreign Office head of security, stated that 'Maclean was not under suspicion' when he was sent home 'for what was considered a nervous breakdown'. That there was considerable confusion at the British end of the 'Homer' investigation appears confirmed by the decision, after he had had six months of sick leave, to offer Maclean the appointment as head of the American department at the Foreign Office in November 1950. Maclean gratefully accepted. He bought a large house in the village of Tatsfield, an hour and twenty minutes from London by commuter train.

The Foreign Office decision must have been only marginally

less explicable in 1950 than it appears with the full knowledge of FBI hindsight.

Yet no one, either in MI5 or the Foreign Office, appears at the time to have taken note that from 1945 on, Maclean had been the UK representative on the Combined Policy Committee that shared information on atomic research. From late 1947 he was the committee's secretary, enabling him to pass the minutes of meetings discussing classification policies and strategic reserves of uranium directly to the Soviets. In his official capacity he also received a pass that allowed him unescorted access – at all hours – to the Atomic Energy Commission's headquarters.

The Foreign Office – presumably with MI5 acquiescence – not only permitted but actively encouraged Maclean to take over the American desk. He may have left his career as a future ambassador in the wreckage of a Cairo apartment, but he was still a valuable Soviet spy. Thanks to the clannishness of the Foreign Office, Maclean continued for another six months to supply Moscow with valuable information on Anglo-American foreign-policy decisions during the first crucial months of the Korean War.

The degree to which His Majesty's Foreign Office protected its own was nothing short of amazing in the cases of both Maclean and Burgess. The most outrageous breaches of diplomatic etiquette and propriety had not brought the irrepressible Burgess anything more than a reprimand. As a member of a sub-committee convened during the 1948 UN General Assembly in Paris, Brian Urquhart, an assistant to the secretary general of the United Nations at the time, vividly recalls his encounter with Burgess at meetings attended by the foreign ministers of Britain, Greece, Bulgaria, Yugoslavia and Albania, 'the latter being eminently conventional, old-fashioned Communists'. They were even more outraged than the Western diplomats by Burgess's appearance one evening 'drunk and heavily painted and powdered for a night on the town.' According to Urquhart: 'When I mentioned this episode to Sir Alexander Cadogan, the head of the British delegation, he replied icily that the Foreign

Office traditionally tolerated innocent eccentricity.'

There was, it seems, a limit even to the Foreign Office's toleration of such eccentricities. Shortly afterward, Burgess was moved to the Far Eastern Division where he helped influence Britain's decision to recognize Mao Tse-tung's Communist takeover of China in the summer of 1949. The 1955 British government white paper on the Burgess–Maclean defection sought to belittle the damage the diplomats had done. But judging by the evidence of Burgess's initials on Foreign Office documents declassified under the thirty-year rule, he avidly devoured a vast range of top-secret information during the critical period running up to the outbreak of the Korean War. What he was able to pass on to the Soviets ranged from military-intelligence reports from General MacArthur's headquarters in Tokyo to Joint Intelligence Committee assessments reflecting Anglo-American intelligence about the disposition of forces in Korea.

Burgess's career as an increasingly outspoken member of the Far Eastern Division came to an end after his autumn 1949 trip to Gibraltar and Tangier. It turned into what Goronwy Rees described as a 'wild odyssey of indiscretions', insults to the local MI6 representative, and homosexual drunkenness that left him either brawling or singing in a loud voice at bars: 'Little boys are cheap today/Cheaper than yesterday.' The protests reached the Foreign Office even before Burgess returned to London. But because he was a protégé of Hector McNeil, George Carey Foster decided to give him one more chance. So instead of getting the sack, which he expected, Burgess was posted, with the rank of second secretary, to the British embassy in Washington.

The appointment was even more extraordinary given Burgess's well-articulated dislike of US global policies, and his ill-concealed loathing of all things American, which he shared with Blunt and the other Cambridge agents.

'Guy, for God's sake, don't make a pass at Paul Robeson' was the advice Burgess said he was given by those who warned him to avoid discussions about communism, homosexuality and the color bar in the United States. The occasion of his celebrated remarks was the bon voyage celebration Burgess threw for himself in July 1950 at his second-floor flat in Bond Street. Packed into the main room, according to Goronwy Rees, was an odd assortment of strange bedfellows including Jackie Hewit, back in residence as housekeeper; the secretary of state for Scotland, Hector McNeil; Guy Liddell, the deputy director of MI5; and 'two working-class young men who had obviously been picked up off the streets that very evening.' The old wartime Bentinck Street crowd showed up in force, led by Patricia Parry, Lady Rothschild, David Footman and Anthony Blunt.

'The only connection between us was Guy,' Rees observed. 'I remember thinking that the oddest thing about the party was that no one seemed to think there was anything odd about it at all.'

Yuri Modin, Burgess's Soviet control officer, was – for obvious reasons – the one missing link in the festivities. But Moscow Center cannot have been pleased at the prospect of this particular agent exhibiting all the symptoms of going wildly beyond prudent control and landing up in Washington, when they knew that the FBI were closing in on Maclean. Because the Cambridge agents knew each other, Burgess was becoming a wild card, an errant joker with the potential to self-destruct – and to take the whole pack with him.

That same sense of unease must have flashed through Blunt's mind. We now know that it concerned Philby, because he accepted responsibility for putting Burgess up as his houseguest in Washington. 'In normal circumstances it would have been quite wrong for two secret operatives to occupy the same premises. But the circumstances were not normal. From the earlier days our careers had intertwined . . .'

The welcome that awaited Burgess at the British embassy on Massachusetts Avenue in the sticky heat of early August 1950 had all the underlying tension that might presage an afternoon thunderstorm sweeping up the Potomac from Chesapeake Bay. With the Soviet controller's assent, Philby quickly took Burgess into his confidence about the steady progress of the 'Homer' investigation.

Time was running out for the Cambridge spies. The FBI was forcing the pace on the Foreign Office. Within a matter of months, possibly weeks, Maclean would be interrogated as a suspected Soviet spy. Philby and the other members of the network would no longer be able to count on protection from what he characterized as 'a genuine mental block, which stubbornly resisted the belief that respected members of the Establishment could do such a thing.'

Guy Burgess arrived at the British embassy in Washington during the first week of August 1950. His official duties as second secretary included serving as an alternate member of the British delegation on the Far East Commission, the eleven-nation UN body set up in December 1945 to monitor the terms by which Japan fulfilled her obligations under the treaty of surrender. State Department officials who worked with Burgess on the War Criminals subcommittee recalled the 'odor of liquor' on his breath and his 'very poor personal appearance in contrast to the usual type of person associated with the British embassy.'

In another official capacity, liaising with the Department of State, Burgess had access to American policy makers and their sensitive documents. He was, therefore, able to pass on to the Soviets much valuable information during the critical opening months of the Korean War when General Douglas MacArthur drove the invading North Korean army back to the Yalu River and was pressing the Truman administration to allow him to carry his counteroffensive across the Yalu and into China.

According to FBI interrogations of Burgess's Washington associates he was deeply concerned that 'the United States might try to control the Chinese situation'. Burgess made no secret of his anti-Americanism, and he was 'very restless and agitated and had a feeling that the United States was headed for doom.' When he was drunk, Burgess was prone to make a pass at any convenient male drinking companion. But he *never* betrayed his Communist sympathies to a single Washington acquaintance. Burgess pined for the trappings of the British Establishment, and he never missed an opportunity to express his disgust for the uncouth and ill-mannered Americans. Ironically he shamelessly cultivated the bluebloods of the Metropolitan Club in hopes of an invitation to join Washington's select establishment.

One aspect of American life that meshed with Burgess's own passions was the nation's love affair with the automobile. He quickly acquired an imposing twelve-cylinder 1941 white Lincoln convertible, which he drove with wild abandon. One of the first trips he made in his new pride and joy was to New York, where he looked up Valentine Lawford. Although the former British diplomat was a fellow Cambridge graduate, the two had never been close, but Burgess insisted on taking him for a spin around Oyster Bay, during the course of which he seemed despondent and said he was 'thinking of leaving the Foreign Office.'

In November 1950, Burgess's spirits were temporarily revived when he was given the task of showing the capital to Anthony Eden, who wrote: 'Truly I enjoyed every moment of my stay in Washington.' An Etonian bond united the elegantly dressed future Conservative prime minister and the disheveled second secretary with his grubby fingernails and his distinctive blue-and-black-striped old-school tie, his only concession to sartorial respectability.

Burgess's habits, the unkempt hair, frequent intoxication and dirty nails, did not escape Dr Wilfrid Basil Mann, a British nuclear physicist. He had worked on the atomic-bomb project in Canada in 1943, and since 1948 had been at the embassy as Ministry of Supply liaison officer with the CIA on atomic-energy intelligence. Burgess occupied the office diagonally opposite his, in the small main chancellery, causing Mann to note him as 'the uncouth character who sported a battered duffle coat.' Burgess purposely kept his own door ajar and sought any excuse for a chat.

Philby and Geoffrey Paterson, the MI6 and MI5 liaison officers in the embassy, occupied adjoining offices on the same corridor with Philby's secretary, Esther Whitfield. A matronly Foreign Office spinster, Whitfield had been in the MI6 office in Istanbul, where she first encountered Burgess on his visit to Turkey in 1948. She lived with the Philby family in the frame house at 4100 Nebraska Avenue in northwest Washington, where Burgess had taken up residence in the basement. According to her, the adult members of the household knew all about his nightly forays.

The FBI file on Burgess makes it plain that Inspector Roy Blick of the Washington Metropolitan Police Vice Squad also knew about Burgess. Blick kept tabs on the Washington bars and rest rooms where Burgess sought out homosexual companionship. The threats of eviction with which Philby faced Burgess whenever he brought male companions back to the family home were never carried out. Philby knew that his own security depended on keeping an eye on his wayward partner in crime. Miss Whitfield also seems to have taken the scene in her stride, showing amused tolerance of the rumors put about by Burgess that she was his office romance. But she vigorously denied that her friendship with Burgess ever extended to telling him about the progress of the 'investigation to identify Maclean'.

What Whitfield did not know was that her boss was keeping both Burgess and Moscow abreast of the developments in the 'Homer' investigation. By December 1950 it became apparent that Patrick Reilly, the newly appointed Foreign Office under-secretary with special responsibility for security and intelligence matters, was taking steps to resolve the case. The unease about events beyond their control in London added to the psychological pressures on Maclean's two co-conspirators in Washington. In turn, this caused considerable concern in Moscow Center, because the unique history of the Cambridge agents made each highly vulnerable to the exposure of a single member.

The errant behavior of Burgess took a dramatic turn on 19 January 1951. He started taking a perverse delight in upsetting the leading members of the US counterintelligence community. On that particular evening, the Philbys were hosting a dinner at home for the CIA's chief Soviet espionage specialist, Bill Harvey, and his wife. Also invited were James Angleton (later to become the agency's counterintelligence chief) and his wife; Robert

Lamphere, from the FBI Soviet Espionage Section; Robert Mac-kenzie, the regional security officer of MI6; and Dr and Mrs Mann. As they sat down to dinner, only Philby knew that the basement beneath them contained the photographic apparatus with which he copied the top-secret Anglo-American intelligence reports on Chinese dispositions in Korea. Philby had been routinely supplying these to the Soviets, along with whatever information he gleaned during his meetings with deputy CIA director Allen Dulles, and his weekly sessions at Harvey's Restaurant with James Angleton.

If Philby had chosen that evening to confess he was a spy, the consternation of his guests could have been scarcely less dramatic than that caused by the appearance around 9:30 of Guy Burgess. Uninvited, and visibly the worse for liquor, Burgess arrived and insisted on drawing a highly unflattering caricature of the wife of the guest of honor, transforming her prominent lower jaw into a 'battering ram'.

'I've never been so insulted in all my life,' Mrs Harvey shrilled, and she stormed out of the house with her equally angry husband. Mann told me how he and Angleton escaped outside to walk around in the relief of the unseasonably warm January night. When they returned half an hour later, they found the normally composed Philby sitting in tears on the sofa, wearing shirt sleeves and red suspenders. Burgess insisted that Mann join him in celebrating his coup against the pompous Harvey with a bottle of Scotch in the kitchen. After downing a tumblerful of whisky, Mann decided he dare not risk driving home because Ambassador Sir Oliver Franks 'had a reputation for being tough on traffic offenses'.

When Mann returned to pick up his car around ten the next morning, he discovered, to his amazement, Burgess and Philby in bed together, downing a bottle of champagne. 'I got the impression that Philby and Burgess were enjoying the situation immensely,' Mann remembered. He told me that he did not think they had spent the night together. But he was sufficiently disturbed by the homosexual overtones of the situation to report his uneasiness to Lieutenant Commander Eric Welsh, his MI6 superior at the Atomic Energy Directorate of the Ministry of Supply, when he returned to England a few months later. But Mann received a brushoff from Welsh. It made him feel an 'outsider' to raise 'doubts about the strange behavior of a senior officer of MI6.'

Angleton was increasingly uneasy about Philby, but the CIA had no solid grounds to suspect him in the spring of 1951. Nor is there any evidence in the declassified FBI files to suggest that Philby's house was bugged, as some have suggested.

Until the end of November 1950, Burgess, as a British delegate to the Far East Control Commission, also had an official pretext for frequent trips to New York. These provided a convenient opportunity for meeting with the Soviet control officer and it allowed him to act as a courier for Philby, too. But the FBI files show that these visits continued even after the ambassador's unhappiness with Burgess's performance cost him his post with the Japan commission. Subsequent investigation of hotel and telephone logs revealed a remarkable regularity in his monthly trips. Burgess would arrive in New York on Friday night, check into the Hotel Sutton, and return on Sunday or Monday to Washington.

Burgess was in New York from Friday, 10 December to Sunday, 12 December 1950; from Saturday, 3 February to Monday, 5 February 1951; and then again from Saturday, 10 February to Monday, 12 February. His final trip recorded by the bureau was from Saturday, 17 March to Monday, 19 March. The close correlation to the sequence of events leading to Burgess's recall and the ongoing 'Homer' investigation in London suggests that the main purpose of these visits was to meet with his Soviet control.

Philby's uncharacteristic tearful collapse on the night of 19 January and the champagne tête-à-tête in bed with Burgess the following morning appear also to be directly related to the realization that the Foreign Office was stepping up its efforts to trace the 1944 spy in the British embassy. They both knew that Moscow could have to find a way to get Maclean out of England before the Foreign Office turned the case over to MI5 for surveillance and interrogation.

There is therefore a special significance to the fact that Burgess made *two* back-to-back weekend trips to New York in February. Both Burgess and Philby were under increasing strain as they pondered what to do about Maclean. Moscow Center was, we now know from the affidavit of defector Vladimir Petrov, equally concerned. Kislitsyn, who was then a member of the First Directorate of Information, responsible for running agents in the Anglo-American territories, told Petrov how he attended a conference called by the First Directorate chief, Colonel Raina, which Anatoli Gorski (Gromov) also attended. As Maclean's US case officer, and the one-time London controller of the Cambridge agents, Gromov understood the peculiar difficulties they faced in rescuing Maclean without blowing the entire network. According to Kislitsyn's account, the 'perils of the proposed operation caused much misgiving, and many plans were put forward and rejected.'

The ruthless arithmetic of Colonel Raina added up to the fact that Moscow realized Maclean was blown. This made Burgess expendable. His usefulness as an agent was coming to an end. His instability threatened the star Cambridge mole, Philby, who might still succeed to the directorship of MI6, providing he could be sheltered from the impending storm. To divert suspicion from himself, Philby tells us how he gave the 'Homer' case a 'nudge in the right direction' by drawing attention to the 1940 claim by Walter Krivitsky that the Soviet spy in the Foreign Office was from Eton and Oxford.

Whether Philby (as he later claimed) or Moscow Center (more likely) decided to use Burgess to effect Maclean's defection, it is evident that Colonel Raina in Moscow gave his final approval to the strategy before the 12 February meeting in New York. In another two weeks Burgess successfully brought about his recall to Britain without arousing suspicion. He accomplished this by exploiting the well-known aversion of Sir Oliver Franks for British diplomats getting ticketed for motoring offenses. The FBI files confirm that Burgess deliberately and calculatingly set out to get himself ticketed for breaking the speed limits. While on an official trip to North Carolina, to compound the offense, he put a hitchhiker named James Turck behind the wheel of his white Lincoln as he headed south from Washington, through Virginia and the town of Fredericksburg on Thursday, 1 March.

'All during the time Mr Burgess kept telling me to step on it,' Turck told the FBI, recalling that Burgess assured him that his DPL license plates guaranteed him freedom from arrest. After they were stopped for a third time, Turck gave a deposition while Burgess remonstrated high-handedly with the county police officer that he was a diplomat and therefore immune from arrest.

The ambassador was already displeased with the 'unsatisfactory work' of his errant second secretary. The formal protest about Burgess's traffic violations, relaying the 14 March letter from Governor John Battle of Virginia, by the chief of protocol at the State Department proved the final straw. Sir Oliver Franks summoned Burgess and told him he was requesting Foreign Office approval for his recall. Burgess had a month in which to pack his bags and leave for England.

That very weekend – 19 March 1951 – Burgess made another trip to New York. His mission undoubtedly was to report to his Soviet contact on the completion of the first stage of the operation. Meanwhile, the embassy booked passage for Burgess on the *Queen Mary* from New York sailing 1 May. This allowed time for his mother, Mrs Basset, to fulfill her plans to visit her son in America during April.

As soon as they had word of Burgess's sailing, the Soviets appear to have alerted Maclean. His friends noted a dramatic change in his behavior around the beginning of April. Since taking on the job of head of the American desk the previous fall, Maclean had been a model Foreign Office commuter. Eschewing cocktail parties and London dinner invitations, he left the office with bowler hat and furled umbrella every evening to catch the 5:19 Kent train from Charing Cross to Sevenoaks. Now he began to stay overnight. He was seen at his old haunt, the Gargoyle

Club, the late-night watering hole for London's intellectual literati throughout the forties and fifties.

Goronwy Rees ran into a 'very drunk' Maclean at the Gargoyle on the night of 2 April – for the first time in fifteen years. 'I know all about you,' Maclean spat at Rees in a slurred voice. 'You used to be one of us, but you ratted,' Maclean ranted, then fell to his knees still pouring out a torrent of drunken abuse. At the end of another of those long evenings, Maclean surprised everyone by stating 'I am the English Hiss.' He made the remark for the benefit of the writer Cyril Connolly, whose friend's neighboring flat enabled Maclean to crash-land during his drinking sprees. The following morning, he challenged Connolly over breakfast: 'What would you do if I told you I was a Communist agent? – Go on, report me.' Connolly would later note in his own memoir how Maclean seemed burdened by some terrible strain.

Connolly put down Maclean's strange outburst to alcoholic befuddlement. But he – and MI5 – might have taken it more seriously had he known that Maclean was renting the darkroom above Ernest White's chemist shop, at Westerham near his Tatsfield home, to develop 'very sensitive' films. Only after Maclean's defection did White tell the police how he had once found a crumpled portion of exposed film on which the pale-blue oval Foreign Office seal could just be made out.

While Maclean hit the bottle to battle against the tightening noose, a chance encounter by Burgess with Michael Straight in Washington raised another threat to the Cambridge spy ring. Straight told me that he could not deny Burgess a ride downtown in his car when he met his fellow Trinityman one morning coming out of the British embassy. But when Straight learned that despite their heated exchange five years earlier, Burgess was still on 'special work' for the Foreign Office, he not only refused to lend his old friend his car, but delivered an ultimatum: Straight told Burgess that he had three months to resign from the Foreign service; otherwise he would 'report him to the authorities'. Reflecting on this last encounter with Burgess some twelve years later, Straight told the FBI that he did not know that Burgess intended to flee to Moscow before his three-month deadline was up.

Although Burgess gave Straight no hint of his intentions, statements he made to others, which are found in the FBI files, suggest that his flight to Moscow was not some last-minute decision taken in London but a carefully planned operation that Burgess knew about long before he left Washington. 'I'm v. depressed,' he wrote to Mrs Nicholas Roosevelt. These distant cousins of President Theodore Roosevelt were acquaintances of his stepfather, Major Basset, and they had put Burgess and his mother up at their South Carolina estate during the first week of April. They also lent him the money to pay his Fort Sumter Hotel bill on the way back to Washington.

Burgess had much to be apprehensive about after he had seen his mother off on the plane to London. While he and Mrs Basset had been sightseeing in Charleston, Philby had also learned that the Foreign Office had narrowed the hunt for 'Homer' down to two suspects – Paul Gore Booth and Donald Maclean. Both had been put under surveillance by MI5 and their phones were tapped as of 17 April. Philby offered odds on the former because *Gomer*, a near anagram of Gore, was Russian for 'Homer'. But he knew that this could not long delay the exposure that he and Burgess understood was inevitable once Maclean's interrogations began.

'Burgess did not look too happy, and I must have had an inkling of what was on his mind,' Philby wrote disingenuously of his final briefing of Burgess the evening before he departed from Washington on 28 April. Over a Chinese meal in the noisy Peking Restaurant, Philby braced Burgess on the need to adhere to the escape plan and not to arouse suspicion by rushing his fences. According to Philby, the instructions were for Burgess to call on Maclean when he reported to the Foreign Office. Burgess would hand him a piece of paper arranging a rendezvous where they could safely go over the details of the escape plan.

'Don't you go, too,' Philby says he reminded Burgess as he drove him to Union Station next morning. In the KGB-approved account calculated to camouflage the true extent of Soviet involvement in the defection, Philby suggests he gave this advice 'half jocularly'. But the FBI file refers to Burgess's depressed state before he left for New York and suggests that he knew that London would be only a brief stopover on the road to permanent exile behind the Iron Curtain. This becomes clear from the FBI record of how he spent his last forty-eight hours in America in a state of semipermanent intoxication, while staying at the New York apartment of his old colleague from Broadcasting House, Norman Luker, who was with the BBC office in Rockefeller Center. In one of his brief moments of sobriety at his farewell party, Burgess prevailed upon Luker to let him use his BBC 'sound mirror' machine (an early tape recorder) to record his well-polished Winston Churchill story for posterity.

President Truman had recalled General MacArthur from Korea three weeks earlier to prevent an escalation of the war, but Burgess left the United States issuing dire warnings that global war was 'inevitable within the next ten days'. Whether this was just gallows humor, or his genuine belief, Burgess's depression was very apparent to Luker, who saw him aboard the *Queen Mary* on 1 May 1951. The American who shared cabin B-130 with Burgess during the five-day transatlantic crossing also recalled little about the British diplomat, except that he drank too much, and that he introduced him to a stocky New Yorker in his mid-twenties, named Bernard Miller, on the last day of the voyage.

Six days later, when Burgess arrived in England, he reported to the Foreign Office. He was warned to expect a request for his resignation. But he made use of that visit to contact Maclean, who conveyed the need for extreme caution. Since 17 April, Maclean said, he had received no top-secret papers. This led him to believe his phones were tapped, and he knew that Special Branch officers were tailing him to and from work. According to what Blunt told Robert Cecil, Burgess mistakenly assumed he, too, was under surveillance and appealed to Blunt to act as a 'cutout' with the Soviet embassy.

'We were longing for the end of three months of suspense,' Sir

Patrick Reilly wrote in 1986. As the undersecretary directly responsible for Foreign Office security, Reilly explained that the 'long delay' before moving against Maclean was unavoidable because coming to terms with the very idea that someone as senior as Maclean 'should be a Soviet spy was something quite horrible and we had been living with this knowledge for months.' But the problem was getting the evidence against Maclean. The Venona decrypts were too sensitive to be used in court. So MI5 had put Maclean under surveillance, hoping a slip would provide the evidence necessary to extract a confession.

Reilly insists there was never any intention to 'hush up his guilt' but rather they 'wanted to get on with his confrontation.' However, George Carey-Foster, then head of Foreign Office security, and Roger Makins (later Lord Sherfield), who was Maclean's immediate superior, have also gone on record as suggesting that the FBI was responsible for the 'disastrous delay' because the Foreign Office had to coordinate 'every detail of this joint Anglo-American exercise' with the FBI, 'down to the actual date of Maclean's interrogation', and that for 'various puzzling reasons, the FBI appeared to be in no desperate hurry.' Reilly therefore finds it 'impossible to understand' why Lamphere says that 'the FO told MI5 not to keep the FBI informed.' Not according to the FBI records which state that Hoover 'possessed no derogatory information re subjects [Burgess and Maclean] prior to their disappearance from England May 1951.'

What this Foreign Office 'insider's account' does not explain is *why* or *how* the FBI kept MI5 from applying to the home secretary for permission to interrogate Maclean until Friday, 25 May 1951. The British government did not speak on the matter until its 1955 White Paper, when it said that Maclean 'was alerted and fled the country together with Burgess.' Expanding on the White Paper version from his intimate inside knowledge of the sequence of events, Sir Patrick Reilly insisted in 1986 that since all the messages from MI5 went through Philby in Washington, 'he could have telephoned Burgess' or used the 'safe channel of his Soviet contacts in Washington, who would have informed their colleagues in London, who must have told Burgess by the morning of the 25th since the latter spent the day preparing for the escape.'

It may be assumed that Philby, for reasons of KGB 'disinformation' rather than 'family' loyalty, concurred with the 'insider's account' by explaining that he wrote a coded warning letter to Burgess telling him to 'act at once or it would be too late' if he did not want his beloved Lincoln Continental, which he had abandoned in the embassy parking lot, sent to the scrap heap.'

Although Burgess's similarly suspect account does not mention this letter, he says that he and Maclean formulated their impromptu escape plans over a lunch in the RAC. He told his biographer, Driberg, that he and a young American he had met on the *Queen Mary* 'were thinking of going off to France for a jaunt, so I booked tickets for a weekend cruise to Saint-Malo and the Channel Islands.' Burgess also arranged to have dinner at Maclean's home on Friday evening. 'But until I got there I didn't know whether I was going to Moscow with Donald or to France with the American for a jolly jaunt. So I told the American to stay by the phone at his hotel until eight-thirty and packed two lots of things suitable for both purposes.'

According to the British 'insider's account' of the defection, MI5 was as vacillating as Burgess. Even after obtaining the Foreign Secretary's approval on the morning of Friday, 25 May to interrogate Maclean, there was some confusion in the Foreign Office over whether they intended to call in Maclean immediately or on the following Monday. Robert Cecil, who was then deputy head of the American desk Department, has also fueled the flames of controversy by saying that his boss, Roger Makins, need not have excused Maclean from his scheduled duty that Saturday morning because he (Cecil) was on vacation that week.

After the defection, when Cecil went through Maclean's office papers, he was struck by how Maclean, an efficient bureaucrat to the last, had made meticulous notes of the Friday visit paid to him by the Argentine Counsellor to discuss an intricate trade issue. Cecil also discovered in Maclean's filing cabinet a numbered copy of the Cabinet paper reporting on Prime Minister Attlee's hurried visit to Washington in December 1950, when it appeared that MacArthur might get permission to use the atomic bomb against the Chinese forces who had joined the Korean War. So contrary to the assertion of some of his former colleagues, that Maclean had no access to very sensitive papers, Cecil says the Cabinet report he found was convincing proof that Maclean had continued to see secret information of great value to the Soviets.

What the Foreign Office officials did not know, however, was that the MI5 watchers who were trailing Maclean shadowed him no farther than the ticket barrier at Charing Cross station. Because his home in Tatsfield exceeded the fifty-mile travel limit imposed on Soviet diplomats, bureaucratic penny-pinching and the risk that Maclean would be 'alerted by surveillance of his home in an isolated part of the country' had persuaded MI5 that it was unnecessary to follow him to Kent.

The Special Branch 'watcher' who waited until the 5:19 to Sevenoaks, with Maclean aboard, rumbled over Hungerford Bridge past the gleaming new exhibition buildings of the Festival of Britain site on the south bank of the Thames did not even guess that he was witnessing the start of a long journey to Moscow. Around the same time, a cream Austin A-40 saloon with Burgess at the wheel was weaving its way through the rush-hour traffic. It pulled up at the twelve-room house in Tatsfield only half an hour after Maclean arrived home. Maclean appears to have known that MI5 had bugged the house through the telephones, because he introduced Burgess to his wife as Roger Stiles, an old Foreign Office colleague.

Melinda later claimed not to have recognized Burgess. Although she was then entering the final month of her third pregnancy, Mrs Maclean did not express dismay when, at the dinner table, her husband informed her he would be leaving the house – or so she would tell the police.

'Mr Stiles and I have to keep a pressing engagement, but I don't expect to be back very late,' Maclean told her. 'I'll take an overnight bag just in case.' They then climbed into the car and drove off. Burgess headed for Southampton, later claiming that Maclean 'dillied and dallied' about leaving his wife, almost making them miss the 11:45 steamer SS *Falaise* for Saint-Malo. But their last-minute dash for the gangplank, abandoning their hired car on the dockside, with a reassuring shout of 'Back Monday!', seems a deliberate ploy to rush through a sleepy immigration post that was about to shut down for the night.

The next morning, when the *Falaise* docked at Saint-Malo around noon, a taxi driver recalled driving the pair to Rennes. There they picked up the Paris-bound express. From there the trail went cold, and there are almost as many theories as there are routes from France to Moscow. Some accounts have them traveling first to Austria, suggesting the fleeing diplomats included a stop in Switzerland, where they obtained Czech passports on the Monday before heading for Prague on Tuesday. But the authoritative account, provided by Kislitsyn, has it that their escape route 'included an air passage over the border into Czechoslovakia'. Kislitsyn then met Burgess and Maclean at the Moscow airport and, as the MVD officer detailed to take care of their 'maintenance and welfare', drove them to a 'comfortable house on the outskirts of Moscow'.

Whatever route Burgess and Maclean took to Moscow is of far less historical significance than the sequence of events that permitted them to escape from Britain. The 'insider's account', which has been generally accepted up until now, is, as the FBI records reveal, nothing more than a travesty of the truth put out by the British government to cover up a chain of bureaucratic bungling and Soviet-inspired conspiracy at the highest levels of MI5.

The oddest aspect of the whole affair is that MI5's decision to move against Maclean came on the Friday, *the day after the final element in the escape plan was in place*. By another uncanny coincidence, the defecting pair was given the entire weekend to effect an escape that new evidence suggests Moscow Center had planned down to the fine details. Furthermore, Blunt, it now emerges, had the primary responsibility for the smooth execution of the cover-up after he had been tipped off by the high-ranking Soviet mole in MI5.

The only justification offered by the 'insider's account' to explain these two coincidences is that the MI5 decision triggering the defection was itself the result of a delay by the FBI. This buck passing by the British is categorically denied by the testimony of the head of the Soviet Espionage Section of the FBI and all the other American counterintelligence authorities I have consulted. Of greater significance is the fact that Hoover was told that the FBI 'possessed no derogatory information' about Maclean or Burgess prior to their defection. The voluminous FBI case records that have been released to researchers under the Freedom of Information Act, from two separate archival sources, and the independent assessments of the affair in 1955 and 1957, confirm that the British *did not* alert the FBI. This explains why the FBI launched its own intensive investigation of Burgess and Maclean *but on a scattershot basis* the moment it knew about the defection.

The British have found it necessary to attempt to denigrate the FBI Burgess and Maclean investigation because it conflicts so dramatically with the 'insider's account' of the Foreign Office. One of the most important reassessments arises from the FBI interviews of Bernard Warren Miller, the young American Burgess met on the *Queen Mary*, who was unwittingly made to play – by both the Soviets and the British – a central role in the defection.

Miller was *not* the owner of an off-Broadway theater as Burgess claimed. This merely fit his convenient account that he was going away for a weekend jaunt with the newly acquired American pickup. Miller told the FBI, during the course of two long interrogations, that he had disembarked from the *Queen Mary* at Cherbourg on 6 May. He then traveled to Switzerland, where he enrolled for a course at the University of Geneva Medical School. He explained that he returned to London on 23 May, after spending a week in Paris, only because Burgess had promised to introduce him to a friend who was a doctor at London's

Middlesex hospital. Miller insisted that he was not a homosexual, although he regarded 'Burgess's sudden efforts on his behalf peculiar'. He also told the FBI he was 'aware of Burgess's general unhappiness and instability bordering on mental illness due to his recall to London.'

Contrary to every account published so far, the FBI records make it clear that Miller never discussed during the voyage, or planned to take, a weekend trip to France with Burgess. There is logic in his claim it was ridiculous to suggest that he would have gone back to Paris only two days after he had come to England from Paris on his way back to New York.

Miller's arrival, it is now obvious, merely gave Burgess a plausible excuse for purchasing the boat tickets to Saint-Malo without arousing suspicion.

Anthony Blunt was in on the plot from the start. That is now clear from Jack Hewit's account. There must have been pressing reasons for Blunt to take the day off on Monday, 7 May to go down to Southampton to pick Burgess up at the Ocean Terminal. Nor did Burgess, his friend of fourteen years, come home to the flat in Bond Street that evening. He spent the night at the director's flat at the Courtauld Institute. Blunt must have already been in contact to discuss the details of the defection scheme with 'Peters' (Yuri Modin, the Soviet control officer) who operated under the cover of an attaché at the Russian embassy.

Moscow Center knew it could rely on Blunt to be a stickler for details. One of the problems that had yet to be taken care of was the possibility that Goronwy Rees would 'rat' to the police when he learned that his old friend Burgess was safely in Moscow. This they decided was a job for Burgess to fix by appealing to old loyalties. So with his bags still unpacked, Burgess headed down to Sonning the next morning to see Rees at home. To reinforce his appeal, Burgess softened up Rees by stressing how McCarthyism was bringing the United States to the brink of war. He read out a long anti-American diatribe that he intended to be his official swan song to the Foreign Office. Rees had no doubt they would fire him. But Burgess told Rees that Michael Berry, an Etonian friend, had approached him in Washington with the suggestion that he might consider becoming a diplomatic correspondent on *The Daily Telegraph*, which the Berry family owned.

For all of Burgess's ebullience and scurrilous stories about Washington adventures, Rees noted he was 'labouring under a tremendous sense of excitement, as if he were under intense external pressures.' A letter in the FBI file from Burgess's step-father to Mrs Nicholas Roosevelt, written that Saturday, 12 May, confirms that Burgess had been out of town for most of the first week of his return. By the second week Burgess was back with Hewit, but he too noted Burgess's violent mood swings. It was not simply alcohol, Hewit said, that made his old daredevil friend 'maudlin one minute and up the next'.

On Saturday 19 May, Burgess visited the home of his wartime friend from MI5, Kemball Johnston, who lived at Henham not far from Cambridge. Timothy Johnson, who was then ten years old, remembers Burgess as a 'fat, smelly, untidy man with a red face and slobbery lips who peed behind a bush in the garden instead of going to the lavatory like normal grown-ups.' Burgess doodled cartoons for the Johnston boys, and the one of Stalin peering over a wall, captioned: 'I wonder what *Kemball* is thinking?', seems to have a sinister purpose: Burgess was intent on reminding Johnston of the need to observe old loyalties. That it was a caution to a Marxist sympathizer is reinforced by FBI files that reveal the extent to which Burgess was already carefully laying the ground for his defection. He was dropping broad hints that weekend about an impending trip abroad.

To preserve the cover story, Burgess did not buy the boat tickets for himself and Bernard Miller until after the American medical student had arrived in London on Wednesday, when he came to cocktails and dinner prepared by Hewit at the flat. Miller's FBI interrogation makes it clear that he never knew about the proposed trip, and Hewit recalls no discussion that evening about a weekend jaunt.

Next morning, Thursday, Burgess announced out of the blue that he was going on a weekend trip to France with Bernard

Miller. This got Hewit's dander up. He told me he created quite a row about Burgess's going off with his 'mousy' American 'pickup'. That morning Burgess made the two-block trip to Thomas Cook's travel bureau, where he booked two tickets for the Friday-night steamer to Saint-Malo, giving his own and Miller's name to the clerk. A twelve-hour crossing would seem an odd choice of escape route to the Continent. But the sleepy fishing port on the Brittany coast had obviously been carefully selected. If a hue and cry erupted in London, they hoped to rely on the British and French officials being less alert at Saint-Malo than at the busier, and more logical, Dover to Calais crossing.

Philby, however, goes out of the way in his account to suggest that Burgess decided to purchase the boat tickets as a result of his letter containing the coded message about Burgess's car being sent to the scrap heap. But it was uncharacteristic of the methodical Soviets in any case to rely on the vagaries of the transatlantic mails. The FBI records demolish the story because they show that Burgess never left his white Lincoln in the embassy parking lot. (Blunt sought to add to the alibi by claiming that he too had seen the letter and that he had snatched it from under the very noses of Special Branch investigators during their search of Burgess's flat the following week.)

The Philby letter now seems to have been a red herring to draw suspicion away from whoever it was in MI5 who tipped off Blunt about the meeting with the Home Secretary to give permission for Maclean's interrogation. Philby would not have been officially notified of the Home Secretary's action until *after* the approval was given on that Friday morning. With the five-hour time difference added to the enciphering and deciphering time required by such a secret message, Philby was in no position to tip off Burgess, even if he had been able to place a transatlantic telephone call, until late Friday afternoon.

Miller's statement to the FBI makes it plain that Maclean was not on the Saint-Malo boat as a result of a hastily cobbled escape plan made by Burgess on 25 May after some last-minute tipoff by Philby. The sequence of events as they can now be reliably reconstructed precludes any involvement by Philby: first, he could not have known that MI5 surveillance did not extend to Maclean's home, making it safe for Burgess to drive there on the Friday evening to collect Maclean. Second, it is unlikely that Philby would have been cabled (if he was) of the Foreign Secretary's approval for MI5 to interrogate Maclean until *after* the decision had been taken on Friday morning. Moreover, several hours would have been taken up by the need to encipher, transmit and decipher the top-secret cable, which (if it was communicated to Philby at all) could not have been in his hands until well into the afternoon, London time, when Burgess was already at the Reform Club with Miller.

All the evidence points to the tipoff about the imminent interrogation of Maclean coming from London, *the day before*, when the brief for the foreign secretary was drawn up by his own staff and the senior MI5 officers involved. Whoever issued the crucial instruction *did so on Thursday at the latest* because of the time needed to draw up the report for Herbert Morrison to sign the following morning.

That Burgess picked Thursday to collect the boat tickets does not therefore appear the result of mere fortuitous circumstances. The decision to submit the papers to the home secretary on a Friday has all the appearances of a carefully timed plan to prime the escape and was calculated to give the birds a two-day window of opportunity to fly the coop.

It was only late on Thursday afternoon, when he returned from work, that Hewit learned that Burgess was not going to France with Miller after all. Hewit thought for a moment he might go instead. But Burgess dashed his hopes by saying he would be taking a friend who was 'in a spot of bother'. Hewit went out to dinner without Burgess. When he came back to the flat after going out to dinner that Thursday night, he found the living-room door shut and sounds of a heated argument taking place in a foreign language. Fourteen years had taught him better than to barge in on Burgess's private affairs, so he went into the bedroom. Burgess poked his head around the door to tell him he was trying to get rid of a drunk friend and not to worry. Hewit described the mysterious man as having a guttural accent, which even he recognized as not being French. But it is most unlikely he was a Russian agent, according to those familiar with Soviet operational practices. They would never have risked entering a house that might be under surveillance.

When Hewit made a pot of tea for his friend the next morning, Burgess seemed in good spirits. When Burgess left the flat around nine, Hewit had no inkling that he might not be back. Burgess had told him about his invitation to dine with Michael Berry on 29 May to discuss the job offer at the *Telegraph*. Hewit says that because of this he expected to see Burgess the following Tuesday at the very latest.

Burgess spent that Friday morning telephoning his old friends. One of those he tried to reach was W. H. Auden, who was staying with Stephen Spender. When Burgess telephoned, Auden was out. But Burgess told Spender how much he agreed with what Spender had said about his dalliance with communism in his recently published memoir *World Within World*. 'It expresses the dilemma of a generation,' Spender recalled Burgess congratulating him.

Burgess then went to Welbeck Motors and hired a small cream Austin A-40 saloon car for the weekend, giving his address as 'care of the Cavalry Club'.

While Donald Maclean went from the Foreign Office to Soho to join his other friends for a lunchtime celebration of his thirty-eighth birthday, Burgess drove the car to the Reform Club, where the barman still served the tumblers full of port that were known as 'Double Burgesses' in his honor.

At three o'clock, Miller arrived at the Reform Club to meet Burgess. He told the FBI that he was expecting to meet the influential medical friend. Instead, Burgess only instructed him not to try to get in touch with the contact at the Middlesex hospital before Monday, 28 May. Miller found these instructions 'strange', because his original understanding was that the introduction would be personal. But, he told the FBI, he did not ask for an explanation.

Burgess told Miller that he was having dinner that evening with an unnamed friend who was 'having marital difficulties', and that he was going away over the weekend 'to help this friend help himself'. After holding forth about the iniquities of General Douglas MacArthur and other unremembered matters, Miller said, Burgess left the Reform around five. They got into a car parked outside on Pall Mall. When Miller commented on the rental sticker on the windshield as they headed to the Green Park Hotel where Miller was staying, Burgess told him that it had been 'rented by a friend who let him use it.' There was no luggage on the backseat, so Burgess must have then returned to his Bond Street flat around 5:30 to pick up the suitcases that he later left behind on the boat to Saint-Malo.

If Miller was telling the FBI the truth – and the declassified record gives no indication that Hoover's experienced interrogators had any reason to doubt his credibility – then Burgess could not have set off for Maclean's home in Kent much before six p.m.

The FBI files also reveal that Melinda Maclean appears to have known more about her husband's abrupt disappearance than she admitted to the British detectives the following week. The next morning, Saturday, 26 May, when Mr and Mrs Robert Oetking, Melinda's American sister and her husband, arrived at Beaconshaw for a weekend visit, Melinda told them her husband would be 'late coming from London'. But when the Oetkings were interviewed by bureau investigators in 1954 – after Melinda had mysteriously vanished from a holiday trip to Geneva – they said it was 'obvious that he was not expected as no place at the table had been set for him.' On Sunday morning, when the two Maclean boys came into the Oetkings' bedroom, they glibly told their aunt and uncle that 'their father would not be coming home'.

Melinda, however, told her sister, Nancy Oetking, later that same day that Maclean had 'disappeared'. She did not know where he was and appeared unconcerned. She said she was not going to advise the Foreign Office, but 'would wait until they contacted her.' Melinda Maclean did not get a telephone call from

Whitehall until the middle of Monday morning.

Melinda's account ties in suspiciously neatly to the 1955 White Paper, which has it that 'Maclean's absence did not become known to the authorities until the morning of Monday 28 May,' when he failed to report for work. But the official version, as Nigel West has pointed out, is 'an extremely misleading account of what had taken place, not least because Maclean *had been spotted leaving for France three days earlier.*'

In 1986, sources formerly inside the British security service leaked to West the details of how an alert immigration official at Southampton had identified the name and number on Maclean's passport with a fresh entry on his 'watch' list. (This standard MI5 practice calls for the circulation of the names of those under particular surveillance to all UK ports of entry and exit.) The Southampton immigration office, following procedure, immediately telephoned the news to the MI5 operational headquarters at Leconfield House. West has assured me he has been told that the still secret office records show the phone call was logged in 'soon after midnight' by the night-duty officer, who passed the word that Maclean had left the country to two of the officers working on the case, who 'by chance, were still in the building conferring about the impending interrogation.'

The Southampton officer had also passed on the information that the *Falaise* would arrive at Saint-Malo just before noon the following day. This appeared to give ample time to arrange for the French police to pick up the two as they came ashore. But West contends on 'reliable authority' that the French police did not receive an alert to look out for the two fugitive diplomats for more than forty-eight hours.

The omission is astonishing and inexplicable. The more so because there are now *two* more corroborative reports that MI6 stations in Europe and North America received the alert within a matter of hours that Friday night.

By Philby's own account, the signal came through at a 'horribly early hour', when Geoffrey Paterson telephoned him at home to ask for Esther Whitfield's help in deciphering the Most

Immediate telegram. Philby fails to identify the day the moment-ous message arrived. But since Washington time was five hours behind London, if the first alarm about Maclean and Burgess had come in midmorning on Monday as the 'insider's account' claimed, then there would have been no need to rouse Philby from his sleep. The cable would have come in during regular afternoon office hours. But 1 A.M. Saturday in London translated to 8 P.M. Friday in Washington. Since London's priorities would be to notify its agents in Europe first and its embassy in Washing-ton second, the likelihood is that Washington *was* notified later during the night, which provides a more rational scenario for Philby's statement.

'The bird has flown,' Paterson told Philby when he came to the office, and he had to feign surprise when he heard that Maclean was missing. Within a matter of hours that Saturday Paterson and Philby had communicated the news to their opposite numbers at the FBI and the CIA. The impact of the message on the American intelligence community was 'electric'. This was the recollection of one American iintelligence officer, who remembered how the news of the double defection shook everyone who heard about it that weekend.

There was little that the FBI or CIA could do except to express amazement and pray that the British would take the necessary steps to apprehend the fleeing diplomats before they slipped behind the Iron Curtain. That was the mission given to MI6 officers all over Europe.

One of them was Anthony Cavendish, who was then stationed in Berlin. Defying an injunction under the Official Secrets Act that forbade him to publish his memoirs, he included his recollec-tions of that dramatic weekend in a privately printed 'Christmas Card' that he sent out to all his friends in 1986.

'The weekend of 25 to 27 May 1951 proved to be a memorable one' for Cavendish and his MI6 colleagues at the Berlin station. They were all roused early from their billets by telephone and summoned to report to the British military headquarters at the Olympic Stadium, which also served as the main SIS office.

'I arrived and was surprised to find that all the officers of the station were assembling,' wrote Cavendish. 'But then our Station Commander began handing out photographs of two men.' They were, he explained, two British diplomats, Donald Maclean and Guy Burgess, who intended to defect and might well pass through Berlin. Cavendish shared this 'forty-eight hours sleepless weekend' with the fifty other officers then stationed as part of the 'enormous' British MI6 presence in Germany. They fanned out to man the crossing points into the Soviet Sector until Monday, when the alert ended.

FBI records also confirm that it was a very busy weekend for Anthony Blunt. His principal mission was damage control. This he did by setting up Bernard Miller to lay down unwittingly a false trail to cover up the real story behind the successful escape.

Many of the names of the leading participants involved in this masterful exercise of deception have been excised in the FBI records to meet the strict requirements of the Freedom of Information Act relating to living persons, or because of official British government requests. But in the thousands of pages that comprise the Burgess and Maclean file, there are scores of near-duplicate interviews and summaries, each of which yields clues to what lies under the censor's pen.

The reconstructed passages of the FBI Teletype report of the 14 June interview conducted by the New York field office reads: ON MAY TWENTY SIXTH MILLER SAID HE RECEIVED A TELEPHONE CALL FROM JACK HEWIT, THE ROOMMATE OF BURGESS, WHO TOLD HIM THAT BURGESS HAD NOT COME HOME THAT NIGHT. HEWIT WANTED TO KNOW IF MILLER HAD INFO REGARDING BURGESS WHEREABOUTS. MILLER TOLD HEWIT THAT HE HAD NO SUCH INFO BECAUSE HE HAD BEEN PREVIOUSLY INSTRUCTED BY BURGESS NOT TO TELL HEWIT OF HIS PLANS FOR THE WEEKEND.

Miller said he had previously met several friends of Burgess at the Reform Club, Blunt and a diplomat friend who 'recently returned from Moscow'. But it was the summary of 18 July, prepared for Hoover, that contains the evidence that implicates the art dealer Harris in Blunt's plot: 'On May 27, 1951 MILLER said that he was contacted personally by PROFESSOR ANTHONY BLUNT and they drove to the home of TOM HARRIS who has been a friend of Burgess for many years. It was only then that MILLER told BLUNT of BURGESS' plan for the weekend. Both BLUNT and HARRIS were disturbed because BURGESS never went away without telling JACK and his mother (Mrs Bassett [sic]). BLUNT and HARRIS seemed to think BURGESS was "going down hill mentally" for a long time. HARRIS said that BURGESS used cocaine for relief from severe headaches, which were the result of a fall. He also said that BURGESS suffered from diabetes.'

Hewit says that the suggestion by Harris that Burgess was a cocaine addict and suffered from diabetes in 1951 was news to him. Hewit also denied that he had any communication with the American medical student after the defection, with the exception of the one telephone conversation.

Miller arrived back in New York on 16 June, and he told the FBI he had received a letter from Blunt shortly afterward. Ten days later, the letter was followed by a cable: WORRIED. NO NEWS. DID YOU GET MY TWO LETTERS A. BLUNT. The FBI account that Miller had destroyed Blunt's letter corroborates that Miller was the innocent dupe. Had he been party to the plot he would have saved the letter as 'evidence' for the FBI. But he did show Blunt's cable to the investigators and his reply advising Blunt that he was OK and telling Blunt his plans to go to the University of Geneva in late August.

To all intents and purposes, the defection of Burgess and Maclean ended the operations of the Cambridge agents. There was still work to be done, however. It involved covering their tracks so that its achievements would be hard to discover, and protection of those who had helped them achieve its goals. This type of rearguard action could have been suicidal. But Anthony Blunt volunteered for the role because he had no intention of going to Moscow.

'I'm certain where Guy's gone. He's gone to Moscow,' Rees said when he came home and was told by his wife that Burgess had called that morning, Friday 25 May, and left the message: 'Tell Goronwy that I'm about to do something almost incomprehensible, but I know he'll understand.'

Burgess could have called Rees at work in the bursar's office of Oxford's All Souls College. Instead of calming Rees, the message had the reverse effect from the one Burgess intended. Rees understood only too well what Burgess was doing. He wanted no part of it. He picked up the telephone and rang David Footman, told him his fears, and asked him to get Guy Liddell to call him. Footman was still with MI6, though under suspicion for his strong pro-Russian attitude. This could explain what Rees called 'extraordinary slowness' in eliciting any response from MI5.

On Sunday afternoon, Rees still had not heard from Liddell. So Rees telephoned Blunt to ask his advice. This was a mistake. Blunt read the signs of incipient panic in Rees's voice and rushed off to Rees's house to forestall a damaging confession from a former member of his network. Arriving in Sonning late that afternoon, he spent several hours talking Rees out of going to the authorities. He played down the idea that *anyone* in MI5 would believe Rees: 'He told me I was a fool even to consider approaching MI5 with an unsubstantiated hunch – and why.' Blunt tried to convince Rees that he would only bring himself under suspicion.

'Blunt's cool reasoning did not deter me,' Rees claimed. But it took another ten days – an astonishing loss of time in the circumstances – before he could get an appointment to see Liddell.

Blunt would admit – twenty-eight years later in his one and only press conference – that he had been in 'direct contact' with the Soviets immediately after the Burgess and Maclean defection. He said: 'It was at that point that I had *orders* to go to Russia and I refused.' It was highly significant that he would use the term 'orders', which contradicted his assertion that he had broken with Moscow six years earlier. He quickly tried to correct this slip by saying that the Soviets 'probably assumed that I was still with them'.

'I was obviously going to be a prime suspect,' Blunt conceded. He assumed that Burgess knew he 'was not going to go' to Moscow. 'I suppose he thought that if the thing got critical, they might simply take me out, not reckoning on the fact that . . .' Blunt checked himself again to say that he had not directly helped the two diplomats to escape.

Blunt was proud of his successful defiance of Soviet orders. He cannot have been unaware of the risk that he might someday be 'burned' to save a more productive agent, or that as ruthless a man as Beria might order a 'wet affair' team artfully to arrange his suicide. But Blunt had no intention of giving up the director's flat at the Courtauld mansion, or his office at the Palace, for a utilitarian flat in one of the bleaker Moscow suburbs, as had Maclean and Burgess.

Blunt was counting on the fact that he could not be arrested on the circumstantial evidence of Rees. Blunt would have reminded his Russian controller that MI5 did not have the facilities of the Lubyanka prison, nor did the gentlemanly British police resort to extracting confessions under torture.

Blunt's friends in MI5, his 'Royal' insurance policy, and his glacial cleverness evidently reassured the Soviets that, of all the Cambridge agents, he was the one least likely ever to find himself in a 'critical' situation. They accepted his persuasive argument that he should remain in England as an immediate and practical one: his effectiveness as a damage-control agent. The defection of two of the prominent members of the Cambridge ring could have numbered his future usefulness in days, but he was able to move swiftly and effectively to seal off the other agents from suspicion.

The audaciousness with which Blunt discharged that damage-
control mission enabled other members of the so-called Cambridge network – such as Alister Watson – to continue usefully
serving Moscow for a dozen more years. But Blunt's greatest
concern, after his preliminary pass at Rees, was to move swiftly
to remove any incriminating paper trail that Burgess might have
left in his flat.

Hewit remembers how Blunt called him and told him that
Burgess probably was not coming back. Then Blunt asked for
Hewit's keys and packed him off to stay with friends near Colchester. Hewit said he did not question this, because he was
used to taking orders from Blunt. Blunt therefore had at least a
day to scour through the closets, drawers and guitar box of old
love letters for any incriminating documents. Twenty-nine years
later, Blunt would drop a hint to Rosamond Lehmann that she
should not believe a word Rees had said about him, because
Rees had helped him with that surreptitious 'housecleaning'.

Whether Rees did participate, or whether it was Blunt's way
of undermining Rees's credibility as a witness, cannot be established. But it was only when Blunt believed that no papers
leading to the other members of his ring remained in the flat that
he offered the keys to MI5 to save them the inconvenience of
having to apply for a search warrant. Blunt was present during
the 'official' examination of Burgess's belongings (when he said
he pocketed a compromising letter that Philby had sent from
Washington).

Blunt's housecleaning was less thorough than he imagined
because Special Branch found a twenty-five-page bundle of
internal Treasury appreciations that dated back to 1940. An
astute MI5 secretary identified them as having been written by
John Cairncross, who was immediately put under surveillance
by MI5. It was evident from Cairncross's wartime service at
Bletchley Park that he should be a prime suspect, and this
appeared confirmed when the tap on his telephone revealed a

summons to a meet with a Soviet embassy official to discuss the Burgess and Maclean defection.

MI5 watchers tailed Cairncross to a deserted wood in Surrey. But no Russian turned up. After several more abortive attempts to catch Cairncross red-handed, Arthur Martin eventually interviewed him. While Cairncross admitted giving nonclassified Treasury documents to his friend Burgess, he denied being a spy. The treasury accepted Cairncross's resignation to go to Canada to take up a teaching post. He eventually went to Rome to work for the UN Food and Agriculture Organization. The failure to trap Cairncross was another indication that the Soviets had a direct line into the upper reaches of MI5 in 1951. The tipoff most likely came via Blunt, who was deeply involved in 'assisting' Guy Liddell in the early stages of investigation into the Burgess and Maclean affair.

It all struck Goronwy Rees as very odd when he arrived in London on 7 June for his long-awaited meeting with Liddell. Rees was 'taken aback' to find that the deputy director of MI5 had not arranged a formal debriefing. Instead there was an informal chat over a lunch that included the intimidating presence of Anthony Blunt.

'The pair of them took up where Blunt had left off' was how Rees recalled his intense discomfort during the lunch that Thursday at Liddell's club. 'They did their level best to convince me that I'd be wasting everyone's time if I went along and submitted the nebulous kind of evidence against Guy Burgess that I seemed determined to offer.'

That the deputy director of MI5 could be involved in Blunt's conspiracy was, on the face of it, ridiculous. But Rees could not forget the 'peculiar circumstances' of that meeting. It convinced him there was 'something sinister about the quiet protectiveness of Guy Liddell.'

That very morning the story of the missing Burgess and Maclean had broken in the British press. The Foreign Office had managed to keep the lid on the incipient scandal for almost two weeks. But the day before, a member of the French Sûreté leaked the details to a journalist. The *Daily Express* and *Daily Herald* did not identify either Burgess or Maclean, but merely noted how 'two British government employees' were 'believed to have left London with the intention of getting to Moscow.'

The cat was now among the pigeons.

Rees was not the only one outside the tight-lipped Foreign Office and intelligence communities who knew the identity of the missing officials. On 7 June, Melinda Maclean received a telegram from France telling her that her husband had to leave 'unexpectedly', and then Mrs Basset got one from Rome saying her son had embarked on a 'long Mediterranean cruise'. So did others.

'Even before their names were published, I was absolutely certain that Guy Burgess was one of the diplomats who had disappeared,' Rosamond Lehmann told me. Sir Stewart Menzies was a friend of her cousin, so she called him from her home that Friday morning to report that she had known since 1937 that Burgess had been a Comintern agent.

'Yes, my dear girl, I would be delighted to talk with you, but it's Friday,' Miss Lehmann recalled C saying. He then asked in his plummy voice: 'Is it about A.B.?'

As a writer, Rosamond Lehmann possesses a remarkable eye for detail. But she was still trying to puzzle out who Menzies was referring to as he ran through a whole string of initials that ended with G.B. It finally dawned on her that the last one was Guy Burgess.

'Yes, it is,' Miss Lehmann said. She asked if she could come up to London to see him on Monday. But Menzies astonished her by saying he would not be in town that day. 'I could scarcely believe it when he told me he was accompanying his daughter to Ascot.'

It seemed odd to Miss Lehmann that the head of Britain's secret service elevated the demands of the social season over matters of national security. She saw her priorities otherwise. She called Harold Nicolson and arranged an appointment at the Curzon Street headquarters of MI5 early the following week. She was interviewed at length by William 'Jim' Skardon, whose success with Fuchs had earned him the reputation of being the service's most skillful interrogator.

'I was very nervous and I told him all I knew about Burgess,' Rosamond Lehmann told me. 'He kept on asking: "What can you tell us about G.R.?"' By then she had grasped that suspects were customarily referred to by their initials. But she stated that she genuinely believed that Goronwy Rees had refused to cooperate with Burgess.

When Skardon, whom Miss Lehmann recalled as a very patient man with a thin moustache, asked her about A.B., she realized that Menzies had been referring the previous Friday to Anthony Blunt. 'I was absolutely astonished. He kept pressing me on what I knew about Anthony – they wanted to know anything and everything,' she said. But she could tell them very little about Blunt. And when she left Leconfield House, Skardon asked her for an assurance she would not tell anyone about the meeting.

The problem was that Rosamond Lehmann had already told her brother John, 'in the strictest of confidence', about Burgess. He had 'let the cat out of the bag' and written to Stephen Spender. The letter had ended up on the front page of the *Daily Express*. Lord Beaverbrook, the crusading newspaper's proprietor, had taken the lead initiating the hunt for the so-called 'Third Man'.

It was to become a sensational Soviet spy story that preoccupied British journalists for the next three decades.

Reports of a Communist connection in the case of the vanishing British diplomats also created a sensation in Washington. Busybodies and crackpots lined up at the British embassy. Among them, however, was one person who had the firsthand knowledge that could have solved the enigma. Michael Straight visited the embassy to tell the Information Service officer that he knew Burgess. But he says the officer on duty told him so dismissively that there were 'so many witnesses' with the same story he decided not to take the matter any further. It would be another twelve years before Straight came forward again to provide the

FBI with the testimony that incriminated Blunt.

The significance of Rosamond Lehmann's account is that she makes it very clear that Blunt was under suspicion in 1951, within two weeks of the defection of Burgess and Maclean. Goronwy Rees also knew about Blunt's role in the conspiracy. In contrast to Straight, Rees did not get cold feet after what he took to be a 'warning' delivered by Blunt and Liddell at their 'peculiar' luncheon. He insisted on telling what he knew to the MI5 investigators in two formal debriefing sessions conducted under the watchful authority of Dick White, the head of B Division and in charge of the investigation.

White is recorded as having said that Rees 'was as slippery as an eel and had a violent antipathy to Blunt.' Rees may have been anxious to downplay his own guilt, but during the second, and more grueling session at MI5, he revealed how the 'tortuous byways' of his friendship with Burgess had led to his discovery, in 1937, that Blunt was a Comintern conspirator. He also named half a dozen of his Oxbridge contemporaries whose secret faith in the Soviet Union, unlike his own, remained unshaken despite the traumatic impact on intellectual Marxist ideologies of the Nazi-Soviet pact and Stalin's bloody purges.

'Goronwy knew the whole business,' Andrew Boyle said. Boyle told me how Rees, even during his deathbed confession, made obscure jokes about the personalities involved. 'I thought he was a four-letter man,' White is on the record as saying of Rees. 'If he had really known all these things, why hadn't he come forward?'

White's attitude is somewhat understandable, given that the allegations made by Rees appeared inconceivable. The very suggestion that White's principal mentor in MI5 – the deputy head of the security service – could be a Soviet agent must have seemed 'obscene'. Rees by his accusations played right into Blunt's hands who salvaged his own credibility by branding Rees as a malicious liar.

Sir Dick White, moreover, asserts that Rees never actually said 'Blunt was our man'. Nor did Rees offer substantiation of Blunt's guilt beyond quoting Burgess's declaration that Blunt was a

Comintern agent. Moreover, Rees was a grammar-school boy, an outsider to the old-boy network of the British intelligence services. The tight-knit community to which White belonged was already too shell-shocked by the Burgess and Maclean defection even to contemplate the possibility that a Soviet spy had made his way undetected into the senior ranks of their exclusive gentlemen's club.

Meanwhile, the FBI had launched its own investigation of Burgess and Maclean. It included surveillance of Philby, and agents tailed him to what appeared to be an empty 'dead drop' in a tree in the Virginia countryside. James Angleton at the CIA had also learned about Philby's experiences in the Communist underground from Teddy Kollek, the future mayor of Jerusalem, who was then a minister at the Israeli embassy in Washington. Kollek had known Philby in Vienna in 1934. But while the FBI and CIA now had good grounds for suspecting that Philby was implicated in the escape of the two British diplomats, they had no proof.

The Americans were hesitant at first to communicate their suspicions to the British. But with Senator McCarthy's hearings making headlines in Washington, both Sillitoe and Menzies appreciated that they would have to move quickly to calm Washington's fears. What they needed was to reassure their transatlantic partners that the 'Homer' investigation had not been bungled.

So when the FBI demanded to know the precise date on which B Division had targeted Maclean for surveillance, MI5 'lied' by putting the date back a fortnight. Liddell and White argued that they had to convince the Americans that their investigation had never produced any actionable suspicions against Maclean. This meant reconstructing the files to that effect. But to play the role of dissembler with Britain's most important ally offended Sir Percy Sillitoe. He protested that it was not his job to lie, no matter how important the purpose. But according to the recollections of one of those who attended the strategy meeting in the director's office, Sillitoe was eventually prevailed upon by senior MI5 officers to put a creative construction on the Burgess/Maclean case so that

MI5 could salvage what little credibility it still had with the FBI.

Sillitoe still insisted he could not carry off the artifice on his own. A decision was taken that an experienced officer would accompany him to help 'sell' the doctored version of the case to the Americans. Significantly, Guy Liddell did *not* accompany Sillitoe on his 11 June trip to Washington. Instead, Arthur Martin was named his assistant. Their mission started off on the wrong foot with the failure of the scheme to get the pair aboard the BOAC flight unnoticed. Sir Percy Sillitoe, the 'honest copper', and Arthur Martin, a former military signals officer, had their photographs plastered all over the front pages next morning.

The *Daily Express* might have had an even bigger field day if the reporters had known that Sillitoe's shoulder bag contained MI5 files on Burgess and Maclean that had been carefully doctored for Hoover's benefit. That the press in London had correctly identified Sillitoe's mission did nothing to modify Hoover's opinion of British ineptness and general untrustworthiness. But the FBI director became even more concerned when he learned that Sillitoe had no real grasp of counterintelligence work. Sillitoe was visibly uneasy at having to lie to Hoover. But Sillitoe had no choice. The embarrassment was even greater for Martin, whose job it was to support him. The FBI officials smelled a rat: they thought it odd that someone of the experience of Guy Liddell had not come to Washington. It was clear to Lamphere that the British were, once again, trying to pull the wool over American eyes.

When the FBI's domestic intelligence chief called the presentation of the British delegation 'horseshit', he was expressing the bitter sentiments of many of his colleagues. It was left to Lamphere to discover in his one-on-one sessions with Arthur Martin why the MI5 delegation had been sent over to lie.

'In our conversation Martin was so open with me, and so upset about having to admit MI5's bad faith, that I was almost sorry for him,' Lamphere records. Martin said the blackout of information on Maclean was the result of instructions from the Foreign Office to MI5. Then Martin turned to the question of Philby, against whom he admitted the British now had 'the gravest of suspicions'. He handed Lamphere a seven-point case against Philby that began with his communism at Cambridge and concluded with the hypothesis that he had played a role in the disappearance of Burgess and Maclean. It was a telling indictment.

'I'd never liked Philby, and now I began to hate him,' Lamphere wrote. He realized that Philby's treachery had compromised the FBI's intelligence advantage with the Venona codebreaking operation, and Philby had probably wrecked a recent FBI request for MI5 to oversee a meet in London between one of the agency's double agents and a Soviet intelligence officer.

At the CIA, Bill Harvey, the ex-FBI rough diamond who was then chief of staff 'C' (Counterintelligence), had no doubt about Philby's guilt. In a cogent five-page memorandum submitted on 13 June 1951, he set out for the benefit of the director of the CIA why he believed Philby was a Soviet agent. Five days later, James Angleton delivered a second assessment to that effect. General Walter Bedell Smith, the head of the CIA, then enclosed both memoranda in a top secret, official communication to the head of the British Secret Intelligence Service. In polite words it amounted to an ultimatum: 'Fire Philby or we break off the Special Relationship.'

The damage triggered by the defection of Burgess and Maclean is clear from declassified American documents. A report prepared for the Joint Chiefs of Staff in 1955 concluded that the Soviets had acquired, through Maclean, a vast amount of intelligence in 'the field of US/UK/Canada planning on Atomic Energy, US/UK postwar planning and policy in Europe and all by-product information.' According to the chairman of the US Atomic Energy Commission, 'practically everything was compromised up to the time of Mclean's [sic] dismissal. A *very* bad situation.' Also compromised was any chance of Britain's sharing atomic energy secrets. Furthermore, as code-room supervisor and head of Chancellery at the British embassy, Maclean 'had access to practically all high level plans and policy information' and 'all UK and possibly some US diplomatic codes and ciphers in existence prior to 25 May 1951 are in possession of the Soviets and of no further use.'

The magnitude of the intelligence disaster was nonetheless carefully concealed from the British public. But the secret record reveals that the timing of the defection was particularly embarrassing because a tripartite team that included British, American and French representatives happened to be conducting an inspection of security facilities in the three countries. Originally set up to probe the leakages in France, their 4 June report focused instead on exposing the deficiencies of the security facilities in the United Kingdom. The full report is still a classified secret, but its contents are summarized in a 1955 report to the US Joint Chiefs that indicated it came down hard on the British for their 'system of personnel clearances for those handling high level information' and their '"old school tie" system in clearing their top people.' The highest military authorities in Washington were told that 'the suggestions made for improving their system were not particularly well received.' Evidently the Americans had good reason to believe that the British had shelved the damaging report because the Joint Chiefs were told that although 'some improvements have been made', 'the current status of security conditions in the United Kingdom is lacking at this time and should be requested.' Significantly, the chairman of the Joint Chiefs was told that both Burgess and Maclean had been able to function as Soviet agents 'for many years prior to their defection' because they 'were apparently protected from exposure and dismissal for a long time by other highly placed officials of the British Government, particularly the Foreign Office.' The report concluded that it was *inconceivable that the pipeline dried up and operations stopped on 25 May 1951. It may be more appropriate to assume total compromise as of the defection date and continue inquiry into present and future security of Joint US/UK projects.*'

The aftershock of the 1951 defections wore the 'special relationship' very thin. Menzies had a keen diplomatic sense and moved swiftly to try to head off the storm building across the Atlantic. He had his deputy, Jack Easton, alert Philby to the possibility of recall in a personal letter of 6 June that was hand-carried to Washington. 'It was an ugly picture,' Philby said of his official order to report to London within a matter of days. During the thirteen-hour flight back to London by BOAC Stratocruiser, he had plenty of time to prepare his defense, confident in the knowledge that the 'strong presumption of my guilt might be good enough for an intelligence officer,' but it was 'not good enough for a lawyer'.

Jack Easton arrived in Washington on 13 July to tell Hoover and Smith that Philby was 'guilty of nothing worse than gross indiscretion, and that an inquiry was being mounted.' He found himself confronting skeptics. When Easton returned home, however, he sat in on Dick White's interrogations and quickly concluded that Philby was 'making no real effort to defend himself', and 'looked and behaved like a rat in a trap.'

'I let him go,' Easton declared. Without a confession, and with nothing but circumstantial evidence, Easton had no choice. 'But his attitude was such that everything being said against him was true and there was therefore a strong presumption of guilt against him,' Easton observed thirty-five years later.

Philby was then summoned to see Sir Stewart Menzies. White had already informed Philby that MI5 had received a strongly worded letter from the CIA that precluded his returning to Washington, so he knew what to expect. With under a year to go before his retirement, it was 'with obvious distress' that C had to ask his onetime protégé for his resignation. The high-flyer who was once considered on his way to becoming the first house-raised director of MI6 was out of a job at the age of thirty-nine. Menzies offered him £4,000 in lieu of his pension, to be paid half down and the rest in six monthly installments to discourage him from defecting.

Six months later, MI5 summoned Philby to Leconfield House for a 'judicial inquiry'. Helenus 'Buster' Milmo was the examiner. A leading barrister with wartime service in the counterespionage section of MI5, Milmo made a formidable interrogator. But according to Philby's account, Milmo let only 'two rabbits out of the bag' that he had not been expecting. One was the 'spectacular rise' in radio traffic from the Soviet embassy in London at the time of the 1944 Volkov affair; the other was a similar increase after Philby's 1949 briefing about the 'Homer' investigation. The chain of evidence assembled by MI5 surprised him. But he was relieved that it was all circumstantial. By meekly parrying Milmo's questions and permitting himself flashes of indignant anger when rebutting attacks on his character, Philby succeeded in what he set out to do: 'to deny him the confession which he required as a lawyer.'

While Philby could not be brought to trial, Sir Jack Easton and Sir Patrick Reilly both agree that there was *no doubt* among senior MI6 officers of Philby's guilt. The same could not be said for MI5 when it came to putting its own house in order and investigating the charges leveled against Anthony Blunt by his close associates Goronwy Rees and Rosamond Lehmann.

We can now see, with the advantage of hindsight, that despite White's skepticism about the reliability of Rees as a witness, Rees had dealt the security service all the cards and it needed to play nothing but high trumps and roll up the so-called Cambridge network. That MI5 and MI6 were familiar with most of the cards in the pack is evident from Rosamond Lehmann's list of their identifying initials.

Yet still MI5 was reluctant to play those cards and launch the same kind of systematic investigation in Britain that the FBI immediately conducted on the Cambridge agents and their connections in the United States. Sir Dick White explained that Rees's accusations lacked both substance and credibility. But Rees *did* implicate Blunt. It is also a matter of record that other MI5 officers – including Dick White, Courtney Young, and Jim Skardon – conducted no fewer than fourteen separate interrogations of Blunt between 1951 and 1963. Blunt considered both White and Young to be friendly, especially Courtney Young, who was his wartime partner in the diplomatic-bag operations, and White himself on occasion had accompanied the two Guys – Liddell and Burgess – to the Chelsea Palace of Varieties during the war. But MI5 insiders have told me that 'cozy chats' would be a more appropriate way to describe these sessions.

Once again, connections and circumstances worked in Blunt's favor. There were also very strong political reasons why senior MI5 officers were reluctant in 1951 to entertain suspicions about their brother officers. An investigation would have smacked of 'vulgar' American McCarthyism, and the consequences of even a limited internal investigation might have proved disastrous. The reputations of Britain's two intelligence services were already on the line with the FBI and CIA because of the successive debacles involving the atomic spies: Nunn May, Fuchs and Pontecorvo. Career officers such as Dick White had to weigh the damaging consequences to the special Anglo-American intelligence relationship if they acknowledged that there were further even more serious internal security problems. Then there was the threat that these twin bastions of the privileged class would face in a 'gloves off' confrontation with the current Labour Cabinet. The very idea that British secrets had been systematically betrayed by this most hidebound of old-boy networks would have ignited in the Labour government a chain reaction of outrage that would publicly explode to nuclear dimensions.

The implications of the allegations Rees made against Blunt and Liddell were just too awful for any senior MI5 officer to contemplate. And so the Committee of Inquiry set up by the Home Office in July 1951 confined itself to the issue of the security clearance of Foreign Office employees. Its recommendation for 'positive vetting' of all new applicants was quickly adopted. The question of what to do about those of questionable loyalty who were already in positions of influence in government was ignored.

James Robertson and Felix Johnston, the MI5 officers who had investigated Burgess/Maclean, concluded that Blunt was a spy, but lacking concrete evidence, they were reluctant to start playing the cards dealt them in 1951. The declassified FBI 'Blunt' file shows, however, that the Bureau wanted to interrogate Blunt in 1953 – but was evidently dissuaded from doing so by the British.

It was ironic that the only MI5 casualty was Guy Liddell. Although his wartime friendships with Burgess and the Bentinck Street set appeared highly incautious, he was never a suspect and never interrogated. But in the corridors of Leconfield House there were whispers that Liddell had 'outlived his usefulness, since the Americans would no longer wish to work for him.' By the time Dick White had leapfrogged into the director general's office in 1953 as Sir Percy Sillitoe's successor (with Roger Hollis as White's deputy), Liddell had already moved on to his consolation retirement posting as security adviser to the Atomic Energy Authority.

In Moscow, according to Kislitsyn, Burgess and Maclean underwent rigorous debriefing and became, for a time, advisers to the Ministry of Foreign Affairs. The Soviets forwarded money for Melinda Maclean through a Swiss bank. Kislitsyn told the defector Petrov about plans to get Mrs Maclean to join her husband. But it was not until she left England to live with her mother in Geneva that Soviet intelligence agents considered it safe to get in touch with her. On 11 September 1953 she disappeared from her mother's house with her three children to go to Moscow.

Despite what the KGB regarded as its generosity to the two defectors, it could not directly support Philby. For four years he had to keep his wife and five children as a free-lance with financial support from Tomas Harris who also paid for the private education of his children.

When Vladimir Petrov made headlines in 1954 with his defection in Australia, Philby had reason to be apprehensive. Petrov testified before a royal commission and might have provided some damning piece of evidence on which Philby could be arrested and tried. But the only light that Petrov shed on the Cambridge agents was what he had learned from Kislitsyn, who had made no mention of a 'Third Man', as the popular press had dubbed the unnamed member of the network who tipped off Burgess and Maclean. The publicity created by Petrov nudged the British government into publishing its own White Paper on Burgess and Maclean. Drawn up as it was by MI5, the official version was ingeniously constructed to absolve everyone from blame and to answer as few leading questions as possible while attempting to counter any criticism of ministerial reticence.

A year before the White Paper appeared in September 1955, Philby received a message from the Soviets. It is not without significance that the chosen messenger was Blunt. At a Courtauld lecture, he recognized his 'old' control, Yuri Modin, who handed him a postcard written by Burgess that fixed a rendezvous at 8:00 the following day in a North London pub. That Blunt responded to this direction shows that he was still under Soviet direction, if not control.

When Blunt arrived at the Angel in the Caledonian Road he was met by the Russian, who asked him to act as an intermediary in fixing a rendezvous with Philby. Moscow was attempting to bring Philby back under direct control just at the time he was getting the break that would rescue his career.

This came on 25 October 1955, when Lieutenant Colonel Marcus Lipton, a Labour member of Parliament, rose to ask the Prime Minister whether he had 'made up his mind to cover up at all costs the dubious Third Man activities of Mr Harold Philby.' Sir Anthony Eden said that he would get an answer from the Foreign Secretary in the following week's debate on the Burgess and Maclean affair. And Harold Macmillan then surprised the House of Commons with his unequivocal assurance: 'I have no reason to conclude that Mr Philby has at any time betrayed the interest of this country, or identify him with the so called "Third Man", if indeed there was one.'

'As far as I am concerned, the incident is closed,' Philby told journalists at a hastily convened press conference at his mother's London home. Some of his former MI6 colleagues, including Nicholas Elliott and Count Frederick Vanden Heuvel, the former station chief in Switzerland, took Philby's public exoneration to mean that he could be reemployed. They arranged with sympathetic friends at *The Observer* and *The Economist* to share the cost of his services. By September 1956 Philby arrived in Beirut on the eve of the Franco-British military operation against Suez.

For the next seven years he operated in the turbulent Middle East. Under his cover as a newspaper correspondent, he also operated as an intelligence agent for both London and Moscow.

The year 1956 also proved something of a watershed for the Cambridge network. Blunt was knighted by the Queen and visited the United States for a lecture tour – prompting another FBI report. Burgess and Maclean reappeared in public at a Moscow press conference. Philby reestablished himself as an MI6 spy aided by his father's extensive Arab network.

The worldwide headlines that greeted the Burgess and Maclean press conference in Moscow rekindled public interest in their case. As a result, Tom Driberg obtained the approval of Burgess – and the KGB – to publish a version of his story. This, in turn, prompted Goronwy Rees to write his own sensational version of events, which was serialized in *The People* that November. Neither Driberg nor Rees could name Blunt, who was protected by British libel law. But anticipation of the possible exposure of his role caused considerable apprehension and discomfort to the central figure in the drama. Sir Anthony Blunt was under such stress that he let his guard slip that memorable night in the taxi in Eaton Square when he broke down in tears before Rosamond Lehmann.

Driberg's memoir of Burgess was a careful pastiche of half-truths and misleading constructions. And Rees's second attempt to set the record straight backfired. The wrath of the Establishment cost him his college job and many of his remaining friends.

Now another botched operation by the secret service almost unseated Phiby from his new respectability. The objective of the ill-planned exercise was to conduct an underwater survey of the hull of the new Soviet cruiser that had carried Marshal Bulganin and Nikita Khrushchev on their state visit to the United Kingdom in April 1956. While the Soviet leaders were in London for a reception at Buckingham Palace – which Blunt, to the surprise of his friends, declined to attend – Commander 'Buster' Crabb, an ex-navy diver, vanished in the murky waters of Portsmouth harbor. The press published the story while the Russian leaders were still in England, to the considerable embarrassment of the government. The head of MI6, General Sir John Sinclair, resigned. White, then head of MI5, replaced him. The unexpected move that put Sir Dick White in charge of both secret services led to his disturbing discovery that Philby was 'back on the books'.

White, whose conviction of Philby's guilt had been unshaken by his public exoneration a year earlier, could have ordered MI6 to sever its connection with him. But the new C decided to troll Philby as a bait to the Soviets in the hope that careful playing of the line would eventually produce the necessary evidence to bring Philby to trial. Philby continued to act in his dual capacity for both British and Soviet intelligence. But his usefulness to Moscow outweighed any contribution he made to MI6.

It was no coincidence that Philby met another member of the Cambridge spy ring that spring. This was Egerton Herbert Norman, the Canadian ambassador to Egypt, who had been named by witnesses as a Soviet agent to an investigating subcommittee of the Senate Judiciary Committee, and had stepped off the topmost ledge of an eight-story apartment building in Cairo on the morning of 4 April 1957.

'I had a chat with [Norman] in Cairo not long before his death. What a shocking affair that was,' Philby confided to Canadian journalist Eric Downton. Philby also said that he had known him 'vaguely' as a brilliant Japanese scholar at Cambridge.

The bizarre circumstances of the suicide of the Canadian diplomat, who had played an instrumental role in General MacArthur's administration in Japan, became the subject of an international controversy. Norman's friends in Canada immediately charged the US Congress with hounding an innocent man to his death. But others have claimed that Norman's suicide note suggests that he took his own life to protect his friend Lester B. Pearson – who was then Canada's external affairs minister and later became prime minister – from exposure as a fellow member of a Soviet network.

Michael Straight, who knew Norman as another underground Trinity cell member, remains convinced that after Norman left

Cambridge, he played a shadowy role as an important agent of influence for Moscow. Not only was Straight well informed but he was no Communist witch-hunter. He had kept the banner of liberalism flying as editor of *The New Republic* and had testified before congressional committees against what he termed the 'spiritual corruption that characterized the McCarthy years.'

From his own experience, Straight was acutely aware of the insidious ways the Soviet intelligence service relentlessly exploited Communist ideologues. He suspected, too, that Blunt still had his lines to Moscow intact. So when he read in a newspaper that a 'British scholar of Cambridge University might become chief of Intelligence' in Britain, his conscience once again moved him into action. Alarmed that this unnamed professor might be Blunt, Straight told the FBI in a 1975 re-interview that he had approached his cousin, C. Tracy Barnes, who was then a senior executive with the CIA, with his suspicions. The FBI could not prove or disprove this statement since Barnes was dead.

The Straight case file shows, however, that the FBI was very keen to know why *The New Republic* had printed a series of articles on the Middle East from Kim Philby in 1957. But Straight pointed out that by then he no longer was editor of the magazine, even though his name was on the masthead. The FBI records also show that they had been told that Blunt made an effort to contact Straight the following year through Sir Philip Hendy, the director of the National Gallery, who was a friend of Straight's mother. Straight could not remember the approach. But he told his interviewer, 'It doesn't mean it didn't happen.' The FBI suggested that Hendy's approach represented an 'attempt by Blunt, under SIS (Soviet Intelligence Service) direction, to reinstitute Straight's association with the SIS'. Straight said this was impossible. He thought it likely that if Blunt was trying to contact him 'it would have been to determine if Straight had informed [the] authorities about him.'

Blunt had every reason to worry about Straight. He shared, with Goronwy Rees, the dark secret that could bring Blunt down. He also may have realized that it would be more difficult to face down Straight's firsthand testimony of his role as the Cambridge recruiter than it had been to dismiss the allegations made by Rees.

The higher Blunt's reputation soared as an art historian, the greater became his fear that his past might surface. There was also the possibility that Burgess would drop some indiscreet hint to the British foreign correspondents with whom he frequently drank in Moscow or, worse still, would carry out his threat to return to England. He confided in Harold Nicolson, who was then in correspondence with Burgess in Moscow, that MI5 had assured him that Burgess would be arrested if he set foot in England. The trial, at which he would be the chief witness, would cost him his job at the Palace and his directorship of the Courtauld. He told Nicolson 'he had conveyed to Burgess that he must not return.'

Blunt, it appears, could still exercise his influence over Burgess *even in Moscow*. But he had no control over the information that other Soviet spies or defectors might provide. The latter threat became more real as the sixties began with a spate of high-level defectors.

In 1960, a colonel named Oleg Penkovsky volunteered himself as an MI6 mole. He was in the GRU, and for the next three years, his Minox camera provided the West with snapshots of the upper echelons of Soviet military intelligence. In 1961 came the defection of 'Sniper', the code name given to Michal Goleniewski, a Polish intelligence officer with KGB affiliations, who helped uncover George Blake, the deep-cover Soviet spy in MI6 who had been captured in Korea and subsequently 'turned' by the KGB. Goleniewski's information also helped MI5 round up the 'Portland Spy Ring', which was run by the KGB illegal Konon Molody. Under the alias of Gordon Lonsdale, Molody had run, via subagents Helen and Peter Kroger, an espionage network at Britain's main antisubmarine-warfare base. But it was another KGB defector, code-name 'Kago' by the British and 'Ae/Ladle' by the CIA, who provided the most damning evidence since Krivitsky of the KGB's extensive high-level penetration of Whitehall.

This was Anatoli Golitsyn who had been named earlier as a potential defector by Peter Deriabin, a KGB officer who defected in Vienna in 1954. Golitsyn spent six years at Moscow Center making mental notes of high-level files. This KGB major turned up at the home of the CIA station chief in Helsinki on the morning of 15 December 1961, asking asylum for himself and his family.

So detailed and extensive was Golitsyn's information on KGB penetration of Western governments that some on the CIA CI (Counterintelligence)] staff under James Angleton suspected he might be an *agent provocateur*. But Golitsyn established a remarkable track record, filling out the details of many cases that Goleniewski had been able only to hint at. His information was supplemented by the leads supplied by two other sources that the FBI and CIA had tapped in the Soviets' UN delegation. One was a GRU officer code-named 'Fedora'; the other was a KGB source known as 'Top Hat'. Both later returned to the Soviet Union and were judged to be plants.

This harvest of Soviet defections resulted in productive spy hunts in more than half a dozen Western countries. Among the agents successfully uncovered were those in the 'Sapphire' network in the French SDECE intelligence organization; Colonel Stig Wennestrom, of the Swedish air force; an American Foreign Service official in Warsaw; and Israel Beer, a KGB mole who had served as an aide to the chief of staff of the Israeli army.

The most dramatic repercussions came in Britain. After the initial debriefing of Golitsyn in the United States, the CIA supplied the British with a list showing he knew of penetrations by at least *ten* Soviet agents. Golitsyn's information was tantalizingly incomplete in many of the cases. One referred to the MI6 spy Blake, who owed his conviction in 1961 and a record forty-two-year prison term to an investigation initiated by Goleniewski. (He was subsequently sprung from prison four years later to resurface as a Moscow-based KGB officer). A second serial led MI5 to John Vassall, a homosexual clerk in the Admiralty, who was arrested for passing on NATO secrets. A third serial pointed to a naval source who was identified as a senior commander who had already retired and against whom there was not enough evidence to proceed. A fourth serial relating to a KGB agent in an RAF missile base in Norfolk was also inconclusive.

Golitsyn's other serials were the most alarming. They appeared to relate to a continuing history of Soviet penetration of MI5. About the Cambridge ring he was able to recall that it was a highly unusual KGB operation because its five members all knew one another and had all, at one time or another, been run by Yuri Modin. He provided positive identifications for Burgess, Maclean, and Philby, whose KGB code-name he said was 'Stanley'. He was able to provide chapter and verse on the damage wrought by Burgess and Maclean. He also said that the Canadian ambassador, Herbert Norman, was 'a long-term Communist and KGB agent'. But when it came to identifying Blunt and Philby, Golitsyn's evidence could not have been used to obtain conviction.

In March 1962 a British team led by Arthur Martin, who, in 1960, had become the head of MI5's D1 investigation division, and his opposite number from MI6, flew to Washington to make their own debriefing of Golitsyn. What gave them real cause for concern was Golitsyn's statement that the safe for British documents at KGB headquarters in Moscow contained recent MI5 technical reports, that Commander Crabb's mission had been betrayed, and that the Soviets were so confident of their sources in London that they had dispensed with the need for a *Soviet Kolony* (SK) agent to organize security at the embassy there. Golitsyn's statements pointed to ongoing high-level Soviet penetration of the British secret services.

The first target was to establish whether Philby really was a mole. Golitsyn had provided no new evidence that would be acceptable in a court of law. But even as Martin was sifting through the Golitsyn material for clues, Flora Solomon provided the breakthrough in the case. In August 1962 she was in Israel, where she ran into Lord Rothschild at the Weizmann Institute at Rehovot and pressed him to 'do something' about Philby's anti-Israel articles in *The Observer*. On his return to London, Rothschild informed MI5. Martin's debriefing of Solomon provided the needed confirmation of Philby's Communist past.

Roger Hollis, now the director general of MI5, and his opposite number at MI6, Dick White, agreed that Philby should be confronted with the new evidence. They also agreed that Philby should be given assurances that he would not be prosecuted if he agreed to return to Britain and cooperate fully with MI5. The intelligence chiefs, and the Conservative government, were anxious to keep the embarrassing scandal covered up. But the offer of immunity in return for exposing the other Cambridge agents was to set a dangerous precedent.

It is difficult not to conclude that the old-boy network once again moved in to protect its own. Arthur Martin, who was originally detailed for the mission, was replaced at the last minute by Philby's friend, the former MI6 station chief Nicholas Elliott. The son of a former Eton master, Elliott, although now persuaded of his friend's treachery, was not the best man for the most difficult of counterintelligence missions: getting a spy to confess and then persuading him to return to face interrogation.

To the dismay of Arthur Martin, who had worked on the Philby case since 1951, Elliott blew it. He succeeded only in getting a general admission of guilt when Philby said he could not deny the long catalog of charges compiled against him. He even asked Elliott to break the news to his wife, Eleanor (an American whom he had married in Beirut in 1959), but he said he needed time to think about the immunity deal. After Elliott returned to London to make his report, Philby vanished from Beirut on 23 January 1963.

21 'The Final Sting'

The news that Philby had been allowed to escape – or as he claimed in his 1987 Moscow interview twenty-five years later, his interrogation 'was deliberately staged so as to push me into escaping' – exacerbated the relations between MI6 and the CIA. The British immediately released their official line on Philby. It sounded similar to what the British had said after the Burgess-Maclean defection in 1951. According to London, the Americans had been kept advised of the decision to interrogate Philby in Beirut.

'Advised? Hell no!' was the uncharacteristically explosive comment of James Angleton. The former chief of counter-intelligence for the CIA believed he had been doubly betrayed, by Philby and by London, because, as he told an interviewer, Verne Newton, in 1986: 'I had an agreement with them [MI6] that Philby would never be interrogated on foreign soil.'

The flight of the so-called Third Man came when Blunt was out of England. His British Council lecture tour of Europe may not have been a coincidence; it was the first extended trip he had made, except for a brief visit to New York the previous September. He had cut back his international travel schedule after suffering a severe bout of Bell's palsy in 1961, a neurological disorder that left him with a droop on the left side of his face.

MI5 had interviewed Blunt more than a dozen times by then. Now the Philby defection prompted more of these polite interrogations. But Blunt knew that it was not only the security service who suspected him. In 1961 there came the first unnerving hint that someone outside the intelligence services had pieced together his complicity.

During an interview at the Reform Club, Blunt was asked: 'Are you the Third Man?' The questioner was Douglas Sutherland, who was writing a book about the Burgess and Maclean affair. 'If you print that I'll sue,' Blunt told the former Foreign Office man turned investigative journalist. Sutherland noted: 'His face was grim and his mouth untypically set.'

Sutherland might have pressed harder with the 'circumstantial evidence' had he known that Blunt's old controller, Yuri Modin, had resurfaced in Beirut at the time of Philby's defection – and that Blunt had visited Lebanon shortly afterward. He had stayed with his old friend Sir Moore Crosthwaite, the British ambassador in Beirut, in March while en route to a lecture at the Weizmann Institute. The possibility therefore exists that Modin met Blunt to alert him of the immunity deal offered to Philby.

Blunt would have returned to London fortified by the knowledge that with Philby in Moscow, if MI5 ever obtained hard evidence against him, it would offer him the same secret deal. The thought would have reassured him. He would never need to flee to Moscow or spend the rest of his life in prison. Blunt may have believed he had weathered another round of crises with his secret still intact and his future secure. His public reputation had soared to new heights the previous year when he stood next to the Queen at the July opening of the Queen's Gallery in the Buckingham Palace mews. Blunt received – and deserved – much of the credit for persuading the royal family of the need for rotating exhibitions that would permit the public to see for the first time sections of the remarkable royal treasure-house of more than 4,500 works of art that had been catalogued and restored under Blunt's supervision.

Art had lofted Blunt to great heights. It was ironic that six months after Philby's defection, it would be an artistic cause, and an American one at that, that would unleash his own Nemesis. At a White House luncheon on 4 June 1963, President Kennedy's special assistant, Arthur Schlesinger, told Michael Straight of his selection to succeed to the chairmanship of the newly created Advisory Council on the Arts. Straight's initial reaction was to accept the challenge of running what would become the National Endowment for the Arts. But when he heard he must undergo an FBI check before his candidacy could be submitted to Congress for approval, the specter of his Cambridge past 'came flooding to the surface through the sinkhole of my memory'.

The next day, Straight told Schlesinger that he wanted his name withdrawn, and that he wanted to tell his story to the FBI. On 7 June 1963 Straight went to the Justice Department for the first of a series of interviews with Bill Sullivan, during which he made a clean breast of his Cambridge recruitment by Blunt, his association with Burgess and his contacts with the Soviet intelligence service in Washington in the early part of World War II. It was, he admitted to the FBI, something 'he realizes he should have done a long time ago.' Straight said that until the presidential appointment came up he 'lacked the resolution' to give his account to the authorities because he knew that it was not merely a matter of sharing his knowledge with a few officials.

'My story would result in a trial in England,' Straight declared, saying that he expected, 'within a few months, I would be facing Anthony Blunt in an English courtroom.' Since having to appear before a congressional committee was his primary concern, it would be surprising if he had not considered himself under an obligation to give Blunt the same sort of warning in 1963 that he had given Burgess twelve years earlier. Straight told the FBI that the 4 June offer from Schlesinger came as a surprise. In his autobiography he says that as early as May 1963, his friend Senator Paul Douglas of Illinois was proposing him for the chairmanship of the Fine Arts Commission. Straight said that he did not know about this recommendation.

Straight made a trip to London from 3 to 12 April that spring. He insists that he neither sought out nor encountered Blunt during this visit. Stella Jefferies, an administrative secretary at the Courtauld Institute, says that Straight appeared unannounced at the Institute one day 'in July 1963' shortly before the director went off to America 'at short notice'. She says that Blunt 'was not keen to see him'. Later she heard Blunt telling someone 'he – meaning Straight – was going to shop them.'

The FBI files make no mention of Straight's April trip, only that he took his family to their summer home on Martha's Vineyard at the end of June. Straight denies *absolutely* that he met Blunt before his FBI sessions that June.

Michael Straight says that he had no contact with Blunt in either Britain or the United States during 1963. To infer that his April visit was in any way connected with Blunt's July decision to go to America, he says is absurd. Mrs Jeffries' claim, he points out, is vitiated by the discrepancy over these dates and her allegations are unsubstantiated. He points out that his passport for 1963 contains no reference to suggest that he was in England or away from the United States when Mrs Jefferies claims that she encountered him in the Courtauld Institute.

It came as a surprise to everyone at the Courtauld, when the director suddenly decided on short notice to accept an invitation the institute had received to send a graduate student to lecture at a six-week summer course at Pennsylvania State University. Blunt's decision astonished – and delighted – the students and staff of the tiny art-history college in the heart of rural Pennsylvania.

'It was a bit like having a Harvard Law School professor come to teach a civics class to a country high school,' recalls Desmond MacRae. He vividly recalls how amazed and delighted everyone was to have someone as grand as Blunt lecture them. They joked that it must have been the $5,000 fee or the Royal Art historian confused their small campus with the more famous University of Pennsylvania. MacRae, then a graduate student of art history, remembers how the lofty Blunt could never get used to the American custom of interrupting the lecturer with questions.

Blunt's hauteur evaporated when his class took him on a tour of the local bars. 'He let his hair down, singing off key some traditional British vaudeville ballads at the Millhein bar, which was decked out as an English pub.' MacRae was surprised to find that the surveyor of the Queen's pictures was far to the left politically. 'He held forth on the extraordinary egalitarian view that all men ought to be treated as equals in every way except intellectual ability,' MacRae recalled. Although they had no idea that Blunt was a Communist, they found his socialist views oddly inconsistent with his intellectual fascination with the France of Louis XIV, in which every subject of the king had an assured place in society. Blunt erupted once in barely controlled outrage when MacRae voiced novelist John Braine's scathing dismissal of the British monarchy as 'a solitary gold filling in a mouth full of decay'.

It was part of Blunt's peculiarly schizophrenic character that while he did not disagree that British society was in a state of decay, he took any attack on the Queen as a personal affront. Although MacRae and his fellow students did not appreciate the paradox, it must have been a bitter irony for their visiting professor that he was in the country that Burgess despised when the news came through that Burgess had died of liver disease on 19 August 1963. At the Moscow crematorium, it was left to Maclean to pay tribute to 'a gifted and courageous man who devoted his life to the cause of making a better world.'

According to MacRae, Blunt was not noticeably moved by Burgess's death, about which several students commented. They knew Blunt's association with Burgess from his dedication to *Artistic Theory in Italy*. But Blunt was a past master at concealing his emotions, and if he was in contact with Straight, he would have known that his own denouement could not be long delayed.

In fact, it did not take place for another nine months. Although Straight agreed to the FBI's request that he meet with representatives of British intelligence that July, Sullivan did not recontact him until January 1964, when he arranged for him to meet Arthur Martin in the Mayflower Hotel. Straight told Martin about Blunt's activities in Cambridge, giving the names of other recruits including Leo Long.

'You may not believe this,' Straight says Martin told him at the end of their talk, 'but this is the first hard evidence that we've been able to obtain on Burgess and Blunt.' Straight did not know that Martin had just finished interviewing John Cairncross at Northwestern University. Cairncross had made what Martin called only a 'partial confession' to passing information to the Soviets. It was Straight's assurances that he would confront Blunt in court if necessary that provided the long-awaited break-through.

Yet another three months elapsed before Blunt was confronted with Straight's confession. Roger Hollis, who had become direc-tor general, apparently wanted to protect MI5's morale and repu-tation following a commission conducted by Lord Denning into the so-called Profumo Affair. The inquiry was ordered after the Prime Minister had been embarrassed that summer by having to admit that John Profumo, his defense minister, had lied to the House of Commons about his sexual liaisons with Christine Keeler and Mandy Rice-Davies. These two 'showgirls', as they were euphemistically described by the press, had been introduced into Profumo's influential circle by Stephen Ward, an artist and 'society osteopath'. In turn, this led to liaisons with Captain Eugene Ivanov, a Soviet naval attaché, during wild weekend parties at Lord Astor's house at Cliveden.

What did not emerge in public, either at Ward's trial at the Old Bailey on charges of procuring, or in the Denning report, was MI5's, or Blunt's role in the affair. Ward committed suicide the night the jury returned a guilty verdict. But it is now known that Ward believed he was assisting MI5 in the entrapment of Ivanov, who was known to be a Soviet intelligence officer and that Blunt had done a service to the Palace by quietly arranging for the purchase of Ward's sketches of members of the royal family, which had been put on sale by Ward to raise money for his defense.

It was not only Blunt's trivial role in this sex-spies-and-drugs scandal that convinced Roger Hollis to tread carefully in per-suading the home secretary that to bring the royal art historian to trial would have public repercussions for the Establishment that would be too awful to contemplate. Professional counter-intelligence officers, such as Arthur Martin, also argued against a trial. They, too, were in favor of an immunity deal that would enable them to extract from Blunt the confession that Elliott had failed to get from Philby: a full list of those recruited and how they operated.

The immunity deal was finally approved by Henry Brooke – himself an old Marlburian contemporary – and it was conditional on Blunt's not having spied for the Soviets after 1945. Reliable sources confirm that Hollis obtained in advance approval for the deal from the Queen's private secretary, because it required the continued presence of a traitor in the Palace. The Queen's private secretary, Sir Michael Adeane, was concerned that at all costs the monarch should not be dragged into the affair, and this would best be served by a secret deal. Adeane knew, even if Hollis did not, that if Blunt ever came to trial, there was the risk of another, even more explosive, royal scandal.

The immunity deal was a convenient but flawed solution for all concerned. It was predicated on the assumption by MI5 that Blunt would live up to his side of the bargain: that he would provide the full and detailed confession that they needed. Once Blunt had been given the guarantee against prosecution, it would be impossible to bring him or any of those he implicated to justice. The price of uncovering the Cambridge network was that none of its members could ever be called to account. But without Blunt's confession, however, there was no way of discovering how deeply the conspiracy had penetrated the British Establishment.

Considering what was at stake in Blunt's confession, it is astonishing that Arthur Martin was sent alone to confront Blunt on the morning of 23 April 1964. (American counterintelligence officers have assured me that the standard practice calls for at least two officers to be present.) Martin still believes that Blunt had been forewarned and held out for the immunity deal.

Martin says that he was met with a blank stare when he informed Blunt that Straight had told him all about his recruitment and dealings with the Russians. Blunt was too smart to be panicked into a confession. It was not until Martin told him that the attorney general had authorized formal immunity from prosecution that there was any reaction. With cool deliberation Blunt got up, walked to the window, and poured himself a drink. Only then did he turn round and say: 'It is true.'

While Martin was relieved to hear this confirmation, he made it clear to Blunt that immunity was conditional on his full cooperation. Blunt confirmed that Leo Long and John Cairncross were Soviet agents. Later, they were both interrogated by Martin, to whom they confessed on the understanding that they would not be prosecuted either. Straight was brought to London to confront Blunt in May 1964, again that September, and again in April 1965, in the hope of stimulating the flow of information. But as Martin affirms, Blunt's first twenty-five-minute confession was more productive than any other session in the more than six years of debriefings that followed.

MI5 was provided with few really fresh leads by Blunt. Apart from Long and Cairncross, he volunteered only the name of the long-dead War Office clerk Tom Wylie as a prewar recruit of Burgess. The security service tried other tactics, which included confronting him with John Hilton, his Marlborough friend in MI6. This meeting ended sourly. So did a confrontation with his Cambridge friend Kemball Johnson.

Arthur Martin, after a disagreement over tactics, had been taken off the Blunt case. Roger Hollis, the head of MI5, had replaced him with Peter Wright. To Wright fell the task of trying to wear Blunt down and persuade him to live up to his side of the bargain. It proved a futile exercise because 'although Blunt under pressure expanded his information, it always pointed at those who were either dead, long since retired, or else comfortably out of secret access and danger.' According to American sources, Blunt's performance conformed exactly to the standard routine that the Soviets drilled their agents to adopt against interrogators.

'I could never be a Whittaker Chambers,' Wright says Blunt told him when he raised the question of Alister Watson. 'It's so McCarthyite, naming names, informing witch-hunts.' Wright says that he reminded Blunt that his acceptance of the immunity deal obligated him to play the role of Chambers. It was no good putting the hood on 'if he would not point the finger'. Notwith-standing Blunt did precious little finger pointing. He gave no evidence against Watson, who fitted Golitsyn's description of the fifth man in the Cambridge ring, and a face to face confrontation between Blunt, Watson and two interrogators resulted only in bitter recriminations. Wright discovered that Lord Rothschild had written to Dick White in 1951 suggesting that Watson should be interrogated because of his Communist affiliations. But he never was. In 1965, Watson, who was still engaged in secret scientific work for the Admiralty, denied the allegations that he was ever a spy, even though he admitted he had met with Soviet agents on several occasions. This admission, and the discovery that he failed to declare his Communist sympathies, were grounds to remove his security clearance and transfer him to nonsecret work at the National Institute of Oceanography.

Blunt was no more helpful when it came to investigating the allegations against Sir Dennis Proctor and Sir Stuart Hampshire. Wright interviewed them both and they vigorously denied that they had ever been involved in any espionage activities. In 1951 Rees had alleged that Hampshire was a part of Blunt's network, but Hampshire had denied this most emphatically in 1965. He did, however, recall a prewar dinner in Paris with Blunt, Burgess and Klugmann, at which the trio might have targeted him for recruitment. But Hampshire insisted that he was never a part of their, or any other, espionage network. Klugmann died before he could be interrogated.

John Peter Astbury, one of the Communist Apostles 'fathered' by Straight in 1937, was also a prime suspect of Wright's. According to his younger brother, Astbury had continued his political activities at London University before being called up to the Royal Corps of Signals. He later worked on radar developing during the war and then at Manchester under Professor P.M.S. Blackett, another Marxist scientist, who made no secret of his sympathy for the Soviet Union. After prewar research at Imperial College, Astbury transferred to CERN in Geneva where he worked for many years on the European nuclear-accelerator project. He would, therefore, have been a valuable recruit for the Soviets. But his brother does not recall that he ever came under suspicion, and he says they were never close, recalling how in the fifties there was a 'kerfuffle' with the press about his brother defecting during an extended holiday trip abroad. Straight told me that he had given Astbury's name to MI5 in 1964 as one of his fellow Apostles who was recruited for the Soviets by Blunt or Burgess. Wright, moreover, confirmed to Chapman Pincher in 1981 that Astbury's scientific work made him an obvious candidate for investigation. But like a number of Cambridge suspects who declined to be interviewed, there was not enough evidence to proceed without their cooperation. Shortly before Astbury died in December 1987, Straight was told by surviving members of their old Cambridge circle, at their Trinity College reunion, that Astbury was studiously avoiding them because MI5 had renewed its investigations of him because of his connections to the CERN project.

Blunt once said cryptically that any friend of Burgess's might be considered a potential recruit. Among the Cambridge contemporaries known to have made Wright's final list of suspects – all of whom denied the allegations – were the following: Ambassador Sir Anthony Rumbold, who was a close friend of Maclean; Sir George Clutton, the former British ambassador in Manila; Rosamond Lehmann's brother, John; Andrew King, a former MI6 officer; the publisher John McGibbon; and Sir Edward Playfair, a former permanent undersecretary, who had just retired as chairman of a major computer company. Permission to interview Rumbold, then ambassador to Austria, was declined although he had been identified through circumstantial evidence to tie him in as one of Krivitsky's Foreign Office sources. But Clutton was dead; Playfair denied he had been a spy, but he admitted he 'had known a lot of Communists'. McGibbon said he never made any secret he was once in the party but that 'doesn't make me a spy'. King's refutation was based on his declaration of Communist party membership when he joined MI6. Lehmann told MI5 that he had rejected an approach made to him in Vienna by a Soviet agent in the 1930s.

One of the few valuable leads Blunt gave Wright was that his former Courtauld colleague Phoebe Pool, with whom he had written a book on Picasso, had acted as his courier in the thirties. MI5 arranged for Anita Brookner, another member of the Courtauld staff, to interview Pool, who confirmed Blunt's story and also said that she had acted as a go-between with Andrew Cohen and the Oxford graduate Jenifer Williams, plus two Oxford-educated brothers, Bernard and Peter Floud. This suggested that the Cambridge ring had spread its tentacles to Oxford, the alma mater of another suspect named Arthur Wynn who was up for appointment as deputy secretary at the Board of Trade.

Wright set out to see all those named. Williams, who had married Oxford professor Herbert Hart, a wartime MI5 officer, admitted being part of the Communist underground. But she declared that she had given up meeting her Soviet control officer when she joined the Home Office in 1938. Peter Floud, a former director of the Victoria and Albert Museum, was dead. Sir Andrew Cohen died from a heart attack before he could be interviewed. Bernard Floud, then a senior Labour MP, committed suicide after his first inconclusive session with Wright. When shortly afterward Phoebe Pool threw herself under a subway train, the new director of MI5, Martin Furnival Jones, became so alarmed that the secret about Blunt would leak out that he summoned Wright to inform him that all the suicides would 'ruin our image'. He ordered Wright to terminate the investigation – and there the matter rested, after some forty potential spies had been identified.

Wright was confident he had exorcised the past and discovered 'how far the conspiracy extended'. But within a few years, another MI5 assessment cast doubt on this claim. Anne Orr-Ewing, another K branch officer, concluded that Blunt's assistance to Wright had been 'entirely insincere'. Nor had Wright discovered the damage that the transatlantic branch of the Cambridge network had caused the Americans – or the instrumental role that Philby had played in assisting the Soviet penetration of US counterintelligence operations.

The damage-control assessments within the CIA were initiated by James Angleton. They followed Golitsyn's defection in 1961. But it was not until after Philby's defection, the Straight confession and the MI5 interrogations of Blunt that the CIA began to appreciate exactly how the sustained, high-level penetration of the British secret services might have affected the security of various American intelligence agencies. The discovery that George Blake was also a mole had serious implications for the CIA because he certainly told the KGB about Operation Gold. This was the successor to the tapping of Soviet telephone lines in Vienna by the British in 1951 – Operation Silver. Operation Gold was a 1,500-foot tunnel under the border into East Berlin. Gold cost $25 million, and it became operational in the spring of 1955. From then until its much publicized 'discovery' eleven months later, in May 1956, the 'Tunnel of Love', as it was dubbed by *The Washington Post*, provided a virtual Niagara of intercepted Soviet military and KGB traffic that kept a factory of translators working around the clock at CIA headquarters. But Blake's exposure five years later raised the question of how much of what had previously been regarded as reliable SIGINT was carefully manufactured Soviet disinformation.

Golitsyn's confirmation that Philby was a spy proved American suspicion that he was responsible for the catastrophes that sabotaged the CIA's operations back in 1949. But since Philby was in the United States until 1951, he could not be held accountable for all the systematic failures that overtook other Anglo-American clandestine operations in Europe during that period.

For example, Anothony Cavendish, who was in R5 counter-intelligence with MI6 in West Germany and Austria, had revealed that the operations he ran from Hamburg, to land émigré Latvian agents ashore, all turned sour. The MI6 men were rounded up. It was later discovered that the KGB then used the captured radio transmitters against the British. A similar fate plagued Project I, II, III and IV, the code name give a series of operations in 1950 that parachuted two- or three-man teams of trained Ukrainian and Byelorussians back into their homeland inside the Soviet Union. Even Cavendish's personal efforts to cultivate contacts with Soviet officers, when he was in Vienna in 1951, seemed mysteriously doomed.

Interestingly enough, Cavendish does not put the blame on the Communists and homosexuals whom he encountered in dis-proportionate numbers within MI6. He blames Philby. Philby was indeed responsible – but not in the way that Cavendish suggested. Philby was in Washington at the time. There is no reason to believe he would have been kept abreast of the details of purely British operations that were run from Europe. But from 1945 to 1947, Philby had been in charge of the MI6 anti-Soviet operations. One of his responsibilities was recruiting and vetting the Ukrainians, Byelorussians and Poles who came from the Intermarium, Prometheus and Abramtchik, factions of the ABN, the Anti-Bolshevik Bloc of Nations. These were the people MI6 trained and pressed into service as Cold War penetration agents.

The background checks on these agents had involved MI5's processing massive volumes of captured German Abwehr, Gestapo and SS files. Many members of these factions had become Hitler's puppet administrators or policemen and had helped enforce the ruthless German occupation in Eastern Europe. These people were thus regarded by the British as good anti-Communists. But as the Abwehr and SS had discovered, many of the émigré groups had been deeply infiltrated by underground agents of the Soviet intelligence service.

Documentation in the formerly top-secret reports that are now in the process of being declassified in the US National Archives, shows the extent to which the OSS and its successor organiza-tion(s) relied heavily on MI5 to weed out these Communists. Contributing to this vetting procedure, which involved checking the captured German counterintelligence files, were intelligence officers on the British Control Commission in Germany. It is significant that among them was Leo Long. And Blunt himself could have been involved because of his wartime operations against the Eastern Bloc governments in exile, and his extensive postwar travel in Germany. Also involved was MI5's F Division, where Roger Hollis and Graham Mitchell had spent the war logging the political connections of both Nazis and Communists.

Agents of the 'Cambridge network' were therefore remarkably well placed at the start of the Cold War to ensure that the MI5 and MI6 vetting slips carried the magic words 'no traces against' when it came to the penetration of the ABN by Moscow. This ensured that a slew of Soviet agents, including the White Russian general Anton Turkul, the Czech Intermarium chief Ferdinan Durcansky, the Ukrainian Stefan Bandera and the Byelorussian leader Mikolai Abramtchik, were either directly involved or had staff members who ended up running and recruiting other agents for covert operations against the Soviet Union.

When Philby came to Washington in 1949, one of the missions he discharged simultaneously for both London and Moscow was to 'sell' Frank Wisner, the assistant secretary of state for refugee affairs, the ABN networks. He claimed it was because the British government could no longer afford to support them. According to one former American intelligence officer, 'the final sting' was that a number of these infiltrated networks were taken on by Wisner, and later passed into the CIA.

After Philby came under suspicion in 1951, a reexamination of the bill of goods OPC had been sold caused it to drop its sponsorship of the Abramtchik faction. But it was not until after Philby defected to Moscow and the Blunt investigations revealed the true extent of the 'Cambridge network' that James Angleton ordered a major reassessment of the CIA's European underground networks. This involved reviewing thousands of previous security checks for agents and sources who had earlier been cleared by MI5 and MI6.

Angleton knew from his own wartime experience in London the damage that double agents could cause. He suspected the British moles had laid the groundwork for a 'Double-Cross' of the West's intelligence services that, if unchecked, would far exceed the disruption the Allies had caused the Germans in World War

II. The new Soviet game would take them deep into what Angleton termed 'a wilderness of mirrors'. This telling and much misconstrued phrase Angleton defined as that 'myriad of stratagems, deceptions, artifices and all other devices of disinformation which the Soviet bloc and its coordinated intelligence services use to confuse and split the west.'

Angleton believed the CIA by the mid-sixties had the resources and experience to navigate in 'the ever fluid landscape where fact and illusion merge' so as to confuse the KGB at its own game. This would be done by turning the infiltrators against the Soviets in a complex web of 'Triple-Cross'. But that involved taking risks. And some American counterintelligence officers lacked Angleton's precise logic. From the outset, they were skeptical of Golitsyn's obsession with the scope and deviousness of Soviet stratagems. For Angleton it became something of a crusade when, in the wake of Philby's defection, Moscow stepped up its assault with a wave of false information and defectors in what Golitsyn warned was a carefully planned effort to protect its still undiscovered moles. The new assault by Moscow reinforced Golitsyn's most stunning allegation: that the KGB already had an agent in the highest ranks of the US intelligence service, and that Soviet defectors would be planted to build up his credibility.

The consequences of Philby's 'final sting', and the appalling dimensions of the success of the 'Cambridge moles', were seen by Angleton as vindications of Golitsyn. 'The Great Mole Hunt' resulted as the British and American intelligence services became preoccupied with the search for the other Soviet infiltrators. George Young, a former senior MI6 officer, suggested that Angleton was a gullible Machiavelli who 'had been completely under Philby's influence and sought to whitewash himself by finding KGB agents in every British department and agency.' But the record, as it has now been uncovered, shows that the CIA counterintelligence chief had good reason for his concern. That was why the highest priority was given to the 'Cambridge connection' in the housecleaning operations conducted by the American counterintelligence agencies in the mid-sixties.

The FBI cooperated by recalling Michael Straight for a further interview in June 1966. He was given a list of eighty-five Americans who had attended Cambridge University between the years 1930 and 1934, from which he picked out one American, whom he knew casually at the Department of State. He then named two more Americans with whom he had studied at Cambridge between 1936 and 1937 and whom he knew to have been Trinity-cell members or Communist sympathizers. Although he did not name any at Oxford, he volunteered to look at any lists. The legal attaché, who was the FBI representative in the US embassy in London, recommended a full review of all Americans who had studied at either Oxford or Cambridge before the war.

Hoover initially balked at the resources needed for the job, and worried about the potential repercussions of an 'investigation of over 500 American citizens with no basis for such inquiry in fact.' But American intelligence officers confirm that he was persuaded by the CIA to change his mind. As a result, the records of nearly six hundred Americans who had attended either Oxford or Cambridge before World War II were carefully compiled, examined and scrutinized.

The British response to the damage they had suffered from the Cambridge moles and George Blake was to set up the so-called Fluency Committee. The need to reassure their American partners that MI5 and MI6 were at last taking steps to put their houses in order prompted the heads of the two organizations to agree to this joint committee whose task was the evaluation of past infiltration and the possibilities of current penetration. An internal investigation code-named Peters was already under way in MI5 to examine the evidence that Arthur Martin had compiled indicating that Graham Mitchell, Roger Hollis's deputy, was a Soviet mole.

Hollis reluctantly agreed to the investigation of Mitchell, but used the word 'Gestapo' to describe the inquiry, when Martin was transferred to MI6 in November 1964. Dick White insisted on nominating Martin as his representative on the Fluency Committee, whose principal contributor from MI5 was Peter Wright. The committee examined some 270 claims of Soviet penetration. After eliminating those that could be attributed to Blake, Philby, Burgess or Maclean, they were left with some two hundred, which were later whittled down to twenty, plus three substantial incidents that could not be accounted for. Two of the three final serials involved the twenty-year-old charges made by Volkov and Gouzenko that pointed to the high-level agent in MI5. The third defector, Goleniewski, had charged in 1960 that there was a middle-ranking agent in MI5 whom the British code-named 'Harriet'. After exhaustive investigation it was decided by the end of 1966 that the Polish defector had probably based his assertion on false information.

The Fluency Committee was then left with the two historical cases. An intensive debriefing of the now-retired Mitchell led the committee to clear him of suspicion for lack of evidence. This wrapped up the 'Peters' investigation, and led to the molehunt code-named Drat, which was led by Wright. Its target was Roger Hollis, the former director general, who was now retired. This investigation uncovered numerous incidents in which Hollis, as head of counterespionage and later director general, had delayed investigations or failed to act with the alacrity that might have been expected. Hollis also fits into two historical serials: as wartime head of F Division he could fit Volkov's reference to 'an acting head' of MI5; and he had traveled home from China in the thirties via the trans-Siberian railway, stopping off in Moscow, which gave him the 'something Russian' in his background that fitted the code name 'Elli.'

Wright was convinced from the evidence he dug up that Hollis was the 'supermole'. But the former director general denied the charges when he was finally brought in to be interviewed. Without a confession, the Drat case collapsed, and the ten volumes of Fluency Committee findings led to no certain conclusion.

In 1981, Wright, then in retirement in Australia, took his case to the public by telling the Hollis story to the journalist Chapman Pincher, who made it the focus of his best-selling book *Their Trade Is Treachery*. The Prime Minister denied in a House of

Commons statement that any conclusive proof had ever been produced to show that Hollis was guilty. From the safety of his Australian retirement Wright successfully defied the Official Secrets Act and a lawsuit brought by the British government to publish his own indictment of MI5 in general and Hollis in particular in *Spycatcher*. The book made him an international sensation and a millionaire, but it did not 'prove' Hollis guilty or shed any more light on the true identity of the supermole in MI5.

The suggestion that the high-ranking Soviet spy was a figment of the feverish anti-Estalishment imagination of molehunters such as Peter Wright and Arthur Martin is flatly rejected by Nigel West. In his book *Molehunt*, which summarizes the investigations and draws heavily on informed security-service sources, West concludes that 'enquiries found overwhelming evidence to show that the original suspicions were amply justified.' He tells us that 'sixteen out of twenty-one molehunters, each an experienced counterintelligence expert, were convinced.' On the basis of his sources, West concludes that either Roger Hollis or Graham Mitchell – or possibly both – was the traitor. He opts for Mitchell on the grounds that he authored the misleading 1955 White Paper.

American intelligence sources, who have studied the cases and who have had links to the British, are not, however, nearly so certain that the answer is that simple. Some of them recall the importance of an observation made by Maurice Oldfield, former MI6 chief, that he would have put his money on the one candidate who escaped investigation altogether because he was believed to be above suspicion. His remark registered in Washington, and not just because of the candor of this unassuming Derbyshire farmer's son, during his tour as liaison officer in the capital in the early sixties at the time of Philby's defection, when he had earned the Americans' respect and helped heal the wounds in the MI6/CIA relationship. They also knew that when Oldfield took over as C in 1973, he reviewed the reports of the Fluency Committee and was struck by what he regarded as a curious and important omission. He duly passed his observations on to some of his

American friends when the conversation turned to the old unsolved cases on a trip shortly before he retired in 1978.

'If I had been in charge of the investigation,' Olfield was recalled as saying, 'I would have put Guy Liddell at the top of the list.'

Oldfield's comment cannot be dismissed as simply another shot in the partisan war with MI5. He was not known for dancing on dead men's graves, and as a staunch patriot, he considered it bad form to snipe at one's fellow countrymen in front of foreigners. That was why his remark stuck in the minds of those who heard him make it in the context of Liddell's suspiciously close association with 'the Cambridges', as some CIA officers refer to Blunt, Burgess, Philby, Maclean and their network of friends.

Within a month of the death of Goronwy Rees in December 1979, the charges of complicity he had made against Guy Liddell twenty-eight years earlier were published in *The Observer*. The reaction of two of Liddell's former protégés was immediate and indignant. TOP SPY MASTERS DENOUNCE NEW 'PREPOSTEROUS SMEAR' was the headline on an unprecedented public statement by two of Britain's most senior MI5 figures, who had 'top level clearance' to speak out in defense of their former boss.

'It was a grotesque charge,' said Sir Dick White, against 'a devoted servant of this country.' Guy Liddell was 'a wonderful man', according to Jim Skardon, who told reporters that 'any suggestion that he was a traitor was preposterous.' He had merely shared 'common artistic and cultural interests' with 'a coterie' of people who included Burgess and Blunt.

Despite their denunciation of Rees, neither White nor Skardon commented on why Liddell might have joined Blunt in trying to persuade Rees to remain silent about Burgess back in 1951. That issue was also sidestepped by Blunt, who wrote a letter to *The Times* about the credibility of Rees's various accounts. Andrew Boyle tartly reminded *Times* readers that Blunt, as a self-confessed liar and traitor, was not a reliable witness. 'May I simply say that Rees had nothing to gain by telling me a pack of lies,' he wrote. 'His aim was to tell the truth and to do so more fully and openly than was legally possible when he published his book.'

'The accusation against Guy Liddell was palpably absurd,' concluded Wright after reading Liddell's office diary, which was considered so secret that it was code-named Wallflowers. Wright, who listened to Liddell's taped historical memories of MI5, in which he made no mention of the Burgess and Maclean defection, thought him a 'tragic figure' who had been 'undone by unwise friendships'.

To Wright – and to Liddell's hand-picked recruits Dick White and Roger Hollis, who were then in charge of MI6 and MI5 – the former deputy director was a revered father figure. To many who served him, Liddell was the epitome of the fictional British spymaster: a thoughtful headmaster whose ruthless professional skills were tempered by artistic and musical sensibilities. The testimony to his universal popularity in the office was the large turnout at his funeral on 6 December 1958. He had died suddenly of a heart attack, but there were those who believed that his spirit had been broken when he was passed over for director general and then betrayed by the defection of his friend Guy Burgess.

Anthony Blunt was a conspicuous presence among the large crowd of mourners. For once he lost control of his emotions and he was observed weeping.

The suggestion that the 'officer and gentleman' who led Britain's secret war against the Soviets for forty years might have been a Soviet agent is still obscene to those who knew him. But in the context of the facts that are now available, Oldfield may have been correct to raise the unthinkable. American intelligence experts who have reviewed the evidence do not find it impossible, or ludicrous, that Guy Liddell *could* have been the MI5 supermole.

The wilderness of mirrors corrodes gentlemanly constraint, and the discipline of counterintelligence theory demands rigorous examination of every potential suspect when penetration by a ruthless and hostile intelligence service is suspected. If possibilities translate to probabilities, then that probability has to be weighed against the facts. By these criteria it is now clear that MI5's lack of any independent research and analysis section contributed to the too-hasty dismissal by Liddell's protégés of the allegations Rees made against him as too absurd to be investigated. It is self-evident after Blunt, Philby and Blake that what seemed an impossibility in 1951 should not have been so lightly rejected by Wright in 1965.

Not only is it *possible* to conceive that Liddell *could* have been recruited by the Soviets, but weighing the probabilities against the newly available evidence, a strong circumstantial case can be made that he was the most successful mole of all. Moreover, when it comes to the key Volkov and Gouzenko serials, Liddell is actually a better 'fit' than either Hollis or Mitchell, the two candidates investigated by the Fluency Committee.

If by '*ispolnyayushchiy nachalnik*' Volkov really did mean 'fulfilling the duties of' – as chief of the department rather than as 'acting head of' – then Liddell, as director of B (Counterespionage) Division, was the obvious candidate for the Soviet source who in 1944 was 'head of a section of the British Counter-intelligence Directorate'.

In the case of 'Elli', the GRU spy in 'one of five of MI' in 1942, Gouzenko's recollection that communication was carried out only by *dubok* in a 'split between two tombstones' once a month suggests that extraordinary precautions were taken to protect a very high-level source. Neither Hollis nor his deputy, Mitchell, was elevated enough in rank to warrant such precautions. But a MI5 director of B Division, with twenty years' experience in anti-Soviet operations, *would* have insisted that this passive role offered him the maximum security because it avoided the risk of face-to-face communications with a Soviet controller or cutout.

A single train journey through the Soviet Union with a stopover in Moscow was considered enough evidence of 'something Russian' in the background of Hollis to make him a good candidate for 'Elli'. Research shows a much more convincing Russian link for Liddell. In his days with Special Branch in the twenties, Liddell had strong contacts in the White Russian émigré community. One was the ubiquitous Anatoli Baykolov. This supposedly White Russian journalist was an associate of Sabline, the tsarist chargé d'affaires who had gone over to the Soviets in the twenties – and it is significant that they were *both* on friendly terms with Liddell. Baykolov continued as a contact until the fifties. In July 1944 he received a dubious communication from Liddell: 'N. and F. have been returned to Paris, ostensibly for further duties, but Soldatenkov has been informed of this move and doubtless he will advise his people to pick them up in Paris.'

Why Baykolov, a supposed anti-Bolshevik, should have been involved with Soldatenkov, the Soviet embassy liaison officer at the War Office, is suspicious. What is more questionable is Liddell's involvement in what has every appearance of a plot to repatriate two unsuspecting Russians to the Soviets. It is difficult to conceive that the long-time head of MI5 counterespionage could have been unaware of Baykolov's Soviet connections. As late as February 1951, Liddell wrote to Lord Vansittart with information he obtained after he had 'seen Baikolof', [sic] who was described as 'very reputable'.

Analysis of Liddell's early performance in the MI5 case files discovered in the US Archives reveals operational mishaps that must be added to the puzzling string of failures that occurred later, when he assumed full responsibility for MI5 counterespionage investigations in 1940. The anomalies are so numerous, and follow such a consistent pattern, that they suggest a prima facie case can be made that Liddell had been leaking information to the Soviets and systematically working to further their interests since the late twenties.

A partial list can now be compiled that raises serious questions about Liddell's competency, bad luck – or treachery. It includes such serials as:

- The allegations that the Arcos house was tipped off before the 1927 raid, and the failure to locate the planted RAF manual, forced the British government to reveal that it had broken the Soviet codes.
- The mishandling of the 1928 arrest of Ethel Chiles, which permitted the escape of Jacob Kirchstein, the Comintern's principal agent.

- MI5's failure to block the visas of Bukharin and the Soviet delegation, which enabled them to propagandize Britain's scientific community in 1931.

- The failure to sustain the wide-ranging surveillance of Cambridge Communists at the same levels as in the mid-twenties, after Liddell joined MI5 in 1931.

- MI5's failure to arrest either Maly (the master recruiter of the Cambridge ring) or his successor, Brandes, who were the Soviet agents running the Woolwich Arsenal spy ring in 1937.

- MI5's failure to keep track of the German Communist émigrés Kuczynski and Fuchs, despite MI6 notification that they were both Communist activists.

- The failure of the MI5 vetting procedure that permitted Fuchs and Nunn May to be given security clearances to work on the atomic-bomb project.

- MI5's failure to 'bag' the Soviet agent running Captain King in 1940 when Krivitsky blew the Foreign Office code clerk.

- Liddell's personal recruitment of Blunt and approval of Burgess for secret-service appointments. Although C Division was technically responsible for security checks, and F Division under Hollis for monitoring subversive activities, Liddell's B Division had an authority that could override negative Registry traces.

- MI5's repeated failures to spot known Cambridge Communists such as Klugmann, Long, Cairncross, Watson et al., who were all cleared for sensitive wartime military and intelligence positions.

- Liddell's failure to investigate the RSS reports on 'Sonja's' radio transmissions or to put her under surveillance in 1947 when her record as a GRU agent runner was confirmed by a British defector from the Lucy Ring.

- Moscow's 1944 alert to Colonel Zabotkin, the GRU chief in Canada, to guard his network against the British 'greens' prior to Liddell's visit to Canada and the United States.

- Liddell's approval of the decision to send F Division chief Roger Hollis to debrief Gouzenko instead of a senior counterespionage officer, and the failure to mount a proper investigation into 'Elli'.

- Liddell's repeated rejection of the reports by his Countersubversion Section chief, Maxwell Knight, that gave detailed warnings of Communist infiltration during World War II.

- The two years that it took MI5 to conduct the 'Homer' investigation, or the Venona serial that exposed Maclean, and the decision to keep the FBI and CIA in the dark.
- The Liddell-Blunt relationship that was the probable source of the Thursday tipoff that the Home Secretary was to give approval on Friday for the interrogation of Maclean the following Monday.
- MI5's failure to maintain continuous surveillance of Maclean, and the lack of an alert to the French authorities to pick up Burgess and Maclean in Saint-Malo.
- Liddell's collusion with Blunt in the aftermath of the defection to dissuade Rees from making a confession to MI5.
- The repeated tipoffs to the Soviets that Cairncross was under MI5 surveillance after the defection.
- Liddell's sanctioning of the 'creative' reconstruction of MI5's Fuchs and Burgess-Maclean files to mislead the FBI in 1951.
- The 1946 warning to Moscow of Skripkin's intended defection, and the significant absence of a single Soviet intelligence-service defector during Liddell's six-year tenure as deputy director of MI5.

There is, therefore, circumstantial evidence to suggest that Guy Liddell was either the 'grandfather' Soviet mole, or was badly compromised by Blunt. Passive spies can be every bit as damaging as active ones. There can be no doubt that Liddell's passivity in the MI5 vetting process let in the Cambridge moles; passivity led to Krivitsky's warnings being ignored – and passivity slowed the 'Homer' investigation into Maclean to a snail's pace. Yet when vital Soviet interests were threatened, as they were during the time of the Arcos raid, the Gouzenko defection and the escape of Maclean, Liddell appears to have played an activist role by discreetly raising the alarm for Moscow with such caution that he never came under suspicion. Yet his astonishing record of passivity, taken together with his compromising friendship with Blunt and Burgess, ought to have given MI5 investigators pause.

That it did not – and still does not – suggests that Liddell's former MI5 colleagues may have too hastily dismissed the probability because they could see no conceivable motive for his betrayal. But, as has been shown with Blunt, the mechanism of intellectual treachery is woven from subtle deceits and resentments. Nor should it be forgotten that the Liddell's – like the Blunts – were a family with aristocratic connections dropping down the social scale. The backbiting cynicism of the homosexual milieu which he enjoyed may have fed a deep-seated resentment against the Establishment, exacerbated by his disastrous marriage. His passion for the cello and his connoisseurship grew in defiance of his stern military father and were nourished by a doting musician mother. Liddell's artistic temperament, like Blunt's, shaped by similar adolescent resentment against the underlying philistinism of British society, may well have sown the seeds of later treachery.

Nor does the probability that the deputy director general of MI5 could have been a deep mole necessarily absolve the two other candidates: Roger Hollis or Graham Mitchell. As the Fluency Committee discovered, incidents such as the Crabb affair and the botched confrontation with Philby indicate that there was an active mole in the upper reaches of MI5 *after* Liddell retired. But even if one – or both – were Soviet spies, their treachery does not explain the earlier series of prewar anomalies.

Espionage networks, like other living entities, have to proliferate to survive. So if Hollis and Mitchell were spies, whoever recruited them must be a prime suspect. Liddell was not only responsible for their admission into the elite ranks of the security service, he directly effected the entry of Blunt and Harris – and it was Harris who maneuvered Philby into MI6. Nor is it insignificant that Liddell's tenure as MI5 counterespionage director coincided with the high tide of Communist infiltration into the upper reaches of the British intelligence services. Only three explanations offer themselves: either Liddell suffered from a run of bad luck that was so disastrous as to be incomprehensible; or he was incompetent to the point of criminal negligence; or he was the granddaddy Soviet mole in the British intelligence services.

Corroboration that Liddell may have been the primary deep-cover Soviet penetration agent is the fact that 'Elli' worked for the

GRU. Blunt and the Cambridge moles started out with the NKVD (later the KGB). In fact, when Philby relayed the news about Gouzenko's defection to his controller in 1945, the telltale Venona decrypt revealed that the 'Chiefs' of the Politburo had to give their permission for Moscow Center to consult its GRU 'neighbors' about the spy whose existence Moscow Center was not aware of.

This indication that 'Elli's' cover was jealously guarded in Moscow is another pointer to Liddell. By the late thirties, when Hollis and Mitchell would have been recruited, they would have worked for the NKVD (later the KGB). Since Elli was GRU, that would seem to rule them out. In the mid-twenties when Liddell was targeted because of his potential, Soviet military intelligence (GRU) was the dominant intelligence force in the UK. As an asset, the GRU would have kept Liddell from all their rivals because his unique position in British counterintelligence enabled him to sound the alarm when Soviet espionage rings were threatened. That could explain why the permission of the Politburo had to be obtained before his very existence could be revealed in 1945, as the result of the emergency caused by Gouzenko's defection.

In practice, unresolved counterintelligence cases are never closed. They still might contain the threat of systemic penetration. As Stalin used to say, 'Espionage is a crime against the people.' But the crime of espionage is difficult to prove in court unless the spy is caught red handed, or can be persuaded to make a confession.

In the absence of incontrovertible proof of guilt, it is rare indeed for a counterintelligence service to develop a case that can be successfully prosecuted in a Western court of law. Occasionally evidence of a substantive nature is found in the reports of defectors and signals intelligence. But the prosecution is frequently inhibited from disclosing its sources and methods in a public trial. The putative cases against Hollis and Mitchell – like the one that can be made against Liddell – arise from careful analysis of their operational histories, their associates, their decisions (or the lack of them), and in the anomalies that come to light after their official service ends.

'Even the mere suggestion of a possible penetration has to be investigated throughly,' a former top-ranked US intelligence officer told me when I asked him to comment on the case against Guy Liddell. This intelligence officer pointed out, with considerable emphasis, that when allegations were made against James Angleton by a disgruntled junior officer, the FBI was immediately brought in to investigate the CIA's chief of counter-intelligence. He also emphasized that it was an independent organization, the FBI and *not* the CIA, that handles internal-security matters.

'In terms of urgency, the report of a bomb aboard an aircraft ranks with information about a possible penetration of the security intelligence services,' the intelligence officer said. 'The bomb may take one hundred lives, but the latter could destroy a nation's capacity to defend itself.'

Guy Liddell and James Angleton occupied similar positions in counterintelligence in MI5 and the CIA. But while the allegations against Angleton in Washington resulted in an immediate investigation, in London the allegations against Liddell were considered too grotesque to warrant any action at all. 'Strange!' my intelligence source mused. 'How very strange!'

Liddell was never caught red handed. He made no confession. The case that he was 'Elli' rests on the incomplete evidence of Soviet defectors. It is understandable that Liddell's former colleagues would rush to protect the reputation of a dead man who could not defend himself against the charges. But as the Blunt case shows, the cost that has been paid because of official rationalization, forgiveness and indulgence has been too high.

A case officer's analysis of Anthony Blunt's life and times provides grim lessons that cannot be overlooked. Perhaps the most telling is the fact that Blunt's involvement in communism was probably known to MI5 as early as 1939, when Blunt was rejected for a post in army intelligence. Yet within twelve months, Guy Liddell personally recruited Blunt into MI5.

From an operational standpoint, American intelligence sources agree that it was unlikely that the Soviets would have told Blunt that his recruitment had been sponsored by one of their agents. If Liddell was indeed the 'grandfather mole', Liddell would have been recruited and run by the GRU, which had good reason in the forties to keep such a deep operational secret concealed from the NKVD.

If so the NKVD recruit Blunt probably never was in a position to know whether his MI5 mentor and friend also served as a Soviet mole. Therefore neither Wright nor any of his MI5 contemporaries had reason to question Liddell's loyalty. Their successors have resorted to scoffing at the very idea that there ever was a 'fifth man' in MI5 by citing Oleg Gordievsky, the former *rezident* in London. He is supposed to have told MI5 that the KGB headquarters echoed with laughter when they learned of the turmoil caused by Wright's belief that the former head of MI5 was a Soviet mole.

Like all such 'official' leaks, close examination reveals it to be more *fabulae facile* than reality. The very idea an interdepartmental joke would echo down the rigidly compartmentalized corridors of the KGB does not ring true to American experts. Nor was it revealed just when, how or by whom the KGB learned of the Fluency Committee's investigations. Also unclear is whether Gordievsky gave MI5 this comforting story before, or after, his spectacular 1985 escape from Moscow that terminated this MI6 penetration of the Soviet Intelligence Service.

Gordievsky has never been permitted to speak publicly. But from what is known of his credentials, he graduated from the KGB training school in 1963 before spending ten years handling Soviet 'illegals'. Sometime before 1978, during his posting as Second Secretary, later press attaché, at the Soviet Embassy in Copenhagen, Gordievsky was recruited by MI6 with the assistance of the Danish Intelligence Services. In June 1982 Britain's mole in the KGB was posted to the London Embassy. He arrived just in time to warn MI5 that one of its members, a thirty-three-year-old misfit named Michael Bettaney, was trying to sell his services to the Soviets.

It proved a bitter irony that Gordievsky managed to 'burn' the relatively unimportant Bettaney, but quite failed – despite his supposed omniscience of KGB operations – to alert the British that an ex-RAF Soviet 'mole' had sold the 'crown jewels' of Anglo-American SIGINT operations to Moscow. This mole was Geoffrey Prime, a Russian linguist in GCHQ whom the GRU had recruited as an informant in 1968. From then until his formal retirement in 1978 from J Division at the heart of the closely guarded Cheltenham complex, Prime had for years been feeding the Soviets the most sensitive data obtained by the NSA's *Big Bird* and RHYOLITE satellite surveillance of the Soviet Union. Moreover, it was the chance investigation of Prime's child molesting in 1982 by local Cheltenham police that led to his exposure as one of the most damaging of all Moscow's postwar British spies.

If Gordievsky had not been briefed while at Moscow Center before he came to Britain about the GRU's star performer Prime, surely it stretches credibility too far to claim that the GRU would have revealed to him the identity of their historic mole 'Elli'. The Soviet intelligence services strict adherence to the 'need to know' principle is a matter of record. So if Gordievsky did not know the identity of 'Elli', he was obviously in no position to give categorical assurances that Wright's quest for Hollis was a wild goose chase.

What is also now a matter of public record is the extraordinary catalogue of blunders for which Liddell was responsible. The MI5 case reports now available show that they cannot all be plausibly explained as the 'manifestation of hindsight' by former British intelligence officials who resolutely dismiss the very possibility that Liddell might have been the fifth man.

'Everyone who knew Liddell thinks this absurd, but then so did everyone who knew Blunt,' Lord Annan allows, despite his own skepticism.

If Blunt ever suspected that Guy Liddell was also working for Moscow, it was a secret he never revealed. But for Andrew Boyle's refusal to be cowed by Britain's strict libel laws, Blunt would probably have avoided public disgrace. The British Establishment moves secretly and effectively to take care of its own – as was evident in 1971 when Blunt was hospitalized. In this instance it was MI5, burdened by Blunt's guilt, who moved swiftly to limit the damage of their ill-judged immunity pact with him.

Just two years after the death in 1969 of his doting mother, Blunt's doctors diagnosed his cancer, the disease that had killed his father forty years earlier. Even as surgeons operated, MI5 was rushing through a top-secret ministerial denial in the event that he died and the scandalous secret leaked out.

Blunt confounded a pessimistic prognosis by recuperating from a colostomy operation. The following year he was fit enough to travel to Berlin to give the 1972 British Council 'Queen's Lecture'. The same year marked his retirement from the Courtauld Institute and as Surveyor, when he was accorded the particular distinction of continuing to advise on the Royal Collection.

Blunt's recovery was a relief to Sir Martin Furnival Jones, Hollis's successor as head of the Security Service, because the guarantee of immunity, which ceased on the death of Blunt, could have leaked. But it must also have been tempered by the realization (confirmed by his death certificate) that Blunt had only been granted a temporary respite by surgeon's knife.

Furnival Jones, a cautious man, had taken the precaution in 1971 of ordering a secret internal review of the Blunt case. His apprehension was only increased when analyst Anne Orr-Ewing's report concluded that Blunt had lied consistently to Wright and only revealed the names of his conspirators who were dead or could not be prosecuted. The ticking down of Blunt's mortality now transformed him into a menacing time-bomb for MI5, Buckingham Palace and all members of the Establishment drawn into his monumental conspiracy.

Yet when the public scandal did explode eight years later, the 'blast walls' of the Establishment once again demonstrated a remarkable capacity for sheltering their own. Although the Prime Minister had rejected the Secret Service and Cabinet Secretary's advice not to admit that Blunt was a spy, once she had let the cat out of the bag she relied on the Conservative hierachy to resist Parliamentary demands for a full inquiry. Blunt was able to escape a full public examination by ducking behind the Official Secrets Act. He emerged without his knighthood, but with his scholarly reputation and authority in the art world virtually intact.

Ironically, the only casualty was the non-Establishment ex-Irish Guards bandsman who was Blunt's intimate companion. William John Gaskin was convinced that Mrs Thatcher's acknowledgement that Blunt had been a Soviet spy would lead to a fresh round of investigations for them both.

Yet neither Blunt nor Gaskin was recalled by MI5. This seems a particularly puzzling omission in the light of the damning Orr-Ewing's report. 'Lady Gasket', as he was contemptuously referred to by the snobbish members of Blunt's homosexual circle, had good reason to be alarmed at the prospect of renewed Special Branch investigation. It was not so much because he could have provided fresh leads into Blunt's treachery, but because of his hushed-up involvement in fraudulent art deals.

This had occurred after Blunt had encouraged Gaskin to expand his small-time jewellery dealing into fine art. To establish him in the business, Blunt allowed Gaskin to dispose of his valuable collection of Poussin and other old-master drawings built up by shrewd purchases over more than forty years.

Unfortunately for Blunt, when Gaskin ran out of genuine works to sell he teamed up with an artist friend to exploit Blunt's august reputation by claiming that he had authenticated old-master drawings that were in fact of doubtful attribution.

So when the press were hounding Blunt after his public exposure, Gaskin became terrified that they would rake up his guilt and this, according to friends, was what precipitated his 'suicide' leap in February 1980. But other members of their homosexual entourage believe that 'Lady Gasket's' guilty know-ledge went beyond fake old master drawings to knowledge of Blunt's double-dealings, because he knew the old spy far better than anyone.

Even if Gaskin was never treated as an intellectual equal, a native intelligence from a youth who survived the rough back-streets of Belfast would have acquired an insight into Blunt's impenetrable mask. Until his death Gaskin still affected the muscularly handsome air of the guardsman dominated by Blunt who, it has now emerged, had no qualms about using his Courtauld subordinates as unwitting couriers. When Gaskin's physical attractions paled, he loyally assumed the procurer's role, supplying the aging Blunt with the soldiers, sailors, plumbers and carpenters who were paid to satisfy his penchant for 'rough trade'.

Since the couple lived together for so many years as 'man and wife' Gaskin must also be presumed to have gleaned a great deal of detailed knowledge through eavesdropping. He always denied knowing that Blunt was a spy, but the traumatic exposure would have enabled Gaskin to piece together a great deal of extremely damaging information he had picked up over the years. At least one member of their homosexual circle believes that it was what Gaskin knew that precipitated the pre-dawn row that led to his near fatal plunge from the fourth floor fire escape on 14 February 1980.

Old friends of Blunt are divided over whether it was loyalty, devotion or remorse that prompted him in July 1981 to draw up a new will that confirmed the ex-Guardsman as his principal beneficiary. This was surprising, since Gaskin had already been provided for as the nominal owner of the lease on their luxury flat at Portsea Place. Now he stood to inherit a rare Poussin painting as part of an estate worth in excess of a million pounds (Blunt's two nieces received only a five thousand pound legacy). When Blunt suffered a fatal heart attack as he sat at the breakfast table on 26 March 1983, under the terms of the will Gaskin had only to survive him by a month to become a millionaire.

Blunt died just three weeks after the death of Donald Maclean in Moscow. The obituary writers' main concern was how to reconcile the damage resulting from Blunt's secretive treachery with his lofty public distinction. It was a dilemma that three years earlier had divided the august of the British Academy. Saying that his fellow academics were taking Senator Joseph McCarthy as their patron saint, the Oxford historian A. J. P. Taylor resigned shortly after Blunt because it was not 'the duty of the Academy to probe into the behaviour of fellows, except on the grounds of scholarship'.

The irreconcilability of scholarship and espionage received official endorsement when the British government rejected as 'inappropriate' the offer by Blunt's executors to bequeath his Poussin painting to the nation in lieu of death duties. After its purchase was rejected by the National Gallery of Scotland the funds to keep *Rebecca and Eliezor at the Well* in Britain were eventually raised by the Fitzwilliam Museum at Cambridge.

Curiosity drew a flock of reporters to the Putney Cemetery on 29 March 1983. But in contrast to Guy Liddell's interment there twenty-five years earlier, on this rainy morning there were no tearful crowds of former MI5 colleagues gathered for Blunt's last rites. The black cortege of cars drove past the press with indecent speed as they bore the spy's corpse and eleven anonymous wreaths through the acres of dripping tombstones.

The thirty mourners in dark coats were outnumbered by the line of police barring the television crews and newspaper photographers from entering the utilitarian crematorium chapel. One of the more diligent reporters noted how fitting it was that Blunt's funeral was taking place on the day of Holy Week traditionally known as 'Spy Wednesday'.

In the brief service held at the crematorium chapel, the Reverend Thaddeus Birchard, incumbent of the parish once ministered to by Blunt's father, admonished the pews of stony faces: 'All have sinned and fallen short of God.' Later Wilfred and Christopher Blunt would make a final pilgrimage to Martinsell Hill above Marlborough. There they cast their brother's ashes to the winds. Winds that Anthony once described as 'more felt than seen', sweeping the 'edge of the abyss', in a schoolboy poem that lovingly portrayed this ridge of Wiltshire downland as 'fixed, immutable/Beyond the power of time.'

John Hilton, Blunt's close friend at Marlborough, suspects that Blunt would have approved of his own epitaph in preference to the Reverend Birchard's apologetic panegyric. Recalling how one of their masters at Marlborough had stressed loyalty to God, king and parents 'in that order', Hilton wryly observed: 'If communism is counted as a religion, Anthony's later practice could be said to conform to this pattern, putting communism ahead of patriotism.'

In this context Blunt would have regarded himself not as a traitor but as a dedicated international Communist. To him this would have been proof of his emotional and intellectual detachment, qualities that he admired in his two great artistic heroes, Blake and Poussin. Their single-minded application of their individual and contrasting visions provided the creative dynamic that elevated them above contemporary moral and social constraints. So, too, did the intense personal revelations of the brooding seventeenth-century Roman architect Francesco Borromini – an icon of Blunt's baroque pantheon. In 1667, Borromini chose to perish in slow agony from a self-inflicted dagger wound rather than concede his subordinate position to his artistic rival Giovanni Lorenzo Bernini.

'To have been under a strain so violent that it drove him to this act of violence – if not madness – and yet immediately afterward to be able to dictate such a lucid account of the event,' Blunt was to write approvingly of Borromini, 'reveals a combination of intense emotional power and rational detachment which are among the qualities which go to make him such a great architect.'

This personal striving to combine 'rational detachment' and 'intense emotional power' was at the heart of Blunt's complex personality. It equipped him well for his role as a Soviet agent. His schizophrenic quest for artistic enlightenment, the intellectual authority that he derived from it, was paralleled by his personal goal of secret authority and power that was realized in his success as a Soviet agent. He was also a master of compartmentalization, in both his personality and his careers, and it made him the supreme Jekyll-and-Hyde character. Unlike the fictional doctor who had to wrestle with his twin identities, Blunt managed to resolve his different personae behind a mask of exquisite detachment that allowed him to live easily with his treachery.

Professor Steiner has pointed out that there is no modern parallel for Blunt's infamous achievement. He was an individual, Steiner says, who, 'as a scholar and teacher, made veracity, scrupulous integrity, the touchstone of his work.' He also managed 'the co-existence within a single sensibility of the utmost truth and falsehood. . . .'

Blunt may have succeeded in reconciling the irreconcilable while he lived. After he suffered the trauma of public exposure, he took comfort that the majority of his former students loyally defended his impeccable scholarship. Only a minority saw a link between his treachery and the self-assuredness of his own judgements – his preference for photographic analysis of a work of art at the expense of the painting itself.

'Arrogance is well known in the academic world and is often inseparable from success in scholarship,' Lord Annan contends. But Blunt's arrogance was so overweening it ensured that after his death, his haughty self-image would tarnish. As Christopher Wright, one of his former pupils, told me: 'Blunt wanted to carve his judgements in stone for all time and could never accommodate easily to criticism – least of all when it involved his beloved

Poussin on whom he wanted to have the final word.'

No history, and certainly not that of such a diffuse discipline as art, can be cast as immutable. Despite the argument that Blunt's academic achievements were separate from and outweighed his espionage, the tarnish has come with the recognition by some of his former colleagues that his inner moral degradation affected his professional judgement. To the dismay of Blunt's ardent admirers, cases have been documented where Blunt suppressed the scholarship of rivals and lent Gaskin his authority on ambiguous attributions for old master drawings. 'Once you get away with lying on one subject, it spills over into the rest of your life – and that is what happened to Blunt' was how his fellow art historian Dennis Mahon chose to put it.

'God dwells in the minutiae,' Blunt was fond of drumming into his art students during lectures at the Courtauld. This dictum, on which he erected his professional reputation, was not his own. He had borrowed it from the pioneer German art historian Aby Warburg, in whose library Blunt honed the skills that launched his professional career. Warburg's recipe for an art historian demanded 'a cool detached serenity which belongs to the categorizing and contemplations of things.'

Blunt's philosophic detachment and his minute attention to detail also account for his astonishing success as a Soviet agent. Ironically, it was the lack of these very qualities that was behind MI5's failure to counter Soviet penetration until too late. Blunt knew, so presumably Moscow did, too, that Britain's intelligence services did not have officers of collective intellectual caliber who could, by 'cool and detached' research and analysis, root out the moles. The career MI5 and MI6 officers, recruited on the old-boy network, unfortunately did not concern themselves with minutiae. They were too easily fooled by the outward appearances of Blunt, Philby and their other wartime recruits from the Cambridge left-wing network.

The assumption that a public-school and Oxbridge education was an automatic guarantee of loyalty to the Crown proved as erroneous and myopically deadly as Senator McCarthy's belief that all American Communists posed a direct threat to national security. But the blind eyes of MI5 in general – and Guy Liddell in particular – were no less disastrous. It is an inescapable fact that Blunt's Marxist record ought to have barred him from MI5. That he gained admission to the inner sanctum of Britain's security service was a result of his cultivation of Liddell, without whom neither he nor Burgess could have engineered the admission of Philby to MI6.

Philby may have been the more dedicated and ruthless professional agent who has attracted the accolade of the 'Spy of the Century'. But his career cannot match the versatility or longevity of Blunt's service for the Soviets, which encompassed three distinct phases:

1. As the principal Cambridge recruiter of the original network of ideologically motivated Soviet moles

2. As an active double agent in World War II, who was instrumental in expanding the Soviet penetration of MI5 and MI6

3. As the unassailable 'agent of influence' who helped thwart later investigations by laying false trails away from Philby and his fellow deep-cover spies who were still operational – and even after they had defected to Moscow.

Each facet of Blunt's treacherous career inflicted a particular harm on his friends, his profession, the Crown, his country and the Anglo-American relationship. On his hands there is the blood of the MI6 agent in the Kremlin he betrayed in 1941 and that spilt by all those Czechs, Poles and Hungarians whose anti-Communist loyalties he betrayed to Moscow during World War II. The extent of the damage that Blunt wrought on a generation of Cambridge contemporaries can never be adequately measured. Treachery by its nature is obscene and shadowy and has no clear-cut boundaries. Investigations (including this one) unavoidably cast a broad shadow of suspicion that taints the posthumous reputations of the innocent along with the guilty.

Blunt's life is an enigma that will never be completely unravelled. But Wright's disclosures show that the sinister web of influence that Blunt wove continues to haunt MI5, the government and the British Establishment.

Blunt's treachery also ultimately proved fatal for Gaskin, the man who was closest to Blunt whose death made him a millionaire. This inheritance may have been intended to buy the silence of the intimate companion of thirty years. With £800,000 in the bank after death duties, Gaskin would not easily be tempted by cheque-book journalists to sell a sensational 'kiss-and-tell' story of 'My Life with the Royal Spy'. As this writer can confirm, Gaskin steadfastly refused all requests for an interview. The only comment he ever made about Blunt's espionage was that it was like a game of 'Cowboys and Indians'.

Blunt's money, however, did not buy Gaskin freedom or peace of mind. Shunned by his dead companion's snobbish homosexual set, Gaskin sold the apartment and moved to a small house in the Dundee suburb of West Ferry where his sister from Belfast had settled. But even in the genteel East-coast Scottish town, he did not escape the consequences of his fatal friendship.

At 8.35 on Monday 18 July 1988 the lifeless body of a well-built man in his late sixties was discovered beside the Ogilvie Road railway crossing at West Ferry. The police, who identified the victim as a William John Gaskin, surmised that he must have died around 7.55 A.M. after being struck by the 7.25 train from Arbroath.

The driver of the commuter train, however, had not reported any incident that morning as he accelerated out of Broughty Ferry station, through a short tunnel and over the crossing. The unmanned pedestrian path was one of many that crossed the line that winds along the picturesque Tay estuary to Dundee past the rolling greens of the renowned Carnoustie Golf course.

In contrast to Blunt's death five years earlier, the demise of his boyfriend was not relayed quickly to the press. Ten days passed before *The Scotsman* carried the story the following Saturday under the headline 'Traitor's Friend Killed.' It reported that a 'fatal accident inquiry will be held' although the Dundee police had 'no reason to believe there were suspicious circumstances'.

To the surprise of some local journalists, the anticipated Fatal Accident Inquiry never took place. In England a Coroner's inquest would have been obligatory, but in Scotland the Crown Office in Edinburgh can waive an inquest if the police and the next of kin are satisfied as to the cause of death. But this was surely one fatal accident where there could be no certainty because no witnesses had come forward and not even the driver could testify if the victim was run down by his train.

The Metropolitan Police report of Gaskin's earlier suicide attempt would have supported the view that he had taken his own life. His death was put down as suicide on official records. And yet – Gaskin knew a great deal of information damaging to both Soviet and British interests. Had the old spy wielded a sinister influence from beyond the grave?

'Anyone can commit a murder, but it takes an artist to commit a suicide', used to be the boast of Stalin's professional assassins in the Soviet Intelligence Service.

Gaskin is now beyond the reach of time – and enquiring journalists. The file on the embarrassing final chapter of Blunt's life is now closed, no doubt to the relief to both British and Soviet intelligence.

Epilogue
The Legacy of the
Cambridge Spies

On 11 May 1988 the Soviet news agency, Tass, announced the death of 'the remarkable Soviet intelligence officer Kim Philby'. Moscow's official news agency referred obliquely to his 'exceptionally delicate work', describing his activities as 'heroic' and his accomplishments as 'multifaceted and vast in their geographic scope'.

The only survivor of the original founding fraternity of Cambridge spies died – probably of heart failure – just three months after he became a bizarre symbol of the new 'openness' that Mikhail Gorbachev is bringing to the Soviet Union. But Philby's startling resurrection led many intelligence authorities to conclude that the KGB was still playing up to Lenin's decree that the key to successfully deceiving the West was to tell them what they want to hear.

Billed as 'the most successful spy the KGB ever had', the seventy-six-year-old Philby understandably chose not to be photographed for the London *Sunday Times* in his Soviet general's uniform. Appropriately for the era of *glasnost*, he wore carpet slippers and a monogramed Cambridge-blue cashmere sweater. Beaming benignly, he mischievously held up a copy of *Spycatcher*. It was an appropriately cheeky gesture for the silver-haired spy – the book was then still banned from publication in England by the British government.

In the wake of the *Spycatcher* affair, the KGB evidently saw an opportunity to have its star spy play a final heroic role in his lifelong saga of deception. Suddenly, the old traitor was again making headlines outside the Iron Curtain. He broke his silence of twenty-five years to tell the world that he was proud of being a spy, that he had no regrets, and that he 'would do it all over again'.

Rescued from the whiskey bottle, and rejuvenated by his fourth wife, a Russian twenty year his junior, Philby spoke of his unshakable faith in communism in six days of cozy tête-à-têtes with Phillip Knightley of the *Sunday Times*. He was the first Western journalist to be invited to Philby's Moscow penthouse apartment. Knightley was shown the spy's trophies – a drawerful of Soviet, Hungarian, Cuban and Bulgarian medals. Philby was especially proud of his Order of Lenin. 'It's the equivalent of a K, [Knighthood] you know!'

One of the reasons Philby gave for the unprecedented 'interview' was his desire to dispel rumors that he was on his 'uppers and abandoned by the KGB and anxious to return to Britain'. Knightley obligingly reported that Philby was 'slim, alert, bubbling with youthful good humor', and that his 'loyalties were always to one side, the KGB.' Philby was confident that he would be proved right by the verdict of history. He was proud to have served the Soviet Union for more than fifty years. 'I want to be buried here,' Philby declared, 'I want my bones to rest where my work has been.'

The verdict that Philby delivered on himself at his final curtain call might have been written in Hollywood. Fate ensured that it was to become his epitaph. Three months later his bemedaled body was lying in state in the so-called Social Club of the KGB before his burial in a Moscow cemetery beneath a black granite headstone adorned by a single gold star.

Philby had delivered his final script and bowed out on cue. And Knightley justified his role in the final act as helping us to 'understand the motives and compulsions of Philby and his ilk'. But no insights emerged from the interviews since he coyly refused to discuss KGB 'operational details'. There was, however, a reference to a Roman engraving that Philby claimed to have received from a fellow Cambridge spy that was significant. He said it arrived shortly after Blunt's exposure in 1979, the inference being that he too still held to the 'faith'. As Philby quipped conspiratorially, 'So like Blunt to have done something like that.'

This, like Philby's contention that his confrontation in 1963 in Beirut with Nick Elliot had been calculated by MI6 to precipitate his flight, was subtly crafted to reopen the old feuds between the British and American intelligence services. As we have seen, there is no substance to Philby's claim that Maurice Dobb was the principal Soviet talent spotter at Cambridge, or in his denial that there was no organized Soviet spy ring at the university. Not surprisingly the verdict of one leading British newspaper on the Knightley articles was 'Philby stirs up old suspicions.'

'In diplomatic circles it is accepted that the Knightley interviews – later to appear as part of a book – were sanctioned by the KGB at the highest level,' observed the *Times* in a caveat that was published after the articles of Philby appeared. 'But opinion is mixed whether the purpose was really to humor an old and much valued operative, or to try and muddy further the intelligence water in Britain.'

There is little doubt in the Western intelligence community that the KGB's intention was the latter, because it later emerged that more than one Western journalist had been promised a 'tell-all' interview with Philby. The Soviet press agency Novosti, itself known to be under close direction by the KGB, had also granted permission 'from the highest level' in November 1987 for an Australian and an American writer in the intelligence field to have an exclusive interview.

Philby had gone so far as to agree to answer a detailed set of written questions based on documentation from the CIA and FBI that exposed just how extensively the British and Americans had recruited ex-Nazi intelligence agents – such as Klaus Barbie – for operations against the Soviet Union during the Cold War. The journalists had even received agreement from Novosti that the session could be taped. They accordingly sent an interviewer over to Moscow who sat out the month of January at Soviet expense while vainly awaiting the promised invitation from Philby that never materialized.

It is perhaps significant that the American writer insisted on videotaping Philby – albeit with the proviso that Novosti would have the right of censorship. In Philby's interview with Knightley, the old spy approvingly noted that the British reporter had 'agreed to come without TV paraphernalia or tape recorders.'

Prior to going to Moscow, Knightley had been publicly skeptical of the Hollis issue during the *Spycatcher* trials. He had written dismissively about Soviet defectors, especially Anatoli Golitsyn. 'The CIA needs the KGB to justify its own existence; and how would the KGB fare without the threat of the CIA?' Knightley opined in his introduction to his book *The Second Oldest Profession*.

A year after Knightley's book was published in the United States, Philby selected him to transmit his story that a deep Communist conviction motivated him to spy for the Soviet Union. This 'made-in-Moscow' myth became Philby's final legacy – and one of the KGB's finer deceptions.

As this account has documented, adequate information has been released from the Western intelligence archives – not to mention the records of Cambridge University and the personal testimony of contemporaries – that exposes the Philby legend as a hoax.

What really caused Philby to become a spy was not his deep political conviction – of which there is scant evidence in his anemic undergraduate socialism – but his calculating self-centered cynicism. That is why he later boasted that he felt no remorse for the victims caught in the web of lies: his first three wives, his children, his friends, his wartime colleagues, and his country – in fact, all who trusted him.

Philby and his Cambridge 'soulmates' – Blunt, Maclean and Burgess – were unashamed elitists. They looked down on their privileged contemporaries and, with the exception of the 'rough trade' preyed upon by the homosexual Blunt and Burgess, they would have nothing to do with the lower classes. Blunt died a millionaire. Even Maclean, the only one of the Cambridge spies who could truly be described as ideologically motivated, once said: 'There's nothing I enjoy so much as the comforts of my wealthy friends.' The florid Burgess continued throughout his exile in Moscow to suck up to Harold Nicolson and his Establishment friends. And Philby's comfortable exile in the workers' paradise was one of splendor, far beyond the dreams of the average Russian.

Snobs as Communists? Elitists as ideologues? Hardly. The Cambridge spies were devoid of political convictions that they were willing to fight and die for. They shared a precocious adolescent rebelliousness and a rootless, elitist contempt for the institutions of democracy that isolated them from their Establishment surroundings.

Philby's admission, 'I never felt I belonged,' is far more revealing of his real motivations than his pretense of being an ardent Marxist. As General Orlov emphasized: the Soviet recruiters in the thirties wanted disaffected, but essentially empty, political vessels who could be molded into the prefect spies. Neither Philby nor Blunt could claim to be Communist, cast in the same heroic mold as John Cornford or Julian Bell. These were Cambridge's passionately motivated left-wing idealists. They spoke out and died for their beliefs; Blunt and Philby did neither. To contend otherwise would be another betrayal of their generation.

If Philby and Blunt had been true Marxist–Leninist converts, their consciences would never have permitted them to take orders from Moscow at a time when Stalin was bloodthirstily liquidating the true adherents of the Marxist faith. 'I do not know what the position of Communist Party members is in ... rabidly anticommunist countries,' observed the Moscow correspondent of *The New York Times* in 1937, 'but it is difficult to believe they face greater hazard than here, for here they are shooting them.'

The Cambridge spies were surprisingly untroubled by Stalin's purges, that made a casualty of Theodore Maly, their venerated controller. They also ignored the Nazi–Soviet Pact of 1939. Of all the conspirators, only Maclean came close to being able to claim he was an ideological convert. That is why the Soviets moved so swiftly to evacuate him to the safety of Moscow in 1951. They had good reason to fear that he might make damaging admissions about his fellow conspirators and give an embarrassing recantation of Stalin's brand of communism in the witness box. Maclean's disillusionment with the Soviet Union in later years was made plain to visitors to his Moscow apartment with its wall plaque announcing 'Anti-Semites not welcome here'.

Nevertheless the KGB has succeeded in promoting the myth of the Cambridge spies as ideological believers as was apparent when Philby's death brought recognition – even in the Western press – that he was a hero of the Communist cause. 'Philby was not blackmailed or bribed into betraying his country,' *The Times* declared solemnly. American newspapers echoed the sentiment that the treachery of Philby and his co-conspirators seems somehow less evil because they had been motivated by political conviction. Was not their spying motivated from high – if misguided – conviction rather than 'cold' cash like the KGB's most recent recruits to be exposed in the United States: the Walker espionage ring?

It is still impossible to give a complete accounting of the damage and casualties inflicted by the Cambridge spies in that tumultuous decade of their operations that began with World War II. But there can be no doubt that one of their most enduring legacies was the shattering of the bonds of Anglo-American trust forged by the wartime 'Special Relationship'.

The British and Americans took a long time to appreciate the Soviet dictum: 'Peace is the continuation of war by other means.' The postwar revelations of defecting Soviet agents, such as Gouzenko and Massing, together with the testimony of former Communist co-conspirators such as Chambers and Bentley, eventually convinced the FBI that penetrations of the US Government were plentiful and deep. But the vulnerability of British bureaucrats and ministers in the postwar Labour government, many of whom had themselves been Communists in the thirties, put the brake on the investigations of Soviet penetration in Britain.

The British government, to the amazement of concerned FBI and CIA officers, conveyed the assurance that it was proceeding with its own investigations – but only at glacial speed. The defection of Burgess and Maclean was followed by the forced recall of their Cambridge contemporary Philby because of American suspicion that he, too, was implicated. But with Blunt assisting – at the request of his friend Liddell, the deputy director of MI5 – witnesses were dismissed or ignored, trials obscured, and other Soviet agents in place were warned or protected.

When the dimensions of the Soviet plot could have been exposed by a thorough investigation of the Cambridge connections in 1951, MI5 continued its ostrichlike indifference. Face-saving half measures created a thirty-year saga of denial of the past. Peter Wright's account clearly indicates that neither he, nor any of the other MI5 investigating officers, ever came close to uncovering the extent, or sophistication, of how the Soviets recruited British penetration agents.

The Establishment and the Oxbridge intelligentsia closed ranks when the press assault in 1955 began to expose the issue. This circling of the wagons was as much to conceal incompetence as from fear of the McCarthy-inspired anti-Communist hysteria erupting in Britain. This enabled Philby to maneuver clear of exposure, and it permitted Blunt to put himself beyond reach of investigation until 1963. Golitsyn's revelations and Straight's accusations *after* Philby's defection finally forced the Establishment to give Blunt his double-edged immunity deal – but at the expense of allowing Blunt and his associates to escape being brought to account for their treachery.

Considering the wartime successes of MI5 – the XX Committee proved how the extensive penetration of a foreign intelligence service can lead to eventual control of any enemy's ability to conduct its own defense – it is inexplicable that this same institution did not grasp the implications of its own discoveries until too late.

Successive British governments, for domestic political reasons, have kept the skeletons in the closet with the now even more restrictive (as far as the intelligence services are concerned) Official Secrets Act. Yet the KGB – from whom few British secrets were concealed – continues to reap additional bonuses from its moles. This was a reward that could not have been foreseen when it launched its Trojan Horse strategy back in the early 1930s. As a result, Britain's intelligence services have been held up to ridicule and contempt. Counterintelligence officers face a difficult enough task as it is in Western societies. It could not be otherwise in governments that believe in individual freedom and democratic rights. Soviet agents, whether native-born or overseas recruits, are, by contrast, well disciplined, carefully trained and rewarded. Compared to the controlled social order of Russia, where even in the age of *glasnost*, freedom is still rationed and secrecy an endemic trait, Soviet and Eastern-bloc agents have a free rein in the countries of the West.

Vigilance, as history shows us, is the price that has to be paid to guard our democratic institutions. Countering persistent Soviet penetration efforts, counterintelligence organizations in Britain and the United States also have to confront Moscow propaganda designed to reduce that vigilance.

This account has detailed the costly miscalculations made by Britain and the United States about the dimensions and effectiveness of Soviet penetration efforts.

If there is one lesson to be drawn from the career of Anthony Blunt and his Cambridge co-conspirators, it is that the ethics of conspiracy – and the motivations for betrayal – are not merely ideological, but timeless and never-ending.

Documents

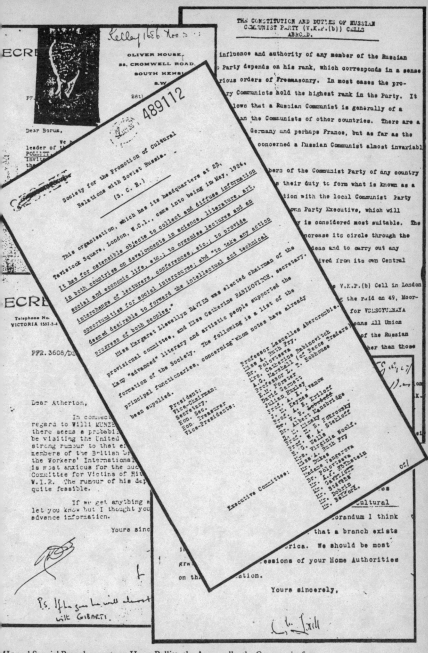

THE CONSTITUTION AND DUTIES OF RUSSIAN
COMMUNIST PARTY (V.K.P.(b)) CELLS
ABROAD.

influence and authority of any member of the Russian
Party depends on his rank, which corresponds in a sense
rious orders of Freemasonry. In most cases the pro-
ry Communists hold the highest rank in the Party. It
lows that a Russian Communist is generally of a
an the Communists of other countries. There are a
Germany and perhaps France, but as far as the
concerned a Russian Communist almost invariabl

bers of the Communist Party of any country
their duty to form what is known as a
tion with the local Communist Party
own Party Executive, which will
y is considered most suitable. The
ncrease its circle through the
deas and to carry out any
ived from its own Central

V.K.P.(b) Cell in London
the raid on 49, Moor-
for VSESOYUZNAYA
ans All Union
of the Russian
her than those

OLIVER HOUSE,
88, CROMWELL ROAD,
SOUTH KENS
A.W

Dear Borus,

We
leader of the
POLLITT,
invite
the

ECRE
Telephone No.
VICTORIA 1557-3-4

PFR. 3608/DS

Dear Atherton,

In connect
regard to WILLI MÜNZE
there seems a probabili
be visiting the United
strong rumour to that ef
members of the British Un
the Workers' International
is most anxious for the suc
Committee for Victims of Hit
W.I.R. The rumour of his de
quite feasible.

If we get anything m
let you know but I thought you
advance information.

Yours sinc

P.S. If the gen he will almost
will GIBARTI.

489112

Society for the Promotion of Cultural
Relations with Soviet Russia.
(S. C. R.)

This organisation, which has its headquarters at 23,
Tavistock Square, London, W.C.1., came into being in May, 1924.
It has for ostensible objects to collect and diffuse information
in both countries on developments in science, literature, art,
social and economic life, etc.; to organise lectures and an
interchange of lecturers, conferences, etc.; to provide
opportunities for social intercourse; and "to take any action
deemed desirable to forward the intellectual and technical
progress of both peoples."

Miss Margaret Llewellyn DAVIES was elected chairman of the
provisional committee, and Miss Catherine BISILOVITCH, secretary.
Many "advanced" literary and artistic people supported the
formation of the Society. The following is a list of the
principal functionaries, concerning whom notes have already
been supplied.

President: Professor Lascelles Abercrombie.
Vice-Chairman: Miss A. Ruth Fry.
Secretary: Dr. Polovtseva Rabinovitch.
Econ. Sec.   Mrs. Catherine (or Secon Traders
Econ. Treasurer   A.G. Marshall: E. Eobhouse
Vice-Presidents: Professor W.
                               E.M. Forster
                               Julian Huxley
                               Prof. M. Koya Ivanov
                               Prof. A. E. Kriloff
                               Prof. Albert Mansbridge
                               Dr. Ginzu SOkrovsky
                               Dr. N. A. Stseloff
                               Prof. V. Wells Woolf.
                               Prof. N.A. Virginia Woolf.
                               Miss G. Roch Fry
                               Madame Yeneorova
Executive Committee: Dr. Polovtseva
                               Mr. Gavitch
                               Dr. L.F. Ehbstein
                               Mr. Starns
                               Mr. Dobrin
                               Mr. Bedforf.

Cultural

orandum I think
that a branch exists
rica. We should be most
essions of your Home Authorities
on th   ation.

Yours sincerely,

The Secret War 1915–69: Summary of the principal events, the rival chiefs of Soviet and British intelligence organizations, and the battles won and lost.

	Bolshevik Revolution		Sov. Trade Mission UK	Lenin's Death			Arcos Raid Labor Govt Sov. Embassy Closed	Rise of Stalin		Sov. Emb. Reopened	Trinity Cell	Hitler in power	Poppy Day Demo		Spanish Civil War	Nazi/Soviet Pact Munich WWII
	Armistice Comintern founded			UK Labor Govt											
1915	1917	1920		1925			1930					1935		1940

Mil. Intel [Red Army 3rd Section   RU (Military and Industrial Espionage)   G R U

Security [– – – – Feliks Dzerzhinski – – – – – – –]|– – – – – V. Menzhinsky – – – – – – – – – G. Yagoda – N. Yezhov – – L. Beria

Apparat ===C H E K A====== G P U======= O G P U=============== N K V D ====

Diplomats   M. Litvinov   A. Rosengolz   Dip. Break   I. Maisky   (S. Kahan)

Rezidentura T. Rothenstein   ++++++++++D. Pestrovsky++++++++++++Theodore Maly+++++ Brandes "Otto"?

Exporting Comintern>>Fronts: Soc. Cultural Relation Int. Workers Relief; Anglo-Soviet Friendship Society
Revolution   CPGB internal subversion>>>>>>>>>>>>>>>>>>>>>

READING SOVIET CODES AND CIPHERS
[– – – – – – – Special Branch – – – – – – – – [Guy Liddell] – – – – – – – – – – – B Division MI5 (Counterintelligence)

                    McCartney Case
                                        Woolwich Case   Krivitsky

MI5 – – – – – – – – – Gen. Sir Vernon Kell DG – – – – – – – – –]
MI6 – – Mansfield Cumming "C" – – –]|– – Adm Sinclair "C" – – – – – – – –]

SECRET US/UK EXCHANGES ON COMMUNIST SUBVERSION

Timeline (1940–1969)

Top events: Dunkirk · Russia attacked · Hiroshima · USSR A Bomb · Korean War · Stalin's death · Burgess & Maclean · Suez Debacle · Cuban Crisis · Philby Defects · Blunt Confesses

Year scale: 1940 — 1945 — 1950 — 1955 — 1960 — 1965 — 1969

2nd Chief Directorate (Soviet Military Intelligence)

- – – L. Beria – – – – – – – – – – – – – – I. Serov – – A. Shelepin – – V. Semichastny – – – – Andropov
- = = = N K G B = = = = = M G B = = = = = = = = = = = = = K G B = = = = = = = = = = = = = = =

GRU

UK Control Officers
[– – – A. Gorski – – –]|– – – B. Krotov – – –]|– – – Y. Modin – – –

Exposed Soviet Spies in UK

| Capt. J. King | D. Springhall | A. Foote | K. Fuchs | | George Blake | Portland Spy Ring |
| | O. Uren | Nunn May | B. Pontecorvo | | | Vassal Case |

Principal Soviet Defectors
Volkov · I. Gouzenko · The Petrovs · A. Golitsyn

MI5
– – – – – – – – – – – Liddell deputy DG – – – – – Harwell Security – – – – – dies.

DG's – – – – Sir David Petrie – – –]|– – – – Sir P. Sillitoe – – –]|– – Sir D.G. White –]|– – – – – – – – – Sir R. Hollis – – – – – – –]|– Sir F. Jones

MI6–"C" – – – Sir Stewart Menzies – – – – – – – – – – – – –]|– – – Sir J. Sinclair – – –]|– – – Sir D. G. White – – – – – –]

Exposed Spies in US
Venona/Bride Sigint (Homer Fuchs & the Rosenbergs . . . . . . still yielding information . . . .)

W. Chambers · H. Massing · The Rosenberg Ring · E. Bentley · M. Straight

PRINCIPAL SOURCES: Corson & Crowley, *The New KGB*; John Dziak, *Chekisty*; Christopher Andrew, *Secret Service*; Nigel West's volumes on MI5 and MI6.

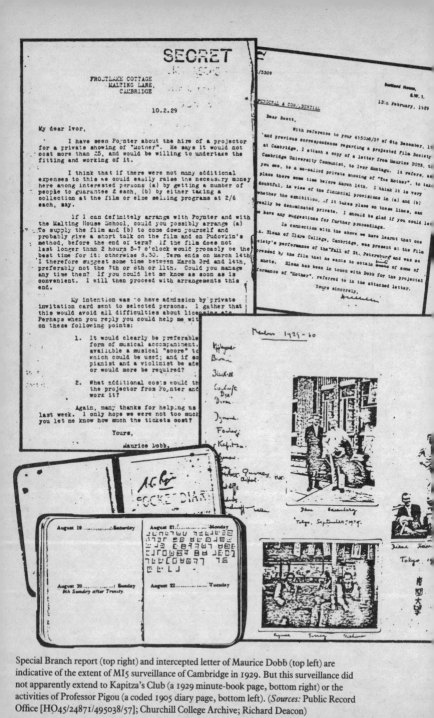

Special Branch report (top right) and intercepted letter of Maurice Dobb (top left) are indicative of the extent of MI5 surveillance of Cambridge in 1929. But this surveillance did not apparently extend to Kapitza's Club (a 1929 minute-book page, bottom right) or the activities of Professor Pigou (a coded 1905 diary page, bottom left). (*Sources:* Public Record Office [HO45/24871/495038/57]; Churchill College Archive; Richard Deacon)

Telephone No
VICTORIA 1555-3-4

P.F.44227/B.4a.

BOX NO. 500 *!L!*
N.D.E
PARLIAMENT STREET, B.O.,
LONDON, S.W.1.

1st February, 1938.

URGENT & PERSONAL.

for Sec'y to Dept

Dear Borum,

      As no doubt you have seen from the newspapers, we have at present four men under arrest here, charged with offences under the Official Secrets Act. These men are all members of a Soviet military espionage organisation operating here.

      We have definitely established that in October, 1937, an important document was photographed at the instigation, and with the assistence of two foreigners who hold Canadian passport No.22247, issued 2nd October, 1936, to Willy BRANDES, native of Rumania, naturalised, aged 35, height 5" 8½", and his wife, Mary, height 5' 4", grey eyes, brown hair, aged 31.

      We have traces of BRANDES and his wife in this country from January 1937 until 6th November, 1937, when they left for Russia via Paris.

      Preliminary enquiries appear to show that ...t No.22247 was unlawfully obtained, ...ther into this.

... this country, BRANDES had
... and posed as an agent of the
...cs Company of New York, and had a
...les of Phantome Pace Powder, the
...eared to be pushing here. He also
...e Charak Furniture Company, 444
...York. The address of Phantome Red
...y also at 444 Madison Avenue, New

... urgently necessary for us to obtain
... data which may enable us to
... entity of BRANDES, I should be most
...d cable an enquiry for us to New
... known both of these two companies

      Yours sincerely,

      Colonel Sir Vernon Kell.

J... B... Brandes.

...hone No.
...RIA 1553-4

BOX NO. 500.
PARLIAMENT STREET, B.O.,
LONDON, S.W.1.
AMERICAN EMBASSY *F!!*
24 SEP. 1935 *C.*
DISBURSING OFFICE

RL.204/11/DS9.

23rd September 1935.

Dear Atherton,

    You may like to know that the following American citizens arrived in London from Leningrad on board the M.V. Smolny on 12.9.35:

      Michael STRAIGHT,
      Joseph LANDER.

    When the Smolny returned to Leningrad on 14.9.35, Ida Sonia SEGAL, an American citizen, was on board.

      Yours sincerely,

      Colonel Sir Vernon Kell.

Roy Atherton, Esq.,
  United States Embassy.

...mmunications to the U.S. State department from MI5 regarding Michael Straight, who
...nt to Russia with Blunt in 1935, and the Soviet illegal Willy Brandes, who was allowed to
...cape the rolling up of the Woolwich Arsenal spy ring in 1938. (*Source:* U.S. Embassy
...ondon, 800 B, R6 84 NA)

The chairman has laid down that, to prevent confusion, but to preserve security, we should forthwith cease referring to A.J.B., but for his eyes only spell out the informant as either A.J. Bennett, or A.J. Bennet, taking great care that we get the spelling of the surname right according to which of the two it refers. The chairman feels this system wou'd be less likely to arouse comment than the use of any code-name. This same method of reference is being used in communications with Balfour, Romnant and Bogovout-Kolomitzov in Paris.

28 / 11 / 28

Most Secret

Maurice Jenks late L.M. of London came to see S.B. to-day on a very Secret & important matter. It transpired at the interview that sometime ago a man Simpson came up for admittance to the Masonic Lodge over which Jenks presides & a message came from H.R.H. P/of/W strongly supporting his Candidature - S he was turned down by the Lodge & Jenks was sent for by H.R.H. who demanded to know the reason. Do you want to hear the Truth I asked? Yes replied the P/of/W.

It is because quite obviously ... husband of your mistress ... in which the fundamental ... sleep with another man ... The P/of/W dines but three ... Mrs S. & gave a pledge to that ... admitted & is now a Mas... how trying this is in the Po... to see Jenks reason - the ... sorrowing & devoted spouse ... wants to marry Mrs S. ... like to have lighted only the ... series - what he wants is in his life back. I suggested he should see the P.M. - S.B. replied to the suggestion with a flat negative. He is the King's chief adviser not Mr S's. In this attitude S.B. is clearly absolutely right.

10 P.M. Clive begins S.B. & I have a frank talk. I am quite convinced that Blackmail sticks out at every step. H.R.H. has already paid large sums to Mrs S. & given valuable presents. I advocate most drastic steps if it is true that S. is an American but if he isn't ... situation is very delicate.

The Masonic man is very clear. The P/of/W put S. in on a lie & is now living in open breach of the Masonic law of Chastity because of the lie he first told. So Mrs S. who is obviously a golddigger has obviously got him on toast. I recommend that if he is an American - the same steps should be taken as were taken in regard to Mrs G. Mrs S. is very close to Stoces and has, if she likes to use them, access to all Secret & Cabinet papers !!!!

Jcc.
4 Feb 1936

Revealing documents discovered in the confidential papers of Tory party chairman J. C. C. Davidson: The SECRET note of November 28, 1928, indisputably refers to Comintern agent Pestrovsky using his alias of A. J. Bennet, which was confusingly close to A. J. Bennett, the Conservative party treasurer. Davidson's SECRET memorandum of February 4, 1936, raises suspicions communicated to the prime minister that Mrs. Wallis Simpson might not only be attempting to blackmail King Edward VII but also be relaying Cabinet secrets to the Germans. (*Source:* Davidson papers, House of Lords Record Office)

27 June, 1953.

My Dear Friend

I have recently had my attention drawn to a
series of telegrams about the attempt of German agents to
bring pressure on the Duke of Windsor in Spain and
Portugal during the summer of 1940. These documents
were found in the German Archives at the end of the war.
All these telegrams are from German sources and represent
Nazi-German intrigue to entangle and compromise a Royal
Prince who had been driven out of France and had taken
refuge in Portugal. If they were to be included in an
official publication they might leave the impression that
the Duke was in close touch with German Agents and was
listening to suggestions that were disloyal. In fact it
was because I foresaw that the Germans would try to entrap
him verbally or even kidnap him especially if they got
him into Spain, that I advised the late King to agree to
his appointment as Governor of the Bahamas and made
strenuous efforts to get him away from Europe beyond the

An exchange at the end of June 1953 between Churchill and Eisenhower that reveals the extent to which the prime minister was prepared to go to prevent the German Foreign Ministry Windsor files from ever being made public. (*Source:* Beaverbrook Collection, House of Lords Record Office)

THE WHITE HOUSE,
WASHINGTON.

July 2, 1953.

Dear Winston,

Your letter of the twenty-seventh just this
moment reached me. I am completely astonished to
learn that a microfilm record was made of the
documents to which you refer.

At the time, in 1945, that the existence of
these documents was called to my attention, I had
them thoroughly examined by Ambassador Winant and by
a member of my own Intelligence Staff. They completely agreed that there was no possible value to
them, that they were obviously concocted with some
idea of promoting German propaganda and weakening
Western resistance, and that they were totally unfair
to the Duke. As a consequence, they were turned over,
upon capture, to the American Ambassador.

At this moment I do not know exactly what it is
possible for me to do because I do not even know in
what classification these microfilms may be kept. I
shall advise you further when I am able to do so.

With my earnest prayers for your early return to
full and vigorous health,

as ever,

IKE.

The Rt. Hon. Sir Winston Churchill,
K.G., O.M., C.H., M.P.

17 April 1944

Dear Colonel Bridge:

I am at length in a position to proceed collecting the British officers for M.F.A.A. duty. Three such officers are likely to become available in the near future. They are, however, much better qualified both as to language and special knowledge to deal with French or Low Countries problems than German.

The officer I would prefer and could most strongly recommend as a capable man, a first rate German scholar and out of the top drawer as an art historian is Major Anthony Blunt, now serving with M.I.5. I have spoken to Major Blunt who promised to make strong representations to his C. O. but did not hold out much hope that he would be released. If there is anything you can do to help us to get the services of this officer I shall be more than gratified, as I am myself very anxious that the German end of this job should be in competent hands and that you should have a British officer in your section.

You will readily appreciate that the difficulties of finding officers among the British art historians is very considerable. At this stage of the war the qualified men are all either crocks or, like Blunt, in responsible jobs in the same time and when they are really good so useful that their C.O.'s are not release them.

Yours sinc...

Col. C. E. D. Bridge,
German Section.

From The Librarian, Windsor Castle, Berkshire.

663 *

November 18,

My dear Passant,

Many thanks for your letter L 5824/2/402 of November 10 enclosi... a copy of Wheeler-Bennett's memoran... of 24 March 1947 concerning Haus Doo... I do not know whether or not you ar... aware that in consequence thereof I ... over to Holland in the following Au... with my colleague Anthony Blunt, to ... the house and its contents on behal... the King. In any case I send you h... my own aide-mémoire on the incident... order that, if necessary, you may br... your file up to date. As this is my only copy may I ask for it back in due course?

Yours ever,

Owen Morshead

PENDANT TO THE DOORN MEMORANDUM.

23 Oct. 1948.

This morning the King came to the Castle and shewed me the Kaiser's two diamanté garter badges from the Cambridge sale, and also his other diamanté one: i.e. the three objects which I had seen at Doorn. The King was delighted with them, and took them away again to house with his others at Buckingham Palace.

His Majesty also brought, and handed to me, the miniature of the Duke of Clarence which I had spotted there. (It has no back, and I am to have a back fitted).

He also received from Doorn the Kaiser's complete Garter robes: not only the mantle and hat, but the full satin breeches etc.

He said nothing about the Field Marshal's baton, and I only remembered it afterwards: I do not know whether or not this has come over.

All these things have been quietly secured by Sir Neville Bland, our Ambassador at the Hague. The King expressly told me that we only hold them on the same footing as we hold the things which I brought back from Frankfurt, i... if the German Family in the future want them back..... well, we have no title to them; we only hold them in security for them, over here in England where things are less unsettled.

O.F.M.

(Doorn itself is to be sold).

Documentation that confirms (top) that Blunt was *not* seconded to the SHAEF art operation in Europe as senior MI5 officers have claimed. The letter of November 18 from Royal Librarian Owen Morshead confirms that as late as 1948 they were still conducting secret missions for King George VI, retrieving documents and artifacts. The 'pendant' of October 23, 1948 confirms that important 'things' were collected from the Hesse archives in Frankfurt, to which the king had only tenuous title. (*Source:* Public Record Office [FO370/1698, paper no. L6634/2/402])

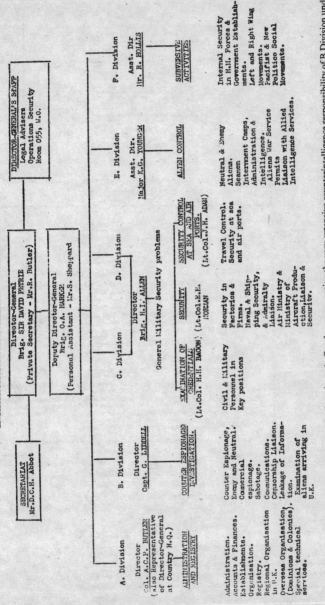

SECURITY SERVICE ORGANISATION

DIRECTOR-GENERAL'S STAFF
Legal Advisers
Operations Security
Room 055, W.O.

Director-General
Brig. SIR DAVID PETRIE
(Private Secretary – Mr.R. Butler)

Deputy Director-General
Brig. O.A. HARKER
(Personal Assistant – Mr.S. Sheppard)

SECRETARIAT
Mr.D.C.H. Abbot

A. Division
Director
Col. A.C.F. BUTLER
(also Representative of Director-General at Country H.Q.)

ADMINISTRATION AND REGISTRY

Administration.
Accounts & Finances.
Establishments.
Organisation.
Registry.
Regional Organisation in U.K.
Overseas Organisation (Dominions & Colonies).
Special technical services.

B. Division
Director
Capt. G. LIDDELL

COUNTER ESPIONAGE INVESTIGATION

Counter Espionage,
Enemy and Neutral.
Commercial espionage.
Sabotage.
Communications.
Censorship Liaison.
Leakage of Information.
Examination of aliens arriving in U.K.

C. Division

EXAMINATION OF CREDENTIALS
(Lt.Col. H.H. BACON)

Civil & Military Personnel in Key positions

D. Division
Director
Brig. H.I. ALLEN

General Military Security problems

SECURITY
(Lt.Col.E.H. KOTAN)

Security in Factories & Films.
Naval & Shipping Security & Admiralty Liaison.
Air Ministry & Ministry of Aircraft Production Liaison & Security.

SECURITY CONTROL AT SEA AND AIR PORTS.
(Lt.Col.J.H. ADAM)

Travel Control.
Security at sea and air ports.

E. Division
Asst. Dir.
Major K.G. YOUNGER

ALIEN CONTROL

Neutral & Enemy Aliens.
Seamen
Internment Camps.
Administration.
Intelligence.
Aliens War Service
Permits with Allied Liaison with Allied Intelligence Services.

F. Division
Asst. Dir
Mr.R. HOLLIS

SUBVERSIVE ACTIVITIES

Internal Security in H.M. Forces & Government Establishments.
Left and Right Wing Movements.
Pacifist & New Politico Social Movements.

The MI5 organization as communicated to the Americans in October 1942, noting the very extensive counterintelligence responsibility of B Division under Captain G. Liddell and that Roger Hollis's F Division was in charge of internal security in the armed forces in addition to left- and right-wing political movements in the civilian population. (*Source:* U.S. Embassy London, R6 84 NA).

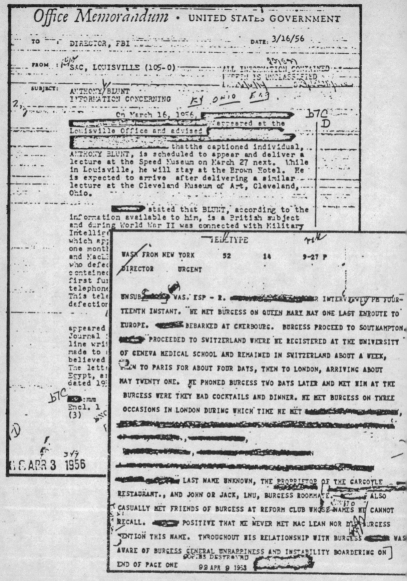

Office Memorandum · UNITED STATES GOVERNMENT

TO : DIRECTOR, FBI   DATE: 3/16/56

FROM : SAC, LOUISVILLE (105-0)   ALL INFORMATION CONTAINED
HEREIN IS UNCLASSIFIED

SUBJECT: ANTHONY BLUNT
INFORMATION CONCERNING

On March 16, 1956, ▮▮▮▮▮▮ appeared at the
Louisville Office and advised ▮▮▮▮▮▮▮▮▮▮
▮▮▮▮▮▮▮▮▮▮▮▮▮ that the captioned individual,
ANTHONY BLUNT, is scheduled to appear and deliver a
lecture at the Speed Museum on March 27 next. While
in Louisville, he will stay at the Brown Hotel. He
is expected to arrive after delivering a similar
lecture at the Cleveland Museum of Art, Cleveland,
Ohio.

▮▮▮▮▮▮▮ stated that BLUNT, according to the
information available to him, is a British subject
and during World War II was connected with Military
Intelligence ▮▮▮▮▮▮▮▮▮▮▮▮▮▮▮▮▮▮▮▮
which ap▮▮▮▮
one month▮▮
and MacL▮▮
who defe▮▮
contained
first fu▮
telephone
This tele▮
defection

appeared
Journal :
line wri▮
made to :
believed
The lett▮
Egypt, a▮
dated 19▮

Encl. 1
(3)

REC. APR 3 1956

TELETYPE

WASH FROM NEW YORK   52   14   9-27 P

DIRECTOR   URGENT

UNSUB ▮▮▮▮ WAS, ESP - R. ▮▮▮▮▮▮▮▮▮▮▮▮ INTERVIEWED RE FOUR-
TEENTH INSTANT. HE MET BURGESS ON QUEEN MARY MAY ONE LAST ENROUTE TO
EUROPE. ▮▮▮▮ DEBARKED AT CHERBOURG. BURGESS PROCEED TO SOUTHAMPTON.
▮▮▮▮ PROCEEDED TO SWITZERLAND WHERE HE REGISTERED AT THE UNIVERSITY
OF GENEVA MEDICAL SCHOOL AND REMAINED IN SWITZERLAND ABOUT A WEEK,
THEN TO PARIS FOR ABOUT FOUR DAYS, THEN TO LONDON, ARRIVING ABOUT
MAY TWENTY ONE. HE PHONED BURGESS TWO DAYS LATER AND MET HIM AT THE
BURGESS WERE THEY HAD COCKTAILS AND DINNER. HE MET BURGESS ON THREE
OCCASIONS IN LONDON DURING WHICH TIME HE MET ▮▮▮▮▮▮▮▮▮▮▮,
▮▮▮▮▮▮▮▮▮▮▮▮▮▮▮▮▮▮▮▮▮▮▮▮▮▮▮▮
▮▮▮▮▮▮▮▮ , ▮▮▮▮▮▮▮▮▮ ,
▮▮▮▮▮▮▮ , ▮▮▮▮▮▮▮▮▮▮N
▮▮▮▮▮▮▮▮▮▮▮▮▮▮▮▮▮▮▮▮▮▮
▮▮▮▮▮▮▮▮ LAST NAME UNKNOWN, THE PROPRIETOR OF THE GARGOYLE
RESTAURANT, AND JOHN OR JACK, LNU, BURGESS ROOMMATE. ▮▮▮▮ ALSO
CASUALLY MET FRIENDS OF BURGESS AT REFORM CLUB WHOSE NAMES HE CANNOT
RECALL. ▮▮▮▮ POSITIVE THAT HE NEVER MET MAC LEAN NOR DID BURGESS
MENTION THIS NAME. THROUGHOUT HIS RELATIONSHIP WITH BURGESS ▮▮▮▮ WAS
AWARE OF BURGESS GENERAL UNHAPPINESS AND INSTABILITY BOARDERING ON
END OF PAGE ONE   COPIES DESTROYED   92 APR 9 1953

A page from the FBI 'Blunt' file (top), revealing that the Bureau was paying serious attention
to his movements as early as 1956. Its suspicions had been aroused within weeks of the 1951
Burgess and Maclean defection after the interrogations of Bernard Miller (below), the
American medical student whom Burgess befriended on the *Queen Mary*. Only partially
obliterated letters indicate Anthony Blunt is one of the blanked-out names.
(*Source:* FOIA FBI files)

He explained that KATZ was a refugee German Jew who left Germany in 1933 to escape punishment by the Nazis because he is a writer and critical of the Nazi regime. According to ISHERWOOD, KATZ first came to Paris where he stayed for a few years and then on to London where he stayed till the late 1930s, and then emigrated to South America in 1939. According to ISHERWOOD, KATZ at the time this interview was conducted, was publishing a news letter, which was in the nature of a financial letter, in Buenos Aires.

With respect to the association between ROLF KATZ and GUY BURGESS, ISHERWOOD believed that BURGESS worked with KATZ "for a while", in 1936 and 1937 or 1937 and 1938, in the publication of a magazine which devoted itself to a survey of economic and political matters. ISHERWOOD stated that he knew of no Communist Party activity or activities on behalf of Soviet Russia on the part of ROLF KATZ, stating that as far as he knew KATZ' field lay more in the line of economics and finance, although he did indulge a bit in political analysis.

ISHERWOOD stated further that as far as he was concerned KATZ was in no way identified with Communist Party activity but was an independent thinker, whom he, ISHERWOOD, very much admired.

On July 17, 1951 CHRISTOPHER ISHERWOOD was interviewed a second time at Laguna Beach, California, by Agents of the Los Angeles Office. At the time of this second interview ISHERWOOD stated that upon reflection he believed that he had met GUY BURGESS through ROLF KATZ in London in the spring of 1936.

With further reference to RUDOLF KATZ, whom he knew as ROLF KATZ, ISHERWOOD stated that in 1929 he went to Germany to live and met ROLF KATZ in Berlin in 1931. With respect to KATZ, ISHERWOOD stated at this time that he was undoubtedly "Leftist" in some of his political thinking and that he believed that at one time had probably adhered to the Communist Party, but that it should be remembered that KATZ had quarreled [...] ints, and [...] KATZ as

8.' *CHRISTOPHER ISHERWOOD, 3000 Rustic Canyon Road, Pacific Palisades, California, advised he met Burgess in London in the late 1930's. He said he also met Burgess again in 1947. Isherwood described Burgess as a drunkard, a homosexual and an emotionally unstable person. He stated he knew of no pro-Soviet acts on the part of Burgess other than his support of the Loyalists during the Spanish Civil War in 1937.*

9. *RUDOLPH KATZ advised that he met Burgess in England in 1936, when he, Katz, was assisting Lord Victor Rothschild. Burgess was a social acquaintance of the Rothschild family. He stated he exchanged letters with Burgess during 1937-38, while Katz was in South America, and upon his return to England again had personal contact with Burgess. He advised the last personal contact with Burgess occurred between 1939 and 1940. Katz stated these contacts were all of a social nature. It is noted that Katz was born in Germany and joined the Communist Party in 1921. He fled Germany to Paris and then to England, and in 1940 he was ordered out of England due to homosexual contacts with British naval personnel. In 1951 he was associated with the Economic Commission for Latin American Affairs, which was a regional body for the United Nations Economic and Social Council, with headquarters at Santiago, Chile.*

page from the July 14, 1951, FBI interrogation report of Christopher Isherwood establishes connection of Rolf Katz (no relation to Otto Katz) to Burgess. The section of the 1955 over report to the White House reveals that the two met through Victor Rothschild. Source: FBI FOIA files, Harry S. Truman Presidential Library)

d. The Federal Bureau of Investigation conducted an investigation at the time of the defection and promulgated a report, the contents of which were used to assist in preparing my memorandum of 18 October 1955. Under date of 19 June 1951, this report was addressed to the Assistant Chief of Staff, G-2, Army, with copies to Navy, State, Special Assistant to the President, Attorney General, Central Intelligence Agency, Atomic Energy Commission, and Office of Scientific Intelligence. Apparently no copy was furnished to the Chairman, Joint Chiefs of Staff, or any Joint Staff Agency. The Federal Bureau of Investigation has indicated interest in the current developments and have been briefed on the contemplated action of the Joint Chiefs of Staff and indicate concurrence therewith.

       Very respectfully,

       EDWIN T. LAYTON
       Rear Admiral, USN
       Deputy Director for Intelligence
       The Joint Staff

THE JOINT CHIEFS OF STAFF
WASHINGTON 25, D. C.

25 November 1955

TOP SECRET

MEMORANDUM FOR: Chairman, Joint Chiefs of Staff

Subject: Safeguarding National Security

Reference: J.C.S. 1712/5

1. In response to your verbal query on 22 November 1955, as to whether any actions were taken by the military security agencies at the time of the Burgess-MacLean defection, or subsequently, the following is submitted:

  a. Apparently no action that can be documented was taken by the Joint Chiefs of Staff subsequent to 25 May 1951 until the current study, which resulted in the report contained in the reference.

  b. In April 1951, a tripartite group of inspectors from US/UK and France was conducting an inspection of security facilities in these three countries and were practically on the spot at the time of the defection. Their report of 4 June 1951, mentioned certain deficiencies in the security facilities in the United Kingdom, especially their system of personnel clearances for those handling classified high level information. Inasmuch as the British had in the past used the "old school tie" system in clearing their top level people, the suggestions made for improving this system were not particularly well received. There is evidence that since the defection incident, some improvements have been made, and are currently being made as a result of the recent publicity given the event in the British and world-wide press. However, definitive information on the current status of security conditions in United Kingdom is lacking at this time and should be requested.

  c. All U. S. diplomatic codes and ciphers were changed immediately following the defection as a precautionary measure, following the same action instituted by the United Kingdom.

TOP SECRET

Rear Admiral Edwin T. Layton's damage-assessment report on the 1951 Burgess/Maclean defection for the U.S. Joint Chiefs of Staff in November 1955. (*Source:* JCS confidential files, National Security.

Notes and Sources

For detailed paragraph by paragraph sourcing and footnotes reference may be made to the hardcover editions published by Wm Morrow (New York 1988); Wm Collins (London 1988) from which this condensed sourcing has been prepared.

Chapter 1 (pp.1–25) 'How Can You Ever Forgive Me?'

Interviews: Guy Rais; Confidential Source New York; Brian Sewell; Rosamond Lehmann; Robert T. Crowley; Arthur Martin.

Published sources: J. R. Ackerly *My Father and Myself* (London: The Bodley Head, 1968) p.135; Andrew Boyle *The Climate of Treason* Preface revised edition (London: Coronet Books, 1980) Preface; Peter Wright with Paul Greengrass *Spycatcher: The Candid Autobiography of a Senior Intelligence Officer* (New York, 1987); Elizabeth Bowen *Death of the Heart* (London: Jonathan Cape, 1938); *The Guardian* 9 December 1986 (Peter Wright affidavit); *The Daily Telegraph* 13 February 1980; *The Daily Mail* 13 February 1986; *The Times* (Transcript of the Blunt Press Conference) 29 November 1979.

Chapter 2 (pp.26–40) 'French Leanings'

Interviews: Nigel West (Rupert Allason M.P.): Arthur Martin; Rosamond Lehmann; Michael Straight; Robert T. Crowley; Robert Cecil.

Published sources: Wilfrid Blunt *Slow on the Feather* (Salisbury: Michael Russell, 1986) p.243; Harry Chapman Pincher *Their Trade is Treachery* (London: Sidgwick & Jackson, 1981) p.90, p.161; Nigel West *MI5* (London: Bodley Head, 1981) p.334; Nigel West *The Circus* (New York: Stein & Day, 1983) p.122; Christopher Andrew, essay 'R. H. Hinsley and the Cambridge Moles' in *Diplomacy and Intelligence in the Second World War* (Cambridge University Press, 1985) p.25; Christopher Andrew *Her Majesty's Secret Service* (London: Heinemann, 1985) p.407; Wilfrid Blunt *Slow on the Feather* p.243; Wilfrid Blunt *Married to a Single Life* (Salisbury: Michael Russell, 1985) pp.8–15; Simon Freeman & Barrie Penrose *Conspiracy of Silence* (London: Grafton, 1986) p.106; Michael Straight *After*

Long Silence (New York: Norton, 1982) p.104. *Studio International* [Anthony Blunt 'Bloomsbury to Marxism'] November 1972; *The Guardian* [Wright affidavit] 9 December 1986; *The Times* [Blunt Press Conference] 29 November 1979; *The Daily Telegraph* 21 November 1979.

Chapter 3 (pp.41–72) Sexual Politics

Interviews: Robert Cecil; John Bowle; Professor Jon Stallworthy; John Hilton.

Published sources: Jonathan Gathorne Hardy *The Public School Phenomenon* (London: Hodder & Stoughton, 1977) p.80; Wilfrid Blunt *Married to a Single Life* p.58; T. C. Worsley *Flannelled Fool* (London: The Hogarth Press, 1985) pp.38–9; Louis MacNeice *The Strings Are False* (London: Faber & Faber, 1982) p.80; Alfred C. Kinsey *The Sexual Behaviour of the Human Male* (Philadelphia: Saunders, 1948); A. L. Rowse *Homosexuals in History* (London: Weidenfeld & Nicolson, 1977) p.167; Tom Driberg *Ruling Passions* (London: Jonathan Cape, 1971) p.15; Robert Wohl *The Generation of 1914* (Cambridge, Mass.: Harvard University Press, 1979); J. M. Winter *World War I and the British People* (London: Macmillan, 1986); Harold Nicolson *King George V* (London: Constable, 1951) p.384; Stanley Hynes *The Auden Generation* (Princeton, N.J.: The Princeton University Press, 1982) p.25; Clive Bell *Art* (London: Chatto & Windus, 1914). *The Marlburian* December 1967; *The Heretick* June 1924; *Studio International* [Blunt] November 1972; *The Marlburian* July, October 1926.

Unpublished sources: MacNeice to Blunt 1926–1938 letters in King's College Archives, Cambridge (hereafter KCA); The MacNeice Papers, Bodleian Library, Oxford.

Chapter 4 (pp.73–107) Exporting the Revolution

Interviews: Robert T. Crowley; Dr John Dziak; Mrs Natale Grant Wraga; Robin Bruce Lockhart; Andrew Barros; Peter J. Liddell.

Published sources: W. Kendall *The Revolutionary Movement in Great Britain, 1900–1921* (London: Weidenfeld & Nicolson, 1964); David Morgan *A Short History of the British People* (Leipzig: VEB, 1979) pp.90–93; Dr L. J. MacFarlane *The British Communist Party: Its Origins and Development* (London: MacGibbon & Kee, 1966) pp.24–5 & 68; William R. Corson and Robert T. Crowley *The New KGB* (New York: Wm Morrow, 1984) p.80; John J. Dziak *Chekisty: A History of the KGB* (Lexington, Mass.: Lexington Books, 1987); Sidney Reilly *Britain's Master Spy: The Adventures of Sidney Reilly* (New York: Harper Brothers, 1933); Robin Bruce Lockhart *Reilly: The First Man* (New York: Penguin Books, 1987); R. H. Ullman *Anglo Soviet Relations, 1917–1921* (Princeton, N.J.: Princeton Univ. Press, 1961); Andrew op. cit.; Joseph Finder *Red Carpet* (New York: Holt

Rinehart & Winston, 1983); Armand Hammer *Hammer* (New York: G. P. Putnam, 1987); Stephen Roskill *Hankey: Man of Secrets* (London: Collins, 1972) Vol. II pp.72–4; Wilfrid McCartney *ZiqZaq* (London: 1937) pp.344–5; Lawrence Badash *Kapitza, Rutherford and the Kremlin* (New Haven: Yale University Press, 1985); Albert Parry (Ed.) *Peter Kapitza on Life and Science* (New York: Macmillan, 1968). *International Journal of Intelligence and Counterintelligence* [Natalie Grant Wraga 'Deception on A Grand Scale'] Vol. 1, No. 4, 1986–7. *The Times* 5 May, 5, 6 December 1927; 17, 18, 19 January 1929 and also *The New York Times* for 'Russia No. 2: Documents'; Commons Paper 2874 HMSO 1927; *The Daily Telegraph* 17 May 1927; *New York Times* 24 May 1927; *Hansard* – Parliamentary Debates (Commons), 5th Series Vol. CCVI, 26 May 1927; *Proceedings of The Royal Society*, London [P. Kapitza, 'Recollections of Lord Rutherford'] 1966.

Unpublished documents: 'Historical Sketch of the Directorate of Military Intelligence During The Great War', 26 May 1921 WO (War Office) 32/10776 Public Records Office (hereafter PRO) Kew, England; Report 9944-A-4 5 April 1918 US Embassy London, Confidential Post Files, Decimal Filing System Ref: 800 B (Bolshevik), Record Group 84, National Archives, Washington DC (hereafter US Emb. Lon 800 RG 84 NA); Cabinet Report 18 August 1918 Cabinet Records (hereafter CAB) 24/52, PRO; CAB 24/118 94308 6 January 1921 PRO; WO 32/3948 Report 14, 2 February 1920 PRO; 'Political Affairs' April 1920 Vol. XLIII US Emb Lon 800 Britain RG 84 NA; Miller to Winslow 4 June 1920. US Emb Lon RG 84, NA. Annual Report of Directorate of Intelligence on 'Revolutionary Movements in Britain' for 1920 Cab 24/118 PRO and Report No. 87 6 January 1921; Memo on 'Messrs Kameneff & Krassin' dated 2 September 1920 Lloyd George Papers F/203/1/4 House of Lords Records Office, London; US Military Attaché London Report 9944-A-166, 15 November 1920, RG 165 NA; Hammer Files US Emb Lon 800B entries: 13 June 1922, 5 March 1924; 9 November 1926 RG 84 NA. War Department G-2 to FBI Military Intelligence Files June–October 1927 RG 165, NA; Cab (24) 166 PRO; Foreign Office (FO) FO 371/1078, PRO; Cabinet Paper 236 (26) 11 and 15 June 1926, Cab 24/180 PRO; 'Communist Papers' HMSO Command Paper 2682 (1926); 'Moness and Chiles' Report January 1923 US Emb Lon 800B RG 84 NA; Special Branch Report 21 July 1927 US Emb Lon, RG 84 NA; Baldwin Papers MSS 113 JDG 10 December 1926 Cambridge University Library; Cab 80 11/5/26 CP 236 (26) PRO; Memos of 27 & 29 March, US Emb Lon, 800B RG 84 NA; 1926 PRO Cab 80 11/5/26 cp 236(26); Report of US Military Attaché in London #19906 20 May 1927 National Archives RG165; Prime Minister's statement dated 24 May 1927 CAB 23/55 PRO; Report 15 November 1927 US Emb Lon 800B RG 84 NA; Report on Communist V(K)b Cells Organization *see* Enclosure 15 November US Emb Lon 800B 15 November 1927; Report on Society for Cultural Relations 18 July 1927 RG 84 NA; Kapitza letters, Papers of Sir John Cockroft CKFT 20/15 Churchill College Archives, Cambridge.

Notes: 1. Lockhart with whom Reilly was involved in the ill-fated 'Envoy's Plot' was arrested – but Reilly managed to slip back to England. 2. Although control of GC & CS passed to the Foreign Office in 1922, the operation was originally established under the aegis of the director of naval intelligence, Admiral Sir Hugh Sinclair, who in 1923 became head of MI6. 5. MacDonald and the Labour Party believed they were the victims of a plot engineered by Conservative Central Office, aided and abetted by right-wing intelligence officers. The Soviets disowned the 'Zinoviev letter' as a forgery from a White Russian émigré 'document factory'. 6. The file draft of the cable telegraphed to the Dominions to coincide with the Prime Minister's 24 May House of Commons statement to the House of Commons on 24 May 1927 was amended to EXCLUDE reference to 'information voluntarily furnished by a person lately in the employment of Arcos.' 7. The functions of the Society for Cultural Relations (founded in 1924) were 'completely in the hands of the Cell' by virtue of its control of executive appointments.

Chapter 5 (pp.108–142) 'Boys of Rough Trade'

Interviews: Michael Robertson; John Hilton; Alistair MacDonald; Jean and Peter Gimpel; Lord Annan; Professor Richard Braithwaite; Richard Deacon; Professor George Steiner.

Published sources: T. E. B. Howarth *Cambridge Between Two Wars* (London: Wm Collins, 1978) p.148; Introduction *The Autobiography of G. Lowes Dickinson* edited by Dennis Proctor (London: Duckworth, 1975) p.24; Kathleen Raine *The Land Unknown* (London: Hamish Hamilton, 1975) p.29; George E. Moore *Principia Ethica* 1903 (Cambridge: Cambridge University Press, 1948); John Jacob Bronowski *The Visionary Eye* (Cambridge, Mass.: MIT Press, 1978) p.25; Cecil Beaton *The Wandering Years* (London: Weidenfeld & Nicolson, 1961) pp.3–6; *Cambridge University Student's Handbook 1926–1927*; Prince Chula Chackrabongse *The Twain Have Met, or An Eastern Prince Came West* (London: G. T. Foulis, 1956) p.132; Christopher Isherwood *Lions and Shadows* (London: Methuen, 1982); M. H. A. Newman *Mathematics* Cambridge University Studies (London: Nicolson & Watson, 1930) p.33; Andrew Hodges *Alan Turing: An Enigma* (New York: Simon & Schuster, 1983) p.60; Charles J. Hessian *John Maynard Keynes* (New York: Macmillan, 1984) p.38; Penrose and Freeman op. cit. p.53; Wilfrid Blunt *Single Life* p.207; Michael Redgrave *In My Mind's Eye: An Actor's Autobiography* (New York: Viking Press, 1983) pp.60–1; Anthony Blunt (Ed.) Introduction *Baroque and Rococo* (New York: Harper & Row, 1978) p.10; Osbert Sitwell *Southern Baroque Art* (London: Chatto & Windus, 1924) p.56; John Lehmann *In a Purely Pagan Sense* (London: GMP Publishers, 1985) p.7; Bertrand Russell *Autobiography of Bertrand Russell, 2 vols* (London: Allen & Unwin, 1967); Richard Deacon *The Cambridge Apostles* (London: Robert Royce, 1985); Michael Holroyd *Lytton Strachey: A Critical Biography, 2 vols* (London: Heinemann, 1977); Paul Delaney *The Neo-Pagans* (London: Macmillan, 1987);

Robert Skidelsky *John Maynard Keynes* (London: Macmillan, 1986) p.266; Virginia Woolf *Roger Fry* (London: Hogarth Press, 1940) p.112; Julian Bell, Quentin Bell (Ed.) *Essays, Poems and Letters* (London: Hogarth Press, 1938) pp.20–1; Roger Fry *Exhibition of Flemish Art* (London: Chatto & Windus, 1927) p.35; A. S. F. Gow *Letters from Cambridge* (London: Jonathan Cape, 1945) p.78; Ben Pimlott *Hugh Dalton* (London: Macmillan, 1985) pp.65–70; George Steiner 'The Cleric of Treason' in *The George Steiner Reader* (London: Penguin, 1985) p.194; Virginia Woolf *The Diary Vol II* (New York: Harcourt Brace Jovanovich, 1980) p.255; Peter Stansky *Journey to the Frontier: A Biography of Julian Bell and John Cornford* (London: Constable, 1970) pp.45–74, 315; Bernard Wall *Headlong Into Change* (London: Harvill Press, 1969); André Maurois *I remember, I remember* (New York: Harper Brothers, 1942) pp.140–3; Nina Lavroukine and Leonid Tchertkov *D. S. Mirsky: Profile* (Paris: Institut d'Etudes Slaves, 1980); Fanya (Feigna) Pascal essay in *Recollections of Wittgenstein* ed. Norman Malcolm (New York: Oxford University Press, 1984); Paul Levy *G. E. Moore and the Apostles* (London: Weidenfeld & Nicolson, 1979) p.270; Sherard Vines, ed. *Whips and Scorpions: Specimens of Modern Satiric Verse 1914–1931* (London, 1932); John Lehmann *The Whispering Gallery* (London: Hogarth Press) pp.137–9. *Studio International* [Blunt] Blunt Obituary by *The Burlington Magazine* [Blunt Obituary by André Chastel] September 1983; *Granta* Cambridge 1 March 1929; *The Experiment* Cambridge 1928; *The Venture* [Anthony Blunt's articles 'Bavarian Rococo', 'Seurat', 'William Beckford', 'The Italian Exhibition', 'Breughel'] Cambridge 1928–30; *The Trinity Review* Cambridge 1929; *The Times* [Andrew Gow Obituary] 4 January 1978.

Unpublished sources: MacNeice Letters KCA; 'The History of the Society' Apostles Paper of 1985; Rupert Brooke letter July 1912, The Berg Collection, New York Public Library NYC; Julian to Vanessa Bell, 14 March 1939, Charleston Collection KCA; Westminster School Archives. John Hilton 'Note' supplied to author; 'The Cult of Homosexuality' unpublished manuscript of Lord Annan; Keynes letter to Vanessa Bell, 24 May 1929; Keynes to Blunt, 19 March 1929, Keynes Papers, KCA.

Notes: 1. Edward, according to MacDonald, was a boy in his house for whom he 'had quite a passion'. In an interhouse boxing match MacDonald had 'clobbered' Edward and he remembered how 'appalled' Blunt had been. Basil, according to MacDonald, was Basil Barr, another Marlborough boyfriend of Anthony's who was a 'rather weak individual whom Blunt easily dominated'. 2. The strong humanist-scientific element of Pontigny 'Decades' – the annual meetings of intellectuals at the Burgundy Abbey of the same name – attracted the attention of the Marxist intellectuals. One of the regular attenders, Prince Dimitrii Svjatopolk-Mirsky, was a graduate of St Petersburg University, who after service in the White Russian Army, was lecturer in Russian Literature and Literary Criticism at King's College, University of London. A frequent guest in Bloomsbury circles Mirsky

618 Mask of Treachery

was not only a committee member of the Comintern-sponsored Society for Cultural relations but he became a full-blown Marxist, joining the British communist party in 1931 before returning to the Soviet Union where he fell victim to the Stalin purges.

Chapter 6 (pp.143–173) 'A World Doomed to Destruction'

Interviews: Dr Arnold Kramish; Felix Cowgill; Natalie Grant Wraga.

Published sources: T. E. B. Howarth op. cit. p.148; *Kapitza in Cambridge* p.17; Arnost Kohlman *We Should Not Have Lived That Way* (New York: Chladize Publications, 1982) pp.176–7; Andrew Sinclair *The Red and the Blue: Cambridge, Treason and Intelligence* (Boston: Little, Brown, 1986); Harrison Salisbury ed. *The Soviet Union: The Fifty Years* (New York: Harcourt Brace & World, 1967) p.12; George Gamow *My World Line* (New York: Viking, 1970); Jack I. Turck 'George Gamow: A Memorial Essay' in *Cosmology, Fusion and Other Matters* (Boulder, Col.: Colorado Associated University Press, 1977) p.192; Neil D. Wood *Communism and The British Intellectuals* (London: Gollancz, 1959) p.120; Charlotte Haldane *The Truth Will Out* (London: Weidenfeld & Nicolson, 1949) pp.25–60; Julian Huxley *If I Were A Dictator* (London: Methuen, 1934) pp.16–19; N. Bukharin, Foreword *Science at the Crossroads* (London: Kniga, 1929); Andrew op. cit. pp.335–7; Philip Spratt *Blowing Up India* (Calcutta, 1955); Robert C. Williams *Russian Art and American Money 1900–1940* (Cambridge: Harvard University Press, 1980) p.211; Arthur Koestler *Darkness at Noon* (New York: Bantam) p.68; L. J. MacFarlane op. cit. pp.206–41 for Petrovsky; Robert Rhodes James *Memoirs of a Conservative* (London: Macmillan, 1970) pp.280–81; Gerald Macmillan *Honors for Sale* (London: The Richards Press, 1954) p.20; Richard Deacon *The British Connection* (London: Hamish Hamilton, 1979) pp.66–7 for Pigou; 'Ypsilon' *Pattern of World Revolution* (New York: Ziff Davis, 1947) p.233; Alexander Orlov *Handbook of Intelligence and Guerrilla Warfare* (Ann Arbor: The University of Michigan Press, 1965); H. A. R. Philby *My Silent War* (New York: Grove Press, 1968) p.14. *The Venture* [Alister Watson 'The Wisdom of Blake'] Cambridge Vol. 1, p.5; *The Times* 24 April 1935; *Pravda* 14 June 1935 quoted in report from British Embassy Moscow of same date PRO FO 371/19470 PRO; *Hearings of House Unamerican Activities Committee* [Walter Krivitisky testimony] Vol. 9, 76th Congress p.5720–; *Report US Senate Internal Security Sub-Committee of the Judiciary Committee* [Testimony of Alexander Orlov] September 1955 and February 1957.

Unpublished documents: Kapitza report 30 August 1930 CKFT 20/15 CCA; Cockroft review *Nature* Vol. 175, 23 February 1957; Kapitza Club Note Books CKFT 7/2, CCA; Bukharin File in Home Office (HO 45/14449 PRO); Unpublished Thesis by Dr Kay MacLeod 'Politics, Professionalization and the Organization of Scientists The Association of Scientific Workers 1917–1942' University of Sussex;

Memorandum 'The Society For Cultural Relations' November 1929 US Emb Lon 800B RG 84 NA. Intercepted letters and reports 9 July 1925, 30 March 1928, 18 February 1929, 10, 16 July in HO 45/24871, PRO; Memorandum 'VOKS' March 1929 US Emb London 800B, RG 84 NA; Reports from Liddell 17 April 1931, 10 May 1931, 8 April 1932 800B. US Emb London RG 84 NA; Sir Edward Brotherton's donation records Davidson papers, HOL; Card Index entries on Bessedovsky; Bogovout Kolomitzev and Baykolov from Wraga Files; 'Internal Security of HM Forces' WO 32/3948 110/Gen/4399, PRO; Report 'Security Intelligence in War' by Capt Eric Holt-Wilson Imperial War Museum, London; Bessedovsky Report US Military Attaché Latvia 15 November 1930 x-1 2037-1552 RG 165 NA.

Notes: 1. 'It is ludicrous to suggest the competence to build a Russian bomb was brought from Cambridge to Moscow by Kapitza' wrote Professor David Schonberg in a letter to *The Washington Post* of 29 April 1987. Dr Zarah Steiner in her well-balanced full page review of *Mask of Treachery* in the *New York Times Book Review* 25 December 1988 asserted there is nothing more than circumstantial evidence that Kapitza was a Soviet technological spy. While Kapitza's defenders are correct to point out that there is no direct connection between his low temperature work at the Cavendish and the bomb, yet it is surely not necessary to show that Kapitza had to be a full-fledged GRU agent to accept the impetus that shipping his laboratory lock stock and barrel gave to Soviet science in terms of prestige and research. According to Dr Arnold Kramish, a leading US physicist and historian, many of those who worked for Kapitza at his Center for Physical Problems did go on to work on the Soviet hydrogen bomb. 2. Confirmation of Oldham's treachery came in 1945 from the debriefing at the Hague of Hans Pieck, a long-serving Dutch Comintern agent. 3. Richard Deacon cites as his sources on Cambridge economist Pigou's links to the Comintern a former Soviet agent code-named 'Roger'. 4. Alexander Orlov, a.k.a. Leon Lazerevik Febin, Lev Lazerevich Kikolsky, served at OGPU Headquarters and the counterintelligence school until 1936, defecting in 1938 to the United States by way of Canada. Fearing retribution he did not make himself known to the FBI until 1953 when he sold his story to *Life* magazine.

Chapter 7 (pp.174–206) 'We Talk Endlessly . . .'

Interviews: Dr George Steiner; Lord Annan; Professor Harry S. Ferns; Professor R. F. Willerts; Sir John Colville; Jack Hewit; Robert T. Crowley; Laughlin Campbell.

Published sources: Steiner op. cit. p.197; Roy Harrod *John Maynard Keynes* (London: Macmillan, 1951) pp.450–1; L. P. Wilkinson *A Century of Kingsmen* (Cambridge: King's College, 1980); Wright op. cit. p.225, pp.252–7, 261–4; Raymond Aron *The Opium of the Intellectuals* (New York: Doubleday, 1957) pp.210–11; Deacon *The Cambridge Apostles* p.217; Steiner op. cit. p.197; Flora Solomon and Barry Litvinoff *A Woman's Way* (New York: Simon & Schuster, 1984) pp.210–16; Fanya Pascal op. cit. p.36; Deacon *The British Connection* p.74; Howarth op. cit. p.198; Harry S. Ferns *Reading from Left to Right: One Man's Political History* (Toronto: University of Toronto Press, 1983) p.222; Philby op. cit.; Goronwy Rees *A Chapter of Accidents* (London: Chatto & Windus, 1972) p.133; Tom Driberg *Guy Burgess: A Portrait with Background* (London: Weidenfeld & Nicolson, 1956) pp.13–21; Boyle op. cit. pp.52–3, p.87, 96–7; Cyril Conolly *The Missing Diplomats* (London: Queen Anne's Press, 1952) p.18; Virginia Cowles *The Rothschilds: A Family of Fortune* (London: Weidenfeld & Nicolson, 1979) p.216; Victor Rothschild *Meditations on a Broomstick* (London: Collins, 1977) p.13; Victor Rothschild *Random Variables* (London: Collins, 1981) pp.203–5; Leonard Woolf *Downhill All the Way* (London: Hogarth Press, 1967) p.18; Orlov op. cit. pp.86–90; Hugh Thomas *John Strachey* (London: Eyre Methuen, 1973) pp.5–17; Haldane op. cit. p.54. *The Times* [Blunt Press] 21 November 1979. *Times Literary Supplement* [Lord Annan's review of *Climate of Treason*] 7 December 1979; *King's College Register* [Alister Watson obituary] October 1983; *The Times* [Richard Llewelyn Davies obituary] 28 October 1981; *Times Literary Supplement* [Charles Madge 'Viewpoint']; *Times Literary Supplement* [Lord Annan 'Scamp into Scoundrel'] November 1972; *Times Literary Supplement* [Lord Annan review of *Conspiracy of Silence*] November 1972.

Unpublished sources: Undated letter from Victor Rothschild to Keynes (putatively late 1933 or early 1934) The Keynes papers KCA; The History of the Apostles; Earl Baldwin letter dated 1 August 1962 Davidson Papers, HOL; St John Philby Foreign Office biography, 7 July 1948 State Dept File 111 20A/7-748 RG 84 NA; Minute book of Trinity Historical Society, CA; MacNeice Letters KCA.

Chapter 8 (pp.207–247) 'I Saw Myself as a Spy'

Interviews: A. L. Rowse; Andrew Boyle; Lord Annan; Robert Crowley; Robert Cecil; Rosamond Lehmann; Arthur Martin; Confidential MI6 Source; Robert T. Crowley; Hayden Peake; Nigel West (Rupert Allason, MP); Christopher Wright; George Steiner; Leonard Miall; Leo Long; Michael Straight; James Barros; Sir Charles Fletcher Cooke; Professor G. M. Wickens; Professor H. S. Ferns.

Published sources: Rees op. cit. p.71–74; A. L. Rowse *A Cornishman at Oxford* (London: Cape, 1965) p.65; A. J. P. Taylor *A Personal History* (London: Hamish Hamilton, 1983) p.78; Stansky op. cit. p.107; Boyle op. cit. pp.116–7, 119; E. H. Cookridge *The Third Man* (New York: Putnam, 1968); Patrick Seale and Maureen McConville *Philby* (London: Hamish Hamilton, 1973) p.67; Lord Vansittart *The Mist Procession* (London: Hutchinson, 1958) p.490; Philby op. cit. p.14; Penrose & Freeman op. cit. pp.106–7; Nigel West *Molehunt* (London: Weidenfeld & Nicolson, 1988) p.65; Phillip Knightley *Philby* (London: André Deutsch, 1988);

Driberg *Guy Burgess* pp.24–6; *The Collected Poems of Louis MacNeice* ed. E. R. Dodds (London: Faber & Faber, 1966) p.22; Williams *Russian Art and American Money 1900–1940* pp.11–31; Michael Straight *After Long Silence* p.104; Steiner op. cit. p.192; Maurice Dobb *Soviet Russia and the World* (London: Wishart, 1932) p.144; James Barros *No Sense of Evil: The Espionage Case of E. Herbert Norman* (New York: Ivy Books, 1987); Wilfrid Blunt *Slow on the Feather* p.295; Christopher Mayhew *Time To Explain* (London: Hutchinson, 1987) p.24; Mac-Neice *The Strings are False* p.161; W. H. Auden, Louis MacNeice 'Their Last Will and Testament' in *Letters from Iceland* (London: Faber & Faber, 1985); Introduction John Cornford *Collected Writings* ed. Jonathan Galassi (Manchester: Carcanet Press, 1986). *The Daily Express* [Boyle Interview] 21 November 1979; *The Observer* [Rees quote] 13 January 1980; *The Times* [Blunt interview] 29 November 1979; *The Spectator* 5 May 1933; *The People* November 1956; *The Sunday Times* [Philby Interviews] 27 March 1988; *The Spectator* [Blunt Art column] November 1934–December 1935; *Studio International* [Blunt 'Blooms-bury']; *The Times* [Blunt letter] 11 April 1971; *Trinity Review* May 1934; *The London Review of Books* [Victor Kiernan 'On Treason'] 25 June 1987; *Toronto Globe and Mail* [Michael Straight 'A Red Mole or Martyr?'] 9 October 1986; *The Canadian Forum* [H. S. Ferns 'For the Record'] November 1986.

Unpublished documents: MacNeice letters KCA; Letter from Lord Thurlow 6 August 1987; Kell letter 26 July, Liddell Report 25 December, US Emb Lon 800B 1935 RG 84 NA.

Chapter 9 (pp.248–269) 'Many a Fickle Makes a Fuckle'

Interviews: Michael Straight; Confidential Source; Leonard Miall; Harry Chapman Pincher; Professor H. S. Ferns; H. R. Astbury; Robert T. Crowley; Dr John Dziak; Anthony Masters; Lord Annan; Robert Cecil; Nigel West; Joan Miller.

Published sources: Straight *After Long Silence* pp.80–1, 98, 101–2, 104–5, 120–2; Cecil Day Lewis ed. *The Mind in Chains* (London: Mueller, 1937) pp.17, 108, 114, 121, 122; Boyle op. cit. pp.98, 120; Pincher *Their Trade is Treachery* p.110; Wright op. cit. p.110, 227; Knightley op. cit.; Elizabeth Poretsky *Our Own People: A Memoir of Ignace Reiss and his Friends* (Ann Arbor: Univ. of Michigan Press, 1963) p.128; Gordon Brooke-Shepherd *The Storm Petrels* (London: Collins, 1977) pp.128, 175–178, 214; Arthur Koestler essay in *The God That Failed* ed. R. H. S. Crossman (New York: Harper, 1950); Anthony Masters *The Man Who Was M: The Life of Maxwell Knight* (Oxford: Blackwell, 1982) pp.30–46; Robert Cecil *A Divided Life: Donald Maclean* (London: The Bodley Head, 1988); West 'MI5' p.83; Joan Miller *One Woman's War: Personal Expoits in MI5's Most Secret Station* (Dublin: Brandon, 1986) pp.106, 154. *The Cambridge Review* 5 February 1937; *Granta* 3 February 1937; *Studio International* [Blunt 'Bloosmbury']; *The Times* 22 November 1979; *The Spectator* 5 June 1937; *The Times* [Blunt interview] 29

November 1979; *The New Statesman and Nation* ['The Revolutionary Movement in Nazi Germany by Ernst Henri'] August 1933; *The Sunday Times* [Knightley Philby interviews] March 1988; *New York Review of Books* [Lord Annan 'Et Tu Anthony'] 22 October 1987; *The Times* 4 February 1939.

Unpublished documents: Cambridge Union Society Debates Minute Book 1937 University Library, Cambridge; MacNeice Letters KCA; Reports on 'Brandes Case' 1 Feb, 15 March, 6 July US Emb Lon 800B RG 84 NA.

Chapter 10 (pp.270–297) Assisting Lord Rothschild

Interviews: Robert J. Lamphere; Robert Cecil; Natale Grant Wraga; Dr John Dziak; 'John Saxon'; Dr Georg Knuppfer.

Published sources: Philby op. cit. pp.189–90; Robert J. Lamphere *The FBI-KGB War* (New York: Random House, 1987) p.242; Lord Inverchapel references *see* Deacon *The British Connection* p.198; Christopher Isherwood *Christopher and His Kind* (London: Eyre Methuen, 1977) p.230; Thomas Whiteside *An Agent in Place: The Wennestrom Affair* (New York: Ballantine, 1983); Pincher *Their Trade is Treachery* pp.138–9; Rebecca West *The Meaning of Treason* (London: Penguin, 1965); Anthony Glees *The Secrets of the Service: British Intelligence and Communist Subversion 1939–1951* (London: Cape, 1987) p.271; Stephen Spender *Journals 1939–1983* (New York: Random House, 1986) p.264; Christopher Isherwood *The Condor and the Crows* (New York: Random House, 1949) p.192; Driberg *Guy Burgess* pp.30–1; Rees op. cit. pp.7, 120–1, 131; Cookridge *The Third Man* pp.23, 78; Koestler *Invisible Writing* pp.197, 210; Babette Gross (Munzenberg's widow) *Willi Munzenberg: A Political Biography* (East Lansing: Michigan State Univ. Press, 1979) p.312; Claud Cockburn *Claud Cockburn Sums It Up* (London: Quartet Books, 1981); W. J. West *Truth Betrayed* (London: Duckworth, 1987); *Der Slanzsky-Prozess* (Prague, 1953) p.253; S. Kuchinski *Memorien* (East Berlin: Aufbau, 1983) pp.270–1; Robert C. Williams *Klaus Fuchs: Atom Spy* (Cambridge, Mass.: Harvard Univ. Press, 1987) p.22; Boyle op. cit. p.122; Nigel Nicolson *Portrait of a Marriage* (New York: Atheneum, 1980) pp.135–137; Harold Nicolson *Diaries and Letters 1930–1939* (London: Collins, 1966) pp.252–361; Driberg *Ruling Passions* pp.32, 233; Page, Leitch, Knightley *Philby: The Spy Who Betrayed a Generation* (London: Deutsch, 1968) pp.89–91, 110; Richard Griffiths *Fellow Travellers of the Right* (London: Constable, 1980) p.52; Sir Henry Channon *Chips: The Diary of Sir Henry Channon* ed. Robert Rhodes James (London: Weidenfeld & Nicolson, 1967) p.248; Simon Haxey (pseudonym) *Tory MP* (London, 1939) p.207; Simon Schama *Two Rothschilds and the House of Israel* (New York: Knopf, 1982) pp.290–93; John Reeves *The House of Rothschild: The Financial Rulers of Nations* (New York: Gordon Press, 1975) pp.168–9; Penrose & Freeman op. cit. p.203; Wolfgang von und zu Putlitz *The Putlitz Dossier* (London: Allen Wingate, 1957) preface, pp.110, 247–9; Anthony Read & David Fisher

Colonel Z: The Secret of a Master of Spies (London: Hodder & Stoughton, 1984); Norman Rose *Vansittart: Study of a Diplomat* (London, 1978); Lord Vansittart *Lessons of My Life* (London, 1944); Dziak op. cit. pp.48–50; Deacon *The British Connection* p.204. *The Daily Express* 14 June 1951.

Unpublished documents: Burgess & Maclean; Philby [Espionage R] FBI Files (hereafter FBI BMP); Isherwood Interviews 15 July 1951 BMP FBI; Blunt's name mentioned in reports 15 July and 4 October 1951 BMP FBI; Stein entries in Shanghai Police Dept Files, NA; 'Katz' 31 July 1951 FBI BMP; *see also* 'Summary Brief' on Burgess, Maclean and Philby prepared by J. Edgar Hoover for President Eisenhower 8 November 1955 FBI Series Box 10 Eisenhower Library (hereafter BMP 1955 EL); Miller letter 2 May 1933 800B 'Wagenknecht' US Emb Lon 800B RG 84 NA; Liddell letter 7 June 1934 US Emb Lon 800B RG 84 NA; Borum to Liddell, 14 June 1939 'Gibarti' US Emb Lon RG 84 NA; FO 371/23058-C20850/645/18 PRO; 'Katz & Breda' US Emb Lon 800B, 1940 RG 84 NA; Fuchs Confession in J. Edgar Hoover to Adm Souers 22 March 1950, President's Secretary Files Harry S. Truman Library (hereafter HST); Rudolph Katz Interview 27 July 1951 BMP FBI; Vansittart Memorandum, 2 October 1939 FO 371/23057-C18620/1645/18 PRO; Memorandum State Department #1437, 29 May 1940 'Putlitz' and FBI reports 11–20 June 1940 800.20211 RG 84 NA; Letter to Vansittart from Putlitz, 1 August 1946, Vansittart Papers (VST II 1/9 CCA; Liddell to Vansittart re Baykolov, 15 February 1950 VST II 1/41 CCA; Most Secret Memorandum 14 February 1936 Davidson Papers HOL.

Notes: 1. Lord Inverchapel's bisexuality was known to Robert Cecil, Dame Rebecca West wrote of Inverchapel in *The Meaning of Treason* of his 'steady passion for the Soviet Union'. Yet Anthony Glees insists that 'there is absolutely no evidence' that Inverchapel was a 'mole' only that the ambassador was 'an eccentric pro-Bolshevik'. 2. Munzenberg was forced to flee from Berlin to France when Hitler came to power in 1933 and in 1938 Munzenberg rashly protested from Paris against the executions of the Communist leaders in the so-called Yezhov purges. In 1940 shortly after the fall of France his decapitated body was found hanging from a tree in a village in the Massif Central. His widow and friends insisted that he had been liquidated by Stalin's agents. 3. Information provided by a former MI6/MI5 officer calling himself John Saxon, currently residing in the United States, who first supplied the information about MI6 pre-war sources on Fuchs to Professor Robert Chadwell Williams. 4. Vansittart – 'Van' as he was known to his admirers – was the outspoken anti-communist and anti-Nazi Permanent Head of the Foreign Office from 1930–38 and then senior adviser to the Prime Minister. 5. Confirmation of Baykolov's suspicious activities is also provided by an article in the 22 October edition of *Vozorozhdeniye*, a White Russian journal that was published in Paris. Deacon asserts (without attribution) that both Sabline and Baykolov 'were on friendly terms with Guy Liddell of MI5'. In support of this contention Deacon cites a communication of July 1944 from Liddell in what he describes as the Baykolov archives.

624 *Mask of Treachery*

Chapter 11 (pp.298–313) 'It Was All a Bit of a Lark'

Interviews: Lord Annan; Confidential Sources; Nigel West.

Published sources: Rees op. cit. pp.126, 131, 140–148; Pertinax (André Géraud) *The Gravediggers of France* (New York: Doubleday, Doran, 1944) pp.49, 100, 431; Philby op. cit. p.132, 189; Page et al. op. cit. p.93; Driberg *Guy Burgess* pp.32, 40, 46; Glees op. cit. pp.391, 264; W. J. West op. cit. pp.33–53, 58–9, 116; Edna Nixon *John Hilton: The Story of His Life* (London, 1946); Telford Taylor *Munich: The Price of Peace* (New York: Doubleday, 1979) pp.134–7, 499; Driberg *Guy Burgess* p.37; Nicolson *Diaries* p.340; Wright op. cit. pp.228, 265; West *Molehunt* p.92; Penrose & Freeman op. cit. p.190; Boyle op. cit. pp.181–4; Spender op. cit. p.214; B. S. Escott *Baker Street Irregular* (London: Methuen, 1965) pp.20–1; Wilfrid Blunt *Single Life* pp.198–231.

Unpublished documents: Blunt Contributors File BBC Written Archives Centre Caversham (hereafter BBCA); Harold Nicolson Contributor Files BBCA; Winston Churchill Contributor File 1938, BBCA; JBC Report FO T 162/858/E39140/4 PRO; Leeper Minute FO 395/647B; P1402/105/150 PRO; Hoover Souers Report 2 March 1950 op. cit. HST.

Chapter 12 (pp.314–331) 'I Can Trust No One'

Interviews: Robert Cecil; A. A. Berends; Malcolm Muggeridge; Lord Gladwyn.

Published sources: Winston S. Churchill *History of the Second World War: Vol. 1: The Gathering Storm* (London: Cassell, 1948) p.391; William L. Shirer *The Rise and Fall of the Third Reich* (New York: Simon & Schuster, 1959) p.721; Rees op. cit. p.149; Penrose & Freeman op. cit. p.218; Malcolm Muggeridge *Chronicles of Wasted Time: The Infernal Grove* (London: Collins, 1972); Pincher *Their Trade is Treachery* p.92; Anthony Blunt *The Writings of Anthony Blunt* (London: Courtauld Institute, 1972); E. H. Cookridge *Secrets of the Service* (London: Sampson Low, 1947) pp.136–146; Corson & Crowley op. cit. p.412; Dziak op. cit. p.64; Isaac Don Levine *Stalin's Great Secret* (New York: Coward McCann, 1956) pp.102, 140; Brooke-Shepherd op. cit. pp.177–82; West *MI5* pp.88–90; Deacon *The British Connection* pp.141–2; Andrew op. cit. p.432; Wright op. cit. pp.265, 325; Philby op. cit. p.175; Chapman Pincher *Too Secret Too Long* (New York: St Martin's Press, 1984) pp.450–52; Nigel West *Friends* (London: Weidenfeld & Nicolson, 1988) pp.153–55. *Hansard* 19 May 1939; *The Times* [Blunt Press] 29 November 1979; *The Sunday Mirror* [interview with John Shearer] 27 November 1979; *The Spectator* [Blunt Art] 22 October 1937, 16 May 1938; *Saturday Evening Post* [Krivitsky] April 1939.

Unpublished documents: MI5 Report on Fifth Column Activities 1 August 1940 800.02 US Emb Lon RG 84 NA; 'The Machine Tool Industry' MI5 report 820 1940

US Emb Lon RG 84 NA; 'Organization of Security Services' Box 9 820.02 1942 US Emb Lon RG 84 NA; MI5 report, 15 March 1938 800B US Emb Lon RG 84 NA; MI5 Report on Liddell's US Visit 1938 Vansittart Papers, VST, I 2.21 CCA; Confidential Report 1 February 1938 800B US Emb Lon RG 84 NA; Liddell report 8 February, Report 5 September 1939 800B US Emb Lon RG 84 NA; Unpublished sections of handwritten diaries of Sir Alexander Cadogan (hereafter MS Cadogan) 4, 15, 25–26 September 1939, 26 January 1940, ACAD 1/8 CCA; Cadogan to Treasury 2 December 1939 T162 574/E40411 PRO; 'The Security Executive' December 1941, Box 9 US Emb Lon RG 84 NA.

Notes: 1. James Dunn was a senior officer in the Department of State and former US Ambassador in Rome who acted as the Washington recipient of the MI5 reports until the mid-forties when pressure from the US Army ended his monopoly of British intelligence dissemination. 2. 'General' Walter G. Krivitsky was the name Samuel Ginsburg adopted (after defecting from the GRU Third Section in 1937) for his sensational *Saturday Evening Post* articles and when he testified before the House Un-American Activities Committee in 1939. 3. Australian-born Charles Howard 'Dick' Ellis had been posted to Berlin in 1924 – fresh from the Sorbonne – as MI6 station chief. His abilities as a linguist and subsequent marriage to Lilia Zelinsky enabled him to tap into the White Russian networks in Europe. His father-in-law, Alexander Zelinsky, one of his sub-agents, was named by an Abwehr (German military intelligence) officer as the source of the MI6 'order of battle' that resulted in the 1940 'Venlo Debacle'. During the war Ellis was with BSC in New York and VENONA decrypts disclosed that there was a Soviet Source in Sir William (Intrepid) Stephenson's organization. According to Wright, Ellis confessed during 1964 interrogation that he had leaked MI6 information to Zelinsky to the Germans – but denied he was a Soviet source. Wright did not believe him.

Chapter 13 (pp.332–363) 'Keep That Man Out of the Office'

Interviews: Alan Berends; West Interviews; Malcolm Muggeridge; Lord Annan; Rosamond Lehmann; Michael Straight; John Hilton; Alistair MacDonald; Timothy Johnston; Jack Hewit; Robert Cecil; Information from Sir Dick White relayed by a confidential source.

Published sources: Anthony Blunt *François Mansart and the Origins of French Classical Architecture* (London: The Warburg Institute, 1941); Penrose & Freeman op. cit. pp.222–37, 249–251; Anthony Blunt preface The Artistic Theory in Italy, 28 June 1940; Chapman Pincher *A Web of Deception: The Spycatcher Affair* (London: Sidgwick & Jackson, 1988) pp.2, 8, 9, 143, 205; V. Rothschild op. cit. pp.29–32; West *MI5* p.246; West *Molehunt* p.85; Martin Green *Children of the Sun* (New York: Basic Books, 1976) p.135; Page et al. 'Philby' op. cit. p.126; Pincher *Their Trade is Treachery* pp.112–3; Wright op. cit. pp.172–3, 220; Driberg *Guy*

Burgess pp.56–8; W. J. West op. cit. pp.192–200; M. R. D. Foote *The S.O.E.* (London: Oxford, 1984) p.15; Sweet Escott op. cit. p.36; Philby op. cit. pp.22–7, 30–31, 49–50; Straight *After Long Silence* pp.129, 134, 141; T. A. Robertson quoted Penrose & Freeman op. cit. p.253; Muggeridge quoted by Boyle op. cit. pp.185, 264; Deacon *The British Connection* pp.174–5; Solomon op. cit. pp.163–9; Nigel West *MI6* (London: Weidenfeld & Nicolson, 1983) p.226; Juan Pujol with Nigel West *Garbo* (London: Weidenfeld & Nicolson, 1985) pp.74–5. *The Daily Telegraph* [George Curry] 17 November 1979; *The Times* [Blunt Press] 29 November 1979; *Baleares*, Palma, 28 January 1964; *The Sunday Times* [Knightley/Philby] March 1988.

Unpublished documents: 'The Machine Tool Industry' MI5 report 4 July 1940 US Emb Lon 820. Box 5 RG 84 NA; 'Gregory Case' File (Elizabeth Bentley) November 1946 FBI; 'Michael Straight' File 25 June 1963 FBI – kindly made available by Mr Straight; *The Observer* Goronwy Rees 13 January 1979; Cadogan MSS 23 December 1943 CCA.

Notes: 1. Wright in *Spycatcher* p.172 says that Solomon, when debriefed in 1962 about her suspicions of Philby's and Blunt's friend Tomas Harris was frightened because Harris had 'recently died in a mysterious car accident in Spain'. In fact that accident did not occur until two years later in 1964!

Chapter 14 (pp.364–382) 'Thwarting a Need to Know'

Interviews: Jack Hewit; Professor Robin Winks; Natalie Grant Wraga; Robert T. Crowley; Felix Cowgill; Leo Long; Malcolm Muggeridge; Peter J. Liddell; Confidential Washington Sources.

Published sources: Winston S. Churchill *History of the Second World War: Vol. III, The Grand Alliance* (London: Cassell, 1950) p.39; Hinsley et al. *British Intelligence in the Second World War* Three Volumes: Vol. 1 (Cambridge University Press, 1979) pp.58–60, 138–9, 205, 368, 435–6, 452, 463–5, 472–3, Cracking the Enigma Machine Appendix 1, pp.491–2, 668; Vol. II pp.20, 59–66; Ronald Lewin *Ultra Goes To War: The Secret Story* (New York: McGraw-Hill, 1978) p.64; Penrose & Freeman op. cit. pp.273–4; Wright op. cit. pp.222, 251, 265; Andrew op. cit. p.460; Pujol & West op. cit. p.74; Robin Winks *Cloak and Gown* (New York: Wm Morrow, 1987) pp.283–77; Sir John Masterman *The Double Cross System in the War of 1939–1945* (New Haven: Yale University Press, 1972) p.168; Dusko Popov *Spy Counterspy* (New York: Grosset & Dunlap, 1974); David Mure *Master of Deception: Tangled Webs in London and the Middle East* (London: William Kimber, 1980) pp.189–90; Krivitsky 'Stalin's Secret Service' op. cit. p.239; Dziak op. cit. pp.96–7; Deacon *The British Connection* pp.177-9; M. R. D. Foote and J. M. Langley *MI9, Escape and Evasion* (London: The Bodley Head, 1979) p.77; Hodges op. cit. p.409; Pincher *Too Secret Too Long* pp.347, 396; Straight *After*

Long Silence p.143; West *MI5* pp.251, 356; Driberg *Ruling Passions* p.178; Masters op. cit. p.178; Miller op. cit. p.64; Philby op. cit. pp.48, 57–9, 79–81; Hugh Trevor-Roper *The Philby Affair* (London: Wm Kimber, 1968) pp.28–9; Muggeridge op. cit. p.126. *The American Historical Review* [J. F. Bratzel and L. B. Rout Jr 'Pearl Harbor, Microdots and J. Edgar Hoover'] Vol. 87, No. 5 pp. 1342–1348.

Unpublished documents: Joint Intelligence Committee (JIC 41) 252 12 June 1941 quoted in Hinsley, Vol. op. cit. p.749; 'The Running of Double Agents' Norman Holmes Pearson Papers, YCAL Box 3, Beinecke Manuscript Library, Yale (hereafter Pearson Yale); Uncensored Typescript of 'Masters of Deception' and David Mure's correspondence with Ewen Montagu, Felix Cowgill and T. A. R. Robertson 'The Mure papers' Imperial War Museum London; Alan Turing letter 26 May 1933 KCA; Vansittart letter on Klugmann VST II 2/23 CCA.

Chapter 15 (pp.383–403) 'Recommended to the Service'

Interviews: Malcolm Muggeridge; Mrs Kemball Johnston; Dr Christine Carpenter; Peter Fairbairn; Felix Cowgill; Robert Cecil.

Published sources: Page et al. op. cit. p.186; Philby op. cit. pp.64, 81, 85, 101, 103, 108–9, 110, 113–4; Winks op. cit. pp.247–321, 322–469 'The Theorist'; David C. Martin *Wilderness of Mirrors* (New York: Harper & Row, 1980); Glees op. cit. pp.279–283; Anthony Cave Brown *C The Secret Life of Sir Stewart Menzies, Spymaster to Winston Churchill* (New York: Macmillan, 1987) Easton quotes pp.474, 623–4; Martin Gilbert *The Road to Victory: Winston Churchill 1941–1945* (London: Heinemann, 1986) p.729; Patrick Howarth *Intelligence Chief Extraordinary* (London: The Bodley Head, 1986) p.63; Penrose & Freeman op. cit. p.286; Pujol & West op. cit. pp.134–6; Wright op. cit. p.228; Pincher *Too Secret Too Long* p.351; Boyle op. cit. p.228; West *MI6* p.386; Muggeridge op. cit. p.250–1.

Unpublished sources: 'British Recruitment and Handling of Agents' Undated Box 2 Pearson Yale. 'Security Arrangements in Govt. Departments 25 June 1942 Box 9 Confidential Files US Emb Lon RG 84 NA; 'Counter Espionage' Undated Box 2, 'Theory of Counterintelligence Operations' Undated Box 2 Pearson, Yale; 'Suggestions for Talks on Russia' Burgess 15 July 1941 R51/520/1, BBC; Cadogan MSS 13 August 1943 ACAD 1/III CCA; Dick White note 31 December 1944 in Assignment of Officers 210.3 SHAEF G-2 Intelligence 1944–5 Box 156 SHAEF RG 331 NA; Administrative Section Subject File 'FORTITUDE' SHAEF G-3 RG 331 NA; Memo 'Planning and Organization' Box 2; Cowgill to Pearson 19 January 1945, Pearson, Yale; Rothschild letter 27 November 1944 Box 71 SHAEF G-3 RG 331 NA.

Chapter 16 (pp.404–437) 'Most Secret Matters'

Interviews: Sir Dudley Forwood; John Loftus; Professor Donald Cameron Watt; Robert Harbinson (Bryan); Philip Ziegler; Jack Hewit; Confidential MI6 source; Andrew Sinclair; Robert T. Crowley; Robert Cecil; Leo Long; Lord Annan.

Published sources: Penrose & Freeman op. cit. pp.286, 292, 298–9; Wright op. cit. p.223; Dieter Rebenstich *Personlichkeitsprofil und Karriereverlauf des national-sozialistischen Adubrungskader in Hessen 1928–1945* (Marburg, 1983) pp.303–5; Hans Phillippi *Das Haus Hessen: Ein europaisches Furstengeschlecht* (Kassel, 1983) pp.152–155; Roger Fulford *Friedrichshof: The Home of the Empress Frederick* (Munich: Schness & Steiner Verlag, 1975); Lady Diana Mosley *The Duchess of Windsor* (London: Sidgwick & Jackson, 1980) p.89; *Documents Relating to German Foreign Policy, Volume I* #5482/E382057 (US Government Printing Office, 1955); Ralph G. Martin *The Woman He Loved* (New York: Simon & Schuster, 1974); Peter Allen *The Crown and The Swastika* (London: Robert Hale, 1983) p.87; Frances Donaldson *Edward VIII* (Philadelphia: Lippincott, 1973) p.385; Charles Higham *The Duchess of Windsor* (New York: McGraw-Hill, 1988); Anthony Blunt *The French Drawings in the Collection of HM The King at Windsor Castle* (London: Phaidon Press, 1945); Sir Kenneth Clark 'Another Part of the Wood: A Self-Portrait' quoted by Kenneth Rose *Kings, Queens and Courtiers* (London: Weidenfeld & Nicolson, 1985) p.111; Philip Ziegler *Mountbatten* (London: Collins, 1985) p.52; Nigel West *Friends* p.23. *The Sunday Times* 25 November 1979; *The New York Times* 10 June 1946; *The New York Times* 23 October 1937; *The Washington Star* 30 April 1945; *The Spectator* 20 September 1986; Anthony Blunt *The Queen's Lecture* (HMSO, 1972); *The Burlington Magazine* 1946 Vol. LXXXVIII p.263; *The Times* 21 November 1979 Blunt transcript.

Unpublished sources: SHAEF G-2 Headquarters Files RG 331 NA; Woolley letter 17 April 1944, Klingender letter 1 August 1944, 12th Army Group HQ File RG 331 NA; Colonel Hesketh letter 27 July 1983; 'Hesse' File entry 254-80 'Operation Ashcan' Box 156 SHAEF G-2 RG 331 NA; Berth Cable 27 January, Zech-Burkesroda 19 February, Stohrer 23 June, 11, 30, 31 July, 3 August (all 1940) taken from Cabinet Memorandum C35 4 Sept 1953 Cab C.53 Box 13 Beaverbrook Papers, HOL; German Foreign Policy documents B15/B002556--B00363; SD reports R SS/1236 and E 035156. Bundesarchiv, Freiberg; Cadogan MSS 25 October 1945 ACAD/1/15 CCA; 'Discovery of Secret Archives of German Foreign Ministry' report, 25 May 1945 'T Force 655' Entry 13 B Box 70 SHAEF G-2 RG 331 NA; Attlee to Churchill 25 August 1945, Churchill–Eisenhower letters July 1953 Box 13 Beaverbrook Papers HOL; State Department Decimal File 1940–5 'Duchess of Windsor' RG 84 NA; Morshead letters, 18 November 1948, 28 September 1947 and pendant of 23 October 1948 FO 370/1698 PRO.

Chapter 17 (pp.438–464) 'An Enormous Amount of Influence'

Interviews: Lord Annan; Judge Robert Morris; David Martin; Hayden Peake; Michael Straight; Andrew Roth; Robert Lamphere.

Published sources: Winston Churchill 'History of the Second World War, Vol. VI: Triumph and Tragedy' (London: Cassell, 1959) p.497; Barros op. cit. pp.20–21; Straight *After Long Silence* pp.229–30, 231, 256–7; Wright op. cit. p.239; Michael Straight *Make This The Last War* (New York: Harcourt Brace, 1943); Hede Massing *This Deception* (New York: Ivy Books, 1987) pp.154, 167, 191–2, 278–9; Christopher Thorne *Allies of a Kind* (New York: Oxford University Press, 1978) p.438; Owen Lattimore *The Solution in Asia* (New York, 1945); *Papers Relating to the Foreign Relations of the United States 1944 Vol. VI China* (Washington US Govt. Printing Office 1963) pp.253, 589–99; Freda Utley *The China Story* (New York, 1950) pp.155, 163; Elizabeth Bentley *Out of Bondage* with a documented Afterword by Hayden B. Peake (New York: Ballantine Books, 1988); 'Silvermaster et al.' Report to J. Edgar Hoover 24 August 1948 in 'Gregory Case' File FBI; Whittaker Chambers *Witness* (New York: Random House, 1952) pp.26, 353; David Rees *Harry Dexter White: A Study in Paradox* (New York: Coward McCann, 1973) p.39; Lamphere op. cit. pp.2, 34–5, 142; H. Montgomery Hyde *The Atom Bomb Spies* (London: Hamish Hamilton, 1980); Barros op. cit. p.145; Boyle op. cit. p.169; John Sawatsky *Men in the Shadows* (Toronto: Doubleday, 1980) p.145; Robert J. Donovan *Conflict and Crises: The Presidency of Harry S. Truman, 1945–1948* (New York: Norton, 1977) p.174; Professor David Oshinsky *A Conspiracy So Immense: The World of Joe McCarthy* (New York: Macmillan, 1983) pp.98–9; *The Specter Original Essays on American Anti-Communism and the Origins of McCarthyism* (New York: Franklin Watts, 1974); E. M. Forster *Two Cheers for Democracy* (New York: Harcourt Brace, 1951) p.67; P. N. Furbank *E. M. Forster: A Life* (Oxford University Press, 1979) pp.224–51; Alger Hiss *In the Court of Public Opinion* (New York: Knopf, 1957) p.307; Alger Hiss *Recollections of a Life* (New York: Henry Holt, 1988) pp.202–11; Professor Herbert Packer *Ex-Communist Witness* (Stanford, Ca.: The Stanford University Press, 1962) p.107. *Hearings before the Subcommittee to Investigate the Administration of the Internal Security Act* Institute of Pacific Relations 1951–52 (hereafter IPR Hearings) 83rd Congress Part 2, p.5, *US Senate Report on the Judiciary* Institute of Pacific Relations (hereafter IPR Report) No. 2050 83rd Congress p.97; *The Saturday Evening Post* 'Muddled Millions, Capitalist Angels of Left Wing Propaganda' 15 February 1941, *La Révue Parlementaire* Paris, 15 December 1949; *The Congressional record* 25 May 1949 82nd Congress p.7764; *The Washington Post* 10 March 1942; *The Saturday Evening Post* 'Must the East Go Red?' 12 May 1945; *Report of the Senate Judiciary Committee* 'Interlocking Subversion in Government Departments' (hereafter InterSubv) (reproducing FBI report of 25 November 1945) 30 July 1953. IPR Hearings pp.491–3; House Un-American Activities, Communist Espionage in the United States Government, *Hearings*, 80th Congress 1948 (hereafter HUAC *Hearings*) p.1180, InterSubv *Hearings* pp.2–5, 20–22, 71, 329; HUAC *Hearings* p.540ff; *Report of the Royal Commission* 'Gouzenko' (Ottawa, 1946) pp.638–640; *The Nation* article by Norman Redlich 30 January 1954 p.86.

Unpublished documents: Petrov Affidavit 'Petrov' docket Senate Internal Security Subcommittee (hereafter SSISC) RG 46 NA; Wittfogel, Budenz; Jaffe, E. H. Norman, Utley, dockets SSISC RG 46 NA; Straight FBI file; War Department Intelligence Summary 'Louis Dolivet 18 May 1943 RG 165 NA; Hoover letter 15 September 1942 in FBI Straight File; 1986 Correspondence between Dr Welderhall and Verne Newton and notes of interview with James Angleton of 23 February 1984. Scott report 6 April 1946 Pearson Yale.

Notes: 1. Louis Dolivet (whose Hungarian name was Ludwig Brecher) continues to deny the charges that he was ever a communist and close associate of Willi Munzenberg. His magazine *United Nations World* began failing when his marriage to Michael Straight's sister collapsed. When he sailed for France on 25 May 1949 the State Department revoked his American visa amid a storm of public allegations in the press and in the House of Representatives of his communist past. 2. Hede Massing, who defected to become an FBI informant in 1947, named Elizabeth Zubilin and William Grienke as the Soviet contacts of Elizabeth Bentley. The Czech with 'stiff blond hair' who looked like 'a ski instructor or storm trooper' whom Straight refused to deal with during Green's absence in 1941 matches Massing's description of 'Anton', the philandering blond Czechoslovak who acted as the photographer of the Golos ring. 3. In his famous essay published originally in the New York *Nation* in 1938 under the title 'Two Cheers for Democracy' E. M. Forster makes it clear, from the contemporary European context, that the State he would betray before a friend was not so much the tolerant Britain for which he had given 'Two Cheers', but totalitarian states, both Fascist and Communist.

Chapter 18 (pp.465–503) 'He Had his Best Man on It'

Interviews: Nigel West; Robert T. Crowley; Hayden Peake; John Dziak; Robert Lamphere; Professor S. F. Ferns; Harry Chapman Pincher; Dr Arnold Kramish; Dr Basil Mann; Verne Newton.

Published sources: Pincher *Too Secret Too Long* pp.105, 111, 112, 204–5, 351, 434–5, 623–5; Penrose & Freeman op. cit. pp.287, 296, 305–6, 334; Oliver Millar *The Queen's Pictures* (London: Weidenfeld & Nicolson, 1977) p.212; Christopher Wright *The Art of The Forger* (London: Gordon Fraser, 1984) pp.142–4; Christopher Wright *Poussin Paintings: A Catalogue Raisoneé* (New York: Hippocrene Books, 1985) p.247; Philby op. cit. pp.115, 126–7, 152, 161, 171, 207, 244–5, 285; Wright op. cit. pp.151, 186, 188–9, 193, 244–5, 280–1, 284–6; Nigel West *The Circus MI5 1945–1972* (New York: Stein & Day, 1983) p.19; Glees op.

cit. pp.279, 309; West *Molehunt* pp.31, 54–61; Cave Brown op. cit. pp.143–4, 693, 696–7; West *Friends* p.145; William Stevenson *Intrepid's Last Case* (New York: Villard Books, 1983) p.74; Montgomery Hyde op. cit. p.42; Solomon op. cit. p.210; Ishmail Akhmedov *In and Out of Stalin's KGB* (Frederick, Md: University Publications, 1984) pp.187–198; Thomas F. Troy *Donovan and the CIA: A History of the Establishment of the Central Intelligence Agency* (Frederick, Md: University Publications, 1981); John Ranelagh *The Agency: The Rise and Decline of the CIA* (New York: Simon & Schuster, 1986) pp.112–5; Nigel West *GCHQ: The Secret Wireless War 1900–1986* (London: Weidenfeld & Nicolson, 1986) pp.202–4, 222–224; Lamphere op. cit. pp.81–3, 87, 88, 132, 240; Williams *Klaus Fuchs* p.23; Rudolph Peierls *Bird of Passage: Recollections of a Nuclear Physicist* (Princeton, NJ: Princeton University Press, 1985) p.148; 1951, Ruth Werner *Sonja's Rapport* (Berlin: Neues Leben, 1977); Alexander Foote *Handbook for Spies* (Garden City, NY: Doubleday, 1949); Kenneth Harris *Attlee* (London: Weidenfeld & Nicolson, 1962) pp.497–8; John Loftus *The Belarus Secret* (New York: Knopf, 1982); Christopher Simpson *Blowback* (New York: Weidenfeld & Nicolson, 1987) pp.269–73; Lord Bethell *The Great Betrayal: The Untold Story of Kim Philby's Biggest Coup* (London: Hodder & Stoughton, 1984) pp.38–9; Rees op. cit. p.7; Brian Urquart *A Life in Peace and War* (New York: Harper & Row, 1987) p.117. *Report of the Royal Commission (Gouzenko)* [see Exhibit 23-J Soviet Embassy Telegram]; *The Toronto Star* 27 March 1981; *Newsweek* ['Cracking Soviet Cipher'] 9 May 1980.

Unpublished sources: Copy of Volkov's Russian wording and translation furnished to the author from a confidential source. Hoover 1955 Memo BMP HST; Souers 6 March 1950 Fuchs Memo HST; Memorandum on Communist penetration of Birmingham University, Vansittart papers VST II 1/41 CCA; Sir Patrick Reilly letter 10 July 1986 reproduced in Glees op. cit. p.359; BMP FBI; Lamphere letter to author 10 July 1987; Records of Joint Committee on Atomic Energy 1956–77 Box 128 RG 128 NA; Head of AEA interview BMP FBI; *The Times*, 2 February 1981 ref. to JIC Memo 'The Nature of Russian Air Assistance'.

Notes: 1. Courtauld Institute Graduates accounted for most of the senior appointments at the National Gallery, The Tate, The Victoria and Albert Museum, The National Museum of Wales, The National Gallery of Scotland, and all the art departments of Britain's universities. See the Courtauld Institute's postwar *Annual Reports* 'Appointments of Former Students'. 2. The Philby story about going to a Buckingham Palace investiture with James Angleton that appears in Leonard Mosley *Dulles* (New York: James Wade/Dial Press, 1978) p.284 was denied by Angleton himself.

Chapter 19 (pp.504–528) 'Something Quite Horrible'

Interviews: Valentine Lawford; Dr Basil Mann; Verne Newton; Robert T. Crowley; Hayden Peake; Michael Straight; Robert Cecil; Robert Lamphere; Timothy Johnston; Dr Christine Carpenter; John Hilton; Jack Hewit; Nigel West; Confidential information from Washington sources.

Published sources: Boyle op. cit. pp.379, 395–6, 401; Wilfrid Basil Mann *Was There a Fifth Man?* (London: Pergamon, 1982) pp.80–81; Philby op. cit. p.176–7; Rees op. cit. pp.191–2; Cyril Conolly op. cit. p.33; Lamphere op. cit. p.176; Penrose & Freeman op. cit. p.340; Glees op. cit. pp.361–3; Driberg *Guy Burgess* p.89; West *Molehunt* pp.135, 185–194; Wright op. cit.; Stephen Spender *Journals 1939–1983*, ed. John Goldsmith (New York: Random House, 1986) p.95. *The Washingtonian* [Verne Newton 'The Spy Who Came To Dinner'] May 1984; 'Report Concerning the Disappearance of Two Former Foreign Office Officials' (HMSO Command 9577 (hereafter Cmd FO 9577) 23 September 1955).

Unpublished documents: BMP FBI; 1955 Hoover BMP Brief HST; PETROV Affidavit 29 March 1956 PETROV Docket SSISC RG 46 NA.

Notes: 1. The FBI assessment in the declassified Burgess/Maclean/Philby Files, Director Hoover was advised on 20 January 1957, states: 'This was primarily a British case and of necessity [a] major portion of the investigation [was] conducted in England. We possessed no derogatory information re subjects prior to their disappearance from England in May 1951. From what we know now of subjects' activities prior to their being assigned to this country, a *routine investigation* would have made them ineligible for government employment, according to our standards.' [Emphasis added] 2. Dr Christine Carpenter does not believe her father (Kemball Johnston) was ever knowingly part of Blunt's conspiracy. She suggests the cryptic Stalin doodle may have been an attempt to discover how much her father knew about Burgess's Communist activities.

Chapter 20 (pp.529–551) 'I Let Him Go'

Interviews: Andrew Boyle; Rosamond Lehmann; Confidential CIA Source; Admiral Edwin T. Layton; Walter Pforzheimer; James Barros; Michael Straight.

Published sources: Boyle op. cit. p.410; Pincher *Too Secret Too Long* pp.394–5; West *MI5* pp.50–51, 84–87, 97; Spender op. cit. pp.95–6; Penrose & Freeman op. cit. p.356; Martin op. cit. p.56; Page et al. op. cit. p.21; Philby op. cit. p.189; Cave Brown op. cit. p.709; Wright op. cit. pp.170–1, 244; West *Molehunt* p.28; Pincher *Too Secret Too Long* p.355; Eric Dowton *War Without End* (Toronto: Stoddart, 1987) p.297; Barros op. cit. pp.120–1, 215–6; Straight *After Long Silence* p.290; H. Nicolson op. cit.; Ranelagh op. cit. pp.564–5; Richard Deacon *The Israel Secret Service* (New York: Taplinger, 1985) pp.164–5; Andrew op. cit. pp.496–7;

West *Friends* p.143. *The Daily Express* 7 June 1951; Cmd FO 9577; *Hansard* 25 October 1955; *The Times* 26 October 1955; *The Observer* (Michael Davie on Philby's 1956 re-employment as a foreign correspondent) 27 March 1988.

Unpublished documents: BMP FBI; Memoranda for the Joint Chiefs from Colonel Totten and Admiral Layton dated 18 October and 25 November 1955 COS Joint Chiefs of Staff 'Admiral Radford 1953–55' Box 46 RG 218 NA; 'Anthony Blunt' SAC Louisville 16 March 1956 FBI; Straight FBI.

Chapter 21 (pp.552–580) 'The Final Sting'

Interviews: James Angleton (interviews by Verne Newton); Michael Straight; Desmond MacRae; Robert Harbinson; Robert Cecil; Alaistair MacDonald; Nigel West; Robert Crowley; Christopher Wright; Lord Annan.

Published sources: Douglas Sutherland *The Fourth Man* (London: Secker & Warburg, 1980) p.12; Straight *After Long Silence* pp.318, 321, 324; Wright op. cit. pp.10, 34, 242, 253, 257, 264–7, 278–86, 302–44; Anthony Summers and Stephen Dorril *Honeytrap: The Secret Worlds of Stephen Ward* (London: Weidenfeld & Nicolson, 1982) pp.228–9; West *Molehunt* op. cit. pp.45, 65, 177–83; Ranelagh op. cit. pp.288–96; Simpson op. cit.; Winks op. cit. pp.536–37; Cavendish op. cit. pp.52–6; George Young's preface to Cavendish op. cit.; Deacon *The British Connection* p.204; Steiner op. cit. pp.191–2; Penrose and Freeman op. cit. *The Times* 20 August 1963; *Sunday Times* 20 January 1980; *The Observer* 20 January 1980; *The Times* letters 23 February 1980; *The Daily Telegraph* 30 March 1983; *The Marlburian* April 1926; *The Daily Telegraph* 4 March 1980; Lord Annan *The New York Review of Books* March 1989.

Unpublished documents: Straight FBI; Letters from Mrs Stella Jeffries to Chapman Pincher 4 May, 19 May 1984; CIC File 'TURKUL' MI5 report KEL 3064, 28 April 1947 IRR Files NA; MI5 letter to Vansittart dated 15 February 1950, VST II 1/41 CCA; Hilton note.

Notes: 1. While it is impossible to do more than speculate what personal motivations and frustrations might have led Guy Liddell to cast his lot with the Soviets, certain obvious factors stand out: his artistic temperament; the scars of his marriage; his contacts with Baykolov and the penetrated Russian émigré community. His son told me that his father suffered from hypertension and high blood pressure, which suggests that his 'ruminative' demeanor concealed bottled up stress. Then too there is the matter of his liaison with a woman in the twenties whose Marxism and connection to the Communist party were well known to her contemporaries. This lead has proved impossible to corroborate, but if true, could explain how a ranking Special Branch officer might have fallen victim to a Soviet 'honey-trap'.

Chapter 22 (pp.581–590) 'Beyond the Reach of Time'

Interviews: Brian Sewell; John Richardson; John Hilton; Nigel West; Robbie Dunwoodie.

Published sources: Penrose & Freeman *Conspiracy* pp.46–47; Peter Wright 'World In Action' Granada Television July 1984 and Nigel West *Molehunt* p.65; Steiner *Cleric of Treason* pp.52–6. *The Times* 24 June 1980; *The Daily Telegraph* 30 March 1983; *The Marlburian* April 1926; *The Daily Telegraph* 4 March 1980; *The Scotsman* 18 July 1988.

Epilogue: 'The Legacy of the Cambridge Spies'

Published sources: New York Times 12 May 1988; *The Sunday Times* 12, 20, 27 March, 20 April 1988; *The Observer* 27 March 1988; *The Times* 12 May 1988; Phillip Knightley *The Second Oldest Profession: The Spy as Bureaucrat, Patriot, Fantasist and Whore* (London: André Deutsch, 1986) pp.8, 77; *The Sunday Times* 20 March, 10 April 1988; *Washington Post* 17 May 1988.

Index

John Costello
Love, Sex and War 1939—45 £3.95

'Explodes whatever myths may still persist' THE LONDON STANDARD

'A fascinating, sprawling book, larded not only with statistics, but also with anecdotes and personal memoirs, and covering an astonishing amount of ground. It has chapters on the ATS and women in uniform generally, on homosexuality in the Forces, on Hollywood's presentation of the war, on "fraternisation", black propaganda and "sexpionage", on VD and on virtually everything else one might thing of' THE OBSERVER

'Racy anecdotes and startling Estatistics from recently declassified Top Secret reports makes for a pretty compulsive read' NEW SOCIETY

'Fascinating . . . throws into new light the well-rehearsed theme of how the war changed the position of women. It is a matter to which Mr Costello gives intelligent and far-ranging attention' SUNDAY TELEGRAPH

'Interesting and entirely readable . . . must have the broadest possible appeal . . . especially to readers for whom the last war is as remote as Agincourt or Jericho' THE YORKSHIRE POST

'It is the memories of ordinary people which make the book a good read' THE MAIL ON SUNDAY

'A comprehensive and highly nostalgic record of the beating of hearts behind the roar of the guns and the crash of the bombs' THE BIRMINGHAM POST

'Compelling social history' DAILY EXPRESS

Sir Basil Liddell Hart
History of the Second World War £7.99

First published in the year after his death in 1970, Liddell Hart's classic history of the Second World War is the work of a leading military analyst, but also of a compassionate and uniquely original thinker.

Sir Basil Liddell Hart was the author of more than thirty books and a world renowned lecturer in strategy and tactics, a man of whom *The Economist* said: 'he is not simply a prophet and a critic but a historian of great rank'.

'The greatest British military thinker of this century' THE SOLDIER

'A work of great length and great learning, illuminated by flashes of insight . . . full of brilliant strategic analysis' A. J. P. TAYLOR

'Unlikely to be surpassed' THE SUNDAY TELEGRAPH

'The book has the mark of the author's genius – a lucidity and insight such as no other military writer can match . . . it will long be read with profit and enjoyment by all interested in the military art' THE ARMY QUARTERLY

'Remarkably good . . . a mine of accurate information'
THE EVENING STANDARD

Milton Shulman
Defeat in the West 4.99

With an introduction by Max Hastings

In 1945, the once mighty Wehrmacht was reduced to pathetic clusters of men in prisoner-of-war camps across Europe and Asia. The Reich that was to endure a thousand years lay in shell-shattered ruins.

Yet the German forces were a superbly armed body of fighting men of incomparable quality. So why did Hitler's Germany go down to such devastating defeat in the West?

In 1945, the man who is today an outstanding critic, commentator on current affairs and broadcaster was a young major with the Canadian Army intelligence on the European battlefront.

In his line of duty, he interrogated many enemy prisoners, including such senior officers as von Rundstedt and 'Sepp' Dietrich, gaining a rare and remarkable insight into the German perspective on defeat in the West.

First published to great acclaim in 1947, his book is now revised and expanded to offer a vivid portrayal of the most awesome war machine the world had known, marching to the tune of a lunatic Fuhrer.

'An absorbing history of the war in the West as it looked to the Germans' WILLIAM L. SCHIRER, author of *The Rise and Fall of the Third Reich*

'One of the most interesting and important books of the war' THE SPECTATOR

'Of permanent value to historians and of absorbing interest to anyone' THE OBSERVER

'This contemporary account, a classic in its time, deserves the reprint it now has' NORMAN STONE, LONDON STANDARD

Hugh Thomas
An Unfinished History of the World £9.99

Following the path of Herodotus, Raleigh and H. G. Wells, one of the foremost historians of the twentieth century surveys the story of humankind from the dawn of man into our own turbulent times. Revised and extended by the author for this Pan edition, including a series of newly commissioned maps.

'What richness it provides. There is scarcely an aspect of human life it does not illuminate' THE TIMES

'Hugh Thomas has laboured hugely to find and fit together all the facts and ideas that constitute not only our history, but our politics as well' ECONOMIST

William L. Schirer
The Rise and Fall of the Third Reich £6.95

The world-famous history of Nazi Germany

'A magnificent work . . . documented, reasoned, objective and never dull . . . the standard, indeed the classic, history of Nazism' HUGH TREVOR-ROPER, SUNDAY TIMES

'I can think of no book I would rather put into the hands of anyone who wanted to find out what happened in Germany between 1930 and 1945' ALAN BULLOCK, GUARDIAN

Phillip Knightley
Philby – KGB Masterspy £4.99

The name Kim Philby has become synonymous with the most amazing exploits in the history of espionage.

Agent, double agent, traitor, enigma. Few knew the real man behind the impenetrable facade that for years fooled British intelligence, the CIA and the FBI. After Philby defected to Russia in 1963 he maintained a code of silence for 25 years – until a few weeks before his death.

Then, in an unprecedented move, he invited journalist Phillip Knightley to his Moscow apartment, and in six days of conversation he bared his soul as never before. He told of his childhood, the influence of his extraordinary father and the events that lead him inexorably to turn traitor.

For the first time, *Philby – KGB Masterpy* tells the full story – before and after defection. Through his views on everything from loyalty and patriotism to pop music and Margaret Thatcher, revelation after revelation combine to build a unique picture of the most notorious spy of the twentieth century, a tale that rivals the best spy fiction.

Lech Walesa
A Path of Hope £5.99

An Autobiography

I regard everything I have achieved in life as merely a sort of loan. After all, from a religious point of view, nothing we receive – be it beauty, happiness or money – is ever worth more than that. If we accept that we are only the temporary guardians of life's various gifts, it's easier not to lose our heads or give way to despair.

For 500 days Lech Walesa was the leader of Solidarity; the revolutionary movement of Polish workers which threatened the stability of Eastern Europe.

Walesa, an electrician from a poor Catholic family, won the Nobel Peace Prize for his attempts to found people's Poland. It was an heroic quest which began when he scaled the railings at the Gdansk shipyard on 14 August 1980 and took charge of the strike committee.

The free trade union was cut short in 1981 by the imposition of martial law. Walesa was imprisoned and vilified.

Yet his intense and enduring courage have enabled him to continue the struggle. *A Path of Hope*, smuggled to the West chapter by chapter, illuminates the driving force of a man whose hopes are part of the fabric of Poland and whose dreams transcend the continuing crisis of the Eastern bloc.

'Reading this book convinced me, once again, that Solidarity wasn't a failed "insurrection". Poland was incomparably lucky to have found Lech Walesa at that moment' NEAL ASCHERSON, THE OBSERVER

'A concise, powerful, and above all sincere account of Walesa's motives and ambitions' RADEK SIKORSKY, THE GUARDIAN

All these books are available at your local bookshop or newsagent, or can be ordered direct from the publisher. Indicate the number of copies required and fill in the form below.

Send to: **CS Department, Pan Books Ltd., PO Box 40, Basingstoke, Hants. RG21 2YT**

or phone: 0256 469551 (Ansaphone), quoting title, author and Credit Card number.

Please enclose remittance* to the value of the cover price plus: 60p for the first book plus 30p per copy for each additional book ordered to a maximum charge of £2.40 to cover postage and packing.

*Payment may be made in sterling by UK personal cheque, postal order, sterling draft or international money order, made payable to Pan Books Ltd.

Alternatively by Barclaycard/Access:

Card No.

Signature:

Applicable only in the UK and Republic of Ireland.

While every effort is made to keep prices low, it is sometimes necessary to increase prices at short notice. Pan Books reserve the right to show on covers and charge new retail prices which may differ from those advertised in the text or elsewhere

NAME AND ADDRESS IN BLOCK LETTERS PLEASE:

Name

Address

3/87